KU-211-140

– arch-back-stabber of political foes and friends alike, arch-womaniser (as when, during an overnight stay at Windsor Castle, he was discovered sneaking into a lady-in-waiting's bedroom, for which he was never to be forgiven by the Prince Consort; or when, in his seventy-ninth year he was cited as co-respondent in a divorce case). But there is much more to the Palmerston era than this. His life (1784–1865) spanned the crucial years between the loss of England's first empire – the American colonies – and the emergence of the second empire 'on which the sun never set', and took in the Napoleonic wars and the Industrial Revolution. Finally, he was in office of one sort or another longer than any other British statesman. *Lord Palmerston*, then, is one of those rare biographies in which not simply the person biographised but also a critical historical period is illuminated.

'Jasper Ridley's *Lord Palmerston* will supersede all previous lives'
Lord Blake The Sunday Times

'Masterly, rich, comprehensive and consistently fair, intelligent and readable. The man and the background become credible despite their incongruity'   *Michael Foot, Evening Standard*

Jasper Ridley gave up his law practice to devote all his time to writing. *Lord Palmerston* is his fourth historical biography. He has also written historical portraits for radio. He has considerable experience of political affairs and has twice stood for parliament in the Labour interest. He is actively concerned in the preservation of our countryside and public footpaths and spends as much time as possible walking.

Jasper Ridley

Lord Palmerston

Panther

Granada Publishing Limited
Published in 1972 by Panther Books Limited
3 Upper James Street, London W1R 4BP

First published in Great Britain by Constable & Co.
Limited 1970
Copyright © Jasper Ridley 1970
Made and printed in Great Britain by
C. Nicholls & Company Ltd
The Philips Park Press, Manchester
Set in Intertype Times

To my daughter Barbara

Contents

List of Illustrations

Foreword

Like other biographers of Palmerston, I must begin by pointing out the impossibility of dealing thoroughly with this enormous subject in a limited space and time. Three years of work, and 793 pages, are not enough in which to write a fully comprehensive life of Palmerston. I can, however, claim that my book covers a wider ground than any previous biography.

I have used, as my chief sources, Palmerston's papers in the British Museum. These papers, which were formerly at Palmerston's country house at Broadlands, consist of 178 letter books,* and one volume of unbound and unsorted manuscripts. The letter books contain Palmerston's original and amended drafts and copies of Foreign Office despatches, copies of his private letters, the text or summaries of despatches received by him, and his account books. There are about 20,000 documents entered in the letter books.

Only three of Palmerston's previous biographers have had access to what were formerly the Broadlands Papers, and none of them made full use of them. In the eighteen-seventies Bulwer suppressed not only Palmerston's strictures of Bulwer's own moral conduct in Constantinople, but also all passages containing criticisms of reigning Sovereigns and of some other living persons. Palmerston's secretary, Evelyn Ashley, who completed Bulwer's work, was equally discreet. Fifty years later, Guedalla used the Broadlands Papers; but though he painted a vivid picture of Palmerston as a personality, he was not really interested in Palmerston's policies. Sir Charles Webster used the Broadlands Papers much more extensively in his *Foreign Policy of Palmerston*; but Webster's book dealt only

*There are in fact 179 letter books, but two of them are identical copies of the same set of accounts.

with the period between 1830 and 1841, and did not cover the whole field of foreign policy even during these years. Palmerston's policy towards China and the United States was left out altogether, and relations with certain other countries were treated much less thoroughly than Belgium, Spain, the Turkish Empire and relations with Russia and Austria. Mr. Brian Connell used the Broadlands Papers for his studies of Palmerston's childhood in his biography of Palmerston's father, and in his book *Regina v. Palmerston*. I have dealt more briefly with Palmerston's relations with Queen Victoria than with some other matters, for this fascinating subject has been covered by recent writers more thoroughly than any other aspect of Palmerston's life.

In quoting passages from Palmerston's manuscripts, I have adopted Palmerston's spelling, punctuation and use of capital letters, both in English and French.

The manuscript sources have made it possible for me to unearth a considerable amount of completely new material in connexion with many aspects of Palmerston's work at the War Office between 1809 and 1827, and with various matters which he dealt with as Prime Minister – for example, the garotting scare in London in 1862, and the attempted expropriation of the absentee landlords in Prince Edward Island. They have also thrown new light on many matters connected with Palmerston's policy as Foreign Secretary – particularly on his relations with Portugal, Spain, and Mexico. The revealing incident of Palmerston's attitude about the execution of Charles Smith the poacher has been ignored by all Palmerston's biographers except Guedalla, who referred to it (in a very misleading manner) in one sentence of his book. The Reverend N. J. Overton, the Vicar of North Baddesley, was kind enough to let me see the papers and correspondence about the case in the parish chest at North Baddesley Church. The greater part of Chapters IV, V, VI, XI, XIII, XIV, XV and XXXV, and large sections of Chapters XVI, XXII and XXVI, are based on unpublished material. Some unpublished material is also used in most of the other chapters. Of the printed sources, the most important are Hansard, the Parliamentary Blue Books, and the memoirs of Palmerston's colleagues.

Her Majesty the Queen graciously permitted me to examine four documents in the Royal Archives at Windsor.

I wish to thank Lord Brabourne and the Broadlands Trustees for permission to see a selected number of documents in that section of the Broadlands Papers which is under their control; Captain R. D. Jeune, Viscount Lambton, the Reverend N. J. Overton, and Mr. John Pointing for entrusting to me the manuscripts in their possession; the Earl of Arran, for private information about Lady Palmerston and her family; Mr. William Collier, for private information about Palmerston's visit to his great-grandfather, Lord Monkswell; Mr. A. G. Geddes, for information about Palmerston's dealings with the local authorities at Romsey; Dr. Michael Smith, for his researches and explanations about the career of Sir William Adams and early nineteenth-century ophthalmology; Mr Peter Grant and my mother, Mrs. Ursula Ridley, for encouragement and advice at the manuscript stage; Mr. Baillie, Miss Felicity Ranger and the staff of the Historical Manuscripts Commission for their help and hospitality; the staff of the Manuscripts Room of the British Museum and the London Library; Mr. Mackworth-Young and the staff of the Royal Archives at Windsor; Mr. John Arnold, Brigadier G. R. Grove, Mr. and Mrs. Henry Hellmann, the Hon. John Jolliffe and Dr. Edmund Ronald for undertaking research and supplying information on various subjects; Mr Antony Evans, for helping me with the proofs; and my son, John Ridley, for his help in arranging my notes and typescript.

The cover illustration has been reproduced by kind permission of Earl Mountbatten of Burma, the Trustees of the Broadlands Collection and the Rt. Hon. Mr. Speaker, House of Commons, where it is on loan (photograph by John Freeman). This was the portrait presented to Lady Palmerston by her husband's supporters in June 1850, at the time of the debate about Don Pacifico. The other illustrations are reproduced by kind permission of the Trustees of the National Portrait Gallery, the Hon. Lady Salmond (plate 2, from the Cowper Collection at Panshanger, photograph by A. C. Cooper), the Trustees of the Tate Gallery, the Mansell Collection, the Trustees of the Broadlands Archives, Lady Brocket, the Victoria and Albert Museum.

Although scholars would doubtless have preferred references in footnote form at the bottom of the page, the majority of readers find footnotes distracting, and they have therefore been placed at the end of the book, despite the slight inconvenience which this may cause to the minority.

JASPER RIDLEY

Chapter One

The Young Harry Temple

On 18 October 1865, two days before his eighty-first birthday, the British Prime Minister, Lord Palmerston, died. His lifetime had been a period of extraordinary change, and a link between two different eras. When the news of his birth reached the tenants on his father's estates at Romsey, the oldest of them could remember hearing Mayor Walter Bell proclaim William and Mary after the Revolution of 1688; when he died, his funeral procession was seen by children who lived to hear Churchill announce over the radio the unconditional surrender of Germany in 1945. When he was born, Louis XVI was King of France, Frederick the Great and Catherine the Great reigned in Prussia and Russia, and the Continental Congress was formulating a Constitution for the United States of America; he died six months after Lee's surrender at Appomatox, when Napoleon III and Bismarck were in power. At his birth the population of Britain was about 9,000,000, of whom over eighty per cent lived in the country and worked in agriculture; at his death it was 25,000,000, of whom nearly sixty per cent lived in towns and worked in industry. Four days before he was born, the people of Romsey saw a glimpse of the future when Jean Pierre Blanchard, one of the first men ever to fly through the air, landed in a balloon in a field outside the town; but no one had ever travelled from London to Edinburgh in less than three days. In 1865 the journey took eight hours. Railways, steamships, gas light, the electric telegraph, the hot-air blast, the steam hammer, the Channel under-water cable, the London Underground, anaesthetics and photography, all came during his lifetime.

As the world changed during Palmerston's life, Palmerston changed with it. He began his political career as a junior minister in a Tory government that was one of the most reactionary and repressive that has ever ruled in Britain. He ended as the darling of at least one section of the Radicals, and one of the founders of the modern Liberal Party. In 1825 he was denounced by Cobbett as a cruel landlord and a brutal oppressor of the poor; in 1850 Princess Metternich thought that he was a more dangerous Red than Louis Blanc. His character, as well as his political complexion, changed over the years. There seem to have been at least three Palmerstons. The young Palmerston is a kind and charming young man, but a little soft and feckless in character; he is liked by everyone, but respected by very few. The middle-aged Palmerston is forceful, arrogant, and supremely competent, intensely disliked by many, but universally respected and feared. The old Palmerston is a great statesman and father-figure, the hero of the nation, who is wise and patient as well as exuberant and gay.

The first Palmerston was painted lolling on a garden bank, with knee-breeches and lace cravat, one stockinged leg crossed over the other, with a lazy, vapid expression on his face; a perfect picture of a young Lord Foppington of Regency days. The portrait of the second Palmerston shows him surrounded by his despatches, able and forceful, with a touch of arrogance about him. The third Palmerston of the daguerreotype photographs is a magnificent old man, with a great head and a noble presence. The first Palmerston was known as 'Lord Cupid'; the second as 'Lord Pumicestone'; the third as 'good old Pam'.

Henry John Temple, the eldest child of the second Viscount Palmerston, was born at his father's town house at 4, Park Street, Westminster – now 20, Queen Anne's Gate – on the south side of St. James's Park, at seven o'clock in the evening of Wednesday, 20 October 1784. He was christened at St. Margaret's, Westminster, on 23 November. Though the family had come to London for Lady Palmerston's confinement, the people of Hampshire, where Lord Palmerston had his country seat of Broadlands at Romsey, were not left out of the celebrations. A great ball was given for the county gentry at Winchester, which impressed the family friend Gilbert Elliot, the future Lord Minto, by its magnificence.

The Temples were descended from an old English family. Seven generations earlier, William Temple, a gentleman of Dorset, had entered the dangerous field of Elizabethan politics, and had emerged in the reign of James I with a knighthood and the office of Master of Trinity College, Dublin. The family thus began a most profitable connexion with Ireland. His son, Sir John Temple, was made Master of the Rolls in Ireland, and a member of the Privy Council of England, by Charles I; but he supported the Parliament in the Civil War, and became one of their leading propagandists. His denunciations of the atrocities committed by the Irish Catholics during their rebellion in Ulster in 1641 were widely used to justify Cromwell's savage reprisals eight years later; and when the Irish Catholic landowners were expropriated, and deported beyond the Shannon, Sir John Temple was granted part of the confiscated lands. This did not prevent him from making a timely change, like so many others, in 1660, and continuing in occupation of his lands and of his official position under Charles II.

His eldest son was Sir William Temple, the famous statesman and author; and a younger son, the second Sir John Temple, also followed successfully in his father's footsteps. Having been appointed Solicitor-General for Ireland by Charles II, he found no difficulty in retaining his appointment under the Catholic James; but when Tyrconnel roused the Irish Catholics in James's support, Sir John departed from Ireland in good time and joined the Revolution of 1688. He was attainted as a traitor, and his lands were forfeited, by the Irish Catholic Parliament next year; but it was William, not James, who triumphed at the Boyne, and Sir John Temple, promoted to be Attorney-General for Ireland and Speaker of the Irish House of Commons, was restored to his lands and granted several more estates which had been forfeited by the defeated Catholics. While the new penal code prohibited Catholics from holding office, disinherited them in favour of Protestant relatives, and even made it a criminal offence for a Catholic

to own a horse, Sir John Temple thrived under the Protestant
Succession; and when he died in 1704, he left a son, Henry
Temple, who carried the family fortunes still further. When he
was a child of seven he was appointed to a sinecure clerkship
worth £2,000 a year in the Court of Exchequer; and in 1723 he
was created Viscount Palmerston of Palmerston in County
Dublin.

The first Lord Palmerston then entered the quieter world
of eighteenth-century English politics. As an Irish peer he was
not eligible to sit in the English House of Lords, but could
enter the House of Commons, where he sat as MP for East
Grinstead in Sussex, Bossiney in Cornwall, and Weobley in
Herefordshire. He lived at his father's house at East Sheen, and
bought Broadlands as a second country estate. He married
as his first wife the daughter of a Governor of the Bank of England. He outlived his son, and when he died in 1757, he was
succeeded by his grandson, the second Viscount Palmerston,
who became the father of the great Lord Palmerston.

The second Viscount Palmerston may be described, much
more accurately than his famous son, as an eighteenth-century
figure. The son was only fifteen when the eighteenth century
ended, and only four when the French Revolution began; he
was in every way a child of the post-1789 world, and was
greatly influenced by the French and Industrial Revolutions.
But his father, the second Viscount, who lived from 1739 to
1802, was a typical eighteenth-century aristocrat. He inherited
from his father and mother an income of about £11,000 per
annum, of which £6,000 came from the rents of some 10,000
acres of agricultural land around Sligo, on the West coast of
Ireland, £2,000 from rents of land in Hampshire, Yorkshire
and Northamptonshire, and nearly £3,000 from sound invest-
ments in stocks and shares. This was not a vast income in comparison with the £100,000 a year which some of the largest
landowners received in rents; but it was more than enough at
a time when he paid each of his servants about £25 a year. His
direct taxes, including the rates on his London house and the
two country mansions, and the carriage tax – the eighteenth-
century equivalent of the modern Road Vehicle Excise Duty
– amounted altogether to £339 a year, or sevenpence in the £.

He lived extravagantly, and enlarged the houses at East Sheen and Broadlands, making Broadlands into a magnificent residence with the help of Capability Brown and at a cost of £23,000. He contributed generously to local charities at Romsey, but he had no feelings of obligation towards his Irish tenants, and never invested any money in his lands in Sligo. These tenants had neither the knowledge, the energy, nor the incentive to improve the land, and, like all the Irish peasantry, lived in great poverty, and came to depend entirely on the potato for their diet. They went short of food every year during the 'meal months' of June, July and August, before the next potato crop was ready; and when the crop failed, they died of starvation. In 1739, one-fifth of the population of Ireland died of hunger. The death of three and a half per cent of the population during the great famine of 1847 shocked Britain, Europe and America; but hardly anyone in England cared in 1739, and historians have hardly troubled to refer to the incident.

The second Viscount Palmerston took part in English politics, but in a desultory way, and more from a sense of public duty than from ambition or interest. At the age of twenty-two he was elected to the House of Commons, and remained an MP till his death forty years later, sitting in turn for East Looe in Cornwall, Southampton, Hastings, Boroughbridge in Yorkshire, Newport in the Isle of Wight, and Winchester. He sat for eleven years on the Board of Admiralty, and was then transferred to the Treasury Board during the American War of Independence. Despite his personal friendship with Charles James Fox, he was always a Government, rather than an Opposition, man, like his son was later to be. His political attitude was very different from that of his Cromwellian great-great-grandfather. He was one of those Whigs who held the view, which seemed so illogical to Disraeli and Bernal Osborne, that Cromwell was bad and William III was good. The Temples and their friends believed firmly in government by aristocracy under constitutional monarchy, and that the Revolution of 1688 was the only justifiable revolution in history.

But the second Viscount was much more interested in literature, art and science than in politics. He was a member of the Garrick Club and the Dilettanti set, a personal friend of Garrick, Dr. Johnson, Sir Joshua Reynolds, Gibbon and Sheridan, and a patron of the theatre and of aspiring playwrights. He was a pall-bearer at the funerals of Garrick and Reynolds. He was a great connoisseur of paintings and sculptures, on which he spent £8,000 during his lifetime, and often went to Holland, Germany and Italy to buy works of art and to enlarge his knowledge and culture. Like all eighteenth-century intellectuals, he was not a narrow specialist, and studied the sciences as well as the arts. He was a friend of Herschel, and installed a telescope at Broadlands in order to watch the stars. He was also a great believer in medical progress, and arranged for all his children to be inoculated against smallpox. The future Prime Minister, who was known as Harry in the family, was inoculated in May 1787, when he was two-and-a-half, along with his younger sister Frances, who was fifteen months old. This was nine years before Jenner first vaccinated a child with cowpox. The Palmerston children were inoculated with a mild dose of smallpox itself, a practice which had been quite widespread among the higher classes in England since Lady Mary Wortley Montagu had introduced it from Turkey sixty years earlier. The chances of dying from the inoculation, though much higher than they would be in the future, with vaccination, were less than five per cent; but when the three younger Palmerston children were inoculated in 1791, the two-year-old Mary died. The second Viscount was deeply grieved, but his faith in inoculation and in medical progress was unshaken.

The second Viscount had married when he was twenty-seven, but his wife had died in childbirth less than two years later, after which he had consoled himself with a series of casual affairs with a succession of English and foreign actresses and women of the town. But at forty-three he married again, after a romantic encounter. He fell from his horse when riding through Dublin, and was carried into the nearest house, which belonged to Benjamin Mee, a wealthy merchant of the City of London. He was nursed by Mee's daughter Mary, and fell in love with her. In January 1783 she became Lady Palmerston, and a month later was presented to the King and Queen.

From her portraits, Lady Palmerston does not appear to

have been a great beauty, but she was generally considered to be so, and had several admirers. She was as popular among the aristocracy in London as she was with her middle-class neighbours in Hampshire. Her active social life and her love of the theatre made her a favourite in society and with her husband's theatrical friends; and the wives of the doctors and curates in the villages near Romsey were delighted at her gracious informality when she dropped in at their houses on her country walks. Some people did not like her. Lord Glenbervie described her as 'a great protectress of the class of demi-rips' because she invited 'women of equivocal character' to her parties in town; but he thought that she was 'a good-natured, obliging woman'. Plumer Ward, who became a political colleague and personal friend of her famous son, said that he detested her because 'she was so fawning and mean', and because she was prepared to resort to any baseness in order to marry off her ugly daughter to 'that monster' Lord Ashburton. But Lady Glenbervie thought that in saying this, Ward had slandered three people in one sentence. When Sheridan and his wife stayed at Broadlands in April 1786, Mrs. Sheridan was impressed, not only with 'a good-natured poetical stuttering Viscount', but with the manners of the merchant's daughter, 'who, tho' she *did* squeeze thru' the City Gates into a Viscountess, bears her blushing honours without shaking them at you every moment'.

Despite Lady Palmerston's exhausting round of social functions, which made Lord Minto say that she made 'such toil of pleasure', she gave birth to five children in just over five years. After Harry was born in October 1784, he was followed by his sister Fanny in February 1786, by William in January 1788, Mary in January 1789, and Elizabeth in March 1790. All the children survived to adult life except Mary. Harry was delicate as a small child, and his parents continued to be anxious about his health even after he went to the university; but he survived the rigours of the first winter of his life, which was one of the coldest on record, and when the future Lord Minto visited Lady Palmerston in London in December 1785 to hear the latest gossip about Mrs. Fitzherbert's secret marriage to the Prince of Wales, he found that Harry was in much better health, and was 'a fine, eager, lively, good-humoured boy.' In September 1789 Harry was taken abroad. The family accompanied Lord Palmerston on a six weeks' journey through the Austrian Netherlands and the German principalities in search of works of art for his collection. They went as far south as Mainz and returned by Düsseldorf and Malines, where Harry celebrated his fifth birthday. In the Netherlands they ran into a revolution, both at Liège on the outward journey and at Brussels on the way home. The repercussions of the French Revolution were already being felt beyond the frontiers of France; but the Palmerstons emerged unscathed, and had reached England by 2 November.

The second Viscount Palmerston was hostile to the French Revolution from the very beginning. His friend Fox had applauded the taking of the Bastille in July 1789; but Burke had immediately denounced the revolution, and Lord Palmerston agreed with him. While many of his Whig friends had their eyes fixed on the attempts of Mirabeau and La Fayette to create a constitutional monarchy on the English model, Lord Palmerston saw the excesses of the mob, the hanging of the most hated *aristos* on the lamp-posts, and the burning of the *châteaux* by the peasants all over France, as a very dangerous threat to peace and order in Europe. It was perhaps with the hope of changing Lord Palmerston's opinions that Fox sent him to Paris in 1791 on a mission to the moderate revolutionary leaders; but his visit only made him more hostile than ever to the revolution. In a letter to Lady Palmerston he described how the inhabitants of a village near Lyons had seized a gentleman in his château, cut him into pieces in front of his wife, and roasted and ate the pieces. He was receptive to every story he was told by the counter-revolutionaries whom he met in France; but he was nevertheless prepared to take his own family into the hornet's nest.

On 20 June 1792 the Paris mob entered the Tuileries Palace, and forced the King and Queen to wear the red cap of Liberty. A few days later, Danton and the leaders of the Jacobin Club decided to seize power, and sent to Marseilles for revolutionary elements of the National Guard to come to Paris to seize the Tuileries and disarm the King's Swiss Guard. On 30 July the Marseillais marched into Paris singing the *Chanson de l'armée du Rhin,* which would henceforth be known as the *Marseillaise*; and two days later Lord Palmerston and his family arrived. Lord Palmerston had sold his London house in Park Street, and bought a larger one on the south side of Hanover Square; and he decided to take his wife and children on a two-year holiday in Italy and Switzerland while his new house was being enlarged. On 27 July 1792 they left London, travelling in a convoy of carriages with their valets, lady's maids, nurses and other servants, and reached Paris on 1 August.

In the Tuileries, Louis XVI and Marie Antoinette, though expecting the worst, carried on their daily lives as far as possible, as if nothing had occurred; and while the Marseillais camped in the Champs Elysées and prepared for the assault on the palace, Lady Gower, the wife of the English Ambassador, presented Lord and Lady Palmerston at Court, as she would have done in normal times. The Queen was particularly gracious to them, and they spoke to the Dauphin, who, Lady Palmerston noted, was a child of about Harry's age; but an officer of the Guard, who was an old friend of Lady Palmerston, showed her the place where the mob had entered on 20 June, and told her that he feared that the National Guard who were defending the palace would desert to the revolutionaries when the attack came. Lady Palmerston decided that the sooner they left France, the better, and that she would view the splendours of Paris at some other time, 'when liberty is not at such a height'. On 6 August they obtained their travel papers from the revolutionary authorities at the Hotel de Ville, who, according to Lady Palmerston, were most courteous and obliging, and next morning they left Paris in their convoy of carriages. They ran into trouble as they approached the barrier in the Faubourg St Antoine, the revolutionary sector on the eastern end of the city. The first coach, containing Lord and Lady Palmerston and Harry, passed safely through, but the other carriages, in which the younger children and the servants were travelling, were stopped by the mob in St Antoine. They were not allowed to proceed until they had been questioned by a revolutionary committee; but thanks to the personal intervention of Santerre, the commander of the revolutionary militia of St Antoine, they were permitted to rejoin their parents and Harry at Charenton. When they reached Lyons, they heard that Santerre's militia and the Marseillais had stormed the Tuileries on 10 August. The National Guard deserted, as Lady Palmerston's friend had feared, but the Swiss fought valiantly. In September the Convention deposed the King and proclaimed a republic. Louis XVI and Marie Antoinette and the Dauphin were sent as prisoners to the Temple and never emerged alive from their captivity.

The events of 10 August shaped the future for young Harry and for all the members of his generation. His politics and his outlook throughout his life were deeply affected by the overthrow of the French monarchy and the events which followed from it, and it is a strange coincidence that, at the age of seven, he should have been almost an eye-witness of this revolution. But it is unlikely that he was personally affected by his experiences in Paris in August 1792. Three years before, an older boy, the sixteen-year-old Count Clemens von Metternich, had been a student at Strasbourg University and had seen the town hall stormed by a revolutionary crowd. He never forgot the scene, and for the rest of his life had a fear and hatred of revolution and mob violence.

As the Palmerstons travelled south through France, they met groups of revolutionary volunteers on the roads marching to the north to join the army which was facing the Prussians near Verdun. A month later, these untrained enthusiasts defeated the invaders at Valmy and saved the revolution; in the words of Goethe, who was present, the cannonade of Valmy announced the birth of a new historical era. By this time the Palmerston cortège had passed safely into Switzerland. They went to Lausanne to see Lord Palmerston's friend Edward Gibbon, who had retired there to write his *History of the Decline and Fall of the Roman Empire*, and then went to Italy for the winter, travelling by Turin, Genoa, Parma, Bologna and Rome to Naples, where they arrived two days before Christmas. They spent the rest of the winter at the Neapolitan Court. The English Ambassador at Naples was Sir William Hamilton, whose wife Emma had not yet met Nelson, but had already been the mistress of several prominent men. Opinions differed widely about Emma Hamilton; many people in so-society were disgusted at the immorality and vulgarity of the blacksmith's daughter, but many others – women as well as men – liked and respected her, and she had won the intimate friendship of the Queen of Naples. Lady Palmerston liked Lady Hamilton, though she thought that her mother, Mrs. Cadogan, was unspeakable. Lady Palmerston herself was frowned upon by some of the straiter ladies at Naples, because she played faro with her husband; but whatever vices the Palmerstons may have had, heavy gambling was not one of them, and Lord Palmerston never lost more than £30 a year at play.

By this time, England was at war with the French Revolution. In November 1792 the National Convention in Paris issued its declaration in which it promised support to all foreign peoples who were struggling to overthrow their tyrants; in January Louis XVI was executed, and war was declared. There was violent indignation in England at the King's execution, and feeling was even stronger at Naples, where the Queen, Maria Carolina, was the sister of Marie Antoinette. Lady Palmerston declared that the execution of Louis XVI was a premeditated murder of which history had no example. Nelson said much the same to the Bey of Tunis; but the Bey reminded him that once upon a time the English, too, had killed their King.

In April the Palmerstons set off for the north, where the climate in summer was more healthy than in Naples. They took with them an additional member of the travelling party, a Signor Gaetano, who had been engaged as Harry's tutor. He taught him Italian, and Harry learned to speak and write it fluently. They stayed in Rome, Verona and Milan, and then went to Switzerland, where they installed Harry and the other children, with the tutor and their servants, in a delightful house on a hill on the outskirts of Berne, while Lord and Lady Palmerston travelled through Switzerland. The children stayed here for a month in August 1793, Year I of the French Republic. While preparations began in Paris for the trial of Marie Antoinette, and Napoleon Bonaparte took up his first command against the counter-revolutionaries and Allied forces at Toulon, Harry studied with Signor Gaetano, learned to ride and picnicked in the sun. When Lady Palmerston returned she found him as brown as a gipsy.

In September they crossed the St. Bernard pass and returned to Italy for another winter; but their journey south was interrupted at Verona, where Harry fell seriously ill with a local fever which was particularly prevalent after hot summers. The services of the best physician in Verona were engaged, the high temperature was brought under control, and after three weeks he was well enough to travel. They had reached Naples by Christmas, and again spent the first four months of the year at the Neapolitan Court. In May 1794 they set out for England, going leisurely by Venice, Innsbruck and Munich to King George III's Hanoverian kingdom in North Germany. From Hanover and Osnabrück they went to The Hague, and visited the British Army under the Duke of York which was defending Holland from French invasion. They reached Harwich on 2 October, shortly before Harry's tenth birthday, after an absence from England of twenty-six months which had cost Lord Palmerston nearly £9,000.

In May 1795 Harry went to Harrow. By this time the great public schools, most of which had been founded two or three hundred years before by wealthy benefactors for the education of poor children, had been taken over by the aristocracy and wealthier classes; but the educational reformers had not yet persuaded the masters to teach discipline and moral values to their charges. The boys learned little except Latin and Greek, and a smattering of English literature. They lived well and drank heavily, and learned to fight with their fists. There were still a few local boys from the poorer classes at Harrow. In 1571 the country yeoman, John Lyon, had left money to found a school at Harrow for the boys of the parish. But Lyon had stipulated that boys from outside the parish could also be admitted; and during the eighteenth century the Governors took advantage of this loophole to admit them, at high fees, in such numbers that they soon constituted a large majority of the boys. By 1795 most of the inhabitants of Harrow were no longer sending their boys to the school, because of the way in which they were treated by their wealthy schoolfellows. The local children were 'being constantly scoffed at and ill-treated by the other boys, and their lives not only rendered uncomfortable but often in great danger, insomuch that parents of such children have been obliged to take them away from the school'. Such, at least, were the allegations made by the church-wardens of Harrow and their witnesses when they brought an action in the Court of Chancery to prevent the Governors from admitting 'foreigners' from outside the parish to the school. The petitioners would have had more sympathy from the Court a hundred and fifty years earlier or later; but in 1810 they had little chance of success, and judgment was given against them.

There is a great deal of information about Harry Temple's life at Harrow, but much of it is rather suspect. Schoolboys do not always tell the whole truth in their letters to their parents, and nor do septuagenarian Prime Ministers when they talk about their schooldays on Speech Day sixty years on. A man's reminiscences of his school-fellows may also be affected by his consciousness of events during the intervening years. The story of Harry's pillow fight with George Gordon, afterwards fourth Earl of Aberdeen, in which the gallant Temple drove the cowering Gordon before him, is vouched for by several eye-witnesses, and may well be true; but the tale was told after the great war leader, Palmerston, had replaced the pacifist appeaser Aberdeen as Prime Minister during the Crimean War. The recollections of old men of young Temple thrashing hefty bullies twice his size may have been coloured by their more recent memories of the cartoons in *Punch* showing 'young Pam, a plucky boy' rolling up his sleeves as he prepares to take on the French bully and the Russian bear. As for Harry's statement in after years that the pleasure of hearing the rebukes and exhortations of his headmaster, Dr. Drury, was almost enough to tempt the boys to do wrong, the pleasure may have been greater seen in retrospect from Downing Street than in anticipation by the Sixth Former in Bromley's house.

But Harry certainly learned to engage in fisticuffs, for it was considered essential for a gentleman to be a competent pugilist, and he could not have survived at Harrow unless he had mastered the art. In September 1870, when Bismarck's armies were marching on Paris, and the crowds of mid-

Victorian holiday-makers were invading the Isle of Wight, a retired Admiral at Ryde wrote an account of his schooldays in less democratic times, seventy-three years before. Sir Augustus Clifford told Bulwer that when he first went to Harrow in 1797, he and two other boys were fags to Harry Temple, Viscount Althorp and Lord Duncannon, who messed together. Temple was easily the most merciful of the three towards the fags, and was considered to be the best-tempered and most plucky boy in the school. Sir Augustus remembered one occasion on which Temple fought a boy named Salisbury 'behind school'. Salisbury was much the larger of the two, but Temple would not give in. Afterwards Mother Bromley had to wash Temple's bloody nose and treat his black eye.

Harry's readiness to fight big bullies is all the more praiseworthy because he was continually being made conscious of the fact that his health was delicate. Lady Palmerston was in the habit of ordering her carriage and driving to Harrow whenever Harry was not well. She had made difficulties about sending Harry to Harrow in the first place, and Lord Palmerston had had to spend a good deal of time assuring her that Harry would have a comfortable room and would be well looked after by a reliable maid-servant. She had wanted to supply him with a special bed and a nightshirt, though her husband had pointed out that these would make Harry feel ridiculous at school. Lord Palmerston got his way about the bed, but had to give in about the nightshirt, because it was very cold for May when Harry first went to Harrow, and he found out that two or three other boys had nightshirts. Lady Palmerston had some excuse for over-anxiety, because Harry had had a good deal of trouble with his skin as a small child, and had been very ill at Verona; and as she had lost one child through Lord Palmerston's belief in inoculation against smallpox, he may have found it difficult to take a tough attitude about Harry's health. Mrs. Bromley, who had taken the black eye and bloody nose so casually, was very alarmed when she heard that he had bathed in the river when he was feeling hot after exercise, for the danger of his catching cold had been firmly implanted in her by Lady Palmerston.

He played cricket, went coursing after rabbits, and took part in the popular, but forbidden, sport of stone-throwing in a place that was said to be an old sea-beach. His physical strength was commemorated in a school song, which refers to 'Temple's frame of iron', a description which would have surprised his mother. On one occasion he took part in a school strike, when the headmaster did not declare a half-holiday which had been expected. The boys refused to go into school after dinner, but when the headmaster threatened to expel the older boys, they held a meeting and decided to give way. A few years later, Lord Byron organized another strike at Harrow. The most serious trouble occurred in 1808, when the boys seized the school, placarded it with the slogan 'Liberty and Rebellion', and set up road blocks on the London road to prevent the authorities from sending messages for help. The ringleaders were expelled, and George III congratulated the headmaster on his firmness.

Harry and his brother William, who joined him at Harrow in 1798, spent their holidays at Broadlands, where Signor Gaetano, who had come to England with the Palmerstons, continued during the holidays to teach Harry the aspects of education which were neglected at Harrow. As the boys grew older, Lord Palmerston brought them to Hanover Square during the Christmas holidays, and introduced them to his society friends, and took them to the theatre; but he does not seem to have succeeded in making Harry share his love of the theatre, for Harry never showed any interest in it in later life. He was much keener to be taught to shoot, because his friends at Harrow went shooting in the holidays.

Lord Palmerston, though he was by now heavily in debt because of his expenditure on works of art and the inability of his agents to collect his Irish rents during the rebellion of 1798, was careful to warn Harry against the evils of gambling and excessive drinking. In fashionable society, and particularly among army officers, it was not unusual to drink between twenty and thirty glasses of claret and port every night at dinner; but Wilberforce and the 'Clapham Saints' were introducing a new morality, or at least a new hypocrisy, among many sections of the aristocracy. Wilberforce had founded a society to prevent the spread of drunkenness among the lower classes,

and he urged men of position, if they did not feel inclined to
renounce alcohol, to drink in secret, so that they might not
set a bad example to their inferiors.

Lord Palmerston was successful in discouraging Harry from
indulging in the delights of the bottle. When Harry was thirteen, he received a letter from a friend of his own age, Francis
Hare, who was living in Bologna. 'I hope you take no part',
wrote Francis, 'in those vices which are common to a public
school, such as I suppose Harrow, as swearing and getting
drunk; but I imagine the son of a gentleman well taught cannot partake in things like these'. His young correspondent
added some more words of advice on another subject: 'I still
persist in my opinion of never marrying, and I suppose you
think the same, as you must have read as well as myself of the
many faults and vices of women'. Harry Temple wrote a letter
of reply from Harrow on 29 March 1798, and reassured Hare:
'I am perfectly of *your* opinion concerning drinking and
swearing, which, though fashionable at present, I think extremely ungentlemanlike; as for getting drunk, I can find no
pleasure in it.' Throughout his life, he always drank very little
alcohol; but he did not agree with Hare about women. 'I cannot agree with you about marriage though I should be by no
means precipitate about my choice.'

During the summer holidays of 1799, Harry went on a riding tour of the south-east coast with his father. They rode to
Walmer, where Harry was to reside, sixty-two years later, as
Lord Warden of the Cinque Ports – a post then held by the
Prime Minister, William Pitt – and on, through Dover, Hythe
and Romney, to Brighton, where they participated in the social
season at the beginning of September. Lord Palmerston
bought tickets for himself and Harry for a fashionable charity
supper and dance; but after Harry had danced, his father removed him before the supper and the heavy drinking began.
Then they went to London, and Lord Palmerston took Harry
and his younger brother to the House of Commons for the
first time, where Harry shook hands with Mr. Pitt himself. In
the members' dining room they found themselves sitting next
to a group of Radical MPs, among whom was Charles Grey,
who thirty-one years later became Prime Minister and chose

Harry as his Foreign Secretary. Grey strongly sympathized with the French Revolution, and was considered by the Government to be dangerous and subversive; and Lord Palmerston was amused to hear Grey and his friends talk with exaggerated concern about the British defeat in Holland, because he was convinced that really they were delighted at the news.

The majority of Englishmen of all classes were aggressively patriotic and anti-French, and the leaders of the pro-French party were often in danger of their lives. The Palmerstons and their circle were enthusiastic supporters of Pitt and the war party, and Lady Palmerston, who had been so favourably impressed with the civility of the local revolutionary leaders whom she had encountered in France in 1792, now referred to them as 'savages' and 'barbarians' in her letters. But occasionally a small incident would restore her faith in human nature. One day she walked, with a companion, across the fields from Hanover Square to Hampstead, and at one point on their journey the two ladies had some difficulty in climbing through a fence. A working man, who was passing, came to their assistance and helped them with the fence. Lady Palmerston was touched, 'as a different demeanour has of late appeared in the lower rank of people since the fatal revolution'.

Chapter Two

Edinburgh and Cambridge: The First Elections

Harry left Harrow in the summer of 1800. At Speeches that year he had recited 'The Bard'; it was not an original choice, for it was one of the favourite poems for the English recitation. Harry declaimed, in appropriate style, Thomas Gray's 'Pindaric Ode' about the old Welsh bard who, standing on a 'rock whose haughty brow frowns o'er old Conway's foaming flood', confronts 'the first Edward' as he descends 'down the steep of Snowdon's shaggy side', after his conquest of Wales. The bard, after proclaiming 'Ruin seize thee, ruthless King', prophesies the downfall of the House of Plantagenet. It was the last time in his life that Harry Temple denounced English imperialism.

Though Harry was to go to Cambridge in due course, his father had decided to send him in the meantime to Edinburgh University to study the new science of political economy with Professor Dugald Stewart. This was a surprising decision for a Tory like Lord Palmerston to take, for Edinburgh University had a reputation for Radicalism, and Professor Stewart had come under serious attack during the anti-Jacobin witchhunt in Britain. But Stewart had been a colleague of Adam Smith's, and, though he is chiefly remembered today as a moral philosopher, was considered to be the leading exponent of political economy. In November 1800 Lord Palmerston took Harry to Edinburgh and entrusted him to Stewart's care.

Harry became a very diligent student, filling many notebooks and imbibing the doctrines of his teacher and Adam Smith. He accepted the doctrines wholeheartedly, and never changed his views on economics. In 1853, when he was Home Secretary, a publisher asked him to act as editor of an edition of Stewart's lectures on political economy which was about to be published. He declined on the grounds that he was too busy, but strongly advised the publisher to bring out the book, and stated that he thought it unlikely that it would be necessary to make any alterations, as Stewart's opinions, 'being founded in Truth', would not be out of date. Throughout all his years at the Foreign Office, he was always ready, at the least excuse, to include in his despatches to foreign governments an exposition of Stewart's views on the merits of free trade.

Dugald Stewart, perhaps because he had been suspected of Jacobinism, refused to be drawn into political or controversial arguments with his students in his home, and confined himself at meals to general conversation and personal reminiscences of Adam Smith. There were, however, a number of active Radicals and advanced Whigs among the students at Edinburgh, including Francis Horner, who like Harry lodged with Stewart; Henry Brougham; Francis Jeffrey, who became the eminent Scottish Judge; and Lord Lansdowne's son, Henry Petty. But Harry Temple remained a Tory, and his closest friend was an old acquaintance from another Tory family, Gilbert Elliot, the son of Lord Minto. He had been sent to Edinburgh University because of Lord Palmerston's favourable reports on Professor Stewart's establishment. Minto, who had been granted his peerage for his services as Governor of Corsica during the two years that it had been British territory, was a close personal friend of Nelson's. He spent a great deal of time with Nelson and Lady Hamilton and her compliant husband at their house at Merton, and in his private correspondence wrote the most caustic comments on Emma's vulgarity and Nelson's vanity.

Both Minto and Lady Minto visited their son in Edinburgh, and were able to send glowing reports on Harry Temple to Lord and Lady Palmerston. They wrote that Harry was a charming, friendly and well-beloved young man, and a great favourite with Mrs. Stewart. Dugald Stewart himself w̲ equally enthusiastic. In April 1801, after Harry had bee̲ him for five months, Stewart wrote to Mr. Blane, wh̲ approached him on Lord Palmerston's behalf, th̲ ple had completely lived up to Blane's recommendation: his talents were uncommonly good, and he did them all possible justice by assiduous application. 'In point of temper and conduct', wrote Stewart, 'he is everything his friends could wish. Indeed, I cannot say that I have ever seen a more faultless character at his time of life, or one possessed of more amiable dispositions.' Lady Minto, it is true, was a little worried that Harry was not more boisterous, and thought that his only fault was ' a want of spirits belonging to his age'. But on one occasion she was pleasantly surprised when Harry, in a rare display of youthful energy, jumped over Mrs. Stewart's sofa and sprained his leg; and Lord Minto assured Lady Palmerston that Harry was a great favourite of his, as he had the two qualities of good sense and good humour.

Harry's excessively staid behaviour in Edinburgh is a little surprising, for he had been energetic enough at Harrow. Perhaps it was to some extent put on for the benefit of his parents' friends, for Harry was not encouraged to be more boisterous by the letters which he received from home. Lord and Lady Palmerston wrote to him regularly, urging him to take care of his health, not to catch cold, and not to eat or drink too much. Lord Palmerston, with his scientific interests, took an interest in up-to-date medicines, and had become a keen believer in the beneficial effect of rhubarb pills. He constantly reminded Harry of the importance of taking them. Harry, in his letters, assured his parents that he was taking rhubarb pills, that he ate nothing except one potato at his evening meal, and that he was, as far as possible, avoiding alcohol, though it was impossible to refuse to drink a glass or two at dinner with Professor Stewart's household. His health was not good while he was in Edinburgh. He was affected by the cold weather in the winter – he disliked the cold all his life – and suffered from headaches and dazzling in the eyes; but he was well enough to indulge in a good deal of shooting, walking and skating, and to play the Scottish game of golf, though he found it a poor substitute for cricket.

In January 1802, Lord Minto came to Edinburgh to see his son and Harry Temple. He must have found the Stewart household a change after the Nelson-Hamilton ménage at

Merton. He wrote to Lady Palmerston that he had never seen anything more delightful than Harry. Both Mr. and Mrs. Stewart had assured him that Harry 'is the only young man they ever knew in whom it is impossible to find any fault'; and he added: 'Diligence, capacity, total freedom from vice of every sort, gentle and kind disposition, cheerfulness, pleasantness and perfect sweetness are in the catalogue of properties by which we may advertise him if he should be lost'. The Foreign Office clerks of future years would not have recognised him from the advertisement.

In April 1802 Harry received an urgent summons to return to London, because his father was very ill. He left Edinburgh at once, accompanied by Gilbert Elliot, but he arrived too late, for Lord Palmerston died of cancer of the throat on 16 April when Harry was on the Great North Road. Lord Minto was with him when he died, and almost the last words which Lord Palmerston spoke were to condemn the peace with France, which he described in the words that Wilkes had used of the treaty which ended the Seven Years War – the 'peace which passeth all understanding'. Minto went to his house at Barnet to meet Harry, so that he could break the news himself; but when Harry and Gilbert Elliot arrived at Barnet at seven o'clock next morning, Minto's plan miscarried. He had given strict instructions to his own servants and the Palmerstons' that they were not to speak to Harry until he himself had seen him. But one of the servants mistook Gilbert for Harry. He brought Gilbert up to his father's room, saying 'Here is Mr. Temple, my Lord', and then ran down to Harry and casually told him of the event as a piece of interesting news. It was a great shock to Harry, for he had no idea that his father, who was only sixty-two, was in any danger; and he took the blow heavily, because he had in recent years been very close to his father. Six weeks later, he was still as dejected as ever, and Lord Minto considered this as a further sign that Harry, despite all his good qualities, lacked a certain resilience and strength of character. 'He is entirely silent', he wrote to his wife on 3 June, 'and at present dejected. He has too little spring for his age; but his heart and disposition, and indeed capacity, are good'.

So the new Lord Palmerston inherited, at the age of seventeen, his father's title, property and debts; but he did not immediately change his way of life. As he was still under age, his father had appointed his old friend the Earl of Malmesbury, and the Earl of Chichester, to be his guardians, and Lord Minto relieved him of his financial difficulties by taking over a lease of the house in Hanover Square, receiving what he called 'a most charming letter' from Harry on the subject. Lady Palmerston, who was deeply affected by her husband's death, was determined that his wishes for Harry should be carried out, and that he should complete his third year at Edinburgh before going on to Cambridge; so he returned to Dugald Stewart's for the autumn term in November.

Lord Malmesbury, though he had originally been a Whig, was now a prominent elder statesman of the Tory Party: after a long and distinguished career in the diplomatic service, which included a residence at the Court of Catherine the Great, he was considered to be a leading consultant on foreign affairs. He nevertheless approved of Dugald Stewart as a tutor for young Palmerston. 'Political economy is a very important and interesting subject', he wrote to Palmerston in November 1802. 'From everything I hear of Mr. Stewart, I have no doubt he will teach it on its right principles, and in the way which can best tend to qualify you to act as becomes you in the rank you hold in life, and in the part you will probably be called upon to act'. Lady Malmesbury was sure that neither Palmerston nor Gilbert Elliot would be corrupted by the political climate of Edinburgh. 'As to Jacobinism', she wrote, 'it is all stuff everywhere. A boy of nineteen may be seduced by a fair face, or led into gaming, or drinking, or racing, but nobody at the age cares about politics that is worth a farthing. It is, like the love of money, belonging to those who have exhausted or left behind them the light and cheerful pleasures of life'. Thus airily she dismissed a movement which was arousing the enthusiasm of many of the most gifted young men of the age.

Palmerston left Edinburgh in the summer of 1803, and after touring the Highlands and Wales, where he fell in love for the first time, he entered St. John's College, Cambridge, in October. He found that the system of education in Cambridge was different from that of Edinburgh. In Edinburgh it was more liberal, for there were no examinations, whereas in Cambridge the education was tuned to the necessity of passing examinations twice a year. In later years, Palmerston wrote that although the detailed facts that had to be learned in order to pass the Cambridge examinations were largely useless, and were forgotten as soon as the examination was over, the habit of mind acquired in preparing for the examinations was very useful. When the plan for establishing colleges in Ireland was discussed in the House of Commons in 1845, Palmerston took part in the debate, and said that, from his personal experiences at Edinburgh and Cambridge, he thought that there were advantages in both systems. Later, as Prime Minister, he supported the introduction of competitive examinations, in preference to patronage, as a method of selection for the civil service, though he was not blind to its defects.

But Palmerston himself encountered a difficulty about the examinations at Cambridge. The University was still governed by the statutes of Elizabeth I of 1570, under which noblemen had the privilege of obtaining their MA degree after two years' residence without passing their examinations. They were also entitled to other privileges. They were free from the discipline of the proctors; they were not obliged to attend lectures; and at dinner, in hall, they sat at a separate table and were served with additional dishes. The sizars, who had won scholarships to the University, were required, as their contribution to the cost of the scholarships, to act as personal servants to the noblemen undergraduates. In the seventeenth century this had caused much resentment and the sizars had been a revolutionary and Parliamentarian element in the royalist universities during the Civil War; but by Palmerston's time the system was generally accepted by a nation which rejected the French ideas of Liberty and Equality as strongly as it believed in the English ideal of Freedom from foreign and domestic tyranny and from governmental regulation.

This state of affairs might suit the ordinary aristocratic student, who had no wish to learn, and had come to Cambridge to get drunk, to incur large debts, and to bully his sizar servant. But Palmerston wished to sit for the examinations. As he was entitled to his degree by right of birth, he asked to be allowed to compete for honours; but this was not permitted. He was, however, allowed to sit for the College examinations, and did very well, winning first-class honours in every examination for which he entered. His general conduct, too, was exemplary. He took part in the social life of the University, and attended the shooting parties on the estates of the noblemen and gentry of Cambridgeshire; but he still avoided excessive drinking, and gambling. The lack of high spirits which worried Lord and Lady Minto were perhaps really only a studiousness and a desire to avoid the excesses of the loud and arrogant young swells of his generation. Palmerston seems to have impressed Dr. Outram, his tutor at St. John's, as favourably as he had impressed Mr. and Mrs. Dugald Stewart.

The war with France had again broken out, and Napoleon was massing his Grand Army at Boulogne for the invasion of England. When Palmerston passed through Doncaster on the journey south after finally leaving Edinburgh, the beacons were lit to warn the people that the French had landed, and a court-martial that was sitting there broke up as the officers ran to the top of the church steeple to see the smoke on Rundlestone Beacon; but it was a false alarm. All over the country, volunteers enrolled in the Militia and the Volunteers, and drilled. A unit was formed at St. John's College, with forty-six volunteers, and Palmerston was chosen as one of the three officers. The appointment may have been partly due to his rank, but this would not have been the only reason. He was afterwards chosen as Lieutenant-Colonel Commander of the Romsey Volunteers. At Romsey, too, there was a false report of an invasion; the Volunteers rounded up the women and children, according to plan, and sent them to a place of safety.

In January 1805 Lady Palmerston died of cancer at the age of fifty. This was another blow to Harry, but he was three years older than when his father died, and seems to have taken it with more composure. Only a few days after her death, he was replying from Broadlands to a letter of condolence from his Cambridge friend, Laurence Sulivan. 'Consolation is impossible: there are losses which nothing can repair; and griefs which time may fix and mellow, but never can obliterate. After the example, however, of fortitude and resignation set us by a being who was the model of every human excellence, it would be criminal in us not to imitate the resignation as well as every other perfection of her character. She was conscious, it is true, that she was but passing to that happiness which her virtues had secured her; and beheld with calmness and composure an event which, to the generality of mankind, comes clad with all the terrors of doubt'. This letter, written by a young man of twenty, may seem pompous to twentieth-century readers, but it shows dignity and self-control, as well as profound grief. His mother's death postponed the taking of his nobleman's degree.

In January 1806 the Prime Minister, William Pitt, died of strain and despair soon after hearing the news of Napoleon's victory at Austerlitz and the defeat of the Coalition which he had raised against France. The Tory Government broke up and resigned at once, and the King reluctantly brought the Whigs back to power after twenty-two years in opposition in Lord Grenville's coalition government. Pitt's death caused a by-election at Cambridge, where he had been one of the two members for the University seat. Lord Henry Petty, Lord Lansdowne's son, was nominated as a candidate by the more Radical section of the Whigs; the more conservative Whigs, who had no liking for the Radicals, put up Lord Althorp, the son of Lord Spencer, who had messed with Palmerston at Harrow. The Tories chose Palmerston as their candidate. He was just old enough to be eligible to sit in the House of Commons, having reached the age of twenty-one on 20 October 1805 – the day before the Battle of Trafalgar; but it was unusual to choose as a candidate for the University seat an undergraduate who had not yet been awarded his degree. He was persuaded to offer himself as a candidate by a group of fellows and graduates of St John's, especially by his tutor Dr. Outram, who was impressed by his intelligence and sobriety.

Petty was expected to win the seat, for the political tide was running in favour of the Whigs. He was only twenty-five, but had been in the House of Commons for the last two years as MP for Calne, the family seat in Wiltshire, and had distinguished himself, a few months earlier, by a powerful attack on

Pitt, in which he demanded the Prime Minister's impeachment. He was appointed Chancellor of the Exchequer in Lord Grenville's coalition Government; the office did not then have the great status that it acquired some forty years later, but it was one of the offices most sought after by rising young politicians, and always carried a seat in the Cabinet. This appointment made it necessary for Petty to seek re-election to the House of Commons, so he stood in the Cambridge by-election. The fact that he was a member of the Government was a great advantage to him, for office gave him the power of patronage. This was an important factor, for the electors did not vote by secret ballot, but openly cast their votes by word of mouth at the hustings. Petty also had the strong support of the Prince of Wales, who had always supported the Whigs in order to annoy his father the King, and the Prince wrote to many University men to urge them, if they valued his friendship, to vote for Petty.

The new government was a coalition of various hostile factions among the Whigs, and Lord Spencer became Home Secretary. It was an accepted tradition that the Home Secretary's son was entitled to be appointed as one of the Junior Lords of the Treasury, and the position was therefore given to Lord Althorp. So the situation arose that the Chancellor of the Exchequer and one of his colleagues in the Government were fighting against each other in the Cambridge by-election, which was almost as strange in 1806 as it would be today. Petty hoped that in view of Althorp's appointment to the Government he would withdraw from the Cambridge contest; but Althorp refused to do so. There was no love lost between the Petty and Spencer families, and Althorp, like Petty, had patronage at his disposal now that he was a minister. When Lord Ellenborough, the Lord Chief Justice, swore him in and gave him the seals of his office, he told him that this would be worth a hundred votes to him in the Cambridge by-election.

The split among the Whigs raised the hopes of the Tories, and some of them who had been prepared to adopt Palmerston in a hopeless contest now regretted that they had not got a stronger candidate than the pleasant and affable young man of twenty-one. But an attempt to nominate Lord Hadley in his place did not materialize, and Palmerston went into the contest with the support of the 'Johnians' of his college of St. John's and 130 promises of support. The election was conducted in a very friendly spirit. No meetings were ever held in contests for the University seat, the candidates relying only on one letter to the electors and personal canvassing. For a fortnight Palmerston, Petty and Althorp went around the colleges soliciting the votes of about six hundred electors, meeting each other continually, and exchanging anecdotes and assessing each other's chances. Lord Byron, who was an undergraduate at Trinity College, and had just celebrated his eighteenth birthday, felt very superior to them all. Disregarding Althorp, who was not expected to take many of the Whig votes, he thought that Petty had nothing to recommend him except his power of patronage as a minister, and Palmerston nothing whatever.

> Then would I view each rival wight,
> Petty and Palmerston survey,
> Who canvass there, with all their might,
> Against the next elective day.
> One on his power and place depends,
> The other on – the Lord knows what!
> Each to some eloquence pretends,
> But neither will convince by that.

The main political issue in the election, apart from the general unpopularity of the late Tory Government, was the slave trade. Fifteen years earlier, Wilberforce had shocked the House of Commons by revealing the inhuman cruelties and the high mortality in the slave ships in which blacks were transported from Africa to the West Indies. His motion for the abolition of the slave trade had been supported by Pitt and Fox, but was lost by 163 votes to 88. The second Viscount Palmerston had been in the House during that debate, and had been very disturbed by Wilberforce's revelations; but he had thought that they must be exaggerated, and that in any case the immediate abolition of the trade would not only injure British commerce, but would be in the worst interests of the slaves themselves. He therefore opposed abolition, but hoped

that the Government would take steps to remedy the worst in-
humanities of the passage. Many things had happened since
the great debate on the night of 18 April 1791. The slave
trade, and slavery itself, had been abolished by the Jacobin
government of France, and restored by Napoleon; a successful slave revolt had occurred in San Domingo, and had resulted in a massacre of all the white colonists in the island; and
Denmark had prohibited the slave trade. A bill to abolish the
slave trade in Great Britain had passed the House of Commons
and had been thrown out by the House of Lords. Pitt had withdrawn his support from the abolitionists; abolition had become associated with Jacobinism and the French Revolution;
and George III had cut Wilberforce at a reception. Abolition
was supported by all the Radicals, but by no means all the
Whigs; it was opposed by most of the peerage, by some of the
bishops, by admirals like Nelson and St. Vincent, and generally by the Tory Party. But some Tories were in favour of
abolition, and Wilberforce himself was a Tory.

The formation of the coalition government was a great
encouragement to the abolitionists. Fox, who became Foreign Secretary and the most powerful man in the Cabinet, was
determined to abolish the trade at once, and public opinion
was at last coming round in favour of abolition. Lord Henry
Petty therefore fought the Cambridge by-election very largely
on the slave trade issue. Palmerston's views on this subject, and
indeed on any subject, were not widely known; but his father
and his associates had always opposed abolition, and it was
assumed that he did the same. Henry Brougham, who was a
Radical and an ardent abolitionist, had known Palmerston at
Edinburgh, and thought of him as a typical young Tory peer
who would obviously be in favour of the slave trade. He wrote
to Zachary Macaulay that Palmerston was utterly unfit to be
an MP. 'I remember him well at Edinburgh, where he was at
college for several years, and what I know of his family and
himself increases a hundredfold my wish for Petty's success.
The family are enemies to abolition in a degree that scarcely
ever was exceeded. I presume that he is so himself. His maxim
is that of all the objects of ambition in the world, the life of
a courtier is the most brilliant. Don't you think that the friends

of the cause have the more reason to support Petty the more strenuously?'

Petty's policy on abolition won him the support of Wilberforce, to the great indignation of Palmerston's supporters. Wilberforce had supported Pitt through thick and thin in his war against the French Revolution and in his repression of Jacobin sympathizers at home, and was a prominent supporter of the Church, to which the Tories were devoted. Only a few days before, he had carried the banner at Pitt's funeral, while Petty had very recently gone as far as to suggest that Pitt should be impeached. He was also, like Palmerston, a Johnian. But for Wilberforce the slave trade question came first. Palmerston's supporters tried to counter the effect of Petty's stand on abolition by accusing him of being a Dissenter and an enemy of the Church. They accused him of having been educated by the hated Priestley, the Nonconformist minister who had been denounced as a Jacobin and atheist by the Tory press, and whose house and chapel had in consequence been destroyed by a 'Church and King' mob.

Petty was elected with 331 votes. Althorp obtained 145, and Palmerston 128. Althorp had done better, and Palmerston worse, than was expected. Palmerston had barely managed to get the votes of those electors who had been already pledged to him some days before, and had made no progress at all during the closing stages of the campaign. Wilberforce considered the result a triumph for abolition. 'Our great cause has been considerably accredited by what has passed at the Cambridge election', he wrote to Gisborne on 11 February. 'Lord Henry Petty got a deal of support, owing to his known zeal in it. His opponent, Lord Palmerston, lost much owing to his being supposed, mistakenly I believe, to be our enemy; and numbers declared they would not, though satisfied in all other points, vote for an anti-abolitionist'.

In view of Palmerston's later achievements in connexion with the suppression of the slave trade, it is strange to read the remarks of Brougham and Wilberforce in 1806. But they can hardly be blamed for their attitude. At Edinburgh, Palmerston had remained a Tory in a Radical atmosphere; and if he had not, perhaps, expressed the views about the desirability of a courtier's life which Brougham had ascribed to him, he had taken part in the social life of the young aristocracy instead of joining the political groups in which Brougham himself, and Horner – Palmerston's fellow-lodger at Dugald Stewart's – had been so active. At Cambridge he was on the point of taking his degree, without any hard work, by privilege of nobility; and he had been put forward as a candidate for Parliament by a group of Tories who were fighting Petty on the slave trade issue. Not everyone knew of his successes in his college examinations, or that he drank much less, and worked much harder, than most of his acquaintances; and no one had troubled to find out whether his ideas on abolition differed from those of his father and his political supporters. In fact, his opinions about the slave trade were changing, as public opinion among the Tories was changing. Palmerston was never a pioneer in support of reforms, but usually came round when public opinion shifted, not because of conscious political opportunism, but because he usually held the same opinions as did other Englishmen of his class, and of most other classes too. In the end, his position and practical experience sometimes enabled him to do more to achieve the reform than any of the Radical reformers who in earlier years had criticized him for his opposition to progress.

But Palmerston cannot have felt strongly about the slave trade in 1806, for he made no reference to abolition in the journal in which he wrote, at some length, his opinions about current affairs and politics. He often referred to party political intrigue and Cabinet-making at home, but was chiefly concerned with international affairs and the military events in Europe. He sometimes shows traces of the splendid self-confidence of youth, and knows much better than the Prussian generals on the spot how the battle of Jena should have been fought; but there are signs throughout of political shrewdness, good judgment and sound sense. His references to Napoleon as 'the usurper' clearly show his patriotic and Tory attitude, but there is no narrow partisanship or party rancour. When Fox died in September 1806 he praised the brilliancy of his genius, and placed him among the 'illustrious patriots whose names are 'consecrated by the applause of a grateful people'; but he thought that 'in the general delirium produced by the French Revolution', Fox had become 'infected with the disorder', and had 'connected himself with the most frantic of the reformers'.

Palmerston was firmly opposed to the peace party. 'Any peace at present would be ruinous', he wrote in his entry for 15 July 1806. 'To disband our forces and dismantle our navy would be, in the existing state of things, impossible, as no reliance could be placed on Buonaparte's pacific professions; and if a large military and naval establishment has to be kept up, we should suffer all the expenses of a war without enjoying any of its advantages'. If this shows a complete disregard of the human element, and assumes that expense is the only drawback to a war, Palmerston's attitude was no different from that of nearly all his contemporaries. The loss of life was considered irrelevant, as the services were manned by officers who cheerfully accepted the risks, with the glamour, of war, and by a rank and file who were regarded as the riff-raff of the nation.

The new Government decided on an early dissolution of Parliament and a general election was held in November 1806. Palmerston was chosen as the Tory candidate for Horsham. This was one of the thirty-seven constituencies in England where the franchise was by burgage tenure, which meant that the only persons entitled to vote were men who held land by burgage tenure from the ancient manorial court. This caused so much resentment among the other freeholders of Horsham that a special Act of Parliament had been passed to appease them in 1771, by which freeholders who were not burgage tenants were granted the right to vote in the town of Shoreham, some twenty miles to the south, and also in the neighbouring constituency of West Sussex, but not in the borough of Horsham where they lived. In 1806 Horsham, with a population of 3,500, had only 73 Parliamentary electors, of whom 14 did not live in the town, but in places as far afield as Godstone in Surrey, or in London.

For the last hundred years, Horsham had been a pocket borough of the Irwin family. The head of the family was Viscountess Irwin, the widow of the ninth Lord Irwin. She had been a society beauty in the days of George II, but was now an old woman living at Temple Newsam in Yorkshire, and rarely visited the family's seventeenth-century manor house on the western outskirts of Horsham. But in recent years the Irwin domination had been challenged by a powerful contender. The Duke of Norfolk, having taken up his residence at Arundel Castle, was eager to extend his local influence to Horsham, and win this Tory stronghold for the Whigs. The Duke was one of the most prominent of the Whig leaders, and combined a capacity to enjoy life to the full with occasional outbursts of radical, and almost revolutionary, behaviour. At the Beefsteak Club, where he was known by the nickname of Silenus, he was in the habit of eating four of the largest beefsteaks at a sitting; and it was said of him that, though he would never use water for any purpose whatever, he fortunately became so drunk every night that his servants could wash him while he was in a state of oblivion. He had formerly been Lord Lieutenant of the West Riding of Yorkshire, but had been dismissed after a great public dinner at the Whig Club at which he had praised George Washington and proposed the toast, not of 'The King', but of 'Our sovereign the people'.

Norfolk had put up candidates in Horsham against the Irwin nominees in 1790, and had succeeded in winning the seat. But Lady Irwin's candidates petitioned Parliament, and the Tory majority in the House of Commons ruled that they had been returned, and unseated Norfolk's candidates. Lady Irwin's candidates also recovered £800 damages against the returning officers for having announced, at the declaration of the poll, that their rivals had been elected. Lady Irwin continued to hold the seat for the next sixteen years, putting in a retired Major-General, a former Governor-General of India, and a West Indian planter who wanted a seat in Parliament from which he could oppose the abolition of the slave trade. But Norfolk worked hard to get Horsham, and often visited the town. He could afford to spend a great deal of money, despite the fact that he had once lost £70,000 in one night at dice; and his sex gave him an advantage over Lady Irwin. He could fraternize with his middle- and lower-class followers in the 'Anchor', while Lady Irwin, as a woman, could not personally participate in the revels of her supporters at the 'King's Head'.

For the general election of 1806, Lord Malmesbury nego-tiated with Lady Irwin to nominate his son, Lord Fitzharris, and Palmerston, as the candidates for the two-member con-stituency. Lady Irwin always charged £5,000 for each of the Horsham seats, though Norfolk, as the challenger, thought it advisable to undercut her and sell his nominations for £4,000. But as it was known that Norfolk would again contest the seat, it was obviously a risky investment to buy the nomina-tion from Lady Irwin. Malmesbury and Lady Irwin therefore agreed that Palmerston and Lord Fitzharris should each pay £1,500 in advance, and the balance of £3,500 only if they won the election and their return was upheld on petition by the House of Commons. The two young noblemen were then nominated by the Vicar of Horsham, and set out to canvass the handful of voters.

The poll opened on 3 November. The candidates stood at the hustings with their agents, solicitors and counsel. As each elector arrived to vote, he was required to produce his title deeds in order to prove his ownership of a burgage tenement, and was cross-examined about it by counsel for the opposing candidates. The two chief points for argument were whether a burgage tenant could increase the number of voters by sell-ing off part of his land to nominees, and whether any votes could be declared void for 'occasionality' if it could be proved that the elector's tenure of his burgage tenement was only a sham. Nearly all the burgage tenements had been bought up by Lady Irwin and the Duke in the name of nominees who had no connexion with the property; and it was unfortunate for Palmerston when even the Vicar of Horsham, who lived and worked in the town, could not remember either the name or the site of his burgage property. As the cross-examinations were sometimes lengthy, the voting proceeded slowly, and when the poll closed on the first day only 17 electors had voted, of whom 8 had voted for Palmerston and Fitzharris, and 9 for their opponents. The voting went a little more quickly next day, with Palmerston and Fitzharris always trail-ing behind, and when polling finally ended, Norfolk's candi-

dates had received 44 votes and Palmerston and Fitzharris 29.
Lady Irwin's agents then challenged the validity of 29 of Norfolk's votes, and called on the bailiffs to declare Palmerston
and Fitzharris elected by 29 votes against 15. The bailiffs, remembering how they had been mulcted in damages for announcing a wrong decision in 1790, took the proper course, in
the circumstances, of declaring all four candidates elected,
thus placing on both sides the onus of petitioning Parliament
to unseat their opponents.

The two petitions were duly presented to the new Parliament in January 1807. The Whigs had won a majority in the
House of Commons and after counsel had argued the case for
eleven days, the House unseated Palmerston and Fitzharris and
declared their opponents elected. Palmerston found that he
had paid £1,500 for the privilege of sitting for six days at the
bar of the House of Commons; but a few months later he
decided that it was a blessing in disguise. The new Parliament
did not last for more than three months, after which another
general election was held. If the House had upheld his election,
the Horsham contest would have cost him another £3,500 for
a few months in Parliament.

At Horsham, Norfolk's triumph over Lady Irwin and her
two 'dapper Lords' was short-lived. At the general election of
May 1807 the Tories obtained a majority in the House of
Commons, and Norfolk's candidates were unseated, and Lady
Irwin's were returned. Six months later, Lady Irwin died, and
in 1811 her son-in-law, the Marquis of Hertford, sold all her
burgage tenements, and influence, in Horsham to Norfolk
for £91,000. Meanwhile an Act of Parliament of 1809 had prohibited the selling of Parliamentary seats by a patron to a candidate, under penalty of a fine of £1,000 on both the seller and
the buyer.

Grenville's Government, after passing an Act which abolished the slave trade, came to grief over Catholic Emancipation. Roman Catholics were prevented from sitting in
Parliament, from holding commissions in the Army or Navy,
or civil offices in the state, or from filling academic posts at
the universities, by the Test Acts of the seventeenth century
which required all holders of these positions to take an oath

repudiating transubstantiation. There was a growing movement among Whigs and many Tories to modify the penal laws; but George III was bitterly opposed to this, and considered that he would be violating his coronation oath if he made any concession to the Catholics. When Lord Grenville proposed to extend to England the rule which already applied in Ireland, and to allow Roman Catholics to hold commissions in the Army up to the rank of colonel, the King not only refused to agree, but demanded that his ministers give a pledge never again during his lifetime to propose any measure of Catholic Emancipation. When they refused to give this pledge, he dismissed them, and called on the Duke of Portland to form a Tory Government. He then asked Portland for the same promise which the Whigs had refused to give, and Portland agreed, although Canning and other Tories were in favour of Catholic Emancipation.

The Duke of Portland found a place in his government for the twenty-two-year-old Lord Palmerston, who in after-life described in his own words how this came about. 'I was at Broadlands at Easter 1807 when, on 1st April, I received a letter from Lord Malmesbury, desiring me to come to town immediately, as he had found me a seat if not in Parliament, at least at the Admiralty. The Duke of Portland had been appointed First Lord of the Treasury. He was an old and intimate friend of Lord Malmesbury, who had been one of my guardians ... Lord Malmesbury had obtained from the Duke that I should be one of the Junior Lords of the Admiralty'.

George III granted Portland a dissolution of Parliament, and at the general election in May Palmerston stood again for Cambridge University. A group of Tories nominated Sir Vicary Gibbs, the Attorney-General, as a candidate, and he and Palmerston, who ran separate campaigns, were opposed by the two sitting members, Lord Henry Petty and Lord Euston, the Duke of Grafton's son. The general election was fought on Catholic Emancipation, and public opinion was against the Whigs, particularly in the universities. At Cambridge the atmosphere was 'all Church and King'.

As all candidates and election agents are well aware, when three or more candidates contest a double-member constituency, the best chance of securing the election of a particular candidate is for his supporters to vote for him alone, and not to use their second vote. A few days before the poll Sir Vicary Gibbs approached Palmerston, and told him that Lord Euston was sure to be elected, but that Petty would probably lose his seat. Several of Gibbs's supporters were therefore thinking of voting only for Gibbs – a 'plumper' vote, as it was called; and Gibbs proposed to Palmerston that they should each of them call on their supporters to vote for them both, in the hope of preventing 'plumpers'. Palmerston agreed; but on polling day, as the voting was drawing to a close, Gibbs came up to Palmerston in the Senate House and accused him of breaking the agreement, as several voters were plumping for Palmerston alone. Palmerston immediately went to the hustings and as his supporters came up to vote, he called on them to vote for Gibbs as well as for himself. His old tutor, Dr. Outram, who was standing there, urged Palmerston to keep quiet. He told him that Euston was well ahead, and Petty far behind, but that Gibbs was three or four votes ahead of him, and that several of Gibbs's friends had been plumping for Gibbs. Outram thought that it would be prudent, and perfectly proper, for Palmerston to allow his voters to exercise their own discretion on the matter. But Palmerston felt that this would be dishonourable, and insisted on urging his people to give their second vote to Gibbs. He was particularly glad that he had done so when he discovered that Gibbs's complaint had been more justified than Outram's, as 12 electors had plumped for Palmerston, and only 7 for Gibbs; but his scrupulousness cost him the election. Lord Euston received 325 votes, Gibbs 313, Palmerston 310, and Petty 265. Euston and Gibbs were in, and Palmerston had been defeated, by 3 votes, for the third time in fifteen months.

But it was essential that the new Junior Lord of the Admiralty should have a seat in the House of Commons, and one was promptly found for Palmerston. It was his father's old seat at Newport in the Isle of Wight. The seat was a pocket borough of Sir Leonard Holmes. Sir Leonard was quite prepared that Palmerston should sit for Newport in Parliament, but he was afraid that the MP would build up a body of supporters and nominees in Newport, which might in time challenge his own power in the borough. He therefore made it a condition of his nominating Palmerston that Palmerston should promise never to set foot in the constituency, not even at election times. Palmerston had no objection to this, as he was in any case intending to fight and win the Cambridge University seat at the first available opportunity. So the bargain was made, Holmes's nominee resigned his seat, and at the ensuing by-election Palmerston was returned unopposed as Member of Parliament for Newport.

Chapter Three

The Admiralty and the War Office

The new Parliament met on 22 June 1807, and Palmerston took his seat in the House of Commons, where he was to remain, except for one interval of six months, until his death fifty-eight years later. In Palmerston's time, Parliament did not ordinarily sit in the autumn, when gentlemen returned to their counties for the shooting season. In 1855, Lord John Russell suggested to Palmerston that Parliament should meet before Christmas for an autumn session; but Palmerston, though he realized that autumn sessions would have many advantages, thought that it would be impossible to have them as a permanent feature, because MPs would insist on spending the autumn in their country houses. If Parliament met regularly in the autumn, thus preventing MPs from shooting, the country gentry would cease to stand for Parliament, and a less desirable class of MP would be returned. Parliament normally adjourned some time in August, and did not meet again until the end of January, except when some national emergency, or a general election, interfered with the usual timetable. This occurred in 1807, and the new Parliament sat throughout the autumn until a week before Christmas.

Palmerston did not address the House during his first six months in Parliament, but in February 1808 he made his maiden speech. In view of what Palmerston was later to become, it was most fitting that his first intervention in Parliament should be, not on some trivial question concerning his department, but on a great issue of foreign policy which aroused violent controversy in England; for Canning's policy in regard to the Copenhagen expedition might well have been called 'Palmerstonian' by later generations.

In June 1807 Napoleon had met Tsar Alexander I on a raft in the River Memel at Tilsit. The Tsar, well chastened by several disastrous military defeats, had made his peace with France, and agreed, in his treaty with Napoleon, to offer to mediate between France and Britain. The British Government knew that there were secret clauses in the treaty, and they were informed by their spies at Tilsit that one of these clauses provided that French troops should invade Denmark and seize the Danish fleet at Copenhagen. Denmark and Sweden were then to join France and Russia in an anti-British alliance, and the Danish fleet – which, since the destruction of the French and Spanish fleets at Trafalgar, was the largest on the Continent – was to be used for an invasion of Scotland and Ireland. In fact, the agent's information was inaccurate. Napoleon had suggested some such plan, but Alexander had insisted that nothing should be done until after his attempt at mediation had been rejected by Britain; and Napoleon had agreed to wait, though he had every intention of carrying out the operation at the earliest opportunity. Canning saw the danger. He sent the fleet and 27,000 troops to the Sound, and invited the Crown Prince of Denmark to join an alliance against France, and to hand over the Danish fleet to British custody for safe-keeping for the duration of the war. The Crown Prince, who wished to remain neutral, refused. Canning then ordered the troops to attack Copenhagen and seize the Danish fleet, and after four days' bombardment of the city, which caused heavy casualties among the civilian population, the fleet was captured, intact, and brought safely to England.

Napoleon's anger when he heard the news is a proof that on military grounds Canning's decision was justified; but it had adverse political repercussions. It caused great indignation in neutral countries. Denmark and Sweden entered the war on Napoleon's side, and the influence of the pro-English faction at the Russian Court was destroyed for the time being. It was strongly criticized by the Whigs in Britain, who attacked Canning and the Government on the moral issue. George Ponsonby said that the same divine Providence which watched the conduct of individuals watched also the conduct of states in international relationships. The Duke of Norfolk declared that whatever military advantage Britain had gained had been more than offset by the harm that it had done to her moral reputation; and Windham and Sheridan accused the Government of entering into a competition in knavery with Bonaparte. The Opposition drew the worst conclusions from the Government's failure to disclose the source of the information on which they had acted; but Canning refused to reveal this, and the secret has never been discovered. It has been suggested that Napoleon's plans were betrayed by his Foreign Minister, Talleyrand; but it is much more likely that Canning's informant was a pro-British member of the Tsar's entourage at Tilsit.

In the debate on 3 February 1808, Canning defended the Copenhagen expedition in a three-hour speech, in which he claimed that he was justified by the imminence of the danger and the success of the operation. He was followed by Robert Pemberton Milnes, who was known as 'Orator Milnes' because of his loud voice and bombastic manner. Milnes denounced the Opposition for trusting to the good faith of Bonaparte, and for putting the interests of Denmark before those of their own country; but his speech did not go down well, not even on the Government benches. Palmerston made a much better impression. He began by justifying the Government's refusal to reveal the source of their information, as this would not only be a breach of faith towards their informants, but would prevent such information from being supplied in future. Then, turning to the moral issue, he said that it was all very well to talk about right, policy and the law of nations, and he was as willing as anyone to pay his respects to these principles, 'and to recommend their application wherever circumstances would permit'; but in the Copenhagen expedition we had applied them 'in conformity to the law of nature, which dictated and commanded self-preservation'. The words 'right' and 'policy' were frequently used by people who did not clearly distinguish them. The Crown Prince of Denmark must have known that 'Buonaparte' would attack, and that the Danes were too weak to resist; yet he had refused the British offer of alliance and protection. 'On this ground, therefore, namely, the weakness of Denmark, and the power of France to force her to become instrumental against Great Britain', he would support the Government.

Thus Palmerston, in his maiden speech, laid down his guiding principle: right, and the law of nations, should be observed in international relations, but only so long as they did not interfere with vital British interests. It was his first clash with that force which he was so often to arouse during his career – the moral conscience of a section of British educated opinion. The British Government, unlike any other government at the time, except possibly the United States, was always hampered by this opposition at home whenever it pursued an aggressive policy abroad.

'My dear Elizabeth,' wrote Palmerston next day to his sister, 'you will see by this day's paper that I was tempted by some evil spirit to make a fool of myself for the entertainment of the House last night; however, I thought it was a good opportunity of breaking the ice, although one should flounder a little in doing so, as it was impossible to talk any very egregious nonsense upon so good a cause'. But his friends thought highly of his speech, which they said was much better than Milnes's; and when Palmerston wrote again to Elizabeth two days later, he was in a much more confident mood. He told her that once he had begun to speak, he did not find it as alarming as he had expected; and though he was glad when it was over, he felt happier when his friends told him that he had not talked much nonsense.

But despite the success of his maiden speech, he did not speak in the House again during the session. He carried on quietly with his duties at the Admiralty. When he was first appointed a Junior Lord, he was still the serious and well-behaved young man that he had been at Edinburgh and Cambridge, and the young ladies who knew him thought him dull. His colleagues at the Admiralty praised him for his abilities and capacity for hard work; but their daughters were less impressed. They thought that he was 'very pedantic and very pompous', and laughed at him, nicknaming him 'Sir Charles Grandison', after Richardson's hero, 'because he was so priggish and so sedate'. But in later years, at least one of these girls was the first to admit that his character had radically changed; for Palmerston soon began to acquire a reputation for gallantry and love affairs.

During the Parliamentary recess he visited his estates in Ireland. He landed at Dublin in September 1808 and drove seventy miles across rough roads and tracks to his estates in Sligo, admiring the beauty of the landscape and staying in the primitive country inns. As word spread that the young lord was coming, hundreds of his tenants came out to stare at him. 'The universal cry was "Give us roads, and no petty landlords",' wrote Palmerston to his sister Elizabeth, and he saw at once that these were the evils which needed to be remedied. His 10,000 acres lay in an area, more than two miles long and six miles wide, between the sea and the barren hills. The soil was boggy and poor, and the area was over-populated, as the peasants had only four or five, or at the most ten or twelve, acres. 'They are too poor to improve their land', wrote Palmerston, 'and yet it is impossible to turn them out, as they have no other means of subsistence. Their position, however, will be improved as I gradually get rid of the middlemen, or petty landlords', who exploited 'these unfortunate devils'. He decided to build roads which would enable the people to get to market; to introduce a Scottish farmer who would teach them improved methods of farming; and to build a little manufacturing village in the centre of the estate, and a little port on Donegal Bay.

He also had plans for education. Education in England and Ireland was among the worst in Europe. In Austria, Maria Theresa had introduced compulsory universal education by autocratic decree in the eighteenth century; but though Scotland, thanks to John Knox and his successors, had had it since 1696, England never achieved it during Palmerston's lifetime. This was partly due to the English devotion to freedom and dislike of government regulation, but chiefly to religious differences, to the opposition of the Church schools to a national system of education, and the refusal of Roman Catholics and Nonconformists to go to Church of England schools. There was, however, a widespread belief in the benefits of popular education, and Palmerston shared the opinion that the education of the lower classes was the long-term solution to the problems of poverty and crime and political disaffection. He was pleased to find that the peasants at Sligo were very eager for education. All over his estates there were schools in the most primitive buildings where not only reading, writing and arithmetic, but Latin and Greek, were taught. The schoolmasters lived in mud huts next to the school, and were paid between ten shilling and £1 a year by the fathers of every boy in the school. Palmerston decided to build three good schoolhouses for the teachers, to give them a small holding on which they could keep a cow and grow potatoes in their spare time, and to pay them an additional salary in cases where the money paid by the boys' parents was insufficient for their maintenance. By these means he intended to bring the schools under his control; but he had no intention of interfering with their religious freedom. 'As the masters will be under my control', he wrote, 'to be turned off at pleasure, I shall have security for their good conduct. I fancy they must be Catholics, for the people will not send their children to a Protestant.'

He returned to London in time for the new session of Parliament, but if Mr. Hansard's reports were accurate – and they were not yet fully verbatim reports – he made only one intervention during the session of 1809. This was during the inquiry into the scandal about the sale of commissions in the Army by Mary Anne Clarke, the mistress of the King's son, Frederick, the Duke of York, who was Commander-in-Chief of the Army. In the course of the examination of one of Mrs. Clarke's servants, Palmerston asked a question which was very much to the point. But he was spending more time in society than in the House, and when, in October, the Duke of Portland resigned, and the Chancellor of the Exchequer, Spencer Perceval, became Prime Minister, there was much surprise when Perceval offered to make Palmerston Chancellor of the Exchequer.

Palmerston himself was as surprised as anyone by the offer. He had just returned to Broadlands from a three-day sailing holiday when he received a letter from Perceval summoning him to come to London immediately, and on arrival was confronted with a gift of the Exchequer a few days before his twenty-fifth birthday. He felt considerable hesitation in accepting. In the first place, he was nervous about speaking in the House of Commons. At this time, a great deal of importance was attached to oratory in politics, and oratory of a dramatic and bombastic kind which no one would take seriously in Britain today. Despite the success of his speech on the Copenhagen expedition, Palmerston felt that he was not an orator, and most of his contemporaries agreed with him. He felt that in the ordinary way it would not matter if he made a bad speech in the House, but that if he did so as Chancellor of the Exchequer it might be disastrous for the Government. Perceval, seeing his hesitation, offered to appoint him as a Junior Lord of the Treasury for a short time as a preparation for taking the Exchequer; but Palmerston still hesitated, and Perceval offered, as a third possibility, the office of Secretary at War. He gave him two days in which to take his choice.

Palmerston discussed the matter with Plumer Ward, his colleague on the Board of Admiralty, as they strolled up to Hyde Park Corner. Ward appreciated Palmerston's nervousness about speaking in the House of Commons, but assured him that in all other respects his colleagues had absolute confidence in his ability to fill the office. He also pointed out that if, as was expected, Perceval's Government would soon be forced to resign, and the Whigs came back, Palmerston's political position in the future would be much stronger if he had once been a Cabinet minister, for however short a time. This argument impressed Palmerston, for neither he nor Ward could have guessed that their party would remain in power for the next twenty-one years; but he consulted Lord Malmesbury, who advised him to refuse the Exchequer. Malmesbury said that, ordinarily, Palmerston's diffidence as a speaker would not have mattered; but as the Government, which had become very unpopular on account of the mishandling of the Walcheren campaign, would be under heavy pressure from Opposition MPs when Parliament re-assembled, he felt that it would not be fair to Perceval, to the public, or to Palmerston himself, if he were to consent to be thrown into the breach as Chancellor of the Exchequer. He therefore advised Palmerston to accept the War Office with a seat in the Cabinet.

Palmerston then told Perceval that he would accept the office of Secretary at War; but against the advice of all his friends he refused the seat in the Cabinet. It was very unusual for the Secretary at War to be a member of the Cabinet, and Palmerston did not feel justified in accepting the honour. 'Considering how young I am in office', he wrote to Lord Malmesbury, 'people in general, so far from expecting to see me in the Cabinet by taking the War Office, would perhaps only wonder how I got there. With the Exchequer it would have been necessary, but with the War Office certainly not; and the business of the Department will, I take it, be quite sufficient to occupy one's time without attending Cabinet councils'.

Malmesbury's advice to Palmerston to refuse the Exchequer was doubtless shrewd, for there was good reason to believe that whoever became Chancellor of the Exchequer would be sacrificed as a scapegoat to popular anger about the Walcheren disaster. The ambitious and self-confident 'Orator' Milnes also refused Perceval's offer of the Exchequer, as did three other politicians; and Perceval, finding no one who was prepared to accept it, became Chancellor of the Exchequer himself, as well as Prime Minister. But in future years Palmerston must often have wondered what would have happened if he had accepted it, or at least, as Malmesbury advised, taken the seat in the Cabinet with the War Office; for his refusal had far-reaching consequences. It delayed his entry into the Cabinet for nearly eighteen years.

The long years which Palmerston spent as Secretary at War have puzzled all his biographers, and after he had become a great Foreign Secretary his contemporaries were equally at a loss to explain why he should have remained for so long in a relatively unimportant office. His wife asked him to explain it, but though he wrote a short autobiographical summary for her benefit, he did not give any clear answer to her question. But it is not perhaps as surprising as it seemed in later years. Palmerston went into politics in a very different frame of mind from that of the middle-class lawyers who would soon be ruling the United States and France and all democratic states. He had been brought up to believe that he was entitled to political power as a right and a duty. Just as the country gentlemen at that time, and for many years afterwards, considered it their business to govern their district at local government level, so Palmerston, as a nobleman, thought that he was expected to govern Britain at a national level. Within the governing circle there was, of course, competition for offices and advancement; but it was possible for a public-spirited peer like Palmerston to enter politics without facing the temptation or the necessity to engage in the single-minded pursuit of power which, for the self-made professional politician, was the only avenue for advancement.

In any case, it was not easy to advance in politics during the eighteen years that Palmerston remained at the War Office. The Cabinet consisted of about a dozen Tories, nearly all of whom were peers, who remained year after year in the same office, and usually only death removed them. It might have been different if Palmerston had become Chancellor of the Exchequer in 1809. Perceval offered him his chance at a time when nearly everyone thought that he was just an agreeable young nobleman; if he had taken it, and survived, he might have convinced the Tories that they had here a third man of the calibre of Castlereagh and Canning. But Palmerston did not seize time by the forelock, and the Tory leaders perhaps came to think of him as a competent and conscientious administrator, rather than the stuff from which Prime Ministers are made.

In 1809, the organization of the War Office was complicated. A senior Cabinet Minister, who by tradition also held the Colonial Office, was responsible in the Cabinet for general questions of military policy and for the strategical direction of the war. He was called the Secretary of State for War and the Colonies, and sat in the Colonial Office; but he had nothing to do with the War Office. The Secretary at War, who was the head of the War Office, was a junior minister who usually did not have a seat in the Cabinet. He was responsible for the financial and general administration of the Army; but all questions of discipline, promotion and the more specifically military side of the Army were under the control of the Commander-in-Chief, who was not under the War Office. This cumbersome organization, which at first sight might seem absurd, was in fact an expression of the British constitutional system of Parliamentary monarchy. The Commander-in-Chief, who was usually a royal Duke, was the personal link between the King and his Army, and was, in theory, subordinate to the King alone, though in practice the King's commands to him were issued on the advice of the Prime Minister; but the Secretary at War's responsibility for all military expenditure ensured that Parliamentary financial control was maintained over the Army. The Secretary at War had a few other duties specifically imposed upon him by statute, including that of ensuring that no military personnel remained in any constituency while an election was in progress; and he answered questions in Parliament as to the activities of the Commander-in-Chief, and was his spokesman in the House.

When Palmerston took up his duties at the War Office at the Horse Guards, he had under him a staff which, including the Accounts Department in Duke Street, numbered nearly two hundred, the numbers having more than doubled, because of the war, from the peace-time establishment of 1792. Palmerston's second-in-command was William Merry, the Deputy Secretary at War, who was the permanent head of the department. As Secretary at War, Palmerston received a salary of £2,480 a year, which, for complicated reasons dating from 1783, was £20 a year less than the salary of £2,500 paid to Merry as Deputy Secretary; but in 1809 a differential salary scale was not needed to maintain the authority and social prestige of Lord Palmerston. The clerks' salaries ranged from £1,400 to £60 per year. A few yards from the War Office, at the Horse Guards, was the office of the Commander-in-Chief, who was assisted by a Military Secretary and a staff of thirty-two.

When Palmerston was appointed Secretary at War, it was generally assumed by the political and social world that this was another case of finding a job for an aristocratic nonentity; for only Perceval, and a handful of people who knew Palmerston well, realized his capabilities. His government colleague John Wilson Croker, the Under-Secretary for Ireland, told Palmerston many years later that it was his impression at the time that Palmerston owed his appointment to 'your station and University character' and to the influence of Lord Mal-

mesbury. Huskisson thought that Palmerston's selection as
Secretary at War was 'a very bad appointment'. 'I suppose
we must be glad of it', wrote young Lady Lyttelton, 'as it may
divert his Lordship from flirting, in the same way as people
rejoiced at his predecessor's appointment because it was to
cure him of gambling.' This continued to be the general impression for some years, because it was not widely known that
Palmerston, almost as soon as he was appointed, had entered
on a serious controversy with the Commander-in-Chief.

It had for long been the practice for the Colonels of regiments to make their own arrangements, through their agents,
with tradesmen for the supply of clothing to the regiment;
the Colonel paid them out of his own pocket, and was entitled
to make deductions from the soldiers' pay in order to recoup
himself. But in 1810 an Act of Parliament was quietly passed,
apparently without anyone really noticing what was being
done, which enacted that tradesmen supplying regiments
should be paid by the War Office, where the deductions from
the soldiers' pay should be made. Palmerston studied the provisions of the Act, and sent out a circular to all Colonels of
regiments, directing them to forward their tradesmen's accounts to the War Office for settlement. He did not consult
the Commander-in-Chief before sending out the circular. He
also wrote to all the Generals asking them for a list of their
aides-de-camp, in order to make sure that they were not receiving allowances for non-existent ADCs.

The Commander-in-Chief was Lieutenant-General Sir
David Dundas. He was the son of a poor tradesman of Edinburgh, and had risen by his own abilities to his present position. It was the proud boast of English society that a man
could climb from the dregs of the gutter to the highest offices
in the state, where he could take his place as the equal of the
most nobly born, and Dundas was one of many public figures
who had proved that this was true. The social inequality lay
in the fact that men like him required ability and years of hard
struggle to achieve what peers like Palmerston were given as
young men without necessarily having any skills at all; in this,
as in so many other things, England stood half-way between
the democratic societies of France and the United States, and

the more rigid aristocratic systems of the old European monarchies. Before the Seven Years War young Dundas had walked from Edinburgh to London, as he could not afford the fare, and bought a commission in the Army with money that he had saved and borrowed. Fifty-five years later he was a respected General. But it was only a freak situation that had made him Commander-in-Chief. The Duke of York had been involved in the scandal about the sale of army commissions by his mistress, Mrs. Clarke, and though the House of Commons had exonerated him, he felt obliged to resign. It was hoped that he would return as Commander-in-Chief when the memory of the scandal had subsided; and in the meanwhile his Quarter-Master-General at the Horse Guards, Dundas, was appointed to fill the vacancy as a stop-gap.

The temporary nature of Dundas's tenure of office, and his relative inferiority in standing as compared with the Duke of York, did not impede him but, on the contrary, increased his determination to prevent any encroachments by the War Office on the position of the Commander-in-Chief. He was determined, as he told Perceval, not to permit any 'supercession of the high office His Majesty has been pleased to entrust to me, and which I shall feel it my duty, at a proper time, to restore unimpaired to him, and on the same honourable footing it stood when he was graciously pleased to put it into my hands'. He agreed that Generals should not receive allowances for non-existent ADCs, but insisted that any orders to this effect should be issued by his own office; and he strongly objected that the Secretary at War should attempt to interfere between the Colonel and 'his tradesmen'. This directive had aroused great resentment among commanding officers; and when Palmerston told Dundas that he was bound by the new Act of Parliament, Dundas retorted that the Act should never have been passed without discussions with the Commander-in-Chief, and demanded that, if necessary, the Act should be repealed. Palmerston and Dundas now embarked on a lengthy correspondence in which they soon passed from 'My dear Lord' and 'my dear Sir' to 'My Lord' and 'Sir', but preserved throughout the most formal courtesy of language.

The controversy was followed with some impatience by the

leading members of the Government at the time, and subsequent historians have dismissed it contemptuously as a petty departmental squabble occurring at a time when the troops in the Peninsula were dying on the battlefields of Talavera and Albuera. But both Palmerston and Dundas felt deeply about the principle involved. Palmerston argued that, quite apart from the recent statute, all questions of finance came under the War Office, and said that if communications to commanding officers on this subject had to be sent through the Commander-in-Chief, the War Office had better close down altogether, and become a sub-department of the Horse Guards. He insisted that the War Office and the Commander-in-Chief's office were two equal and independent bodies, the one dealing with finance, the other with discipline: Dundas, on the other hand, unequivocally asserted that the Secretary at War was subordinate to the Commander-in-Chief; and he justified this novel proposition by the words of the King's commissions to the Commander-in-Chief and the Secretary at War. The commission appointing the Commander-in-Chief directed him 'to observe and follow such instructions, orders and directions from time to time as you shall receive from Us'; the commission to the Secretary at War stated: 'You are to observe and follow such orders and directions as you shall from time to time receive from Us or the General of Our Forces for the time being according to the Discipline of War'. Palmerston now felt that he was fighting for Parliamentary control over the Army and for the principles of 1688. He did some historical research, and countered Dundas's claim with the argument that the words of the commission, 'the General of our Forces', which had been unchanged since the seventeenth century, did not refer to the Commander-in-Chief, but to the obsolete office of Captain-General which had existed in Charles II's time.

Dundas referred the dispute to the Prime Minister. Perceval decided that it could only be ended by an official order from the King; and as George III had again relapsed into final insanity, the case was submitted to the Prince Regent, who asked Perceval to deal with it. Both sides submitted written arguments to Perceval. Palmerston, with the energy and inexperience of youth, tried the patience of Perceval by submitting a 30,000-word document in which he examined at length the differences in the powers of Charles II's Captain-General and the modern Commander-in-Chief, and quoted 495 cases since 1669 which established the independence of the Secretary at War. His treatise was remarkably clear and thorough. His marshalling and presentation of the precedents were worthy of a trained lawyer, and his summary of his basic principles was equally lucid. He stated that the office of Secretary at War was established 'as a sort of barrier between the military authority of the officer in command of the Army and the civil rights of the people', as a Parliamentary check on military expenditure, and as a protection for the property rights of civilians.

At the height of the dispute, Dundas resigned to make way for the Duke of York, who felt able to resume his old office in May 1811. Palmerston continued the struggle against his royal adversary with as much determination as he had shown against Dundas, though his language was more respectful. 'Lord Palmerston', he wrote to the Duke, 'feels great embarrassment in the execution of this part of his task, because on the one hand he should conceive that he deserted his official duty if he did not make the reply which the facts seem to call for, he at the same time is not without apprehension that in attending to the force and conclusion of his argument he should appear to overlook the respect which is due from him to His Royal Highness, and it certainly would be a great relief to him if he could feel himself at liberty to have treated these observations as those of His Royal Highness's advisers rather than of His Royal Highness himself'. But Frederick would not shelter behind his royal rank, or allow Palmerston to take advantage of it. 'The Commander-in-Chief', he replied, 'cannot but regret that the Secretary at War should even for a moment have felt any embarrassment or hesitation in the mode of conveying his sentiments under the apprehension that his observations might be considered as anywise wanting in respect.... The Commander-in-Chief begs at the same time to complain to the Secretary at War that nothing can be further from his idea than that of ever shrinking from the responsibility which he holds, or of arrogating to himself such a monarchical distinction as would attend his allowing it for a moment to be supposed that he acts under the influence of advisers and not upon his own judgment'.

In December 1811 Perceval reached his decision, after consulting Lord Eldon, the Lord Chancellor, and Lord Liverpool, the Secretary of State for War and the Colonies. He agreed with his two colleagues that the Secretary at War was not subordinate to the Commander-in-Chief, and that any attempt to make him so by a new Act of Parliament would cause great resentment and encourage anti-militarist and Radical agitation. But it was advisable, in the interests of the service, that the Secretary at War should not, in future, issue any orders to the Army, even on matters which were under his control, without first submitting them for approval to the Commander-in-Chief. If the Commander-in-Chief objected to them, and the Secretary at War insisted on issuing them, the dispute was to be referred to the Prime Minister. Perceval's ruling was embodied in an order issued by the Prince Regent in the name and on behalf of His Majesty on 29 May 1812. Palmerston's official biographer, Henry Bulwer, and some of his later biographers, have given the impression that the decision was made by the Prince Regent personally; but in fact he delegated the matter to Perceval, and his final order was identical with Perceval's draft. Palmerston had succeeded in defeating the attempt to place the War Office under the control of the Commander-in-Chief; and for the time being he obeyed the Prince Regent's order to consult the Commander-in-Chief before issuing instructions to the Army.

Chapter Four

Lord Cupid

Palmerston's most important duty as Secretary at War was to introduce the Army estimates in the House of Commons in March every year. He did this very competently, having prepared for it by drafting many lists and carefully tabulated memoranda, and by having all the figures and facts at his finger tips. As long as the war lasted, there was not much controversy about the estimates, and the short debates on them gave Palmerston very little opportunity of distinguishing himself in the House; so most people continued to think of him as a man about town who had some position or other in politics. But even as a social figure he was not prominent in the public eye. His name is often found in the society columns of the newspapers among the other Viscounts in the lists of those present at some great ball or reception; but although these newspapers told their readers that the Duke of Norfolk came to a party dressed as Silenus, and that Lord Buckingham had had the first dance with Lady Jersey, they never described the fancy dress costume that Palmerston was wearing, or gave the names of his partners.

He was more at home in the private and select atmosphere of Almack's than at the big functions. Almack's, in St. James's, was the most exclusive club in London. A lady or gentleman could only be considered for membership if they were proposed by a member of the opposite sex; but the final decision as to whether to admit them rested with the seven Lady Patronesses who ruled the club. The seven were the gay and flirtatious Countess of Jersey; the sedate and virtuous Countess of Sefton; the Countess Cowper, who had been Emily Lamb, and would one day be Lady Palmerston; the Viscountess Cas-

tlereagh, the Foreign Secretary's wife; Mrs. Drummond Bur-
rell, who later became Lady Willoughby; and the Princess
Esterhazy and the Countess Lieven, the wives of the Austrian
and Russian Ambassadors. Almack's was described as being
the ambition and despair of the middle classes. Every parvenu
manufacturer who tried to gain admission found the door
firmly closed against him; and only a handful of the three hundred officers who applied were successful. But rank and breeding were not the only criteria adopted by the Lady
Patronesses; they were largely influenced by their personal
likes and dislikes. The Duchess of Bedford and Lord March
were refused admission; but the witty, overdressed Jew, Benjamin Disraeli, was accepted in 1834. Palmerston had no difficulty in entering, and was probably the lover of three of the
Lady Patronesses. There is reason to believe that Lady Cowper, Madame de Lieven and Lady Jersey each in turn became
his mistress.

Sarah Sophia Fane, the daughter of the Earl of Westmorland and the granddaughter of Child the banker, who had
married the Earl of Jersey, was aged twenty-five in 1810, and
the most famous society beauty of the day. She had succeeded
in eclipsing her mother-in-law, who was the mistress of the
Prince Regent, and whom she cordially disliked. She was
proud and domineering, and was hated by most of her women
acquaintances, including the other Lady Patronesses of Almack's, for Lady Jersey attempted to rule over their Committee as autocratically as their Committee ruled over the
club; but she was capable of acts of great kindness to her
friends of either sex. Her easy-going husband, to whom she
had brought a vast fortune and the ownership of Child's Bank,
made no difficulties about her love affairs, and resolutely refused to fight duels in defence of her honour; he said that if he
once started doing this, he would have to fight every gentleman in town. At various times during the next twenty-five
years, the rumour-mongers said that she was having a liaison
with Palmerston. Evidence of this is not likely to be forthcoming. Palmerston and his contemporaries conducted their
affairs discreetly, and carefully burned any love letters which
they found; if any still exist, they are probably hidden among

the archives of those families which still today, a hundred and fifty years later, hide their family secrets and scandals from the eyes of prying historians.

Dorothea von Benckendorff was the daughter of a famous German family from Latvia. She had survived an adolescence spent at the Court of the mad Tsar, Paul I, and had married Count – later Prince – Lieven, who in 1812 arrived in London as Russian Ambassador, when Napoleon's march on Moscow converted Russia from a hostile neutral into a valuable ally. The Countess Lieven became very popular in London society, as was shown when she was invited, along with the Princess Esterhazy, to be the first foreign Lady Patroness of Almack's. A close friendship developed between Madame de Lieven and Lady Cowper. Some people thought that Madame de Lieven was ugly, because her nose was too long, and in later years, at least, her complexion was coarse. The hostile caricaturists, exaggerating these defects, made her look horrible; but Lawrence in his portrait emphasized her long, elegant neck and beautiful eyes, and presented her as a fascinating, if not a pretty, woman. She was very intelligent, and a skilful political intriguer. She made many enemies by her plots, by the scandalous things that she said about her friends behind their backs, and by the merciless way in which she snubbed any attempt at intimacy by those whom she considered to be her social inferiors, but who, in the less rigid graduations of English society, considered themselves to be her equals. She showed greater tact in the way in which she repulsed the amorous advances of the English royal Dukes.

She became Metternich's mistress at the Congress of Aix-la-Chapelle in 1818, and twenty years later, at the age of fifty-two, she became Guizot's. In London she may have had an affair with Palmerston, for though there is no clear evidence of this, the tone of their letters makes this not unlikely. They attracted attention by waltzing together at Almack's. Until 1814 the dances at Almack's were all English country dances and Scottish reels; but Lady Jersey introduced the quadrille after her visit to Paris at Napoleon's downfall. The waltz, originally a German country dance, appeared in revolutionary France in 1793, and spread from Napoleon's Court to St.

Petersburg and Vienna. Madame de Lieven brought it to England in 1812, but did not venture to dance it at Almack's until Tsar Alexander, on his visit to London in 1816, danced it there with her. A dance in which the man seized his partner round the waist and clasped her to him, in public, had not been known in polite society since the sixteenth century, and it naturally created a sensation; and in the atmosphere of Almack's in Regency days, it could hardly have the innocent significance which it had, as an already established custom, in staid Victorian times. Even after the Tsar had set an example, most members hesitated to dance the waltz; but Captain Gronow states that in course of time Palmerston might be seen 'describing an infinite number of circles with Madame de Lieven', and the Austrian chargé d'affaires, Baron Neumann, waltzed regularly with the Princess Esterhazy.

Palmerston's connexion with Lady Cowper was more lasting. She was three years younger than he, the daughter of Lord Melbourne and his brilliant and beautiful wife, and the sister of William Lamb, the rising Whig MP, who later became the great Lord Melbourne. Emily Lamb had married Earl Cowper in 1805, when she was eighteen and he was twenty-seven. Cowper was a quiet, pleasant man who was not as stupid as he was often thought to be, but took no part in public life and disliked society; his wife was gay and beautiful, and liked society very much. Her portrait painters have captured her in various moods – gay and flirtatious, superbly arrogant, bored and languid, weak and yielding. She was considered to be the most approachable and amenable of the Lady Patronesses of Almack's. Her kindness and even temper made her a very popular mistress with her servants, and with the tenants of her estates, whom she often visited, bearing gifts, at Christmas and other times. Nearly every day, her house was beset by villagers with requests for charity and favours, for it was said that Lady Cowper was so kind-hearted that she was incapable of saying no. It was also rumoured that she was equally incapable of refusing more passionate demands from gentlemen of her own class. She acquired the reputation of having many lovers. Palmerston may have been the father of some of her children, and another is said to have been the child of Pozzo di

Borgo, the Corsican friend of Napoleon's, who broke with him and came to England as a refugee in 1796, and returned, many years later, as Russian Ambassador to London. Lady Tankerville – the former Corisande de Grammont – who was one of Lady Cowper's closest friends, told Canning's daughter, Lady Clanricarde, that Lady Cowper had been the mistress of Charles Greville, the Clerk to the Privy Council, who wrote such amusing and spiteful things about Palmerston in his diary. Lady Granville stated that all the men 'were more or less in love with Emily Cowper' at the succession of house-parties which she attended, where Lady Granville could always recognize the voices from the drawing room – 'Lady Cowper loud yet languid, Madame de Lieven dry and conclusive'.

In view of the moral tone of society in Regency days, and the reputation of Palmerston and of the Lady Patronesses, there can be very little doubt as to the nature of his relationship with Lady Jersey and Lady Cowper, though he may have found the Princess Lieven more difficult. Although the popular tradition of the period represented English women as being virtuous, proud and unattainable, as compared with the weak and dissolute foreign ladies, this did not apply in the case of these three. Neither Palmerston nor Lady Cowper expected to have a monopoly of each other's favours, and Palmerston doubtless had a number of other affairs which escaped the attention even of the gossip-writers. On one occasion he looked in at a party given by Harriette Wilson, the famous society courtesan, and her more respectable sister, Amy. Harriette was the daughter of a Swiss clockmaker in Mayfair, and had risen to become the mistress of the Duke of Argyll and to rebuff the Duke of Wellington. Palmerston arrived from Lady Castlereagh's just as Harriette was twitting her admirer, Beau Brummell, with the fact that his father had been a valet. 'I vote for cutting all the grocers and valets who intrude themselves into good society', she said. Brummell looked at Palmerston, who was just making his bow to Amy, and said: 'My father was a very superior valet and kept his place all his life, and that is more than Palmerston will do'. Harriette Wilson wrote in her memoirs that Palmerston had given her money, though she did not accuse him, as she did so many other men, of having tried to make love to her.

Palmerston was also devoting a good deal of his time to politics. He often attended the small political dinner parties where some half a dozen of the ministers, with no ladies present, discussed the best way to defeat the machinations of the Whigs, the alignments within the Cabinet, and the bitter feud which had developed between Canning and Castlereagh, which culminated in a duel in 1809. He indulged in some desultory journalism and other writing, contributing satirical verse and short stories to the *New Whig Guide*, the *Courier*, and other pro-government publications. These literary efforts were neither brilliant nor profound, but were of moderate ability, and, though a little supercilious, were never malicious. The style of humour was Tory. Palmerston poked fun at well-meaning and woolly-minded Radicals, at clumsy servants and at imaginary pompous negro chiefs presented at the Court of St. James's; but he never laughed at the Regent, Castlereagh, Lord Ellenborough, or any of the other persons in authority who were the target for the mockery of Byron and Shelley and the Radical writers.

He did not really share his father's love of the theatre, but he kept up his acquaintanceship with some of the dramatists and authors who had been his father's friends. He remained friendly with Sheridan, who was his political opponent, after Sheridan had lost his seat in Parliament, his place in society, and all his money. Palmerston, Sheridan, Canning and some others formed a kind of literary club for the improvement of the English language, and decided to hold dinners in turn at each other's house. The first dinner was held at Sheridan's house. The bailiffs had taken possession of the house at the insistence of Sheridan's creditors; but Sheridan persuaded them to act as waiters during the meal. When Palmerston was asked, in later life, whether he and his friends had in fact improved the English language at these dinners, he replied: 'Not, certainly, at that dinner; for Sheridan got drunk and a good many words of doubtful propriety were used'.

On one occasion, Palmerston intervened with Sir Robert Peel, the Chief Secretary for Ireland, on behalf of the Irish dramatist, Maturin. Maturin was a Protestant curate in Dublin, and the Archbishop of Dublin was threatening to take action against him because he had written a play, *Bertram*, which the Archbishop considered was immoral. Palmerston pointed out that the play was not a farce, but a 'Legitimate Tragedy, in Five acts, of the full standard length & weight, in which all the rogues & whores are brought to the most condign and Exemplary punishment in a Manner that must be admitted to be Most Edifying even by the Most active & zealous Member of the Vice Society'. He said that the Archbishop's attitude was a disgrace to the nineteenth century. But Palmerston was a patron, rather than a devotee, of the arts. He enjoyed music, particularly good concert singing; but he grew bored with people who asked him to express an opinion on Sir Walter Scott's latest work. His interests lay, not in literature, but in politics, field sports and women.

Palmerston was very often in Cambridge. Immediately after the election of 1807, when he had lost at Cambridge by three votes, he began nursing the constituency, for Lord Malmesbury was convinced that he would win the seat next time, and he was eager to sit in Parliament as MP for his University instead of for the pocket borough in the Isle of Wight. He regularly attended University functions, and spent much time in his college, drinking – though as little as possible – with the Fellows, and playing whist. In March 1811 the Duke of Grafton died, and as Lord Euston succeeded to the peerage, there was a by-election at Cambridge. Palmerston resigned his seat at Newport, and stood for the University. He had a straight fight with John Henry Smythe, the nephew of the new Duke of Grafton, and was elected by 451 votes against 345. He retained his seat at Cambridge in the general election the next year, when he was elected unopposed, as he was again at the elections of 1818 and 1820.

As MP for the University, Palmerston watched carefully over the interests of his constituents. He used his patronage and influence as a member of the Government in favour of his college and University colleagues, provided that he felt that he could properly do so. He entertained the University representatives to dinner at his house in Stanhope Street whenever they came to London on official business, and impressed them with the variety and quality of his wines. In the House of Commons, he championed the University's interests in connexion with the Copyright Bill of 1817. The bill abolished the obligation of publishers, under the Acts of 1709 and 1814, to supply a free copy of every book to the University libraries. Several MPs, who were representing the interests of authors and publishers, argued that the Universities should pay for their copies; but Palmerston opposed this, and succeeded in defeating the bill. The obligation on publishers to supply a free copy has continued to the present day.

But on another, and more important, question, Palmerston came into conflict with many of his Tory supporters at Cambridge. The issue of Catholic Emancipation had divided the Tories throughout the country. Pitt had always been in favour of relaxing the penal laws against Roman Catholics, and Canning and his followers still supported this policy; but many influential Tories opposed it, and the opposition was particularly strong in the Universities. It therefore needed some degree of political courage for Palmerston to speak in favour of Catholic Emancipation in the debate in the House of Commons on 1 March 1813.

The debate took place on a motion by Henry Grattan, the Irish leader, to set up a Committee to consider what degree of emancipation could be granted to the Catholics. In Ireland, Catholics were already entitled to hold commissions in the Army up to the rank of Colonel, and Grattan and his supporters now demanded that they should also be eligible for the higher military ranks, and argued that the State had no right to interfere with freedom of religious worship. Palmerston opposed this argument. 'Although I wish the Catholic claims to be considered', he said, 'I will never admit those claims to stand upon the ground of right. To maintain that the legislature of a country has not a right to impose such political disabilities upon any class of the community as it may deem necessary for the welfare and safety of the whole, would be to strike at once at the fundamental principles on which civilized government is founded. If I thought the Catholics were asking for their rights, I for one would not go into the Committee'.

But viewing the question 'entirely upon the grounds of expediency', he did not think that the penal laws were necessary now, as they had been in the seventeenth century. He thought that it was absurd to exclude Catholics from the higher Army commands while they were admitted to the lower ranks; for the higher ranks would be filled by the higher classes of society, who, because of their superior education and higher sense of professional honour, were less likely than the lower classes to be disloyal to the State. Nor would there be any danger in admitting Catholics to Parliament, for he did not think that Catholic MPs would form themselves into a Catholic Party. They were much more likely to attach themselves, according to their political inclinations, either to the Whigs or to the Tories.

'Is it wise', he asked, 'to say to men of rank and property, who, from old lineage or present possessions, have a deep interest in the common weal, that they live indeed in a country where, by the blessings of a free constitution, it is possible for any man, themselves only excepted, by the honest exertions of talents and industry, in the avocations of political life, to make himself honoured and respected by his countrymen, and to render good service to the State; that they alone can never be permitted to enter this career?' He reminded the House what the country would have lost if Nelson, Wellington, Burke, Fox or Pitt had happened to be Roman Catholics. 'The question is not whether we would have so large a part of the population Catholic or not. There they are, and we must deal with them as we can. It is vain to think that by any human pressure we can stop the spring which gushes from the earth. But it is for us to consider whether we will force it to spend its strength in secret and hidden causes, undermining our fences and corrupting our soil, or whether we shall, at once, turn the current into the open and spacious channel of honourable and constitutional ambition, converting it into the means of national prosperity and public wealth.'

Palmerston's attitude on Catholic Emancipation displeased many of his Tory supporters; but it was fundamentally a Tory attitude. He rejected the principle of religious liberty, and opposed the penal laws only because they deprived the Catholic members of the upper classes of the opportunity for advancement in public life, and prevented the State from enjoying the benefit of their services. On other issues, he was stoutly Tory; otherwise he could not have remained a member of Lord Liverpool's Government. He had, of course, social connexions with some of the Whigs. Lady Jersey was a Whig, and could at times be passionately anti-Tory; and Lady Cowper and the Lambs were also Whigs, though they represented the extreme Right wing of the Whig Party. William Lamb was one of the Whigs who supported the suspension of habeas corpus and the other repressive measures of the Tory government in 1817, and Lady Cowper was violently anti-Radical. Her hostility to the Radicals was increased by the love affairs of her two sisters-in-law. She liked Caroline Rosalie de St. Jules, the French-born wife of her brother George Lamb, but she was annoyed when Caroline had an affair with Brougham which caused a scandal. Lady Cowper expressed herself strongly about Brougham and his Radical friends; but perhaps she did not dislike Brougham as much as she sometimes made out, for, though she hinted that he had made advances to her, she kept up an acquaintanceship with him. She had a low opinion of her other sister-in-law, Lady Caroline Ponsonby, the wife of William Lamb. She was shocked that Lady Caroline had demeaned herself by becoming the mistress of a Scottish doctor, and disapproved of Lord Byron, whose affair with Lady Caroline Lamb caused an even greater scandal than Brougham's relationship with the other Caroline Lamb; but here again, Emily Cowper's bark was worse than her bite, for she used her influence to get Lady Caroline into Almack's in the face of strong opposition. Lady Cowper became more incensed than ever with Byron when he broke off his affair with Caroline and fell in love with Lady Melbourne, Lady Cowper's mother. The Lamb connexion increased Palmerston's opposition to the Radicals, especially to Byron and the Radical artistic intelligentsia. Byron, on his part, hated Palmerston. This must have been something more than a political objection, because Byron liked Peel, who was just as much of a Tory as Palmerston. But Lady Melbourne had a great affection for Palmerston.

During the nineteen years that Palmerston was at the War Office, particularly in the years between 1811 and 1822 when Castlereagh dominated the Government, there was a good deal of popular discontent and government repression. Only about two per cent of the adult male population had the right to vote for their MPs, and the middle classes of the great industrial towns of the north were not entitled to send members to Parliament. The stamp duty on newspapers made them so expensive that the lower classes could not afford to buy them, which seriously curtailed written propaganda among the people; and political prosecutions for libel, sedition and blasphemy were common. In Ireland, where there had been revolutionary excesses and savage reprisals in 1798 and 1803, there was great resentment at social and religious injustice. Trade unions had been prohibited by the Combination Act of 1799, and many strikers were in prison. The criminal law had been made much more severe during the previous hundred years, and was now the harshest in Europe; whereas in France, under the Code Napoleon, there were six offences punishable by death, in Britain there were 223, though this was so ineffective in preventing crime that in 1820 there were nearly four times as many of these offences committed among the 12,000,000 inhabitants of Britain as among 27,000,00 Frenchmen. The slave trade had been abolished, but slavery still existed in the British colonies in the West Indies, and Wilberforce and his colleagues were once again beginning an agitation about it. There was also a great deal of economic misery in the country, which was made worse when the Corn Laws of 1815 prohibited the importation of corn in order to keep up the price of corn for the benefit of the farmers and of the landowners to whom they paid their rent. In 1811 the outbreak of the Luddite riots in Yorkshire and the Midlands had led to the enactment of legislation which punished frame-breaking by death.

Palmerston fully supported the Government policy. His biographer, Henry Bulwer, who himself entered the House of Commons as a Radical in 1830, and became a great admirer of the Palmerston of later days, tried to make out that Palmerston did not really approve of the policy of the Tory government in which he was a minister for twenty-one years; but there is no reason whatever to believe that this is true, and according to Madame de Lieven he was, when she first knew him, 'very attached to Tory policy, and particularly to Lord Castlereagh'. Like other Tories, he disagreed with the Government on Catholic Emancipation; but he had no other criticism of the policies of Castlereagh and Sidmouth, as he showed by his attitude in the House of Commons. The Whig Opposition was hopelessly split, for its leaders, though they periodically opposed the Government in the lobbies, were much closer to the Tories than to their own Left wing; but the Government was persistently attacked by a handful of Radical MPs – the Honourable Henry Bennet, Sir Francis Burdett, Sir Samuel Romilly, Joseph Hume, Sir Matthew White Ridley, Lord Cochrane – until his imprisonment and expulsion from the House – John Cam Hobhouse, and above all Henry Brougham. Nearly every week these MPs – or those of them who were not in prison – divided the House on capital punishment, flogging in the Army, slavery in the West Indies, the deportation of foreign refugees from Britain, Parliamentary reform, freedom of the press, or on some case of injustice to prisoners or other humble victims of tyranny. On all these occasions Palmerston voted with the Government against the Radicals; and on the question of flogging in the Army, he was chosen, as Secretary at War, to be the chief spokesman for the Government.

Flogging had been almost unknown in the British Army before 1688, but it was introduced immediately afterwards by William III as a punishment for his Dutch soldiers, and was soon applied throughout the British Army. On one occasion Bernal Osborne, a witty and brilliant Whig MP, pointed this out to the Radicals in the House when they were denouncing flogging, reminding them that revolutions can sometimes have harmful consequences, as flogging had been one of the results of the Revolution of 1688. It first became a controversial issue in 1810, when William Cobbett, who had himself served in the Army as a Sergeant-Major, protested in his *Political Register* against the flogging of five militiamen at Ely. These English militiamen had organized a protest demonstration in their unit when their pay was stopped to cover the cost of their knapsacks. They were awarded five hundred lashes each, and the sentence was carried out by German soldiers of the German Legion Cavalry at Bury St. Edmunds. There was already a good deal of ill-feeling about the employment of foreign units in the British Army, and Palmerston had had to defend the practice in the House of Commons in the face of strong criticism from MPs of all parties. Now the flogging of free-born Englishmen by Germans caused great anger, which was not diminished when Cobbett was prosecuted for his article and sentenced to two years' imprisonment for seditious libel.

Flogging was part of the price which Britain paid for its military system. It was a matter of pride to Englishmen that, instead of the slavery of conscription which Napoleonic tyranny imposed on France, the British Army was raised by voluntary methods. But only men from the lowest class volunteered for the Army. The ordinary Englishman, staunch patriot though he was, was not eager to join an army where he would never, except in the most extraordinary cases, be able to win promotion from the ranks; where he would be subjected to military law and deprived of his legal rights as an Englishman under the law; where he would be sent to die on the battlefields of the Peninsula, to have his limbs amputated without an anaesthetic, and to face the far greater risk of disease in camps and hospitals where the organization was even worse than Florence Nightingale was afterwards to encounter in the Crimea; and where, if he survived, he would be discharged from the service at Dover, and left to walk, begging his way, to his home village, and if permanently maimed, left without any pension whatever – until 1811 – to face destitution and the penalties of the Vagrancy Laws. Patriotism was not enough to drive men into such an army, especially as there was no moral pressure upon anyone to join up. It was thought no more discreditable for a man of the middle classes to continue managing his business, or for an artisan to continue at his daily labour, than it was for Lord Palmerston and other young nobles, in perfect physical health, to spend the war at Almack's, or shooting on their country estates. It was an Englishman's privilege that his country could fight, and win, its wars without calling on him for military service, unless he was one of the young aristocrats who chose to purchase a commission and run all risks for glory, or a poacher, convict, vagrant or dare-devil who joined the ranks to escape from the village constable or from the irate father of a pregnant girl. The majority of Army leaders and politicians were firmly convinced that fear of the lash was the only way of preserving discipline in an army composed of criminals.

The question of flogging was raised four times in the House of Commons in March and April 1812. Brougham attacked a system which 'had its principle in torture', and declared that death would be a more merciful punishment than a sentence of a thousand lashes. Burdett referred to three cases where soldiers had died from flogging, and another where a man of seventy was flogged after fifty years of blameless service; and he said that the British soldier was in a worse position than the negro slave in Jamaica, where there was a limit to the number of lashes which could be imposed, and the sentence could not be awarded at the arbitrary will of one officer. A number of members, including several Army officers, spoke in favour of flogging. Their arguments varied from those of General Porter, who claimed that Army discipline had been getting milder and milder since 1775, to Mr. Charles Adams, who declared that if Cobbett had 'felt the terror of the lash when he was in the Army, he would have been deterred from publishing many of those opinions which since he left the Army had involved him in so many awkward predicaments', and had now landed him in prison. Palmerston defended flogging on the grounds of necessity: no other punishment was so effective. He indignantly rejected the comparison between English soldiers and negro slaves. It was true that flogging was not used in any foreign army, but this was because 'there existed what was still more degrading to the men – a system of wanton and capricious ill-usage'. In the English Army, a sentence of flogging could only be imposed by a court-martial, or by the commanding officer, under proper legal procedure; and he dismissed as absurd the suggestion that death was a more merciful punishment than flogging.

The frontal attack on flogging having failed in 1812, the Radicals came back next year with a more moderate proposal.

They urged that when a sentence of flogging had been suspended, at the orders of the surgeon, before the full number of strokes had been inflicted, the soldier should not be brought out again, after his wounds had healed, to complete the punishment. They referred to a case in which a soldier was sentenced to a flogging, and the surgeon intervened and stopped the punishment before the full number of lashes had been received. The soldier recovered, and served well for several years. He was then accused of some offence by his commanding officer, and sent for trial by court-martial, and acquitted, whereupon his commanding officer ordered him to receive the remaining lashes which had never been inflicted under the sentence passed some years before. Even the most ardent supporters of flogging admitted that, in this case, the action of the commanding officer had been improper; but Palmerston, replying for the Government, refused to order that a suspended sentence of flogging should never be resumed, as this would encourage the deliberate feigning of unconsciousness by soldiers undergoing a flogging. His attitude shocked the Radical MPs, and Bennet declared that it was 'indecent'. Palmerston replied that 'when he should find it necessary to take lessons of decency, he would not, from the specimens which he had seen of the honourable gentleman, think of applying to him'.

On 21 June 1815, Bennet raised in the House of Commons the activities of Colonel Quentin and the floggings in the 10th Hussars. It was three days after the soldiers whose punishments they were discussing had won the battle of Waterloo, and rumours of the victory had reached London on the previous day. Bennet told the House that in the Peninsula in 1813 Quentin had sentenced 63 men in the 10th Hussars to receive 14,000 lashes between them, many of the men being given between four and six hundred lashes at one time; and in 1814, in the whole Army, more than 18,000 men had been flogged. Burdett, as usual, supported him. 'No man would deny', he told the House, 'that punishment, even severe punishment, was necessary; but was there no other fit punishment but that of stripping a man naked, tying him to the halberts, and treating him like a beast?' He said that this punishment was a national disgrace, as no foreign army used it, and asked: 'Why should the British soldier be alone liable to this ignominious torture?'

Palmerston opposed the motion. The Commander-in-Chief, he said, was a merciful man, and so were most officers who sat on courts-martial. They normally limited the number of lashes which were to be inflicted to the greatest extent compatible with the public service; and when a sentence of flogging was interrupted at the surgeon's intervention, the man was no longer brought out to be flogged a second time, except in very grave cases, where a severe example was necessary. But these questions should be left to the discretion of the military authorities; Parliament should not intervene, as the power to award the most extreme punishments should be available as a deterrent. He denied the suggestion that the foreign soldiers serving in the British Army were treated more leniently than the English troops. They were just as liable, in law, to be flogged as English soldiers; and if the Portuguese and other foreign soldiers in our pay were in fact flogged much less often than our men, this was because the English, like all soldiers from Northern lands, were more likely to get drunk than men of Southern nations, and were therefore more liable to commit offences.

Next day the newspapers confirmed the news of Waterloo, and fires were lit and windows illuminated in every town and village of England. A week later, the war ended with the capture of Peronne. It was the last of 182 engagements in which the British Army had fought since the first action at Valenciennes in July 1793. Palmerston, with his usual methodical habits, tabulated all the battles and the losses sustained in each: in the twenty-one years of war, including the war against the United States of 1812–14, the British Army had suffered a total of 920 officers and 15,214 other ranks killed, of whom nearly one-sixth had fallen in the last week in Belgium. In the Navy, the total losses were 3,662, the combined losses of both services in twenty-one years of war being less than one-third of the number who fell in one day's fighting at the Somme in 1916. The Government proposed a grant of £300,000 to the Duke of Wellington; and the leaders of the Opposition, who were particularly anxious just then to dissociate the Whig Party from its Radical and pacifist section, carried an amendment increasing the figure to £400,000. As usual, very little attention was paid to the rank and file; even the war memorial erected at Waterloo bears the names of the officers only, and refers merely to the numbers of the other ranks who fell.

But one man in authority remembered the common soldier. On 3 July 1815 Palmerston suggested to the Duke of York that every soldier who had served at Waterloo should be entitled to count it as two years' service for the purposes of qualifying for increases in his pay and pensions, though it would not be reckoned as such in calculating the time that he was required to serve before being entitled to his discharge. He also proposed that, in commemoration of Waterloo, the pensions of wounded officers should henceforth be increased whenever the officer was promoted in rank, and not always remain at the level fixed for the rank which the officer had held at the time when he was wounded. The Duke of York welcomed Palmerston's proposal and the Prime Minister, Lord Liverpool, agreed. It was also at Palmerston's suggestion that the men who had served at Waterloo were entered on the pay-roll of their regiments as 'Waterloo men', for this, he wrote, 'would constantly keep alive in the minds of the Soldiers of the Army the memory of this unexampled victory'.

Chapter Five

Lord Pumicestone

In August 1815, after Parliament had risen for the recess, Palmerston went to France. The peace terms dictated after Waterloo had been more severe than those imposed before the Hundred Days, and France was saddled for three and a half years with the presence, and the cost, of the Allied armies of occupation; but official relations between the Allied commanders and Louis XVIII's government were friendly, and despite a few incidents, the British troops were popular with the French people, as were the easy-going Russian troops. The French were impressed with the restraint and discipline of Wellington's men, which they contrasted with the revengeful brutalities of the Prussians.

Palmerston went to Paris, and spent five weeks taking part in the gay social life of the headquarters of the army of occupation, with the English and foreign visitors who had gathered around Wellington and the Allied sovereigns. As he spoke perfect French, he could converse with people of all classes. As soon as he landed at Le Havre after a twenty-four-hour crossing from Southampton, he noted that though the white flag was flying everywhere, and all officials had a dirty piece of white ribbon in their hats, the tricolour was in their hearts. He made another journey to France in the autumn of 1818, visiting Wellington's headquarters at Cambrai, and watching the joint manoeuvres of the British, Prussian and Russian armies near Laon. He dined with Wellington, Tsar Alexander and the King of Prussia at field headquarters, and travelled with them from St. Quentin to Sedan, and then returned to England by way of Brussels and the battlefield of Waterloo.

He kept a diary of his French travels, and his comments

show his pride in the achievements of the British Army, and a
certain vindictive satisfaction at the humiliations inflicted on
the French. He was very pleased when the Allied troops removed from the Louvre the art treasures which Napoleon had
brought there from conquered countries. This caused the
greatest resentment among the French, who claimed that it
was a violation of the surrender terms; but Palmerston was
glad that the Allies had had an opportunity to resort to an
open display of armed force, because this was something
which the French could not explain away as having been
achieved by voluntary negotiation, but would bring home to
them the fact that they had been defeated in war. During a
third visit to France in 1821, he was more sympathetic to the
French people. He wrote to his sister Elizabeth: 'With all my
prejudice against the French, I must own that there is a great
deal of natural good manner and civility among the lower
classes, and particularly the women, which one does not meet
with in England'. But he was not surprised when he heard
a boy of eight singing an anti-English Bonapartist song.

In his first six years at the War Office, Palmerston encountered very little opposition when he introduced the Army estimates in Parliament; but it was a different matter after 1815.
The end of the war had made it possible for the Government
to reduce the size of the armed forces, but the reduction in
military expenditure did not go fast enough to satisfy public
opinion. From 1816 onwards, the estimates were regularly
attacked, year after year, by Joseph Hume, the Radical MP
for Aberdeen, who demanded a return to the peace-time establishment of 1792. Palmerston argued that this was quite impossible, in view of the new commitments abroad and the social
unrest at home. Britain had acquired new colonies and protectorates at Malta, the Ionian Isles, and in the West Indies; it
was necessary to guard Bonaparte on St. Helena; and with
Luddite violence and Radical agitation in London and the
North, the army in England must be kept in a state of readiness.

This last argument did not go down well with the Radical
MPs or with larger bodies of opinion in and out of Parliament.
The Government was accused of trampling on the liberties

of Englishmen and threatening the constitution by keeping a standing army. But Palmerston rebutted these accusations in his speech on the estimates on 8 March 1816. He said that England was not a state like ancient Rome, where 12,000 praetorian bands could rule an empire; for a standing army could only overthrow the civil constitution of a country which had become degenerate, whose martial spirit had been destroyed, and which had been brought to a state of political degeneration 'such as few countries experience which have once known the blessings of liberty'. He claimed that this could not happen in England, which 'enjoyed the practical blessings of freedom in a greater degree than had ever been done by any other country', or than England itself had ever experienced at any time in its history.

The Army estimates for 1816 were grudgingly accepted by the House of Commons; but even the Tories were dissatisfied that expenditure was not being more drastically reduced, and some of them blamed Palmerston personally for the refusal to cut military costs, and held him chiefly responsible for the high taxation, the economic distress, and public discontent. Palmerston reminded them that the Army always became unpopular after every war was over, and told the story of the soldiers who marched out of London against the Jacobites in 1745. 'There go our brave Guards! There go the pillars of the State!' cried the people. 'Aye', said one of the soldiers, 'but when we have licked the enemy, the cry will be: "There go the caterpillars of the State".'

But Palmerston was determined to do his best to reduce unnecessary expenditure, and in 1821, in response to a circular from the Treasury insisting on government economies, he drew up a plan for saving nearly £18,000 a year in the administration of the War Office. He planned to reduce the numbers of persons employed at the War Office from 136 in 1821 to 77, as compared with 57 in 1797, and proposed substantial cuts in all salaries except his own. He proposed to remove the anomaly by which the salary of the Secretary at War was £20 per year less than that of the Deputy Secretary, by maintaining his own salary at £2,480 and reducing the Deputy Secretary's from £2,500 to £2,000. He proposed similar reductions all the way down the scale as far as the Junior Clerks, whose salaries were to be reduced from £250 to £90 a year. These proposals caused some resentment in the War Office, as did the new disciplinary rules which Palmerston introduced. He put a stop to visitors calling during office hours to talk to the clerks on personal matters, and in other ways tightened up the running of the office by a series of new regulations. He threatened instant dismissal of any clerk who contravened these regulations.

When Palmerston had become Secretary at War in 1809, he had immediately found a position in the War Office for his friend Laurence Sulivan, who had been very intimate with him when they were undergraduates at Cambridge, and two years later married his sister, Elizabeth Temple. In his plans for reducing the War Office staff in the autumn of 1821, he decided to promote Sulivan to be Superintendent of Accounts in the place of Mr. Foveaux, who had been at the War Office since 1782, and was now to be retired on pension. Foveaux wrote a long letter of protest to Palmerston; he accused Palmerston of favouring his brother-in-law at the expense of a man like himself who had had thirty-nine years' service in the War Office, and complained of the injustice of promoting Sulivan, with his large private income, to the higher paid post, whereas Foveaux, who had always had difficulty in subsisting on his War Office pay, would now have to live on the reduced income from his pension. In his reply, Palmerston coldly and inexorably informed Foveaux that he had taken the decision because Sulivan was efficient and Foveaux was not. Foveaux had objected to the fact that, some time before, Sulivan had been placed in charge of the Department of Current Accounts and Foveaux transferred to the Arrear Accounts; but Palmerston pointed out that Sulivan had succeeded in ending the chaotic state which had existed in the Current Accounts Department when it had been under Foveaux's management.

'I have no hesitation', he wrote to Foveaux, 'in declaring my firm and perfect conviction that such a result could not by possibility have taken place if the Department of Current Accounts had been placed under your superintendence. I am on the contrary fully satisfied, from a long observation of your habits of business and turn of mind, that if you had been left upon the Current Accounts, and Mr. Sulivan had been transferred to the Arrear, the Arrear might possibly have been by this time nearly in as satisfactory a state as the Current Business now is. But the Current Business from 1810 downwards would, on the other hand, have been fast approaching to the state in which those for the previous years now are. . . . I have high opinion of your integrity, and I believe you to be a jealous and very laborious Public Servant; but I have had occasion to remark that you do not possess that activity of Mind which presses forward to the attainment of results – that however sedulous your application to business, you have not the faculty of disposing of it with perspicuity and despatch; and that your want of arrangement and method not only mars your own labors, but defeats to a considerable degree those of the persons under you'.

But there was worse to come for Foveaux. When Foveaux came back with another long, indignant letter, Palmerston told him that he had used a tone which was improper from an inferior to his superior in an office, and that he was herewith dismissed from the War Office. This brought Mrs. Foveaux into action. She wrote to Palmerston in a style which was a shrewd mixture of respect and reproof, and told him that he would fall short of the nobility of nature which was to be expected in one of his rank if he punished Foveaux for his impropriety by depriving him of his post and his pension. Palmerston answered with a most courteous letter. He said that she had done no more than her duty as a wife in interceding with him on her husband's behalf, and that though it was impossible for him to reinstate Foveaux, he had never had any intention of depriving him of his pension.

In later times, when Palmerston's uneventful years at the War Office seemed to form such a contrast to his brilliant achievements at the Foreign Office, it became fashionable to say that he did nothing for nineteen years except introduce the Army estimates and sign orders for the supply of greatcoats to the army in the Peninsula. This overlooks the bold and visionary schemes which he put forward, and carried through, for improving the conditions and prospects of the soldiers. Like most of his contemporaries, Palmerston accepted the eighteenth-century view that the common soldier was the scum of the earth, who could only be kept in order by fear of the lash; but he was also a member of the generation which had been influenced by the Evangelical movement, by Wilberforce's 'Clapham Saints' and Raikes's Sunday School Movement. He believed that the army ruffians could be made into better men by educating them and keeping them sober.

He did all he could to further education in the Army. He interested himself in the schools for army orphans at Chelsea, Gibraltar, and in Canada, and in the face of considerable opposition from Hume and other advocates of Army economy, he persuaded Parliament to grant funds for establishing a military college for officers at Sandhurst. He was able to win the sympathy of the House of Commons for this project by pointing out that British officers were obliged to go abroad to foreign military academies to learn their profession; and he assured those MPs who had so often criticized him for employing foreign soldiers in the British Army that he 'wished to see the British soldier with a British character, with British habits, with a British education, and with as little as possible of anything foreign'. It was a welcome assurance from a Secretary at War who had been identified with the flogging of English militiamen by German Hussars.

Palmerston, like all the army officers, attributed the crime and indiscipline in the Army to drunkenness. He always suggested, whenever possible, that the men should be given more regular pay or allowances, rather than larger cash payments as bounties which they were sure to spend on drink. In 1825 he urged General Taylor, the Commander-in-Chief's Military Secretary, to set up savings banks in the Army, into which the soldiers could pay part of their pay, which they would otherwise spend in getting drunk. Many army officers were opposed to the scheme, because they thought that if a soldier had accumulated some money in a savings bank, 'he would begin to think himself independent of his officers and become insubordinate'. Palmerston appreciated the force of this argument, but thought that it overlooked the great moral improvement which must have taken place in any soldier who could manage to save, out of his meagre pay, any substantial sum in a savings bank, instead of spending it on alcohol. 'Property which is acquired by chance or by a blow, like a prize in the lottery or a prize in War, is apt to unhinge the mind, and tempt to irregularities. But property acquired by long continued industry or frugality necessarily, and by the laws of human Nature, improves the character of the man who has acquired it'. Taylor and the Army leaders were unenthusiastic, and argued that if soldiers wished to save their money, they could invest it in the ordinary civilian savings banks; but Palmerston pointed out that 'the lower classes feel confidence in the Savings Banks in their respective neighbourhoods because they are under the superintendence and management of the gentlemen of the district, but that Soldiers would not feel the same Confidence in such Banks because they would not have the same sentiments towards the Directors and Managers, and that none but officers of the Army can stand in the same relation to Soldiers in which the gentlemen stand with respect to the lower Classes'.

When it came to dealing with the black troops in the West Indies, Palmerston tried to prevent the military authorities from issuing them with the rum ration which was given to the white soldiers. 'We have at last nearly succeeded', he wrote in 1817, 'thru' the force of institution, regulation and example, in making our black Soldiers almost as drunken and depraved as the Whites, altho' the Negro Tribes, of all the varieties of the human race, savage or civilized, are the least addicted to the vice of drunkenness. A more cruel experiment (however differently meant) than that of serving a full ration of rum upon the new Negro, along with his food, can scarcely be imagined'. It was said that the black troops might resent it if they were not given the same rum ration as the British soldier; but Palmerston thought that they would be equally happy if they were given 'a small portion of sugar or syrup instead of rum to mix with the water', and this would be much better for their health.

His concern for the welfare of the soldier involved him in a medical controversy, and a struggle with the whole of the Army medical establishment. The subject of the controversy was a brilliant but exasperating doctor, who aroused strong passions during his lifetime, but is almost entirely forgotten today. William Adams was a village boy from Cornwall who took employment as a lad with a doctor in Barnstaple, was sent by him to London to study medicine, and by the time he was thirty had become the personal oculist to the Prince Regent and two of his brothers, and had been awarded a knighthood for his services. He claimed to have discovered, or to have developed, a cure for 'Egyptian ophthalmia', an ailment which seems to have been a form of trachoma, and which was prevalent in the Army at the time. His claims were ridiculed by Sir James Macgregor, the head of the Army Medical Department, and by many other eminent doctors; but Adams, through his influence at Court, was able to obtain permission to experiment on some Chelsea pensioners, and soon afterwards exhibited to the Duke of York and Palmerston some patients who had formerly been unable to see a post, but could now, as a result of his treatment, read the tiny print of an early nineteenth-century newspaper. In the face of strong opposition from the Army Medical Department, Palmerston vigorously backed Adams. Whether Adams was in fact the inventor of the cure, or had merely developed the invention of his teacher Saunders, was irrelevant for Palmerston: it sufficed that here was a treatment which could restore to old soldiers the eyesight that they had lost in the service of their country, could check a highly infectious disease which was spreading among the lower classes, and could save the Exchequer the cost of paying pensions to the blind soldiers. At Palmerston's suggestion, many victims of Egyptian ophthalmia were placed under Adams's care in the military hospital at Chelsea. Adams was not given any military rank or official position, and carried out his work without fee.

Adams's appointment was bitterly resented by the Army medical officers. They did not like to see this civilian put in charge of a military hospital, and they disapproved of Adams's methods. At a time when most doctors were very secretive about their discoveries, Adams developed a flair for public relations which he could have used to greater effect in the days of television and the popular press; and his vanity and self-advertising technique exasperated many members of the

medical profession. The Army doctors at Chelsea criticized
him at every opportunity. One of them even went so far as to
advise, in a letter which by chance fell into Palmerston's
hands, that Adams's patients should be made drunk in order
to retard their cure. In May 1819, Adams's appointment was
raised in the House of Commons by several MPs, who had
been well primed with medical data by Adams's enemies
among the doctors, and were able to quote cases where
Adams's treatment had not cured the patients, but had actually made them worse. They represented the case as one in
which Palmerston was arrogantly overriding expert opinion
on a subject about which he knew nothing, and was promoting a fashionable and influential doctor over the heads of men
who had spent their lives in the service of the Army Medical
Department. But Palmerston strongly defended his conduct,
and claimed that Adams's treatment had been very successful.
Hume, who as usual was one of Palmerston's chief critics, later
withdrew his allegations against Adams; and when, in June
1820, Palmerston asked Parliament to grant £2,000 to Adams as
an ex gratia payment for his free services to the Army, he had
little difficulty in persuading the House of Commons to agree.

Though Palmerston was always eager to develop beneficial
schemes for the welfare of the troops, he had the rigidity and
hardness of the well-meaning bureaucrat when it came to individual 'hard cases'. He had little sympathy with applications
for pensions, or for other favours, from people with a grievance. He was more ready to grant such indulgences to the
families of officers of higher rank, because, as he explained in
a memorandum in 1815, he considered that the basis on which
pensions and allowances should be granted was not the merit
of the service performed, but the desirability of maintaining
an ex-serviceman and his dependants at the appropriate standard of living for persons of their social class. An example of
his cold, hard logic in his attitude when Major Forneret of the
1st Battalion of the 60th Regiment asked him for permission
to pay a higher bounty to the foreign troops who re-enlisted
after seven years' service, similar to the bounty which was
paid to English troops on such occasions. Palmerston, who
was always watchful about public expenditure, waited for

two and a half years before definitely replying to the suggestion, and then refused. When the Commander-in-Chief supported the proposal, and pressed him on the matter, Palmerston not only argued that an increased bounty would be spent on drink, but pointed out that if the foreigners left the Army, they would have difficulty in paying their fare home to their own countries, and it was therefore unnecessary to offer them any incentive to re-enlist. This was at a time when he was often explaining to the House of Commons the necessity of using foreign troops in the British Army, and the value of the services they rendered. Only four months later, in December 18132, he told the House of Comomsn that 'our foreign troops, and particularly the German Legion, merited all the rewards that could be bestowed upon them'.

This element of hardness in Palmerston's character was becoming increasingly marked, and showed itself in his private life as well as at the War Office. He had changed a good deal between the ages of twenty-five and thirty-five. In 1810 he was regarded as a quiet, considerate and studious young man, but lacking in drive and push; he was almost universally popular, but few people had a high opinion of his abilities. By 1820 he was respected, but was widely disliked because of his high-handed behaviour, his quarrelsomeness, and his lack of consideration for others. Perhaps he felt that his former modesty had not been properly appreciated, but had been mistaken for inadequacy. Perhaps he had gained in self-confidence now that he was free from the protective influence of his father and mother, and was the lover of at least three of the most famous society beauties in London.

He showed signs of hardness, or at least of arrogance, in his attitude towards his creditors, though in this he was not very different from many other young noblemen of the time. Tradesmen were kept waiting for many months before he paid them, although he did not dispute that he owed them the money, and could well afford to pay. It was difficult for these creditors to press him for payment, because of his social position, and the fact that he understandably refused to be troubled with small financial matters which he left to be handled by his servants and agents. William Day, whose father trained Palmerston's racehorses, mentions that on one occasion a butcher, who had waited a long time for payment of his account and had repeatedly made unsuccessful applications to Palmerston's agents, forced his way into Palmerston's presence and insisted on immediate satisfaction. Palmerston wrote out a cheque for the amount, and then, putting on a glove in the butcher's presence, picked up the pen with which he had written the cheque and threw the defiled object out of the window.

But the butcher was luckier than many other creditors, for at least he got paid without going to court. On twenty occasions in thirty years, Palmerston was sued by hatters, coachmakers, chandlers, moneylenders and other creditors. In eighteen of these cases judgment with costs was awarded against him. In the nineteenth case he settled out of court by paying the amount claimed and the plaintiff's costs. Apart from one case in 1836 when some bankers obtained judgment against him for £4,895 7s. 6d. on a dishonoured promissory note, the sums recovered by the creditors varied from £298 7s. 5d. to £2 12s. 0d. The first case in which he was sued was in November 1811, which may be taken as an indication of the approximate date at which the abstemious young paragon of Edinburgh and Cambridge Universities was transformed into a Regency rake, though it is only fair to point out that many of his financial difficulties were due to his expenditure on developing his Irish estates. In the course of the next six and a half years to April 1818, he was sued nine times. After being taken to court only twice in the next fifteen years, he was then sued six times between June 1833 and October 1836, and three more times in fifteen months at the height of his triumphs as Foreign Secretary in 1840 and 1841. There was also an occasion in May 1835 when the landlord of Palmerston's house at No. 122 Piccadilly, sent in the bailiffs to levy a distress for the year's rent of £105 which Palmerston owed him. The bailiffs were in the house for three days before Palmerston paid the rent and the bailiffs' costs.

His attitude towards his private creditors stands in great contrast to the sentiments which he expressed in his memor-

anda to commanding officers in the Army, when he urged
them to establish savings banks in their regiments in order to
encourage the virtues of thrift among their men. Perhaps the
troubles of Palmerston's creditors were partly due to the obstinacy and dilatoriness of his agents, for Palmerston left the
handling of his private affairs to Messrs. Oddie, Oddie and
Forster – later Oddie, Forster and Lumley – and only examined their accounts once every four or five years. But when
the time to do this came round, he spent four or five days
looking very closely into their figures, and spotted the smallest
discrepancies; so he must have been well aware of these repeated judgments against him, which unnecessarily involved
him in additional expense as well as giving him a bad name in
certain circles.

He was a good and popular employer and landlord in
Hampshire, as well as in Ireland. He paid his labourers and
servants the average wage rates, or occasionally a little less,
but he was generous in supplying them with beer and other
conventional perks, and cared for old servants after their retirement. He did not press his farmers unduly for their rents,
and was always reluctant to evict them. He took a personal
interest in the well-being of his servants and tenants. On one
occasion, when he was very busy working on his despatches at
Broadlands, he heard that one of his tenants had been very
badly injured in an accident, and immediately left his work to
ride over to visit the dying man. He contributed to local
charities, and helped the Baptist chapel in Romsey as well as
the Anglican church in the old abbey, where he himself attended divine service with moderate regularity. He paid for
the installation of gaslight in the buildings, and for structural
repairs to the abbey to make it warmer for the congregation.
He instituted a school for poor children in the town, and paid
a salary of £10 a year to the teacher. The repairs to the school
building, and other expenses in connexion with the school,
cost him between £75 and £100 every year. In later years he
built a number of model workmen's cottages for his tenants
and employees; but these well-built, mid-Victorian red-brick
houses date from the fifties and sixties, when such beneficial

projects had become the vogue. Palmerston also carried out extensive alterations, from 1808 onwards, to the big house at Broadlands.

His largest single items of expenditure were on the maintenance of his gardens at Broadlands, and on game, which cost him about £550 and £340 a year. He hunted with the Putney Hounds when he was living in London, and with the local Hunts in Hampshire, but preferred to go shooting with his gamekeepers, or with a few of his London friends, on his own estates. On one occasion in about 1812 this involved him in an incident which caused some ill-feeling in the neighbourhood. He went out shooting with his gamekeepers, and found himself on the edge of his property, next to the cottage and garden of Mr. Webb, a local brickmaker. Palmerston jumped over the hedge into Webb's garden, which he was entitled to do, under the Game Laws, when in pursuit of game, and was confronted by a savage bulldog, which Palmerston thought ought to have been kept chained up. He immediately stepped back over the hedge on to his own property, but the dog leaped up and put his front paws on the top of the hedge. Palmerston, thinking that the dog was about to attack him, shot the dog. Webb's little girl was heartbroken. She nursed the dog, but though her beloved Lion seemed to recover, it worsened again, and eventually had to be destroyed.

Palmerston's action may have been necessary, as he claimed, in self-defence to save himself from serious injury, or it may have been an error of judgment in a moment of panic; but it could be represented by Palmerston's local enemies as a typical example of aristocratic oppression, and fitted well into the appealing, sentimental and downtrodden style of English Radical propaganda, which was so different from the defiant, aggressive, revolutionary line of continental Radicalism.

Chapter Six

The Tory Landlord

The years which followed Waterloo were a time of acute economic distress in Britain, and of increasing bitterness in public life. In 1815 there had been riots in London against the Corn Laws, when the householders barricaded their doors and windows, and Palmerston ordered his servants to 'pepper the faces of the mob' with small shot as a warning that they would be fired at with more deadly ammunition if they persisted in their threatening attitude. Next year there was a great demonstration at Spa Fields in London, which was broken up by the police, and there were frequent riots, one of which engulfed Lady Cowper on her way to Almack's. The Government passed legislation which prohibited public meetings of more than fifty persons, making attendance at such meetings punishable with death, and placed more restrictions on the freedom of the press. They suspended the Habeas Corpus Act, to allow imprisonment of political agitators without trial for one year, and a number of prosecutions for sedition and blasphemy were instituted. These measures aroused much resentment among the Opposition, as did the use by the Government of spies and *agents provocateurs* – a practice which even Palmerston found a little distasteful, at least in non-political cases, for he was not pleased when he found that a Colonel had employed an *agent provocateur* to catch a man who was receiving stolen equipment from the Army.

Some of the less balanced critics of the Government, having no vote for Parliament, and frustrated by the restrictions on public meetings and the liberty of the press, resorted to assassination. In 1812 the Prime Minister, Perceval, who had made himself unpopular with the Radicals by the manner in which he had conducted political prosecutions as Attorney-

General in Pitt's Government, was shot dead in the lobby of the House of Commons by a man named Bellingham, who was probably mad, but was considered sane enough to hang. Palmerston was the next victim. On 1 April 1818, a Lieutenant Davies, a retired officer on the half-pay list, who seems to have had some grievance about the manner in which the War Office had treated his claims for a pension, and was completely mad, waited for Palmerston on the staircase at the War Office and shot at him as Palmerston walked up the stairs to his room. Davies fired just as Palmerston was turning the corner, and the bullet grazed his back just above the hip, and only inflicted a slight wound. Palmerston, being informed that Davies was insane, paid for a barrister to appear in his defence at the trial. Davies was found to be mad, and sent to Bedlam, from where he wrote humble and contrite letters to Palmerston, begging for forgiveness and release. Two years later Arthur Thistlewood and other Radicals planned from their headquarters in Cato Street to murder all the ministers while they were attending a dinner at Lord Harrowby's house in Grosvenor Square. The Cato Street conspiracy was betrayed by a government spy, and the plotters were executed.

In August 1819 came the 'massacre of Peterloo', when a peaceful but alarming demonstration of thousands of factory workers in St. Peter's Fields in Manchester was charged and sabred by the cavalry of the Hussars and the Yeomanry, at least a dozen people being killed and more than five hundred seriously injured. The Prince Regent sent a message of congratulation to the Manchester magistrates who had ordered the Yeomanry to charge. The Radical leader, Henry Hunt, who had addressed the Manchester meeting, was sentenced to two years' imprisonment, and other agitators in the North were arrested. The Radicals and many Whigs were indignant at the massacre of Peterloo, but had few opportunities to express their anger, as Parliament was not in session, and all public meetings were banned, and could only be held with the consent of either the Lord Lieutenant or the High Sheriff of the county. The Opposition supporters therefore petitioned the Lord Lieutenant or High Sheriff for permission to hold County Meetings, and prepared to use this one available opportunity to protest about Peterloo. They applied for permission to hold County Meetings in Essex, Hampshire, Berkshire, Wiltshire and Cornwall; but in every case some of the landowners who supported the Government sent in a counter-requisition asking the Lord Lieutenant or Sheriff not to permit the meeting to be held. In Hampshire, where Wellington was the Lord Lieutenant, and the requisition was therefore sent to the High Sheriff, the counter-requisition against the meeting was signed by many landowners, including Wellington himself, and Palmerston. In all five counties the Lord Lieutenant or Sheriff refused to allow the County Meeting to be held. In the West Riding of Yorkshire the Lord Lieutenant, Lord Fitzwilliam, agreed to call a meeting, at which he criticized the action of the magistrates at Manchester. He was immediately dismissed from his office of Lord Lieutenant by the Government.

In November the Government recalled Parliament to pass a Seditious Meetings Prevention Bill, which imposed stricter restrictions on public meetings, and other legislation – the famous Six Acts – restrained the freedom of the press, and enacted other measures to suppress seditious and blasphemous activity. When Lord Sidmouth, the Home Secretary, disclosed the terms of the bills to the junior ministers at the Cabinet dinner given by Castlereagh on the eve of the Parliamentary session, there was general agreement among Palmerston and his ministerial colleagues that the bills did not go far enough to restrict the freedom of the press; but the Opposition bitterly attacked the bills in the House. During the debate Brougham denounced Palmerston for his part in banning the County Meeting in Hampshire. The Hampshire case appeared to the Whigs to be worse than any of the others, because in Hampshire two of the signatories of the counter-requisition, Wellington and Palmerston, held official positions in the Government, and while purporting to act as the owners of Stratfieldsaye and Broadlands, had really been carrying out government policy. Palmerston defended himself in a short but powerful speech, in which he went out of his way to praise the action of the authorities at Peterloo. He argued that the fact that he was Secretary at War did not prevent him from exercising his rights as a Hampshire landowner, and said that he and his fellow-signatories had signed the counter-requisition in order to prevent the outbreak in Hampshire of disorders like that which had been so properly suppressed by the Manchester magistrates.

As Secretary at War, Palmerston had some responsibility for the use of troops to suppress internal disorders, and he threw himself with great energy into this part of his official duties. In April 1820 a revolutionary group in Glasgow constituted themselves as a provisional government, and though they urged their followers to avoid violence and excesses, they called on them to fight for their freedom. Troops were sent to suppress the movement, and several of the leaders were executed for high treason. Palmerston showed great interest in the deployment of the troops, and carefully studied the proclamations of the revolutionaries, marking those passages which could be held to be treasonable.

He was particularly anxious to ensure that the troops did not come into contact with the people in disaffected areas. This was a lesson which the Government had learnt from the French Revolution, when the National Guard had fraternized with the revolutionaries and gone over to them. In July 1820, Palmerston asked the House of Commons to grant supplementary estimates of £70,000 to enable barracks to be built, where the soldiers could be confined and segregated from the local population. The Radicals attacked the whole idea of having troops in barracks as a plot to overawe freeborne Englishmen, and Cobbett singled out Palmerston as being responsible. Palmerston undoubtedly attached great importance throughout his life to the need for this precaution. He mistrusted the Volunteers, remembering how in 1810 the London Volunteer Infantry had been on the point of joining the rioters who had attempted to stop Burdett being sent to the Tower. The Volunteers were part-time volunteers drawn largely from the class of small shopkeepers. The Yeomanry, on the other hand, were mounted troops, also part-time volunteers, but composed of country gentlemen and farmers. They were a reliable anti-revolutionary force, but had become very unpopular in many quarters as a result of their action at

Peterloo. Palmerston recommended that the Volunteers should be disbanded, and the Yeomanry strengthened.

The Government also decided to increase the size of the standing army in Britain to nearly 60,000 men, as compared with 15,000 in 1792. They were bitterly assailed for this by the Opposition in the House of Commons, and in June 1820 Lord Nugent called on the Government not to resort to repression, but to remedy the causes of discontent. 'Would a large standing army give bread to starving labourers?' he asked. Palmerston said that Nugent's speech 'was more fit for the audiences that assembled in Covent Garden, in Smithfield, and Palace Yard, than for those that were to be found' in the House of Commons. The Army, he claimed, was necessary to defend the constitution from traitors, for the country was on the verge of civil war. He stoutly denied that the Government was aiming at military dictatorship; if anyone was doing this, it was 'those self-called, but misled, reformers' who wished to have a more democratic electoral system, for this would lead, as history had proved, to military dictatorship.

The Government's measures to maintain order were popular, at least among the small class of Parliamentary voters; and in the general election of 1820, which followed automatically on the death of George III, the Opposition failed to repeat their electoral successes of 1818. But soon a new issue split the nation, and endangered the Government, as the country divided into supporters of the King and of the Queen. The attempts of George IV to divorce Queen Caroline on the grounds of her adultery with some of her servants, and with other men, had angered the people, who were disgusted with the King's hypocrisy, in view of his own moral record and his treatment of his wife and children in the past. The Opposition leaders rallied to the Queen's support, and Brougham became her counsel in the divorce proceedings. When the House of Lords passed the divorce bill by only nine votes, the Government persuaded the King to withdraw it, amid great popular rejoicings. Palmerston, as a Tory and a member of the Government, supported the King, and his friends the Lambs also sided against the Queen, Lady Cowper declaring that she had disgraced herself by having an affair with a courier, though if

he had been a gentleman it would have been perfectly understandable. When Queen Caroline died soon afterwards, her
death was thought by many to have been caused by her anxieties and ill-treatment; and an incident at her funeral involved
Palmerston in a violent altercation about one of the most colourful of the Radical leaders.

General Sir Robert Wilson had had a distinguished career
in the Army and in the diplomatic service. He had fought in
the Peninsula, had been expelled from Russia as a spy after
Tilsit, and had returned there in 1812 to fight alongside the
Russians at Smolensk and Krasnoye. But in the course of the
years he had developed Radical views; and in 1815, when he
was in Paris with the British army of occupation, he became
involved in the escape of General Lavalette. Lavalette was
sentenced to death by the French courts for having deserted
to Napoleon during the Hundred Days; but his wife arranged
a sensational escape from his prison a few days before his execution was to take place. While the authorities were searching
for Lavalette in Paris, Wilson obtained a British officer's uniform and papers for him, and took him in his coach past the
barrier, and to safety in Brussels. Wilson's part in the escape
was discovered, and he served three months in a French prison
and received a public censure from Wellington which was read
out to the assembled troops in every unit. Wilson returned to
England and became an MP and a prominent spokesman for
the Radicals in the House of Commons. He was particularly
active in denouncing flogging in the Army.

On 14 August 1821 Queen Caroline's funeral procession
passed through London. As it entered Hyde Park, the crowds
clashed with the Household Cavalry, who were thought to be
trying to prevent them from following the hearse. The crowd
threw stones at the troops, the Life Guards galloped around
with swords drawn, and shots were fired by the infantry over
the heads of the crowd. General Wilson was there with
Brougham and the other Opposition leaders, and as the shots
whistled past his ears he strode up to the soldiers, who were re-
loading their pistols. 'It is quite disgraceful', he told them, 'to
continue firing in this manner, for the people are unarmed.
Remember you are soldiers of Waterloo; do not lose your

honours gained on that occasion. You have had cannon shot at your head, never mind a few stones'. The soldiers, who recognized Wilson, put up their pistols, and the Major commanding them decided to withdraw his unit, after Wilson had pointed out a way that they could retreat up the Edgware Road without meeting the angry crowds who might have attacked him. A few weeks later, General Wilson received a curt note from the Duke of York, informing him that he was dismissed from the Army, as His Majesty no longer required his services.

The matter was raised in Parliament in February, and Palmerston replied for the Government. The Opposition claimed that it was a tyrannical exercise of the royal prerogative, because Wilson had been dismissed, and had forfeited all his pay and privileges, without any kind of trial, or having been charged with any offence; and they said that it was a case of political victimization of a prominent Opposition MP. Palmerston made a very strong speech. He maintained that the Crown had a right, under the prerogative, to dismiss any officer without giving a reason, for if officers could only be dismissed after being tried by a court-martial composed of other officers, the Army would be a privileged and irremovable military caste. He ridiculed the idea that Wilson had been dismissed because of his political opinions, for if the Government had wished to get rid of him on these grounds they would not have waited till 14 August 1821; nor had they taken any action against General Sir Ronald Ferguson, who was also an active Opposition MP. Then he turned to deal with Wilson's behaviour at the Queen's funeral, and said that by joining with a number of persons engaged in illegal proceedings, and opposing the legitimate orders of the King his master, Wilson was guilty of a gross insult to the Sovereign whom he served. This in itself fully justified his dismissal. Wilson had found the Life Guards 'venturing their lives in an attack on a furious populace; he found these brave men, who had so gallantly fought for their country, in a situation of considerable jeopardy. What did the honourable gentleman do on the occasion? He must have been aware of what was the duty of an officer under such circumstances. If he was not aware of that duty, he was unworthy of the commission which he bore'. Speaking amid loud interruptions from the indignant Opposition MPs, he accused Wilson of having urged the soldiers to disobey orders, and said that he was guilty of a gross breach of military discipline, which made it necessary to remove him from the Army.

Palmerston's speech caused much resentment among Wilson's supporters. John Lambton, afterwards Earl of Durham, who was Lady Jersey's nephew and was known as 'Radical Jack', expressed his disgust at the 'sneering style' which Palmerston had adopted towards Wilson, and suggested that Wilson's military services would bear favourable comparison with Palmerston's exertions in civilian life. Nor was General Ferguson mollified by Palmerston's reminder that he himself had not been dismissed from the Army for his opposition to the Government in Parliament. Palmerston had throughout his speech referred to Wilson as the 'honourable gentleman', not as the 'honourable and gallant gentleman' – the usual designation for an MP who was also an officer. Ferguson warmly praised the conduct of 'his gallant friend – gallant he still would call him, for, though no longer a General in the British Army, the remembrance of his deeds could not be obliterated'.

A month later, Bennet and Burdett moved an amendment to the Mutiny Bill, which would have restricted the prerogative power of the Crown to dismiss any officer without holding an inquiry or assigning a reason. Palmerston resisted the amendment in a more philosophical and less bellicose speech than he had made during the Wilson debate. 'However dangerous might be the existence of a standing army', he said, 'it would be infinitely more dangerous to have no army at all. . . . If the Army was not to be erected into a Fourth Estate, it must be placed under some species of control. The honourable baronet [Burdett] objected to that control being vested in the Crown. Was Parliament, then, to have the control of the Army? Whenever popular assemblies had attempted to command a military force, the thing had usually ended by that force commanding them'. He ended by pointing out that the King of Prussia also possessed this power over his army. It is significant that he should have cited, as an example to be followed, the powers exercised by a foreign sovereign who was consistently refusing to grant a constitution to his subjects. Palmerston was not yet the Palmerston of 1850,

It was just at this time that Palmerston became involved in an incident on his estates at Broadlands which for several years was used against him by some of the Radical politicians. The right to shoot game was governed by the Game Laws of Charles II's reign, which granted the right as an exclusive privilege to peers, and to the larger and medium-sized landowners. Even for this purpose the laws were unsatisfactory. Whereas peers and their eldest sons were allowed to shoot game, their younger sons, on a strict interpretation of the law, were not; nor were foreign Ambassadors, or Irish peers in England, though Palmerston, as the owner of more than a hundred acres of land, could legally indulge in his favourite hobby. As most peers and landowners ate their own game, or gave them as presents to their friends, the urban middle classes had to rely on poachers to stock their tables. Poaching became widespread throughout the country. Some of the poachers were desperate labourers who, in a time of falling wages and economic distress, stole an occasional hare to feed their hungry families; but most of them were well-paid members of an organized poaching gang which was supplying the London market.

In their war against the poachers, landowners placed hidden steel traps and spring guns in the undergrowth in their woods, in the hope that they would catch, maim or even kill the poachers. This had been upheld as legal by a much disputed court decision, and it was not until 1826 that it was prohibited by an Act of Parliament. It added an element of risk to the sport of shooting, for landowners were often caught by their own traps and guns. On one occasion, in 1810, Palmerston went shooting on the estates of Mr. Conyers in Essex in a party which included William and Lady Caroline Lamb. Conyers' sons had insisted, against the wishes of their cautious father, on putting spring guns in the woods, and Palmerston stepped on one of them; but it failed to go off, and he was unhurt, though for the rest of the shoot he was nervous whenever a bramble caught his legs.

Parliament had passed a series of laws increasing the penalties for poaching, and a poacher could now be sentenced to seven years' transportation to the convict settlements of Van Diemen's Land for the first offence, though he was much more likely, in practice, to receive a few months in prison. This encouraged poachers to resort to violence to escape arrest, and led to further legislation to protect gamekeepers. By Lord Ellenborough's Act of 1803, any poacher who wounded a gamekeeper, with malicious intent, was liable to be hanged. The Game Laws were unpopular, and Radical MPs had made several attempts to abolish them; but the Government and their supporters argued that, without the Game Laws, game would become extinct. Then the landed aristocracy, unable to shoot, would cease to reside on their country estates; they would forget the art of hunting and riding, which had trained them to be cavalry leaders in war; and the government of the countryside would pass from the hands of gentlemen to those of professional politicians and other undesirables.

In the village of Toothill, on the southern edge of Palmerston's Broadlands estate, there lived a twenty-six-year-old labourer named Charles Smith, who had a reputation of being a poacher, though his friends denied that this was true. In the early evening of 22 November 1820 he called at the cottage of his brother-in-law, John Pointer, and persuaded the reluctant Pointer to come poaching with him in Palmerston's woods. They entered Hough Coppice, where Smith shot at a hare, and missed. The sound of the shot was heard in the cottage of young Robert Snelgrove, a lad of seventeen who had just been engaged by Palmerston as an assistant gamekeeper; and being more eager and courageous than many older members of his profession, he at once set off in the direction from whence the shot had been fired. As he approached Hough Coppice, Smith's dog began to bark, and the poachers decided to depart; but they emerged from the wood into a turnip field, in the full light of the moon, to find themselves face to face with Snelgrove. Smith was well clear of him, and might perhaps have escaped unrecognized; but Snelgrove seized Pointer, and struggled with him. Smith then advanced to within a few yards of Snelgrove, and, taking careful aim, fired and wounded him in the thigh; and both the poachers made off.

As soon as Palmerston heard what had occurred, he made

determined efforts to catch the criminal. Snelgrove, who knew Smith well, and had been on friendly terms with him, at first refused to give him away; but eventually he told Martin, the head gamekeeper, that it was Smith, and Martin told Palmerston. Smith fled from his house, and hid in the woods, where he remained for some time. Palmerston repeatedly sent out parties of gamekeepers to search for him; but though he was spotted on several occasions, the gamekeepers kept their distance, as he was known to be armed and desperate. Once they came close enough to shoot at him, and wounded him, but he fired back at them, and escaped into the woods. Palmerston offered a reward of thirty guineas for information leading to his arrest. This must have been a temptation to agricultural labourers earning nine shillings a week; but Smith and his family were very popular in the district, and he almost certainly had some assistance, as well as sympathy, from the local residents, as he managed to live in the woods for several months, despite his wound, at the height of the winter.

Smith eventually got clear away from the district, and moved to another part of England; but after a few months he returned to the neighbourhood, and took a lodging in Southampton, where he joined a well-known poaching gang. In November 1821 the authorities succeeded in capturing him, probably with the assistance of an informer in the gang, for the circumstances of his arrest were not revealed at his trial. He was tried at Winchester Assizes in March 1822 before Mr. Justice Burroughes for 'wilfully, maliciously and unlawfully shooting at Robert Snelgrove' under Lord Ellenborough's Act of 1803. He was unlucky in his Judge, for Burroughes, who had been promoted to the bench at the age of sixty-six after more than forty undistinguished years at the bar, was unimaginative, inflexible and severe, and a personal friend of Lord Eldon's, to whom he owed his Judgeship. The key witness against Smith was his brother-in-law, whom he had been rescuing when he shot Snelgrove. Pointer, who had been arrested in November 1820 and later released, at first refused to testify against Smith; but when the Judge warned him that he could be prosecuted for perjury, he told the whole story. Smith was found guilty, and sentenced to death.

The criminal law was not only severe, but uncertain. In nearly all the 223 offences punishable by death, the death sentence was discretionary, and a Judge, having before him two men guilty of the same offence, might sentence one to be hanged, and the other to a week's imprisonment. Under the pressure of public opinion, the law was becoming more lenient; whereas in 1770, nearly three-quarters of those convicted of capital offences had been executed, by 1810 the figure had fallen to less than ten per cent. Even when the Judge had passed sentence of death, he might commute it to a term of imprisonment before the end of the Assizes; but Mr. Justice Burroughes, in sentencing Charles Smith to be hanged, had spoken of the need to protect gamekeepers from poachers, and had warned him to expect no mercy; and when the Judge left for Salisbury without altering his sentence, the authorities at Winchester prepared to carry out the execution in the course of the next fortnight.

Palmerston was immediately approached on Smith's behalf, and was asked to intervene in his favour with the Judge. He wrote at once from London to Burroughes at the Judge's lodgings at Salisbury; but his plea for Smith was somewhat restrained. 'The Man most undoubtedly deserves the full extent of the Punishment which the Law most justly assigns to the Offence which he has committed, and I am afraid that the general Character of the Man, and his conduct upon the occasion and Matter which brought him under the Sentence of the Law, afford no extenuating Circumstances upon which I could venture to found any application to your Lordship on his behalf'. But he suggested that though Smith was 'morally guilty of the full intention to Murder', nevertheless, as Snelgrove had fortunately escaped without any permanent disablement, it would be possible to commute Smith's sentence to transportation for life. 'Whatever your Lordship's better Judgment may lead you to determine upon this matter, I am persuaded that you will at least pardon the liberty which I have taken in thus addressing you'.

Burroughes was not to be moved. 'It would have afforded Me the greatest pleasure', he wrote to Palmerston, 'could I consistently with my Duty to the public have given your Lordship any Hope of any Interference from Me to prevent the Sentence from being carried into Execution. My Rule is that when a Man is convicted of a Capital Offence attended with Circumstances of wanton Cruelty never to extend favour to the Convict'. The local inhabitants then organized a petition to Palmerston, which was signed by the Mayor of Romsey, by the Town Clerk and the Vicar of Romsey, and more than 180 other petitioners. They expressed their horror at Smith's crime, but asked for the death sentence to be commuted.

Palmerston wrote next day to the Mayor of Romsey and asked him to state the reasons why the petitioners thought that Smith was entitled to mercy. 'I take for granted', he wrote, 'that the Petitioners do not mean to question the justice and expediency of that Protection which the law extends to the Members of the Community, by declaring a Malicious attempt to take away life equally criminal, whether the victim of the attack Shall recover from his wounds or Shall die under them. ... I imagine further that it is not disputed that Smith has for a long period of Time been engaged in that Systematic course of nightly depredation which has led to So many Similar outrages against Servants while employed in the performance of their legitimate Duty'. This brought a most apologetic letter from the Mayor, disclaiming all responsibility for organizing the petition; but he did venture to point out that Smith had been so close to Snelgrove when he fired that he could easily have aimed for a fatal part of the body had he wished to kill him. Palmerston then sent the petition to Sir Robert Peel, the Home Secretary, but Peel refused to advise the King to exercise the prerogative of mercy.

On 20 March, Palmerston wrote a very long letter to the Mayor of Romsey, which he asked the Mayor to communicate to the petitioners. He warned them not to think 'that the Execution or remission of a sentence of death passed by a Court after a verdict found by a Jury, can depend upon private Influence or personal favor or that the intention of the Law can be stayed in compliance with the mere wish of any Number of Individuals. If such were the Case, the Criminal law of England, instead of being the most perfect system which has ever yet been established in any Country would deserve to be ranked with the worst abuses of the most capricious Institutions'. It was the duty of the Government to enforce the laws which the Legislature had enacted for the general good. 'The Capricious remission of Punishment out of regard to private favor and personal affection was one of the great abuses of Prerogative complained of at the period of the Revolution, and provided against by the Bill of Rights'. He obviously felt that Smith's execution was necessary to uphold the rule of law and the principles of 1688.

Three days later, Smith was hanged. Cobbett published an article about the case in his paper, and strongly attacked Palmerston; and next year the case was raised by Radical MPs in the House of Commons. The incident has been completely ignored by all Palmerston's biographers, but it is still clearly remembered in the district, where local residents can point out the spot in the turnip field where Snelgrove was shot. At the time it aroused a good deal of feeling, for Smith had been a popular dare-devil. There was sympathy for him on account of his youth, because he had committed his crime, not to save himself, but to rescue his brother-in-law, whose evidence convicted him, and because he had fired low, at Snelgrove's legs. Snelgrove had recovered from his wound before the trial took place, though he walked with a limp until he died more than sixty years later. He forgave his assailant, and helped canvass for signatures for the petition in Smith's favour. Cobbett and his supporters erected a tombstone in Smith's memory in the churchyard at North Baddesley, which was then the parish church of Toothill, with the inscription: 'In Memory of Charles Smith who suffered at Winchester on the 23rd March 1822 for resisting by firearms his apprehension by the game-keeper of Lord Viscount Palmerston when found in Hough Coppice looking after what is called game. Aged 30 years. If thou seest the oppression of the poor and violent perverting of judgment and justice in a Prince, marvel not at the matter for he that is higher than the highest regardeth and there be higher than they. Eccl. 5'. It is indicative of the local feeling that it was possible to erect such an inscription in a public place on the edge of Palmerston's estates. It was only after Palmerston's death that Evelyn Ashley, who was Lady Palmerston's grandson, the owner of Broadlands, and a biographer of Palmerston's, erected another tombstone immediately adjoining the other in North Baddesley churchyard, which states that Smith was convicted of the attempted murder of Snelgrove, and points out that in 1822 attempted murder was a capital crime. This statement is not strictly accurate, for Smith was convicted, not of attempted murder, but of unlawful wounding under Lord Ellenborough's Act.

Charles Smith was to some extent a victim of the English devotion to the rule of law. It was easier for a Russian serf to win his pardon by petitioning the Iron Tsar, Nicholas I, on the highway, than for a Radical or Young Tory MP to persuade Peel or Lord John Russell to allow political prisoners to read books or newspapers, or to permit a little girl of seven to have a doll in her cell during her sentence of three years' solitary confinement; for British Home Secretaries believed, as an article of faith, that they must not arbitrarily interfere with the prison regulations. Palmerston shared this respect for the rule of law. He did not wish to be vindictive, and made two pleas for Smith; but he did so with some reluctance, because he did not wish to weaken the deterrent effect of the law against violent poachers, or to encourage the Radical agitation against the death penalty. He made this very clear for the benefit of the Romsey petitioners. His references to the desirability of maintaining hanging as a punishment for attempted murder, to the criminal law of England being the 'most perfect' which had ever existed in any country, and to the Game Laws as having been enacted 'for the general good', show that he had firmly nailed his colours to the Tory mast against the reformers. It was well worthy of a ministerial colleague of Lord Eldon's.

Chapter Seven

The Canningite

In August 1822 Castlereagh cut his throat with a razor in a fit of insanity. For twelve years he had dominated the Government, and had been held responsible by the Opposition for all the evils of the times. He had been an object of special hatred to the Radical intelligentsia; and Byron, who described him as a 'cold-blooded, smooth-faced, placid miscreant', openly rejoiced at his miserable end. 'As to lamenting his death', he wrote, 'it will be time enough when Ireland has ceased to mourn for his birth'. But Palmerston deeply regretted Castlereagh. 'There could not have been a greater loss to the Govt.', he wrote to Sulivan, his brother-in-law, 'and few greater to the country at the present moment; in the House of Commons we cannot replace him. I conclude Canning must come in'. His forecast was correct, and Canning succeeded Castlereagh as Foreign Secretary.

Castlereagh's foreign policy had been as anti-liberal as his policy at home. Under his leadership, the war against France had ended, as it had begun, as an anti-Jacobin and anti-Radical crusade; and the forces of Liberalism, who had risen against the tyranny of Napoleon, had received no reward or thanks for their efforts. In their proclamation to the French people a month before Waterloo the Allied sovereigns had declared their aim 'of punishing the factious horde by which the present troubles have been fomented, and which has dared to pronounce against the unanimous wish of all the European monarchies'. The Allies had replaced Louis XVIII 'on the throne of his ancestors and proclaimed the reign of the family of Bourbon, until its extinction, over the French people. They now take up arms to restore and confirm that dynasty – to support the cause of Kings, to consolidate the Government, to secure the repose of mankind, and to give an imposing example of sovereign authority to all nations'. In reply, the French people rallied to Napoleon's support with an enthusiasm which they had not shown since 1793. Their defeat at Waterloo seemed to mark the end of that new historical era which Goethe believed had begun at Valmy.

Palmerston supported Castlereagh's foreign policy as completely as his policy at home, and fully endorsed the war aims of 1815 and the Treaty of Vienna. But the strains of the alliance, and British distrust of Continental absolutism, soon led to a shifting in Castlereagh's position. The disagreements were brought to a head by events in Spain. The Spanish Liberals had come off worst during the long struggle with Napoleon. After being persecuted by their Government for sympathizing with the French Revolution, they enthusiastically embraced the cause of popular national resistance when Napoleon invaded Spain, and at the height of the struggle proclaimed a democratic constitution at Cadiz in 1812, which for thirty years was accepted throughout Europe as the model for Radicals and Democrats. But victory over Napoleon, thanks largely to Wellington's influence in Spain, brought back Ferdinand VII, who abrogated the constitution, which he had promised to maintain, and restored the Inquisition. There followed six years of absolute monarchy, with censorship, imprisonment without trial, and religious persecution, until in 1820 a military coup d'état overthrew the absolutist regime and re-established the Constitution of 1812. The King pretended to accept the Constitution but appealed to foreign powers for help.

Metternich, Tsar Alexander, the King of Prussia and Louis XVIII united to suppress Liberalism. While Austrian troops suppressed a rising in Italy, and delivered over the Liberals to the vengeance of the King of Naples, Louis XVIII asked permission of the Allied powers to invade Spain and restore Ferdinand as an absolute monarch. At the Congress of Verona in 1822 only Britain opposed the proposal, and worked for a compromise. The British Government, in a formal note to Spain, demanded that the democratic Constitution of 1812 be modified, and that many of the King's powers should be restored, in the hopes that this would appease the reactionary sovereigns and prevent the French invasion. At the same time, they warned the Spanish Liberals that Britain would remain neutral, and not intervene in their support, if the French troops marched. The Spanish Liberals indignantly rejected the British proposal. The French Army thereupon crossed the frontier and overran Spain without much difficulty. The Liberal leaders surrendered to Ferdinand on promise of their lives; but Ferdinand broke his word, and Riego and other leaders were shot. Ferdinand now established an even more brutal police state than that which had existed before 1820.

In Britain, the Opposition denounced the Government's policy, and initiated a debate in the House of Commons in which, on 30 April 1823, Palmerston made his first speech on foreign affairs since his maiden speech on the Copenhagen expedition more than fifteen years before. The debate followed lines which were to become very familiar in the next hundred and twenty years. The Radicals, who hated war and militarism, called for action to help democracy in Spain; the Tories, with their Army connexions and military traditions, accused the Radicals of being warmongers, and refused to go to war to help foreign Liberals unless vital British interests were involved. The Radicals complained that the Government, which had sent an army to prevent the French from conquering Spain in Napoleon's time, had now permitted France to do this under the reactionary monarchy of Louis XVIII; and to the accusations of the Government supporters that the Opposition were clamouring for war, they replied by denying that they wished to send a British army to the interior of Spain, but merely urged that the Navy should be sent to the Mediterranean, and that the French merchant ships and colonies in the West Indies should be seized, as a reprisal against France.

Palmerston said that the Government deplored the fact that French troops had invaded Spain, but that it was absurd to make out that this invasion by the armies of the peaceful Bourbon monarchy constituted a threat to British interests comparable to that which existed when Spain was invaded in 1807 by Napoleon, who at the time was already at war with

Britain. The Opposition had criticized the Government for having announced in advance that they would remain neutral if the French marched in; but Palmerston said that it would have been cowardly to bluff, and to lead the Spanish Liberals to believe that we would help them, if we had no intention of keeping our word and giving them the promised aid. No aid, however, would have been effective unless a British army had been sent into Spain; for it would have done no good to have sent the British Navy to the Mediterranean. As for the Opposition proposal that we should seize the French colonies in the West Indies, the Spaniards would then have accused us of being more interested in gaining territory for ourselves than in helping them. Nor should the Government be criticized for having urged the Spaniards to modify the Constitution of 1812, because this was a most unsatisfactory constitution.

Although the Government did nothing to help the Spanish Liberals, the French action aroused anger in Britain, and led to a change in British foreign policy. Canning decided, as he told the House of Commons, that if France were to have Spain, it should be Spain without the Indies, and he called the new world into existence to redress the balance of the old. The British Navy prevented Ferdinand VII from crushing the revolts in South America; and when he tried to overthrow the constitutional monarchy of Queen Maria in Portugal, and to put her uncle, the absolutist Dom Miguel, on the throne, the British Government sent troops to defend Maria's government under the old alliance with Portugal. The new alignment in foreign policy had its influence at home in Britain. While Canning separated from Metternich and the Holy Alliance in international affairs, Peel, as Home Secretary, modified some of the rigour of the criminal law and of the Game Laws.

Steps were even taken to restrict the severity of flogging in the Army, and Palmerston played a leading part in this. The Commander-in-Chief had already issued an order which prevented a regimental court-martial from awarding more than three hundred lashes; but in April 1823 Palmerston suggested to the Duke of York's Military Secretary that the maximum should be reduced from three hundred to two hundred. As regimental courts-martial could only deal with small offences, and all serious offences had to be tried by general court-martial, he thought that this limitation on the powers of a regimental court-martial was reasonable, and wished 'to submit to the consideration of His Royal Highness whether 200* lashes might not be deemed an adequate Punishment for a *small*' offence'. He hoped that by announcing this further concession he would be able to forestall Burdett, who had given notice that he was going to raise the question of flogging again in the House of Commons. On one occasion Palmerston, reversing his usual role, had to argue in the House against the supporters of flogging. The Government dismissed a Colonel from the Army for excessive flogging, in particular for having ordered a soldier to receive twenty-five lashes for holding his firelock at a slightly wrong angle at inspection. Palmerston defended the Government's action, and pointed out that the Colonel had been allowed to retire on half-pay. He still in general defended flogging, which he thought was more than ever necessary now that so many soldiers came from the towns. 'Where large masses of people were collected together in the manufacturing districts', he said, 'they had not the same simplicity of manners which distinguished the agricultural part of the population; and that therefore punishment was more likely to be deserved by the former than by the latter class'.

The Government was advancing, too, on the question of slavery. Although the slave trade had been abolished, slavery still existed in the West Indies, and from time to time Brougham and Fowell Buxton and other abolitionist MPs drew the attention of the House to cases of horrible cruelties to slaves. In 1823 they persuaded the Government to declare themselves, in principle, in favour of gradual abolition of slavery. Palmerston's attitude to slavery had changed since the days in 1806 when he stood at Cambridge as the anti-abolitionist candidate. By 1820 he had gone so far as to become a supporter of the Anti-Slavery Society which Wilberforce, Brougham and Buxton had formed. Palmerston did not think that it was possible for him, as a member of the Government, to support the Society openly; but he entirely approved of the idea of forming a branch of the society in Hampshire, and wrote to various

*Palmerston's italics.

prominent local personalities to urge them to join, and support the branch financially.

But his opposition to slavery seems to have been inspired more by a theoretical belief in freedom than by any strong emotional detestation of the cruelty practised on the negroes in the West Indies. In April 1825, he had to deal with the case of Lieutenant Vaughton, who had been dismissed by the colonial authorities from his post as Superintendent of Negroes. This raised the question as to whether Vaughton should be removed from the half-pay list. In the ordinary course of events, an officer was placed on the half-pay list on his retirement from full-time service; but if he was cashiered by sentence of a court-martial, he might be removed from the list. As this was a financial matter, it concerned the Secretary at War as well as the Commander-in-Chief. Palmerston was always inclined to take a severe attitude on this question. In several cases where officers were convicted by court-martial of defalcation of funds, and cashiered, Palmerston refused requests from the Commander-in-Chief or other persons that, in view of the delinquent's years of service and previous good conduct, he should be allowed to remain on the half-pay list. In 1824 and 1825 Palmerston was engaged in a long controversy about one particular case in which both the Judge-Advocate-General and the Duke of York made repeated intercessions on behalf of an officer who had embezzled the Army funds. Palmerston absolutely refused to permit him to remain on the half-pay list, though General Taylor, the Duke's secretary, said that 'the poor man is reduced to extreme distress and quite bereft of the means of supporting himself and his family,' and was living on charity. Nor was Palmerston mollified when the Judge-Advocate-General told him that he believed that the case had not been properly investigated at the trial. Palmerston, with his rigid belief in the rule of law, declared that he could not see that there was anything which gave the man 'any claim to more favour than the sentence of the Court carried with it'.

Yet Palmerston adopted the opposite attitude when Lieutenant Vaughton was dismissed from his post as Superintendent of Negroes. 'Do you not think', he wrote to General

Taylor, 'that it would perhaps be rather a severe measure to strike this Officer off the half-Pay List upon the grounds contained in these Papers? The Offence with which he is charged is cruelty and fraud towards certain Negroes in his capacity of Superintendent of Pensioners'. Here again, Palmerston's attitude was partly determined by his strict legalism: Vaughton had not been tried by court-martial, but had been dismissed by administrative action of the colonial authorities acting on unsworn testimony. But Palmerston had another reason as well. Assuming that Vaughton was guilty of the offence, 'he has already been punished once for it, by being dismissed from the appointment which he held, and because the offence not having been committed in his Military Capacity, it may perhaps be doubted whether it is of so flagrant a Character as to render it absolutely necessary to deprive the Lieutenant of his future means of support'. This seems a long cry from the Palmerston of the next decade who suppressed the slave trade of foreign nations, and was said to be so passionately indignant at the wrongs of the negro as to be almost unbalanced on the subject. In 1825 he thought that the offence of 'cruelty and fraud towards certain negroes' was one which was not 'of so flagrant a character' as to render the offender liable to the deprivation of his livelihood, to which Palmerston so remorselessly condemned any officer who was guilty of fraud – without cruelty – in other circumstances.

Nor did Brougham forget, in after years, how Palmerston had voted in the debate on the atrocities in Demarara on 11 June 1824. When the news reached the slaves in the colony that the House of Commons had passed a resolution in favour of emancipation, they believed that slavery had been ended, refused to work, and rose in revolt and killed three whites. The rising was suppressed with great severity. More than a hundred and fifty negroes were put to death, and John Smith, an English Methodist minister and prominent abolitionist, was arrested and sentenced to death. He died in prison before his pardon arrived from England. The planters drew the conclusion that the insurrection was the result of the anti-slavery agitation in Britain and the ill-judged Government declaration on the eventual abolition of slavery; the abolitionists deduced that slavery should be abolished immediately. Brougham and his colleagues moved a resolution in the House deploring the treatment of Smith and the repression in Demarara, and urging that steps should be taken to educate the slaves in the West Indies with a view to abolishing slavery as soon as possible. The resolution was defeated by 193 votes to 146. The abolitionists were indignant that Palmerston had voted against the resolution, in view of the support which he had given to the Anti-Slavery Society.

But Palmerston continued to advocate gradual abolition. On 28 February 1826 he presented a petition from his constituents at Cambridge in favour of such a scheme. He said that it was most natural that the University, with its strong tradition of devotion to the Christian religion and the Church of England, should object to so un-Christian an institution as slavery. 'No man', he said, 'thought that, in the present state of the West Indies, slavery could be at once abolished. Such a sudden abolition, besides the sacrifice of other interests, would be most injurious to the negroes themselves. But if the resolutions of 1823 were steadily carried into effect, the gradual abolition would take place. It was a matter of great regret that the colonial legislatures should have shown such a disposition to resist the operation of those resolutions'.

Palmerston had meanwhile re-opened his quarrel with the Duke of York about the powers of the Secretary at War and the Commander-in-Chief. The Duke was now the heir to the throne, as George IV had no surviving children; and many men in public life were already preparing, as Palmerston put it, to be the ministers of King Frederick I. This did not stop Palmerston from doing battle with him once again. For eleven years Palmerston had faithfully adhered to Perceval's decision of 1812, by which all orders to commanding officers concerning financial or general administration were to be transmitted to them from the War Office through the office of the Commander-in-Chief. But when the Treasury decided to reduce the number of clerks in the military establishments in the West Indies, Palmerston sent out circulars in January 1823, direct to the commanding officers in the West Indies, ordering them to dismiss thirty of their clerks, and then informed the

Commander-in-Chief's secretary of what he had done. A few days later, an officer who had returned from Chatham to his unit in the Isle of Wight sent his application for the refund of his travelling expenses to the Commander-in-Chief's office, in the usual way, and the Commander-in-Chief forwarded it to the War Office. Palmerston ordered that the application should be returned to the commanding officer in the Isle of Wight, and informed him that in future such applications must be sent direct to the War Office, and not to the office of the Commander-in-Chief.

The Duke of York reacted immediately. He drafted a circular to the commanding officers ordering them to disregard Palmerston's instructions, and directing them to pay no attention in future to any orders which they received from the War Office unless they were transmitted through the Commander-in-Chief; but he postponed issuing the circular for the time being. Palmerston replied with a 'most respectful but strongest protest' to the Duke against this attempt to subvert the authority of the War Office, which he said was most harmful to the public service. When the Duke pointed out that Palmerston, by his action, had violated the Prince Regent's order of 1812, Palmerston refused to discuss this matter until the Duke had withdrawn his circular. The Duke appealed to the Prime Minister, Lord Liverpool, who censured both the protagonists. He said that it was wrong of Palmerston to send out his instruction to commanding officers without first submitting it to the Commander-in-Chief; that it was wrong of the Duke of York to issue an order to the commanding officers to disobey the Secretary at War; and that it was wrong of Palmerston to refuse to discuss the merits of the case until the Duke's circular was withdrawn. This last action, he said, put the Duke in an impossible position. 'I should not think such a proposition just', wrote Liverpool, 'as between any two individuals, and it is not too much to say that somewhat more of courtesy is due where one of the individuals is of the rank of the Commander-in-Chief'. He hoped, however, that the Duke would agree to withdraw the circular of his own free will. There was more trouble in January 1826, when a Colonel stationed at Paisley, who had had some minor altercation with the civil authorities there, wrote to Palmerston about it. The Duke of York informed the Colonel that it was improper for a serving officer to communicate directly with the Secretary at War, as all such communications must be sent through the Commander-in-Chief. Palmerston protested to the Duke against this.

It was perhaps partly because of these difficulties with the Commander-in-Chief that Liverpool tried from time to time to persuade Palmerston to leave the War Office and take on some other post. As early as 1812 Palmerston had been offered the position of Chief Secretary for Ireland; but he refused it for reasons which he did not specify in the autobiographical memorandum that he wrote for Lady Cowper, where he merely stated that 'particular circumstances and considerations' led him 'to decline it at once and without the least hesitation'. A few years later, he was offered the Governorship of an East Indian territory on the understanding that he would be made Governor-General of India at the next vacancy; but he refused it. When the Marquis of Hastings ended his term as Governor-General of India in 1822, the post was offered to Palmerston; but again he refused it.

One of his reasons for refusing these offers was undoubtedly his liking for London society, and his reluctance to leave it for Dublin or Calcutta; for he was as much a social figure as ever, and in 1823, when he was thirty-eight, he was even thinking of marrying. He proposed to Lady Georgiana Fane, the daughter of the Earl of Westmorland, who was Lady Jersey's younger sister; but she refused him. Georgiana's cousin, Mrs. Arbuthnot, the Duke of Wellington's great friend and confidante, did all she could to encourage the project. She was convinced that it would be a splendid match for Georgiana, and that the silly girl was longing to marry Palmerston, and was only waiting to be asked a second time. Mrs. Arbuthnot's chief motive in her match-making was to annoy Lady Jersey, who was telling everybody that Palmerston was madly in love with her, and for this reason would not marry her sister or anyone else. Two years later, on a very hot night in July 1825, Palmerston proposed again to Lady Georgiana at a ball at Devonshire House; but she refused him again. Mrs. Arbuthnot was convinced that it was all Lady Jersey's doing. A few months later, when she attended a house party at Broadlands, she found Palmerston charming and 'very gentlemanlike', and she thought, more than ever, what a fool Georgiana had been.

Meanwhile Palmerston resumed his relationship with Lady Cowper. In March 1829 Creevey met them at Lady Sefton's. 'I must be permitted to observe', Creevey wrote in his diary, 'that considering the rigid virtue of Lady Sefton and the profound darkness in which her daughters of from thirty to forty are brought up as to even the existence of vice, the party was as little calculated to protect the delusion of these innocents as any collection to be made in London could well be.' The people present included Lord Chesterfield and his mistress, the Princess Esterhazy, and Palmerston and Lady Cowper. 'Anything so impudent ... or so barefaced as the whole thing I never beheld', wrote Creevey, for these were 'by far the most notorious and profligate women in London'.

In November 1821, Liverpool tried to tempt Palmerston to leave the War Office by offering him a position which would not require him to leave London. He offered him the post of Postmaster-General with a peerage of the United Kingdom, which would have given him a seat in the House of Lords. Palmerston once said that an Irish peer was in a particularly fortunate position, being able to enjoy the social advantages of a peerage without the political drawback of not being able to sit in the House of Commons; but not many of his contemporaries agreed with him, and in 1821 it did not appear to be politically disadvantageous to be in the House of Lords. During thirty out of the first thirty-five years that Palmerston was in politics, between 1806 and 1841, the Prime Minister sat in the House of Lords; and during nearly the whole of this period the majority of the Cabinet were in the upper House. Although to the general public a lord was a lord, most Irish peers resented the fact that they were not peers of the United Kingdom, and were very eager to obtain a seat in the House of Lords. The second Viscount Palmerston, at the time of his death, had been trying very hard to obtain a United Kingdom peerage from Pitt or Addington. Yet Palmerston refused Liverpool's offer. He liked the work at the War Office and the atmosphere of the House of Commons, and felt that it would be considered to be a step down if he now became Postmaster-General.

The gradual softening of the Government's policy on such questions as slavery and the criminal law caused misgivings among many Tories, and before long the Government and the Tory Party were dividing into a progressive and a reactionary section. The progressives were led by Canning. Canning had always been an enemy of Radicalism, and had built his political career on his scathing denunciations of Jacobins and Radicals in his paper, the *Anti-Jacobin*; but he had throughout favoured Catholic Emancipation, and had never been trusted by the extreme Tories. The reactionary section of the Tories was led by Lord Eldon. Fifty years before, Eldon had been a romantic young man who had waited beneath the window of his sweetheart's house in Newcastle and had eloped with her; but he had now, for many years, been hard, dour and rigid, and the slowest Lord Chancellor in history in conducting legal business. When he supported a bill which abolished the right of a convicted criminal to demand trial by combat – a right which had been considered obsolete, but of which a murderer had recently availed himself – it was said that this was the only reform that he ever supported during his twenty years on the woolsack.

In earlier years, Palmerston had not been particularly close to Canning in politics. When he had first joined the Government in 1807, Canning and Castlereagh had been engaged in the bitter feud which culminated in their duel. Palmerston had been in the anti-Canning set with Plumer Ward and the others who despised Canning as the son of an actress, and spread hostile stories about him at the dinner tables. But Palmerston was comparatively free from the extreme social snobbery which was so common among the upper classes of the period. He had always admired Canning, and had known him in Sheridan's literary circle; and he agreed with him about Catholic Emancipation. Now, after 1822, he moved, with public opinion, away from extreme Toryism. He became a Canningite.

Palmerston himself did not have strong religious opinions or feelings; but as an Irish landlord and English Tory he nat-

urally adhered to the Church of England, and never under-
estimated its importance in maintaining the established order.
He showed this in his speech on the Building of New Churches
Bill in April 1824. The building of churches had become a
political issue. In 1818, at the height of the economic distress
and social unrest, the Government had angered the Radicals
and Nonconformists, as well as the Irish Catholics, by devoting £1,000,000 of public money to building new Anglican
churches throughout the country. They justified this on the
grounds that the spread of Anglican religious teaching would
counter the growth of Jacobin and Radical doctrines among
the lower orders. In the more liberal atmosphere of 1824, the
question of building new churches was raised again, and the
grants for this purpose were considerably reduced. Palmerston protested against the reduction. The national finances
were now, he said, in a much better condition than they had
been in 1818; yet Parliament, which had then granted
£1,000,000 without demur for the building of new churches,
was now quibbling about giving £500,000. He said that
although he was opposed to subjecting Roman Catholics and
Nonconformists to political disabilities, he regretted that the
number of dissenters was growing. He wished to see the
Church of England as the predominant Church in the country,
because nothing contributed more to the general tranquillity
and happiness of a people than religious unity. This speech
must have pleased many of his High Church supporters in
Cambridge; but the good effect was undone, as far as they were
concerned, when he once again voted in favour of Catholic
Emancipation in the great debate of May 1825, when the Irish
MPs persuaded the House of Commons to pass their resolution, only to see it thrown out by the House of Lords.

Palmerston's colleague as MP for Cambridge University
was William Bankes. Bankes had become unpopular at Cambridge, and his moral conduct was causing concern. Dr. Wood,
the Master of St. John's, who had been appointed Dean of Ely
thanks to Palmerston's patronage, and was perhaps unaware
of his patron's behaviour in private life, told Palmerston that
Bankes had shocked the University by his pursuit of Lady
Buckinghamshire. In November 1825, when it became obvi-

ous that a general election would be held next summer, Sir
John Copley, the Attorney-General, informed Palmerston
that he intended to stand as a candidate against Bankes at
Cambridge, though he would not be opposing Palmerston.
Copley, who later became Lord Lyndhurst, and Lord Chancellor, had begun his political life as a Jacobin; but now he was
a rabid Tory, and a supporter of Eldon's faction. Soon afterwards Goulburn, the Chief Secretary for Ireland, who was also
a supporter of Eldon's, announced his candidature for the
University seat at Cambridge. Though neither Copley nor
Goulburn was officially standing against Palmerston, there
were only two MPs to be elected for the seat, and it soon became clear that these two High Tory members of the Government were standing together against their Canningite colleague from the War Office.

The candidates began their campaign at once, and for the
next six months spent a great deal of time in canvassing in the
University. Palmerston's first action was to write to Eldon for
support. Eldon replied in a typical short, dry letter, in which
he said that he had been under the impression that Palmerston
would soon be joining him in the House of Lords, and that he
had no influence in Cambridge which he could usefully apply
in Palmerston's favour. This was a clear refusal, and Palmerston prepared for a tough fight with his ministerial colleagues.
He tried in vain to enlist the support of Lord Liverpool. He
wrote to Liverpool, and told him that if he were defeated in
the election he would resign as Secretary at War; but the
Prime Minister continued to adopt a neutral attitude between
the two factions in his Government, and merely urged Palmerston not to take any hasty action. Eldon openly backed
Copley and Goulburn, as did the Duke of York, who, apart
from his other difficulties with Palmerston, was a staunch opponent of Catholic Emancipation, and had made it clear that
he would oppose it when he came to the throne. But Palmerston had two advantages. Copley, Goulburn and Bankes were
all opposed to Catholic Emancipation, so the High Tory vote
was going to be split between them; and the Whigs decided
not to contest the seat. Palmerston had therefore the united
support of the Canningite Tories and the Whigs.

As usual, the candidates' only official statement of policy was their personal letter to every voter. Palmerston's letter was very short, and said nothing except that he wished 'to promote the welfare of the Empire and to maintain and strengthen the Constitution in Church and State'; but the Whigs threw themselves energetically into the campaign to elect Palmerston. Sedgwick, a keen Whig, wrote to the Radical leader, Hobhouse: 'I can hardly yet reconcile my position as a committee man in the interests of a Tory and a King's minister. But these are evil days, in which we do not fight so much for honour as contend against disgrace'. He told Hobhouse that if Palmerston lost his seat, 'it will be entirely in consequence of his acts on the Catholic question. A defeat will be a complete triumph for the *no Popery* faction, it will consolidate their interests, and the noise of it will ring through every corner of the kingdom. If the Catholic question be an important question, it is important for us to defeat the country parson and the bigot who at this moment are dishonouring the land we live in'. Palmerston, as usual, was confident of victory from the beginning. 'I think I shall have all the Johnians and most of the Trinity men', he wrote to Sulivan as early as 4 December 1825, 'the Protestants will support me as a Tory, and the Whigs as a Catholic'.

Polling took place on three days in June 1826. Palmerston urged all his supporters to wait until the last day before voting, unless they had to leave Cambridge or were going to plump for him alone, so that they could judge the state of the votes, and cast their second vote in such a way as would not injure Palmerston. Bankes adopted a different tactic, and called on his supporters to vote early, in the hopes that he would get an early lead, so that the anti-Catholics who had not yet voted would vote for him, thinking that he had a better chance than Goulburn of beating Palmerston. Nevertheless, on the evening of the second day, Palmerston was ahead of Bankes, and he knew then that he had won. Copley obtained 772 votes, Palmerston 631, Bankes 508 and Goulburn 437. 'The Whigs have behaved most handsomely to me', wrote Palmerston to his brother William, 'they have given me cordial and hearty support, and, in fact, bring me in. Liverpool has acted as he always does to a friend in personal questions – shabbily, timidly and ill'.

But on other issues than Catholic Emancipation, Palmerston seemed to be more Tory than ever. He had never put the case for flogging in the Army as strongly as he did in March 1827, when the question was raised as usual on the Army estimates and the Mutiny Bill. He castigated the 'crude and visionary theories' of the opponents of flogging, and told Dr. Lushington, an able lawyer and leading Radical MP, that he had 'wasted a vast deal of very respectable and constitutional indignation, which he might better have reserved for some ocassion on which it would be more necessary or useful'. He angered the Radicals by claiming that there was no difference in principle between the practice of French Army officers of administering random blows with a cane or the flat side of a sword to fully dressed soldiers, and the flogging in the British Army, where several hundred lashes with a cat-o'-nine-tails were laid on the naked back of a man strapped to the halberts. He said that if flogging were abolished, some other punishment would have to be devised, and this would mean building military prisons at a considerable cost; and he ended by asserting 'that if the infliction of corporal punishment were abolished, it must be followed by the abolition of the Army itself, which, without it, would soon become the most dangerous establishment in the Empire'. General Duff supported him, and expressed the view 'that it was as easy to chain the North wind as to manage British soldiers without the aid of corporal punishment'.

At the same time Palmerston, who usually kept his temper in the House, became involved in bitter personal exchanges with Hume. The Opposition had raised the case of two quarrelsome officers, Colonel Bradley and Major Arthur. When Major Arthur was sent from Jamaica to replace Colonel Bradley as the commander of the troops in Honduras, Bradley disputed the validity of Arthur's commission, and refused to hand over his command, whereupon Arthur had him arrested and imprisoned him for 312 days in a small stuffy room in the heat of the Honduras climate, while executions and floggings were carried out under his window. Then Bradley was released, and sent home to England. The Radicals did not like Arthur, because he had invented the illegal practice of flogging 'by tap of drum', under which each stroke of the lash was administered to the accompaniment of a drum-beat at intervals of precisely one minute, thus prolonging the duration of a sentence of a hundred lashes from five minutes to more than an hour and a half; but the Duke of York and the Government backed Arthur to the full, and paid his costs when Bradley sued him for damages in the Court of King's Bench. Bradley lost on the main issue, but was awarded £100 on a subsidiary point. The Government then appointed Arthur as Governor of Van Diemen's Land, and Bradley was unable to recover the damages or the costs which he had been awarded.

Palmerston was the Government spokesman in three debates about Bradley, and in one of them, in December 1826, he was repeatedly interrupted by Hume, who pressed him for further details about Arthur's commission to replace Bradley in Honduras. Turning to Hume, he said that 'it was impossible for him to be answerable for the extreme obtuseness of understanding possessed by the honourable member. He would venture to say that no other man in the House entertained any doubts as to the clearness of the explanation which he had given.... If the honourable gentleman's intellects were so deeply obtuse as to require these numerous repetitions and explanations – repetitions and explanations more numerous even than those in which the honourable gentleman was in the habit of indulging – if it were necessary by these means to soak into his understanding, as it were, the comprehension of the most simple fact, he must leave the honourable gentleman to that impenetrable darkness which dwelt within the interior of his brain, and leave his statements to the judgment of other gentlemen whom he had the honour of addressing. It was a matter of indifference to him whether the honourable gentleman understood him or not. He addressed himself to the House of Commons, not to the honourable member for Aberdeen'. The Tories cheered, but Hume replied that an angry tone was not an answer, and if he was obtuse in his understanding, it was his misfortune, not his fault, and this had nothing to do with the case of Colonel Bradley. Palmerston's words still rankled with Hume two months later. In another debate about Bradley in February 1827, Hume insisted that one of Palmerston's statements about the case was untrue. Palmerston icily inquired whether Hume was calling him a liar. Hume replied that Palmerston had no right to expect any courtesy from him, after he had, during the previous debate, 'so notedly declined acting as a gentleman'. The Speaker intervened, and Hume withdrew the remark.

Events were pushing Palmerston into a breach with the Tories; but he went slowly and reluctantly. He himself wrote in later years that the Tories 'were the aggressors' in his quarrel with them in connexion with their contest at Cambridge in 1826; and now again it was they who forced the issue. In February 1827 Lord Liverpool had a stroke, and resigned. After some weeks of negotiations, Canning became Prime Minister, and Wellington, Eldon and Peel, and most of the Tory leaders went into Opposition. Palmerston, Huskisson, Lord Dudley and Charles Grant remained with Canning, who brought William Lamb and other Whigs into his Government. Canning offered Palmerston the post of Chancellor of the Exchequer with a seat in the Cabinet; but at this time a minister had to resign his seat in Parliament and contest a by-election if he was appointed to a new office in the Government, and as it was not convenient for Palmerston to spend a fortnight in Cambridge fighting a by-election during the Parliamentary session, it was agreed that he should remain as Secretary at War for the time being, and that his appointment as Chancellor of the Exchequer should be postponed until the beginning of the Parliamentary recess.

But before the session ended, Canning withdrew his offer of the Exchequer. This was partly because of the opposition of George IV, who did not like Palmerston; and Canning himself did not have a high opinion of him. He was glad to have him in his Government at a time when he was being abandoned by so many Tories; but he did not agree when Lord Granville suggested to him that Palmerston had hidden abilities which had not yet been revealed. Nor was Palmerston generally considered to be of sufficient standing for the Exchequer. *The Times* wrote that 'nothing so ridiculous can have been thought of' as the idea of appointing him as Chancellor of the Exchequer, and attributed the fall in Consols to the rumour of his impending appointment. Canning was also influenced by the fact that Palmerston had just been involved, though only indirectly, in a financial scandal as a director of the Devon and Cornwall Mining Company.

Palmerston had been in financial difficulties for some time. His father had died heavily in debt, and when Palmerston inherited Broadlands it was encumbered with a mortgage for £10,000. He paid off part of the mortgage in 1811, but in 1817 he had to borrow another £8,000, bringing the total amount of the mortgage on Broadlands to £14,000. He also raised a mortgage on some of his Irish lands. He sold the family house at Sheen in 1806, and let his London house in Hanover Square to a succession of tenants, who included Sir Robert Peel, the Duchess of Brunswick, and the Bishop of Durham. He himself took a lease of a house at 9, Stanhope Street – now Stanhope Gate – having decided that a nice house in Manchester Square was too far west, and 'sadly out of the way'. In 1839 he sold the house in Hanover Square, and with the proceeds he was able to pay off half the mortgage on Broadlands.

Although he had an income of £12,000 a year, his expenses were heavy. Apart from the cost of his life in London society, and the upkeep of his estate at Broadlands, he had taken to buying racehorses; but his chief liabilities were in connexion with the developments of his Irish estates. With the money that he borrowed on mortgage, he carried out his plans for building schools, roads and a harbour at Sligo. Unlike his father, he regularly visited his Irish estates, and by 1825 he was going there every year in September to supervise the works in progress. He also visited the lime works which his father had begun at Fairburn in Yorkshire, and his slate quarries in Tan y Bwlch in Caenarvonshire, and invested money in developing them a good deal further than in the days of the second Viscount.

In 1825 Palmerston became a director in two companies, both of which involved him in some difficulties. He formed the Welsh Slate Company in order to raise capital to develop his slate quarries, while John Wilks, the MP for Sudbury, invited him, and a number of other peers and MPs, to become directors of the Devon and Cornwall Mining Company, which Wilks had promoted to purchase a copper mine in Cornwall. It was a time of heavy speculation on the Stock Exchange, with investors making great profits and ruinous losses, particularly in mining shares. The shares of the Welsh Slate Company and of the Devon and Cornwall Mining Company were quickly taken up, and were sold just as quickly when a scare succeeded the original confidence. The value of the shares fell rapidly, and the shareholders lost a great deal of money. Palmerston felt that, as a director of the companies, he had a duty to retain his shares, and bought the shares of several of the other shareholders in the Welsh Slate Company who were anxious to sell.

In the case of the Devon and Cornwall Mining Company, some of the shareholders presented a petition to Parliament accusing the directors of fraud. They alleged that Wilks and some of the other directors had made a secret profit by buying the mine from the former owner and re-selling it to the company for £45,000 more than they paid for it. The petition was debated in the House of Commons on 9 April 1827. Palmerston made a brief statement at the beginning of the debate. He explained that he had had nothing to do with the formation of the company, but had only afterwards become a shareholder and director; that he had only attended five meetings of the board of directors; and that he had made no profit of any kind from his position, but had paid up his share capital in full, and had lost, not gained, by the transaction. He then said that he would take no further part in the debate, though Wilks defended the action of the directors in a long speech. In due course the panic subsided, and, in the case of the Welsh Slate Company, the company prospered. Palmerston, like the other shareholders who had kept their heads and their shares, made a considerable profit out of his holdings.

The scandal about the Devon and Cornwall Mining Company had touched Palmerston closely enough to give a handle to his political enemies, and may well have affected Canning in his decision not to make him Chancellor of the Exchequer. Many people considered that there was something improper in the very fact of a peer engaging in Stock Exchange speculations. Mr. Cobbett, riding past Broadlands on his rural rides on 16 October 1826, noted in his diary that evening at Ringwood that he had passed

the sort of park called *Broadlands*, where poor Charles Smith (as mentioned above) was hanged for *shooting at* (*not killing*) one Snelgrove, an assistant gamekeeper of Lord Palmerston, who was then our Secretary at War, and who is in that office, I believe, now, though he is now better known as a director of the grand Mining Joint-Stock Company, which shows the great *industry* of this noble and 'right honourable person', and also the scope and the various nature and tendency of his talents. What would our old fathers of the 'dark ages' have said if they had been told that their descendants would at last become so enlightened as to enable Jews and loan-jobbers to take away noblemen's estates by mere 'watching the turn of the market', and to cause members, or at least one member, of that 'most honourable, noble and reverend body' to become a director in a mining speculation! How one *pities* our poor, 'dark-age, bigoted' ancestors, who would, I dare say, have been as ready to *hang* a man for proposing such a 'liberal' system as this, as they would have been to hang him for *shooting at* (not killing) an assistant gamekeeper! Poor old fellows! How much they lost by not living in our enlightened times!

Chapter Eight

The Road to the Foreign Office

In 1827, as in 1809, Palmerston failed to get the Exchequer, and he was destined never to hold the office. Instead, Canning offered to make him Governor of Jamaica; but Palmerston roared with laughter at the very idea, and told Canning that he 'preferred England and the War Office to Jamaica and the negroes' – a statement which in itself seems to dispose of the legend that Palmerston was a fanatical devotee of the cause of the negro slave. A few weeks later, Canning offered him the post of Governor-General of India, but for the third time he refused this offer. In the end, Canning kept Palmerston at the War Office, but gave him for the first time a seat in the Cabinet; and as the Duke of York had died in February, he appointed him as acting Commander-in-Chief until a successor was appointed. Palmerston had always been fond of dressing up in the regimentals of the Hampshire Volunteers and attending military parades in the county; and he now caused great amusement among Army officers by turning up in uniform at a review of the Coldstream Guards. But Palmerston was the first to realize that the office of Commander-in-Chief should be filled by a military man, and in the summer of 1827 it was given to Wellington.

The funeral of the Duke of York was not the last state funeral which killed, as well as buried, a public figure. Canning caught cold attending it, and by the time he became Prime Minister he was already a dying man. When he died in August 1827 he was succeeded by Goderich, who offered the Exchequer to Palmerston; but again the offer fell through, owing to the objection of George IV. Canning's death, however, broke up the Government as effectively as Liverpool's death had split the Tory Party. Goderich carried on for a few months as Premier, but it was clear that the Government could not continue, and in January 1828 the King dismissed him and invited Wellington to form an administration.

No one believed that Wellington would succeed. A government based only on the High Tories could not hope to survive for long; and it seemed out of the question that the Canningites, having been violently denounced by the Tories for joining a coalition with the Whigs less than nine months before, could now unite with the Tories again. But for six days in January 1828 the political world waited in amazement as Palmerston, Huskisson, Lord Dudley and Charles Grant called on Wellington at Apsley House and bargained with him as to the terms on which they would leave the Whigs and rejoin the Tories. They demanded that Catholic Emancipation should be left an open question, on which members of the Government should be free to speak on either side, as they had been under Lord Liverpool's government; and Wellington agreed. They also insisted that Dudley should remain at the Foreign Office, where he could continue to follow Canning's principles in foreign policy; and to this, too, Wellington agreed. The Canningites then decided to join his government, and Palmerston continued at the War Office with a seat in the Cabinet. Canning's widow was enraged at their conduct, and 'very violent' about it; and Charles Greville wrote that behaviour such as that of Palmerston and Huskisson would in private life 'look very like a fraud'. On the other hand, many of the High Tories were angry with Wellington for having made concessions to the Canningites, and for having excluded Eldon from office.

But Palmerston regarded the situation with the utmost cheerfulness. On 18 January 1828 he wrote a letter to his brother William Temple, for whom he had obtained the post of chargé d'affaires in St. Petersburg a month before. The letter is very revealing of two facets of Palmerston's character: it shows his breezy optimism and his ability to move with the tide of public opinion without feeling any regrets for the past, or any need to explain the inconsistencies between his past and present actions. Wellington, he wrote, would form a strong, liberal government. 'Eldon and Westmorland will not be in it, though I fear Bathurst is inevitable, but he will be President of the Council, or hold some other office which gives no departmental influence.' Canning's principles would be carried on by Dudley in foreign policy, and by Huskisson and Grant in colonial and commercial affairs; and 'Peel will probably return to his Home Office, where he will prosecute his system of reform. All this, instead of a pig-tail Tory Government, shows the great strides which public opinion has made in the last few years. Such a Government as Liverpool's even cannot now be established; and such a one as Perceval's could not be for a moment thought of.' Palmerston had been a member of both Liverpool's and Perceval's governments, and yet, without ever having clearly broken with the principles which he had then held, he now considered such governments to be unthinkable. On the other hand, he was quite unperturbed by the anger of the Whigs. 'The Whigs of course will be furious and violent, and lay about them to the right and left. I very sincerely regret their loss, as I like them much better than the Tories, and agree with them much more; but still we, the Canningites, if we may be so termed, did not join their Government, but they came and joined ours; and whatever regard we may feel for them we have not enlisted with them, so as to be bound to follow their fate and fortunes, or to make their retention a condition of our remaining; and, indeed, if we had all gone out I should certainly not have sat with them in the House of Commons, but should have taken an independent and separate position.'

Not for the last time, his optimism was unjustified. Wellington's government was rent with bitter political and personal controversies. In foreign policy, they divided about the policy to be pursued towards Greece. The Greek struggle for freedom and independence from Turkey had aroused the greatest sympathy in Britain, and British volunteers joined the Greek guerrilla armies; but the Greek leaders had from the beginning looked primarily to Russia for assistance, and the British Government did not wish to see Russian expansion into the Balkans and the dismemberment of the Turkish Empire. Canning had solved this dilemma by offering to mediate, and by aligning Britain with France and Russia in order to assist the Greeks by peaceful means.

Wellington was much less sympathetic to Greece than Canning had been, and far more eager to maintain the position of Turkey against Russia. But Palmerston was even more pro-Greek than Canning. His devotion, as a Canningite, to the memory and policy of Canning; his sympathy with a free people struggling against an Oriental despotism; and his pro-Russian sympathies, which he had derived from his intimacy with the Princess Lieven, all led him to clash with Wellington inside the Cabinet. Palmerston thought that Wellington's anti-Russian policy was partly due to personal factors. 'A great many little things', he noted in his diary, 'have contributed to set him against the Lievens. Mrs. Arbuthnot and Lady Jersey, who have both influence over him, both hate Madame de Lieven.' Wellington did not openly repudiate Cannings policy towards Greece, but he adopted an anti-Greek and pro-Turkish attitude on all controversial issues; he wished to reduce the size of the new Greek state by limiting it to the Morea peninsula south of the Isthmus of Corinth, and he argued in favour of a higher figure as the compensation which Greece would pay to Turkey for having seized Turkish property in Greece. Palmerston, on the other hand, argued in favour of placing the frontier further north, on a line between the gulfs of Arta and Volo – which still left more than half of present-day Greece under Turkey – and of fixing a lower figure as the amount of compensation. He supported the Russian position in the negotiations, and urged Wellington to agree that Kapodistrias, the Greek national leader who had formerly been Russian Foreign Secretary, should become the first head of a provisional Government of Greece. He went so far as to write to his brother William in St. Petersburg, urging him to drop hints to the Russian Government about the opposition to Wellington's policy inside the British Cabinet, in order to encourage Russia to hold out for better terms for Greece. News of Palmerston's activities inside the Cabinet also reached the Russian Government through the Princess Lieven.

Yet Wellington sometimes put up Palmerston to defend the Government's policy about Greece in the House of Commons. In October 1827 the Greek War of Independence was effectually decided when an accidental collision between the British and Turkish fleets at Navarino gave Admiral Codrington the opportunity to sink nearly all the Turkish navy, though Britain was not at war with Turkey. There was great rejoicing in Britain; but when the new Wellington Government met in Parliament in January, the King's speech referred to Navarino as an 'untoward event'. The Opposition denounced the use of this expression, and moved a resolution congratulating Codrington on his brilliant victory. Palmerston opposed the motion on behalf of the Government. He said that it was quite impossible to congratulate Codrington for a victory over a nation with which we were not at war; as for the words 'untoward event', 'untoward' was merely another word for 'unexpected', and no one could deny that the engagement at Navarino had been unexpected. He made up for any lukewarmness in his defence of the Government by an extravagant eulogy of Wellington, whom he warmly defended from Brougham's attack.

The quarrels in the Cabinet soon became known outside, not least to the Princess Lieven, who wrote to her brother, General Benckendorff, that the 'ministers blackguard one another like draymen'. The political disagreements were made worse by personal ill-feeling. Wellington expected from his Cabinet the loyalty which he had received from his staff in the Army, and he resented criticism. He developed an intense dislike for Palmerston, who stood up to him in the Cabinet much more than any of the other Canningites, and annoyed him in many ways. When Palmerston replied for the Government in the debate on Lord John Russell's bill to abolish the disabilities imposed on the dissenters by the Test Acts, he called on the House to reject the motion, but angered the Tories by doing so for the wrong reasons. He said that as the restrictions on the Nonconformists were much less onerous than those resting on the Catholics, it was right that Catholic Emancipation should be granted before the dissenters were relieved. He also displeased the High Tories by his praise of Canning when he spoke on the bill to provide an annuity for Canning's widow.

But Palmerston, though he was prepared to resist and provoke Wellington, did not wish to leave the Government. In
March 1828 Charles Grant, his fellow-Canningite, became so
disturbed by Wellington's commercial policy, which was a re-
versal of the free trade policy which Canning had inaugurated,
that he resigned as President of the Board of Trade. But Palmerston succeeded in persuading Grant to withdraw his resignation. He stated his motives very frankly in his private
journal. If Grant, a young man with his career to make, were
to resign a good Cabinet post rather than defend a policy of
which he did not approve, it would be very difficult for the
older and more prominent Huskisson to remain in the Government without being accused of having betrayed his principles.
But if Huskisson resigned, it would be almost impossible for
Palmerston to stay, for without Huskisson the remaining
Canningites would be swamped in an otherwise High Tory
Government.

Palmerston's tactics against Wellington were very similar to
those in which he later indulged against foreign Governments
as Foreign Secretary. He tried to pursue the policy which is
now known as 'brinkmanship' by going as far as he could
venture with impunity, but no further. But in May 1828 he
miscalculated, in connexion with the East Retford Disfranchisement Bill. The Whigs had for some years been stepping
up a campaign for Parliamentary reform. They had taken up
the cause of the middle classes in the large industrial towns in
the North, who could not send an MP to Parliament, although
the rotten boroughs returned nominees of the landed aristocracy. They demanded an end to a system whereby Lancashire,
with a population of one and a quarter million, had 14 Parliamentary seats, whereas 44 MPs represented the 290,000 inhabitants of Cornwall. Faced with increasing demands for
Parliamentary reform, Lord Liverpool's Government, under
Canningite pressure, had modified a few of the most glaring
anomalies by introducing an occasional bill to disfranchise
some notoriously rotten borough; but instead of giving the
vacant seat to one of the new industrial towns, they transferred it to the neighbouring hundred.

In the spring of 1828 the Government introduced a bill to disfranchise Penryn and East Retford, which had only about a hundred inhabitants. The Canningites wished to give the two seats to Manchester and Birmingham; but the High Tories, including Peel, wished to transfer them to the neighbouring hundreds. A compromise was reached in the Cabinet, by which it was agreed to give the Penryn seat to the hundred, and East Retford to Birmingham; but in the course of the debate, a Tory backbencher moved an amendment to give East Retford to the hundred of Bassetlaw. Peel and the other Tory ministers told the Canningites that they would support the amendment. Huskisson had the greatest difficulty in making up his mind what to do; but Palmerston persuaded him to vote against the amendment. Palmerston later told Hobhouse that Huskisson had still been hesitating when the division was called, and kept asking Palmerston: 'What shall I do?' The supporters of the amendment had to walk into the lobbies, and the opponents had to remain seated. Palmerston persuaded Huskisson to remain in his place, but told Hobhouse that he was sure that if Huskisson had had to move, instead of sitting still, in order to vote against the amendment, he would have voted the other way.

A few weeks later, Palmerston explained in the House the reasons why he favoured giving the East Retford seat to Birmingham. Hansard reported that he 'expressed his wish that the franchise should be extended to a great town, not because he was a friend to reform in principle, but because he was its decided enemy. To extend the franchise to large towns, on such occasions as the one in question, was the only mode by which the House could avoid the adoption, at some time or other, of a general plan of reform. It appeared to him very inconsistent in the enemies of reform to oppose the transfer of the franchise to a large town. When people saw such populous places as Leeds and Manchester unrepresented, whilst a green mound of earth returned two members, it naturally gave rise to complaint. The House ought, therefore, to take advantage of every case of delinquency, to apply a gradual remedy to the defective state of representation.'

Wellington described the action of Huskisson and Palmer-

ston in one word – 'mutiny'. Immediately after the debate,
Huskisson, still uncertain whether or not he had done the right
thing, wrote a letter to Wellington which any reasonable person would have interpreted as being a letter of resignation.
Wellington accepted the resignation, and informed the King.
This was not at all what Palmerston had wanted and he persuaded Huskisson to write again to Wellington a few hours
later, to say that he had not intended to resign. Palmerston
hastened to find Wellington at the House of Lords, and tried
to persuade him to allow Huskisson to continue in the Government. As they could not find a vacant committee room,
they walked up and down the gallery for half an hour discussing the situation; but apparently Palmerston did most of the
talking, for Wellington afterwards told Lord Ellenborough:
'I said nothing; it was not for me to fire great guns at small
birds'. According to Mrs. Arbuthnot, Wellington was 'very
dry and cold' to Palmerston. In view of Wellington's attitude,
Palmerston and the other Canningites decided that they had
no alternative but to resign, as they could not stay in the Government without Huskisson; and Palmerston left the War
Office after more than eighteen years.

His last encounter with his old staff at the War Office was
unfortunate. At the end of 1827 the Deputy Secretary, Merry,
who had held the post for all the years that Palmerston had
been Secretary at War, retired from the civil service to a small
estate in Bedfordshire. Palmerston appointed his brother-in-
law Sulivan to succeed Merry. No sooner had Palmerston
joined Wellington's Government than *The Times,* which was
a strong anti-Tory paper and had always taken every opportunity to attack Palmerston, accused him of having forced
Merry to resign so as to make way for Sulivan. Palmerston
wrote to Merry in his retirement, and asked him to write a
letter to *The Times* denying the truth of the allegation; but
Merry found one excuse after another for not doing so,
though Palmerston asked him on more than one occasion.
Palmerston reminded Merry that it was Merry himself who
had first suggested that the time for his retirement had come,
and that 'it is due both to yourself and to me, it is due to truth,
that this statement be contradicted'; but Merry could not be

prevailed upon to write to *The Times*. Perhaps Foveaux was not the only member of the War Office staff who had resented Sulivan's successive promotions in defiance of the rules of seniority; or perhaps some of Palmerston's autocratic and arrogant memoranda had rankled with Merry for many years. At any rate, they were glad to see the last of Palmerston at the War Office. Mrs. Arbuthnot wrote that the clerks were so pleased to get rid of him that they would have liked to illuminate the building – for putting candles in the windows was the recognised way of celebrating a military victory or some other joyous event. 'It is quite extraordinary', she wrote, 'how he was detested.' But Mrs. Arbuthnot was not an impartial witness. Since Palmerston had split with the High Tories, she no longer considered him to be 'very gentlemanlike', but 'the shabbiest of all' the Canningites.

Palmerston now found himself on the Opposition benches for the first time since he had entered Parliament, and was in a somewhat isolated position. He and the other Canningite ex-ministers did not join the Whigs, but remained in the middle between both the contestants, ready to join either side, but running the risk of being rejected by both. But from a long-term viewpoint, his expulsion from the Government by Wellington was to prove to be a blessing in disguise. Palmerston rose enormously in political stature during the two years that he spent in opposition; in particular, he managed to live down his reputation of not being a good Parliamentary speaker. 'He has been twenty years in office', wrote Charles Greville in his diary, 'and never distinguished himself before.... The office he held was one of dull and dry detail, and he never travelled out of it. He probably stood in awe of Canning and others, and was never in the Cabinet; but having lately held higher situations, and having acquired more confidence, and the great men having been removed from the House of Commons by death or promotion, he has launched forth, and with astonishing success'. But Greville had probably not hit on the true explanation of Palmerston's emergence as an orator. As Secretary at War, he could do the job that needed to be done by a cool and logical exposition of the facts. Now this was not enough to attract attention, to become a prominent political figure, and to establish himself in the eyes of both Whigs and Tories as someone worth wooing. Palmerston acquired the art of Parliamentary eloquence in 1829 because it had suddenly become essential for him to do so.

His first venture in Opposition oratory was on the subject of Ireland. He had prepared himself for speaking with authority on Irish questions, by spending two months in Ireland in the autumn of 1828, when he not only visited, as usual, his estates in Sligo, but held political discussions with the Lord Lieutenant of Ireland and other leading figures. The question of Catholic Emancipation had brought Ireland to the verge of civil war. A great Irish leader, Daniel O'Connell, had united the forces of Radicalism and Catholicism, and given them brilliant political direction. By mixing daring with caution, and by strict adherence to legality with a clear threat of violent revolution, O'Connell aroused all Ireland against the Protestant landlords, and forced Wellington at last to grant Catholic Emancipation. In March 1829, Palmerston spoke strongly for Catholic Emancipation in the House of Commons in a great speech in which he vividly described the horrors of civil war, which was bound to ensue if the Government did not give way. 'I will grant, if you will, that the crimsoned banner of England would soon wave in undisputed supremacy over the smoking ashes of their towns and the bloodstained solitude of their fields. But I tell you that England herself would never permit the achievement of such a conquest: England would reject, with disgust, laurels that were dyed in fraternal blood'. His clear call for religious toleration, which was no longer trammelled by the qualifications which he had expressed in the days when he was a Tory minister, delighted the Opposition. A few weeks earlier, he had spoken against the bill to suppress O'Connell's Catholic Association, which a few years before he would certainly have considered to be a seditious organization. 'Put down the Association? They might as well talk of putting down the winds of Heaven, or of chaining the ceaseless tides of the ocean'.

But he opposed the Radicals and Irish MPs in their demand that the English Poor Law should be extended to Ireland. There had never been any system of poor relief in Ireland; if the Irish labourer was out of work, he had to rely on the charitable contributions which the English aristocracy in Dublin provided from time to time in periods of acute distress. But the English Elizabethan Poor Law was under strong attack in Parliament from MPs who believed that it pampered the working classes, and Stuart Villiers and Grattan had no chance of getting it introduced into Ireland. In the debate on 7 May 1829, Palmerston opposed the motion on classical Malthusian grounds. He said that any Poor Law was always a tax on industry in favour of the idle and improvident, and tended 'to diminish the wages of labour, by the stimulus they gave to population.... The introduction of English capital would be a greater benefit to Ireland than of these poor laws, which, if hastily put into operation, might make of that country one vast poor-house'.

It was Palmerston's speech on foreign policy on 1 June 1829 which really established him as a great political and Parliamentary figure. Though the attendance in the House was poor, as it always was when foreign affairs were discussed, he had the speech printed, and circulated it not only to Hansard but to MPs and newspapers. He attacked the Government's policy on Portugal and Greece. Wellington's Government had not only allowed Dom Migue to overthrow the Government of Queen Maria and seize power in Portugal by a coup d'état; they had also allowed Miguel's fleet to capture Madeira, although the British Navy had prevented Maria's followers from seizing the island of Terceira. Dom Miguel had instituted a police state, with arbitrary arrests and executions, and some British subjects had been caught up in his police net. Palmerston denounced the failure of the Government to compel Miguel to make proper compensation for the ill-treatment of British subjects, and for having accepted the sum of £56 17s. as compensation for the illegal arrest of five of them. He reminded the House how the British naval commander in the Tagus had demanded from the Miguelite authorities that a British subject, who had been imprisoned, should be released within forty-eight hours. 'The time elapsed,' said Palmerston, 'the answer arrived; it was a positive and categorical refusal. What followed? Any assertion of national dignity?

Was Fort St. Julien laid in ruins? Was the Miguelite squadron burnt, sunk, and destroyed? ... Nothing of the sort. Our naval commander puts his answer in his pocket, and in dignified silence proceeds to sail away'. We did not even impose a blockade against Miguel. 'Buonaparte in the plenitude of his power never treated the humble representatives of a petty German principality with more contemptuous disregard than that which our remonstrances have met with at the hands of Don Miguel'. He rejected the Government's argument that Britain should not interfere in the internal affairs of other nations. 'If by interference is meant interference by force of arms, such interference, the Government are right in saying, general principles and our own practice forbade us to exert. But if by interference is meant intermeddling, and intermeddling in every way, and to every extent, short of actual military force; then I must affirm that there is nothing in such interference which the laws of nations may not in certain cases permit'.

Palmerston could not have realized, when he spoke these words, that they would be quoted by all his biographers, more than a hundred years later. It is unlikely that he had any other thought, when he uttered them, than to impress the audience which he was addressing; and when he became Foreign Secretary, he was to discover that the aggressive doctrines which he had advocated in his speech could not always be applied in practice. But this vigorous denunciation of Miguel, whom he called 'this royal poacher', and his upholding of Britain's right to intervene against foreign tyrants, was just what the Whigs in the House of Commons wished to hear. He hit the right note, too, in his strictures on the Government for their proposals that the territory of the new Greek state should be limited to the area south of the isthmus of Corinth and a few islands, denouncing the idea of 'a Greece which should contain neither Athens, nor Thebes, nor Marathon, nor Salamis, nor Plataea, nor Thermopylae, nor Missolonghi'. He ended by accusing the Government of having aligned England with the forces of absolutism in Europe. Instead of being looked up to as the patron of constitutional freedom, and the shield against oppression, England was considered to be the ally of Miguel and Sultan Mahmud, and the governments of Austria and Spain. Under Canning, England had been regarded by Europe as the friend of liberty, 'because it was thought that her rulers had the wisdom to discover that the selfish interests and political influence of England were best promoted by the extension of liberty and civilization'. But now it seemed that she considered 'her advantage to lie in withholding from other countries that constitutional liberty which she herself enjoys'.

The success of his speech of 1 June decided him to concentrate almost exclusively on foreign affairs in his Parliamentary interventions in 1830. Apart from one speech against an unsuccessful bill to impose a property tax on land, which Palmerston opposed on grounds of principle, he spoke about nothing except Portugal and Greece during the session, though he invariably voted with the Opposition minority in the proposals to give the seats of various rotten boroughs to Birmingham and Manchester. He enhanced his reputation with another successful speech on Portugal on 10 March 1830. It was a fine oratorical effort, with lofty sentiments, forceful phrases, and those quotations from Shakespeare and other poets which were considered so appropriate in great Parliamentary orations. He denounced Miguel in the strongest terms, and praised the doctrines of Liberalism; and though he described the Constitution of 1812 as 'crude' and 'ill-digested', he spoke in favour of a constitution in principle, thus associating himself with the main demand of the Continental Liberals and their Radical supporters in Britain. He referred to the events of the Napoleonic Wars in very different terms from those which he had used at the time, and accused the European rulers of having broken the promises which they had made to their peoples when they had invoked their aid against Bonaparte 'in the sacred names of Freedom and National Independence'. But he disclaimed any intention of wanting war. Peel, in a speech which might have been made by Palmerston in 1823, accused Palmerston and his supporters of urging England to go to war to defend the Portuguese Constitution. 'I am neither mad', said Palmerston, 'nor destitute of ordinary sense; how, then, is it possible I could wish to plunge my country into unnecessary war?' He said that 'none are really fond of war but those who are ignorant of its evils'. In any case, the trophies of the war that ended at Trafalgar and Waterloo were enough to satiate the most ardent imagination, and reconcile it to a century of peace.

He helped to familiarize himself with international affairs by visiting Paris, where he spent three weeks in January 1829. He attended the soirées of the leading Parisian hostesses, and met Talleyrand, Sébastiani, Casimir Périer, Pasquier and Benjamin Constant; and he developed a friendship, which was to last for many years, with Napoleon's aide-de-camp, General Flahaut. He also had a long talk about the problems of the Balkans with Pozzo di Borgo, who was now the Russian Ambassador in Paris. He returned to Paris ten months later. He took a room high up in the Hotel de Rivoli – he did not mind having to climb the stairs – with a fine view south over the Tuileries Gardens and the Seine to the houses on the left bank. He stayed there for the whole of December, and attended public lectures given by various eminent professors on the State of Liberty and Wealth in the World, on the Progress of Modern Languages, and on the Progress of Civilization in Europe. One of the lecturers was the eminent historian Guizot, who had not yet gone into politics. During his stay in Paris, Palmerston noticed the rising political dissatisfaction in France, and the increasing unpopularity of the reactionary government of Prince de Polignac, whom Wellington had advised King Charles X to appoint as his Prime Minister. In his letters to his brother he foretold that unless Polignac was got rid of, the King himself might well be overthrown by a revolution, as the loyalty of the army could no longer be counted upon. On his way back from Paris, he crossed from Calais in the same ship with Hobhouse, and discussed politics with him. Hobhouse noted that Palmerston 'talked Liberal just as well and as freely as if he had played the part all his life'.

The revolution in France came in July 1830. After three days of street fighting in Paris Charles X abdicated and fled to England, and his cousin the Duke of Orleans became King Louis Philippe. If the revolution had come ten years earlier, the Allies might have intervened to crush it; but by 1830, though they were profoundly disturbed, they would not contemplate the use of force against France. The only ruler who favoured such a course was the former French revolutionary General, Bernadotte, now King Charles XIV of Sweden, who had turned so violently against his native land that he refused to speak French at his Court, and offered to march an army to the gates of Paris to restore Charles X to his throne. But Wellington, Metternich and Tsar Nicholas I agreed that this was out of the question. The Tsar withdrew his Ambassador from Paris; but the other powers contented themselves with warning France that they would go to war if the new French régime attempted to export the revolution on their soldiers' bayonets, or to challenge the Treaty of Vienna.

Palmerston applauded the revolution of July 1830. It had overthrown a reactionary and autocratic régime, it had been led by constitutional and moderate Liberals, and the extremists never threatened to take control, as they did in the French revolutions of 1789 and 1848. Nor had it led to the establishment of a republic, but to a constitutional monarchy, though it was regrettable that the new King should have adopted the Bonapartist practice of calling himself the King 'of the French', and not by the traditional title of King of France. Palmerston considered that it was a revolution of the same type as the Revolution of 1688 in England. 'What a glorious event this is in France', he wrote to his Canningite colleague Charles Grant on 17 August 1830, 'how admirably the French have done it! What energy and courage in the day of trial; and what wisdom and moderation in the hour of victory! Who that remembers the excesses and outrages and horrors and insanity of 1792 and 93 could have expected to see, in so short a time, a nation of maniacs and assassins converted into heroes and philosophers? And what has wrought this miraculous change? Not any change of climate or soil; not even the infusion of Cossack blood produced by international gallantries during the three years of occupation; nothing but a short and imperfect enjoyment of a free press and a free constitution'. He wrote that this would teach 'the Metternichs and Wellingtons' that they could not 'down the mind of man to the scale of their police regulations and military codes', and would force Wellington to change his reactionary policy in Portugal and Greece. 'We shall drink the cause of Liberalism all over the world', he wrote to Sulivan on 1 August. 'The reign of Metternich is over and the days of the Duke's policy might be measured by algebra, if not by arithmetic.' When Palmerston changed his political line, he always changed with a vengeance, and expressed his new ideas with great intensity, not only in speeches in Parliament, but also in his private letters. It could be said of Palmerston, as it was said of a twentieth-century statesman: 'How he meant it, how he meant it – at the time'.

But the spirit of 1830 not merely forced Wellington to change his policy; it got rid of him altogether. The death of George IV in June 1830 caused a general election in Britain, as this followed automatically on the demise of the Crown. The Whigs won many seats, and came back to Westminster with a larger Radical minority in their ranks, and pledged to introduce a great comprehensive measure of Parliamentary reform. It immediately became very doubtful if Wellington's Government could survive. The Duke's only hope was to gain the support of the Canningites. Some of his followers had made advances to Palmerston some months before the general election, with a view to getting him to rejoin the Government as Secretary of State for the Colonies, and they had offered him the leadership of the House of Commons; but Palmerston, though he had not rejected the proposal out of hand, eventually turned it down. He had made up his mind that he would not go alone into a Tory government; he would go in, or stay out, with the other Canningites. This was his justification, in his own eyes at least, for the conflicting political attitudes which he adopted between 1827 and 1830. He was no longer a Tory, and he had never been a Whig; he considered himself to be a loyal Canningite.

The possibility of the Canningites rejoining Wellington was not to be excluded. This was perhaps the reason why the Tories did not fight Palmerston at Cambridge in the general election of 1830, as they had done in 1826. Peel thought that Palmerston was 'too discreditable and unsafe' to have in the Government; but in September, Wellington sent Lord Clive to Palmerston to offer him a seat in the Cabinet. Again Palmerston did not at once refuse, but carried on the negotiations for several days while Clive journeyed between Apsley House and Stanhope Street. But a few weeks later an accident put an end to the last hope of a reconciliation between Wellington and the Canningites. Huskisson, who had always been the most pro-Tory, as well as the most eminent, of the Canningites, was run over and killed by a train at the official opening of the Manchester to Liverpool Railway. He had stepped on to the railway line in order to talk to Wellington, and with his usual indecision had hesitated when the train approached, and had not immediately jumped clear. Huskisson's death made a rapprochement with Wellington much more difficult, and by threatening the very existence of the Canningite party, drove the remaining Canningites towards the Whigs. Meanwhile, as Wellington's difficulties increased and the political crisis deepened, Palmerston went off to Paris. Perhaps this was a way of 'playing hard to get'.

As soon as he returned at the end of October, Wellington invited him to Apsley House and offered him a seat in the Cabinet. But Palmerston now demanded that not only the Canningites, but the Whig leader, Lord Grey, and Lord Lansdowne – the former Henry Petty – should accompany him if he entered Wellington's Government; and Wellington would not consider this. As it became increasingly obvious that Wellington could not go on, and that William IV would soon be compelled to send for Lord Grey, William Lamb – who had now become Lord Melbourne – and his sister, Lady Cowper, began to think of finding a place for Palmerston in a Whig Government. In this situation, Palmerston was prepared to sever his last links with the Tories. On 6 November Croker called on him with a renewed offer from Wellington. After a short while, Croker suddenly said to Palmerston: 'Well, I will bring the matter to a point. Are you resolved, or are you not, to vote for Parliamentary Reform?' 'I am,' replied Palmerston. 'Well, then,' said Croker, 'there is no use in talking to you any more on this subject. You and I, I am grieved to see, shall never again sit on the same bench together.'

Apart from Melbourne and Lady Cowper, Palmerston had another ally working for him – the Princess Lieven. The Princess was a very intimate friend of Lord Grey, and she urged him to choose Palmerston as his Foreign Secretary. Earlier in the year, she had tried to persuade George IV to make Wellington give the Foreign Office to Palmerston, which enraged Wellington so much that he thought that he would be justified in demanding that Lieven should be recalled as Ambassador. Apart from her close friendship with Lady Cowper, and her old relationship with Palmerston, Madame de Lieven considered it her duty to work for Palmerston's appointment, for Palmerston had strongly supported Russian policy in Greece, and had a reputation of being very pro-Russian in foreign affairs. 'Lord Palmerston, Cabinet Minister and *our* Minister', she described him in a letter to her brother in May 1828; and during Palmerston's negotiations with Wellington in the autumn of 1830, of which he kept her fully informed, she expressed the opinion that his presence in the Government was necessary 'to keep down English Jacobinism'. In later years, when she had quarrelled bitterly with Palmerston, she accused him of base ingratitude, as she claimed that it was she who had been responsible for his appointment to the Foreign Office. She said that both Palmerston and Lady Cowper had urged her to use her influence with Lord Grey, that Palmerston had several times galloped over from London to her house at Richmond to press her to continue with her efforts, and that she at length succeeded in persuading Grey to offer the Foreign Office to Palmerston, though Grey had at first rejected the idea as absurd. The account which she wrote to her brother at the time is probably much nearer the truth. 'As there is no rule without its exception, I thought that I was entitled to make one to the rule I have always observed of never meddling with the political matters of this capital. Lord Grey wished to give the Foreign Office to Lord Lansdowne. I suggested Palmerston, and Grey consented in the hope that the choice would be agreeable to our Court'.

Her story has been strongly denied by the admirers of both Palmerston and Grey. There is no doubt, as they claim, that Grey first offered the Foreign Office to Lord Lansdowne, and that Lansdowne refused it, and advised Grey to give it to Palmerston. It is also obvious that Grey was not the man to be

unduly influenced in his Cabinet appointments by the persua-
sions of a woman friend. It is nevertheless clear that the Princess Lieven had every reason to exert herself on Palmerston's
behalf, and that her influence must have counted for something
with Grey. Even if his personal feelings for her played no part
in his decision, he cannot have ignored her argument that the
appointment of Palmerston as Foreign Secretary would have
a very beneficial effect in St. Petersburg and at the other European Courts. The governments of the absolutist monarchies
had been alarmed at the results of the British general election
and the prospect of the formation of a Whig government in
Britain. They felt that such an event, coming on top of the
July Revolution in France, meant that Western Europe was
taking the road of Liberalism and Jacobinism. Madame de
Lieven urged that the best way to reassure them, and to avoid
considerable difficulties for Lord Grey's new Government in
foreign affairs, would be to counter the appointment to the
Cabinet of notorious Radicals like Brougham and Lord Durham by entrusting the Foreign Office to a man like Palmerston, who had always been so far removed from the Radicals
and who was still at heart a Tory.

On 15 November, Palmerston and the Canningites voted in
the House of Commons in favour of Brougham's resolution
for a general measure of Parliamentary reform. The motion
was carried, Wellington resigned, and Grey became Prime
Minister; and on 22 November 1830 Palmerston became Secretary of State for Foreign Affairs at the age of forty-six. Princess Lieven was delighted. Palmerston's appointment was 'perfect in every way', she wrote on 20 November; and three days
later, she stated that 'it is impossible to display better judgment, juster views and greater propriety than does Lord Palmerston'. Outside the Russian embassy there was no great
enthusiasm about the appointment. No one suspected that he
would be a great Foreign Secretary.

Chapter Nine

The Foreign Secretary

When Palmerston, at the age of nine, returned with his parents from his travels in Italy and Switzerland, he completed the longest foreign journey that he was ever to make in his life. Never again did he go as far away as Naples from the shores of Britain. Apart from his many visits to Ireland, he went to France ten times; and in 1844 he travelled through Belgium, Germany and the Austrian Empire, going as far as Prague and Berlin. But he never went to any other foreign countries. Those other places about which he repeatedly wrote in his despatches, and the fate of whose inhabitants he influenced so greatly – Spain and Portugal, Constantinople and Alexandria, Greece and the Balkans, China, Persia, Abyssinia and the River Plate – he knew only from maps.

Palmerston could only travel when he was out of office. In the nineteenth century, the Foreign Secretary did not attend conferences and meetings abroad, and was expected to spend nearly all his time at his desk in the Foreign Office and in his place in the House of Commons. When Palmerston was Foreign Secretary, he very rarely left London. He remained there throughout the Parliamentary recess, when no other Cabinet minister was in town, attending to his despatches, usually on seven days in every week. He hardly ever managed to be at Broadlands for the shooting, and considered himself lucky if he was able to spend three or four days there at Christmas, or Easter, or occasionally at other times in the year. Once every five or six years he went electioneering, but normally did not visit his constituency at any other time. He never made public speeches outside Parliament, except in his constituency at election times, or, on exceptional occasions, at a banquet in the City. It was only after 1847, when the railway came to that part of Hampshire, that he could pay frequent visits to Broadlands while he was in office. When he was Prime Minister he often went there for a few days or weeks, and acquired the habit of going all over England and Scotland to open new mines and railways, and to make political speeches at public meetings.

When Palmerston first became Foreign Secretary, communications were still very slow, as neither railways, steamships nor the electric telegraph had been widely developed. The despatches from the embassies in Paris and Brussels took two days, or sometimes three, to reach the Foreign Office; those from The Hague took three days, those from Vienna, Lisbon, Madrid, St. Petersburg and the German and Italian states between ten days and a fortnight, and those from Constantinople and Washington about a month. Despatches from Montevideo took three months, those from Teheran might take four months, and those from Canton between five and seven months. This meant that Palmerston had to leave a great deal of discretion to his representatives on the spot. Sometimes it was the military and naval commanders who had to take important political decisions; but usually these were left to the diplomats, or to politicians specially sent out to the sphere of action with proconsular powers. On several occasions, at times of international crisis, the British Ambassador at Constantinople was given power to summon the Navy to the Dardanelles in order to reinforce his diplomatic démarches, although on one occasion, in 1853, the Government well knew that such a step would be tantamount to an act of war; and the High Commissioner in the Far East was given power to make war against China.

But Palmerston always kept the general direction of policy in his own hands. When envoys took up their posts abroad, they received, in their first despatch from Palmerston, a full statement of the aims of British foreign policy in connexion with the country to which they were accredited and the situation which confronted them, and similar statements were sent to them from time to time as the situation changed. These despatches were unambiguous and forceful. They left an intelligent Ambassador in very little doubt as to what action to take as each new development arose, and provided future historians with the clearest indication of Palmerston's policy in each successive crisis during his term of office. With a Foreign Secretary as lucid as Palmerston, and Ambassadors as able as Granville, Clarendon, Ponsonby, Frederick Lamb, William Russell and Howard de Walden, the system worked very well. Some of these diplomats did not like Palmerston, but they knew what he wanted them to do, and they did it efficiently. Palmerston nearly always approved of the steps which his Ambassadors took whenever they had to take emergency action on their own initiative.

Within a very short time of becoming Foreign Secretary, Palmerston was as much hated at the Foreign Office as he had been at the War Office. The chief reason why the Foreign Office clerks disliked him was that he made them work very hard. The clerks were appointed by patronage and personal recommendation from influential friends, and were all men of good family. A few stayed at the Foreign Office for a lifetime of service, rising perhaps to be one of the Under-Secretaries; but most of them were young men who had met Palmerston at a house-party, or had been recommended to him by a friend, and intended to spend a few years at the Foreign Office before settling down on their country estates, or perhaps entering Parliament. They wanted to rag about in the Office, to play practical jokes on each other, to smoke cigars in the Nursery, as the clerks' room was called, and to ogle the pretty girls who worked in the dressmaker's establishment in Fludyer Street, at the back of the Foreign Office building in Downing Street.

Palmerston made his Chief Clerk put a stop to the ragging, and whenever there was any fooling in the Nursery, the sound of a footstep in the passage was always enough to send them scurrying back to their desks in panic. Palmerston forbade the clerks to smoke in office hours. Like most people of his generation, he thought smoking was ungentlemanlike. After 1770 the upper classes gave up the pipe-smoking in which their fathers had indulged, partly to please Beau Brummell and his fastidious society friends, and partly at the exhortations of Wilberforce and the Society for the Suppression of Vice; but daring young men liked to smoke in the privacy of their homes, or in smoking saloons. Palmerston, whose gay and dashing habits never led him to violate the accepted canons of social conduct, strictly prohibited smoking in the Foreign Office, and on one occasion made a great fuss because a despatch which he received from the Embassy in Vienna had smelt of tobacco.

But it was the residents in Fludyer Street, not Palmerston, who objected most strongly to the wavings and shouting between the Foreign Office clerks and the young women in the dressmaker's establishment. When they complained to Palmerston that the clerks had been flashing mirrors at the girls, Palmerston ordered his staff to desist from 'casting reflections on young ladies opposite'.

The clerks objected to the modern innovations which Palmerston introduced in the interests of efficiency and economy. They disliked being summoned to his room by bell instead of by messenger; and they resented the reduction in their salaries, and in the amounts spent on coal and candles, which Palmerston imposed in 1841 in order to save public money. But their chief objection was that Palmerston made them work late hours, which seriously interfered with their social life. He often kept them at work until ten o'clock at night, and sometimes on Sundays. Once Palmerston arrived at the Foreign Office with Lady Cowper on a Sunday morning, and became very annoyed when he found that several of the clerks were not at work; but Lady Cowper, to the delight of those who were present, interrupted Palmerston's scoldings in order to remind him that some people went to church on Sundays. In October 1832 he received an anonymous letter, in which the writer complained of the late hours that the Foreign Office clerks had to work. The letter stated that this was injuring the clerks' health, and meant that they were unable to get home to their lodgings in time for their evening meal, but had to dine at the Foreign Office, or at their club, which came very expensive for young men living on a modest clerk's salary, and was much resented by the wives of the married clerks. The writer suggested that instead of having to work half the night, the clerks should begin earlier in the morning, and finish at 6 p.m.,

as they had always done until Palmerston became Foreign
Secretary.

The clerks were employed largely on copying duties. They
had to make tidy copies of Palmerston's drafts, to make pré-
cis of the despatches received from British Ambassadors, to
prepare memoranda to be secretly printed in time for the next
Cabinet meeting, and to write out a daily information bulletin
about developments in foreign affairs for the use of the King,
the Prime Minister and members of the Cabinet. For this it
was necessary that their handwriting should be easily legible.
Clear handwriting was an important qualification for a clerk
in any office before the days of the typewriter; but Palmerston
was more insistent than most heads of offices on this point.
He had a tendency all his life to suffer from dazzling and
fatigue of the eyes; it was the only defect in a splendid physical constitution until he developed gout in his old age. It was
therefore essential for him that the many documents which he
had to read should strain his eyes as little as possible, and he
ordered his clerks to write as large and as clearly as he did himself. He was famous among his acquaintances for his handwriting. It was not always quite as clear in his rough drafts of
despatches, or in hurriedly written notes, especially at the end
of the line, when he tried to compress all the letters of the last
word into the available space; but in any letter or document
which he wrote for despatch, the writing was faultless. It was
large and well-spaced even by modern standards, and seemed
very large to his contemporaries, most of whom wrote in a
much smaller handwriting than is usual today.

If the Foreign Office staff, and British representatives
abroad, disobeyed Palmerston's orders to write in a large and
clear handwriting, they ran the risk of receiving a sharp reproof. 'Has the Writer of this Letter lost the use of his right
hand?' Palmerston wrote on one occasion. 'If not, why does he
make all his letters slope backwards like the raking masts of
an American Schooner?' One offending diplomat was informed 'that the person who copies out his despatches should
form his letters by connecting his slanting down strokes by
visible lines at top or bottom according to the letters which
he intends his parallel lines to represent'. On one occasion, a

clerk at the Foreign Office ventured to play a joke on Palmerston, and copied out a document in exaggeratedly large writing. But Palmerston rose to the occasion. He wrote on the document. 'The Writer of this Paper would write an excellent hand if he wrote a little larger'.

Palmerston was equally insistent that his clerks and diplomats should use black ink, as pale ink strained his eyes as much as illegible writing. In January 1851, towards the end of his last term at the Foreign Office, he wrote a minute to his Under-Secretary: 'These Consuls are too bad; there is hardly one of them that writes a decent hand and with readable Ink. Write to each of the offenders that if they do not write larger and more legibly, and with black Ink, I shall be obliged to send all their despatches back to them to be written over again; and if they do not pay more attention to their Instructions, other persons will be found who will do so. This is not to be a Circular, but special to those who deserve it. Life is not long enough to decipher their scribbling'. He did in fact send back a despatch to the Consul at Massowah for it to be written out again in blacker ink, although despatches took between three and four months to come from Massowah. Edward Hertslet, who worked at the Foreign Office under Palmerston, thought that Palmerston had perhaps not realized the difficulties involved in obtaining ink at Massowah, because Hertslet remembered that on one occasion, when events at Massowah were being discussed, Palmerston had asked: 'Where exactly is Massowah?' But despite his real, or feigned, ignorance as to its precise location, Palmerston knew well enough that this island off the coast of Abyssinia, at the southern extremity of the Turkish Empire, was an important base for British traders who were hoping to establish commercial relations with Abyssinia.

Palmerston also strongly objected to an improper use of language by his clerks. He directed them to be brief, and not to use two adjectives where one would do; though a modern reader who encounters, in Palmerston's own despatches, such phrases as 'I am of opinion that', and 'to evince a desire', may think that Palmerston was as bad as any of his clerks in this respect. From time to time he flared up when his subordinates used words which he thought were of foreign origin. He insis-

ted that they write 'interference', not 'intervention', which was
a French word. He could be equally particular about spelling.
When he received a despatch in which 'battalion' was spelt
'batallion', he told the writer that these battalions should be
placed on the English, not on the French, footing. But he was
so inconsistent about the use of Gallicisms that it is difficult
to avoid the impression that he was merely being awkward,
and finding excuses to be unpleasant to his staff. He himself
very often used French words and phrases in his private correspondence, and sometimes wrote whole sentences in French.
He was particularly fond of quoting French proverbs in the
original.

When he was annoyed, he did not mince his words. Once
when he was irritated by a stupid despatch from an envoy in
South America he wrote on the docket: 'Goose, goose, goose'.
At other times, he was more subtle in his reproofs. Soon after
Christmas 1839, there was a fire at the Foreign Office, because
of the negligence of a little boy who was employed as a chim-
ney-sweep. Palmerston went into an attic at the top of the
building where an elderly German, who was employed as a
translator, was engaged in his work. 'Have you any valuable
books in this room, Mr. Huttner?' said Palmerston. Huttner
did not look up from his work to see who had asked the question, but answered casually: 'And what if I have?' 'Oh, nothing if you have', replied Palmerston, 'but I suppose you know
that the house is on fire'; and thereupon he left the room and
closed the door, leaving Huttner excitedly shouting: 'Mein
Gott, mein Gott!' One of the clerks took advantage of the
confusion caused by the fire to play a daring prank on Palmerston. Palmerston was often nicknamed 'Protocol Palmerston' in
the Office. During the fire, the clerk opened the door of the
room in which Palmerston was waiting and called out im-
pudently: 'Take care of the protocols!' Palmerston was furious, but the clerk ran quickly down the stairs before Palmerston could identify him, and no one ever found out who the
offender was.

Palmerston behaved rather differently towards those diplomats whom he respected because of their high rank or ability. Only four of the British Ministers abroad held the rank of

Ambassador – those in Paris, Vienna, St. Petersburg and Constantinople – and these posts were always given to men of aristocratic families, and usually to peers. Palmerston treated these Ambassadors, and some of the other Ministers, with respect. Even here he was guilty of occasional lapses, one of which caused Ponsonby to complain to Lord John Russell that he had received letters from Palmerston to which no man could submit; but at least Palmerston never commented on the English, the use of Gallicisms, or the handwriting of these eminent Ambassadors, though some of them, like Lord Howard de Walden, wrote in a very illegible hand; and the wording of his official despatches and private letters to them was much less peremptory than those which he sent to less exalted diplomats. He was particularly courteous in his language to Frederick Lamb, the Ambassador in Vienna, who was the brother of Lord Melbourne and Lady Cowper. Palmerston and Frederick Lamb were by no means on friendly terms. Lamb was not pleased that his sister was Palmerston's mistress, though he himself had been involved in nearly as many love affairs as Palmerston. But Palmerston respected Lamb's great abilities as a diplomat, and Greville thought that he did everything that Lamb suggested for fear of offending Lady Cowper. 'The Chief is devoted to the sister, and the sister to the brother', Greville wrote in his diary, and added that Lady Cowper would not hesitate to put the brother before the lover, and would make Palmerston suffer if he annoyed Lamb in any way. All this was an exaggeration. Palmerston does not seem to have treated Lamb with any greater deference than he showed to Lord Granville, Lord Durham, Lord Clarendon, Lord Howard de Walden or Lord Ponsonby. He was equally considerate to his colleagues in the Cabinet. When Greville travelled up by train from Stoke to London with Lord Melbourne, soon after the railway was first built, Melbourne was very surprised to hear Greville's complaints about Palmerston's arrogance, and told him that Palmerston was particularly polite and accommodating at Cabinet meetings, though he could be obstinate.

But even those noblemen whom Palmerston treated with an outward show of respect sometimes felt that his courtesy was only a cover for underhand intrigue. According to the Duchess of Dino, who was Talleyrand's daughter-in-law and acted as his hostess at the French Embassy in London, Lord William Russell told the Princess Lieven that Palmerston was prepared to resort to any means to discredit diplomats who annoyed him. 'If you display any independence, whether of language or of opinion, it irritates him', said Lord William. 'His one thought is how to get rid of you and bring about your ruin. When I was at Lisbon, my views did not agree with his, so he attacked my wife's reputation. . . . No gentleman can in the end consent to do business with him'. Madame de Dino almost certainly exaggerated, and to some extent distorted, what Lord William Russell had said, and it had doubtless already been exaggerated and distorted on the way to her by the Princess Lieven.

The clerks at the Foreign Office might have been less dissatisfied if they had been given more responsibility; but even the Under-Secretaries had very little opportunity to exercise their own initiative. Palmerston once told Queen Victoria that as the Foreign Secretary was liable to be questioned in Parliament about all aspects of his department, it was essential that he should be thoroughly familiar with all the details, and that the only way he could achieve this was to do all the work himself. He drafted all important despatches himself, and assured the Queen that this system worked much better than the practice adopted in the Foreign Ministries of the Continental states, where despatches were drafted by underlings and only approved and signed by the Foreign Minister. Palmerston was wrong when he said that he was the only Foreign Minister in Europe who wrote his own despatches, for Metternich drafted the more important Austrian ones; but Palmerston drafted more despatches than Metternich did, and many more than any other Foreign Minister. Despatches about claims against the Mexican Government by British business men in Oaxaca, or the cost of repatriating an English sailor who had deserted from an American ship at Vladivostock, were all drafted by Palmerston. After writing his first draft, he inserted corrections and additions – these were often numerous – and gave the document to a clerk to be copied out neatly. Palmerston then often made further alterations, and the despatch was finally copied out neatly once again by a clerk for signature by Palmerston and submission to the King before being delivered to a King's messenger to carry by ship and coach to the British Embassy abroad.

Some matters of minor importance were left to the Under-Secretaries to deal with; but generally speaking, the only aspect of Foreign Office business which Palmerston did not handle himself was the Secret Service work. It would have been inappropriate for the Foreign Secretary to be personally involved in this. There was much less espionage activity in Palmerston's time than there had been two or three hundred years earlier during the religious struggles of the Reformation period, and would be again in the ideological contests of the twentieth century. There was less scope for espionage in the detached and gentlemanly atmosphere in which foreign policy was conducted between states in the early nineteenth century, though there was a good deal of police spying on revolutionary organizations. Palmerston believed that the development of a free press in many countries had rendered espionage superfluous, as foreign governments had only to buy the newspapers of a country in order to learn everything that was going on there. The only Secret Service work in which his Under-Secretaries engaged was occasionally to make payments to British firms abroad to reimburse them for expenses which they had incurred in buying secret information in the countries where they were stationed. These payments sometimes amounted to about £100, but were usually nearer £20. The Secret Service, like every other Government department, was run on the cheap, with a consciousness of the paramount need to prevent wastage of public money.

Apart from drafting most of the despatches himself, Palmerston spent a considerable amount of time writing directives and articles for the press. Most newspapers were prepared to advocate any political line if they were paid sufficiently. It is hardly accurate to call them corrupt, because the practice was as well recognized as it is today for a newspaper to sell advertising space, or for an advocate to place his forensic ability at the service of a client in return for money. Palmerston paid the

Observer, out of the Secret Service money, to support the Government's foreign policy, and himself wrote memoranda to the editor laying down the political line that was to be followed in the paper. He similarly directed the policy of the *Courier* and the *Morning Chronicle*; but the chief organ of Government foreign policy was the evening paper, the *Globe*. Palmerston not only sent general directives on policy to these newspapers, but often wrote their unsigned articles and editorials himself. He did not, however, exercise any direct censorship over the papers which supported the Government; and he told the Princess Lieven that though he could force the editors to publish an article defending his foreign policy, he could not prevent them from attacking him in another article next day. 'I can compel, but I cannot control', he wrote. 'The only communication that takes place is that every now and then, when we have any particular piece of news, it is given to the editor, and he thereby gets a start of his competitors, and on the condition of receiving these occasional intimations he gives his support to the Government'. Other papers, like the *Morning Post*, the *Standard*, the *Morning Herald* and the *Morning Advertiser*, were Tory, and attacked Palmerston's foreign policy, as did *The Times* after 1834.

Although the clerks in the Foreign Office complained that Palmerston made them work long hours, he himself worked harder than any of them. He needed eight hours' work every day to deal with the routine business of his office, apart from the time which he spent in the House of Commons. When he was an undergraduate at Cambridge, he made it a rule never to go to bed later than one, or get up after seven. He tried, as far as possible, to keep to this routine throughout his life, though when the House of Commons was sitting late, he often did not get to bed till three or four o'clock in the morning. But even then he was up again by seven and went for a ride in the park, or, when out of London and the circumstances permitted, went swimming or rowing. He returned in time to read a few despatches before breakfast, and would arrive at the Foreign Office at about ten o'clock, where things went ill for any clerk who was not already hard at work by the time he arrived. He worked on his despatches throughout the morning

and early afternoon, without taking any break for a midday
meal; and even when he was entertaining friends to luncheon
at Broadlands or in London, he himself ate nothing except an
orange. Whenever possible, he went for a ride or a walk in the
afternoons, but pressure of work sometimes prevented this.
The meetings of the Cabinet were held in the afternoons. He
made it a general rule, except in emergencies, never to grant
interviews before 5 p.m., by which time the Cabinet meeting
would be over; and Ambassadors and other persons with
whom he had matters to discuss were invited to attend on him
between 5 p.m. and dinner at 6 or 6.30 p.m. After eating a large
meal, he went to the House of Commons. He would go home
as soon as he was able to leave the House, and work on his
despatches till 1 a.m., not sitting, but standing at a special desk,
because he was afraid that he would fall asleep if he sat down.
He then retired for his six hours' sleep.

But the day's routine did not often run to schedule, and
Palmerston, who was overwhelmed by the amount of work
which he had taken on, became notorious for his unpunctuality. This developed into a really serious defect, and was one
of the reasons why he was as unpopular with the diplomatic
corps as he was with his own staff. He often kept Ambassadors
waiting at the Foreign Office when they came for interviews.
This was partly because of the well-established British system
by which persons attending for interviews with the Secretary
of State were kept waiting, however eminent they might be,
until it was their turn, as the Secretary of State always received
his callers in the order of their arrival. Thus the famous interview between Nelson and Wellington, a few weeks before Trafalgar, took place in the waiting room of the Secretary of State
for War and the Colonies, where the Admiral and the General
were kept waiting for a long time. But in other countries, great
dignitaries expected to jump the queue over less important
personages; and Talleyrand, the French Ambassador, was
very annoyed that Palmerston often kept him waiting between
one and two hours. When Palmerston heard that Talleyrand
was angry, he coolly commented that Talleyrand was being
unreasonable, as Talleyrand had nothing else to do except to
conduct his business with the Foreign Secretary, whereas Pal-

merston had all the other Ambassadors to deal with, and the
Foreign Office to administer. 'Other diplomats who want me',
wrote Palmerston, 'come and pop into my room at Stan. Street
at 12 and come in and go out in a short time; he does not
weigh anchor till after 1 or near 2; and what he likes to do is
to come and establish himself in the armchair at the office
about 4, just as I want to go away to eat something before I
go down to the He. of Commons. This I always try to fight
off; for his visit never lasts less than an hour including getting
up and sitting down and that throws us out as to everything to
be done afterwards'. But Talleyrand was not the only Ambassador who was made to wait. The Belgian Minister, Van de
Weyer, stated that he had read the whole of Richardson's
Clarissa while he was waiting in Palmerston's anteroom; and
Palmerston once kept the Russian Ambassador, Pozzo di
Borgo, waiting for two hours. Pozzo wrote that he had never
known a minister, or an English gentleman, carry his insolence
to such lengths as this. Perhaps the fact that Pozzo had once
been Lady Cowper's lover made Palmerston the more ready to
inconvenience him.

　Palmerston's unpunctuality, and his unusual hours of work,
did not always improve the efficiency of the Foreign Office.
Lord Granville's son, Lord Leveson, who was Under-Secretary for Foreign Affairs under Palmerston in Melbourne's
Government, and later, as the second Earl Granville, became
Foreign Secretary himself, thought that he fulfilled a useful
function at the Foreign Office because he had opportunities
for meeting Palmerston, and was not 'so dreadfully afraid of
him. It is impossible to have a glimpse of him in the office', he
wrote to Granville in March 1840. 'He comes down very
late, having kept quantities of people waiting for him; and
before he has seen them all, goes down to the House. The
clerks detest him, and have an absurd sort of fancy that he
takes pleasure in bullying them'.

　Palmerston sometimes went to his house in Stanhope Street
in the middle of the day so that he could work undisturbed.
On one occasion soon after he became Foreign Secretary, he
arrived at the Foreign Office at half-past six, having kept the
King's Advocate waiting for an hour and a half for an inter-

view which had been fixed for five o'clock. He explained to the perturbed Under-Secretary that he had been working at home on an important despatch, which he had been unable to draft for several days owing to constant interruptions at the Foreign Office, and that he had therefore taken it home to work on it there, and that he had to finish it without further delay, however long the King's Advocate waited. He was nearly always late for social engagements. It so happened that Lady Cowper was as bad as he was in this respect, so he got no encouragement from her to be punctual, either before or after he married her. She nearly always arrived late for church, and on one occasion, when Queen Victoria was staying at her house, she kept the Queen waiting for their afternoon drive. When she and Palmerston were invited out, they usually arrived late for dinner, and there was a saying in London society that the Palmerstons always missed the soup. This also applied at great official banquets when members of the royal family were present. Palmerston would walk in breezily half-way through the meal, and make the most perfunctory of apologies, saying 'Public business must be attended to, Your Royal Highness'. He arrived at a dinner at the Duchess of Kent's after the meal had started, and at the first state banquet which Queen Victoria gave at the beginning of her reign, he arrived after all the guests had sat down. A diplomat who arrived at Palmerston's house for a formal diplomatic dinner found Palmerston mounting his horse in the courtyard; and Palmerston explained to him that he was just going for a short ride to get some exercise before the dinner. Palmerston once arrived three-quarters of an hour late for a dinner at the Turkish Ambassador's, who made all the other guests wait until he arrived. But Palmerston did not have a high opinion of this Turkish Ambassador. He told Ponsonby, the British Ambassador at Constantinople, that he was just 'a greasy, stupid old Turk,' 'like a Turk in a melodrama on the stage, one of Bluebeard's attendants'.

However harassed and overworked Palmerston may have been, he could have arranged, like other busy men, to be punctual for his public and private engagements if he had really wanted to. Only twice in his life did he fail to be in his place in

time for a debate, or to answer questions, in the House of
Commons. His unpunctuality did not spring from fecklessness
or from a slapdash inability to plan his affairs, for he showed,
by his capacity for work and the orderliness of his mind, that
he was quite free from these defects of character. It resulted
from his arrogance and lack of consideration for others, or
rather, to put it in a fairer way, from a conviction that his own
work and time were more important than other people's and
that he would not suffer any adverse consequences if he inconvenienced a King's Advocate, a foreign Ambassador, or a
royal Duke. He knew that foreign diplomats, however much
they might resent his conduct, were eager to have friendly
relations with Britain, and would therefore continue to woo
the British Foreign Secretary. It was one of his maxims that
the foreign policy of a nation was determined, not by temporary passions, but by basic long-term interests; and on several
occasions when his worried diplomatic agents or ministerial
colleagues remonstrated with him for having whipped up anti-
British feeling in some foreign country by his provocative
attitude, he would calmly assure them that the ill-feeling
would soon subside, for the economic and diplomatic interests
of the foreign state were bound to lead to a rapprochement.

People who had been inconvenienced by Palmerston's unpunctuality were particularly resentful because they knew
that, despite his claims to be overworked, he still found time
to enjoy himself in society. No one who knew the number of
despatches which Palmerston wrote could ever have accused
him of putting pleasure before work; but those who saw him
in the company of some beautiful woman, not realizing that it
was perhaps the first time for many weeks that he had taken a
few hours off from his work, spread the rumour that when he
was late for official appointments it was because he had been
making love to one of his mistresses. His pleasures and habits,
as he approached the age of fifty, were the same as when he
was a young man. He still dressed in the height of fashion,
and had grown side-whiskers down the whole length of his
face, just like any up-to-date young buck. When Henry Bulwer met him for the first time, a few weeks after he became
Foreign Secretary, at a party at Lady Cowper's, Bulwer noted

that 'his air was more that of a man of the drawing-room than of the senate'. But Bulwer was struck by his 'clear short, decisive way of speaking on business', and by the questions which Palmerston put to him about Belgium, from which Bulwer had just returned.

It was probably largely because of his appearance and manner that Palmerston struck observers as being a playboy; and the illusion was fostered by the hostile Tory papers, especially by *The Times,* which referred to him as 'Lord Cupid'. It was an open secret that he was Lady Cowper's lover, and some of the foreign embassies made use of this knowledge by inviting Lady Cowper to functions in order to ensure that Palmerston would accept the invitation, though this bait did not always succeed in catching Palmerston. When Lady Cowper went abroad for a few months in 1833, Palmerston spent a great deal of time with Lady Jersey. She was still a handsome woman, with her black hair and perfect complexion and haughty manner, though she was now nearly fifty, like Palmerston and Lady Cowper. A few years later, Balzac described her as the perfect type of English aristocratic beauty when he saw her at the opera in Paris. The society gossips made much of her association with Palmerston.

He was less successful with Mrs. Stanley, later Lady Stanley of Alderley. She was Henrietta Maria Dillon-Lee, the daughter of Lord Dillon, and before her marriage had been the leading beauty of the season at Florence, where she became a supporter of the cause of Italian liberation, and created a sensation by refusing to dance with Austrian officers. She had strong Radical sympathies, and was probably the Lady Daisy – 'half Jacobin and half coquette' – of William Mackworth Praed's poem. Many years later, she told Chichester Fortescue that, soon after her marriage in 1826, Palmerston had made love to her 'in his impudent, brusque way, with a "Ha, ha! I see it all – beautiful woman neglected by her husband – allow me, etc." ' Stanley became a Whig MP in 1831, and Chief Whip in 1839, when Palmerston described him as being 'joint whip with Mrs. Stanley'. When Palmerston became Foreign Secretary for the last time in 1846, he chose Stanley as his Under-Secretary.

Palmerston also showed interest at this time in another woman of a very different type from his usual mistresses. She was Mrs. Laura Petre, a young widow of twenty-two, who, though she had never played a prominent part in society, was an intelligent and cultured woman, and a Roman Catholic. In 1833 and 1834 the rumour spread that both Palmerston and Lord Brougham, the Lord Chancellor, were pursuing Mrs. Petre, and that she had rejected Brougham and become Palmerston's mistress. Her relations with two Cabinet ministers caused some comment in political circles on account of her religion. Greville complained that Palmerston was spending his time making love to Mrs. Petre instead of doing his work, and that he brought her down to the House of Commons in order to parade his conquest. But the extent of the conquest was probably less than Palmerston hoped and Greville believed, for Mrs. Petre was famous for her virtue as well as for her intellect, and soon afterwards entered a convent and became a Prioress.

Another minor cause of irritation between Palmerston and the foreign Ambassadors was the fact that in regard to certain customs and courtesies, Britain did not observe the internationally accepted rules. This was not primarily due to Palmerston, but to the increasing insularity and dislike of foreign practices which was felt by the British public. It was an accepted practice for sovereigns to confer their national orders and decorations on foreign statesmen and diplomats as a mark of friendship and respect, when international relations were reasonably friendly; but the British Government refused to permit its servants to accept foreign decorations except in very exceptional cases, and even then the decoration could only be worn in Britain by special leave of the King, and on special occasions. Palmerston enforced this rule very strictly. The only British subjects who were permitted to accept foreign orders were those who had been in the employment of foreign governments, or officers who had served in the field in joint military operations conducted by Britain and the foreign state. Apart from these cases, Palmerston made only one exception, when he allowed Lord Durham to accept the Order of St. Andrew from the Tsar which was conferred on him in

1837 after he completed his term as Ambassador in Russia; but the many requests which he afterwards received from other British Ambassadors for permission to accept a foreign decoration convinced him that Durham's case had been an unfortunate precedent which must on no account be followed. Several foreign governments offered their highest decorations to Palmerston, but he always politely declined them, explaining that he was not allowed to accept.

Britain did not conform to the usual international rules about attending royal funerals and coronations. When the King of Denmark died in 1839, Queen Victoria was one of the few foreign sovereigns who did not send an envoy to congratulate Christian VIII on his accession, and Palmerston thought it advisable to explain to the Danes that this was not through any lack of respect or friendship, but only because it was not the practice of British monarchs to do so. Palmerston initiated another departure from recognized diplomatic practice in 1834. It had for long been accepted among all nations that diplomatic notes from one government to another were written in French. Palmerston instructed British ministers abroad that in future all official diplomatic despatches sent to foreign governments must be written in English. He explained that apart from any other advantages, they had to be in English so that they could be laid before Parliament whenever the House demanded to see them, though there was no reason why British diplomats should not continue to write in French or any other foreign language in their private letters or unofficial correspondence with foreign governments. Palmerston also put a stop to the practice by which the Foreign Office and British embassies exchanged gifts at Christmas and on other occasions with foreign governments and embassies, and ordered that in future no British representatives were either to give or to accept such gifts, except in a purely private capacity. This regulation was doubly popular with the British public, as it saved the taxpayer's money as well as preserving diplomats from corruption by foreigners.

Although Palmerston, like all other society gentlemen of the period, behaved with a courtesy which may appear stiff and formal to people in the twentieth century, there was a certain

frankness and easy-going casualness in British conduct which
sometimes struck foreign diplomats as a lack of decorum.
Princess Lieven was shocked when her friend Lady Cowper
told her that the British naturally disliked having Lieven as
Russian Ambassador, because he represented the interests of
his country with such great ability. Madame de Lieven thought
that this remark was in very bad taste. The Duchess of Dino
was disgusted, when Palmerston invited her to a banquet at
the Foreign Office, to find that hardly anyone present came
from the higher ranks of English society, but that someone as
low class as Mrs. Petre was present, and signalled out for such
attention by Palmerston. Mrs. Petre would have been considered acceptable everywhere in British society; but the Duchess
of Dino thought that even Lady Jersey was middle class, because her grandfather was Child the banker.

But in the Duchess of Dino's eyes, Palmerston could do
nothing right. She hated him because of the way he treated
Talleyrand. Talleyrand himself was more forgiving, and could
not hide his respect for Palmerston. 'Lord Palmerston', he
wrote, 'is certainly one of the most able, if not the most able,
man of business whom I have met in my career'; though he
added: 'One feature in his character dissipates all these advantages, and prevents him, in my opinion, from ranking as
a real statesman. He feels passionately about public affairs,
and to the point of sacrificing the most important interests to
his resentments. Nearly every political question resolves itself
into a personal question in his eyes, and in appearing to defend the interests of his country, it is really the interests of
his hate and vengeance that he satisfies'. Talleyrand gave Palmerston the credit of being friendly in social life, and having
elegant manners; but Madame de Dino was not convinced.
'M. de Talleyrand may say what he likes', she wrote, Palmerston 'may have a gift for the despatch of business; he may
speak and write French well; but he is a rude and presump-
tuous person, his behaviour is arrogant, and his character not
upright'.

Chapter Ten

The Belgian Crisis of 1831

Palmerston had only one principle in foreign policy. As he told the House of Commons in 1848, he believed that the furtherance of British interests should be the only object of a British Foreign Secretary. He added that it was a British interest to preserve the balance of power in international affairs, and that Britain had no permanent friends or permanent enemies. On several other occasions he declared that constitutional states were the natural allies of Britain, and that it was therefore Britain's interest to maintain constitutional governments throughout the world; but this doctrine, as he showed repeatedly in practice, was qualified by the more fundamental principles that he laid down in his speech in 1848.

In the ideological struggle between absolutism and liberalism in Europe, Palmerston pursued a policy of neutralism. He allied Britain first with one state, then with another, sometimes with liberal constitutional governments, and sometimes with absolutist monarchies. He supported the bourgeois constitutional monarchy of Louis Philippe, and then inflicted on it a number of calculated humiliations. He alternately helped and thwarted the policies of Metternich and Tsar Nicholas of Russia. He encouraged Liberalism in Germany in 1832, and hampered it in 1848. He sometimes praised Polish nationalism in words, but never helped it with deeds. He sometimes helped, and sometimes hindered, the cause of Liberalism and nationalism in Italy and Hungary. He supported moderate constitutionalism in Portugal and extreme Radicalism in Spain. He denounced the despotism of Miguel in Portugal, of King Ferdinand of Naples, and of King Otho in Greece; but he supported dictators like Napoleon III, Milosh in Serbia, Rosas in Argentina and Maximilian in Mexico. He waged a long war for the suppression of the international slave trade, but did his best to injure the cause of the North, and to help the cause of slavery, during the American Civil War. In every situation he thought only of one thing: British interests. A policy of neutralism, or ideological non-alignment, can be dangerous, unless the nation which pursues it has three necessary qualifications to ensure its success: military or naval superiority, a sound and thriving economy, and skilful direction of its foreign policy. In Palmerston's time, Britain possessed all three of these requirements.

Palmerston was not one of those statesmen, like Bismarck, Cavour or Abraham Lincoln, who had one great political objective to which he dedicated his life and for which he worked on a long-term strategical plan. His policy was merely to preserve the status quo, to prevent any power from becoming so strong that it might threaten Britain, to prevent the outbreak of major wars in which Britain might be involved and weakened, and to obtain any incidental advantages for Britain which might happen to accrue out of any passing situation, and to protect the lives and property of British subjects all over the world. His foreign policy was therefore a series of tactical improvisations, which he carried out with great skill. He was as opportunistic, and as free from entanglements, in working for Britain in international affairs as he was in furthering his own political career in British internal politics. He was almost always successful in both fields.

Palmerston's policy of first supporting, and then abandoning, an ally caused him to be very unpopular with foreign governments, apart from the fact that foreign statesmen and diplomats who had to do with him also disliked him personally because of his arrogance, his unpunctuality and other private characteristics. This did not worry Palmerston at all. It seemed to him perfectly natural that he should be hated by the Foreign Ministers and by the people of other nations. Palmerston was very conscious of the advantages of international co-operation in certain fields, particularly in regard to trade, for he was firmly convinced that free international trade brought mutual benefits to all nations who practised it. He was also eager to avoid wars, especially major wars, and was on the

whole successful in achieving this. No major war broke out in
Europe during the sixteen years that he was at the Foreign
Office, and it is very likely that he would have prevented the
Crimean War if he had been in charge of British foreign policy
in 1853. But he also believed that there were conflicts of interests between states, and when a conflict arose between Britain
and a foreign country, and he furthered British interests at
this other country's expense, he expected to be hated by his
adversary. From time to time, when he was violently attacked
in the press of some foreign nation whom he had thwarted, the
British Ambassador reported the fact in great indignation.
Palmerston usually told the Ambassador not to worry, as such
a thing was perfectly natural, and the press campaign would
be sure to subside when the interests of the foreign power led
it once again to pursue a policy of friendship with Britain. It
is easier for the victor than for the vanquished to be generous
to his enemies, and Palmerston could usually afford to smile at
the rage of his discomfited adversary. On the few occasions
when Britain got the worst of an international encounter, or
when he was beaten in the political game at home, he sometimes indulged in an outbreak of childish anger and recrimin-
ations; but these soon passed, and in general he accepted the
few defeats of his career with complete equanimity.

In December 1830, Palmerston told the Sardinian Government that Britain would not go to war 'except for the vindication of National honour, or in defence of the possessions of
the Crown'. In Palmerston's time, states sometimes went to war
merely to vindicate their honour and prestige. In earlier and
later eras, wars were waged in too horrible a manner to be
embarked on lightly; but in the eighteenth and early nineteenth centuries, the gentlemanly wars of the period were considered a suitable way of revenging insults to nations, as the
duel avenged insults to individuals. When a great power had
been slighted by a little country, its honour required it to extract an apology, often in the most humiliating circumstances,
by threat of force; and a great power, on the other hand, was
reluctant to undergo the humiliation of having to make an
apology, even if its representatives had misbehaved themselves towards another country. This practice of compelling

weaker states to make humiliating apologies was begun in 1684 by Louis XIV of France, when he forced the republic of Genoa to pay an indemnity, and send envoys to Paris to ask forgiveness, at the foot of his throne, for an insult to the honour of France. Britain took over the practice in the eighteenth century. In 1769 Captain Jervis – later Lord St. Vincent – insisted that the Government of Genoa should send an official on board his ship to apologize, in front of the assembled ship's company, for having removed a Turkish slave who had escaped to a British ship in the port of Leghorn. In 1804, when the Dey of Algiers expelled the British Consul for having allegedly violated a native girl, Nelson sailed with the fleet to Algiers and required the Dey to sign an apology which he had drafted, informing the Dey that this was the least humiliating form of apology which the British Government was prepared to accept.

This method of vindicating the national honour could only be enforced by a navy. A powerful land army was almost useless for the purpose, as states with strong armies could only threaten their neighbours, unless they were prepared to march through neutral territory and precipitate a major international war. Russia could only bully the Shahs and Emirs of Persia and Central Asia, and the people of Poland and certain parts of the Balkans; and even here, the movement of great land armies was likely to arouse fears and provoke counter-action from other great powers, like Britain. But the British Navy could sail to any part of the world, or blockade or bombard the Piraeus, the River Plate or Canton, if a British subject had been injured or the British flag insulted there, without any other great power having any apprehensions that Britain was threatening its security or upsetting the balance of power. In the first half of the nineteenth century, there were only three powers which possessed a navy which was capable of carrying out such actions – Britain, France, and the United States. It so happened that in all three countries there was a free Parliament and a free press, where MPs and journalists could arouse national passions, and make it much more difficult for the Government to overlook the insult to the national honour than it would have been for an absolutist Tsar or King. So all three powers used their navies to bully smaller countries. Britain, under Palmerston, bullied them a little less than France, and a little more than the United States.

Today this gunboat diplomacy is particularly associated with Palmerston; but Palmerston did not start it, and was merely the instrument of British public opinion. In 1858, this British public opinion drove Palmerston from office because it was thought that he was knuckling under to a foreign government. It is usually considered to be an irony that Palmerston should have been forced to resign as Prime Minister because he was not sufficiently Palmerstonian for the British people; but in fact the British people were always more Palmerstonian than Palmerston. When he sent a gunboat to coerce a foreign government, it was usually only after he had spent many weeks urging patience and excusing his inaction to an angry House of Commons. When he first became Foreign Secretary, he was accused of appeasing France; some years later, he was accused of appeasing Russia; and he was twice driven from office for appeasing Napoleon III. He owed his political success to the fact that he nevertheless managed to persuade the British public that he was the greatest Palmerstonian of them all.

When Palmerston first became Foreign Secretary, he was confronted almost immediately with five major international problems. The troubles in Greece and Portugal, about which he had spoken so often as an Opposition MP during the previous two years, were still unsolved; and within a few weeks of taking office he was also facing the problems of Belgium, Poland and Italy. When Palmerston became Foreign Secretary, the Greeks had already won their war of independence against Turkey; but the questions of the frontiers of the new Greek state, the settlement of its financial obligations to Turkey, and its internal form of government, had been referred to an international conference of the great powers which was meeting in London under the chairmanship of the British Foreign Secretary. In Portugal, Miguel was still in power, and the Liberal forces of Maria da Gloria and Dom Pedro held nothing except a foothold on the island of Terceira in the Azores. In Belgium, a revolution had broken out in August 1830, and the people were demanding independence. Dutch rule; this problem, too, had been referred to a conference of the great powers in London. A week after Palmerston took office, a revolt against Russia broke out in Poland; and in February 1831 the Italians rose in revolt against the Pope, the Duke of Modena and Marie-Louise, the Duchess of Parma.

Of these problems, the Belgian and Italian situations were the most dangerous, as both of them might have led to war between France and the three absolutist powers – Russia, Prussia and Austria – who, in the English diplomatic language of the period, were known, somewhat inappropriately, as the Northern Powers. Palmerston intervened between France and the Northern Powers in order to prevent war. In Belgium, with the British Navy in the background, his intervention was decisive; in Italy, it was much less effective, but nevertheless played a useful part in preventing war.

Until 1790, the modern state of Belgium was still part of the Habsburg territories, and under the rule of the Emperor of Austria. Then, at the beginning of the French Revolution, the Belgians proclaimed their independence, and soon afterwards the French armies drove out the Austrians and united the country to France. At the peace treaties of 1814 and 1815 the Allies gave it to Holland. No sooner had the Revolution of 1830 broken out in Paris than it was followed in Brussels by a nationalist and Liberal rising against the reactionary autocratic government of the King of Holland. The revolution was successful, and the Dutch garrisons were driven out. The King of Holland prepared to send troops to suppress his rebellious subjects. The French Government prepared to send an army to liberate the Belgians from the Dutch. Prussia prepared to go to war in support of Holland, and Russia and Austria were preparing to support Prussia. But neither Wellington nor Metternich wanted a European war, so they favoured the idea of erecting Belgium into a new independent state, which should be pledged to neutrality in European conflicts by the decision and guarantees of the great powers.

It was decided to refer the problem to a conference of the great powers. A conference, in the diplomatic practice of the age, was different from a congress. At a congress, all the powers were represented by their Foreign Ministers or heads of government, or by other special plenipotentiaries; but at a conference, only the country in which the conference was held was represented by its Foreign Minister, who presided at the conference; all the other powers were represented by their resident Ambassadors. This made the venue of the conference an important factor. It was agreed to hold the conference on Belgium in London, because of all the great powers Britain was the least committed in the dispute. The Conference assembled on 4 November 1830, and had only held a few sessions when Wellington's Government gave way to Grey's, and Lord Aberdeen was replaced as Foreign Secretary by Palmerston. Within forty-eight hours of taking office, Palmerston was presiding at a session of the Conference. At his side at the conference table sat Talleyrand, the French Ambassador; his old acquaintances Prince Lieven and Prince Esterhazy, the Ambassadors of Russia and Austria; the Prussian Ambassador, Baron Bülow; and the Dutch Ambassador, Baron Verstolk. The Belgian rebels, whose Committee in Brussels had not been recognized by any foreign government, were not officially represented at the Conference; but the Conference had decided, against Verstolk's protests, to invite them to send observers, and Baron Van der Weyer attended the Conference on their behalf.

Palmerston had firmly decided, from the very beginning, that Belgium should become an independent and neutral state. Nine days after taking office, he wrote to Ponsonby, the British representative in Brussels: 'His Majesty's Government consider the absolute and entire separation of Belgium from Holland to be no longer a matter for discussion, but to have become, by the course of events, an established, and as far as can at present be foreseen, an irreversible fact'. This was not because Palmerston had any sympathy with the national aspirations of subject peoples, or the right to self-determination, which came to be accepted as a desirable objective in the twentieth century. But he was convinced that there was no other way of avoiding war and preserving the balance of power in Western Europe. He explained this in a despatch to Prussia on 31 December 1830. 'It was for the interest of both England

and Prussia that Belgium and Holland should have remained united, if their union could have been maintained; but that union having become impossible by the force of events, it is obvious that the independence of Belgium is the only means of preventing another union, which would be in the highest degree objectionable to Prussia and England, and which could not even be attempted without involving Europe in war'. His chief aim, throughout the Belgian crisis, was to prevent the union of Belgium with France.

It took only a month to persuade the London Conference to agree to the independence of Belgium, which was formally settled by the Conference on 20 December 1830. The two remaining problems were to fix the frontiers of the new state, and to find a King to rule it. Palmerston was determined that the frontiers should be settled by the great powers, and did not feel that either the Dutch or the Belgians had any right to be consulted. The Dutch had been unable to suppress the revolt in Belgium, and had referred the matter to the London Conference; they had therefore abdicated their sovereign rights over Belgium in favour of the great powers. As for the Belgians, Belgium had never at any time in history existed as an independent state, but was now being given sovereignty by the great powers; so the Belgians should accept any gift which the great powers chose to give them, and not ask for more. Palmerston believed that the London Conference should draw the frontiers of Belgium in accordance with the strategic interests of the great powers with a view to preventing a European war; such questions as ethnic or language affinities, or the wishes of the inhabitants of a region, were of no importance. When the French wanted Bouillon to be restored to France, he could not understand it. The fact that Bouillon had always been linked to Sedan for centuries before 1814 – the link still exists today, after a hundred and fifty years of legal separation – meant nothing to Palmerston. 'It really disgusts one', he wrote to Lord Granville, the Ambassador in Paris, 'to see the government of a great country in a great crisis of affairs, when such great interests are at stake, scrambling and intriguing for such pitiful objects as the ruined castle of Bouillon and its little circumjacent territory'.

He strongly maintained this attitude in the House of Commons on 18 February 1831, when Hume and the Radicals denounced the great powers for interfering with the freedom of the Belgian people to choose their own King and to fix their own frontiers. Replying to Hume as 'the humble representative in that House of the five great powers whom the honourable gentleman had been pleased to attack', Palmerston declared that 'the doctrine that every state had a right to fix its own limits was set up by Buonaparte, and upon it there was a slight difference between him and the rest of Europe; he contended that the limits of France ought to be the confines between Europe and Asia. The rest of the world thought it more convenient that those limits should be somewhat nearer Paris. The majority was against him, and he lost Belgium in the quarrel. When he was conquered by the Allied Powers . . . the Powers of Europe disposed of Belgium by uniting it to Holland, not for any purpose of advantage to Holland, not as an act of grace and favour to the Netherlands, but for the purpose of making the appropriation of Belgium contribute to the peace and security of Europe. . . . The other powers of Europe, and England among them . . . had a right to say to Belgium: "You, never having been an independent state, have no right to despoil Holland of its ancient and historical boundaries. Holland is a state whose independence concerns the security of the other countries of Europe; you are but a power of yesterday, and have no right to convert yourselves into aggressors and to claim as yours that which belongs of right to another" '.

The most serious bone of contention was Luxemburg. Luxemburg had never been officially part of Holland, but the King of Holland was also Grand Duke of Luxemburg, and in this capacity was one of the sovereigns in the German Confederation, and a member of the Diet at Frankfort. The people of Luxemburg had joined the Belgian revolt in 1830, and troops of the newly formed Belgian army had occupied Luxemburg; so the Belgians demanded that Luxemburg should be included in the new Belgian state. The French, after toying with the idea of seizing Luxemburg for themselves, decided to back the Belgian demand; but the King of Holland was determined that if he must lose Belgium, he would at least keep Luxemburg. The fact that Luxemburg was in the German Confederation made the conflict much more dangerous, for the Confederation was dominated by Austria, and an attempt to give Luxemburg to Belgium directly involved Austria as well as Prussia.

At first it seemed as if the question of the frontiers would be settled comparatively quickly. The principle of Belgian independence having been agreed on 20 January 1831, frontier line was accepted by all the plenipotentiaries in London after one month's hard bargaining on 20 January 1831, when they signed a protocol which became known as the *Bases de Séparation*. The frontier between Belgium and Holland was fixed along the line which had been the frontier before 1790 between Holland and the Austrian Netherlands. The King of Holland was to retain Luxemburg. Talleyrand, who had tried to obtain either Luxemburg, or Philippeville and Marienburg, for France, was eventually persuaded to accept the protocol in circumstances which Palmerston described in a letter to Granville. 'At last we brought him to terms by the same means by which juries become unanimous – by starving. Between nine and ten at night he agreed to what we proposed, being, I have no doubt, secretly delighted to have got the neutrality of Belgium established'. The Dutch reluctantly accepted the protocol. Their position had been weakened by the outbreak of the revolution in Warsaw, as Palmerston was at pains to point out to them. It took the Russians ten months to suppress the revolt, and they had no desire to be entangled in hostilities in the West while the fighting was continuing in Poland. Prussia was chary of supporting Holland when they could not rely on Russian help. As for the French, Palmerston told Talleyrand that he ought to be very satisfied with the position, as it was a great gain for France to have Belgium neutral instead of a bastion of the Allies against France; and it followed, from the fact of Belgian neutrality, that the fortresses which the Allies had built in Belgium after 1815, as a defence against French invasion, would now be demolished.

But public opinion in France was not satisfied with a neutral Belgium. Louis Philippe himself was far from being a warlike character: it was said of him that while Napoleon had ruled

France with the sword, he ruled it with the umbrella. But the Revolution of 1830 had revived the martial and revolutionary spirit in France. Public opinion was urging the Government to take firmer action in support of their French-speaking brothers in Belgium, and popular singers were proclaiming that only the Rhine could temper the steel of the French weapons. Talleyrand found that the concessions that he made in London were disapproved of in Paris. The Foreign Minister was General Sébastiani, one of Napoleon's old commanders, and he periodically pandered to the patriotic passions of the nation by indulging in bellicose talk which alarmed the Northern Powers. In Belgium, the people looked to the French to liberate them from the Dutch, and there was a strong body of opinion in favour of union with France.

The Belgians had set up a provisional administration, and their elected National Congress was discussing the form of government which should be established in the new independent state. A few of the delegates to the National Congress wished to set up a republic; but this would have been unacceptable to the Northern Powers, and to Palmerston, and was opposed just as strongly by Louis Philippe, who did not wish to see a republic established in France, and refused to encourage republicanism in Belgium. So the majority of the Belgian MPs decided to choose a King. Palmerston ordered Ponsonby to use his influence in Brussels to persuade them to choose the Prince of Orange, the King of Holland's eldest son, who held far more Liberal opinions than his father, and had always been in favour of making concessions to the Belgians. He felt that this would go far to reconcile the Dutch, and the Northern Powers, to Belgian independence, and would be the best means of preventing Belgium from falling under French influence. But this proposal was absolutely unacceptable to the Belgians, and to the French, as it would have meant that Belgium would be independent from Holland only in name. Palmerston therefore agreed, without much argument, to abandon this idea. There were in fact only two candidates who had strong support in the Belgian Congress – the Bonapartist Duke of Leuchtenberg, and Louis Philippe's son, the Duke of Nemours.

None of the great powers, least of all Louis Philippe, was prepared to have a Bonapartist as King of Belgium; but as it became increasingly clear that Nemours was the most popular candidate in Belgium, Louis Philippe became more and more tempted to obtain the throne of Belgium for his younger son, and French public opinion demanded that he should do so. But when Talleyrand sounded Palmerston on this possibility, Palmerston made it clear that Britain would regard this as a union with France, and would never consent to it. On 3 February 1831, the Belgian Congress elected Nemours as King. On the previous day, the British Cabinet decided, in Palmerston's words, 'to require France to refuse acceptance at the risk of war'. Palmerston made this perfectly clear to his old friend Flahaut, who had been sent on a special mission to London. The purpose of Flahaut's mission was to propose to Palmerston that Britain and France should form a secret defensive and offensive alliance; but Palmerston was determined to adhere to his policy of neutralism. He told Flahaut 'that our position at present ought, I conceive, to be that of impartial mediators between France on one hand, and the three other powers on the other; that as long as both parties remain quiet we shall be friends with both; but that whichever side breaks the peace, that side will find us against them'.

Palmerston took the opportunity of warning Flahaut against the consequences of permitting Nemours to accept the crown of Belgium; and he reinforced these warnings by a technique which he was often to adopt in the future. He did not wish to embarrass the French Government by sending them threatening despatches; so he wrote private letters to Lord Granville, and asked the French Embassy to transmit them to Granville in Paris, knowing that the letters would be opened and read in the French Foreign Office. On 2 February, he wrote in a private letter to Granville: 'We are reluctant even to think of war, but if ever we are to make another effort this is a legitimate occasion, and we find that we could not submit to the placing of the Duc de Nemours on the throne of Belgium without danger to the safety and a sacrifice of the honour of the country'.

These warnings had a wonderful effect. At 1 p.m. on 4 February, Sébastiani had adopted a very aggressive tone towards Granville; but at 5.30 on the same afternoon he visited Granville to tell him that although the Belgians had elected Nemours, Louis Philippe had refused the offer. Palmerston was convinced that Sébastiani's change, during these four and a half hours, had been caused by the urgent warnings which he had received from Flahaut that Britain would go to war if Nemours accepted the Belgian crown.

Louis Philippe's refusal to allow Nemours to accept the crown caused great resentment in France, and the people, as Sébastiani angrily told Granville, accused the Government of having been duped by Britain. Palmerston used the medium of the private letter via the French Foreign Office to reply to Sébastiani. 'Pray take care', he wrote to Granville on 15 February, 'in all your conversation with Sébastiani, to make him understand that our desire for peace will never lead us to submit to affront either in language or in act'. And two days later he again wrote to Granville through the French Foreign Office: 'Sébastiani really should be made to understand that he must have the goodness to learn to keep his temper, or, when it fails him, let him go to vent his ill-humour upon some other quarter, and not bestow it upon England. We are not used to being accused of making people dupes'.

Palmerston achieved another success when the Belgians were persuaded to elect Prince Leopold of Saxe-Coburg as their King. Leopold was not officially connected with any of the royal houses of the great powers, but he had formerly been the husband of Princess Charlotte, George IV's daughter, and would therefore have been the husband of the Queen of England if Charlotte had survived. He had lived for some years in England, and had pro-British sympathies; but he was engaged to be married to Louis Philippe's daughter, so Palmerston and Talleyrand agreed, as a satisfactory compromise, to have him as King of the Belgians. The Northern Powers and Holland reluctantly agreed, as there was no chance of having the Prince of Orange or the Archduke Charles of Austria, and Leopold was better than Nemours or a Bonapartist. As it turned out, Leopold, who was able and conscientious, devoted himself to the interests of Belgium and was quite prepared, when necessary, to stand up both to Palmerston and to the French Government; but Palmerston was very satisfied with him. There could be no better solution, from his point of view, than to have a neutral, but Anglophile, Prince ruling Belgium as a constitutional monarch; and his satisfaction was complete when Belgium, almost alone of all the countries of Europe, was free from revolutionary troubles in 1848.

But Leopold's first show of independence caused Palmerston a great deal of trouble, and postponed the final settlement of the Belgian question for nearly eight years. The Dutch had accepted the *Bases de Séparation* of 20 January, but the Belgians rejected it, chiefly because they insisted on having Luxemburg. Palmerston had made up his mind from the beginning that they should not have Luxemburg. On 1 December 1830 he informed the Belgians that Britain entirely agreed with the Northern Powers about 'the unreasonableness and injustice of any attempt on the part of the Belgians to deprive the King of the Netherlands of the Grand Duchy of Luxemburg. . . . His Majesty's Government would consider any attempt of the Belgians upon that Duchy as an act of aggression which the [German] Confederation would be justly entitled to repel'. But five weeks later he thought of another solution. On 7 January he suggested that if the Belgians would accept the Prince of Orange as their King, the King of Holland might be persuaded to give Luxemburg to his eldest son. Not even Luxemburg was a big enough bribe to induce the Belgians to accept the Prince of Orange, and when the proposal was rejected, Palmerston reverted to his opinion that Luxemburg should stay under the King of Holland, and persuaded Talleyrand to accept it in the *Bases de Séparation* of 20 January. After three more months of hard work, Palmerston persuaded the French Government to ratify the *Bases de Séparation* on 17 April. As British interests were not directly concerned in the fate of Luxemburg, Palmerston was prepared to throw it either way as a bargaining counter.

But Leopold, having been chosen as King by the Belgian Congress, decided to act like a King of Belgium before becoming one. He announced that he would not accept the offer of the crown unless his new kingdom included Luxemburg and other areas claimed by his subjects. This completely upset all the plans of the great powers; but Palmerston was eager to have Leopold as King of the Belgians, and, confronted with this unexpected obstacle, gave way. His chief anxiety was that if Leopold did not become King, the Belgians would establish a republic, and with the help of foreign volunteers would launch a revolutionary war against Holland. He wrote to Granville on 17 May that Ponsonby had come specially from Brussels to tell him 'that if a Republick were established, Belgium would become the centre of action of all the revolutionists of Europe, and would be likely to disturb the internal tranquillity of France, Holland, and the Rhenish provinces of Prussia. That the best and almost only chance of averting these mischiefs would be the appointment of a Sovereign, and that consequently it is most important to facilitate that appointment by all possible means'. He therefore persuaded the London Conference to rescind the *Bases de Séparation*, and put forward eighteen articles which gave Luxemburg to Belgium and made other proposals more favourable to Belgium than those contained in the protocol of 20 January.

He then explained to the Dutch Government why it had been necessary to make this volte-face. He deeply regretted, he wrote, that he had been forced to approve proposals which weakened Britain's ancient ally, Holland; but as the Belgians refused to accept the *Bases de Séparation*, the great powers had only three courses open to them. They could wash their hands of the problem, and leave Holland and Belgium to fight it out; in this case, he warned the Dutch, Belgian enthusiasm might prove more than a match for Dutch military superiority, and thousands of French volunteers would rush to the aid of Belgium. The second course was for the great powers to use force to coerce the Belgians; this was 'entirely out of the question. . . . Such a course would have been War, and War undertaken for the professed purpose of preventing War'. The only remaining possibility was to put forward a scheme which was acceptable to both parties; for any other course was more likely to lead to the annexation of Belgium by France than to a settlement on the lines of the *Bases de Séparation*.

The King of Holland drew a different lesson than Palmerston intended from the surrender of the great powers to Belgian intransigence. On 1 August 1831 he repudiated the armistice, and his troops invaded Belgium next day. King Leopold placed himself at the head of his army, but the Belgians fell back rapidly, and were routed at the battle of Louvain. By this time a French army had crossed the frontier. As the French approached, the Dutch retreated as fast as they had advanced, and within ten days were back where they had started.

Palmerston was deeply disturbed by these events. The greatest evil which was likely to result was that French troops would overrun Belgium; and meanwhile everyone, both at home and abroad, was blaming him. He tried to dissuade both the Dutch and the French from marching. On 5 August, he sent a despatch to Holland urging the Dutch to withdraw from Belgium at once, and above all not to carry out their threat to bombard Antwerp. 'His Majesty's Government', he wrote, 'cannot persuade themselves that the Netherlands Government can contemplate such an outrage as the Bombardment of the city of Antwerp; so unprovoked a Devastation of private property, and so unjustifiable a destruction of human life, would incalculably increase the obstacles to Peace, and would draw down upon its Authors the universal indignation of the civilized world'. On the same day he wrote to Granville: 'The great thing to be done now is to prevail on the French Government to prevent the French soldiers from running into Belgium, and to induce them to stick to the alliance and concur in the decision of the Conference'. He suspected that the French had secretly incited the Dutch to invade in order to provide an excuse for the French to march in. But the French declared that they had only entered Belgium for the purpose of expelling the Dutch, and would withdraw as soon as peace had been established; and on the strength of this assurance Palmerston and the Ambassadors of the Northern Powers agreed to endorse the French invasion, declaring that France had acted in the matter as the agent of the London Conference.

The Tory Opposition attacked the Government policy. The Tories, and their press, had tended to support Holland ever since the Whig Government had taken office, and Wellington and Londonderry spoke strongly in the House of Lords about the French invasion of Belgium. In 1815, they declared, the battle of Waterloo had been fought to prevent the French armies from overrunning Belgium; now Palmerston had allowed them to do this without protest, and indeed with his moral support. They accused Palmerston of inaction, and of being caught napping by the Dutch and the French.

Palmerston defended himself by saying that the Dutch had invaded Belgium without giving any prior notice to the London Conference and that their action was quite unexpected; and Grey stated in the House of Lords that the Government immediately took action to put the Navy in a state of readiness as soon as they heard that the Dutch had marched. But Palmerston's explanation involved him in an incident which caused him some embarrassment. The Dutch Army had attacked on 2 August. On 1 August the Dutch Government had addressed a note to Palmerston informing him that their troops would march next day, but it had only been delivered to him by the Dutch Minister in London, Zuylen de Nyevelt, at twelve noon on 3 August. The Tories asked why the Government had not announced the news until 4 August. Palmerston then explained that though he had received the Dutch note at midday on the 3rd, he had not read it until next day. The Tories made great play with this statement, and hinted that Lord Cupid had been neglecting his duties as usual : while the telegraph signals were already busy carrying orders from the French Ministry of Defence to the Army headquarters at Lille, Palmerston was walking about with the unopened despatch in his pocket. Palmerston then explained that as the despatch had been addressed to him as chairman of the Conference, he had thought that he should not open it until he could do so in the presence of the Conference next morning; he would, however, have read it at once if Zuylen de Nyevelt had given him any indication as to what it contained. Sir Charles Wetherell, in the House of Commons, was very scornful of this explanation. He said that any of the Opposition MPs would have opened the Dutch despatch in these circumstances, and that if Palmerston had been sitting with them on the Opposition benches he, too, would have appreciated the urgency of the situation; but he added, amid loud Tory laughter, that he realized that Palmerston was not in the habit of sitting on the Opposition benches.

The Tory criticism mounted when the Dutch withdrew but the French remained. The French action put Palmerston in a very difficult position in the House, and convinced him that British interests were threatened. He strongly pressed the French to withdraw without delay. But Talleyrand used the presence of the French troops in Belgium to bargain about the Belgian fortresses. The Allies had decided to demolish most of the fortresses, for their upkeep was expensive, and less essential if Belgium was to be a neutral state; but they were not prepared to discuss with France which of the fortresses should be demolished, and which retained. When Talleyrand tried to discuss this with them in April 1831, Palmerston argued that France had no right to be consulted. The fortresses had been erected after 1815 at the expense of the Allied powers in order to protect Belgium from French aggression, and the French had no more right to decide which of the fortresses were to be demolished than a housebreaker had to decide which of the locks on a house should be removed.

In August, the French, with their armies deep in Belgium, opened direct negotiations with Leopold about the fortresses. Leopold was not unwilling to discuss the question with France, but Palmerston warned him very firmly that he must not do this: the Allies had borne the bulk of the expense of erecting the fortresses, and the question as to which were demolished, and which were retained, must be decided between them and Belgium without consulting the French. He insisted that the French troops must be withdrawn at once, and without any *quid pro quo*; and he supplemented his courteous official warnings to the French Government with more forthright threats in letters to Granville sent through the French Foreign Office. 'Even if the Cabinet had the slightest wish to give way', he wrote on 13 August, 'which they have not, public opinion in England would prevent them. It is, then, a question of war or peace. On Thursday next Vyvyan renews his motion on Belgium. On that day at latest I shall be compelled to give the House of Commons a categorical answer, Yes or No, to the question, Do the French troops evacuate Belgium or not? Pray enable me to give an answer by that day, and let not the French Government mistake the import of the answer which they may enable me to give. The Yes or No which I shall have to utter will imply events of most extensive consequence to the two countries and to all Europe'. Four days later, he wrote to Granville again: 'One thing is certain – the French must go out of Belgium, or we have a general war, and war in a given number of days'.

Again his firmness succeeded, for the French withdrew their troops before the end of August. In December, Britain, Holland, Belgium and the Northern Powers signed an agreement to demolish all the fortresses except Charleroi and Tournay, and informed Talleyrand. There was great indignation in Paris that the agreement had been signed behind France's back; and in Parliament, Wellington and the Tories criticized Palmerston, and argued that all the fortresses should have been retained. But Palmerston was very satisfied with the position.

Palmerston now set out for the third time to find a solution to the frontier problem. Leopold's determination had led to the abrogation of the *Bases de Séparation* of 20 January; his defeat in battle at Louvain caused the withdrawal of the Eighteen Articles of 26 June. Palmerston showed complete mastery of all the details of the negotiations. His despatches to Brussels, Paris, Berlin and The Hague dealt with the line of the proposed frontier through the various villages, with the navigation rights on the Scheldt and the level of the tolls on various articles of merchandise, with the rights of the Belgian authorities to fell timber in the forests of Limburg, and to assimilate the institutions in occupied Luxemburg with those of Belgium. He urged moderation on both sides. He prevented the Dutch from punishing as deserters those captured Belgian prisoners-of-war who had formerly been soldiers in the Dutch Army stationed in Belgium, and had joined the new Belgian Army after the revolution; and he persuaded the Belgian Government to forbid the inhabitants of Luxemburg to fly the Belgian flag in their villages.

The London Conference was meeting several times a week, and often sat late into the night. The pressure of work began to tell on Palmerston. He found it difficult to get as much exercise as he would have liked, and as he never left London he missed the country air. One evening in late October, after he had had dinner, he suddenly put his despatches in his pocket, mounted his horse, and rode through the night to the 'Star and Garter' at Richmond, where, after working till 1 a.m. on his despatches in his hotel bedroom, he had a good night's sleep, and rode back to the Foreign Office next morning feeling much refreshed by his excursion.

On 15 October 1831 the London Conference agreed on Twenty-Four Articles which they declared were final and irrevocable. They gave Belgium more than the *Bases de Séparation*, including the western part of Luxemburg, but less than the Eighteen Articles. The Belgians were to evacuate Eastern Luxemburg and Limburg; the Dutch were to evacuate Antwerp; nearly half of the national debt of the former kingdom of the Netherlands was to be assumed by the new Belgian state; there was to be free navigation of the Scheldt for all nations, but tolls were to be paid to Holland. On 15 November, Palmerston persuaded all the Ambassadors, including Talleyrand, to sign the final treaty embodying the frontiers agreed in the Twenty-Four Articles. After a year's exhausting work, Palmerston could relax, and spent a whole day in bed.

The Belgians were indignant at the decision about Luxemburg and Limburg, and at the size of the debt which they were to pay. They instructed Van de Weyer to refuse to sign the treaty, but Palmerston badgered him until he disobeyed his instructions. Palmerston described this in a private letter which he wrote on the night of 11 November, when the terms of the treaty were finally settled at three o'clock in the morning. 'I have been at Van de Weyer all yesterday and today and have persuaded him that the only use of a plenipotentiary is to disobey his instructions, and that a clerk or a messenger would do, if it is only necessary strictly to follow them. I have got him, therefore, to throw overboard most of what he was ordered to do.... I am writing in the Conference, Matuszevic copying out a note for our signature, old Talley jazzing and telling stories to Lieven and Esterhazy and Wessenberg ... and the patient Van der Weyer in the adjoining room waiting to know his fate and scratching out and altering just as we tell him to do'. King Leopold persuaded the Belgian Government to accept the treaty by threatening to abdicate if they did not.

But there was still trouble ahead. It took another six months before Palmerston could persuade all the great powers to ratify the treaty which their plenipotentiaries had signed in London. He eventually persuaded all the Northern Powers to accept it by warning them that if they delayed the ratification much longer, the French Government would repudiate the treaty, and the French troops would march again. But the King of Holland refused to agree to the treaty. He was not satisfied with having destroyed the Eighteen Articles by the Ten Days Campaign in August; he would yield nothing beyond what had been agreed in the *Bases de Séparation*.

Palmerston's policy in the Belgian question had been strongly criticized in the House of Commons and in the British press. The Radicals had denounced him for being pro-Dutch, and the Tories for being pro-Belgian and pro-French. But although his line had been neutralist and shifting, his Belgian policy, during his first year in office, had been chiefly directed to thwarting France. He had threatened war to prevent the son of the King of France from being elected King of Belgium, but had proposed that the throne should be given to the son of the King of Holland. He had excluded France from all share in the consultations for the demolition of the fortresses, but had settled the matter with the Northern Powers. He had deplored the Dutch invasion of Belgium in August, but his threats of war had been directed only against the presence of the French troops in the country. Now it was the absolutist King of Holland, not the nationalist and revolutionary elements in France or Belgium, who was the stumbling block to a final settlement of the Belgian question. By the time that Palmerston had to grapple with this problem, a fundamental change had taken place in his foreign policy.

Chapter Eleven

1831: Italy, Poland, Spain

In February 1831, revolution broke out again in Italy. The people rose in revolt against the Papal Government in the Romagna and the absolutist governments of Parma and Modena. All Liberal sentiment throughout Europe was behind the rebels' demand for constitutional freedom, and many already sympathized with their more distant aim of the national liberation of Italy. In Britain there was the additional factor of Protestant sentiment. Anti-Catholic feeling was strong in Britain; it was the age of the Duke of Cumberland and the Orange lodges, of popular editions of Foxe's *Book of Martyrs,* and the lurid publications which revealed the horrors of life in convents and the tortures of the Spanish Inquisition. Few Britons could fail to sympathize with Liberals in the Papal states, where all government administration, and the courts of law, were staffed exclusively by priests, and where there were no representative institutions, or any freedom of the press.

But Metternich reacted as firmly as he had done in 1821. It was a fixed maxim of his policy that though he was powerless to prevent revolution in Paris and Brussels, he would not allow it to take place in Italy; and when he saw that the Papal government was unable to suppress the disorders in the Romagna, he sent an Austrian army to Bologna at the Pope's request, and crushed the revolt. This aroused violent indignation in Paris, where La Fayette declared that 200,000 Frenchmen were ready to march to the assistance of the Italian Liberals. Louis Philippe and Sébastiani did not wish to encourage revolution in Italy, because they were afraid that it might prove to be contagious, and spread to France; but they were unable to resist the pressure of La Fayette, 'the Clubs', and 'the Propaganda', and in January 1832 French troops seized Ancona, the Papal port on the Adriatic, as a counter to the presence of the Austrian army at Bologna.

In Italy, as in Belgium, Palmerston adopted a neutralist position; but in Italy he was much less effective. He was as strongly opposed to popular revolution as he had been in the days when he was Castlereagh's colleague in a Tory Government; but, as a Whig Foreign Secretary and a staunch believer in the principles of 1688, he supported the Liberal demands for constitutional government and freedom of the press, and he knew the strength of anti-Papal feeling in Britain. On the other hand, he did not wish to encourage the growth of French influence in Italy, least of all at the expense of Austria, who had been Britain's most constant ally in the war against Napoleon, and was the only great power whose interests did not conflict with Britain's in any part of the world. On 11 March 1831 he wrote to Granville: 'It will be impossible for England to take part with Austria in a war entered into for the purpose of putting down freedom and maintaining despotism; neither can we side with France in a contest the result of which may be to extend her territories; we shall therefore keep out of the contest as long as we can'.

But Palmerston was determined to play some part in the affairs of Italy. He thought it essential for British prestige that he should have a finger in the pie, and he intervened repeatedly with counsels of moderation to all the parties. He urged the Papal Government to grant concessions to the rebels, to offer them an amnesty, and to reform the administrative system. He urged Metternich not to send troops to Bologna, and after Metternich had done so, he urged him to withdraw them as soon as possible; and he asked him to release the Romagna rebels who had been captured by an Austrian ship on the high seas, in defiance of international law, and transported to prison in Austria. He urged the French Government not to retaliate by seizing Ancona, and afterwards to withdraw their troops; and he asked them to do all they could to prevent further revolutionary outbreaks in Italy. These exhortations were all couched in the most courteous language, as friendly advice, and without any hint of a threat. Palmerston did not often make threats when he was not in a position to carry them out.

But Palmerston's policy was in fact less neutral than it appeared to be, or than he himself perhaps intended. His object was to prevent the outbreak of war between France and Austria, and to lessen the dangers of war by persuading both sides to withdraw their troops as soon as possible. This was much more likely to be achieved if there were no more disorders in Italy. Palmerston therefore supported the *status quo* in all the Italian states, and worked to prevent fresh revolutionary outbreaks from taking place. He wished to see the authority of the Papal Government re-established in the Romagna, though he hoped that they would introduce reforms which would appease the popular indignation and make revolutions less likely in future. The British diplomats at the Italian Courts, who had less sympathy than Palmerston for constitutional government and freedom of the press, were even more eager than he to see the defeat of the Italian revolutionary movement. But when it was suggested that Britain should join with Russia, Prussia, Austria and France in a guarantee of the maintenance of Papal authority in the Romagna, as a condition for the withdrawal of the Austrian troops, Palmerston refused to join in the guarantee, though he assured the Papal Government and the envoys of the great powers that 'His Majesty's Government feel a sincere desire to see the Papal states secured against the evils which the prevalence of a revolutionary spirit may produce'. He knew that public opinion in Britain would never permit him to guarantee the Pope.

In March 1831, Palmerston persuaded France and Austria to join with Britain in an attempt to solve the Italian problem by peaceful means. He sent Sir Brook Taylor to Rome with instructions to work with the French and Austrian Ministers to settle the difficulties between the Pope and his subjects. Taylor did not have diplomatic status, because, as the Protestants in Britain were constantly reminding Palmerston, it would have been a breach of the statutes of Henry VIII and Elizabeth I for a British subject to take any action which could be deemed to be recognizing that the Bishop of Rome was entitled to exercise any authority; but Palmerston told him to work unofficially, and whenever possible to make verbal, rather than written, representations.

On 2 April 1831, Palmerston sent Taylor his first instructions. 'The Basis of the arrangement to be effected', he wrote, was 'that on the one hand the people of Romagna should return to their obedience to the temporal Authority of the Pope, and that on the other, the Pope should grant to his subjects such improvements in their Institutions and in the Form and administration of their government, as may remove the main part of those practical grievances which they have hitherto suffered'. He did not urge the Pope to grant representative institutions to his subjects, for he thought that this would be premature; but he hoped that he would abolish the Inquisition, and appoint laymen instead of priests to judicial tribunals. He repeatedly stressed that Taylor must not appear to be interfering in the internal affairs of the Papal territories, and must make it clear that he was merely offering friendly advice to the Pope. He asked the Pope to show leniency to the rebels of Romagna. 'Although it is impossible to deny that the people of Bologna', he wrote to Rome in February 1832, 'have rendered themselves liable to the Penalties which attach to armed resistance to legal authority, yet, under all the circumstances of the case, it would be far wiser as well as more honourable for the Roman Government to view with an indulgent eye the offences which its subjects have committed'. He reminded the Papal authorities of the atrocities committed by their soldiers at Casena and Forli, and suggested that 'the innocent Blood which was wantonly shed in the streets of those Towns might well be accepted as full atonement for the political offences of the people of Romagna'.

The Papal Government did not follow Palmerston's advice. Palmerston urged Metternich to use his paramount influence with the Pope to induce him to grant concessions to his subjects; but though Metternich promised to do this, there was no improvement in practice. In August 1832 Palmerston ordered the British representative, Seymour, to leave Rome; as British advice was flouted, Seymour should not, by his presence at the Papal Court, appear to approve of the repression in the Romagna. Before the end of the year, the Liberal movement had been defeated throughout Italy. The Austrian troops withdrew from Bologna and the French from Ancona, leaving the absolutist governments in power and the prisons full of Liberals. Palmerston had achieved much less in Italy than in Belgium; but he had played his part in preventing a war between Austria and France, and this had been his only object. 'I should myself say to France', he wrote to Granville on 1 March 1831, 'that it would not be worth her while to risk involving all Europe in war for the sake of protecting the revolutionists in Romagna. If we could by negotiation obtain for them a little share of constitutional liberty, so much the better; but we are all interested in maintaining peace, and no one more than Louis Philippe'.

In one way, the contrast between Belgium and Italy emphasized the power of Britain. In Belgium, where Britain considered that her vital interests were concerned, the French troops had withdrawn from Belgium within a fortnight in the face of Palmerston's threats; in Italy, where Britain had made it clear that she was not directly concerned, and only intended to give friendly advice, both the Austrian and French armies of occupation had remained for many months at Bologna and Ancona, and had refused to be dislodged by the requests or remonstrances of any power.

Palmerston had even less opportunity for effective action in Poland than in Italy, though he had more legal justification for intervening. The Kingdom of Poland, after being partitioned between Russia, Austria and Prussia in 1772, 1793 and 1796, and resurrected into a pseudo-independent Grand Duchy by Napoleon, had had its fate determined by the Congress of Vienna in 1815. The part of Poland held by Russia was to be ruled by the Tsar as Grand Duke of Poland, but was to be administratively independent of Russia and preserve its national privileges. When Tsar Nicholas I succeeded his brother Alexander, the régime in Poland became much less Liberal, and the Poles revolted in November 1830. Palmerston claimed that Britain, as a signatory of the Treaty of Vienna, had a right to be consulted on the fate of Poland. Neither the Tsar nor Metternich was prepared to take this claim seriously.

The news of the revolt at Warsaw caused great enthusiasm in France, where a committee was set up to help the Poles. In

Britain, too, there were a number of individuals who were very sympathetic to Poland, the most prominent of whom was Lord Dudley Stuart, the MP for Arundel. This was one of the first examples in British history of a group of MPs and other eminent personages being formed to canvass support for some foreign country which is the victim of oppression by a powerful state, the members of the group being influenced not by personal advantage, by a consideration of British interests, or even by ideological bonds, but purely by sentiment and sympathy for the victims of injustice. Lord Dudley Stuart and his colleagues put a great deal of pressure on Palmerston in the House of Commons to help the Poles; and the French Government, which was under very much stronger pressure from public opinion in France, also urged him in this direction. But Palmerston was much more cautious, and his feelings with regard to the Poles were mixed. He sympathized with their demands for constitutional freedoms, and he was assured by the British Minister in Berlin that the revolt was supported by the upper classes in Poland, and that one of the nationalist leaders, Count Pac, was very English in his tastes and habits. But the news which he read caused him some anxiety that the Radical extremists might gain control. He was alarmed at the activities of 'the Clubs' in Warsaw, and noted, in a summary of a despatch which he received, that 'The attainment of National Independence seems to be but a secondary object with the Jacobins at Warsaw – their principal aim is to propagate their levelling system'.

He was also anxious to maintain friendly relations between Britain and Russia, and was conscious that any action which he might take over Poland, while it could do little to help the Poles, might easily anger the Russians. He looked on the fighting in Poland chiefly as a useful diversion which would prevent the Russians from being troublesome about Belgium; but even on this point his feelings were mixed, because of his neutral position between the protagonists in Belgium. On 9 March 1831, he told Granville that he feared 'that when the Russians have reconquered Poland, which (were it not for the ill-concealed spirit of aggrandizement of France) I should say I am afraid they will, the tone of Russia about Belgium will be different from what it has been, and that Prussia and Austria will probably be swayed by her influence'.

In the summer of 1831 the Polish poet, Niemcewicz, came to England to enlist sympathy for the Polish struggle. He had an interview with Palmerston, who offered him no encouragement. 'Palmerston found me too hot', he wrote, 'and I found him colder than ice'. Niemcewicz then asked leave to present a letter to William IV from Prince Adam Czartoryski, the former Russian Foreign Minister who had joined the revolutionaries and become President of the Provisional Government of Poland. Palmerston strongly advised that the King should refuse to receive the letter; but Lord Grey was more doubtful, and asked his Cabinet Ministers to give him their opinion in writing. All of them except Lord Holland thought that the King should refuse to recognize the Polish Government, or to receive a deputation from the Poles; but Lord Lansdowne, Lord Carlisle and Charles Grant, as well as Lord Holland, thought that it would be in order for Czartoryski's letter to be received. 'To refuse receiving it', wrote Grant, 'would, I think, be a proceeding of a harsh, and even hostile, character. It would show too much of a Russian inclination'. Graham, Goodrich, Lord John Russell, Stanley and Melbourne all felt that the King should not receive the letter, though none of them opposed it as strongly as Palmerston. 'The King', wrote Palmerston, 'cannot well receive So formal a Letter addressed to him by the President of a Govt. not as yet acknowledged, and Established by Insurrection in the Territories of an allied Sovereign – would not the Emperor of Russia have reason to complain that the English Government, while professing to take no Part in the Contest, was giving Material Encouragement to the Poles.' Czartoryski was disgusted with Palmerston, and the Polish supporters in Britain were even more angry. Henry Hunt, of Peterloo fame, who had been elected an MP in 1830, complained that Palmerston had refused to receive a petition from the Westminster Political Union on behalf of the Poles, and had worded his refusal in a most offensive manner, which Hunt contrasted with the courteous way in which Grey had rejected a similar petition from the Birmingham Political Union.

Palmerston also did his best to discourage the French from helping the Poles. As early as January 1831, Sébastiani expressed his anxiety to Lord Granville that the Russians, after suppressing the revolt, would incorporate Poland into Russia in contravention of the Treaty of Vienna. Palmerston agreed that this would be a violation of the Treaty of Vienna, but said that there was no reason to believe that the Tsar intended to do so. The French Government continued to urge that something should be done to help the Poles. In July, Talleyrand proposed to Palmerston that Britain and France should make a joint offer of mediation between Russia and Poland. Palmerston said that the time was not yet opportune. As the Russian armies slowly fought their way towards Warsaw, and news came in of their atrocities in the Polish villages, the French proposed that Britain and France should protest to Russia; but Granville said that it would be wrong to threaten when they were in no position to carry out their threats. Sébastiani said that as the Poles still held a part of the sea-coast, and the British and French navies were unchallengeable, they could send money and munitions by sea to the Poles; and Louis Philippe told Granville that he regretted that Palmerston had prevented them from taking any action to put an end to the 'barbarous warfare' carried on by the Russians in Poland. The French press and Parliament then demanded that their Government should act alone, without British assistance; but Louis Philippe and Sébastiani had no intention of doing this, and found Palmerston's attitude a good excuse for their inaction.

Warsaw surrendered on 8 September 1831, and the last Polish stronghold fell on 21 October. Many Poles were sent to Siberia, all traces of freedom were stamped out, and Poland was completely incorporated into Russia. Palmerston and the French Government pointed out that this was a breach of the Treaty of Vienna; but the Tsar replied that the Poles had repudiated the treaty by revolting, and deposing the Tsar as Grand Duke, and that now, after the ten months' war, he held Poland by right of conquest. Metternich supported this view. Palmerston sent a number of despatches to the Russian Government during 1832. He disclaimed any wish to interfere in Russian affairs, but advised them, as a friend, to show leniency to the Poles. Nesselrode, the Russian Foreign Minister, assured him that they fully intended to do so; but the reports from the British Consul in Warsaw belied the assurances. When Lord Durham visited Russia, Nesselrode told him that Palmerston's friendly advice was unwelcome. In view of this, Durham did not present Palmerston's latest despatch about Poland. Palmerston told him that he had acted rightly, and made no further representations on behalf of the Poles. Madame de Lieven still had no reason to regret that she had helped Palmerston to become Foreign Secretary, and she made this clear in her letters to her brother and to Nesselrode.

After the collapse of the Polish resistance, Prince Czartoryski escaped to London. On 29 December 1831, he had his first interview with Palmerston. 'Lord Palmerston', he wrote, 'struck me as a man of very cold temperament, who, having made up his mind on the Polish question, only thought of rebutting our arguments on the other side'. Palmerston told him that 'if the fate of Poland depended on his personal wishes and those of Englishmen generally, their struggle for independence would not have had such an unfortunate result'. But Palmerston would offer no hope to Czartoryski. 'It is a principle among states', he said, 'not to interfere between a government and its subjects, except in cases where a state has a direct interest in so interfering, or is distinctly authorized to do so by treaty'. When Czartoryski referred to the Treaty of Vienna, Palmerston said that it was very doubtful if this really justified British interference in Poland. After a while Palmerston looked at his watch, but said that Czartoryski could call again whenever he wished to do so, and that he would be at the Foreign Office every afternoon.

Czartoryski had several other meetings with Palmerston, who always adopted the same attitude. Britain could do nothing to help the Poles except go to war, and this the British people were not prepared to do. In any case, even war would not help the Poles. 'We cannot send an army to Poland', he told Czartoryski, 'and the burning of the Russian fleet would be about as effectual as the burning of Moscow.'

Czartoryski took up his residence in Paris, where he lived

till his death in 1861, and often visited London. He was very
popular in London society, and despite the protests of the
Lievens he was received everywhere; but he got no further
with Palmerston than at his first interview. When Austria occupied the free state of Cracow in 1836 – the last remaining
independent Polish territory – on the grounds that Cracow
had sheltered Polish refugees from Russian-occupied Poland
who conducted revolutionary agitation there, Palmerston protested to Austria against this violation of the Treaty of Vienna;
but there was nothing he could do for Poland. From time to
time, Czartoryski urged him to resist Russia in some part of
the world, arguing cogently that British interests in India or
elsewhere made it essential for Britain to send military aid to
Persia or Circassia; but Palmerston always had an equally
convincing answer to everything Czartoryski said. He would
not go to war with Russia to help Poland, and every step
which Czartoryski urged him to take would mean war. 'Now
the English nation is able to make war', said Palmerston, 'but
it will only do so where its own interests are concerned. We are
a simple and practical nation, a commercial nation; we do not
go in for chivalrous enterprises, or fight for others as the
French do'.

Palmerston showed an equal lack of enthusiasm for the
cause of Liberalism in Spain, where the firing squads were
busy and the prisons full of the opponents of the despotism
of Ferdinand VII. On 9 February 1831, he wrote to the British Minister at Madrid that he wished to see internal tranquillity in Spain and the suppression of revolutionary activity there, and added that he hoped that Ferdinand would
realize that this could best be achieved by granting an amnesty
to his political opponents and allowing the Liberal refugees to
return to Spain. In 1823, Palmerston had defended the Government's inaction when French troops crushed constitutional
government in Spain and reimposed the rule of Ferdinand VII;
in 1831, he used all his influence to prevent a new French government from reversing the process and assisting the Spanish
Liberals. When Ferdinand complained of the revolutionary
propaganda which was emanating from Spanish Liberal refugees in France, Palmerston urged the French Government to

prevent the refugees from plotting against Ferdinand, and suggested that they should forbid the refugees to reside near the Spanish frontier, and should move them to the North of France.

He adopted the same attitude in 1831 when the Spanish Government objected to the propaganda activities of Spanish refugees in Gibraltar. Palmerston believed that a state should permit foreign political refugees, whatever their political opinions might be, to reside peacefully within its territory, provided that they did not engage in any hostile political activity against any foreign government. If people had appreciated his consistency on this point, they would not have been surprised at the attitude which he adopted at the time of the Orsini plot in 1858. He refused to expel all the Spanish Liberal refugees from Gibraltar, but ordered the Governor to suppress all plots of the refugees against Ferdinand's Government, and to expel any of them who had been engaged in any such plots. Palmerston did exactly the same in the case of the Neapolitan Liberal refugees at Malta in 1837. But in 1831, the Spanish Government was not satisfied with Palmerston's attitude, and imposed a trade embargo against Gibraltar until the Liberals were expelled. Palmerston then expelled a number of the refugees who had plotted against Spain. Addington, the British Minister at Madrid, tried to get the Spanish Government to pay for the cost of expelling them; but Palmerston did not agree with this. 'The Refugees were sent away from Gibraltar upon grounds of good faith towards Spain', he wrote to Addington on 9 December 1831, 'and His Majesty's Government do not feel that they can call upon the Government of Spain to pay the expenses incurred in doing that which His Majesty's Government considered to be no more than an act of duty on their own part. You will accordingly desist from your demand, and acquaint M. Salmon that you are instructed to do so'. It was not often that Palmerston missed an opportunity of saving the British tax-payer money; but on this occasion he would do nothing which could throw any doubt on his determination to prevent refugees from using British territory as a base for their activities against the government of their own country.

On 30 November 1831, a small group of Spanish Liberals, who had been living illegally at Gibraltar, set out by sea from Gibraltar, together with an English Radical sympathizer, intending to sail a few miles along the coast and to enter Spain secretly in order to join revolutionary guerrillas. The ship which they had fitted out was in need of repairs, so they engaged an English carpenter in Gibraltar to do the work; but as he took longer than was expected, and they were pressed for time, they put to sea with him still on board, telling him to complete the work during the voyage. They were intercepted by a Spanish warship, which drove them on to the coast of Spain at a spot where they had not intended to land. After barricading themselves in a farmhouse, they surrendered to the troops who surrounded them, and were taken to Malaga, where five days later all of them, including the two British subjects, were shot without trial. Palmerston sent a protest to the Spanish Government against their rigour in executing the two British subjects without trial, especially the carpenter, who had known nothing of the revolutionary intentions of the others; but he did not make any demand for compensation, or take any further action, for he admitted that the Spanish Government were justified, in international law, in enforcing the law of Spain against revolutionary sympathizers. On 27 February 1832, he wrote to Addington that if the group 'were proceeding at the time with an intention of making an attack upon the Spanish Government, the fact that they were driven on shore at a different point of the coast from that at which they meant to land, cannot alter the character in which they presented themselves; and being taken in arms in the course of effecting an hostile enterprise against the Spanish Government, they were liable to be dealt with as such circumstances might justify, and it would be difficult to find any ground upon which a distinction in this respect between Mr. Boyd and his Spanish companions could properly be founded'. He adopted the same attitude during the upheavals of 1848. British Radicals who took part in revolutions abroad would get no help from Palmerston.

Chapter Twelve

The Reform Bill:
The New Foreign Policy

The Whigs came to power in November 1830 pledged to introduce a reform of the Parliamentary franchise; but the struggle for the Reform Bill was a long one, and the Government were reluctant to force the issue. There was great unrest throughout Britain. The Government suppressed the agricultural riots in Sussex and Hampshire with considerable severity, and prosecuted Cobbett for inciting them; but Cobbett maintained that several members of the Whig Government had said as much as he had done when they were in Opposition. This at least was an accusation which he could not level at Palmerston; but he subpoenaed Palmerston, along with the other Cabinet ministers, as witnesses for the defence, and Palmerston had to sit for four and a half hours in Court, listening to Cobbett's speech in his own defence. He was released when the Judge refused to allow Cobbett to call the ministers to give evidence as to why they had advised the King to pardon one of the rioters who was alleged to have been a police spy. Cobbett was released after the jury had disagreed.

There was also trouble in Ireland, where O'Connell and his followers, having obtained Catholic Emancipation, were agitating for the repeal of the Union, or, as it would later be called, for Home Rule. Palmerston opposed this demand when he spoke for the Government in the House of Commons in the debate on 8 February 1831. He stated that in Ireland 'the wretched creatures who submitted to the guidance of a demagogue' were in favour of the repeal of the Union, but not 'the intelligence, the property, and respectability of the country', for 'he could safely state to the House that all persons of property, and all those who had any stake, or anything to lose, in the country, were opposed to the repeal of the Union'.

On the question of the Reform Bill, there were strong disagreements inside the Government itself. Palmerston was far from enthusiastic about the bill, and in this he was encouraged by Lady Cowper, who, according to Greville, was 'a furious anti-reformer'. The ministers were divided into what would now be called the Right, Left and Centre. The Right wing, consisting of Palmerston, Melbourne and the Duke of Richmond, wished to introduce the very minimum of change, and to disfranchise only a few of the worst of the nomination and rotten boroughs. The Left wing, under Althorp, Lord John Russell and John Lambton – who was now Lord Durham – were in favour of sweeping them all away; and the Centre, led by Grey and Brougham, adopted a half-way position. Thanks chiefly to the determination and skilful manoeuvring of Durham, the Left wing got their way in the Cabinet, and on 1 March 1831 Lord John Russell introduced a Reform Bill, which provided for the disfranchisement of 168 nomination and rotten boroughs. There followed three weeks of bitter debates in the House of Commons, which ended with the second reading being carried by 302 votes against 301 – a majority of 1.

On 3 March, Palmerston made a speech in favour of the bill, in which he explained his attitude to reform. He was not a very enthusiastic supporter. 'He must be a bold, or a very unshrinking man', he said, 'who did not contemplate the measure with the deepest solicitude and the greatest anxiety; who could calmly and carelessly look at a measure calculated to effect a great change in the character and constitution of the House of Commons – a House of Commons which, in spite of its defects, had for many years contributed so effectually to promote the happiness of the people'. He said that the English people were not fond of political change. 'They formed a striking contrast to their neighbours on the Continent . . . who boasted of the newness of their institutions, while the English were proud of the antiquity of theirs'. But he explained that unfortunately there were some anomalies in the existing system. If the worst of these had been reformed in time, the present extensive measure might have been avoided; but now it was necessary. The great merit of the bill was that it admitted the middle classes to a share in political power; for despite all the taunts with which the middle class was assailed, 'there never was a time when it contained so many men of intelligence, when its opinions were more entitled to confidence and respect, or its members more distinguished by morality and good conduct, by obedience to the laws, by the love of order, by attachment to the throne and the Constitution'. He was confident that if the bill were passed, 'property, rank and respectability would still maintain the same influence in representation – an influence of which he should be the last man to deprive it'; but it was also necessary to have good conduct, morality and intelligence, as 'it was the provision of those qualities, united with rank and station, which commanded admiration and respect'.

In April the Government was defeated on the Committee stage of the bill, and Grey persuaded the King to dissolve Parliament amid scenes of violent uproar in both Houses. When a royal salute was fired in honour of the King's arrival at the House of Lords for his dissolution speech, Sir Henry Hardinge declared, in the Commons, that the next time the guns sounded they would be loaded and would shoot off the ministers' heads. At the general election of May 1831, fear of popular violence was stronger than fear of the landlords, and even in the rotten boroughs Whig candidates were elected. The Government was returned with a greatly increased majority, but Palmerston lost his seat at Cambridge University. Goulburn and Peel stood against him as the Tory candidates, and were elected with 805 and 804 votes. Palmerston's colleague, Cavendish, who had been elected with him in 1830, received 630 votes, and Palmerston was bottom of the poll with 610. A seat was found for him at Bletchingley in Surrey, where he was returned at the by-election. Bletchingley, like Horsham and Newport, was a borough where voting was by burgage tenure. It was scheduled for disfranchisement in the Whig Government's Reform Bill; but in the meantime it could provide the Foreign Secretary with a Parliamentary seat.

The new House of Commons passed the Reform Bill by a

large majority, but in October the bill was thrown out by the House of Lords. This caused an outburst of popular indignation. Burdett and Attwood formed political organizations to put extra-Parliamentary pressure on the Lords, and riots broke out all over the country. The Government were almost as alarmed as the Tories at these developments, and talk of revolution was in the air. If the Tory majority in the House of Lords refused to pass the bill, the measure could not become law unless the King could be persuaded to create new peers to outvote them. The majority of the Cabinet, spurred on by Durham, Althorp and Hobhouse, were strongly in favour of creating new peers; but Palmerston, Melbourne and the Duke of Richmond were equally strongly against it, and so was Lord John Russell, in spite of his enthusiasm for reform. William IV was very reluctant to create the peers, and in view of the King's opposition, Grey and Brougham began to waver; and while the Radicals demanded 'the Bill, the whole Bill, and nothing but the Bill', the Government became increasingly convinced of the necessity of reaching a compromise with the Tories in the House of Lords.

Palmerston was one of the members of the Cabinet who was most strongly in favour of compromise, and carried on a series of private negotiations with some of the Tories. In this he had the strong support of the King, and of the King's private secretary, General Taylor. But it was not easy to arrange a compromise when die-hard Tories were insisting that there should be no concessions, and Radicals on the Government benches were demanding that the bill should be forced through the Lords without further delay. Palmerston's Tory past, and his inherent Toryism, made him eager for compromise, but it also made him an unsuitable person to achieve it. Old Whigs like Brougham, Durham and Hobhouse were suspicious of his compromising attitude, and the Tories distrusted him as a turncoat, and assumed that he was acting from the worst motives. When, in December 1831, Taylor arranged a meeting between Palmerston and the Tory Lord Chandos at the King's request, Mrs. Arbuthnot deduced that the Whigs were on the way out, and that it was a case of the rats leaving the sinking ship. The King, however, was grateful to Palmerston, and in June 1832 insisted on giving him the Order of the Bath.

In March 1832 a modified Reform Bill passed the House of Commons, but was thrown out by the House of Lords on 6 May. Two days later, with the country on the verge of revolution, the Cabinet met to consider what to do. The only solution now was to ask the King to create new peers; but the Whig ministers shrank from such a step, which would anger the King and outrage the constitutional conventions. As soon as the Cabinet met, Palmerston proposed that the King should be asked to give an undertaking that he would create new peers if the House of Lords rejected the Reform Bill; and all the ministers, except the Duke of Richmond, agreed to his proposal. The King refused, the Government resigned, Wellington became Prime Minister, and Palmerston left the Foreign Office for nine days. Wellington did not survive any longer. While serious violence broke out in many towns, Francis Place, the Radical tailor of Charing Cross, conceived the idea of sticking up posters overnight in London containing seven effective words: 'To stop the Duke, go for gold'. A run on the bank followed, and the Bank of England paid out £1,800,000 in three days. Faced with a grave financial crisis and the possibility of revolution, Wellington resigned and Grey came back. The King agreed to Grey's demand that he should promise to create new peers; and the threat was sufficient, for the Lords gave way and passed the bill.

Palmerston was one of the most Tory-minded of the Whig ministers. He had never been enthusiastic for reform and had tried harder than anyone to get the bill withdrawn and compromise proposals accepted. But at the crucial moment, it was he who first proposed to take the extreme measure. When the pressure of public opinion became irresistible, Palmerston always gave way to it, and did so without reservations. He had followed the advice which he always gave to foreign governments, and yielded to popular clamour when there was no other way of preventing revolution. As long as it was possible to suppress disorder, Palmerston was the most determined upholder of the rule of law; when it became impossible, he surrendered to the course of events.

As soon as the Reform Bill was passed, the Government dissolved Parliament and fought an election on the new franchise. As Bletchingley had been disfranchised, Palmerston had to find a new constituency, and was adopted as a candidate for Penryn and Falmouth; but he later withdrew, and stood for South Hampshire. The constituency consisted of the polling districts of Southampton and Portsmouth – outside the borough constituencies – and of Fareham, Romsey, and Lymington, and included Palmerston's estates at Broadlands. He had in his favour his local influence, and the political popularity of the Whigs. The constituency returned two MPs, but the Tories nominated only one candidate against Palmerston and his colleague, Sir George Staunton.

It was the first time in his life that Palmerston had fought a county constituency, having hitherto contested only burgage boroughs and the University seat. After holding a number of meetings and canvassing throughout the constituency, he was nominated with the other candidates at Southampton on 15 December 1832, when in accordance with the usual practice he took his place on the hustings and made the main speech of his election campaign. His nomination was seconded by William Nightingale of Embley Park, the father of Florence Nightingale, who was a social acquaintance, as well as a political supporter, of Palmerston. The meeting was very stormy, and Palmerston was shouted down by hecklers who accused him of making war against Holland and of having used 'undue influence' during the election. This meant that his agents were alleged to have used bribery and intimidation, and was a charge levelled against nearly every candidate at nearly every election. The heckling was so loud that Palmerston was inaudible, though he continued with his speech.

After all the candidates had spoken, the election was held by show of hands. Palmerston and Sir George Staunton were declared elected but the Tories demanded a poll, as the party which was defeated at the hustings always did. The Sheriff ordered the poll to be held on the next two days, and the result was that Palmerston received 1,625 votes and Staunton 1,539, while Fleming, the defeated Tory candidate, received 1,276 votes. After the result was declared, Palmerston appeared on the balcony of the George Inn in Southampton, and was loudly cheered by the Whigs. In the country, the Whigs were returned to power with a large majority.

The passing of the Reform Bill had an influence on British foreign policy. It aroused deep misgivings in the courts of the Northern Powers, who were convinced that the English Revolution had begun; and the hostility of the reactionary governments and the enthusiasm of the Liberals drove the British Government to re-align its foreign policy on more Liberal ideological lines. It also affected Palmerston's personal position in British politics. The fight for the bill had embittered political life, and had hardened the divisions between the parties. This had the effect of eliminating the Canningites as a separate body, of merging them completely with the Whigs, and removing any possibility of Palmerston rejoining the Tories. The Tories, in fact, hated Palmerston more than any other member of the Government, and attacked him incessantly. Talleyrand thought that one of the reasons why they denounced his foreign policy so violently was because they hated him personally, and regarded him as a traitor to their cause.

The Tory MP and author, Winthrop Mackworth Praed, whose satirical verse was an entertaining feature of political controversy, enjoyed himself at Palmerston's expense in October 1832:

> *There was a time when I could sit*
> *By Londonderry's* side,*
> *And laugh with Peel at Canning's wit,*
> *And hint to Hume he lied;*
> *Henceforth I run a different race,*
> *Another soil I plough,*
> *And though I still have pay and place*
> *I'm not a Tory now.*
>
> *I've put away my ancient awe*
> *For mitre and for crown;*
> *I've lost my fancy for the law*
> *Which keeps sedition down;*

*This is a reference to Castlereagh, who inherited the title of Marquis of Londonderry a few months before his death.

> *I think that patriots have a right*
> *To make a little row;*
> *A town on fire's a pretty sight:*
> *I'm not a Tory now...*
>
> *I learn to be extremely shy*
> *With all my early cons;*
> *I'm very cold at Trinity,*
> *And colder at St. John's;*
> *But then, my Falmouth friends adore*
> *My smile, and tone, and bow;*
> *Don't tell them what I was before —*
> *I'm not a Tory now! ...*
>
> *If Harvey gets Brougham's seals and seat,*
> *My friend will Harvey be;*
> *If Cobbett dines in Downing Street,*
> *He'll have my three times three;*
> *If Hunt in Windsor Castle rules,*
> *I'll take a house at Slough;*
> *Tories were always knaves and fools.*
> *I'm not a Tory now!*

In the House of Commons, the Tories never missed a chance to jeer at Palmerston. They had a good opportunity in a debate on Ireland in July 1834, when a Government MP enthusiastically declared that the Government contained no Radicals, but consisted entirely of 'pure old Whigs'. Peel commented, in an audible aside, that there were at least two Tories in the Government, and pointed at Palmerston and Charles Grant. Palmerston rose and defended his own political consistency, and attacked Peel's shifts of policy; but at this Sir Henry Hardinge commented that as Palmerston had been a member of every Tory Government for twenty years, he could hardly be described as a 'pure old Whig', but might be called 'a juvenile Whig – a pure juvenile Whig'.

But Palmerston was also very unpopular with the Radicals and many other MPs of his own party, who not only disapproved of his attempts to compromise with the Tories on the Reform Bill, but were also very critical of his foreign policy.

His reputation at this time was almost the reverse of what it later became. Many people regarded him as a weak and ineffectual Foreign Secretary. The Tories accused him of yielding to France, and the Radicals of yielding to Russia. They did not know how skilfully he handled an international conference, and how firm he could be in diplomatic negotiations. They judged him only by his performance in the House of Commons. His chief object here was to avoid giving offence to foreign powers and exacerbating delicate international situations, or prejudicing the success of his secret diplomacy. He no longer indulged in the stirring speeches which he had made in Opposition, with his ringing denunciations of Miguel and tyranny in Europe; he now made halting apologies for foreign despots, and evasive excuses for his own inaction. He quickly lost his short-lived reputation as a Parliamentary orator, and MPs now had an even lower opinion of his Parliamentary abilities than they had had when he was Secretary at War. Few of them would have given him the credit, which he had when he was at the War Office, for uninspiring efficiency in speaking to his official brief.

The lobby correspondent, James Grant, who in later years became a great admirer of Palmerston, had a low opinion of him at this time.

The situation he fills in the Cabinet [wrote Grant in 1836] gives him a certain degree of prominence in the eyes of the country, which he certainly does not possess in Parliament. His talents are by no means of a high order. Assuredly they would never by their own native energy have raised him to the distinguished position in the .councils of his Sovereign in which a variety of accidental circumstances have placed him. He is an indifferent speaker. I have sometimes seen him acquit himself, when addressing the House, in a very creditable manner; but he often stutters and stammers to a very unpleasant extent, and makes altogether an indifferent exhibition. His voice is clear and strong, but has a degree of harshness about it which makes it grate on the ear. He is very indolent. He is also very irregular in his attendance on his Parliamentary duties.

It was at this time that he definitely established the reputation, which he never lost, of being a bad speaker. He would become hopelessly lost in his own sentences, break off, hesitate, say 'hum' and 'er', and flourish his handkerchief in the air

while he tried to remember what to say. His critics complained
that when he did utter an impressive sentence, he ruined it by
an anti-climax in the peroration, which seemed a more serious
defect to nineteenth-century listeners than it would today. 'He
would say, for instance', wrote Sir William Fraser, ' "The language of the honourable gentleman is unusual, unparliamen-
tary, violent, discreditable, and ahem!" – a pause – "to be
deprecated".' One of the reasons why everyone was so impressed by Palmerston's Don Pacifico speech in 1850 was that
it was so unexpected.

The MPs would have forgiven him for his lack of eloquence
if they had not been so exasperated by his manner in the
House. His fastidious dress and supercilious attitude gave
them the impression that he was an arrogant and ineffectual
dandy. Disraeli, writing in *The Times* under the name of Run-
nymede, called him 'the Lord Fanny of diplomacy', and
mocked him for 'cajoling France with an airy compliment
and menacing Russia with a perfumed cane'. *The Times* was
even harsher in its editorials. 'What an offensive union is that
of a dull understanding and an unfeeling heart!', they wrote
of him. 'Add to this the self-satisfied airs of a flippant dandy,
and you have the most nauseous specimen of humanity – a
sort of compound which justified Swift in the disgusting exhibition of the Yahoos'. MPs felt that he despised them. He
tried, as far as possible, to prevent the House from debating
foreign policy, and if he had to take part in a debate, he said
as little as he could. In August 1831, when the Dutch and
French armies were marching into Belgium, he told MPs that
as long as they had confidence in the Government they should
not expect him to defend its foreign policy.

He found it easier to persuade the members to accept this
argument during his first two years at the Foreign Office than
he would have done in normal times, because the controversy
about the Reform Bill was taking everyone's mind off other
topics. Princess Lieven wrote that whenever questions of foreign policy were discussed in the House of Commons, all the
members rose and trooped out, except the front bench, and a
handful of Tories. But a few people in Parliament were very
interested in foreign affairs, and nearly all of them had a low

opinion of Palmerston. His chief Tory critics were Wellington and Londonderry in the House of Lords. Wellington's position gave the greatest weight to his views. The Marquis of Londonderry, who was Castlereagh's brother, had been a General in Spain and had represented Britain as a diplomat at international conferences when Castlereagh was Foreign Secretary. He was bitterly hated by all Whigs and Radicals. When his employees in his Durham mines went on strike, he forced them back to work by calling out the troops as Lord Lieutenant, by turning them out of their houses, which he owned, and by threatening to do the same to any shopkeeper who supplied the strikers with food; and by such actions he had come to be regarded as the archetype of reactionary Tory. In the House of Commons, Peel echoed the criticisms of Wellington and Londonderry about Palmerston's pro-French foreign policy; but his more vociferous critics in the Lower House were the Radicals in his own party – Burdett, Hume, Hunt, Colonel de Lacy Evans, Cutlar Fergusson, Attwood, and Daniel O'Connell, whose sympathies with oppressed nations were not limited to his own people of Ireland.

On 28 June 1832, the Radicals attacked Russian policy in Poland, describing the horrors on the long march on foot of the deportees from Poland to Siberia, and the suicide of women on the road. O'Connell denounced the Tsar as 'this Attila, this scourge of God', who had separated wives from their husbands, and sent a hundred thousand children to the interior of Russia, to forget their language, their kindred, and their country. Evans declared that he would not shrink from going to war for Poland if it were necessary. Palmerston said very little, beyond expressing the mild hope that the Tsar would be lenient. When the Tory MP, Sir Robert Inglis, said that he was shocked that ministers permitted such language to be used of a foreign sovereign, Palmerston said that he, too, deeply regretted it, but did not feel justified in interrupting the speakers. This was not good enough for the Radicals, who were increasingly convinced that Palmerston was a Russian tool. They were particularly indignant that Palmerston had agreed that Britain should undertake to pay the interest due from Holland to Russia on the loan that Russia had made to

Holland during the Napoleonic Wars. Britain had assumed this liability as part of the Belgian settlement, when the former Kingdom of the Netherlands was divided. Palmerston defended his action by referring in the warmest terms to the debt which Europe owed to Russia for her part in overthrowing Napoleon.

On the same day that the House of Commons was debating Poland, the German Diet discussed a recent incident at Hambach when Radical students, at a rally, had drunk the health of La Fayette, and made revolutionary speeches. The Diet passed six resolutions which ordered the governments of the German states to ban revolutionary meetings and badges, to restrict the freedom of the press, and to tighten the discipline in the Universities. They also proclaimed the right of the Diet to enforce obedience to these orders if the sovereigns of the German states refused to obey. William IV, as King of Hanover, was a member of the Diet, and his representative cast his vote in favour of the Six Resolutions. The action of the Diet aroused great resentment among the Liberals everywhere. The French Government proposed to Palmerston that Britain and France should make a joint protest against the Six Resolutions, arguing that such an intervention would be justified because the German Confederation had been established by the Treaty of Vienna, to which both Britain and France were signatories. Palmerston rejected the proposal. Sébastiani then sent a formal protest to the Diet on behalf of France alone, though Palmerston tried to prevent him from doing so. Palmerston's silence about the Six Resolutions, combined with the fact that Hanover had voted in favour of them, convinced everyone in Europe that Britain, unlike France, approved of the suppression of political freedom in Germany.

On 2 August 1832, Henry Bulwer moved a resolution in the House of Commons deploring the Six Resolutions and the action of Hanover in supporting them. There was the usual lack of interest in a debate on foreign affairs, and only eleven MPs were present; but Palmerston, in his speech, took the first step on the road which led him to become the accepted champion of Liberalism in Europe, the darling of the Radicals, and the bugbear of the absolutist sovereigns. He defended the

vote of the Hanoverian delegate, and argued that the Six Resolutions did not threaten constitutional freedom in Germany;
but he declared that if Bulwer thought that German freedom
was threatened, he was justified, as a British MP, in being
alarmed at the situation. 'For I am prepared to admit that the
independence of constitutional states, whether they are powerful like France or the United States, or of less relative political
importance such as the minor states of Germany, never can be
a matter of indifference to the British Parliament, or, I should
hope, to the British public. Constitutional states I consider to
be the natural allies of this country; and whoever may be in
office conducting the affairs of Great Britain, I am persuaded
that no English ministry will perform its duty if it be inatten-
tive to the interests of such states'. He stated that the Government had never held the view that Britain should adopt a
policy of non-interference in regard to such matters in foreign
countries, though this interference would be by words, not by
arms. When he said that an MP had talked about 'non-interference', the MP corrected him, and said 'Non-intervention'.
'I will not talk of non-intervention', said Palmerston, 'for it is
not an English word'.

This linguistic patriotism was not enough to appease the
Radicals, especially when, five days later, in another debate on
Poland, Palmerston defended Russia from Evans's attack, and
claimed that in the last three wars in which Russia had engaged, it was not Russia, but the Persians, the Turks and the
Poles, who had been the aggressors. But if he had not gone far
enough for the Radicals, he had gone much too far for the
Northern Courts. The Austrian chargé d'affaires, Baron Neumann, who had a somewhat stormy interview with Palmerston
after his speech, was incensed that Palmerston had not prevented the debate from being held, as he could have done, by
asking for a count of the MPs present. Madame de Lieven was
also becoming very dissatisfied with Palmerston. She told her
brother that because the Radicals had called Palmerston a
Russian tool, he was now afraid to say anything in support of
Russia. Palmerston tried to repair relations with the Russian
Government by assuring Nesselrode that he had stated that
constitutional states were the natural allies of Britain only in

order that these states would cease to look to France for support.

The debate of 2 August had persuaded Palmerston that he must do something, however ineffectual, about Germany, and on 7 September he sent a despatch to the President of the Diet protesting against the Six Resolutions. He drafted it after lengthy consultations with Grey, and despite the disapproval of the King. In the despatch, he justified his intervention on the grounds that Britain was a party to the Treaty of Vienna – that charter of reactionary Europe – and stressed that his object was to uphold the existing system by dissuading the Diet from taking a course which would provoke revolution. He stated that many people in Germany felt that the Six Resolutions threatened their freedom, and that this feeling was not 'confined to noisy agitators, declaiming at public meetings or acting by means of a licentious press', but was causing great anxiety 'in the minds of all classes, including the most wealthy and the most intelligent. He argued that concessions and constitutional government were a more effective barrier than repression against the influx of revolutionary doctrines from France into the Rhineland and other parts of Germany. 'When the bulk of a people are contented, partial insurrections, of which all countries furnish occasional examples, are easily put down; but instances are not wanting to show that where discontent is general and deeply seated, a casual conflict, or the rash act of a few desperate individuals, may involve a whole nation in a bloody civil war'. If the Diet were to try to enforce its decrees by the use of Austrian and Prussian troops, 'it might produce a general convulsion in Europe, from which the soundest institutions and the most firmly established Thrones might not escape unharmed. His Majesty's Government, therefore, actuated by Conservative principles in the strictest sense of the expression', and by 'sincerest friendship', asked the Diet not to enforce the Six Resolutions.

The note of 7 September enraged the absolutist Courts. The Prussian Chancellor, Ancillon, refused to receive it, but was eventually persuaded to do so by the British Minister in Berlin. Munch, the Austrian President of the Diet, was insulting when the British Minister at Frankfort delivered it to him, and spoke about oppression in Ireland. William IV was angry, and told Palmerston that if freedom of the press were permitted in Germany, the whole country would be inundated with scurrilous papers like *The Times*. Metternich wrote a strong reply, denying Britain's right to intervene in an internal German matter, and threatened to publish his note if Palmerston published his despatch of 7 September. Palmerston had no intention of engaging in a public controversy with foreign governments; he did not even send the despatch of 7 September to the smaller German Courts, which would really have angered Metternich. The Germans, however, could read his speech of 2 August in Hansard; and 200,000 copies of a German translation of the speech were printed and circulated in Germany.

It was in this new situation, with the estrangement between Britain and the Northern Powers which followed the despatch of 7 September, that Palmerston had to deal with the King of Holland's refusal to accept the Belgian Treaty. The Dutch were now the only obstacle to the final settlement of the Belgian question, and Palmerston was determined to make them give way. The French wished to compel them to submit by the use of force. The Northern Powers, though they had at last accepted the treaty, and urged the Dutch to do the same, were opposed to the use of force against Holland, and would only agree to 'pecuniary measures' – or, as we would say today, to economic sanctions. Palmerston adopted a midway position. He believed that economic sanctions would be slower than the use of force, and would, on the other hand, inflict greater suffering on the innocent Dutch people; and he considered, at first, the possibility of joint Anglo-French military and naval operations against Holland. But he did not wish to see a French army march into Holland, and knew that many other people in England would like it even less than he. The King was violently against it. William IV, who was a true Tory, and had been a naval officer in two wars against France, detested the French. He was very disturbed by Palmerston's policy of alliance with France, and absolutely refused to agree to an invasion of Holland by an Anglo-French force. 'The King cannot for a moment admit the possibility', he wrote to Palmerston on 18 September 1832, 'of Great Britain being forced into a war against Austria, Prussia and Russia in conjunction with revolutionary France. . . . His Majesty is also of opinion the British nation is decidedly against war with Holland'. Palmerston therefore proposed that force should be used by the French alone against the Dutch garrison in Antwerp, but that only economic sanctions should be applied against Holland itself.

Palmerston allied himself again with the French, whom he had threatened with war a year before, and called back the French armies into Belgium from which he had then compelled them to withdraw. With Palmerston's approval, a French army marched to Antwerp and besieged the Dutch garrison there; and the British and French navies enforced a joint blockade of the coast of Holland, especially of the Scheldt and the port of Rotterdam. Palmerston did not find it easy to persuade the House of Commons to accept this policy, as the Tories disapproved of the coercion of our ancient Dutch ally in collaboration with the hated French, and claimed that these hostile acts against Dutch shipping were illegal in time of peace; but Palmerston was ready with his quotations from Vattel on international law. There was also considerable opposition to Palmerston among naval officers, who carried out their orders to help the French blockade Holland with the greatest reluctance. This did not greatly worry Palmerston, who cheerfully pointed out to Lord Howard de Walden that 'Tories abound in the naval and military service'.

The Dutch garrison in Antwerp surrendered after a month's siege. In Holland, public opinion rallied behind the King and a policy of resistance; but before long, the business interests began to suffer from the blockade, and to demand a change in Dutch policy. In May 1833, the King of Holland agreed to withdraw from all the territories which had been assigned to Belgium by the treaty of November 1831, and to refrain from any hostile acts against Belgium; but he refused to sign the treaty. Britain and France then raised the blockade, but would not compel the Belgians to withdraw from the territories which they occupied until Holland had signed the treaty. So the Belgian question was thus settled on a *de facto* basis, though not a *de jure* one, and on a basis which gave the Belgians nearly all they had claimed. They remained in possession of Luxemburg and Limburg, and assimilated the administration with that of the rest of Belgium. But when the Belgian problem was finally settled in 1839, Palmerston was on the point of making another complete volte-face in his foreign policy, and the Belgians were the sufferers.

Palmerston's attitude about Germany in August and September 1832 had strained relations with Austria; but relations with Russia were still reasonably satisfactory. Palmerston had refused, despite great pressure, to condemn Russian action in Poland, or to repudiate Britain's liability with regard to the Russian-Dutch loan; and the Russians had at least acquiesced in the British and French attempts to coerce the King of Holland. In July 1832, Lord Durham was sent on a special mission to Russia. He was an important member of the Cabinet, and the Prime Minister's son-in-law; but at first sight, Radical Jack hardly seemed to be an ideal envoy to the Tsar. Princess Lieven had reported that he was more pro-Polish than anyone else in England. His consistent Radicalism, both in opposition and in office, had made him the hero of the Radicals, who felt that he would be a much better Foreign Secretary than Palmerston. Unfortunately, as is often the case with men of his type, his ability, sincerity and charm were marred by great personal vanity and susceptibility to flattery. Palmerston was suspicious of Durham, though he treated him with the respect and consideration which he showed only to Lamb and a few of his most eminent Ambassadors. Durham's mission to Russia was a political godsend to Palmerston. At his first meeting with the Tsar on the imperial yacht at Reval, Nicholas was charming, and Durham was completely won over. Madame de Lieven declared that 'we drowned him in courtesies'. When Durham returned to England, he was prepared to defend everything Russian, especially Russian policy in Poland, where the Tsar was posing as the champion of the peasant against the Polish aristocracy who had led the national revolt. The Radicals lost their faith in Durham, and Palmerston had nothing more to fear from this rival.

Anglo-Russian friendship was wrecked by an Albanian adventurer. Mehemet Ali began life selling tobacco in a village in Thrace, then entered the Turkish Army, and succeeded by his military prowess and his ruthless massacres of his enemies in making himself ruler of Egypt as Pasha, or Viceroy, for the Sultan of Turkey. He quarrelled with the Arabian chiefs and seized Mecca and most of Arabia. Soon afterwards, his son-in-law penetrated far to the south into the Sudan, where he was captured by a local chief and burnt alive, whereupon Mehemet Ali exterminated the population of the region, and extended his dominions to the boundaries of Abyssinia. When the Greek revolt broke out, the Sultan called in Mehemet Ali to assist him, and Mehemet Ali sent his son Ibrahim, who was the General of his forces, to massacre as many Greeks as possible. As a reward, the Sultan gave Mehemet Ali the government of Crete, but as he failed to give him certain other benefits which Mehemet Ali said he had been promised, Mehemet Ali sent Ibrahim and his army to seize Syria, and threatened to march on Constantinople.

Sultan Mahmud appealed to the great powers to protect him from his rebellious Pasha. The Tsar, who had so recently been at war with Turkey, offered in the name of monarchical solidarity to protect the Sultan against the rebel, and assembled an army in the port of Odessa ready to occupy Constantinople if Ibrahim advanced. Mahmud preferred to be saved by someone else, and asked the British Government to send the Navy to the Dardanelles and to Alexandria to threaten Mehemet Ali. Palmerston was in favour of doing this, but the rest of the Cabinet would not approve, partly because the Navy was already busily engaged in enforcing economic sanctions against Holland. Palmerston was therefore obliged to write a despatch to Constantinople saying how sorry he was that Britain was unable to help. Five years later, on 22 May 1838, he wrote to Frederick Lamb: 'There is nothing that has happened since I have been in this office which I regret so much as that tremendous blunder of the English government. But it was not my fault; I tried hard to persuade the Cabinet to let me take the step. But Althorp and Brougham and others, some from ignorance of the bearing of foreign affairs, some for one foolish reason, some for another, would not agree.

Grey, who was with me on the point, was weak and gave way, and so nothing was done in a crisis of the utmost importance to all Europe, when we might with the greatest of ease have accomplished a good result'. And on 8 March 1840 he wrote to Lord Holland : 'I humbly venture to think ... that no British Cabinet at any period of the history of England ever made so great a mistake in regard to foreign affairs'.

In view of Britain's refusal, the Sultan asked the Tsar to save him. The Tsar responded at once, Mehemet Ali drew back, and Ibrahim retreated from Anatolia. As a reward for his assistance, the Tsar made the Sultan sign the Treaty of Unkiar Skelessi on 8 July 1833, in which Turkey and Russia agreed not to take any step in foreign affairs without first consulting each other. By a secret clause in the treaty, the Sultan agreed to modify Turkey's traditional policy of excluding all foreign warships from the Sea of Marmora in peace time, by allowing Russian ships to enter whenever they wished.

Lord Ponsonby, the British Ambassador at Constantinople, found out about the treaty and the secret clause at once, through a spy, and told Palmerston. Palmerston was very alarmed at the news. It was not the secret clause to which he objected so much as to the provision by which the two powers agreed to consult each other on their foreign policy; this meant that 'the Russian Ambassador becomes chief Cabinet minister of the Sultan'. The fact that he realized that it was all the fault of his own colleagues, who had forced Mahmud to turn to Nicholas by refusing the Turkish request for aid, did not make him any less angry.

Palmerston was all the more incensed with the Russians because in the week in which the Treaty of Unkiar Skelessi was signed, he had twice defended Russia from vicious attacks by the Radicals in the House of Commons. On 9 July, Cutlar Fergusson and Attwood launched a violent denunciation of Russian policy in Poland. Fergusson described the abduction from Warsaw of the screaming children, with the mothers hurling themselves on the railway line in an attempt to stop the departing trains. Attwood referred to 'the horrible cruelties of the Emperor Nicholas', and said that although the English people would be prepared to give £40,000,000 in taxes in a war to liberate Poland as willingly as he would offer the lives of his four sons, all that he asked was that the House should pass a resolution condemning Russian actions in Poland.

Palmerston admitted that atrocities had been committed in Poland, but thought that they had been exaggerated. He referred to the detested Nicholas, the Iron Tsar, as 'a man of high and generous feelings', and said that he was sure that the Emperor was not to blame for any of the cruelties which had been committed against the Poles. He was scathing about Attwood's speech. Attwood's 'voice was all for war – a general war; and he was generous enough . . . to offer the Government what he considered ample means for the prosecution of such a war. He offered the whole of the National Debt, £40,000,000 a year of additional taxes and his four sons'. But Palmerston had grave doubts 'whether the people of England were prepared to pay £40,000,000 a year of fresh taxes for the purpose of carrying on a war in favour of the Poles; nor did the warlike member for Birmingham state whether he had consulted his four sons about the sacrifice which he was ready to make of them upon the altar of Liberty'. He pointed out that if the Western allies went to war to liberate Poland, the three Northern Powers who had partitioned Poland would unite to crush the Poles long before Britain and France could bring them aid; and he then appealed to Fergusson to withdraw his resolution criticizing Russia, because no vote of the House would have the slightest effect on Russian policy. After Palmerston had sat down, O'Connell declared that he 'would as soon keep company with a thief who had been tried at the Old Bailey as with Nicholas', and traced all the present evils to the first partition of Poland in 1772 by 'that outrageous public prostitute, the notorious Catherine, the grandmother of this Emperor,' with her 5,000 lovers; but Lord John Russell deplored the use of such language about 'a sovereign with whom His Majesty was on terms of amity'.

Fergusson refused to withdraw his motion deploring the Russian conduct in Poland, and it was defeated by 177 votes to 95, with Palmerston and the Government, and Peel and the Tories, voting against the motion, and the Radicals and other members on the Government back-benches voting for it. Two

days later, there was another debate on the Russian intervention in Turkey. Palmerston again defended the Russians, and
expressed his certainty that they would withdraw their troops
from Turkey as soon as Mehemet Ali had been checked. But
though he had said enough to forfeit whatever Radical support he had won since August 1832, the Tsar and Nesselrode,
who were sensitive to criticism in the House of Commons, were
angry that he had not supported Russia more whole-heartedly,
and complained to the British chargé d'affaires.

When Palmerston heard the news about Unkiar Skelessi, he
said nothing in public against the treaty or against Russian
policy, and again defended Russian intervention in Turkey in
the debate in the House of Commons on 24 August 1833. But
he ordered Ponsonby to urge the Sultan to refuse to ratify the
Treaty of Unkiar Skelessi; and after he had failed to prevent
the ratification of the treaty, he sent a strong protest to Turkey
and to Russia, which annoyed Metternich, who said that Palmerston's arguments were untenable. It also angered the Tsar
and Nesselrode, particularly as Palmerston, after sending the
protest, petulantly ordered the chargé d'affaires in St. Petersburg to refuse to discuss it with Nesselrode.

In October 1833, the Tsar, the Emperor of Austria and the
King of Prussia met at Münchengrätz in Bohemia, with Metternich in attendance, and issued a declaration of solidarity
against revolution. They proclaimed that every sovereign had
not only a right, but a duty, to assist other sovereigns to suppress revolutions in their territories, and announced that they
would intervene, by force if necessary, to suppress Liberal
movements at the request of the ruler of a territory. It was a
challenge to Liberalism and constitutional movements everywhere, and a disguised alliance against Britain and France.
Palmerston, as Foreign Secretary in a Whig Government,
could not fail to react. He could do nothing against the Northern Powers in Poland, in Italy, or – for the moment – in the
Dardanelles. But he could, and did, strike back in the West.
He replied to Münchengrätz and Unkiar Skelessi in Spain and
Portugal.

Chapter Thirteen

The Quadruple Alliance

In the two years before he became Foreign Secretary, Palmerston's chief attack on Tory foreign policy had been directed at their action in Portugal. In 1826, Canning had sent troops to protect the Liberal constitutional Government of the infant Queen Maria, and had saved it from the counter-revolutionary rising under her uncle, Miguel; but Wellington's Government withdrew the troops, and allowed Miguel to seize the throne. When Palmerston went to the Foreign Office, Miguel was in complete control in Portugal; his prisons were full of his political opponents; and the eleven-year-old Maria II was a refugee in France. But Maria had the support of her father, Dom Pedro, who had become constitutional Emperor of Brazil after leading the Brazilian national movement for liberation from Portugal. In 1831, Pedro resigned the throne of Brazil in favour of his infant son, and returned to Europe in order to lead a revolution against his brother Miguel and restore his daughter Maria as Queen of Portugal. Maria's supporters still held the island of Terceira in the Azores, and from this base prepared to attack Miguel in Lisbon. The Portuguese Navy was divided between Pedro and Miguel; part of it was at Lisbon, and part at Terceira. In Portugal, Pedro had the support of the middle classes, of the intellectuals, of many of the aristocratic families, and of small groups of revolutionary artisans in Lisbon and Oporto; Miguel was supported by the Army, by the great wine monopoly, by the Catholic Church, and by the overwhelming mass of the peasantry, who followed the directions of their priests. When Miguel appeared in public, he was received with great shouts of *'Viva Dom Miguel I, rei absoluto'*

Palmerston's sympathies in the Portuguese political conflict were well known: in 1829 he had declared in Parliament that 'the civilized world rings with execrations upon Miguel'. But when he became Foreign Secretary, he did not intervene in support of the Constitutional side, as Canning had done in 1826. He did not, like Canning, find a constitutional government in power in Portugal, which he could protect against counter-revolution on the grounds that he was defending Portugal under the ancient treaty of alliance; it would have been another matter to assist a rebellion against the established government of Miguel, even though Wellington's Government had broken off diplomatic relations with Miguel because of the imprisonment of Englishmen by Miguel's police. Palmerston therefore decided to pursue a policy of strict neutrality, while vigorously defending the rights of British subjects in Portugal.

As usual, he paid careful regard to the forms of international law. The Anglo-Portuguese treaties of 1667 and 1810 gave many privileges to British subjects in Portugal – privileges which were not reciprocated for Portuguese in Britain. They were exempted from Portuguese taxation, and any litigations between Portuguese and British nationals were to be tried by a Judge Conservator in special courts. The Judge Conservator was a Portuguese lawyer whose appointment had been approved by the British Government. Palmerston was prepared to use the full might of the Royal Navy to enforce every letter of these treaties, and to avenge every breach of them, or any insult to the British flag; but he would do nothing to help an Englishman who had violated Portuguese law by committing criminal acts, by smuggling, or by committing political offences in support of Maria.

Palmerston appointed Sebastian Hoppner as British Consul at Lisbon, and directed him to act as spokesman for the British Government while official diplomatic relations with Portugal were suspended. On 14 January 1831 he sent Hoppner his first instructions. Hoppner was to maintain the strictest neutrality between the contending parties in Portugal; but 'the deep interest which England has always taken in the welfare of Portugal' made it his duty to urge Miguel to adopt a conciliatory policy towards his political opponents. Hoppner was to tell Miguel's Government that, though Britain would forbear from insisting on the grant of an amnesty as a condition for re-establishing diplomatic relations with Miguel, such an amnesty would certainly facilitate this, and Miguel was therefore urged to permit the Liberal refugees to return, and to stop confiscating the property of political opponents of the régime. 'You will not fail, in the meantime, to inculcate upon all British subjects in Portugal the necessity of abstaining from all interference in its political dissensions, and to explain to them that they must abide by the consequences which might attend any violation on their part of the Laws of that Country'. But Hoppner must prevent any violation of the rights of British subjects, 'giving the Portuguese Government to understand that His Majesty's Government will not permit such acts to be committed with impunity'.

From time to time, Miguel's police arrested an English resident on a false charge, and sometimes the naval authorities seized a British ship. Hoppner reacted strongly in every case, and always obtained not only an apology and compensation, but the dismissal of the Portuguese officer who had been responsible for the outrage, though he sometimes complained that the culprit was shortly afterwards reinstated, or appointed to a higher post. On the other hand, Palmerston paid no attention whatever when the Portuguese Government complained of misconduct by English officials, and when in August 1832 they complained that a Portuguese port regulation had been broken by an English naval officer, Palmerston immediately demanded that the Portuguese official who had raised the matter should be dismissed for making untrue allegations against an Englishman.

In the summer of 1831, the Miguelite authorities arrested and flogged a Frenchman. The French Government sent Admiral Roussin and a fleet to the Tagus, and demanded compensation; and Liberal opinion in France suggested that Roussin should take this opportunity to get rid of Miguel. The British Tories raised a cry of alarm at the French fleet in the Tagus, and called on Palmerston to protect the ancient ally from French aggression, as we had done in the days of Napoleon. Palmerston refused to defend Miguel against the French, and upheld the right of the French to protect their nationals in Portugal; but he urged them not to overthrow Miguel, or interfere in any way in Portuguese internal affairs. As Miguel refused the French demands for satisfaction, Roussin forced his way into the Tagus, and seized several Portuguese ships after an exchange of fire with Miguel's land batteries. When Palmerston heard the news, he called Talleyrand to the Foreign Office, and warned him that Britain had refused to support Miguel against the French only because he felt convinced that France had no other object than to obtain compensation for wrongs done to Frenchmen.

But in France, Liberal opinion was strongly against Miguel, and under this pressure the French Government introduced ideological factors into the dispute. Roussin actually offered to restore the Portuguese vessels which he had seized if Miguel would release four hundred of his twenty thousand political prisoners; but Miguel refused. As the situation developed, Palmerston became increasingly worried. 'England is upon very ticklish grounds in this dispute between France and Portugal', he wrote to Granville on 10 June 1831. 'If the French were to attempt to land in Portugal, or to threaten to bombard Lisbon, we might find ourselves compelled, very unwillingly, to interfere and to assist the Portuguese; and it is unneccessary to say how much we should regret any event which could place us in collision with France. A bombardment of Lisbon seems not an appropriate measure of retaliation for the offence: it would be punishing the innocent inhabitants for the sins of the guilty Government; and besides, if we stood by and allowed such a thing, we should have an immense outcry in this country on behalf of the English in Lisbon, whose property the French shells would not distinguish from that of Don Miguel himself'. On 22 July he wrote to Granville: 'We shall get into hot water with France if she attempts anything like occupation of any part of Portugal. The French Government may be driven by public opinion at Paris, but we could not in that case resist public opinion in London'. And three days later he told Granville to warn the French Government 'that the English Government and Parliament will begin to be jealous of the French occupation of the Tagus if the French fleet should remain there. England would never stand the occupation of the Tagus by the French; and no Government here could be allowed to connive at it'.

On 27 July, Sébastiani proposed to the British Government that Britain and France should act jointly against Miguel, that they should recognize Maria and Pedro as the Government of Portugal, and that the Portuguese ships which Roussin had seized should be handed over to Pedro at Terceira. Sébastiani said that if Britain was not prepared to support France in this move, he was nevertheless ready to act alone and to do it on his own responsibility, provided that Palmerston did not object; but if the British Government did not approve of this course, France would not pursue it. Palmerston replied in a despatch to Granville on 10 August. He stated that the British Government deeply regretted 'the existence of that system of misgovernment by which the Portuguese nation have been for the last three years oppressed'; but 'Governments are not at liberty to act solely from motives of generous sympathy for the sufferings of an oppressed people, they are bound by the severer rules of general principles, to respect rights which are inherent in other nations'. Britain and France had proclaimed the principle of non-interference in the internal affairs of independent states, and they should be bound by this principle. 'Whatever then may be the opinion of His Majesty's Government as to the present condition of Portugal, so long as the people of that country submit to the existing order of things, it does not appear that any other Prince ought to use active interference to work a change, even though such change might be for the evident advantage of the Portuguese nation. Every people ought to be left to judge for itself upon matters connected with its internal Government, and any departure from the principle of non-interference in such affairs, even tho' directed for the attainment of objects demonstrably benevolent, would establish a precedent liable to be perverted, to serve the worst purposes of ambition and injustice'. He thanked the French Government for the frankness with which they had confided in him, but stated 'unreservedly and unequivocally, that His Majesty could not feel himself justified in uniting with France to effect by force a change in the Government of Portugal'. Miguel gave in and paid the required compensation, and the French fleet withdrew.

The French action in Portugal had caused great alarm to the Tories. It was just at the time that the French troops marched into Belgium to expel the Dutch after the Ten Days' Campaign, and the Tories made much of the double danger in Portugal and Belgium. Wellington's men had fought in the Peninsula to save Portugal from the French, and at Waterloo to prevent the French invasion of the Netherlands; yet here was Palmerston conniving at the presence of a French navy in the Tagus and a French army in Belgium. This argument was particularly effective when it was put forward in the House of Lords by Wellington himself. Palmerston was also bitterly attacked in the House of Commons by his old friend Croker, and by Lord Brudenell, the Tory MP for Fowey, who later acquired fame and notoriety as Lord Cardigan of the Light Brigade. Brudenell said that Palmerston 'had been guilty of the grossest injustice towards our old and faithful allies, the Portuguese in the South and the Dutch in the North – a French fleet occupied the Tagus, and the tricoloured flag was planted in the soil of Holland'. Yet Palmerston, he said, had pursued a different policy with regard to Poland, because 'there it would seem that we should have had to deal with a different sort of enemy. It was one thing to abandon a weak country like Portugal or Holland, and quite another to encounter so formidable a power as that of Russia'. Brudenell reminded the House that in the debates on the Reform Bill, the Government spokesmen were very fond of quoting Chatham's statements in favour of reform; but the bare mention of Chatham's name was a reproach to Palmerston's foreign policy. 'In the days of Lord Chatham, England was respected by all the nations of Europe; but in these days she had abandoned all her ancient principles, and ought to blush at the name of Chatham – she had abandoned her old and faithful allies, rushing forward to grapple with the weak, and perfectly ready to truckle to the strong. If this system were continued, the English name would be a byword for all that was base and dishonourable'.

In the spring of 1832, Dom Pedro fitted out a fleet in the

Azores for an invasion of Portugal. He collected an international body of men, some of them enthusiastic Radicals and others mercenary-minded adventurers, including many Polish refugees and Englishmen. He placed them under the command of Captain Sartorius, a retired British naval officer, who was afterwards replaced by another British naval officer, the brilliant and unorthodox Captain Charles Napier, who temporarily resigned from the British Navy, and assumed the name of Carlos Ponza, in order to serve with Pedro. The volunteers somehow managed to find loopholes in the British foreign enlistment laws, and Palmerston did nothing to stop them, as their actions were legal and in line with public opinion in Britain. In view of the marked hostility which Britain was showing towards him, Miguel asked Palmerston to withdraw the British fleet from the Tagus, and turned for help to the absolutist government of Ferdinand VII of Spain. Palmerston agreed to withdraw the fleet, as he would not have been justified under international law in remaining in Portuguese waters against the will of the Portuguese Government; but he told Admiral Parker to wait just outside the three-mile limit. He also sent Lord William Russell on a special diplomatic mission to Portugal.

Palmerston gave Russell his instructions on 23 May 1832. 'His Majesty has declared it to be his intention to preserve a strict neutrality in the approaching contest between Don Miguel on the one side, and Don Pedro on behalf of his daughter Dna. Maria on the other, provided other Powers pursue the same course. But His Majesty could not remain an indifferent spectator of the Interference of any other Power, by force of arms, in the Internal affairs of Portugal'. Although the Spanish Government had announced that they, too, would be neutral, there was reason to believe that 20,000 Spanish troops had been assembled on the Portuguese frontier. 'If Spain should so depart from her promised neutrality, and interfere by force of arms on one side, His Majesty would consider himself absolved from his own declaration of neutrality; and a due regard to British Interests would require that Great Britain should in such a case afford counterbalancing aid to Don Pedro'. Palmerston impressed on Russell the need to be very

cautious before ordering Admiral Parker into action, even if
he should hear that the Spanish troops had crossed the frontier; he was to give the Spaniards the benefit of every doubt.
As Admiral Parker would be ready to act on the shortest notice, 'less inconvenience would arise from your delaying to announce to him the advance of the Spanish troops, for some
short time after they had actually entered Portugal, than from
your making to him the announcement in consequence of information which might afterwards prove to be erroneous'. He
ended by telling Russell to give 'the strictest orders' to his subordinates not to do 'anything which might appear like partiality or Interference in the political differences which divide
the Portuguese nation, so long as you continue to act in the
Character of an agent of a neutral Power'.

Palmerston was certainly not looking for an excuse for intervention in Portugal. He wrote to the Spanish Government,
not in the harsh, threatening language that he used to Miguel,
but in the courteous style in which he addressed the governments of the great powers. He told them that Parker's fleet
would remain off Lisbon in order to protect British life and
property in Portugal, but would not intervene on Pedro's side
unless the Spanish Army crossed the frontier. Otherwise the
marines would only land if this were necessary to protect
British subjects, and would in this case return to their ships as
soon as they had accomplished this task. He told Russell not
to call in Parker's force if the Spanish troops should cross the
border by inadvertence, or on some short foray, unless he was
convinced that a serious invasion of Portugal had begun. He
also took steps to prevent Pedro from offering any provocation to Spain. The Spanish Liberals, who had been unsuccessfully attempting to revolt against Ferdinand's police state ever
since the French troops of Louis XVIII had restored him as an
absolute monarch, were greatly encouraged by Pedro's expedition, and hoped that the liberation of Portugal would be followed by the liberation of Spain. But Palmerston warned
Pedro not to give any encouragement to the Spanish Liberals.
On 7 June 1832, he wrote to Pedro's adviser, Palmella, that if
Pedro's followers made any attempt to excite disturbances in
Spain, the British Government would consider that this gave

the Spanish Government 'a legitimate ground for armed interference against a party by which its safety was thus threatened, and that no co-operation would in such case be afforded
to Don Pedro by His Majesty's Forces'. He urged Pedro not
to permit any Spaniard to accompany his expedition, for fear
that this might alarm the Spanish Government.

In July, Pedro's forces seized Oporto, and proclaimed the
government of Queen Maria. The Portuguese people remained loyal to Miguel, and very few of them joined Pedro;
but Pedro managed to hold Oporto for a year with his 8,500
trained men against Miguel's besieging army of 80,000 soldiers. The French Government proposed to Palmerston that
Britain and France should recognize the Liberal Government
in Oporto; but Palmerston refused, and said that even if Britain recognized Maria as Queen, they would still feel obliged to
preserve strict neutrality in the Portuguese Civil War. But once
the fighting had started – which was just about the time of Palmerston's change of policy towards the Northern Powers, and
his speech of 2 August 1832 about the Resolutions of the
German Diet – Palmerston managed to be neutral on the side
of Dom Pedro. He made things as difficult as possible for Miguel. When Miguel, who was in bad financial straits, raised
money to pay his troops by a forced loan from all the inhabitants of Portugal, Palmerston refused to listen to his
arguments about the necessity of war and extraordinary circumstances, and insisted – successfully – that British residents
in Portugal should be exempted from the loan. When Miguel's
troops damaged British-owned property in the course of their
military operations against Oporto, Palmerston demanded
compensation in his most threatening style. When Miguel imposed a strict inspection of all boats entering and leaving the
port of Lisbon in order to prevent communications between
Pedro's fleet and his secret sympathizers in the capital, Admiral Parker, with Palmerston's approval, refused to allow
British boats to submit to the inspection when they entered or
left the harbour with letters between him and Russell and the
British Consul, Sorrell. Sorrell warned Miguel's ministers that
the British fleet 'will avenge any insult or damage to British
property', or to the British flag.

British policy aroused resentment in Portugal, and only the strictest orders of Miguel's Government prevented British subjects in Lisbon from being lynched. Miguel suggested to Palmerston that all British subjects should be placed in one area where they would be effectively guarded from popular anger. Palmerston refused, and said that if any Briton were injured or insulted, the Navy would act against Miguel. Parker's tugs were sometimes detained by the Portuguese authorities, and occasionally fired upon. In every case Britain demanded, and obtained, the punishment or dismissal of the Miguelite officer who was responsible.

On 29 August 1832 – four weeks after the speech of 2 August on the Six Resolutions of the German Diet – Palmerston sent a despatch to Russell which initiated a new departure in British policy towards Portugal. Russell was to offer to mediate between Miguel and Pedro's forces at Oporto, and arrange for Pedro to evacuate the town and return unhindered, with all his forces, to the Azores. If Miguel refused to accept this offer, the British Navy would cover Pedro's embarkation and protect him on his journey back to the Azores, on the strict understanding that Pedro did not attack any Portuguese territory on the journey. Palmerston told Russell to tell Miguel's Foreign Minister, Santarem, 'that His Majesty's Government cannot permit so wanton and unnecessary a sacrifice of life to take place as would be the result of the capture of Oporto by storm, when the Portuguese Government had the power of obtaining possession of that place without giving a single shot – and that when Don Pedro and his adherents are willing peacefully to depart from Portugal, His Majesty's Government cannot allow them to fall victims to the vindictive proceedings which would probably follow upon their being captured. That consequently though the British Government have scrupulously abstained from affording Don Pedro any assistance in his offensive operations, yet they feel themselves perfectly at liberty to obey the dictates of humanity, by protecting his retreat from Portugal, as they would have been prepared to do by that of Don Miguel, if the fortune of war had proved adverse to him. He added that Britain would greatly regret having to enter into hostilities with the Government of Portugal as a result of any incident which occurred while the Navy was covering Pedro's embarkation.

Pedro was no more willing than Miguel to accept Palmerston's offer, as he had no intention of evacuating Oporto. A fortnight later, Palmerston took another step against Miguel. The winds and stormy seas in the Atlantic made it dangerous for Parker's fleet to stay out at sea. Palmerston therefore told Miguel's Government that the British ships would enter the Douro, as this was necessary in order to protect British subjects at Oporto and to receive them on board if Miguel's troops attacked the town. He warned Miguel not to resist this entry of the British Navy into Portuguese waters. 'Any insult offered to His Majesty's flag', wrote Palmerston, 'however small the vessel which bears it, would be resented and avenged by all the means which Great Britain can command', and 'any hindrance opposed to the execution of these orders will be considered as an act of hostility'.

Pedro surprised Palmerston as well as Miguel. With one-tenth of Miguel's force, he held Oporto for a year, and in July 1833, after a brilliant victory at sea by Napier, his supporters seized Lisbon by a military coup. The young Queen was brought back from France, and Miguel and his Government withdrew to the country districts, where he still had the support of nearly all the peasants, and carried on the war with great savagery. But Pedro, as well as Miguel, was having his differences with Palmerston. Palmerston did not approve of Pedro's policy of confiscating the property of the Jesuits, of the monasteries and convents, and of Miguel's supporters. There was occasional friction when Pedro's forces seized a British ship, and Palmerston remonstrated in language almost as haughty and threatening as that which he used to Miguel on such occasions. Pedro showed a disposition to adopt the Constitution of 1822, which was based on the Spanish Constitution of 1812 and too democratic for Palmerston's liking, instead of the Charter which Pedro had issued in 1826, which was much nearer the British system, with a limited franchise and a hereditary Upper House. In August 1833, Russell asked Pedro's Foreign Minister, Xavier, to include more aristocrats in the Government; but though Xavier promised that this would be done, the new ministers whom Pedro appointed were members of the Democratic Party, and in November Russell complained that 'the war has now assumed an appearance of a struggle between the Church party and the Democrats'.

On 29 September 1833, the whole situation was transformed by the death of Ferdinand VII of Spain. He was succeeded by his daughter Isabella, who was aged three. Ferdinand's fourth wife, Maria Cristina of Naples, had mildly Liberal leanings, and before Ferdinand's death had introduced Liberal ministers into the Government. She now became Regent, and declared her intention of establishing constitutional government in Spain. Isabella's uncle, Don Carlos, stood for absolutism and the Catholic Church, and claimed the throne under the Salic Law which debarred women from succeeding. He and his supporters crossed the frontier into Portugal and linked up with Miguel and his army.

Palmerston did not, at first, have any great sympathy for Isabella and her cause. In October 1833 he was present at a dinner party when a lady asked whether they should drink the health of the King Don Carlos or the Queen Isabella. Palmerston replied: 'For my part, I drink to the health of the one who gets the better of the other'. But his attitude changed when Carlos joined Miguel and intervened in Portugal. This development made it possible for Palmerston to achieve a great diplomatic success. On 22 April 1834, he and Talleyrand and the Spanish and Portuguese Ambassadors in London signed the Quadruple Alliance, by which Britain, France, Isabella's Government in Spain and Maria's Government in Portugal agreed to act together to re-establish peace in the Iberian Peninsula. Palmerston annoyed Madame de Dino by keeping the three Ambassadors waiting for several hours before he arrived at the Foreign Office to sign the additional articles of the treaty, which was signed, as a result, in the middle of the night; but he knew that the Ambassadors would be prepared to wait for more than a few hours to get the signature of the British Foreign Secretary to what was, in effect, an agreement to impose constitutional Liberal Governments in one corner of Europe in defiance of the absolutist Governments of the Northern Powers. It was the greatest success which the Liberals had gained anywhere in Europe since 1815. 'I should like to see Metternich's face when he reads our treaty', wrote Palmerston to his brother William the day before the treaty was signed. Under the terms of the treaty, Spanish troops were to march into Portugal to defeat the forces of Miguel and Carlos, and to establish the Government of Donna Maria, while the British Navy was to co-operate for the same end. As the Spanish armies advanced, Miguel and Carlos surrendered to the British Admiral, and were received on board a British ship.

The Spanish Government asked Palmerston to surrender Carlos to them. Palmerston refused, and said that it would be breaking faith with him after he had surrendered to the Royal Navy. Palmerston hoped to bribe both Miguel and Pedro into giving up politics and retiring into exile on some large pension which would enable them to live in a manner appropriate to their rank. Miguel accepted the offer, and retired to Rome, and lived quietly abroad for the rest of his life, though from time to time his opponents felt an unnecessary anxiety that he was attempting to return to Portugal. Carlos was brought to England. When he reached Portsmouth, Palmerston sent his Under-Secretary, Backhouse, to see him without telling Talleyrand that Carlos had arrived. This omission angered Talleyrand, and was probably deliberate, so that Britain could get in ahead of her French ally. Backhouse offered Carlos a pension of £30,000 a year if he would renounce his claim to the Spanish throne and promise never to return to Spain or Portugal; but Carlos refused, and talked about his rights as a sovereign and his duties to his brave followers in the mountains of Northern Spain. The Spanish Ambassador became alarmed, and asked Palmerston to arrest Carlos. Palmerston told him that this was impossible under English law, but that Carlos would be prevented from leaving England. 'The Spanish Government need give themselves very little uneasiness about Carlos', he wrote to Villiers, the British Minister in Madrid, on 17 June 1834, 'besides, his personal character is a security against much danger from him. He will not land like Murat with half a dozen followers, nor march like Bonaparte in triumph from a sea-port to the capital'.

Carlos came to London, and rented Gloucester Lodge. But

after spending a few weeks there, and having talks with Wellington and Londonderry, he slipped out of the house while his servants pretended that he was ill in bed – one of them impersonated him from under the bedclothes – and left the country, which was not difficult in the days when passports were not required in Britain. Palmerston was not alarmed, even when he heard that Carlos had gone. 'I shall believe him in Spain when I know the fact', he wrote to Villiers on 15 July. Eight days before, Carlos had reached the hills near San Sebastian, and had placed himself at the head of a growing band of guerrillas; and before the end of the year the Carlists and Isabelinos were engaged in an exceptionally savage civil war. The Spanish Government blamed Palmerston for allowing Carlos's escape.

Palmerston had now emerged, without really intending it, as the champion of Liberalism in Europe. He still lagged behind the French Government in almost every arena where the battle between absolutism and constitutionalism was being fought; but his assistance to the Liberals, being more unexpected, was the more appreciated. By 1834 he was taking up the cudgels on behalf of the Poles. After the defeat of the Polish rising in 1831, 7,000 Polish refugees crossed the border into Prussia, Saxony and Austria. Some went on to Frankfort and Paris, and to Brussels, where they joined the Belgian Army and provided a revolutionary leaven in the Belgian nationalist movement; and some joined Pedro's forces in Portugal. In 1833 the Tsar asked the King of Saxony to hand over the most prominent of the refugees who had remained in Saxony. Palmerston and the French Government interceded with the Saxon Government on behalf of the Poles, urging that the dictates of humanity forbade the surrender of the refugees to the vengeance of the Tsar. The Saxons refused the Tsar's request, but expelled all the refugees from Saxony. Most of them went to Switzerland.

A few of the Poles in Switzerland came into contact with Mazzini and the Italian Radical refugees. On 1 February 1834, about a hundred Italian and Polish refugees seized a boat on Lake Geneva, crossed the lake to the Sardinian province of Savoy, and marched against a Sardinian army outpost. Before they reached their objective, their leaders quarrelled amongst themselves, and the party abandoned their project and retreated into Switzerland; but the 'invasion' was greatly magnified by Metternich and the absolutist Governments. The Sardinian Government and the Diet of the German Confederation accused the Swiss of harbouring revolutionary elements who menaced their security, and demanded that all the Polish refugees be expelled from Switzerland, along with all the German Liberals who had taken refuge there. Palmerston adopted the same attitude which he always took with regard to political refugees. He urged the Swiss to refuse the request of Metternich and the Diet for the expulsion of all the refugees. He advised them to expel only those who had been engaged in the raid on Sardinian territory, or had otherwise taken part in revolutionary or subversive conspiracies, and to compel the other refugees to leave the frontier districts, and to live in the centre of Switzerland. He also urged Metternich and the Diet to desist from their demand, and to require only the expulsion of the guilty individuals. When Metternich imposed economic sanctions against the canton of Berne, where most of the refugees resided, and massed some troops on the Swiss frontier, Palmerston protested and reminded Metternich that Swiss neutrality had been guaranteed by the Treaty of Vienna.

Palmerston had an ulterior motive for his attitude: he did not wish the Poles to come to England. In the summer of 1833, when the Government of Saxony decided to expel the Polish refugees, Palmerston ordered the British Minister at Dresden to refuse to grant them passports to come to Britain; and he hoped that the Poles in Switzerland would go to the United States if they were compelled to leave. 'It is extremely desirable that the Poles now in Switzerland should not come to England', he wrote to Cartwright, the Minister in Frankfort, in September 1833. 'It is understood that they have no adequate means of subsistence for their support after they come here, and it would be very difficult to find any way of affording them assistance at the publick expense. Their removal to this country therefore would be equally embarrassing to them and to us. His Majesty's Government Consequently hope that if these Poles are to leave Switzerland, arrangements will be made for removing them at once into the United States of America'.

The Swiss Government was forced to comply with the request of the German Diet, and all the refugees were expelled from Switzerland. Some of them went to France, some to America, and some came to Britain. Lord Dudley Stuart and his Committee pressed the Government to provide for their relief; but the Government refused, and on 25 March 1834 the Polish supporters attacked Palmerston for this in the House of Commons. They accused him of having refused relief to the Poles at the request of the Russian Government, and Attwood stated that he had 'apologized to the brute who kicked his country'; but Palmerston denied that the Russian Government had intervened in the matter. Eventually, the eloquence and determination of Lord Dudley Stuart and his friends persuaded the Government and Parliament to vote £7,000 for the maintenance of 466 Polish refugees for one year. Next year, in 1834, the grant was increased to £10,000 a year, and in 1837, after the Austrian occupation of Cracow, to £15,000 a year, on condition that no refugee who arrived in future would be eligible for the grant. In 1840, Parliament decided that they had done enough for the Poles, as a total of nearly £80,000 had been paid to them in seven years, and no further payments were made. The bulk of the money for Polish relief came from private charity. It was a great achievement of the Polish lobby to obtain anything from the Government, in view of the accepted attitude at the period about public expenditure on charitable objects.

On 3 April 1833, a group of German and international Radicals, including a good sprinkling of Polish refugees, tried to start a revolution in Germany by seizing control of Frankfort. Metternich had been warned about the plot, but he allowed it to mature, and utilized it to the full. He raised the matter in the German Diet. The Diet, which met at Frankfort, and consisted of representatives of all the states included in the German Confederation, was dominated by Austria; and at Metternich's direction, the Diet accused the Frankfort authorities of connivance in the outbreak at Frankfort, and asserted its right to exercise its sovereign control of members of the Confederation. Frankfort was occupied by Austrian and Prussian troops, supported by token forces from other German states, and the Diet assumed the temporary government of the city.

Palmerston took no action about the occupation of Frankfort for more than a year. Apart from his new policy of opposition to absolutism, he was interested in Frankfort from the point of view of British trade, for Britain had signed a commercial treaty with Frankfort, and Palmerston hoped that it would be possible to open new markets for British goods in Germany. The situation had therefore to be handled with some care. In April 1834 Cartwright warned Palmerston that Austria and Prussia were putting pressure on Frankfort to enter the German Customs Union – the *Zollverein* – which would mean that Frankfort would be obliged to impose tariffs against British goods in violation of their treaty with Britain. At the same time, the Government of Frankfort, on the anniversary of the occupation of the town by the Federal troops, asked the Diet to withdraw the troops; and when the Diet refused, Palmerston sent a despatch to the Diet protesting against the military occupation of Frankfort.

In his despatch of 15 May, he explained that his long delay in sending a protest was not due to lack of concern, but solely to the fact that he had hoped that unofficial hints would be enough to cause the Federal forces to be withdrawn. He argued at length that the Diet had contravened several articles of the Constitution of the German Confederation by forcibly intervening in the internal affairs of one of the members of the Confederation; and as the Confederation and its constitution had been established by the Treaty of Vienna, Britain had a right and duty, as a party to the treaty, to prevent this violation of the constitution. His despatch caused great anger in Austria and Prussia and in the absolutist German states. The Austrian President of the Diet, Munch, sent a strong reply, in which he protested against Palmerston's interference in the internal affairs of the Confederation, and expressed his resentment at the language of Palmerston's despatch.

Palmerston's reply was almost apologetic in tone. 'You will state', he wrote to Cartwright on 13 July, 'that His Majesty's Government regret very much to perceive from an expression

in Monsieur de Negler's Note, that the communication which
you were instructed to make to the Diet upon the subject of
the military occupation of Frankfort has been considered by
the Diet as not having been couched in language sufficiently
friendly. It was far from the intention of His Majesty's Government to give anything like an unfriendly character to the
expressions of that communication, and with regard to its
substance they are of opinion that there is nothing inconsistent with the offices of friendship in timely remonstrance, between contracting Parties, against an apprehended departure
from the stipulations of a Treaty'. But he reiterated his arguments as to the illegality of the Federal intervention in Frankfort. Instead of replying to this despatch by a diplomatic note
to Cartwright, the Diet passed a resolution in which they rejected Palmerston's arguments and protested against his conduct, and handed a copy of the resolution to Cartwright. On
16 November – his last day at the Foreign Office – Palmerston sent a note to the Diet, declining to continue the correspondence, in view of the fact that the Diet had adopted this
improper way of communicating their views to the British
Government.

Palmerston had obviously had the worst of the encounter,
as the Federal troops remained in Frankfort; but Germany
was not Portugal, and Frankfort was far beyond the reach of
the British Navy. No one appreciated this better than Palmerston, with his realistic understanding of the balance of power
in any situation; and he realized that he was powerless to act.
In 1835, the Government of Frankfort felt reluctantly compelled to agree to the demand of the Diet that they should join
the German Customs Union, and they asked Palmerston to relieve them from their obligations under their commercial
treaty with Britain. Palmerston agreed, having been advised by
Cartwright that if he refused, British goods would be excluded
from Germany altogether.

In January 1839, there was an unpleasant incident at Frankfort, when Mr. Cole, a British subject, who was crossing a
bridge in the town, kicked some snow at an Austrian sentry
posted on the bridge. Cole claimed that it was unintentional,
but the sentry struck him and arrested him, and he was sen-

tenced by a Frankfort court to six months' imprisonment
for insulting a soldier of the occupying forces. He was allowed
to commute the sentence by paying a large fine. Palmerston
protested strongly to the Frankfort authorities; but they
claimed that it would be derogatory to their dignity to alter
the decision of their judicial tribunals at the request of a foreign power. Palmerston took up the question with Metternich.
Metternich adopted his usual evasive and dishonest tactics; he
said that he had no power to intervene, and threw all the
blame on the Judge at Frankfort, adding that this incident
proved how necessary it was that Austrian troops should occupy a town where justice was so badly administered. Palmerston thereupon told Abercombie, at Frankfort, to show the
despatch of the British chargé d'affaires in Vienna, containing
the account of his talk with Metternich, to the Frankfort Government. This would show them 'how little the City of
Frankfort is likely to gain by the subserviency which its Tribunals have shown to Austria by the gross injustice which
they have practised upon Mr. Cole'.

Eventually the Government of Frankfort offered to refund
Cole's fine. Abercombie demanded that they should also pay
the heavy legal costs which Cole had incurred, and compensation for the wrongs which he had suffered; but Palmerston
ordered Abercombie to accept the offer to refund the fine, to
tell Cole to leave Germany immediately, and to take no further action.

While Palmerston was quarrelling with Austria over Austrian policy towards Switzerland and Frankfort, he became
involved in another conflict with the most absolutist of the
Northern Powers. It arose on a trivial issue, and led to more
serious consequences than anyone intended. In the summer of
1832, the British Ambassador to Russia retired, and Palmerston proposed to appoint Sir Stratford Canning, who was the
cousin of the former Prime Minister, in his place. Stratford
Canning had just returned from a diplomatic mission to Constantinople, where he had impressed Palmerston by his ability,
but greatly annoyed the Russians; though according to one
story, the Tsar's dislike of him arose, not from his diplomatic
activities in Turkey, but from a personal quarrel which had

arisen between them in 1823, when Nicholas had been the heir
to the throne and Canning an attaché in St. Petersburg. At any
rate, Nicholas refused to receive Canning as Ambassador.

It was the accepted practice on the Continent for no Ambassador to be appointed by his Government until the Government of the country to which he was accredited had been
notified and had expressed their willingness to accept him. But
Palmerston would not agree to conform to this practice. He
took the view that as the business of an Ambassador was to
act as vigorously and effectively as possible for the interests
of his country, it was natural that, if he were successful at his
job, the Government to which he was accredited would object
to him. If foreign governments were to be allowed to veto the
appointment of British Ambassadors, they would obviously
refuse to receive any good ones. For this reason, he refused
to protest when the Greek Government appointed a notorious
enemy of Britain to be their Ambassador to London in 1837,
and wrote to Lyons, the British Minister in Athens: 'Every
Independent State has an indisputed right to judge for itself
as to the persons whom it may choose to select to represent it
at Foreign Courts, and no Government has a right to object
to receive a person so accredited to it, unless in a very extreme
case'.

After consulting the King, Palmerston inserted an announcement in the London Gazette on 30 October 1832, announcing that Sir Stratford Canning had been appointed
Ambassador to St. Petersburg. The Tsar was very angry. He
let the British Government know that he would not allow
Canning to cross the Russian frontier. Both sides had now
committed themselves, and could not retreat without loss of
face. Canning could not go to Russia, and Palmerston refused
to revoke his appointment and appoint another Ambassador. The protagonists tried to avoid making the quarrel worse
by keeping it as private as possible. Palmerston refused to say
anything about it in the House of Commons, though he was
often pressed to do so by the anti-Russian Radical MPs; and
the correspondence between the two governments was conducted by private letter, not by official despatches. Palmerston
suggested, as a compromise, that both governments might

agree to be represented by chargés d'affaires for a time. The Tsar did not accept this suggestion, but it was obvious that he could not keep an Ambassador in London indefinitely while Britain had only a chargé d'affaires in St. Petersburg.

This caused great anxiety to Princess Lieven. She had lived in London for more than twenty years, and was very distressed at the prospect of Lieven being recalled, and of her having to leave Almack's and her friends in London society. She asked Lady Cowper to intervene with Palmerston, to urge him to reach some compromise solution which would enable her to stay; and she herself wrote a personal appeal to him from Lady Cowper's country house at Panshanger in Hertfordshire in January 1833. Palmerston did all he could to help her. In December 1832, he sent Canning on a special mission to Spain to persuade Ferdinand VII to remain neutral in the Portuguese civil war, and on his return suggested to Lord Grey that Canning should take up a permanent appointment as Minister to Madrid instead of going to St. Petersburg; but Canning refused, and said that his honour made it necessary for him to be sent to Russia. Palmerston then proposed a compromise to Nesselrode: if the Tsar would receive Canning, Palmerston would withdraw him within a few months, and appoint another Ambassador in his place. The Tsar refused, but offered, instead, to confer one of the highest Russian orders on Canning if Palmerston agreed to revoke his appointment as Ambassador, an offer which Palmerston likewise refused. Palmerston was meanwhile showing every consideration to Madame de Lieven. He was particularly attentive to her at a dinner party in March 1833; and later in the year, after the Lievens returned from a visit to Russia, he visited Madame de Lieven at her house in Richmond and invited her and Lieven to stay at Broadlands.

At last, in May 1834, the Tsar ordered Lieven to leave London. This was largely due to the machinations of the Lievens' personal enemies in the Russian Foreign Office, above all to Count Orlov, who had recently distinguished himself by negotiating the treaty of Unkiar Skelessi. Many people in Britain were delighted to see Madame de Lieven go. William IV, who according to Madame de Lieven had once unsuccessfully tried to seduce her in his carriage in the streets of Brighton, was very glad to see the last of her, and so was Wellington. *The Times* exulted, and published an offensive article referring to her love affairs and the shape of her nose, which Madame de Lieven believed was due to the fact that she had once refused to give a ticket for Almack's to a journalist on the staff of *The Times*. But many of her friends in London society were sorry that she was leaving, and went out of their way to show their sympathy after *The Times* article appeared.

The incident soured Madame de Lieven, and she never forgave Palmerston for his part in it. She fell ill on the journey to Russia, and soon after she arrived there, her son died from the harsh Russian winter climate, to which he was not accustomed. A few years later, she separated from Lieven, and went to live in Paris, where she became the mistress of Guizot, who whetted her dislike of Palmerston. She repeatedly accused Palmerston of having engineered the whole incident of Canning's appointment as Ambassador with a view to procuring Lieven's recall and driving her out of England. Talleyrand said the same. Their accusations came to be believed by the Radicals and anti-Russian groups in Britain, and when Palmerston had become the hero of the Radicals, they gave him all the credit for expelling the Princess Lieven.

Palmerston himself was prepared to accept the credit which his Radical supporters bestowed upon him. But the story told by Talleyrand and Madame de Lieven is obviously untrue. Palmerston had become irritated at Madame de Lieven's activities, but he could hardly have foreseen the consequences when he gazetted the appointment of Canning to St. Petersburg; and in any case, such devious tactics were more in keeping with the methods of Metternich, and of Talleyrand himself, than with Palmerston's character and diplomatic practice. He did, at one point, propose to Nesselrode that Britain and Russia should for the time being be represented only by chargés d'affaires; but this was one obvious solution of the problem which Palmerston put forward along with several others, and would in any case have occurred to the Tsar as a way of solving the dilemma.

'I am very sorry on private grounds to lose old friends and

agreeable members of society', he wrote to his brother William in June 1834, a fortnight before the Lievens left England, 'but on public grounds I do not know that their loss will be great'. He added that Madame de Lieven 'has done much mischief here by meddling and intriguing; a busy woman must do harm because she cannot do good'. But he had nevertheless done all that he could, conformable with his public duty, to enable Madame de Lieven to stay in London. Palmerston was a gentleman, and he played fair with his old mistress. Both Englishmen and foreigners came in time to think of Palmerston as the very personification of John Bull; but he was a John Bull with the most polished manners, who spoke perfect French, and was always at home in the cosmopolitan *milieu* of the international aristocracy, where personal friendships were not unduly affected by political and national disagreements.

Chapter Fourteen

The Difficulties with Portugal

In June 1834, Lord Grey resigned as Prime Minister, and was succeeded by Lord Melbourne. Melbourne had serious disagreements with the King about the formation of his Government, and in November William suddenly dismissed him – the last time in British history that a sovereign exercised his right to dismiss a Government that had not decided to resign. William IV was always a Tory, and hated nearly all his Whig ministers. The only one he liked was Palmerston. He disapproved of Palmerston's foreign policy, especially of his alliance with France; but, personally, the King and the Whig Foreign Secretary got on well, like the two old Tories they were.

On 16 November 1834 – four years almost to the day after he had first become Foreign Secretary – Palmerston left the Foreign Office, to the delight of all his staff there. They were able to do him a small disservice at his departure, by refusing to supply him with copies, for his letter books, of the despatches which the Ambassadors abroad had written to him before they heard of the change of government, but which arrived after he had surrendered the seals of office. On his last day in office, he wrote to Fox-Strangways, the chargé d'affaires in Vienna, informing him of his departure from the Foreign Office. 'Tell this immediately to Metternich', he wrote, 'it will gladden his heart and be the most agreeable thing he has ever heard from me'. Fox-Strangways passed on this message to Metternich in a modified form; but he said enough to draw the icy comment from Metternich that this was yet another example of Palmerston's utter misunderstanding of the true situation.

Peel became Prime Minister, and appointed Wellington as Foreign Secretary. As he could not govern with the existing House of Commons, in which the Whigs had a majority of over 350, he asked the King to dissolve Parliament, and a general election was held in January 1835. Palmerston was opposed in South Hampshire, and fought a fierce election campaign. It cost him £1,390, and though he considered that this was cheap for a county contest, he had to borrow £1,000 from his brother William, because he was, as usual, in debt. He rode all round the county canvassing, and addressed meetings of freeholders at the local inns. His friend Admiral Osmaney, who was on leave from the Navy, came with him, with the object, as Palmerston put it, of helping him canvass and of acting as his second in any duel in which he might be involved. After the election, the Tories asked questions in Parliament as to how it came about that Osmaney had been granted leave from the service in order to assist Palmerston in his election campaign; but Palmerston assured them that no impropriety had been committed, and that nothing exceptional had occurred in Osmaney's case.

The local Tories worked hard against Palmerston in South Hampshire, and brought all their influence to bear on the voters. Palmerston thought that he would do better if voting were by secret ballot; but this did not alter his opinion, which he held all his life, that the ballot should not be introduced, for an individual case did not make a bad principle good. He thought that electoral reform had gone quite far enough with the Reform Bill, and was anxious that it should go no further. On the day that he left the Foreign Office he had written to William Temple about his fear that at the general election the candidates would be 'tempted on the hustings to pledge themselves chin-deep to most extravagant measures. Triennial Parliaments, ballot, and universal household suffrage will be the cry on almost every hustings, and no man who does not bid as high as that will have any chance in the great towns. The Tories will be turned out; and then it will be difficult to make a Government which shall be acceptable to the Commons, and shall not at the same time consist of men pledged to all sorts of extreme measures'.

Palmerston, to his great surprise, was defeated in South Hampshire. He had, as always, been very optimistic as to his chances of success; but though he obtained a small majority in the rural districts, he lost in the south coast towns. After the first day's poll, he was 150 votes behind the second Tory candidate; and the final result was that Fleming and Compton, the Tories, were elected with 1,765 and 1,683 votes, whereas Palmerston received only 1,512 votes and Sir George Staunton 1,474. According to Greville, when the Foreign Office clerks heard that Palmerston had been defeated, they wanted to illuminate the Foreign Office, though this was perhaps merely a new version of the old story about the War Office staff wishing to illuminate the War Office when Palmerston resigned in 1828.

Palmerston was the only one of the former Whig ministers who lost his seat, and the Tories were still hopelessly outvoted in the House of Commons. After a number of defeats in the House, Peel resigned in April 1835, and Melbourne formed a government. He had to decide what to do about Palmerston. Palmerston wanted to return to the Foreign Office, and both Melbourne and Lady Cowper were anxious to oblige him; but an influential body of opinion in the Whig leadership did not want him back there. So Melbourne offered him the Colonial Office. Palmerston refused, and said he would take nothing except the Foreign Office. The Austrian and Prussian Ambassadors told Melbourne that relations would be more friendly if Palmerston were not given the Foreign Office; but this only had the effect of annoying Melbourne, and when Metternich heard of what Esterhazy had done, he described it as a great blunder. A rumour spread that Palmerston had been offered, and had accepted, the important post of Ambassador to Paris; but on 26 April Palmerston was appointed Foreign Secretary.

His first business was to find himself a seat in Parliament. On 22 May – nearly four weeks after he took office – Lord Darlington asked Lord John Russell, the Leader of the House of Commons, whether Palmerston was going to be made a peer of the United Kingdom and sent to the House of Lords, as he ought not to continue as Foreign Secretary much longer without a seat in Parliament. Arrangements were in fact already being made for him to become MP for Tiverton in Devonshire. He paid the Whig MP for Tiverton £2,000 to re-sign his seat and in June 1835 he was elected unopposed at the by-election. The by-election cost him £300, so the total costs of his two elections in South Hampshire and Tiverton amounted to £3,700; but he was confident that he could pay all his creditors out of his salary as Foreign Secretary.

Palmerston found that things had changed very little at the Foreign Office during his five months' absence, for Wellington had not made any change in British foreign policy – a fact which Palmerston was to emphasize in the next few years in answer to his Tory critics. In Spain, the civil war was raging, with the Carlists entrenched in the north with the support of the Basque separatists and led by a gifted general, Zumala-carregui; and in Portugal, whose civil war had ended as Spain's began, Queen Maria da Gloria seemed to be firmly established. Pedro had died in September 1834, leaving Marshal Saldanha and the Duke of Palmella as the main sup-ports of the young Queen's Government. In the tussle be-tween Palmerston and the Northern Powers, Portugal was Poland in reverse: Russia, Austria and Prussia could do no more to help their adherents in Portugal than Palmerston could do to help the Poles.

Britain's influence in Portugal was stronger than in any other foreign state. The two countries were tied by treaties going back several centuries; British troops had saved Portu-gal from Napoleon, and from the French and Spanish threat in 1826; and British policy had been decisive in holding Fer-dinand VII in check, and in determining the result of the civil war of 1832–4. Palmerston, with his usual appreciation of the realities of power relationships, exploited his position to the full against the Portuguese. He treated them in a more high-handed way than he treated any other government, and never used such bullying and insolent language to anyone else as he used in his despatches to the Portuguese Foreign Minis-ter. But Portugal never became a British satellite state in the full political sense. Palmerston prevented any other foreign power from supplanting Britain's influence in Portugal; but he

never seriously tried to determine the composition of the Portuguese Government, or to control its internal policy. He abstained from political interference to a much greater extent
than most other governments would have done in similar circumstances. He knew that the British Navy was strong enough
to compel any Portuguese Government to respect the life and
property of British subjects and to pay its British creditors;
so he did not greatly care about the party affiliations or
opinions of the government with which he had to deal.

By 1835, the only power whose influence Palmerston had
to fear in Portugal was France. The Northern Powers had
lost whatever interest they had had in Portugal after the defeat of their favourite, Dom Miguel; but France, the ally
in the Quadruple Alliance, had shown more enthusiasm than
Palmerston for the cause of Maria and Pedro, and was represented in Lisbon by a very active Ambassador, Monsieur
de St. Priest. In May 1835, the Portuguese Foreign Minister,
Moncorvo, went to Paris, and discussed with the French
Government the possibility of a marriage between Queen
Maria and Louis Philippe's son, the Duke of Nemours,
who, having failed to become King of the Belgians, was hoping to become King Consort of Portugal as a consolation
prize. British intelligence learnt what was going on. When
Moncorvo came to London after leaving Paris, Palmerston
had an opportunity not only for an exchange of civilities with
the Foreign Minister, but also for a franker talk with Moncorvo's subordinate, Lavradio, whom Palmerston had met
during his visits to Paris before he became Foreign Secretary.
He told Lavradio that he knew that Moncorvo had gone to
Paris to discuss the Queen's marriage to Nemours. Lavradio
eventually admitted that this was true, but said, as Palmerston
expressed it to Lord Howard de Walden, the British Minister
in Lisbon, 'that the alliance with England is too necessary for
the existence of Portugal to allow any Portuguese government
to risk that alliance by a matrimonial Connection displeasing
to us'.

Palmerston could be as tactful on some occasions as he
could be provocative on others. He told Lavradio 'that I did
not pretend to say that an alliance with England is at all neces-

sary for the political Existence of Portugal. That on the Contrary the alliance between the Two Countries has been founded upon their material interests and on that account it is that the alliance has continued so long. That I did not think that Portugal would be a gainer by transferring to France the connexion which she had hitherto had with England, But that such a transfer must necessarily be the result of a marriage with a French Prince. That one great Reason why Canning had preferred the separation of Brazil from Portugal was, that our engagements with Portugal could not be continued, if Portugal was liable by its connexion with any other state to be thrown into war upon interests and quarrels not really Portuguese. That the same reason applied equally to a connexion with France, and that if such a connexion were established, we should declare our treaties at an end'.

This was enough to end the negotiations for a marriage with Nemours; but Palmerston wished to see Maria safely married, and suggested Prince Ferdinand of Saxe-Coburg-Gotha. Some of the Portuguese ministers would have preferred some other Prince, instead of either Nemours or Ferdinand; but on 18 December 1835, Palmerston told Howard de Walden firmly that 'it is too late now to revert to any other choice than that of P. Cobourg'. Ferdinand and Maria were married in April 1836. Palmerston had thwarted Nemours as effectively in Portugal as in Belgium.

In 1836, British-Portuguese relations deteriorated, as conflict arose on four different questions. The first was the slave trade. By the Treaty of Vienna, Britain had been given the duty by the great powers of suppressing the international slave trade; and the growth of public opinion in Britain in favour of abolition, which led to the abolition of slavery itself in the British dominions in 1833, gave new impetus to the efforts of the British Government to suppress the slave-trading activities of nationals of other countries. Palmerston threw himself into this with great energy, and acquired a reputation of being a great champion of abolition. It was in fact said of him and Brougham, the Lord Chancellor, that they were not quite sane where the sufferings of the black man were concerned. Palmerston's concern for the cause of the black man was not only of much more recent origin than Brougham's, but even now was more pronounced when it came to suppressing the slave trade of foreign nations than abolishing slavery in the British dominions. As late as 1830 he voted against Brougham's motion in the House of Commons for the immediate abolition of slavery.

When slavery was abolished in 1833, Parliament substituted a system of apprenticeship, which, while relieving the blacks from some of the worst incidents of slavery, compelled the former slaves to work for their former masters, and punished them for absenteeism and other offences by flogging and imprisonment. Soon the abolitionists in Britain discovered that the number of floggings of negroes had greatly increased since the abolition of slavery, and that in other ways their condition was worse than before. In March 1838, the abolitionists moved a resolution in the House of Commons urging that the apprenticeship system, which was due to continue until 1840, should be ended immediately; but Palmerston and the majority of members voted against the resolution. Palmerston also voted against a resolution prohibiting the flogging of apprentices without an order of a magistrate, which was likewise defeated. Six weeks later, a resolution calling for the immediate ending of the apprenticeship system was passed by a majority of three in a depleted House of Commons. This resolution was rescinded a week later by another resolution which Palmerston supported; but the news of the earlier resolution had already reached the West Indies, and as the apprentices thereupon refused to work, the colonial legislatures reluctantly enacted a bill to abolish apprenticeship after 1 August 1838. Palmerston was criticized for his voting record on negro apprenticeship by some of his Liberal supporters at Tiverton during the general election of 1841. He justified it by the argument that the Government could not break faith with the slave-owners, who had been promised that they should have the apprenticeship system at the time of the abolition of slavery in 1833.

But no abolitionist could quarrel with the zeal that Palmerston showed in suppressing the international slave trade. He denounced the horrors of the passage and the cruelty of the slavers in his speeches in the House. British ships patrolled the west coast of Africa to prevent the traders from carrying their human cargo to Brazil, to the Spanish colony of Cuba, and above all to the slave states of the USA. Palmerston was restrained only by his respect for international law. The British Navy could not stop and search a ship which was flying the flag of a foreign nation without the permission of that nation; so Palmerston tried to negotiate treaties with all foreign governments giving the mutual right of search of each other's ships to the navies of both nations. As British traders no longer engaged in the slave trade, which was severely punishable under British law, and as the British Navy was the only one which was active in suppressing the slave trade, this face-saving formula in fact meant that British ships would have the right to search the foreign ships. France, Holland, Denmark, Sweden and Spain were prepared to grant the right, and signed treaties of mutual right of search with Britain; but Portugal and the United States were not, and made various objections to negotiating a treaty with Palmerston. In Portugal, the more idealistic Liberals were in favour of banning the slave trade; but the slave-trading lobby opposed this strongly, and worked up feelings of patriotic resentment against Palmerston's attempts to bully their Government and subject Portuguese crews to the indignity of being searched on the high seas by foreign warships. The result was that the Portuguese Liberal Government opposed the slave trade in theory, but not in practice.

The second cause of dispute with Portugal was over the Portuguese commercial policy. Palmerston objected to the Portuguese tariffs against British goods, and put pressure on the Portuguese Government to negotiate a commercial treaty. 'It rests with the Portuguese Government', he wrote to Howard on 25 April 1836, 'to make their own Decision on this Matter, but Your Lordship will distinctly and most unequivocally declare to that Government that the Political relations of the Two Countries are inseparably connected with Commercial Intercourse, and that if Portugal should determine to put an end to the latter it must not be surprized if Great Britain should become extremely indifferent to the former. Political Connections between Governments are neither useful nor lasting, unless they are rooted in the Sentiments and Sympathies of Nations; and it is only by extensive Commercial Intercourse that a Community of Interests can be permanently established between the People of different Countries'.

As always, he demanded no special privileges for British traders, but only free trade and a treaty with 'the most favoured nation' clause, under which no other nations' traders would be granted any privileges which British traders did not enjoy. This was all that British exporters needed, for British goods were of such good quality, and so cheap, and the reputation of British business for reliability and performance of contracts was so high, that Britain could always hold her own in international trade unless discriminated against by foreign tariffs. Palmerston strongly favoured free trade. For political reasons, neither he nor the Whig Government had so far ventured to urge the repeal of the Corn Laws, which restricted the import of foreign corn into Britain; but he worked as far as possible for tariff reductions, and was always reluctant to yield to the clamour in the House of Commons for the Government to impose retaliatory tariffs against states which maintained tariffs against British goods. On the other hand, he insisted that foreign powers should strictly adhere to their commercial treaties with Britain; however old such treaties might be, he felt that they gave him the legal right to enforce Britain's demand by the threat, and ultimately by the use, of force.

Another cause of friction arose from the legal privileges of British subjects in Portugal. After the overthrow of Miguel the new régime, under popular pressure, was eager to abolish the right of Englishmen to be tried in the Court of the Judge Conservator. Palmerston agreed, in principle, that such privileges were undesirable, because they tended to create ill-will; but he never gave anything vital away if he could avoid it, and was only prepared to agree to the Portuguese alternative of a jury composed of six British and six Portuguese jurors, on condition that the jury was required to be unanimous. 'If a bare Majority are enough', he wrote to Howard on 14

December 1835, 'then six Portuguese and one spiteful Englishman might condemn one of our People against five honest Men'. Palmerston never missed a point of detail.

But the chief cause of dispute was, as usual, over debts due to British subjects. The Portuguese finances were in a bad state, owing to the civil war and general administrative incompetence; but Palmerston would accept no excuses, and whenever he had international law on his side, pressed the British case like the most ruthless debt-collector or solicitor. He demanded payment of the debts due to British officers who had claims for wages and pensions for their services to Portugal during the Peninsular War twenty-five years before, to the British sailors who had fought for Pedro under Sartorius and Napier, and for compensation for losses suffered by British subjects during the civil war. This last demand was resented by the Portuguese, for Palmerston asked for compensation for British property which had been destroyed by the military operations of either side, and for the sufferings of Englishmen who had been arrested or maltreated by Miguel's police. He always insisted that any government in a country was liable for all the debts and misdeeds of former governments, whatever the political differences between them and their predecessors, and whatever changes of régime had occurred in the meantime.

The cases that caused most ill-feeling were those of Wellington and Lord Beresford, who had been granted the rank of Marshals in the Portuguese Army, and large grants of lands and pensions by Juan VI for their services to Portugal in the Peninsular War. The Portuguese Radicals did not relish the idea of paying large sums of money, in the impoverished state of Portugal, to a very wealthy English Tory like Wellington, whose vast income had often been adversely commented upon by English Radical writers like Byron, or to Beresford, who had suppressed a democratic rising in Portugal for Juan VI in 1817, and had been dismissed from the Portuguese service after a successful revolution two years later. They were particularly angry because Wellington and Beresford had both made frequent speeches in the House of Lords, supporting Miguel and attacking Pedro and the new régime in Portugal.

But Palmerston insisted that the pensions should be paid. 'My dear Howard', he wrote in a private letter on 20 February 1836, 'make Soulé understand that we shall not allow the Portuguese Government to break faith with British officers who have performed useful and distinguished services to Portugal, merely because in their character as English Politicians They may afterwards have espoused the cause opposed to that of the Queen. Wellington and Beresford owe no allegiance to Portugal, and their Pensions were not coupled with engagements of Fealty to the Portuguese Crown'. But the pensions remained unpaid, the slave-trade treaty remained unsigned, and anti-British feelings rose in Portugal. 'My dear Palmerston', wrote Howard on 23 January 1836, 'what are we to do to keep these fellows in order?"

In September 1836, a Left-wing revolt broke out in Lisbon, when King Ferdinand and his German adviser, Dietz, tried to ban a Radical demonstration. Howard offered to land a detachment of marines from a British warship to protect the palace and to receive the Queen on board if she wished to leave the country; but to his disappointment she agreed to accept a democratic Government and proclaim the democratic Constitution of 1822, though she made a secret declaration to the diplomatic corps that she had done this under duress. After their September coup, the democratic party became known as the Septembrists; their opponents, the Right-wing Liberals, were called the Chartists, because they stood for the Charter of 1826 with its restricted franchise against the democratic Constitution of 1822. Lord Howard de Walden wanted Britain to intervene by force to overthrow the Septembrist Government and replace the Chartists in power; but Palmerston was much more cautious. He received a stream of letters from Howard and from his nephew Stephen Sulivan – the son of his old friend and of his sister Elizabeth – for whom he had found a place in the Legation in Lisbon. Howard and Sulivan told Palmerston about the iniquities of the Democrats and Red Republicans who now ruled Portugal; but Palmerston took it much more calmly than his envoys.

'This is a very unfortunate thing', he wrote to Howard on 19 September, 'but there is no help for it.... As far as we are concerned this Revolution makes no Material Change in our Relations with Portugal. Our Treaties remain unaltered by it. In fact it is one of those Internal or if you wish infernal Changes which happen in friendly Countries and with which we do not meddle'. He said that Howard had done right in offering protection to the Queen on a British ship, but he was glad that she had not accepted, as it might have been taken as an abdication 'as in the case of our James 2nd'. Twelve days later he wrote to Howard: 'As to any assistance which we can give, you know that sending troops is out of the question'. He did, however, send two more warships and more marines to the Tagus, raising the British strength there to six ships and 900 marines, and gave Admiral Gage some discretion as to how he used them. 'Of course he must protect the Person of the Queen', he told Howard, 'and if in order to do so, in a Case of real necessity, it should be requisite to put any men on shore, why all I can say is, that he must *take care to succeed*'.

Palmerston was under strong pressure from many quarters to do more than this to help the Queen. Howard assured him that all men of property were for the Queen, and that only 'the rabble' supported the new Government, and asked permission to announce that any restraint on the Queen's person or threat to her safety would be instantly answered by the King of England with 'assistance, and to the extent if required of war'. Palmerston fully supported Howard in this, but he would not sanction any action to overthrow the democratic Government of Portugal. King Leopold of the Belgians, who was on a visit to England, was alarmed at the danger to his nephew Ferdinand, and when he met Palmerston at Windsor he suggested that two thousand Belgian troops should be sent to protect him. But Palmerston thought that 'the Reaction ought to be brought about by the Portuguese themselves'. When, to his disappointment, the Portuguese Army declared for the Constitution of 1822, he decided that nothing could be done. 'It seems to me', he wrote to Howard on 13 October 1836, 'that unless the Queen should find a sufficiently strong Physical Support from a Body of armed Portuguese, whether Troops of the line or National Guard to give a fair Prospect of succeeding in an attempt at Counter Revolution, The wisest Course for her to pursue is to let Things go on quietly; to endeavour to moderate and restrain the Party now in Power, and to lie in wait for better Times. As to sending a Belgian Force to conquer Portugal that is wholly out of the Question. There are twenty Impossibilities which would prevent the Execution of such a Plan'. He was ready to send the Marines to protect the Queen if she wished, but he hoped that she would not be in a hurry to accept his offer. 'She had better by far make the best of Things as they are and wait till the Tide turns. The moment she threw Herself upon us for Protection unless to defend her against actual or threatened attack, from that moment she would cease to be Queen of Portugal: because all Parties would then turn against her and our force would be too weak to keep her on the Throne and could only be strong enough to bring her away. If we had Clinton's Division of 6,000 men at Lisbon Things would be different, but we have no Chance of being able to send Troops; and our Ships and Marines are all we can afford to give'.

Two days later, Palmerston was almost induced to change his mind by that persuasive dare-devil, Captain Napier. Napier called at the Foreign Office and assured Palmerston that from his experience of affairs in Portugal he was certain that he could carry out a rapid and successful coup d'état against the Septembrists without the help of any other force than the British ships in the Tagus and a few of his friends in Lisbon. 'I am half disposed to believe him', wrote Palmerston to Howard, 'think this over, and let me know what you think of it; but do not mention the Idea to any other human being, because if it is not done, nobody should know it was thought of; and if it is done its success would depend upon previous secrecy'.

Before Napier's scheme could materialize, the Portuguese Chartists made their own attempt at a counter-revolution at Belem. It failed, and Palmerston told Howard of his disgust 'at this stupid foolish cowardly attempt at a counter revolution. People who deal in revolutions should have either force enough or courage enough; Force may do with little courage, or courage may do with little force; but those who are wanting in both had better remain quiet.... The Queen having foolishly played her hand she must abide by the chance of the game and pay her stake, and she ought to abandon and discourage any further attempt at violent Measures with a view to changes of Ministers or institutions. She must now make all her efforts by legal means, and endeavour to make the best of a very bad bargain'.

Palmerston's attitude to the revolution of September 1836 is very revealing of his character. It shows his anti-democratic sympathies, his relative indifference to the form of government in foreign countries, his caution and his shrewd appreciation of the realities of the situation, and his cheerful optimism. When all his advisers were getting excited about the spread of Anarchism, Palmerston was sure that everything would turn out all right. His optimism was justified. Before the end of the year the Septembrists were quarrelling among themselves, and the Clubs in Lisbon and Oporto were accusing the Septembrist ministers of betraying the revolution. 'I am glad to hear', wrote Palmerston to Howard on 3 December, 'that Papos and Sà de Bandeira are quarrelling with their Club friends and becoming moderate and monarchical. But so it happens with all men when they get into Power. We were told that Freire and Carvalho were the types of Democracy – When in office they had no fancy for destroying the authority from which They derived their own Power. Next came Papos and Bandeira, the former of whom was the child of many Parents, the creature of all the clubs. He turns out tolerably inoffensive as a Minister. Moncorvo tells me that Papos and Bandeira will soon be obliged to resign and fly and that Barristo Feio and men of his stamp will succeed to office; well, if They do, we shall only see another conversion, and Feio will probably try to fill his pockets as fast as he can, and to maintain the monarchy till he has done so to his satisfaction, which would be giving the monarchy a longish lease'.

But Palmerston was not prepared to tolerate the slightest interference with British rights. When the democratic Government of Portugal, under strong pressure from the Clubs, announced that it would comply with the new Constitution by prohibiting the grant of privileges to foreign nationals,

Palmerston informed the Portuguese Government that Britain 'will not permit the Rights and Privileges of British Subjects to be violated with Impunity'. Arguments about the Portuguese Constitution did not interest him at all, any more than did the objection of the Portuguese Democrats to be made responsible for debts and misdeeds of the Chartist and Miguelite régimes. 'His Majesty's Government can enter into no Distinctions', he wrote on 13 May 1837, 'with Regard to the Character of the Portuguese Authorities by whom those Treaties may be violated. The Portuguese Nation is bound by the engagements which it has in former Times Contracted, and the Portuguese Nation will be held answerable for any violation of these Contracts'. When the Portuguese Government, having argued that it was prevented by the Portuguese Constitution from paying Wellington's pension, eventually offered in 1839 to ask the Cortes for power to pay part of the pension, Palmerston was not impressed. He directed Howard to tell the Portuguese Government 'that it is a matter of entire indifference to Her Majesty's Government whether the Cortes do or do not sanction the payment of the sums due to the Duke of Wellington and to Lord Beresford and to other British Subjects, because the British Government holds the Portuguese nation responsible for the full and honest payment of these sums and will know how to enforce that Payment if it shall be refused either by the Executive Government or by the Cortes'.

In September 1837, the Chartist Generals organized a counter-revolution in the provinces against the Septembrist Government in Lisbon, and civil war broke out. Palmerston would not assist the counter-revolutionary forces, but was quite prepared to administer as many pinpricks as possible to the Democrats. As soon as the counter-revolution broke out, the Government suppressed the Opposition newspapers, including the British community's English newspaper, the *Lisbon Mail*. On 9 September, Palmerston informed the Portuguese Foreign Minister 'that the Portuguese Government must be held responsible for any Insults or Injuries which may be suffered by Her Majesty's Subjects in Portugal in consequence of the Calumnies which are daily circulated by

Papers published under the sanction of that Government while the freedom of the Press is suspended and which are directly calculated to excite unfounded and unjust Hostility on the Part of the Portuguese against England and British Residents in Portugal'.

A fortnight later, he explained at greater length his attitude towards anti-British propaganda in foreign newspapers. In a country where freedom of the press was permitted, Palmerston would not object to attacks on Britain, because the British Government could defend itself by inserting articles in other newspapers, or by publishing its own newspapers in the country in question; but if a Government did not permit freedom of the press, it must be held responsible for anything which was permitted to appear in its newspapers. The Portuguese Government permitted violent anti-British propaganda in the press, and when Palmerston asked them to permit the publication of the *Lisbon Mail*, replied by stating that the press in England was as free to attack Portugal as the Portuguese press was to attack Britain. This did not satisfy Palmerston. If the Portuguese Government had allowed the *Lisbon Mail* to appear, 'the Editors of that Newspaper would have had the means of vindicating their Country and their Countrymen; and Her Majesty's Government would have had no Ground for making any Representation to the Government of Portugal'. But as this had not been permitted, 'it now becomes Necessary therefore for Her Majesty's Government to call upon that of Portugal no longer to permit its own organs to continue their present System of libels upon England', and to insist that henceforward 'nothing in the slightest Degree offensive or disrespectful to the British Nation or hostile to British Interests will appear in any Newspaper published in Portugal'.

But the attacks on Britain in the Portuguese press continued, and a few weeks later, General das Antas, the Commander-in-Chief of the Portuguese Government's forces, issued an order of the day in which he blamed Britain for inciting the Chartist counter-revolution, and denounced the 'infamous' policy of the British Government. King Ferdinand and Dietz sent a secret message to Palmerston, urging him to make the most of this incident in order to embarrass and humiliate the democratic government, and Palmerston demanded an apology in the strongest terms. The Portuguese Government made Antas write a letter of apology, but Howard returned it as not being a sufficiently ample apology. Antas then wrote a fuller apology, which Howard sent on to Palmerston. Palmerston after threatening to blockade Lisbon unless Antas was dismissed from his post, told the Portuguese Foreign Minister that though 'this Apology falls short of that Satisfaction which the British Government is entitled to demand and which it would be justified in resorting (if necessary) to force, in order to exact, for so flagrant an affront offered to it by a responsible officer acting under the orders and actually in the Employment of a Foreign Power', he was nevertheless prepared to accept the apology, and regard the incident as closed.

Palmerston had conceived the idea of turning Portugal's difficulties to good account by acquiring Goa for British India. In 1835, the East India Company had notified him that they would like to purchase Goa from Portugal, and he had sounded the Portuguese Government about it. The offer was refused, though Howard thought that the Portuguese had acted purely out of national pride, as Goa was of no value to Portugal. In March 1839, Palmerston began to pile on the pressure. He protested to Portugal against the fact that rebel tribes in British India were using Goa as a base for their operations, and argued that if these activities continued to be tolerated in Goa, Britain would be justified in invading Goa and annexing it to British India; but at the same time he renewed his offer to buy Goa and all the other Portuguese colonies in India and the East Indies for £500,000, deducting from the purchase price the sums owed by Portugal to all her British creditors – Wellington and Beresford, Napier's volunteers, and the victims of Miguel's tyranny and of war damage. Meanwhile he pressed his demands more strenuously than ever, insisting on five per cent interest on the arrears in payment of Wellington's pension, and refusing all offers of compromise, even though the payment of interest was prohibited, as usury, under Portuguese law. He insisted on payment of all debts, in full, with interest, to the last penny.

The democratic sentiments of the Portuguese Septembrists

had led them to pass a law prohibiting the slave trade within a few months of coming to power. But thanks to the inefficiency and corruption of their leaders, no attempt was made to enforce the law, and the trade continued unchecked under the Portuguese flag. The Septembrists were no more ready than the Chartist Government to sign a treaty with Britain providing for the right of mutual search; and Palmerston eventually decided, under pressure from the abolitionists in Britain, that the British Navy should act without the consent of the Portuguese Government. He introduced a bill in Parliament which gave the Government power to direct the Navy to stop and search Portuguese ships on the high seas, and seize any which were found to be carrying slaves. The ships were to be confiscated, and compensation paid to their owners. The bill was strongly condemned by Wellington and Londonderry as being a violation of international law and an affront to a foreign nation, and it was thrown out in the House of Lords, to the annoyance of Palmerston, who thought that it would encourage the Portuguese to resist the British Government's demands; but the bill was re-introduced in the next session in a slightly amended form, and passed. This aroused the greatest indignation in Portugal; but Palmerston told the Portuguese Government that if they were dissatisfied they could declare war.

In November 1839, Ferdinand and Dietz engineered a coup d'état in Lisbon which overthrew the democratic government. They acted because they believed that, unless the Septembrists were removed from power immediately, Goa and all the Portuguese possessions in Asia would be seized by Britain. Howard had refused their request that Britain should assist the coup d'état, but told them that they were right in thinking that Portugal could never re-establish friendly relations with Britain as long as the Septembrists remained in office. A Right-wing government was formed under Marshal Saldanha and the Duke of Palmella. Palmerston had more respect for Saldanha and Palmella than for any other Portuguese politician, and he much preferred the Chartists to the Septembrists; but it made very little difference to his attitude about the Portuguese debts.

Palmerston made this clear when, after congratulating Howard for his refusal to play any part in overthrowing the Septembrist Government, he instructed him on 7 December as to the line which he should take about the debts. 'Although Her Majesty's Government must require an early and complete settlement of the various British claims which Portugal has allowed to remain so long unsatisfied, yet undoubtedly Her Majesty's Government would deal with this matter if they should have to treat it with a friendly and honest administration in Portugal in a different manner from that in which they would deal with it if they were treating with an administration whose guiding sentiment was hostility to England and whose determination was to defraud the claimants and to refuse to make any settlement unless compelled to do so by force'. But he said that Portugal's reputation was now so low, because of the behaviour of the Septembrist Government, that Britain would not be satisfied with assurances, but required performance. 'The Portuguese Government should be made clearly to understand that British Claims were not put forward for the purpose of effecting a change of Government at Lisbon but for the purpose of obtaining satisfaction for the claimants, and that consequently although Her Majesty's Government rejoice at the change of Administration which has happened at Lisbon because that change will tend to improve the relations between the Two Countries and to promote the best interests of Portugal herself yet Her Majesty's Government cannot accept that change as an equivalent for the settlement of the Claims'.

The Chartist Government, on coming to power, had hastened to announce that the chief object of its foreign policy was to improve relations with England; but the ministers soon discovered that they were unable to pay their debts. They proposed to Palmerston that Portugal would agree to sign a treaty for the right of mutual search of ships if, in return, Britain would cease to press for immediate payment of the debts. Palmerston rejected the offer out of hand. He pointed out that the British Government now had legal powers, under English law, to stop and search Portuguese ships without the consent of the Portuguese Government, and had the naval power to carry it out. Portugal was therefore offering nothing when they said that they would sign a treaty for mutual search. On 31 January 1840 he wrote to Howard: 'Your Lordship cannot too strongly impress upon the Portuguese Government that the conclusion of a Slave Trade Treaty is a matter which now concerns Portugal only but that the British Claims are a matter upon which Her Majesty's Government cannot admit any further delay. I have to remark to Your Lordship that as yet the new Portuguese Ministry differs from the preceding one in words only; that Her Majesty's Government expects deeds; and that evasion and delay cannot be accepted from Count Villa Real any more than from Baron Ribiera de Sabrosa'.

The Portuguese, playing desperately for time, sent Marshal Saldanha to London to negotiate about payment, and at the same time put forward, for the first time, counter-demands for compensation for damage done to certain factories in Portugal by British troops during the Peninsular War. Palmerston would not even consider these claims. He said that it was strange that they had never been mentioned before, and insisted that Britain was not liable for damage done by British troops in Portugal during operations undertaken for the joint benefit of Britain and Portugal, and that Portugal must pay her debts in full, at once. Any new Portuguese claims against Britain could then be looked into, but he would not discuss them now. The Portuguese protested against the tone of Palmerston's despatches. 'Her Majesty's Government have to observe', replied Palmerston on 8 February 1840, 'that so far from having made those demands in too peremptory a manner as asserted by Count Villa Real, they have on the contrary shown too much forbearance in allowing them to remain unsettled so long'. The Portuguese protest did not cause him to moderate his language. On 4 April he told Howard: 'I have to state that it is quite apparent that there is no use in appealing to the reason, the justice, the good faith or the honour of any Portuguese Minister upon any question whatever and Your Lordship therefore need not discuss these claims any further with Count Villa Real'. He also brought forward a whole batch of new claims against Portugal for losses by Bri-

tish merchants in the Portuguese colonies and at sea through
the misconduct of Portuguese officials, and asked for interest
at five per cent on all the debts which had not been paid on
time.

On 7 March 1840, Palmerston sent a note to the Portuguese
Government, stating that unless he heard from Howard, by
the next packet after Howard received the letter, that Portugal would pay all the debts, with the interest, immediately,
Britain would seize the Portuguese colonies in satisfaction of
the debts. To Palmerston's great annoyance, Howard refused to present the note. 'I have to express my hope', Palmerston told him, 'that Your Lordship will not again embarrass
Her Majesty's Service by a similar neglect of the Instructions
which you may receive from me'. He later accepted Howard's
excuses as satisfactory; but on 18 April he sent another ultimatum to Portugal, saying that if the debts were not paid
within a fortnight, 'Her Majesty's Government will then proceed to take such steps as may appear to them to be most
proper for the purpose of obtaining redress'. But Palmerston
was combining threats in Lisbon with affability in London.
In May he reached agreement about the debts with Saldanha.
Portugal was to pay the private creditors in four instalments
within three years, and its public debt to the British Government within six years. Interest was to be paid; but Lord Beresford's claim was to be reduced by £8,000. 'This is a Relaxation
of our last Terms', wrote Palmerston to Howard, 'and is something for Saldanha to have obtained'.

Chapter Fifteen

The Spanish Civil War

The Governments of the Quadruple Alliance had pledged themselves to ensure the defeat of Don Carlos in Spain. Portugal sent 6,000 troops to help the Isabelinos. Britain and France sent their fleets to the north coast of Spain to give them moral support, and any assistance that might be necessary; but Palmerston did not permit the Navy to engage in direct operations against the Carlists. He disappointed the Spanish Government by refusing to agree to their request, and to the French Government's proposal, that Britain and France should enforce a blockade of Carlist territories and stop ships from bringing arms and other supplies to Carlos's troops. Palmerston had been eager to do this, but was advised by the King's Advocate that it would be illegal under international law. Ships with supplies for Carlos were being fitted out in the ports of Holland and the Italian states, and as the French had closed the land frontier across the Pyrenees to the Carlists, a blockade of the Carlist ports would have rapidly ended the Spanish Civil War; but Palmerston firmly refused to commit a violation of international law which might have involved Britain in incidents with ships of the Northern Powers. He had declared in his maiden speech in Parliament, at the time of the Copenhagen expedition, that international law should only be violated when the survival of Britain was at stake; he was not prepared to break it to ensure the triumph of constitutionalism in Spain. He would not even prohibit Carlos's agents in England from chartering a British ship to carry arms to Carlos, claiming that the Government had no powers under English law to prevent this. On the other hand, he encouraged the French Government to send troops to assist the Isabelinos; but Louis Philippe refused to do so, and declared that the victory of the Government forces in Spain was not worth the life of a single French soldier.

But Palmerston thought out an effective way of helping the Liberal forces in Spain which had the advantage of not costing anything to the British taxpayer. He not only permitted, but gave every encouragement, to British volunteers to go to Spain to fight for the Isabelinos. The volunteers were to be paid by the Spanish Government, at rates of pay negotiated between them. With some difficulty, Palmerston persuaded the Cabinet and William IV to agree to the scheme, to pass the necessary legislation to amend the Foreign Enlistment Acts, and to give facilities for recruiting officers for the Spanish Government to visit army and naval barracks in Britain. Any British officer who wished to volunteer was given assurances that his pension and promotion prospects in the British service would not be endangered. The British Legion was placed under the command of Colonel de Lacy Evans, the Radical MP for Westminster. Palmerston himself chose Evans for the post, because he thought that 'it is only men of ardent minds who are fit for difficult enterprises'; though afterwards, when he realized how much William IV and the British Tories disliked Evans and the Legion, he thought it might have been wiser to have allowed the Horse Guards to choose the Legion commander. Only a minority of Evans's men were inspired by the revolutionary enthusiasm which moved their successors, a hundred years later, to participate in another Spanish Civil War. Many of the volunteers were poverty-stricken Irish labourers, who were encouraged to join by the prospect of pay and plunder, as well as by the passionate exhortations of O'Connell.

Palmerston gave his full support to the British Legion in Spain, and helped them as much as he could without charging the British tax-payer. He defended them in Parliament from the attacks of Londonderry and Lord Aberdeen and other Tories, who strongly disapproved of sending British subjects to fight as mercenaries abroad, and who denounced the men of the Legion as the lowest dregs of the population. Lord Mahon, opening a debate in the House of Commons on 24 June 1835, 'thanked God our people were not Swiss' who fought as mercenaries in other people's quarrels. Palmerston, in reply, said that the volunteers were 'brave and honourable men', and asked Mahon if he would 'not conceive that some other motive might lead Englishmen to fight under the banners of a constitutional sovereign except the lucre of pay'.

Palmerston took up their cause with the Spanish Government. He treated their claim for pay from the Spanish Government as a debt owing to British subjects and safeguarded by treaty, and therefore pursued it with the usual vigour that he showed in protecting the just rights of British subjects against foreign governments. He followed their military operations with great interest, and when Evans complained that his men in the Legion were not being given adequate support at the siege of San Sebastian by the Spanish units in the Government armies, Palmerston urged the Spanish Government to be more vigorous in their prosecution of the war, and gave them advice as to the military measures which could be taken to relieve the danger which threatened the British Legion before San Sebastian. But he was insistent that the Legion was a Spanish, not a British, liability. When a ship carrying soldiers of the Legion was forced to take refuge in the port of Lorient, Palmerston refused to pay the French Government for the cost of their keep in France, as he claimed that they were in the employ of the Spanish Government.

To send Liberal idealists and hungry Irish labourers as volunteers was the cheapest way of helping the cause of Liberalism in Spain, and Palmerston was determined that the British tax-payer and business man should gain, not lose, from the transaction. He virtually forced the Spanish Government to place the contract for supplying the equipment to the Legion with a British firm; he pestered them continually for payment of the wages of the volunteers and for the arms supplied by Britain to the British Legion and to the native units in the Spanish Government army; and he used the services of the Legion, the supply of arms, and the limited assistance given by the Navy, as a lever to extort the payment of Spain's debt to British creditors and in his negotiations for a trade agreement with the Spanish Government.

In 1835, the Queen Regent appointed Mendizabal as her

Minister of Finance. He was a middle-class Jewish financier of great ability, who had just arrived from England, where he had lived as a refugee in the days of Ferdinand VII. He was politically Left-of-Centre in the Liberal Party. Palmerston approved of Mendizabal. He always tended to like Jews, for with his tolerant attitude in religious matters he did not share the religious anti-Semitism which was strong among ardent Roman Catholics and Anglicans, and the Jewish qualities of business energy and individual self-help appealed to Palmerston. The British Minister at Madrid, George Villiers, afterwards Earl of Clarendon, was disturbed at Mendizabal's tolerance of stockjobbers and financial adventurers; but Palmerston was sure that he was the only able politician in Spain, and much the best Prime Minister available – for Mendizabal dominated the Spanish Cabinet under the nominal Premiership of the Count of Toreno. There were other political aspects of the Spanish situation which Palmerston found less satisfactory. The war against the Carlists aroused revolutionary feeling among the working-class population of the towns in Isabelinos territory. Revolutionary organizations demanded more energetic and Radical measures in the struggle against the Church and the peasantry who supported Carlos, and answered the Carlist atrocities with massacres of monks and other acts of revolutionary violence. In the summer of 1835, Barcelona and other towns in the provinces were under the control of self-appointed revolutionary committees. Palmerston and Villiers were alarmed at this development, and used their influence to prevent Mendizabal from introducing the Constitution of 1812, which the Spanish Radicals were demanding. Mendizabal promised that he would not adopt the Constitution of 1812; but under Radical pressure he proposed an electoral franchise which he admitted was 'too democratical', and which Villiers criticized as excluding men of property and including too many others.

The 'mob' demanded that the existing Parliament, which had a moderate Liberal majority, should be dissolved, and in January 1836 Mendizabal agreed to this demand, and dissolved the Cortes, despite the fact that Villiers resorted to what he called pleas and 'even threats' to dissuade him from doing so. Meanwhile the civil war was becoming more and more savage. In the summer of 1835, Don Carlos issued the notorious 'Durango decree' from his headquarters at Durango near Bilbao, in which he announced that he would shoot all foreigners whom he captured fighting for the Government forces; and this decree was carried out against the soldiers of the British Legion who were taken prisoner by the Carlists. In revenge for the cruelties committed by the Carlist General Cabrera, who had shot many Isabelinos prisoners and several Radical Mayors, the Government troops shot Cabrera's mother as a hostage, whereupon Cabrera executed 1,100 prisoners and the wives of four prominent Radicals. Palmerston protested to Carlos against the Durango decree and to Mendizabal against the killing of Cabrera's mother. Mendizabal deplored the fact that she had been executed, but said that public opinion would not permit him to punish the officer responsible. Nor would he agree to a plan put forward by Villiers for the exchange of seventeen Carlist prisoners, which he said would be ascribed by the people to the pressure of some pro-Carlist ladies and gentlemen in London.

The Spanish Civil War split political opinion in Britain. Many of the Tories supported Carlos, and two of their MPs visited his headquarters near Bilbao, where, according to Villiers, 'they were treated like two babies, and sent home to repeat the lesson that has been crammed into them'. In the House of Commons, the Radicals denounced the cruelties of the Carlists, and the Tories the excesses of the revolutionary Spanish Radicals on the Government side. Although the Tories were always ready to complain about any case in which the Spanish Government neglected or illtreated the men of the British Legion, they also denounced the Legion, especially de Lacy Evans, and accused them of committing atrocities in Spain. When Evans returned to England to defend his seat in Parliament at the general election of 1837, he was subjected to the most violent abuse by his Tory opponent at Westminster in an exceptionally bitter campaign. Evans had spoken and voted in the House of Commons in favour of the abolition of flogging in the Army; but the Tories accused him of flogging women in Spain, as well as sending out a reconnoitring party at San Sebastian on a Sunday. Evans reminded the Tories that Wellington had fought the battle of Waterloo on a Sunday.

On 5 February 1836, Mr. Fector, the MP for Dover, opened a debate on Spain, declaring that the Government 'had virtually sent out, by their connivance at a public enlistment, hordes of ruffians from the purlieus of London to wage war against a nation with whom we professed to be at peace. By this act they degraded the character of the British officer and the British soldier'. He was followed by his colleague, Mr. Grove Price, the MP for Sandwich, who excused the atrocities of the Carlists, but condemned those of the Isabelinos as being carried out in 'cold, predetermined and savage imitation of the demon cruelties committed at Nantes under that minister-ial apostle of democracy, Fouché'. He said that Palmerston must be aware that the Isabelinos had shot their wounded prisoners, and had massacred whole villages; but 'notwith-standing all this . . . the noble Viscount had come down, with his bland and dulcet voice, to inform the House of Commons that the prudent and vigorous conduct of the Queen's Govern-ment would soon restore tranquillity to Spain'. Palmerston stoutly defended Evans and the British Legion. He said that he regretted what certain speakers in the debate had said 'with regard to those members of the House who have so nobly, as I contend, volunteered their services in the cause of the Queen of Spain. . . . I think that the honourable and gallant member for Westminster, who is now serving at the head of a large body of our countrymen in Spain, deserves well of his country for having undertaken the service in which he is engaged; and I can assure the honourable member for Sandwich that the hopes and feelings and wishes and prayers of a great por-tion of the people of this country are embarked in the success of his cause'.

But the Radicals were still far from satisfied with Palmer-ston. They defended the actions of the British Legion, but could not defend the policy of the Foreign Secretary. Palmer-ston's policy in Spain, like his policy in Belgium five years earlier, came under fire from both sides. It was not until 19 April 1837 that he at last gained the support of the Radicals.

It was the last day of a four-day debate on Spain in the House of Commons. Roebuck, the Radical MP for Bath, criticized Palmerston for not sending the British Army to help the Isabelinos, and for doing 'neither one thing nor the other'. He also condemned Palmerston for not having spoken in the debate, which had already lasted for three nights. 'The noble Lord seemed to think that there was a sort of bush-fighting going on, and to be afraid lest he should be hit down the moment he ventured to show himself. It was most outrageous that when an important question of foreign policy was before the House the Secretary of Foreign Affairs should so long decline to come forward and let the House understand what it was he proposed to do. Not, for that matter, that he (Mr. Roebuck), even when the noble Lord did enter into his explanations, could very well make out what the explanation was, for the noble Lord had a peculiar faculty of making a long speech without letting the House know in the slightest degree what he was talking about. The noble Lord had almost invariably contrived to wrap up his replies in so peculiar a phraseology as to put in despair all those who sought an elucidation of the mysteries of his foreign policy. There were three nights of the public time wasted in hopeless discussion, solely because the noble Lord had not the courage and the manliness to come forward at once and explain in clear terms what his policy really was.'

Roebuck's resentment was understandable, in view of the great reluctance which Palmerston had always shown, ever since he became Foreign Secretary, to explain anything to the House. But Palmerston remedied this before the night was out. He spoke for three hours, and did not sit down until half past one in the morning. He not only dealt with the events in the Peninsula, but surveyed the whole field of his foreign policy since 1830, laying particular stress on his solution of the Belgian crisis, and the Quadruple Alliance. He characterized the Carlist rising as a fight 'for Carlos and despotism against Isabella and constitutional government', and was loudly cheered by the Radicals. His speech was ably answered by Peel; but the Government had a majority of thirty-six in the division, and all the Radicals voted with them.

For the first time in his life, Palmerston had won the good-will of the Radicals; and Spain was the only place in the world where they had any reason to be satisfied with him. He had given very little help to the cause of freedom in Poland and Italy, and had supported only the most moderate constitutionalism in Germany and Portugal; but in Spain, he championed the forces of Radicalism. He was led against his will into this position by his suspicions of France. In Portugal, Lord Howard de Walden was sure that the French Minister in Lisbon, Bois-le-Comte, was behind the Septembrist revolution; but in Spain the position was reversed. In Portugal, Britain backed the moderate Chartists and France the revolutionary extremists; but in Spain the French supported the Right-wing Liberals against the pro-British Mendizabal, and this drove Palmerston reluctantly to support the Left-wing Spanish Radicals – the Exaltados – in what was the strangest ideological alignment in foreign policy since Cardinal Richelieu supported the German Protestants in the Thirty Years War.

In June 1836 Mendizabal, under pressure from the Radicals, asked the Queen Regent to dismiss some Right-wing officers from the Army. The Queen Regent had come to hate Mendizabal because he had led her to believe that he was in love with her, and then, when she offered herself to him, he drew back and laughed at her. She refused to remove the Right-wing officers, and dismissed Mendizabal; and the Right-wing Isturiz was appointed Premier. Villiers was sure that the French Ambassador had engineered the change of government; but Palmerston, though he was sorry to see Mendizabal go, told Villiers to cultivate friendly relations with Isturiz, not to show any signs of resentment at the change of government, and not to permit this development to upset his amiable relations with the French Minister.

In August, a Radical revolution broke out throughout Isabelinos territory. Next month, two Radical sergeants in the Queen's Guard carried out a military coup d'état at the royal palace at La Granja in the Guadarrama mountains, proclaimed the Constitution of 1812, and installed a new government in place of Isturiz. The French believed that Palmerston and Villiers had instigated the coup. This was quite untrue, but Palmerston was not sorry to see the Radicals in power instead of the French party, though he was eager to prevent the revolutionary spirit from going too far. On 12 September 1836, he instructed Villiers to warn the Spanish Government against revolutionary excesses if they wished to preserve the Anglo-Spanish alliance. 'The objects which Great Britain had in view in entering into that alliance, were to uphold the succession of Queen Isabella to the Throne, and to assist in restoring internal Peace, order and Tranquillity in the whole Peninsula; but not to associate the British Name with acts of Insurrectionary violence; nor to protect and sanction outrage against the Royal family of Spain'. The whole trouble had arisen because the Queen Regent had dismissed Mendizabal. 'His Majesty's Government have long had reason to think that the advice upon which the Queen Regent was acting in the Dismissal of M. Mendizabal, in the Dissolution of the Cortes, and in the system which Her Government has since pursued, was suggested from without, and did not proceed wholly from Spanish Councillors. The present ministers seem to take a more national view of affairs, and to consider it their first and most important Duty to direct the excited Energy and Patriotism of the People to put an end to the Civil War'. Rather than have Spain under a moderate government controlled by his French ally, Palmerston preferred to have a Radical government which was restrained by British pressure. On 31 October he again warned the Spanish Government, more explicitly, that Britain would withdraw from the Quadruple Alliance if murder, rapine and the guillotine were established in Spain.

Having reconciled himself, in the autumn of 1836, to Radical governments in both Spain and Portugal, Palmerston set out to badger the Exaltados Government in Spain, as well as the Septembrist Government in Portugal, into paying their British creditors, without any regard to their internal difficulties, or even to the effect on the Spanish civil war. He refused to assist in the overthrow of the democratic régimes, but saw no reason why he should help them in their troubles at the expense of British subjects. He acted like a zealous solicitor

for his client – the British public – by pressing the debtor all
the harder as he got into greater difficulties, and was particularly anxious to ensure that the French and other creditors
did not get preferential treatment through adopting a tougher
attitude than the British Government. He felt that Britain's
forbearance, and French bullying, would lead foreign governments to think that it was wiser to pay the French, and let
the British cry for their money; and he was determined to
show them that failure to pay the British would lead to consequences just as disastrous as failure to pay the French.

The civil war was placing the greatest strain on Spanish
finances; but the British Government would not help. In
December 1835, Villiers negotiated a trade agreement with
Mendizabel's Government, under which the British Government was to guarantee a loan to Spain in return for the
abolition of Spanish tariffs on British goods. Palmerston,
under instructions from the Cabinet, refused to ratify the
agreement, and firmly rejected Mendizabel's request for a
loan. He persisted in this refusal when the successive Spanish
Governments repeatedly asked him for financial aid. He told
them that if they wanted a loan, they must apply to British
capitalists – the word had not yet acquired a pejorative meaning – but that the British Government would neither guarantee
the loan, nor put any pressure on British capitalists to grant
it; and he added that the best way of persuading the British
investor to trust the Spanish Government with his money
would be to abolish the Spanish tariff. He also discouraged the
French Government from granting or guaranteeing a loan to
Spain, for he did not want the Spaniards to find them more
generous than the British. In 1839, there was a rumour that
France would grant a loan if Spain mortgaged the Philippines
to France. Palmerston advised the Spanish Government to reject the offer. Next summer, he heard that Belgium had made
the same offer to Spain on the security of the Philippines.
Palmerston warned the Spanish Government that the Belgians
were acting as agents for French capitalists, who would thus
get control of the Philippines. The only financial aid which
Palmerston was prepared to give to Spain was to ask Rothschild to lend £5,000 to the Spanish Government to enable

them to pay arrears of wages to the soldiers of the British Legion who had already returned to Britain.

While refusing financial help to Spain, Palmerston pressed harder and harder for payment of the interest owing to the British creditors who had subscribed to the Spanish Government loan in the days of Ferdinand VII in 1823 and 1828. He also pressed, though less insistently, for payment for the supply of arms sent by Britain to the Spanish Government forces during the civil war, for satisfaction of the payments due to the soldiers of the British Legion, and for compensation to British subjects who had been maltreated by Ferdinand's police, or whose property had suffered in the course of military operations in the civil war. By October 1837 he was threatening to withdraw British military aid to Spain if the interest to the bondholders was not paid. At the same time, he insisted on the strict observance of British treaty rights. He insisted that British residents in Spain should be exempted from the forced loan raised for the war, and compelled the Spanish Government to release the horses of British subjects which had been taken when all horses were requisitioned for the war. He warned them that if this 'plundering' of British property in Spain continued, Britain would withdraw from the Quadruple Alliance and seek redress by her own strength. This was at the most critical moment in the civil war, when Don Carlos had advanced to the outskirts of Madrid, and was so near that Villiers could see Cabrera's staff through his telescope.

Relations between Britain and the Spanish Government got worse in the summer of 1838. At the end of March, Palmerston again refused a Spanish request for financial aid. A fortnight later, he heard with indignation that the Spanish troops were preparing to evacuate San Sebastian to the Carlists, and warned them that if they did so, the British fleet would be withdrawn from the north coast of Spain. On 3 May, he asked the Spanish Government for immediate payment of the interest due to the British bondholders of 1823 and 1828, and suggested that the revenues of the Spanish colony of Cuba should be appropriated for this purpose until the debt was paid. On 26 July, he announced that all further military aid to Spain would be suspended until the Spanish Government had paid for the arms already supplied. On 16 August, he suddenly put forward a new demand – that Spain should compensate British subjects for losses suffered when Spain was Napoleon's ally in 1804 and 1805.

Meanwhile another dispute had arisen over the rights of British residents in Bilbao. Bilbao had been the scene of heavy fighting during the previous three years; it had twice been besieged by the Carlists, and twice relieved by the Government armies after actions in which the British Legion had greatly distinguished themselves. By an ancient privilege, certain citizens of Bilbao were exempt from the obligation to pay a particular tax imposed by the Spanish Government. Palmerston demanded that British merchants in Bilbao should also be free from this tax, and based his demand on a clause in the treaty of 1706 by which Englishmen in Spain were not to be placed in a more disadvantageous position than the native Spaniards. When the Spanish Government argued that the treaty did not refer to special privileges held by a limited class of Spaniards, and that all other Spanish subjects, except a small number of Bilbaoans, were liable to the tax, Palmerston insisted that every British subject living in Bilbao should be in as favourable a position as any group of inhabitants of the port. He reminded the Spanish Government that the British Navy was stationed off Bilbao, and threatened to use it to enforce his demand. It is not unusual for allies to quarrel in wartime; but it is not often that a Foreign Secretary has threatened to use armed force against an ally, in the middle of a war, in order to obtain a trivial advantage for a handful of British subjects on the basis of a far-fetched interpretation of a treaty more than a hundred years old.

Meanwhile Palmerston was trying from time to time to mediate between the Spanish Government and the Carlists. Villiers sent an emissary to the Carlist headquarters to attempt to negotiate an armistice, and sometimes tried to arrange an exchange of prisoners. Palmerston also tried, without much success, to mitigate the cruelties committed on both sides. He persuaded Metternich, who supported Carlos, to urge his protégé to tell his Generals to be a little less savage; and Palmerston warned the Spanish Government that British help would be withdrawn if their Generals continued to carry out reprisals against the Carlist sympathizers. Then suddenly the civil war came to an end. Villiers's agent, Lord Edmund Hay, arranged a secret meeting between the Government General, Espartero, and the Carlist General Marota. After lengthy negotiations, the two Generals reached an agreement in August 1839, by which Marota agreed to seize Carlos and hand him over to the Government forces, and to end the war and submit to the Government's authority, on condition that he and his men were granted an amnesty and employment in the Spanish Army with the same rank that they had held in the Carlist forces. Carlos escaped to France, where he was interned by the authorities, and eventually allowed to go to Austria.

This made Espartero the hero of the nation, and soon his portrait was hanging in every cottage, and adorning every packet of the most popular brand of cigars. He joined the extreme Radical Party, was immediately chosen as its leader, and mobbed by the people of Madrid whenever he appeared at the opera or in the streets. The Queen Regent was forced to accept him as Prime Minister, and granted him the superb title of Duke of the Victory. When she tried to replace him with a Right-wing Liberal Premier, a revolt broke out in Barcelona, and in October 1840 the Queen Regent fled to France, and Espartero became Regent for the infant Queen. The French believed that Palmerston and Villiers were plotting every move that Espartero made; but in fact, both of them regretted the flight of the Queen Regent, which weakened the royal authority in Spain, sowed the seeds of fresh conflict there, embittered relations between Britain and France, and compelled Britain to rely on the extremist Exaltados in Spain.

The political developments in Spain were far from pleasing to Palmerston. The mutiny of La Granja, the democratic Constitution of 1837, and the coming to power of Espartero and the Exaltados, offended all his political sympathies; but it was better than having a French puppet government in Spain. With his usual ability to believe what he wanted to believe, he reconciled himself to the situation by propounding the theory that there was something peculiar in the Spanish character which made democracy a suitable form of government for Spain, alone among all countries in Europe. He put forward this view in a despatch to Prussia on 4 December 1840. 'The Prussian Court no doubt disapproves of the political principles upon which the present order of things in Spain is founded; and perhaps even Her Majesty's Government may think some parts of the Constitution of 1837 different from that which according to the notions and experience of affairs in England would seem to be the best. But each Nation has its peculiar character and what may be objectionable for one may be without inconvenience for another. There seems in fact reason to believe that there is something in the character of the Spanish Nation which enables them to bear without anarchy or derangement of the social system domestic institutions which carry political power lower down in the scale of 'society than could safely be done in many other countries. At all events the Constitution of 1837 is now established and cannot be overthrown without force and convulsion; and the Majority of the Nation seem to be attached to it and averse to any change'.

Palmerston was quite prepared to have Espartero as the ruler of Spain provided that he paid his debts. A few weeks before the end of the civil war, Palmerston threatened to seize Cuba and the other Spanish colonies if the bondholders of 1823 and 1828 were not paid immediately. The Spanish Government played for time. They sent delegates to London to negotiate the details of payment; but when they arrived, they informed Palmerston that they had no authority to act. Palmerston did nothing for another two years, during which time he continued, on the one hand, to threaten the Spanish Government, and on the other to assure the indignant MPs in the House of Commons that he was sure that Spain would honour its obligations and that all outstanding questions would soon be satisfactorily settled in the most friendly manner. He did not give the slightest hint in public of the menacing tone in which he was addressing the Spanish Government, and many people in Britain thought that he was doing nothing at all for the British bondholders.

On 5 April 1841, he told the Spanish Government that 'Her Majesty's Government now for the last time' demanded payment to the British creditors, and that if 'Spain shall not immediately and without any further delay whatever, comply with this Demand, the British Government must resort to other means to obtain justice'. The Spanish Government declared that they had no money to pay, pointing out that the salaries of their civil servants were more than a month in arrears, and offered to cede the islands of Fernando Po and Annobon in the Gulf of Guinea to Britain in discharge of the debts. Palmerston accepted the offer, and the Spanish Government introduced a bill in the Cortes to cede the territory; but a wave of patriotic indignation swept through Parliament and the press, and the Cortes threw out the bill. Palmerston accepted the situation without even a protest. On 2 September 1841, he told the Spanish Government that he regretted that the bill had been defeated, but realized that the Spanish Government had tried most honourably to fulfil their undertaking in the matter, and asked them to put forward new proposals for settling the debts. Next day Palmerston resigned as Foreign Secretary, and bequeathed his debt-collecting duties to his Tory successor, Lord Aberdeen.

During his last winter at the Foreign Office, Palmerston was able to demonstrate the extent of British influence in the Iberian Peninsula. By the autumn of 1840 both Spain and Portugal were quiet at last for the first time for more than a decade, with Spain settling down under a Radical, and Portugal under a Liberal-Conservative, government. They thereupon began a dispute with each other which nearly led to war. Spain accused Portugal of violating Spanish treaty-rights in the River Douro, Espartero made provocative speeches, and Spanish troops were massed on the frontier. Portugal appealed to Palmerston for help under the Anglo-Portuguese treaty. Palmerston was quite happy about the situation. 'I do not apprehend any serious annoyance to Portugal from Spain', he wrote to Howard on 5 December 1840, 'and it is not amiss that the Portuguese should be a little frightened and should be brought to remember their political Connexion with England'. He warned Spain that if Spanish troops invaded Portugal, Britain would be forced to go to war on the Portuguese side, and urged Espartero to do nothing to encourage the Septembrists in Portugal who, as the Spanish-Portuguese dispute developed, had appealed for help to the Radical Government of Spain; and he offered to mediate between Spain and Portugal. He then made the Portuguese yield to nearly all the Spanish demands. The Portuguese forgot all their recent resentments against Palmerston, and offered him the Grand Cross of the Order of the Tower and Sword for his services in saving Portugal from Spanish invasion – an offer which he could not, of course, accept, owing to the rule which restricted British subjects from accepting foreign decorations; and Espartero was perfectly satisfied at having obtained nearly all that he had wanted. But the quarrels of the last few years had left a strong undercurrent of resentment against Britain in Spain, as Palmerston was to find when he returned to the Foreign Office in 1846.

Chapter Sixteen

Mehemet Ali: The Crisis of 1839

The crisis in the Middle East – which was then called the Levant – in 1839–41 produced a diplomatic success for Palmerston which has been generally regarded, both by his contemporaries and by historians, as the greatest triumph of his career. He sent British troops to intervene by force in the internal troubles of the Turkish Empire – a course which he had always refused to adopt in Spain or Portugal or anywhere else – and by this use of force, and by his diplomatic activity, he bolstered up for another eighty years a régime which could not have survived without his support. He also successfully accomplished a complete volte-face in British foreign policy by breaking the alliance with France, and aligning Britain with the autocratic Northern Powers. But he did not set out with any intention of doing either of these things. He played the whole game by ear, allowed events to take their own course, and then intervened decisively at the right moment with the object of obtaining the maximum possible advantage for Britain from a complex international situation.

The events of 1833 had left Mehemet Ali as ruler of Egypt, Syria and Crete, and Russia as the sole effective protector of the Sultan. This was a very undesirable state of affairs from Britain's point of view. Britain wished to have a powerful Turkish Empire as a bulwark against Russian expansion into Asia and India; instead, she now had half this Empire controlled by a rebel at Alexandria, and the other, and the central government, by the Russian Ambassador at Constantinople. Palmerston had no plan for remedying the situation, and for six years did nothing but wait for the situation to develop. In the end, the development benefited him and Britain more than anyone else.

In later years, it was natural that Palmerston's actions in 1840 should have been seen in the light of his policy at the time of the Crimean War. His admirers of a later generation, who had been brought up to regard him as the leader of the national resistance to Russia, thought that his object, in the days of Mehemet Ali, was to prevent the disintegration of the Turkish Empire in order to preserve it as a check to Russia. If this had been Palmerston's only object, he could have achieved it best by allying himself with Mehemet Ali against Russia. The Russian presence at Constantinople had aroused patriotic and religious resentment in Turkey, and many Turks regarded the Viceroy of Egypt as the only leader who could deliver them from the oppression of the foreign infidel. Mehemet Ali thought that Russia was his greatest enemy, and directed his propaganda against her.

In June 1833, Mehemet Ali proposed an anti-Russian alliance to Palmerston. He said that if the British Navy would prevent Russia from breaking out into the Baltic, he could handle the Russians in Turkey. Palmerston politely declined the offer. When rumours of Mehemet Ali's proposal leaked out, and the question was raised in the House of Commons, Palmerston refused to admit that any such offer had been made, but said that the British Government could never make an alliance with a ruler who was a vassal of the Sultan and not a sovereign power. This answer displeased the anti-Russian MPs who were indignant that Palmerston refused to condemn Russian policy in Turkey, or to admit that he was displeased with the Treaty of Unkiar Skelessi. They accused him of appeasement towards Russia. 'Two years ago', said Attwood, 'if this country had held up its finger, Poland would have been saved; and six months ago, if it had held up its finger, Constantinople would have been saved too; but now it might cost hundreds of millions to save Constantinople, unless indeed we were prepared to surrender the Thames to the Russians'.

But Palmerston, unlike the Radicals, was not looking for excuses to go to war with Russia in order to be able to liberate the Poles and other victims of Russian oppression. He wished, on the contrary, to maintain a strong Turkey so that it would deter Russia from embarking on ventures which might involve her in war, and would induce the Tsar to pursue a policy which would be compatible with British interests. He was suspicious of Russia, but wished to avoid a direct confrontation with her; and he knew that if he backed Mehemet Ali, he would come face to face with Russia across the corpse of the Turkish Empire. There were also ideological factors involved. Sultan Mahmud was a sovereign, and Mehemet Ali was a rebel, and this was a very important consideration, not only with the Tsar, but also with Metternich. Austria was suspicious of Russian designs in Turkey and the Balkans, but was too strongly influenced by the principles of the Holy Alliance to feel justified in opposing the Tsar's attempts to maintain the Sultan against his rebel subject. Palmerston, too, preferred a hereditary monarch to an upstart usurper; but in his case this was not a very important factor. Though he once referred to Mehemet Ali contemptuously as a former 'waiter at a coffee shop', he was always prepared to support a self-made military adventurer if British interests required it, as he showed in the case of Espartero in Spain and Milosh in Serbia. But Palmerston did not want a war with Russia, and still less with Russia and Austria together. There was also the fact that France, who had alarmed the British Government by seizing Algeria in 1829, might be tempted to expand eastwards along the North African coast if the Turkish Empire foundered. Palmerston's chief object in wishing to preserve the Turkish Empire in 1840 was not to stop Russian expansion, but because he feared that the collapse of Turkey would lead to a scramble for the pieces which would trigger off a major European war.

There was another factor which influenced Palmerston's attitude to Mehemet Ali. It was useful for Britain that there should be one central authority ruling over the Turkish Empire, even if that authority was only nominal. When British engineers wished to explore the possibilities of erecting a telegraph line across Syria and Arabia to India, when British traders wished to develop contacts with Abyssinia at Massowah, when British missionaries, archaeologists and other travellers wished to venture into Palestine, Tunisia or Serbia, the Ambassador at Constantinople could obtain permission from the Government of the Porte without having to ask the consent of local chiefs. Once Palmerston had obtained the Sultan's authority, the British Navy could compel the provincial Pashas and local chieftains to obey it without transgressing any rule of international law. But permission and authority might be harder to obtain if Mehemet Ali were either the sovereign of an independent Egypt, or installed at Constantinople as the Sultan's Grand Vizier and de facto ruler of the whole Ottoman Empire.

Palmerston strongly objected to the economic system which Mehemet Ali had imposed in his territories. It was a kind of simple State Socialism. Mehemet Ali granted monopolies of production and trade in various commodities to government agencies, in which he and his family, and his subordinate rulers, had large personal interests. He also embarked on great enterprises such as the building of dams, bridges and public buildings which impressed European visitors even more than did the iron steamer in which the Viceroy travelled between his capitals of Cairo and Alexandria, and persuaded them that Mehemet Ali was a great progressive ruler who was converting Egypt into a modern state. Palmerston viewed the situation differently. 'The fact is', he wrote to Ponsonby on 23 June 1838, 'that Mehemet Ali has divided the population of Egypt into two classes, the Rich and the Poor. The rich class consists of Mehemet Ali himself singly and alone; the poor class of all the other inhabitants of Egypt.'

Mehemet Ali raised large sums of money from his taxes and monopolies, paid tribute to the Sultan, and kept the bulk of the money for the expenses of his administration and the personal use of himself and his family. He maintained a large standing army by a system of conscription, which the people resented as much as the forced labour which the Pasha used for his great building projects. Palmerston strongly disapproved of all these aspects of Mehemet Ali's régime, as he did of the slave-trading activities which the Viceroy's troops carried out among the negro population in the Sudan. He pro-

tested against the system of monopolies which Mehemet Ali
had established in Egypt, and which he extended to Syria after
he conquered it in 1833. Palmerston declared that these monopolies contravened the commercial treaties between Britain
and Turkey. This argument, of course, could only apply if
Mehemet Ali's territories were part of the Turkish Empire.

In Crete, Mehemet Ali introduced a régime of which
Palmerston disapproved in every particular. He suppressed
the revolts of the Greek population with savagery, stamped
out all forms of political freedom, and introduced a socialistic
land reform which shocked Palmerston. Commissioners were
appointed to survey all agricultural land in Crete, to transfer
a proportion of the land of the rich to the poorer farmers, to
re-settle the population of overcrowded areas into districts
where there was a labour shortage, and to banish all idle
people who refused to work. On 23 November 1833, Palmerston protested to Mehemet Ali against the regulation. 'Nothing
but the total inability to resist would induce the Inhabitants
of any country to submit to such a system as this', wrote
Palmerston. He then condemned the way by which the Commissioners in Crete were to ascertain whether each landowner cultivated his land efficiently, and if he did not, were
to fine him; after he had been fined three times for this, 'if
his system of cultivation still falls short of the expectations
of these Commissioners, his lands are to be taken from him
and are to be transferred to some other person, considered
more capable of rendering them useful to society, the former
proprietor receiving one fourth of the profit of the lands for
his support. Such a regulation, so far from tending to encourage Industry as it professes to do, appears to be founded
upon violence and injustice, and to be calculated only to legalize oppression and spoliation'. Palmerston advised Mehemet
Ali, if he wished the Cretans to be prosperous and contented,
'to allow every man to employ his labour and cultivate his
land as may appear best to himself, to secure to every man
the undisturbed enjoyment of the fruits of his own Industry,
to abstain from extending to Candia [Crete] the system of
monopolies which prevails in Egypt, but on the contrary to
let every man sell his Commodities to those who will give him

the best price for them, and purchase what he wants from those who will sell the cheapest'. It did not occur to Palmerston that many of these regulations would be introduced in Britain within a hundred and twenty years.

In 1833, Mehemet Ali had retreated from Anatolia because Russia had threatened him with war if he marched on Constantinople. For six years, the Taurus mountains remained the unrecognized boundary between the territories of the Sultan and those of Mehemet Ali. Both Palmerston and the French Foreign Minister tried to redeem their shaken credit with the Sultan by associating themselves belatedly with Russia in a defence of his territories, and announced that if Mehemet Ali broke the peace they would intervene by force in defence of the Sultan. But Mehemet Ali had no intention of re-opening hostilities. Although on one occasion he threatened to proclaim the independence of Egypt, he was really aiming at controlling the Turkish Empire through his influence at Constantinople, where he had bribed several of the Pashas and government officials, and had won the support of the masses by his stand for Turkey and Islam against the Russian infidels. It was Sultan Mahmud who was planning to resort to force by sending his troops across the Euphrates and driving Mehemet Ali out of Syria, which he was encouraged to do by the reports which he constantly received of resistance and rebellion by the Syrian tribes against the oppressive taxation and wholesale conscription which was enforced by Mehemet Ali's son, Ibrahim, who governed Syria for his father.

Palmerston received contradictory advice from his subordinates as to the policy which he should pursue. The Consul at Alexandria, Colonel Campbell, had a high opinion of Mehemet Ali, for the illiterate Albanian, with his courteous manners, his lively wit, and his great personal charm, made a favourable impression on all the Europeans who came into contact with him. But Lord Ponsonby, the Ambassador at Constantinople, strongly supported the Sultan. He urged Palmerston to re-establish British influence at Constantinople by vying with the Russians in support of the Sultan, and to go the whole hog by offering him military assistance if he marched across the Euphrates and attacked Mehemet Ali in

Syria. Palmerston rejected this advice, and adopted a policy
of pro-Turkish neutrality. If Mehemet Ali attacked the Sultan, Britain would intervene on the Sultan's side; if the Sultan
attacked Mehemet Ali, Britain would remain neutral, but
Palmerston strongly urged the Sultan to do no such thing.
This policy succeeded in keeping peace in the Middle East
for six years, because Mahmud knew that without the support of the European powers he had no chance against Mehemet Ali.

But Britain lost more ground at Constantinople with an
incident for which Ponsonby himself was largely responsible.
In May 1836, a British journalist named Churchill, living at
Galata, went out shooting quail, and accidentally shot and
wounded a Turkish boy. Churchill was seized by the furious
villagers, and removed to the nearest police station, where he
was bastinadoed on the soles of his feet. Ponsonby protested
to the Turkish Government, demanded compensation for
Churchill, and insisted that all the policemen who had bastinadoed Churchill should themselves be bastinadoed much
more severely than they had bastinadoed him. The Sultan's
favourite, Achmet Pasha, and his placeman, Akif, refused
these demands, and endorsed the action of the local police.
Palmerston was as indignant as Ponsonby about the way in
which Churchill had been treated; but he warned Ponsonby
against making too much of the matter for fear of antagonizing the Turkish Government. Ponsonby believed that a firm
stand, though it might temporarily annoy the Sultan, would in
the long run have a beneficial effect by convincing him of
Britain's strength and determination, and peremptorily demanded the dismissal of Achmet and Akif as well as the local
police officials. He was supported by Achmet's enemies at the
Turkish Court, and the Sultan acceded to his demands; but
at this point, the Russian Ambassador intervened in Achmet's
favour, and forced the Sultan to reinstate him. Palmerston
then told Ponsonby not to demand the dismissal of either
Achmet or the local police officials, but to be content with
the resignation of Akif, to which the Russians had not objected. Eventually Ponsonby managed to persuade the Sultan
to compensate Churchill out of his private purse.

Despite all the criticisms of his pro-Russian sympathies in the House of Commons and the British press, Palmerston was opposing Russian policy as best he could along the whole length of the Russian border. In the north, he was very successful. The Tsar was eager to win over Sweden, and made repeated advances to Charles XIV. He paid an impromptu visit to Stockholm, and embraced the King as a beloved royal brother – a rare compliment for Nicholas to pay to the French solicitor's son, Bernadotte, in view of the fact that he was refusing to treat the usurper Louis Philippe as an equal, and afterwards adopted the same haughty attitude towards Napoleon III. Bernadotte was filled with hatred for his native country, and quarrelled violently with France in 1833 when a play was put on in a Paris theatre in which Bernadotte figured as one of the characters. The play, which had the promising title of *Le Camarade du Lit*, was not complimentary to the King of Sweden; and when the French Government refused to ban the play, Sweden broke off diplomatic relations with France. Palmerston immediately stepped in to prevent developments which might have thrown Sweden into an alliance with Russia. He patched up the quarrel between Sweden and France, and persuaded the Swedish Government not only to reject the Russian proposal to buy a strategic strip of land in Northern Norway, but also to declare its neutrality in the event of a war between Britain and Russia.

In the south, Palmerston was less successful, for he was not able to do much to counter Russian designs in the Balkans, the Caucasus, or in Central Asia, while in Persia the complicated situation between Britain and Russia eventually involved British India in an unsatisfactory war in Afghanistan. In the Balkans, Russian influence was predominant as a result of the war of 1828 and the Treaty of Adrianople. Serbia, the most northern province of the Turkish Empire, was ruled by Milosh Obrenovitch, a shepherd boy who had been one of the chief lieutenants of Karageorge in the national revolt against Turkey at the beginning of the century, and had been accepted by the Turkish Government as hereditary ruler of Serbia owing only a nominal allegiance to the Sultan. Milosh ruled as an autocrat. He owed his position, and the semi-independence of his country, to Russian intervention; but he had no wish to be a Russian pawn. He not only entered into friendly relations with Austria, who was interested in the area and very suspicious of Russian intrigues on her southern frontier, but also invited Britain to appoint a Consul in Belgrade, and to develop trade with Serbia. The Russians then turned against Milosh. They encouraged the landowners and the middle classes in Serbia to demand that Milosh grant a constitution, and that he should rule as Prince with the assistance of a Council of Boyars, elected for life by their fellow-landowners and not removable at the will of Milosh.

In ordinary circumstances, Palmerston would have supported this proposal, and preferred government by a constitutional Prince and conservative landowners rather than the dictatorship of a shepherd boy who had become an autocrat as a result of being a revolutionary guerrilla leader; but as Russia supported constitutional government, Palmerston supported Milosh. 'The British Government has Two objects in view with Respect to Servia', he wrote in October 1837. 'First that Servia should form a Barrier against the further Encroachments of Russia; Secondly that Servia should afford an opening for the extension of the Commerce of Great Britain'. Whatever might be the position elsewhere, in Serbia these objects would not be achieved by supporting constitutional government. He therefore warned the Turkish Government not to grant the demands of the Serbian constitutionalists for an irremovable Council of State. This was exactly the opposite line to that which he had taken in Spain, where he had unsuccessfully urged Mendizabal to appoint a hereditary Upper House of landowners instead of one composed of removable government nominees. In 1839, a revolution broke out in Serbia, with Russian support; Milosh abdicated and fled abroad, and a pro-Russian constitutional government of Conservative landowners was established. In Serbia, the Tsar's policy was as flexible as Palmerston's.

In the principalities of Wallachia and Moldavia – the modern Rumania – Russian influence was almost supreme, for though the Hospodars and their Council of Boyars who ruled these Turkish provinces were nominally vassals of the

Sultan, the treaty rights which Russia had obtained after the war of 1828, and which she periodically enforced by military occupation of the principalities, made the Russian Consul in Bucharest the real ruler of Wallachia and Moldavia. The treaties with Turkey gave Russia control of the mouth of the Danube at Sulina, and the duty of keeping it clear for shipping; and the dilatoriness of the Russians in dredging it, and the other obstructions which they periodically placed on shipping, led from time to time to minor conflicts between Palmerston and Nesselrode. There was more serious trouble in 1833, when an Ionian in Bucharest, who was a British subject, complained to the Russian commander that Russian soldiers had forced their way into his house, and was sentenced to a short term of imprisonment by a Russian court-martial for making untrue allegations against the occupying forces. Palmerston made a strong protest to both Russia and Turkey against the proceedings of the Russian military authorities in Bucharest, and used harsher language to Nesselrode about this incident than he usually used towards Russia; but he obtained no redress of any kind.

From 1831 to 1839, Russia waged a war against the Circassian tribes on the Black Sea coast. The British press warmly praised the heroic Circassians who were defending their country against overwhelming odds; but in the end their guerrilla warfare proved ineffectual. The Radicals in England urged Palmerston to send military aid to the Circassians, as did Prince Czartoryski, to whom a European war would have been a small price to pay for the liberation of Poland; but Palmerston told Czartoryski that 'John Bull will not go to war to save Circassia'.

In 1836, an anti-Russian English shipowner fitted out a ship named the *Vixen* to sail from Constantinople to Circassia carrying salt for the Circassians, with the connivance of David Urquhart, an attaché at the British Embassy at Constantinople. The Russians seized the ship in a Circassian port. There was a storm of indignation and anti-Russian propaganda in Britain, and Palmerston sent a demand to Nesselrode for compensation for the shipowners; but there was considerable doubt as to the legal rights of the parties, which involved complicated points of international law about blockades and the power to enforce them on the high seas. Palmerston played down the incident as much as possible, and when the Tsar denied all liability but offered to make an ex gratia payment to the shipowners as a contribution to friendly relations with Britain, he accepted the offer with thanks. Soon afterwards Ponsonby complained to Palmerston about Urquharts' insubordination in the Embassy, and Palmerston recalled Urquhart. He did not directly pronounce on the merits of the dispute, but decided, as he did on other occasions, that if an Ambassador and an attaché were at loggerheads, the attaché had better be transferred elsewhere. Urquhart left the foreign service, and published a newspaper, the *Portfolio*, in which he denounced Palmerston as a Russian agent.

Palmerston was strongly criticized by the Radicals in Britain for his conciliatory attitude about the *Vixen*, and for his policy of appeasing Russia. On 14 December 1837, Attwood opened a debate in the House of Commons in which he denounced the Government for neglecting the Navy, and asserted that the Russian fleet could sail into the Thames, or burn Sheerness, whenever they wished, even if Palmerston brought back the six ships of the line which had been sent to Lisbon to protect the Queen of Portugal from her Septembrist Government. 'The ostensible excuse for maintaining so many ships there', said Attwood, 'was to protect the life of the Queen of Portugal; but they did not care so much about the life of the Queen; the real object was to put down liberty, to support despotism and fraud, and to destroy the Constitution which the Queen of Portugal had sworn to defend and maintain'. Attwood summed up Palmerston's policy in a phrase which expressed the view of many Tories as well as Radicals: 'Bully to the weak, and coward to the strong'. In his reply, Palmerston defended Russia more strongly than he had ever done, and declared: 'I say that Russia gives the world quite as much security for the preservation of peace as England'.

The Tsar never abandoned the hope that he would be able to improve British-Russian relations and eventually detach Britain from the alliance with France, which in Nicholas's view was giving so much encouragement to the revolutionary forces in Europe. But Palmerston was slow to respond, chiefly because he was suspicious of Russian ambitions in Persia and Central Asia. In 1835, Lord Durham was sent on a second embassy to Russia. Durham was as sympathetic as ever to the Tsar, even after Nicholas had enraged Durham's Radical associates by a very provocative speech in Warsaw in which he said that he would answer any Polish complaints by bombarding the city. Durham assured Palmerston of Russia's good intentions and desire for friendship with Britain; but Palmerston remained sceptical, and proceeded almost automatically to counter every Russian move wherever he could.

But the Anglo-French alliance was showing signs of strain. Paradoxically, French relations with Palmerston grew worse as the revolutionary mood of 1830 ebbed in France, and the Left-wing French governments were succeeded by more Conservative ones. As long as the Government – or rather, public opinion – in France felt strong sympathy for Liberal movements in Belgium, Italy and Portugal, Palmerston was able to manipulate the French Government as he pleased, and could send their armies in and out of Belgium at his will. He knew that France would go no further than he wished them to go against the Northern Powers for fear of antagonizing Britain, but that French public opinion would always force the French Government to go as far as Palmerston permitted. When Right-wing governments came to power in France, they were less eager to be used by Palmerston to fight for Liberalism against the Northern Powers, and were as ready as Palmerston himself to subordinate ideological sympathies to their national interests. In 1836, French agents in Spain and Portugal worked against the pro-British governments of the Portuguese Chartists and Mendizabal in Spain, and Howard de Walden and Villiers told Palmerston that Bois-le-Comte and Latour-Maubourg were responsible for the coming to power of the Left-wing Septembrists in Portugal and the Right-wing Isturiz in Spain.

The alliance with France had always been unpopular in Britain, for Englishmen, from William IV downward, had never liked the French. The view of the Tory politicians was expressed in the House of Commons by Grove Price, when he stated that the Anglo-French alliance could never last, because 'one country had been at the head of the Revolutionary Movement for years, as the other had been the leader of the Conservative Party in Europe'; but a more general, and simpler, attitude was described by Praed in his poem, 'The Old Soldier'. The old veteran, sitting before his cottage door, proposes the toast: 'Sorrow take the French!' On being told that he is out-of-date, because 'Lord Palmerston and Mr. Grant can find no fault with France', he merely knocks out his pipe, and remembers a time when Palmerston, too, disliked the French. '"God bless the Duke", so ended he, "How he did beat the French!"'

Palmerston was eager to preserve the alliance. When Howard complained to him that the French Minister in Portugal, St. Priest, was intriguing against Britain, and had ordered a French frigate to the Tagus in order to strengthen his hand, Palmerston wrote on 20 May 1836:

My dear Howard, Never mind St. Priest and his Frigate, remember that it is of great importance to us, not only to be well with the French Government, but to appear to all Europe to be so. England alone cannot carry her points on the Continent. She must have allies as instruments to work with. We cannot have the cooperation of our old allies the 3 Powers, because their views and opinions are now a days the reverse of ours. France thinks with us, and from their peculiar position is compelled to work with us and by her assistance, whether willingly given or extorted by the force of circumstances, we are enabled to control the 3 Powers, and to give what direction we wish, to Many of the great events of the day. We must not then lay too much stress upon the folly or vanity or impertinence of individual agents whom the French Government may employ, but rather try to overlook these little ebullitions of national conceit, and take care that Europe shall see us everywhere united as far as Circumstances allow us to be so.

But the French successes, within a few months, in overthrowing the Governments of Spain and Portugal caused Palmerston some annoyance, and when William IV opened Parliament in January 1837, the speech from the throne contained no reference to the French alliance. This was intended by Palmerston as a warning to France, and was much resented by Louis Philippe. Palmerston did not care. He had, as usual, correctly calculated the relative strength of himself and his adversary. The French could not afford to break the alliance with Britain, and Louis Philippe told Granville that the incident would not affect his pro-British foreign policy.

The chief strain to the alliance came over Spain. After Isturiz was overthrown by the Exaltados – a coup which the French were sure had been engineered by Villiers – the French enthusiasm for the Isabelinos' cause cooled noticeably. Louis Philippe refused the Spanish Government's request that he should send a French army across the Pyrenees, partly at least because he feared that the French soldiers would be contaminated by revolutionary propaganda in Spain. Palmerston was not sorry about this, for no British Foreign Secretary ever wished to see a French army enter Spain; but he was quite willing that the French Government should fulfil its pledge to send the French Foreign Legion, which had been formed a few years before to fight in Algeria, to help the Spanish Government. But the French made one excuse after another, and only about four thousand men of the Foreign Legion arrived – less than half the numbers in the British Legion. Even more serious was the fact that French frontier officials often winked at the efforts of Carlist sympathizers in France to smuggle arms across the frontier into Carlist territory, which bordered on the Pyrenees. Palmerston repeatedly drew the attention of the French Government to the activities of the Carlist smugglers, and was sometimes able to supply them with details in advance of the Carlists' smuggling operations; but the French authorities took no action, and Palmerston became convinced that the smuggling had the unofficial approval of Louis Philippe.

In the autumn of 1838, when the relations between Britain and France were worse than they had been at any time since 1830, the Tsar made an overture to Palmerston. At Russia's suggestion, a meeting was arranged at Milan between Frederick Lamb, the British Ambassador in Vienna, and Nesselrode, the Russian Foreign Minister, both of whom were on holiday in Italy. Nesselrode made no concrete proposal, but in effect

invited Palmerston to break the Anglo-French alliance. Lamb
and Palmerston did not give a definite reply; but Palmerston
kept the Russian option open, although he hesitated to break
the alliance with France. Next summer the Tsar sent the
Tsarevitch – the future Alexander II – to England on a mission of goodwill. Palmerston entertained him at a banquet at
the Foreign Office, and sat him next to Lady Seymour, one
of the prettiest women present, though the young Prince was
too shy to make the most of his opportunity. He was also
taken to the races at Newmarket, where, in his honour, an
annual event was henceforth known as the Cesarevitch.

It was in this climate, with Palmerston warming a little towards Russia and cooling more than a little towards France,
that Palmerston and the London Conference were suddenly
called upon to arrange the final settlement of the Belgian
question. For six years the de facto settlement had continued
on the basis of the status quo. From time to time the Dutch
Ambassador in London had made a new offer of a compromise solution, and Palmerston convened a meeting of the
London Conference to consider it; but though the representatives of the Northern Powers urged him to accept a compromise, he refused to agree to any modification of the treaty
of November 1831. Then suddenly in March 1838 the Dutch
accepted the treaty. It was now the turn of the Belgians to
resist. They had been in occupation of Luxemburg and Limburg since the armistice of January 1831, and had integrated
the system of government in these provinces with the government of Belgium. They claimed that it was too late for Holland
to accept the treaty, and thereby undo a system which had
worked satisfactorily for so long. Palmerston agreed to change
the treaty to the extent of reducing the Belgian share of the
national debt; but he refused to allow any modification of the
territorial terms, and after indignant protests and demonstrations in Belgium, the Belgians evacuated Luxemburg and Limburg. The treaty was finally accepted by Holland and Belgium
in May 1839.

But neither the events in Belgium and Spain, nor the
friendly gestures of the Tsar, would have disrupted the
Anglo-French alliance if the issue had not been forced by

Sultan Mahmud. The old Sultan knew that he was dying, and
was determined, before he went, to regain Syria from Mehemet Ali. Early in 1839, the Turkish ministers again asked
Ponsonby if the British Government would support the Sultan
if he attacked Ibrahim in Syria. If Ponsonby had been a free
agent, he would eagerly have promised British support, but
he was too conscientious a public servant to pretend that the
extensive powers which had been granted to him could be
stretched to such a length. He referred the decision to Palmerston. Palmerston told him that he must not encourage the
Turks to cross the Euphrates. 'I have to instruct Your Excellency', he wrote to Ponsonby on 12 April 1839, 'to continue
to cooperate actively with your colleagues in endeavouring
by all means in your Power, to prevail on the Sultan to abstain from any hostile proceedings against Mehemet Ali'.

The Sultan now had to weigh the risk. Ponsonby had told
his ministers that if he attacked Mehemet Ali, Britain would
stay neutral and not help him; but if the fighting once began,
and Ibrahim got the best of it, Russia or Britain might well
be forced to enter the war on the Sultan's side in order to
prevent the dissolution of the Turkish Empire. On 22 May,
Ponsonby was invited to meet four of the chief Turkish ministers. They told him of Ibrahim's misdeeds in Syria, and argued
that his punitive operations against certain rebellious tribes
constituted aggression against the Sultan. Then they put a
number of questions to Ponsonby, which Ponsonby answered
with a dutiful determination to fulfil Palmerston's instructions, but perhaps also hoping to give the Viziers a different
impression from that which he was supposed to give. They
asked him how Britain would react if they attacked Ibrahim;
Ponsonby said that Britain had always advised them to abstain from war. They mentioned that some of the great powers
– they meant France – were earnestly pressing them not to go
to war with Mehemet Ali, and asked if Britain would permit
these powers to use force to prevent them from attacking
Mehemet Ali. 'I said', wrote Ponsonby to Palmerston, 'I could
not suppose Her Majesty's Government would sanction any
attempt to deprive the Porte of the exercise of any rights of
sovereignty, so long as it was an ally of the Porte'. Finally,

they asked whether the British Navy would prevent the Turk-ish fleet from attacking Syria or Egypt, and Ponsonby replied that he had heard of no orders to this effect. The Sultan de-cided to risk the gamble. Without consulting his ministers, he ordered his army in Syria to advance against Ibrahim.

As soon as it was known that hostilities had begun, the Russian Government immediately announced that Mehemet Ali was the aggressor. All the reports from the British agents in Syria denied that this was so, and showed that Ibrahim, under orders from Mehemet Ali, had gone to every length to avoid hostilities or provocation along the Euphrates. Colonel Campbell, in Alexandria, wrote to Palmerston, assur-ing him of Mehemet Ali's peaceful intentions, and indignantly denying the Russian allegations; but Palmerston continued to be neutral on the side of the Sultan, as he had been before hostilities had begun. On 25 June he ordered Admiral Stop-ford, who commanded the fleet in the Mediterranean, to pre-vent naval hostilities between the Turkish and Egyptian fleets. Stopford was to urge both commanders to refrain from attack-ing the other. If the Sultan's Admiral disregarded this advice, Stopford was to take no further action; if Mehemet Ali's Admiral disregarded it, Stopford was to prevent him by force from attacking the Sultan's fleet. As it turned out, Mehemet Ali achieved his aim by bribery and propaganda. The Turkish fleet deserted to Mehemet Ali. It sailed to Alexandria and placed itself under his orders.

Palmerston's chief concern was to prevent the conflict in Syria from leading to a European war. If Ibrahim defeated the Turks, and marched on Constantinople, the Russians would intervene; but France was not prepared to see Russia gain control of the Turkish Empire. The French Government therefore suggested to their British ally that the French and British fleets should sail to the Dardanelles, as a warning to the Russians. Palmerston agreed, and the two fleets went to the Dardanelles; but at the same time Palmerston proposed that an international conference of the five great powers should be held to settle the fate of the Levant.

France, Russia, Austria and Prussia accepted the proposal. Palmerston naturally suggested that the Conference, like the

Greek and Belgian Conferences, should be held in London, where he would preside and be the only Foreign Minister among the Ambassadors; but Metternich wanted the Conference to be held in Vienna. On the advice of Frederick Lamb – who had been created Lord Beauvale – Palmerston immediately accepted Metternich's proposal. To hold the Conference in Vienna would flatter Metternich, and as Metternich would be chairman, it would involve Austria more closely in the Middle Eastern crisis, which was desirable, as Austria's interests in the area did not conflict with Britain's, as French and Russian interests did. There was also the important advantage that Vienna was only a week or ten days' journey from Constantinople. It took three weeks for news to reach London, for after the despatches had been carried from Constantinople to Trieste on a steamship of the Austrian Navy, and had reached Vienna, it took another ten days or a fortnight for them to travel to London, even if the electric telegraph was used between Strasbourg and Paris. Palmerston also knew that he could rely on Beauvale to represent British interests at the Conference with great ability. His personal relations with Beauvale were worse than usual at the moment, for Beauvale knew that Lady Cowper was on the point of marrying Palmerston, and strongly disapproved of the marriage; but neither man allowed their personal differences to impede the public service.

Palmerston now carried out a diplomatic coup in which he succeeded in preventing a European war about the Levant, and in getting the best of both France and Russia. When the Russians heard that Palmerston and the French Government had sent their fleets to the Dardanelles, they drew back. Instead of sending an army to support the Sultan, they proposed that Mehemet Ali should be granted Orfa and Dioubehin, on the eastern bank of the Euphrates and beyond the borders of Ibrahim's territory. But on 9 July, Palmerston instructed the British Ambassador in St. Petersburg to make a new proposition to Nesselrode, which he had already put forward to Metternich on 28 June. 'It seems to the British Government, that there can be no security for permanent peace between the Sultan and Mehemet Ali, as long as they have both of

them an army in Syria; for neither of them can look upon
their present state of occupation as permanently satisfactory.
Mehemet Ali has too much, not to wish for more; and the Sultan has lost too much, to be able to sit down contented with
his loss. Each party, therefore, must consider his present position in Syria, as a starting point for an attempt to accomplish
the object of his desire; the one for further encroachment on
the Turkish provinces; the other for the reconquest of Syria.
... The only arrangement, therefore, which could appear to
Her Majesty's Government to be calculated to secure peace
for the future, would be the evacuation of Syria by Mehemet
Ali, and the withdrawal of his authorities, civil and military,
into Egypt. By such means, the Desert would be interposed
between the two parties; and the chances of conflict between
them would be almost entirely prevented. But Mehemet Ali
would justly require some counter-balancing advantage, in return for such a concession on his part; and Her Majesty's
Government conceive, that this might be given him by making
the Pashalic of Egypt hereditary in his family'.

It would hardly be possible, in 1970, for a British Foreign
Secretary, on the outbreak of a local war, to propose, without
raising a storm of protest, that the aggressor should be rewarded by the gift of a large tract of the victim's territory
which he was quite incapable of conquering for himself; and
even in 1839, as Palmerston was soon to discover, it encountered considerable opposition. But Palmerston was convinced
that he had made a very advantageous move for Britain in the
diplomatic chess game, and nothing would deter him from
carrying out his policy of expelling Mehemet Ali from Syria.
As the Consul at Alexandria, Colonel Campbell, continued,
in his despatches, to argue Mehemet Ali's case, Palmerston
decided that the time had come for Campbell to retire, and
appointed Colonel Hodges to succeed him; and though the
British merchants in Alexandria strongly supported Mehemet
Ali, Palmerston was not to be moved. He had an answer to
every argument which was put forward on Mehemet Ali's behalf. He paid no attention to the argument that Mehemet Ali,
as the champion of Islam, could arouse the religious zeal of
Moslems against the infidels; but he was equally unimpressed

by the fact that Mehemet Ali employed more Christians in his service than did the Viceroys in any other part of the Turkish Empire, despite the fact that the discrimination against Christians in Turkey had for long been a cause of resentment in Europe. 'It is indeed remarkable', he wrote to Beauvale on 16 October 1839, 'how contradictory are the assertions which the partizans of Mehemet Ali are driven to have recourse to; for while at one time and for one purpose they represent him as the great champion of Mahommedan feeling, at another time, and for another purpose, they extol him as the subduer of Mahommedan prejudice, and as a man who has had energy enough to coerce that religious fanaticism which rendered the Mahommedans so overbearing and intolerable to the Christians in all the transactions and intercourse of life'.

Palmerston would hear no good of Mehemet Ali. On 10 June 1839, he wrote to Granville: 'I hate Mehemet Ali, whom I consider as nothing better than an ignorant barbarian who by cunning and boldness and mother wit has been successful in rebellion. . . . I look upon his boasted civilization of Egypt as the arrantest humbug, and I believe that he is as great a tyrant and oppressor as ever made a people wretched'. So he proposed taking Syria away from Mehemet Ali, and giving it back to Sultan Mahmud, whom ten years before, in his speech of 1 June 1829, he had bracketed with Miguel as the two greatest despots in Europe. The Governments of Mehemet Ali and Mahmud were equally tyrannical, but one was an efficient military dictatorship, and the other the corrupt and incompetent rule of a decadent Court. But for Palmerston, such matters were almost irrelevant, except, perhaps, that a decadent and corrupt régime was easier to manipulate than an efficient one. All that concerned him was to strengthen Britain's position in the Middle East. 'No ideas therefore of fairness towards Mehemet', he wrote, 'ought to stand in the way of such great and paramount interests'. He had no doubt where British interests lay. 'Egyptian civilization must come from Constantinople, and not from Paris, to be durable or consistent with British interests of a most important kind'.

He was not affected by arguments about Mahmud's misgovernment, or by the current political jargon in which the Turkish Empire was compared to a rotten tree. 'As to the Turkish empire', he wrote to Bulwer, the chargé d'affaires in Paris, on 1 September 1839, 'if we can procure for it ten years of peace under the joint protection of the five Powers, and if those years are profitably employed in reorganizing the internal system of the empire, there is no reason whatever why it should not become again a respectable Power. Half the wrong conclusions at which mankind arrive are reached by the abuse of metaphors, and by mistaking general resemblance or imaginary similarity for real identity. Thus people compare an ancient monarchy with an old building, an old tree, or an old man, and because the building, tree, or man must from the nature of things crumble, or decay, or die, they imagine that the same thing holds good with a community, and that the same laws which govern inanimate matter, or vegetable and animal life, govern also nations and states'. There was no comparison, because, while buildings, trees and people decayed, 'the component parts of a community are undergoing daily the process of physical renovation and of moral improvement. Therefore all that we hear every day of the week about the decay of the Turkish empire, and its being a dead body, or a sapless trunk, and so forth, is pure and unadulterated nonsense'. There was very little sign of moral improvement in the Turkish Empire during the next ten years, or during the next seventy years; but Palmerston, as usual, saw the realities of power. As long as the great powers were prepared to uphold the Sultan's régime by armed force, it would remain in power, however much politicians and journalists talked about sapless trunks, or the Christian Churches deplored the Sultan's tyranny.

Nesselrode welcomed Palmerston's proposal that Mehemet Ali should be expelled from Syria. Metternich proposed that he should be permitted to retain it for life, and that it should revert to the Sultan at his death; but Palmerston and Nesselrode rejected this concession, which in any case would hardly have been accepted by so devoted a father as Mehemet Ali. Then, on 22 July 1839, Palmerston heard the news of two shattering events of which he knew nothing when he put forward his proposal on 9 July. On 24 June, the Sultan's army had attacked Ibrahim at Nezib in Syria, and had been utterly routed; the men had fled in panic, and many deserted to Ibrahim. Six days later – on the day that the news of the battle reached Constantinople – Mahmud II died without knowing of the defeat of his army. He was succeeded by the young Abd-ul-Mejid. Mahmud had often considered promulgating political reforms in Turkey, but had always postponed doing so, and his death opened up the possibility of modifying the despotism of the Sultan; but Palmerston felt only regret that Mahmud had died, because he thought that the authority of the Turkish Government would be weakened by the change from a despot who was respected and feared to an inexperienced youth of eighteen. His fears were justified. Mehemet Ali ordered Ibrahim not to pursue the Turks across the Euphrates, and set out to achieve his aims by intrigue at Constantinople. With their army shattered and their Sultan dead, the Turkish ministers had no wish to carry on the struggle on which Mahmud had embarked without consulting them, and Mehemet Ali's supporters among the Viziers soon won over the rest. On 27 July, they decided to recognize Mehemet Ali as Viceroy of Syria, and ordered the messenger to leave Constantinople for Alexandria next day to take the news to Mehemet Ali.

The Turkish Viziers had thus settled by themselves the crisis of the Turkish Empire which had troubled Europe for six years; but they were foiled by Metternich. When Metternich heard, on 10 July, the news of Nezib and of the Sultan's death, he realized the urgency of the situation, and acted quickly. He proposed to the Conference in Vienna that the powers should deliver a joint note to the Porte, requiring them to leave the settlement of the Syrian dispute to the great powers, and not to negotiate with Mehemet Ali. There was no time for the Ambassadors to consult their governments, but they agreed that the Austrian Ambassador at Constantinople should present a note to this effect to the Turkish Government on behalf of the five powers, and if possible persuade the other Ambassadors to join him in his démarche. Ponsonby and the French, Russian and Prussian Ambassadors at

Constantinople had had no instructions from their governments, but they agreed to sign the Austrian note, which was presented to the Turkish Government at 5 a.m. on 28 July, a few hours before the Turkish messenger was due to leave for Alexandria with the offer to Mehemet Ali. On receiving the Ambassadors' note, the Turkish Government countermanded the orders to the messenger; Mehemet Ali's enemies won over the waverers; and the offer of Syria to Mehemet Ali was withdrawn. Mehemet Ali had been foiled by a few hours.

Chapter Seventeen

Mehemet Ali: The Crisis of 1840

After 27 July, the urgency went out of the situation. Mehemet Ali gave Ibrahim the strictest orders not to pursue the defeated Turks across the Euphrates, and went out of his way to placate the great powers, particularly Britain, in every possible way; and Ponsonby, realizing that time was on the side of the Porte, persuaded them not to attack again. Palmerston had thus all the time available to persuade the other great powers to agree to expel Mehemet Ali from Syria. Russia, Austria and Prussia agreed, but France made difficulties. This was because of the strong sympathy for Mehemet Ali in France. Palmerston was a firm believer in the freedom of the press, but if a free press had not existed in France, he would have avoided a great many troubles in 1839.

The French press, like the British press, was for sale to the highest bidder, and Mehemet Ali bought up several French newspapers. It was a sound investment, for there were factors in France which made it more likely that he would get a response there than elsewhere. Forty years before, Napoleon had hoped to conquer Egypt, and now that France had annexed Algeria, they looked with favour on the prospect of having Mehemet Ali as an independent ally in Egypt. It was also possible to present Mehemet Ali to the French in an ideologically favourable light. An efficient dictator who had risen from the lowest social origins to modernize a backward and barbarous nation, and who was hated by the Tsar as a rebel against his sovereign, was more likely to appeal to a French Jacobin than to Palmerston. His oppressive rule over subject peoples, and his slave-trading activities in the Sudan, were not mentioned by the French journalists in his pay.

Meanwhile his opponents were also angling for the sympathy of progressives in Europe. On 3 November 1839, the new Sultan promulgated a decree, the Hathi Sheriff of Gulhané, which introduced many reforms into the Turkish administration, and modified the despotism of Mahmud II. Palmerston was delighted. 'Your Hathi Sheriff', he wrote to Ponsonby, 'was a grand stroke of policy, and it is producing great effect on public feeling both here and in France'. But Metternich thought that it was absurd to suppose that these reforms could be introduced in practice in Turkey; and he was right. The Hathi Sheriff of Gulhané proved to be only window-dressing.

The French Government played their cards very badly throughout the crisis in the Levant. They were guilty of all the blunders that Palmerston never committed, and by their evasions and duplicity angered foreign powers without deterring or frightening them. If they had clearly backed Mehemet Ali before 28 June 1839, Palmerston would probably not have suggested that he should be expelled from Syria; and even later than this, Palmerston might have abandoned the plan if France had made this clear at any time in the next six months. But at the Conference in Vienna in July 1839, the French Ambassador agreed without qualification to Palmerston's proposal, despite the fact that a large section of the French press and public opinion was vigorously supporting Mehemet Ali. This action of the Ambassador's seriously weakened the French position in the subsequent negotiations.

In August and September, as the French press worked up pro-Egyptian feeling in France, the French Government began to draw back from the position which it had taken at the Vienna Conference. Sébastiani, who had succeeded Talleyrand as French Ambassador in London, told Palmerston that France would like to see Mehemet Ali withdraw from Syria, but did not think that he would agree to do so, and that France could not be a party to expelling him by force. Palmerston replied by stating that if France did not wish to be a party to the use of force against Mehemet Ali, Austria, Russia, Prussia and Britain would be willing to act without France. He compared the situation to that which had arisen with regard to the coercing of Holland about the Belgian settlement: all the great powers had approved the settlement, but the three Northern Powers had refused to apply force to compel Holland to submit to it, and had left Britain and France to enforce the decision without their assistance. The French Government did not like Palmerston's suggestion, and stated that France would have the strongest objection to a Russian army entering Turkey to fight Mehemet Ali. Palmerston said that if Russia acted with the consent of all the powers, it would be very different from Russia acting alone; but that in any case, there would be no need for the Russians to march. He did not believe that Mehemet Ali would defy a threat of force from all the great powers, but if he did, the French and British fleets could attack him in Alexandria without Russian troops being involved. The French Government seemed more sympathetic to this idea; but they would not amplify their position.

Of the four other great powers, Prussia was not really interested in the Levant, and only took part in the negotiations so as not to be left out, and to establish its great power status. Metternich was not unwilling from time to time to consider the possibility of a compromise solution. It was the Tsar and Palmerston who were determined to drive Mehemet Ali out of Syria. Neither the defeat of the Turkish army at Nezib nor the death of Mahmud II made Palmerston waver in this determination. 'The result of that battle', he wrote to Beauvale on 26 July 1839, 'cannot entitle Mehemet Ali to any greater favour from the Five Powers, rather the contrary, as it was fought in defiance of the remonstrances made by them; his Army being assailant, and the Field having been beyond the Frontier of Syria'. This completely overlooked the circumstances in which the two armies came to be engaged at Nezib. 'That Battle has not diminished the force of the political considerations which have led the powers to think the evacuation of Syria by Mehemet Ali essential to the maintenance of the Turkish Empire, and to the peace of Europe'.

The fact that Turkey was now governed by a young and inexperienced Sultan, and was therefore weaker than when Mahmud was alive, only made it more necessary for the great powers to intervene to maintain the Turkish Empire. This was their object, and their only object.

If indeed [wrote Palmerston to Beauvale on 1 August] the only object of the Five Powers was to determine how Syria could best be administered, and if they had any right to take on themselves the settlement of such a question, much might be said both ways, as to whether it would be most for the advantage of Syria to be governed by a Pasha appointed directly by the Sultan, or to be governed by a Person appointed by Mehemet Ali, under an authority delegated to him by the Sultan, although it may be safely said that little doubt could exist on this point, if Mehemet Ali were to continue to subject the Syrians to the many and severe oppressions which they have hitherto suffered under his rule. This is not the question before the Powers, their object is the mainten-ance of the Turkish Empire; and they have a Right to maintain that Integrity because its maintenance is necessary for upholding the Balance of Power in Europe, and is essential to the Peace of the world. The Five Powers ought not therefore it seems to Her Majesty's Government to consider the integrity of the Turkish Empire as less important, merely because for the moment the throne happens to be filled by a Minor. They should look to permanent Interests and not to temporary accidents, and as they possess the means of effectually supporting Turkey, they ought to employ those means for that purpose.

But even Palmerston had not yet taken up a final position about Syria; for while the Tsar hoped that Mehemet Ali would be the cause of a rupture in the Anglo-French alliance, Pal-merston did not want this to happen. He did not wish to join in an anti-French alliance with the Northern Powers; he wan-ted to drag France behind him, as a complacent junior partner, into an alliance with the Northern Powers against Mehemet Ali, and then perhaps walk out, taking the French with him, at some future time, if this should turn out to be desirable. So he was still eager, in the autumn of 1839, to reach an agreement with the French; and in October he offered a compromise to France. He proposed that Mehemet Ali should surrender only the north of Syria to the Sultan, and should retain Southern Syria for his life, except for the fortress of Acre. Neither Russia nor Austria were pleased when they discovered what Palmerston had done, and Palmerston was much relieved when the French rejected the proposal. Palmerston told Sébastiani that, in view of the French refusal, the offer was withdrawn, and he refused to discuss it when Sébastiani tried to raise it again.

On 16 December, Palmerston took the day off from the Foreign Office to marry Lady Cowper. Earl Cowper had died in June 1837, two days after William IV died and Victoria succeeded to the throne, and Palmerston had thereupon asked Lady Cowper to marry him. She had hesitated for a long time before accepting. There was a strong feeling in nineteenth-century Britain that a loyal widow ought never to re-marry, and as Lady Cowper was already fifty when her husband died, and could certainly not re-marry immediately, she was afraid that she might be laughed at for marrying at an advanced age. Apart from this, her family had objections to her marrying Palmerston. Melbourne, who had a high opinion of Palmerston as a Foreign Secretary, was not so eager to have him as a brother-in-law; and Beauvale was even more strongly opposed to it. In that age of extreme social snobbery, the Lambs could not forget that if Emily married Palmerston she would be reduced in rank from a Countess to a Viscountess, that Palmerston was only an Irish peer, and that even with Broadlands and £12,000 a year his income was considerably lower than Emily would have a right to expect. Though these objections were freely voiced by Emily's relations and friends in their letters, their real objections undoubtedly went deeper: they were worried because of Palmerston's reputation as a spendthrift and a philanderer. It was known that Palmerston was heavily in debt, and at this very moment he was being sued in the courts by several creditors; while they obviously feared that tongues would wag more than ever if Emily married her old lover now that her husband had died.

All these objections only strengthened Emily's resolve to accept Palmerston. She always took the view, where match-making was concerned, that much the most important factor was that the man should be handsome and the woman beautiful, and tended to brush aside less romantic considerations. She made Palmerston woo her for two years before accepting him. This may have appealed to her vanity and sense of propriety, and certainly the account which she wrote to her friends of his courtship was calculated to obscure the fact that she had been his mistress for nearly thirty years. Eventually she accepted him, informing everyone that her hesitations had been overcome by the fact that her children had strongly encouraged her to marry Palmerston. This was quite untrue, for at least one of her daughters was strongly opposed to the match.

They were married on 16 December 1839 at St. George's Church in Hanover Square. Palmerston was fifty-five, and Lady Cowper fifty-two. The wedding of the Foreign Secretary and the Prime Minister's sister was a great social occasion, and no traces of resentments in the family were allowed to appear on the surface. There was no time for any sort of honeymoon, for as soon as the wedding festivities were over, Palmerston returned to his desk at the Foreign Office and the problem of Mehemet Ali. But a week later, he spent a few days at Broadlands at Christmas, and Lady Palmerston gave her first house party there. It was a momentous one. Palmerston invited Baron Neumann, the Austrian chargé d'affaires, and Baron Brunnow, who had been sent on a special mission to England by the Tsar. Palmerston had decided not to wait any longer for the French, but to settle the problem of Syria without consulting France. He invited Neumann and Brunnow to spend Christmas at Broadlands in order to lay the foundations for an alliance between Britain and the Northern Powers.

On 23 December, and on the morning of Christmas Eve, Neumann went shooting on the Broadlands estate while Palmerston and Brunnow stayed in the house and discussed Palmerston's proposition. They reached complete agreement. On the afternoon of Christmas Eve, it was Brunnow's turn to go shooting while Palmerston put the same proposition to Neumann, who also agreed. On Christmas Day, all three statesmen stayed indoors and discussed the situation together, and agreed, subject to the consent of their governments, that they would expel Mehemet Ali from Syria, by force if necessary, with or without the participation of France. Brunnow and Neumann returned to London in very optimistic mood.

They believed that the Anglo-French alliance was over. But Palmerston had not consulted the Cabinet about this move, and Brunnow and Neumann also needed to obtain the ratification of their governments; and Palmerston was also determined that the Turkish Government should be involved at every stage of the proceedings. He did not have a high opinion of Turkish statesmen – least of all of Nourri Pasha, the Turkish Ambassador in London; but he thought it essential that he should appear to be consulted. 'Poor old Nourri', he said, 'is a perfect cypher, but he can hold his pen and sign his name'.

Sébastiani had heard rumours about the meeting at Broadlands. He also knew that Palmerston had gone on from Broadlands to spend a few days at Lord Tankerville's house at Watton in Hertfordshire. Fortunately for Sébastiani, Lady Tankerville was Madame Sébastiani's sister; so he invited himself to the house-party at Watton, and spent the time pumping Palmerston about what had happened at Broadlands. Palmerston was most affable, but told him practically nothing. But a week later, Palmerston made one of those surprising moves by which he from time to time baffled the people with whom he had to deal. He wrote to Sébastiani on 5 January, and told him everything that had been agreed at Broadlands. He showed him a copy of the agreement which he had signed with Brunnow and Neumann, though he would not allow him to take a copy of it. He then told Brunnow and Neumann what he had done. Brunnow was furious. Neumann was less incensed, but believed that Palmerston had made a great blunder in telling Sébastiani, for it would now be possible for Sébastiani to contact the pro-French element in the British Government, and work up opposition to the Broadlands agreement in the British Cabinet. This was in fact exactly what happened. While the Austrian and Russian Governments each confirmed their envoy's action, and waited impatiently for Palmerston, the British Government would not endorse the agreement. Meanwhile Palmerston was still hoping that the French would join the other great powers in coercing Mehemet Ali, which was doubtless the reason why he had told Sébastiani about the talks at Broadlands. He made his position quite clear to the French Government: he would much prefer France to join in the common action of the powers, but if France refused to come in, the other powers would act without France. The French Government were much less forthright in declaring their position; while some of the French papers and politicians proclaimed that France would never permit the great powers to drive Mehemet Ali from Syria, the French Government merely stated that France would not join in any coercive action against Mehemet Ali.

While he marked time about the Levant, Palmerston forced on another smaller crisis in which he offended Austria and relied on French collaboration. In 1837 the Government of Naples passed a law which granted a monopoly in the exploitation of the Neapolitan sulphur mines to an international cartel, in which the leading shareholders were members of the French Bourbon family of the Legitimist branch which had gone into exile with Charles X in 1830, and was bitterly opposed to Louis Philippe and the Orleanist régime. Palmerston protested that this violated the Anglo-Neapolitan commercial treaty of 1816, which, as usual with commercial treaties negotiated by Britain, provided that British subjects should have 'most favoured nation' treatment, and not be placed in a less advantageous position than the nationals of any other country. He demanded that the Neapolitan Government revoke the grant of the monopoly, and as the Neapolitans refused, and the months passed by, Palmerston added a demand for compensation for British traders for what they had lost during the time that the monopoly had been in force. Having been assured by the Queen's Advocate that his position was justified in international law, he became more and more threatening.

The Radicals in Britain and Italy were delighted at Palmerston's stand. The King of Naples was a reactionary autocrat; his prisons were full of Radicals; his police practised inhuman tortures on political oppositionists; and both in Sicily and on the mainland revolutionary outbreaks recurred quite frequently, and were savagely suppressed by the Neapolitan Government. The tyrannical régime had been saved in 1799 when Nelson and the British fleet intervened to crush the

Jacobin revolt, and hand over the rebels to the vengeance of the King; and it was a gratifying change for the Italian Radicals to see a British Foreign Secretary threatening the King of Naples and not his oppressed subjects. The English Tories, on the other hand, condemned Palmerston's attitude as high-handed. The King of Naples' sympathizers obtained a learned opinion from Sir Frederick Pollock, the former Attorney-General, and Dr. Phillimore, a leading English lawyer, that, contrary to the view of the Queen's Advocate, Palmerston's action was illegal under international law.

In April 1840, Palmerston sent the fleet to the Bay of Naples, and ordered the Admiral to seize Neapolitan ships and blockade the port. He said that he would only release the ships and raise the blockade when the Neapolitan Government abolished the sulphur monopoly and compensated British subjects for what they had lost in the way of prospective trade profits. It was the first time that he had carried out his threats to resort to force since he became Foreign Secretary. He thought that the time had come to emulate the French action against Portugal, Mexico and Argentina.

Metternich was very disturbed at Palmerston's policy. He warned Palmerston that if Britain continued to humiliate the King of Naples and strangle Neapolitan trade, this might provoke revolution in Naples and Sicily which could have disastrous consequences for all Europe. Palmerston replied that if revolution broke out in King Ferdinand's dominions, this would be the result of the King's misgovernment, and that he would not forbear from enforcing the rights of British subjects in order to save the King of Naples from the effect of his own tyranny. Palmerston had never played so openly for Radical support, though he was still, as always, much more restrained in his public statements in the House of Commons than in his despatches to foreign powers. Metternich then told him that if revolt broke out in Italy as a result of Palmerston's action against Naples, Austrian troops would have to march in to suppress it, and would do so whatever French reaction might be; and he asked Palmerston to spare him from the embarrassment of having to do so. Palmerston replied that the only thing that interested him was to vindicate the rights of

British subjects. To Metternich's great annoyance, Palmerston asked France to mediate. He explained to Metternich that France was the most suitable mediator, as the monopoly was held by French monopolists. In fact, he knew that Louis Philippe and his Government would be the last people to sympathize with the French Bourbon Legitimist shareholders.

Palmerston made it clear to the French Government that he was submitting to mediation, not to arbitration. The distinction was well understood. Arbitration was when a third power was asked to judge the merits of a dispute between the two others, and to give a decision which the two contestants agreed in advance to accept. In mediation, the third power tried to negotiate a solution acceptable to both sides. When, as often occurred, one great power mediated in a dispute between another great power and a weaker one, the task of the mediating power was to persuade the weaker power to surrender. The mediator tried to persuade the stronger power to make a few minor concessions, and the weaker power of the folly of resisting a stronger adversary. The advantages of mediation were that, for the stronger power, it saved them from the trouble of war or enforcing a blockade; for the weaker power, that it might gain them a few concessions, and saved them from the humiliation of submitting openly to force; and for the mediating power, that it gained them the credit for having settled the dispute, and enabled them to boast of their influence over both the contestants. In the dispute with Naples, the usual course of mediation was followed. The French asked Palmerston not to seize any more Neapolitan ships while the mediation took place, and Palmerston agreed on condition that Naples gave way in principle, and that the negotiations over the details were not too prolonged. The French then persuaded the King of Naples to agree to revoke the sulphur monopoly, and to pay compensation for the loss of profit by British sulphur merchants since 1837, Palmerston agreeing to reduce the figure which he had originally claimed. By inviting France, and not Austria, to mediate, Palmerston denied Austria the opportunity of showing its power to make Naples submit, and gaining credit with the Neapolitan Government for extorting a few concessions from Palmerston; and he gave the prestige of a successful mediation to France. This was a rebuff to Austria, just at the time when Metternich was hoping that he had detached Britain from the Anglo-French alliance. Palmerston had learned, from his wide experience of diplomacy and his love affairs, the advantages which could be gained by being difficult, and hard to get.

But Metternich, too, could see the advantages of not appearing to be too eager. In May 1840, Neumann proposed to Palmerston that Britain and the Northern Powers should renew their offer to France to give Southern Syria to Mehemet Ali for life, and to improve on it by offering to let him retain the fortress of Acre and other territory in Southern Syria which had not been included in Palmerston's offer in the autumn of 1839. Neumann had objected to the previous proposal as offering too much to Mehemet Ali; now he himself was offering even more, and it was Palmerston's turn to tell Neumann that he was offering too many concessions. But Palmerston agreed to put the suggestion to Guizot, who had succeeded Sébastiani as French Ambassador in London. The French were unenthusiastic about the plan, but agreed to consider it, and to submit it to Mehemet Ali, explaining that they would not be able to know for sixty days how Mehemet Ali would react to it. The Austrian, Russian and Prussian Ambassadors immediately protested against this reference to Mehemet Ali. They said that Mehemet Ali, as a mere subject of the Sultan, had no right to be consulted; and if France consulted Mehemet Ali before replying, the great powers would in fact be negotiating with Mehemet Ali, and not with the French Government. Palmerston told the Ambassadors that he agreed with them in principle, but pointed out the practical advantages of inducing Mehemet Ali to consent to a peaceable solution. The situation was becoming a little embarrassing for Palmerston when suddenly, without consulting Mehemet Ali, the French Prime Minister, Thiers, rejected the plan out of hand. Britain and the Northern Powers would henceforth stand fast on the decision of the Vienna Conference to expel Mehemet Ali from Syria.

After waiting patiently for six months for France to join the other great powers in carrying out this policy, Palmerston heard reports from Ponsonby which persuaded him not to delay any longer. A French agent at Constantinople made secret approaches to the Turkish Government to persuade them to settle the question by direct negotiations with Mehemet Ali, without informing the other great powers, and suggested that Mehemet Ali should make a few concessions, but that he should retain nearly all his conquests in Syria. Palmerston was indignant at the French attempt to exclude the great powers from the settlement and to encourage the Turks to renew the negotiations with Mehemet Ali which had been so narrowly frustrated by Metternich on 27 July 1839.

He was now firmly convinced that Britain must act at once with the Northern Powers and without France. As the Cabinet still hesitated, Palmerston wrote to Melbourne on 5 July 1840 and offered his resignation. He reminded Melbourne that he had been overruled by the Cabinet in 1833 when he had wished to send the fleet in response to the Sultan's appeal for help against Mehemet Ali; but this time he would resign rather than accept the Cabinet policy. If his advice was not followed, it would lead to 'the practical division of the Turkish Empire into two separate and independent states, whereof one will be the dependency of France, and the other a satellite of Russia; and in both of which our political influence will be annulled, and our commercial interests will be sacrificed; and this dismemberment will inevitably give rise to local struggles and conflicts which will involve the Powers of Europe in most serious disputes'. Melbourne had hitherto been very lukewarm about expelling Mehemet Ali from Syria; but he was sure that if Palmerston resigned, it would break up the Government. He therefore decided to support Palmerston's policy in order to avoid serious political troubles at home. He persuaded the Cabinet to agree, and though Lord Holland and Lord Clarendon, and later Lord John Russell, threatened in their turn to resign if Palmerston's anti-French policy were adopted, Melbourne talked them out of it by telling them that the Government would fall if they did.

On 15 July 1840 Palmerston and the Ambassadors of Austria, Russia, Prussia and Turkey initialled a treaty at the Foreign Office by which the powers agreed to instruct their

Consuls at Alexandria to require Mehemet Ali to withdraw from Syria and Crete. If Mehemet Ali agreed to the demand within ten days of receiving it, the four great powers would advise the Sultan to confer the Pashalik of Egypt on Mehemet Ali and his family hereditarily, and to appoint him Viceroy for life of the Pashaliks of Southern Syria, including the fortress of Acre, but excluding the Holy Cities of Jerusalem, Mecca and Medina. If Mehemet Ali did not accept the offer within ten days, the offer of Southern Syria would lapse; but he would still have another ten days in which to accept the offer of the hereditary government of Egypt. He must restore the Turkish fleet to the Sultan, and agree to pay whatever tribute for Egypt the Sultan might decide, without deducting the expenses which he had incurred in maintaining the Turkish fleet while it was in his possession. If he had not accepted these conditions within twenty days of receiving the ultimatum from the powers, the Sultan would dismiss him from the post of Viceroy of Egypt if the great powers so advised. At Palmerston's suggestion, the treaty contained the most unusual provision that the powers should begin to carry out the treaty before it was ratified by their governments; and Palmerston, after attending a Cabinet dinner, sat up late into the night writing instructions for the treaty to be put into effect at once.

Two days later, Palmerston informed Guizot of the terms of the Treaty of London. He said that all the powers regretted that France was not associated with them, but that as France preferred to have no part in the coercion of Mehemet Ali, the other powers would handle this matter without her, which would not in any way lessen their friendship with France or the prospects of their collaboration with her in future. Guizot's reception of the news was stony, but was nothing to the reaction of Thiers when he was informed by the British chargé d'affaires, Henry Bulwer. Thiers immediately declared that the Anglo-French alliance was dead. Next day, the French papers violently attacked Britain; they promised aid to Mehemet Ali, and denounced the Treaty of London as a renewal of the Grand Alliance against France. In the cafés, people sang the *Marseillaise*, and shouted 'To the Rhine', and the British Ambassador's carriage was stoned. This provoked equally passionate anti-French demonstrations in Germany, where the people were singing the new song by Becker, *Sie sollen ihn nicht haben, den freien deutschen Rhein*. The German sovereigns invited the Duke of Wellington to take command of their armies. It was widely believed that a major European war was about to break out.

Palmerston was surprised at the violence of the French reaction, but, almost alone among diplomats and politicians, he treated it all very calmly. He was convinced that France would give in, and that there would be no war. He based this conviction on his analysis of the nature of Louis Philippe's régime. The government and the influential classes in France were no longer revolutionary enthusiasts or military adventurers who thirsted for glory, but stolid bourgeois who wanted peace and were not prepared to take undue risks. It would have been different if vital French interests had been involved; but France would not go to war with all Europe for the sake of Mehemet Ali. The war talk in France was just patriotic froth. Many years later, when Palmerston was discussing the crisis of 1840 with his private secretary, Charles Barrington, at Broadlands, he said that he had been influenced by his knowledge of the unpopularity of Louis Philippe in France, and believed that Louis Philippe would soon be forced to abdicate. Barrington wrote that Palmerston added 'with one of his pleasant laughs, "I knew besides that the French were in no condition at the time to go to war" '.

On 18 July, he wrote to Colonel Hodges in Alexandria, and told him to inform Mehemet Ali about what had been decided. 'Mehemet Ali must necessarily feel ... that successful resistance on his part is impossible; and that any attempt at it would only lead to his losing the advantages which the Sultan and his Allies are willing to offer. The only chance of success which Mehemet Ali could have, would be from the assistance of France; but France will not help him. France would, indeed, oppose a hostile coalition of the Five Powers above-mentioned, if those Powers were to threaten to invade France, to insult her honour, or to attack her Possessions; but France will not go to war with the other Great Powers of

Europe in order to help Mehemet Ali, nor has she the means of doing so'.

Very few people shared Palmerston's optimism. The Ambassador in Paris, Lord Granville, believed that the French would go to war, and urged Palmerston to make concessions. In the Cabinet, Clarendon, Lansdowne and Holland were in favour of appeasing the French anger. Lord and Lady Holland continued the pro-French tradition of their family and the Foxite Whigs, and at their receptions at Holland House Guizot received many expressions of sympathy and support from his host and hostess and their guests. He received equal hospitality, without the political sympathy, from Lady Palmerston, who warmly supported Palmerston's policy, but told many of her friends, at the height of the crisis of 1840, that Monsieur Guizot was a most charming man. Soon they were dining alone together, and carrying on a more or less serious flirtation. Guizot had become the lover of her old friend, the Princess Lieven, who, despite her estrangement from Palmerston, still maintained a friendly correspondence with Lady Palmerston, and had congratulated her on her marriage. Madame de Lieven visited England with Guizot, in the summer of 1840; and for a few days after 15 July, a certain personal coolness developed on their side, in their relations with Palmerston. 'Guizot and Madame de Lieven have looked as cross as the devil for the last three days', wrote Palmerston to Bulwer on 21 July. Palmerston thought that this was perfectly natural.

The prominent Whig politician, Edward Ellice, was also strongly opposed to Palmerston's policy. Ellice, a self-made man who was always known as 'Bear Ellice' because he had hunted bison in Canada, was an unpopular, but formidable, political personality. He now spent much of his time in Paris, where he did his best to encourage the French to resist Palmerston's policy. Palmerston knew that all these politicians, including many of his Cabinet colleagues, were working to frustrate his policy; but though he sometimes gave vent to his indignation at being thus double-crossed by his colleagues, he bore them no ill-will. He continued to maintain friendly relations with them, though he was careful not to trust them, as he cheerfully assumed that they would reveal his secrets to Guizot. On the other hand, for the first time for many years he had won the support of the Tory Opposition, who supported his policy of alliance with the Northern Powers against France. He told Lord Ashley – the future Lord Shaftesbury – that the support of the Tory press had eased ten thousand difficulties; and the Tory support in Parliament and in the country was undoubtedly an important factor in strengthening his hand against the opposition in his own party. The Tories would have agreed with Metternich, who wrote to the King of Prussia that, for the first time since he became a Whig, Palmerston was on the right side.

Palmerston was also confronted by noisier, though less effective, opposition from Radical agitators. The Radicals sympathized as usual with France, and they admired the rebel Mehemet Ali, the son of the people who was modernizing Egypt and resisting the decadent tyranny of the Porte; though Liberal support for Mehemet Ali was weakened after Ibrahim had connived at a pogrom of Jews in Damascus in April 1840, which aroused great indignation in the House of Commons and a more restrained condemnation by Palmerston. The Radicals' sympathy for Mehemet Ali was increased by the propaganda line which the Tsar and Metternich, and even Palmerston, were putting forward, that they were intervening to defend their ally, the Sultan of Turkey, against a rebellious subject. Here was Palmerston, who had always refused to send troops to help the Liberals in Spain or Portugal on the grounds that it was improper for a foreign state to intervene in a civil war, now intervening by force to help the Sultan against his rebel Pasha in a new revival of the old Holy Alliance. Now that Palmerston had openly allied himself with the Northern Powers, they were firmly convinced that he was a Russian agent, as they had always claimed.

On 6 August 1840, David Urquhart sent a memorandum to Melbourne in which he accused Palmerston of high treason, and demanded that the Prime Minister conduct an inquiry into Palmerston's treasonable negotiations with the Russian Government. When the Cabinet met for the first time after the summer recess on 28 September, they found, to their consternation, that copies of Urquhart's memorandum had been laid on the table in front of each minister's place; and Palmerston used the incident to warn Lord John Russell and his other colleagues how easily their disagreements, and other Cabinet secrets, could leak out to foreign embassies. Attwood went to Paris to see Thiers, but Granville persuaded Thiers that it would be improper to receive him, even unofficially. Julian Harney and the Chartists in Britain allied themselves with Attwood's movement, and large demonstrations were held against Palmerston's policy in Birmingham and elsewhere in the North and Midlands in the autumn of 1840. Palmerston, despite his cheerful optimism, was too much a child of the Peterloo era not to take revolutionary agitators seriously. He hired agents, at his own personal expense, to attend Attwood's meetings, and take verbatim reports of everything that the speakers said. He sent copies of these speeches, and articles in Chartist newspapers, to the Attorney-General, and asked him to consider whether Urquhart and Attwood and two other Radicals could be prosecuted for sedition. He explained to the Attorney-General that he had no wish to stifle criticism of his policy, but objected to these atrocious calumnies against him. The Attorney-General advised him that it would be very unwise to prosecute the Radical leaders.

As the clamour in France got louder and louder, many members of the Cabinet, especially Lord John Russell, became increasingly alarmed at the danger of war. But Palmerston remained convinced that the French were bluffing. On 22 September he wrote to Bulwer: 'Notwithstanding the mysterious threatening with which Thiers has favoured us, I still hold to my belief that the French Government will be too wise and prudent to make war; and various things which come to me from different quarters confirm me in that belief. Besides, bullies seldom execute the threats they deal in; and men of trick and cunning are not always men of desperate resolves. But if Thiers should again hold to you the language of menace, however indistinctly and vaguely shadowed out, pray retort upon him to the full extent of what he may say to you, and with that skill of language which I know you to be the master of, convey to him in the most friendly and unoffensive manner possible, that if France throws down the gauntlet we shall not refuse to pick it up; and that if she begins a war, she will to a certainty lose her ships, colonies and commerce before she sees the end of it; that her army of Algiers will cease to give her anxiety, and that Mehemet Ali will just be chucked into the Nile. I wish you had hinted at these topics when Thiers spoke to you; I invariably do so when either Guizot or Bourqueney begin to swagger; and I observe that it always acts as a sedative'.

The Consuls of Britain and the Northern Powers at Alexandria presented Mehemet Ali with the ultimatum of 15 July. The Pasha was as cool and courteous as ever, but the Consuls knew him well enough to detect his anger and emotion from the way in which he plucked at the hairs of his white beard. He refused the terms, and said that he would fight against all the great powers. He said that he treated the statement as a declaration of war, and ordered the Consuls to leave Alexandria. This they refused to do, claiming that as they had been appointed Consuls in Egypt with the consent of the Sultan, Mehemet Ali, as the Sultan's Viceroy, had no right to compel them to leave; but soon afterwards they received orders from their governments to withdraw from Egypt. After the expiry of the twenty days' ultimatum, the Sultan carried out the threat contained in the Treaty of London. He deprived Mehemet Ali of the Pashalik of Egypt, and appointed a new Viceroy in his place.

When news of the deposition of Mehemet Ali reached Paris, the French Government, for the first time, took a really firm and unequivocal stand in his support. On 8 October, Thiers sent a note to Palmerston in which he declared that France considered the rule of Mehemet Ali as a vassal Prince in Egypt to be as essential to the balance of power in the Levant as the continued existence of the Turkish Empire; France, he stated, 'could not consent to the Act of deprivation decreed at Constantinople being carried into execution'. Thiers had at last made the French position clear: France would fight to retain Mehemet Ali in Egypt, but not in Syria. The British Cabinet, who were less confident than Palmerston that France was bluffing, were impressed by Thiers' determination; and

Palmerston, too, always had more respect for firmness than for a conciliatory policy. On 15 October, Palmerston wrote to Ponsonby and told him that, while he approved of the Sultan's deposition of Mehemet Ali as Viceroy of Egypt, he hoped that the Sultan would offer to reinstate him if he agreed within a reasonable time to evacuate Syria. This was not really a great concession on Palmerston's part, because on 3 October, a week before he received Thiers' note, he had written to Bulwer: 'Though it certainly would be a good thing if Mehemet Ali could be got rid of altogether, yet I look upon that as a very improbable event, because he will give in long before matters come to such a point.... We do not want to oust him from Egypt if he is content to spend the rest of his days there as a faithful servant'. Meanwhile, the French press became more belligerent, and the French fleet in the Mediterranean was reinforced.

At this point, Melbourne suddenly intervened. Without consulting his colleagues, he wrote a personal letter to the King of the Belgians, which Leopold, as Melbourne certainly intended, sent on to Louis Philippe. The original letter has not been found, but we know of its contents from a report of it at the time by the Austrian Ambassador in Brussels, to whom Leopold showed the letter, and from the subsequent memoirs of a French Foreign Office official who also read it. Both accounts agree that Melbourne warned Leopold that if Thiers continued his policy, and French naval rearmament continued, it would lead to war between Britain and France. This scared Louis Philippe, and when Thiers refused to modify his policy, the King dismissed him and recalled Guizot from London to appoint him as Prime Minister and Foreign Minister. Thiers denounced the King's policy as appeasement in the Chamber of Deputies, and rallied the support of the Left Opposition in France; but the resistance had gone out of French policy. The new French line was for Louis Philippe to point out to Leopold that if France were humiliated by the great powers, it would lead to an upsurge of patriotic fury in France which would sweep away Louis Philippe and his régime and lead to the establishment of a revolutionary republic. Leopold was alarmed, and passed on the message to Queen Victoria and Prince Albert, whom Victoria had married in the previous February. They, too, were impressed by this potential danger, and used their influence with Melbourne to induce Palmerston to make face-saving concessions to France.

But Palmerston had already disposed of this argument nine years before, when Granville had used it at the time of the Belgian crisis. 'I never can admit', he had written to Granville on 22 April 1831, 'that it can be wise to give way to the unjust pretensions of France for the purpose of gaining for the French Government, be it Périer or Sébastiani, the support of the violent party, or even of the moderate encroachers.... What is the use of having a moderate and pacific administration in France if, for the purpose of keeping them in the good graces of the violent and warlike, we submit to the demands of the latter instead of having the benefit of the good faith of the former? It is a contradiction in terms, and when such arguments are used, distrust the sincerity of those who employ them'.

He reassured the Queen on this point in a letter of 11 November 1840. 'There is no doubt a large party among the leading politicians in France who have long contemplated the establishment of a virtually, if not actually, independent State in Egypt and Syria, under the direct protection and influence of France, and that party feel great disappointment and resentment at finding their schemes in this respect baffled. But that party will not revenge themselves on the four powers by making a revolution in France, and they are enlightened enough to see that France cannot revenge herself by making war against the Four Powers who are much stronger than she is'. He stated that France was a very different nation now from what she was in 1792. 'France then imagined that she had much to gain by foreign war, France now knows that she has everything to lose by foreign war.... Upon all these grounds Viscount Palmerston deems it his duty to Your Majesty to express his strong conviction that the appeals made to Your Majesty's good feelings by the King of the French, upon the score of the danger of revolution in France, have no foundation in truth and are only exertions of skilful diplomacy'.

Meanwhile Palmerston combined friendly gestures to France on matters which did not affect British interests with ceaseless activity to frustrate France wherever he considered that this would benefit Britain. He willingly acceded to the French request to return the body of Napoleon from St. Helena for a great state funeral in France, which he hoped would 'make those full grown children think less of other things'; but he insisted that the Belgian Government abandon its plan for a commercial union with France by a virtual threat of war, despite the fact that the Belgians asserted that this was the only way of ending the acute economic distress in Belgium; and he interfered to prevent the French from using force in Morocco to obtain compensation for injuries to French subjects.

Despite all his confidence, Palmerston had been a little worried as to how Ibrahim's armies were going to be driven out of Syria if Mehemet Ali could not be persuaded, in the last resort, to give way to the threats of the great powers. This problem was suddenly solved. In the autumn of 1840, revolts broke out all over Syria against Ibrahim's tyranny. Turkish agents stirred up the tribesmen, and Palmerston sent arms, for which he insisted on prompt payment from the Turkish Government. The British Navy, assisted by a small Austrian flotilla with the Archduke Charles on board, conducted operations along the coast of Syria against Ibrahim's garrisons and interrupted his communications with Egypt. They were under the command of Commodore Charles Napier, who had returned to the British Navy after winning the Portuguese civil war for Pedro. He captured Beirut and Acre, and in less than three months Ibrahim was trying desperately to retreat overland to Egypt, with the Syrian tribesmen mercilessly murdering all the stragglers from his retreating army.

The only question now was whether Mehemet Ali would be allowed to retain Egypt. Ponsonby was furious when he received Palmerston's despatch of 15 October with the suggestion that the Sultan should reinstate Mehemet Ali as Viceroy, and when he broached the matter with the Turkish ministers, he found that they were even more indignant than he was. The collapse of Ibrahim in Syria and the fall of Thiers in France made it much less necessary in December than it had been in October to make any concessions to Mehemet Ali. But in the end Mehemet Ali was saved by his personal charm. On 25 November Napier arrived with the fleet at Alexandria and demanded that Mehemet Ali surrender the Turkish fleet which had deserted to him, submit to the Sultan and the great powers, and evacuate Syria. He was fascinated by the personality of the old military adventurer whose character was not so very different from his own. He urged Mehemet Ali to submit to the overwhelming force of the British Navy which confronted him, and told the Pasha's chief minister how reluctant he would be to have to fight him. 'I am a great admirer of His Highness', he told him, 'and would much rather be his friend than enemy'.

Without any authority from Admiral Stopford or Palmerston, Napier negotiated an agreement with Mehemet Ali. In return for the surrender of the Turkish fleet, and the acceptance by Mehemet Ali of the Treaty of London, Napier agreed to send the British Navy to evacuate Ibrahim's men from Syria – thus saving them from the marauding tribesmen and the horrors of a march across the desert – and undertook that the Sultan would confer the hereditary Pashalik of Egypt on Mehemet Ali and his family. Ponsonby was very angry with Napier, and urged Palmerston to repudiate the agreement. Palmerston was displeased with Napier, but he had already decided to let Mehemet Ali keep Egypt; and though Ponsonby tried to influence him by sending him a hair-raising account of the cruelties committed by Mehemet Ali's troops in their slave-trading operations against the negroes of the Sudan, he was not to be moved. The four powers ordered their Ambassadors at Constantinople to advise the Porte to grant the hereditary Pashalik of Egypt to Mehemet Ali. Ponsonby refused to join his colleagues in this démarche on the grounds that his instructions from Palmerston were ambiguous; but Palmerston, after irritating Metternich by trying to throw the blame for Ponsonby's obstruction on the Austrian Government, ordered Ponsonby to join in putting pressure on the Sultan. The negotiations as to the terms of the grant of the Pashalik went on until the summer of 1841. It was necessary to devise face-saving formulas to emphasize the Sultan's sovereignty over Egypt, and Mehemet Ali was forced to agree to pay a higher annual tribute and to limitations on the size of his army; but on 13 February 1841 he was granted the hereditary governorship of Egypt, which his family ruled until 1952.

Guizot tried hard to persuade Palmerston to agree to let the great powers sign a declaration stating that it was at the request of France that they had urged the Sultan to allow Mehemet Ali to retain Egypt. Despite pressure from King Leopold and Queen Victoria, Palmerston refused to throw this sop to French pride, and alleviate what he called the 'salutary humiliation' of France; but he was equally firm in rejecting the Prussian proposal that Britain and the Northern Powers should sign a permanent anti-French alliance. He adopted the attitude that France, having refused to join the great powers in their coercion of Mehemet Ali, should have no say in the settlement of that issue; but as soon as this had been settled, France should be brought back into the concert of the great powers. He persuaded the Northern Powers to agree to this, and in July 1841 France joined with Austria, Russia and Prussia in signing the convention about the navigation of the Dardanelles. By this convention, the powers agreed that no foreign warships should enter the Dardanelles while Turkey was at peace. Russia thus relinquished the advantages which she had gained under the Treaty of Unkiar Skelessi in 1833. The Tsar thought it worth while to make this great concession in order to win Britain's goodwill. His expectations did not materialize. This was a mistake which Palmerston would not have made.

Chapter Eighteen

The Opium War

While Palmerston was collaborating closely with the Tsar against France and Mehemet Ali, he was busily engaged in resisting Russian policy in Asia. Like all other British statesmen, he was afraid of Russian designs against India, and believed, in the words of Lord John Russell, that 'if we do not stop Russia on the Danube, we shall have to stop her on the Indus'. The great Indian Empire belonged in theory to a private trading organization, the East India Company, and was governed by the company's Governor-General in Calcutta and Court of Directors in London; but the Governor-General, though formally chosen by the directors, was in fact appointed by the Crown, and acted on the instructions of the British Government in London and a Cabinet minister holding the office of President of the Indian Board of Control. In 1835, the Court of Directors selected Lord Heytesbury, a former Ambassador to Russia, to be the Governor-General of India; but Peel's Government, who had favoured Heytesbury, went out of office before the appointment could be made; and when Palmerston became Foreign Secretary, he refused to have Heytesbury on the grounds that he was too pro-Russian. To the great annoyance of the directors, he insisted on appointing Lord Auckland, who had for many years been a prominent Whig politician.

The British rulers of India were very conscious that every conqueror of India – except the British themselves – had entered from the north; and in the first half of the nineteenth century, they saw Russia expanding southwards along the shores of the Black Sea and the Caspian, and extending their influence over the petty khanates of Central Asia. India was separated from Russia by two thousand miles of territory belonging to Persia, Afghanistan and the independent Sikh state of the Punjab; and Palmerston was determined to do all he could to prevent this distance from being shortened. In February 1840 he wrote to Hobhouse that it was inevitable that Britain and Russia – 'the man from the Baltic and he from the British islands' – should meet in the centre of Asia, and that his job was to see that this clash occurred as far as possible from the frontiers of India.

Persia, Afghanistan and the Punjab were not only continually troubled by civil wars between various claimants to the throne, but were also often engaged in wars with each other for territorial aggrandizement. Palmerston's policy towards these states was always to support the south-east against the north-west. When armies marched south-eastwards, they approached India; when they marched north-westwards, they went away from India. So Palmerston wished to see the south-eastern states advance against their north-western neighbours. He supported Persia against Russia; he supported Afghanistan against Persia; he supported the Punjab against Afghanistan. But in the case of the Russo-Persian disputes, another factor was involved. Palmerston did not wish to become involved in a serious conflict with Russia, particularly at times when he was seeking Russian support in Europe or the Middle East; and he did not wish to see a weak state like Persia gain any advantage from playing off two great powers against each other. He therefore tried to cooperate as far as possible with Russia in Persia, while preventing Russia from acquiring a dominant position there, or expanding south-eastwards.

In 1834, the Shah of Persia died, and two of his relations immediately claimed the throne. One of them asked Russia for help, and the other appealed to Britain. Palmerston proposed to Nesselrode that they should agree on a candidate and compel the Persians to accept him. They chose a third claimant who was installed as Shah, and at the suggestion of the British and Russian ministers at Teheran, the pro-British pretender was exiled to Turkey, and the pro-Russian one to Russia.

Next year, Palmerston sent Mr. Ellis to Teheran to congratulate the new Shah on his accession. Ellis had the rank of a special Ambassador, but he was to propose that in future Britain should be represented by a minister in Persia, instead of by an agent of the East India Company. Ellis sailed from Falmouth on 28 July, and reached Teheran on 3 November. Before he left, Palmerston instructed him as to the attitude which he should pursue with regard to Russia.

As England and Russia are for the moment acting in unison, you should be careful that your Deportment towards the Russian Mission should neither indicate unfriendly Feelings, nor unnecessarily imply Suspicion; but on the other hand you should not allow the Russian Minister to suppose that the British Government does not attach the greatest Importance to the maintenance of the Independence and Integrity of Persia; or that England is not firmly resolved to uphold that Integrity and Independence. In your Confidential Intercourse with the Persian Government you must not conceal the opinion entertained by His Majesty's Government that however cautiously Russia may be acting at present, it is from Her that the great Danger to Persia must arise; and against Her that the Defensive arrangements of Persia should be directed. You will especially warn the Persian Government against being made the Tools of Russian Policy, by allowing themselves to be pushed on to make war against the Afghans. Russia has objects of Her own to gain by exciting the Persian Government to quarrel with its Eastern Neighbours. The attention of Persia is thus turned away from what is passing to the North and the West, and the Intrigues by which Russia is paving her way to future encroachments upon Persia have a better Chance of being carried on unobserved.

Palmerston urged the Shah to remain on friendly terms with Turkey. He suggested that it would be unwise for Persia to alarm the Russians by making a formal alliance with the Sultan; but he worked continually, and on the whole successfully, to smooth out any difficulties on the Turco-Persian border, and any other cause of resentment; and he stopped the Turkish Government from giving any encouragement to Persian political refugees in Turkey, or from permitting them to plot against the Shah. But Persia's relations with her eastern neighbour were less friendly. Persia coveted the Afghan province of Herat; and Russia encouraged the Persians to move south-east. Palmerston supported the Afghans over Herat. He sent the Navy to seize the Persian island of Kharak in the Persian Gulf, and threatened to act against the port of Bushire if the Persians continued to attack Herat. The Afghans forced the Persians to abandon the siege of Herat, and this defeat, as well as British pressure in St. Petersburg, persuaded the Tsar to advise the Shah to abandon his designs against Herat.

. The Tsar was not much more successful in his projects against Khiva, seven hundred miles north of Herat. The independent Khan of Khiva had for many years been in the habit of raiding the caravans of the nomadic tribes who lived across the Russian frontier, and removing some of the inhabitants as slaves. In 1839, the Russian Government decided that it must prevent this outrage against Russian subjects by conquering Khiva. Palmerston urged Nesselrode not to invade Khiva, and offered to mediate and to obtain the release of the Russian nomads held as slaves. The Russians refused mediation, and sent an army into Khiva; but it got bogged down in the wild mountainous country, and when Palmerston sent an envoy to the Khan of Khiva, and persuaded him to release the Russian slaves, the Tsar abandoned his military campaign. The Russians did not conquer Khiva for another thirty years.

Afghanistan was ruled by the formidable Dost Mahommed. Lord Auckland sent Sir Alexander Burnes as the British envoy to Dost Mahommed in Kabul. Burnes was almost the only man in Britain who knew anything about Afghanistan. He had travelled there, and in Khiva and Bokhara, and on his return to England had published a book about his experiences which had made him famous before he was thirty. He had lectured about Afghanistan all over Britain, and had talked about it to William IV at the Brighton Pavilion. Burnes established very friendly relations with Dost Mahommed. But Britain had also established equally friendly relations with Dost Mahommed's eastern neighbour, the Sikh Maharajah of Lahore, Ranjit Singh, who ruled the Punjab with his powerful army. Thirty years before, Ranjit Singh had seized Peshawar from Afghanistan, and was now giving asylum, and every encouragement, to Shah Shujá, the former ruler of Afghanistan – an exceptionally vicious despot who was in the habit of blinding his political opponents. Dost Mahommed was eager to

regain Peshawar. He proposed to Burnes that India and Afghanistan should make an alliance against the Punjab, under
which he could attack Peshawar with British approval. Burnes,
who had a high opinion of Dost Mahommed's ability, urged
the British Government to accept the offer.

Palmerston consulted the President of the Board of Control, Sir John Cam Hobhouse, who had formerly been a Radical MP, and had actually been imprisoned for his political
activities at the time of Peterloo; but since he had become
Palmerston's colleague in a Whig Government, he had repudiated nearly all his earlier opinions. They were advised by
Lord Auckland that they could not possibly abandon Ranjit
Singh and the Sikhs of the Punjab, who had been faithful allies
of the Indian Government for many years. Ranjit Singh, on
the other hand, asked the Indian Government to assist him
in overthrowing Dost Mahommed in Afghanistan and replac-
ing Shah Shujá in power there. Lord Auckland urged the British Government to back Ranjit Singh to the full, and to act
with him against Dost Mahommed. The matter was discussed
in great secrecy, not at a full meeting of the Cabinet, but only
by Melbourne, Palmerston, Hobhouse, Lord John Russell,
Glenelg, Lansdowne, and Lord Cottenham, the Lord Chancellor, at a meeting at Windsor Castle on 24 October 1838.
They agreed to pursue the course which Auckland advised;
and Auckland had already acted on his own authority. The
monstrous Shah Shujá entered Afghanistan from the Punjab
accompanied by British and Sepoy troops of the Indian Army.
After some sharp fighting, they were victorious. Shah Shujá
was installed as Emir of Afghanistan, and maintained in power
by a British army of occupation in Kabul; while Dost Mahommed was sent as a prisoner to India.

The policy of the British Government was strongly criticized in the House of Commons by several Radical and other
MPs, who objected, chiefly on moral grounds, to the British
intervention in Afghanistan, and especially to the imprisonment without trial of Dost Mahommed in India, though this
could be legally justified as Dost Mahommed was a prisoner of
war, like Napoleon at St. Helena. The task of defending the
Government's policy fell chiefly to Hobhouse, as President of

the Board of Control; but Palmerston occasionally intervened
to support him in the House, and was his most ardent supporter in the Cabinet.

As usual in such cases, the MPs demanded that the relevant
papers be laid before the House. Palmerston prepared the
despatches for publication, devoting a great deal of personal
attention to this matter, as he had done in the case of the
despatches relating to the Middle Eastern crisis. On these occasions, he had to strike the balance between satisfying the
desire of the House of Commons for full knowledge of the
facts, and the need to avoid causing international complica-
tions by publishing statements which might be resented by
foreign powers. When he published the documents on the
Middle Eastern crisis, he omitted not only those passages
which contained adverse comments on Louis Philippe personally, but those in which Ponsonby had warned against the
danger to British interests from Russian influence at Constantinople. The published papers nevertheless contained some remarkably frank disclosures, and gave an accurate general picture of the development of the crisis.

But it was another matter with the papers on the Afghan
war. Palmerston published several of Burnes's despatches, but
cut out all the passages in which Burnes had praised the wise
government and pro-British sympathies of Dost Mahommed,
and had urged the British Government to make an alliance
with him. This gave a very misleading impression about
Burnes's attitude. By publishing Burnes's despatches in this
mutilated form, Palmerston succeeded in suggesting that the
Government had consulted the greatest expert on the Afghan
problem, without giving any idea that they had acted in flat
contradiction to his advice; and Dost Mahommed, who was
condemned to silence in his Delhi prison, was represented in
a much less favourable light than he had been regarded by
the British agent who knew him best. Burnes was very angry
when he read the printed despatches, and realized what
Palmerston had done; but as a Government servant, he could
make no comment, and he was far away in Kabul, trying duti-
fully to carry out a policy of which he disapproved.

Palmerston and the Whig Government had gone out of office before the next stage in the events in Afghanistan. In November 1841, the Afghans rose in revolt, under the leadership of Dost Mahommed's son, against Shah Shujá and the British garrison in Kabul. Shah Shujá was killed, and Burnes, who had come to be regarded as a traitor by the Afghans, was murdered by a mob when he was trying to reassure them as to British intentions. The British troops were surrounded, and surrendered on being granted a safe-conduct to return to India; but the terms were violated by the Afghans, who attacked them in the mountain passes, and exterminated them. Only one survivor escaped and reached India out of the force of 15,000 men.

Auckland and Hobhouse bore the brunt of the blame for the disaster, but some of it was thrown on Palmerston. Next year, Britain avenged the humiliation by sending another army from India to Afghanistan. They captured Kabul, burned a bazaar and two mosques, and removed the sacred gates of the city which they falsely claimed were those which had been taken from the people of India eight hundred years before, and which Britain was now supposed to be restoring to the rightful owners. Having thus vindicated British honour, and aroused a great deal of criticism in the Moslem world and in Britain, the British Government released Dost Mahommed and restored him to the throne of Afghanistan.

The relatives and friends of Burnes, whose brilliant career had been cut short at the age of thirty-six, were indignant that Hobhouse and Palmerston had suppressed the fact that their disastrous policy had been pursued against Burnes's strong advice. They enlisted the support of a number of MPs who in 1842 demanded that the Conservative Government should publish those parts of Burnes's despatches which had been suppressed. The Government argued that this would be against the public interest, and the MPs agreed to abandon their demand for publication after Hobhouse had given a personal assurance that the despatches which he and Palmerston had published did not misrepresent Burnes's views. But the criticism continued outside Parliament. In 1851 Colonel Sir John Kaye published his *History of the War in Afghanistan*, in which he revealed the truth about Burnes's despatches, and accused Hobhouse and Palmerston of falsifying the despatches and misleading the House of Commons about them. Eventually, in 1859, the Government gave way, and the suppressed passages in the despatches were published.

By this time Palmerston was Prime Minister, and his opponents re-opened the question of Burnes's despatches in order to discredit him. In March 1861 they moved in the House of Commons for the setting up of a Committee of Inquiry into the circumstances of the publication of the Parliamentary Papers on Afghanistan in 1839. Palmerston opposed the motion, and defended his actions twenty-two years before. He said that Burnes, though an excellent public servant, had misjudged the situation in Afghanistan, and that as the Government had not acted on his advice, but on the wiser advice of Lord Auckland and the Government of India, there was no point in publishing those parts of Burnes's despatches which had not affected the Government's decision. He said that the demand for a Committee of Inquiry was pointless, as the events of 1839 had no relevance for the present time. This did not appease the anger of Palmerston's critics, least of all John Bright, who by 1861 had become Palmerston's most bitter political and personal enemy. Bright declared that it was still relevant to examine what had happened in 1839, in order to know 'whether there was and is a man in high position in the Government ... who had so low a sense of honour and of right that he could offer to this House mutilated, false, forged opinions of a public servant who lost his life in the public service'. But the motion to set up the Committee was defeated by 159 votes to 49.

In the Far East there were no great powers, or satellites of great powers, who could threaten British strategical interests; for the empires of China and Japan were completely isolated from the rest of the world. But here Britain became involved in conflict because of that other vital British interest – free trade. China contained one-third of the total population of the world: it had more than 350,000,000 inhabitants, at a time when the population of Russia was 50,000,000 and the United States 13,000,000. British merchants were not permitted to trade with any Chinese port except Canton, and all trading there had to be conducted by the East India Company with a guild of Chinese merchants – the Co-Hong; but China was Britain's biggest supplier. One-sixth of the total British overseas trade was with China. China exported tea to Britain, where it had recently become the most popular drink with the British working classes. In the eighteenth century, the tea had to be paid for largely in silver; but in 1773, the first cargo of Indian opium was sent to China. The importation of opium was illegal by Chinese law, but the opium trade grew enormously, and silver, instead of flowing into China, flowed out of it. By 1833, fifty-five per cent of British exports to China was illegal opium. Next year, the British Government, to the annoyance of the Chinese, abolished the East India Company's monopoly of trade with China; and individual British merchants carried on a growing trade with Canton, though on the Chinese side it had still to be conducted exclusively through the Co-Hong guild.

No foreign nations had diplomatic relations with China. The Chinese believed that the Emperor of China was ruler of the world, and that all foreigners were 'outer barbarians' who should approach the Emperor as suppliants, not presume to send him Ambassadors as equals. Two British attempts to send an Ambassador to Peking had broken down when the Ambassador refused to perform the kowtow, and prostrate himself nine times, when he was received by the Emperor. Foreign residents in Canton were not allowed to enter certain streets, to walk in the park except on special days in the month, or to ride in sedan chairs, which was a privilege reserved for the higher-class Chinese; and they were repeatedly forbidden to have sexual relations with Chinese women. These regulations were not always strictly enforced; but the Chinese attitude was very irritating to British merchants, who knew that their country could thrash the Chinese in war without the slightest difficulty.

The ordinary English trader in China despised the Chinese as much as the Chinese mandarin despised the English. It was a common occurrence if a Chinese annoyed an Englishman by making a noise in front of his house, or in some other way, for the Englishman to seize him and flog him without more ado. One of the most forward in resorting to self-help was the British opium trader, James Innes. Innes took action against a Chinese who disturbed him by cutting wood near his house, and in the ensuing controversy Innes was wounded in the arm with a chopper. He thereupon called on the local magistrate, at 2 p.m., and told him that unless he had arrested the assailant by sunset he would burn down the magistrate's house. Innes carried out his threat that night, and the magistrate was so impressed that he arrested Innes's assailant next day, and sentenced him to be cangued. This meant that he had to walk around the town for a month with his head stuck through an enormous board. But even when the Chinese gave concessions and indulgences to the British, they did it in a condescending and patronizing manner which caused resentment. Their attitude that the barbarians must be forgiven for their misconduct because they were too ignorant and uncouth to know any better, angered the British, and at the same time caused them to despise the Chinese for their weakness.

Conflict between China and Britain was inevitable. On the one side was a corrupt, decadent and caste-ridden despotism, with no desire or ability to wage war, which relied on custom much more than force for the enforcement of extreme privilege and discrimination, and which was blinded by a deep-rooted superiority complex into believing that they could assert their supremacy over Europeans without possessing military power. On the other side was the most economically advanced nation in the world, a nation of pushing, bustling traders, who had been brought up to believe, as an article of faith, in the merits of self-help, free trade, and the pugnacious qualities of John Bull.

As the Chinese Government refused to enter into diplomatic relations with foreign powers, Britain was not able to have any diplomatic or consular official at Canton. Negotiations between the British merchants and the Chinese authorities were carried on between a selected British spokesman and the Co-Hong merchants, who were appointed by the Chinese Government to deal with the barbarians. All communications from the British merchants to the Chinese authorities had to be in the form of a petition, beginning with the word 'Pin' used by an inferior to a superior. Palmerston thought that British prestige required that British relations with China should be on a higher than Chamber of Commerce level; and in 1834 he sent Lord Napier to Canton to negotiate with the Cantonese provincial government on behalf of the British Government. In his instructions to Napier, Palmerston emphasized that he must behave with the utmost courtesy to the Chinese, and avoid doing anything to offend their susceptibilities; but Palmerston included one sentence in his despatch which, as the Tories afterwards pointed out, ordered Napier to do a thing which would offend the Chinese more than anything else could do: 'Your Lordship will announce your arrival at Canton by letter to the Viceroy'. This meant that Napier was to claim to come as an envoy from the King of England, and to write as an equal, not as a petitioner. The Tories also thought that even a Western government might take umbrage if a representative of a foreign power arrived uninvited at one of its ports on an official mission.

Lord Napier's mission got off to a bad start. As the Chinese would only communicate with him through the Hong merchants, he invited them to meet him in the British factory. When they arrived, a long argument developed as to the seating arrangements for the meeting, for the Chinese insisted on re-arranging the chairs so that Napier and his staff should sit on the north, or inferior, side, whereas Napier was adamant that he, as host, should sit at the head of the table, with the Chinese visitors in the place of honour on his right. Napier got his way, but then proceeded to give the Chinese a sharp dressing down for having arrived two hours late, which he said was an insult to the King of England. There is no record of what Palmerston thought when he received Napier's despatch containing this interpretation of the significance of arriving two hours late for a meeting with a foreign envoy. A few days later, Napier was unceremoniously ordered to leave Canton. He went to the Portuguese colony of Macao, where he died, according to his doctors, of the strain brought on by his exertions at Canton.

Palmerston made no further efforts to establish official re-

lations with China; but he sent Captain Elliot of the Royal
Navy to Canton to act for the British Government and to
safeguard the interests of British subjects there. Elliot was the
cousin of Gilbert Elliot, who had been Palmerston's closest
friend at Edinburgh University. Palmerston repeatedly told
Elliot not to write 'Pin' on his letters to the Cantonese authorities; but Elliot knew that if he followed this directive, the
Chinese would not receive his letters, so he wrote 'Pin' like
a petitioner.

The main cause of conflict between China and the British
traders was opium. Opium had been grown and consumed in
China for many centuries; but it was only after the Spaniards
had introduced tobacco smoking that the Chinese began to
smoke opium, which then rapidly became a grave social
menace. In 1729 an Imperial decree prohibited the growth,
importation or smoking of opium, under pain of flogging or
canguing; but the traffic grew unchecked, as nearly every
Chinese official, from the highest to the lowest, connived at
the importation of opium, after accepting a bribe appropriate
to his station. In 1796, the Emperor imposed the death penalty
– a rare punishment in China – for growing, importing or
smoking opium; but the law was a dead letter, and the trade
continued to grow. If the people of Britain were to have tea,
the smuggling of opium into China had to continue.

In 1836, the Chinese Government decided to grapple with
the opium problem. Some of the ministers advised the Emperor to accept the fact that it was impossible to suppress the
habit, and urged him to regulate and control it. They suggested
that the growth of opium in China should be permitted, that
the import of Indian opium should be legalized subject
to the payment of customs duties, and that the Hong
merchants should be compelled to pay for the opium in tea
and other goods, so as to stop the export of silver. But other
ministers advocated that a more determined attempt should
be made to stamp out opium. They claimed that opium
smuggling was ruining the health of the whole population,
especially the army, and thought that the British were trying
to weaken the Chinese by introducing opium as a preparatory
step to conquering the country, like the Dutch had done in

Java. The Emperor decided to adopt this policy. He sent Lin Tse-sü to Canton with orders to suppress the opium trade by all the means at his disposal. The British merchants now found that when the opium was landed at Canton it was no longer passed by smiling officials with itching palms, but was seized and burned by angry officers of Lin. The British merchants defeated Lin's efforts by storing the opium, as it arrived from Calcutta, on receiving ships lying off Canton, just outside Chinese territorial waters. From there the opium was run in at night on small sailing ships and steamers up the Canton river, or to other places on the coast. Chinese coastguards seized and destroyed many cargoes of smuggled opium, and sometimes engaged in violent clashes with the smugglers. Nearly all the British traders at Canton were connected with the smugglers, or very sympathetic to them. Elliot tried to collaborate with the Chinese authorities in suppressing the illegal trade, and became very unpopular with the British community in consequence.

But Elliot got no assistance from Palmerston. Palmerston was, as usual, overworked and busy with the great problems of Europe and the Middle East. He did not hurry unduly in replying to Elliot's despatches, and this, combined with the slowness of transport, meant that it was usually about ten months before Elliot received a reply to his letters. When the replies came, Elliot did not find them helpful. Palmerston said that British subjects must not expect to receive any help from the British Government if they were caught and punished by the Chinese for breaking the laws of China; but he pointed out that Elliot had no legal powers to punish Britons for offences in China or on the high seas, and was not entitled to interfere with their property, or to help to enforce Chinese laws against British subjects. He advised British ships to submit to inspection by Chinese coastguards in Chinese waters, but to resist it on the high seas. Above all, he ordered Elliot not to take any arbitrary or illegal action against British subjects in order to suppress the opium smuggling. 'In the present state of our relations with China', he wrote to Elliot on 22 July 1836, 'it it especially incumbent upon you, while you do all that lies in your power to avoid giving just cause of offence to the Chinese authorities, to be at the same time very careful not to assume a greater degree of authority over British subjects in China than that which you in reality possess'. This meant that Elliot could do nothing against the receiving ships off Canton.

The only action which Palmerston was prepared to take was quite inadequate to deal with this problem. He introduced a bill in Parliament to enable Elliot to set up a law court at Canton, and to deport from China any British subject who was convicted before his court of an offence against Chinese law. But the bill aroused great opposition in both Houses, where members were indignant that an officer of the Crown should be given powers to deport British subjects from anywhere. So the bill was withdrawn, and Elliot was powerless to do anything against the opium smugglers.

Palmerston showed the same respect for international law when the Chinese authorities confiscated a cargo of opium which James Innes was smuggling into Canton. Innes told them that unless they released the opium, his boats would retaliate against Chinese shipping wherever they had the opportunity to do so. Palmerston instructed Elliot that if Innes carried out this threat, he would be guilty of piracy, and as Britain was entitled and bound, under international law, to suppress piracy, Elliot was to use his naval forces to seize or destroy Innes's pirate boats.

In December 1838, Lin decided to make an example of both a British and a Chinese opium smuggler. He expelled Innes from Canton, and though Innes at first flatly refused to leave, he eventually departed when the Chinese threatened to burn his house over his head if he stayed. Lin was more drastic with the Chinese smuggler. He ordered that the man should be publicly strangled in the square immediately in front of the British factories. The British were indignant, and when the scaffold was being erected, they ran out of their factories and tore it down. The Chinese officials then ordered the execution to take place in another part of the town; but while the man was being strangled, the British merchants arrived on the scene, and, charging into the crowd, dispersed the onlookers with whips and lathis. Palmerston did not approve of such lawlessness. 'I ... wish to know', he wrote to Elliot on 15 April 1839, 'upon what alleged ground of right those persons considered themselves entitled to interfere with the arrangements made by the Chinese officers of justice for carrying into effect, in a Chinese town, the orders of their superior authorities'.

Eventually, Lin demanded that the whole stock of opium held in the receiving ships should be surrendered. When Elliot refused to do this, Lin interned two hundred British merchants in their factories at Canton, and threatened to hold them there until the opium was handed over. He also ordered the Chinese servants to refuse to work for the British, and cut off all supplies of food to them. Elliot went to the factory to see what was happening to the British subjects, and raised the Union Jack over the factory; but he was himself detained by the Chinese as a prisoner with the others. He then agreed to sign a document in which he promised to surrender the opium; and although he had no power to compel the merchants to give it up, they agreed to do so after Elliot had unofficially given them to understand that they would be compensated by the British Government. The prisoners were then released and after some delay the whole stock of opium in the receiving ships was handed over – 20,291 chests worth more than £1,250,000. It took four months to pour it all into the sea. But the British merchants began almost immediately to smuggle opium into China again.

In July, a group of drunken English sailors attacked a Chinese village, assaulted several of the inhabitants, and killed one man. Lin asked Elliot to hand over the murderer. Elliot paid compensation to the relatives of the murdered man, and tried several of the sailors for riot, and sentenced them to fines and terms of imprisonment to be served in Britain – a sentence which was later quashed by the British Government on the grounds that Elliot had exceeded his jurisdiction. But Elliot told Lin that he was unable to discover who had committed the murder. Lin demanded that the whole of the crew of the ship be delivered up to him, and promised that after making inquiries he would select one man for execution and return all the others to Elliot. This seemed perfectly reasonable to Lin, because the idea of collective responsibility was clearly accepted in Chinese criminal law, and they had often punished an innocent neighbour when they could not discover the identity of the murderer of a British subject. But the British had always been reluctant to surrender British subjects for trial by the Chinese, because though the Chinese punishments for murder were in some respects milder than in Britain, and fewer crimes were punishable by death, the Chinese used torture to extract confessions, and the British had no faith in their system of justice. Elliot refused to hand over any of the sailors. On 3 November 1839, Lin sent twenty-nine war junks to surround two English ships and demand the surrender of the murderer. The British Captain replied by opening fire on the junks and sunk four of them. The war had begun.

On 20 February 1840, Palmerston wrote a note to the Chinese Government in Peking. He assured them that the British Government had no wish to protect British subjects who contravened the law of China by smuggling opium; but he protested against the fact that the Chinese Government should suddenly have enforced the law so drastically after they had for so long allowed it to be broken with impunity. He also complained that the Chinese Government had enforced the law against British subjects, but had not punished the Chinese who had broken it – a strange contention, in view of the fact that a Chinese smuggler had been strangled for his offence despite the attempts of British merchants to prevent it by force, while nothing worse had been done against any British subject than expulsion from China and the confiscation of his opium. Palmerston protested against the imprisoning of innocent merchants and an official representative of the Queen – he did not mention the fact that the Chinese had never accepted Elliot in this capacity – and against the attempt to starve the British residents into submission in order to compel Elliot to surrender the opium, which he had no legal power to do. He praised the patriotism of the opium merchants who had voluntarily surrendered their opium in order to save their imprisoned fellow-countrymen, and told the Chinese Government that he fully approved of the action of the British ships in firing on the Chinese junks on 3 November.

Palmerston therefore demanded that the Chinese Government pay compensation in full for the confiscated opium, which the British Government would pay over to the owners. As compensation for the insult to Elliot, he demanded the cession to Britain of some island off the China coast. He demanded that the debts owing to the British merchants by the Hong merchants should be paid by the Chinese Government, because the Chinese Government had compelled the British merchants to do business with the Hong merchants, instead of permitting them to trade freely with any Chinese of their own choosing. He demanded that British merchants should be permitted to trade at Amoy, Foochow, Ningpo and Shanghai as well as Canton. He then explained that in view of the great distance between England and China, and the time that it took for communications to travel between them, he was sending a military and naval expedition to China, which would immediately begin to blockade the Chinese ports and to occupy strongpoints on the mainland before receiving the Chinese Government's reply to this note, and he demanded that China pay the cost of these operations. 'The British Government', wrote Palmerston, 'fervently hopes that the wisdom and spirit of Justice for which The Emperor is famed in all parts of the World, will lead the Chinese Government to see the equity of the foregoing demands'.

On the same day, Palmerston wrote to Elliot and told him that if the Chinese were reluctant to cede any island to Britain, he was to accept, instead, a treaty which gave to British subjects complete freedom of trade with China. Palmerston explained that such a treaty would in fact be preferable to acquiring an island, and that Britain did not demand any special privileges for British subjects, but only freedom of trade for every nation in the world. But Elliot was on no account to depart from any of the other demands; and if, in the meantime, he had negotiated any treaty with China which contained less favourable terms, he was to tell them that this treaty had not been ratified by the British Government. He ordered Elliot to occupy the island of Chusan at once, and to retain it until all the demands had been complied with.

On 7 April 1840 the Tories moved a vote of censure on the Government's policy towards China. The motion condemned

the Government for having brought Britain to the verge of
war with China by its negligence in failing to take steps to
deal with the smuggling of opium. The speeches in the debate showed the great clash of principles which had arisen —
a clash between international morality and British honour,
which would often recur during the century in debates in the
House. Peel and the leading Opposition spokesmen did not
deny that a situation had now been reached in which it was
necessary to begin hostilities in order to vindicate British prestige; but they claimed that this rupture with a friendly nation
and our best business customer would never have occurred
if Palmerston had not been so dilatory in dealing with the
situation instead of sending orders to Elliot to suppress the
opium-smuggling.

The Government spokesmen did not defend the traffic in
opium, but said that a desire to suppress the opium trade
could not justify the Chinese authorities in imprisoning British merchants and insulting the Queen's representative; and
they denounced the decree which forbade the Chinese to sell
provisions to the British — a measure which was utterly barbarous, as it deprived starving women and children of food,
and in itself justified war. They also said that the Chinese had
poisoned the wells to prevent the imprisoned British from having water, which the Opposition MPs denied; and in fact the
Chinese had allowed the prisoners to have water. Sir George
Staunton, Palmerston's former colleague in South Hampshire, said that if we submitted to the 'degrading insults of
China' we would soon lose our Indian Empire. Macaulay
stated that the Chinese, in trying to suppress the evils of
opium, had committed an even greater evil — an interference
with private property and free trade; and he reminded the
House 'that they belonged to a country which had made the
farthest ends of the earth ring with the fame of her exploits in
redressing the wrongs of her children; that made the Dey of
Algiers humble himself to her insulted Consul', and had not
degenerated since Cromwell 'vowed that he would make the
name of Englishman as respected as ever had been the name
of Roman citizen'.

The most pro-Chinese speech was made by the thirty-year-old Tory MP for Newark, William Ewart Gladstone. He denounced 'this unjust and iniquitous war', and accused Palmerston of hoisting the British flag 'to protect an infamous contraband traffic, and if it were never to be hoisted except as it is now hoisted on the coast of China, we should recoil from its sight with horror'. Gladstone made one slip. 'The Chinese', he said, 'had no armament ready wherewith to expel us from Lintin. They therefore said, "We will resort to another mode of bringing you to reason. We will expel you from our shores by refusing you provisions", and then of course they poisoned the wells'. As the Government MPs roared at him, he hastily corrected himself, and added: 'I have not asserted – I do not mean to assert – that the Chinese actually poisoned their wells. All I mean to say is, that it was alleged that they had poisoned their wells'. It was many years before Gladstone was allowed to forget this unfortunate statement.

Palmerston replied to the debate late on the third night, when he spoke for two hours. He did not reach the lofty heights on which Macaulay had defended, and Gladstone had attacked, the principles on which the Government had acted; but his speech was loudly cheered by the Government supporters, who were delighted with his cheerful pugnacity. He criticized the arguments of the Opposition speakers, and made great play with Gladstone's statement that 'of course they poisoned the wells'; and he spent a great deal of time in showing that he had replied to Elliot's letters as rapidly as Wellington had done when he was Foreign Secretary. He claimed that it would have been improper 'to put down the opium trade by acts of arbitrary authority against British merchants. . . . Any Government would have been greatly to blame, which, without taking the sense of Parliament, would upon its own responsibility have invested a consular officer, at 15,000 miles' distance, with powers so arbitrary'. Nor would the House have tolerated such a policy. 'It was said that it was our duty to cooperate with the Chinese Government in putting down this contraband trade. He wondered what the House would have said to Her Majesty's ministers if they had come down to it with a large naval estimate for a number of revenue cruisers to be employed in the preventive service from the river at

Canton to the Yellow Sea for the purpose of preserving the morals of the Chinese people, who were disposed to buy what other people were disposed to sell to them'.

He claimed that the Chinese Government had not acted out of any moral objection to opium, as they wished to encourage the consumption of home-grown opium, and had acted under pressure from the Chinese opium-growers, and in order to prevent the export of silver. A careful perusal of the official papers which Palmerston had prepared for Parliament shows that this argument was most misleading. There was certainly a section of opinion in the Chinese Government which favoured pursuing such a course; but the policy of Lin, and the party which had prevailed at Peking, was to suppress the smoking of opium of all kinds and at all costs, because of its deleterious effect on the health and morals of the Chinese people; and Palmerston must have realized that Lin's decrees, which punished opium-smoking by death and set up reformatories where addicts could be cured of the habit, could not be part of a policy to encourage the consumption of the home-grown opium.

Palmerston disclaimed all feelings of hostility to the Chinese people. It was irrelevant whether the Chinese were a cruel or a kind-hearted people. 'He believed that both cruel men and benevolent men were to be found among them, as among all other nations. . . . On the whole, he should say, that the Chinese were not a cruel people, and there was one feature in their character which was very commendable – their aversion to capital punishment'. But if Britain had a quarrel with another country, 'it never entered into their consideration to make their measures stronger if they thought the people were of a ferocious disposition, nor to make them less decided because they thought the inhabitants of a milder character'. The vote of censure was defeated by 271 votes to 262 – a majority of 9. The division was more or less on party lines, with all the Tories voting against the Government, and most of the Whigs for them; but many Government supporters abstained. All the Radicals except Attwood voted for the Government.

The British forces had no difficulty in defeating the Chinese, who sometimes fought bravely, but were always badly led and incompetent, as the financial rewards offered by the Chinese Government for the heads of English soldiers could not succeed in converting them into a match for the British Army. Elliot captured Canton, but allowed the Chinese to ransom the city for 6,000,000 Spanish dollars. He also seized the island of Chusan. But Elliot was worried by the spread of disease among his soldiers and sailors at Chusan, who were short of supplies and medical assistance and were dying in large numbers. In August 1840 he opened peace negotiations with the Chinese delegate, Kishen. Both Elliot and Kishen departed from their instructions. Kishen agreed to cede Hong Kong to Britain, and to pay 6,000,000 dollars as compensation for the opium, in return for the evacuation of Chusan by the British forces. Elliot thought that he had made a good bargain, as he would in any case have been unable to remain in Chusan in view of the infection which was exterminating his men there; and he had also obtained the release of the British civilian prisoners, who had been very badly treated by the Chinese. But Palmerston was very angry when he heard about the peace terms, and his indignation was shared by his Cabinet colleagues, and especially by Queen Victoria, who strongly supported Palmerston's policy towards China.

Palmerston did not allow his close connexion with Elliot's family to influence his attitude. He persuaded the Cabinet to repudiate the peace treaty, and to remove Elliot from his command. On 21 April 1841, he broke the news to Elliot in a private letter. 'It is with great regret that I have to express to you my extreme disappointment at the Result of your Negotiations, and my disapproval of the manner in which you have conducted them'. Elliot had flagrantly departed from his clear instructions, and had utterly failed to appreciate the strength of his bargaining position. He had not insisted on an indemnity for the expenses of the war, on payment of the debts of the Hong merchants, or any of the other terms on which Palmerston had insisted; he had evacuated Chusan before the terms had been ratified, and all he had obtained was 'the cession of Hong Kong, a barren Island with hardly a House upon it'. Nor had he insisted on the use of words denoting his equality with the Chinese delegate. 'You will no doubt, by the time

you have read thus far, have anticipated that I could not conclude this Letter without saying that under these circumstances, it is impossible that you should continue to hold your
appointment in China. I can assure you that it is with great
and sincere regret, that I find myself unavoidably led to this
conclusion; but being convinced that I cannot consistently
with my public Duty continue to place in your Hand the public Interests with which you have been charged, I think it but
right towards you to take the very earliest opportunity of
telling you so'. Elliot remained in the Government service,
and in due course became an Admiral. His opposite number,
Kishen, suffered a worse fate for having exceeded his instructions and agreed to the cession of Hong Kong. He was carried
in chains through the streets of Canton, and exiled to the
Amur region.

Palmerston sent Pottinger to replace Elliot and to continue
the war. Chusan was taken a second time by storm, and several
towns on the mainland were captured and released on payment of a ransom. Palmerston ordered Pottinger to insist on
the original terms, and the indemnity claimed from China was
fixed at 21,000,000 dollars – three and a half times greater
than the sum which Elliot had agreed to accept. The Government were criticized in the House of Commons for demanding
compensation for the confiscated opium; but Palmerston
would not budge from this, nor from his insistence that the
Chinese Government should pay the debts of the Hong merchants. This demand was particularly resented by the Chinese
Government, because they had forbidden the Hong merchants to incur the debts; and Elliot thought it unjust. 'The
arrangements for the payment of the Hong debts', he wrote,
'were consented to by the Foreigners, and they have always
been faithfully observed on the other side; and I do not think
they can be disturbed without such a shock to confidence in
our justice and good faith, as it would be most unfortunate
to induce'.

Palmerston did not insist that the peace terms should contain anything about opium; but on 26 February 1841 he wrote
to Elliot and ordered him to try to persuade the Chinese
Government to legalize it. When Pottinger replaced Elliot,

Palmerston sent the same instructions to Pottinger on 31 May 1841. He used the same arguments that had been put forward by those ministers in the Chinese Government who supported the legalization of opium – that as it had proved impossible to suppress it even by the most draconian legislation, it would be better to legalize it and obtain customs revenue by importing it. He added the further argument that the legalization of opium would improve Anglo-Chinese relations, because as long as it continued to be banned, there would inevitably be clashes between the Chinese authorities and British smugglers. But the Emperor of China was absolutely determined on this point, and would not relax the laws against opium.

In August 1841, the Whig Government, and Palmerston, went out of office, and left the continuation of the war and the peace negotiations to Peel's Foreign Secretary, Lord Aberdeen. The Tories forgot the pro-Chinese arguments which they had used when in Opposition, and in August 1842 signed the Treaty of Nanking on the terms which Palmerston had laid down. It was Palmerston's war, and Palmerston's peace.

A year later, on 4 August 1843, the treaty was debated in the House of Commons. From the Opposition front bench, Palmerston defended the treaty against the critics, though he complained that the Government had not obtained a high enough figure as compensation for the opium merchants. He admitted that in the ordinary way Britain would not be entitled to demand compensation for opium which had been seized under the provisions of Chinese law; but 'what the late Government demanded was satisfaction for the injured honour of the country'; and 'one of the ways in which satisfaction was to be given was payment for the opium'. The demand that the Chinese should pay the cost of the war 'was certainly unusual in European warfare, but it was not unusual in Asiatic warfare; and under all the circumstances, in order to make the Chinese sensible of the extent of the outrage they had committed, and that they might sufficiently feel the exercise of the power of Britain in vindication of their honour, it was thought expedient and proper to make them pay the expenses of the war, in addition to compensating the injured parties'.

In demanding that China pay the cost of the war, Palmerston was departing from the principles which he had put forward a few years earlier when he was trying to persuade the Russian Government to abandon its demand for a war indemnity from Persia. On 16 June 1834, he told Lieven that he had heard 'that by the Treaty of Durkmanchay a large sum of money was stipulated to be paid by Persia to Russia for the expenses of the late War. That the British Government certainly never can admit the equity of principle upon which the exaction of such payments is made to rest. That when a powerful State gets into war with a weaker one and is as it must be victorious, it seems unjust that the beaten party should in addition to its own losses in the war be crushed by the overwhelming weight of a pecuniary burden from which it has no adequate means of relieving itself. That such a mode of dealing with a discomfited power would be almost as fatal to its Independence as territorial cessions would be, because the resources of a State may be crippled and its freedom of action taken away by the want of pecuniary means, as well as by a curtailment of territorial extent'. But if anyone had put these arguments to Palmerston on behalf of China in 1841, he would no doubt have brushed them aside as impatiently as Nesselrode did when the British chargé d'affaires read Palmerston's despatch to him. Palmerston never intended to apply these principles to Britain's disadvantage, and did not expect Nesselrode to accept them to Russia's detriment. As Florence Nightingale said of Palmerston in later years, 'he was a humbug, and knew it'.

The object of Palmerston's policy in China was not to acquire what he called 'the desert Island of Hong Kong', or any other territory; and the vindication of the honour of the Queen's envoy was only a secondary consideration, a means to an end. His chief aim was to secure and enlarge the Chinese market for the British trader. 'The rivalship of European manufactures', he wrote to Lord Auckland on 22 January 1841, 'is fast excluding our productions from the markets of Europe, and we must unremittingly endeavour to find in other parts of the world new vents for the produce of our industry. The world is large enough and the wants of the human race ample enough to afford a demand for all we can manufacture; but it is the business of the Government to open and to secure the roads for the market. Will the navigation of the Indus turn out to be as great a help as was expected for our commerce? If it does, and if we succeed in our China expedition, Abyssinia, Arabia, the countries on the Indus and the new markets of China, will at no distant period give a most important extension to the range of our foreign commerce'. It needed two more wars with China before Palmerston's objective was achieved.

Chapter Nineteen

The United States: The McLeod Case

In 1858, Palmerston declared that there were only three countries in the world which were capable of threatening the naval supremacy of Britain, and throughout his life he considered that the aim of British foreign policy must be to thwart the designs, and weaken the power, of these three states. The three countries were France, Russia and the United States. During the thirty years that Palmerston controlled British foreign policy, Russia was the only one of these three powers with which Britain went to war; but Britain was twice very near to war with both France and the United States, and in some ways Palmerston's policy was more hostile to the United States than to either of the other two rivals.

A year before Palmerston was born, the thirteen British colonies in North America had won their independence after the only war in which Britain has been defeated during the eighteenth, nineteenth and twentieth centuries. Palmerston was already Secretary at War when Britain went to war for a second time with the United States. The war of 1812 came about because Britain had claimed the right to stop and board American ships on the high seas and haul off deserters from the British Navy – including four thousand naturalized American citizens, who had lived for many years in the United States – to hang them at the yard-arm, or flog them around the fleet. The Whig Opposition had opposed the war; Palmerston and the Tories had supported it. In the course of the fighting, the British forces had done great damage to the east coast towns of America, and had burned the city of Washington and the White House as a reprisal for American raids in Canada. In the end the two belligerents made peace at Ghent at Christmas 1814 on terms which neither side could claim as a victory. A fortnight later, before the news of the peace had crossed the Atlantic, the British Army had suffered a signal defeat at the hands of Andrew Jackson at New Orleans. The Americans had thus twice humbled the British forces – the only nation to do so in a hundred years of warfare.

There was another factor which influenced Palmerston and his contemporaries in their attitude to the United States. It was a republic and a democracy, and even more alien to the spirit of British constitutional monarchy and aristocracy than were the absolutist monarchies of Europe. The feelings of many Englishmen were expressed by Lord Brougham in the House of Lords in 1843, long after Brougham had ceased to be a Radical, or even a Whig, and had become very close to the Tories. 'There was something in the establishment, for the first time in modern ages, of a great democratic government, of a purely republican constitution, which had an inevitable tendency to beget soreness of feeling on our side of the water. We, with ... our natural abhorrence of the levelling system and a democratic form of government', were alarmed to see the rise of a great empire which was a level republic, 'ruling, and conquering, and flourishing, without a King to govern, without a prelate to bless, without a noble to adorn them – we saw all this affected at the point of the sword after a series of defeat, disaster and disgrace to the British arms'.

From the many passing remarks about the United States which Palmerston made in his private correspondence, it is clear that he shared these feelings, though Van Buren and other American ministers in London were sometimes deceived by his courtesy into thinking that he bore no resentment against the United States. His dislike of the American system was increased by the accounts which he received from Vaughan, the British minister in Washington, of the mid-term elections of 1830. A month after he became Foreign Secretary, he noted in his summary of a despatch from Vaughan: 'Even the Politicians of the Jefferson School begin to be alarmed at the great extension of the right of voting, in a majority of the States amounting to Universal Suffrage. The combinations of the lower Classes and their desire for influence at the Elections, are a cause of apprehension to the more respectable part of the Community. An Association is now formed in almost every principal Town throughout the United States, under the denomination of "the Mechanics' and Working Men's Party". Their object is political influence, and their support is anxiously courted at all sorts of Elections, and they are invited as a Body to assist at all publick Processions'.

But the United States did at least have the merit of being a good trading customer and supplier, a profitable field for British investment, and a useful dumping ground for European trouble-makers. Palmerston thought that any turbulent working-class Englishman with democratic ideas ought to emigrate to the United States; and he had hoped that the revolutionary Polish refugees would go there instead of coming to England. He also encouraged the more youthful and enterprising of his Irish tenants to go and seek their fortune in America if they encountered bad times at home.

It did not seem to augur well for Anglo-American relations when Andrew Jackson was elected President of the United States in 1828. Jackson had hated the British ever since he was a boy of eleven when his brother was killed and his house burned by British forces during the War of Independence. He had emerged as the hero of the War of 1812 by his victory at New Orleans; and three years later he had become the most hated man in England when, in conducting operations against the Seminole Indians in Florida, he had captured two Englishmen who were fighting with the Indians, and had had them shot after a trial by drumhead court-martial in defiance of the orders of the United States Government. He also introduced a much more democratic element into American political life. His inauguration ball on 4 March 1829, when hundreds of his supporters swarmed through the White House clutching whisky bottles and chewing tobacco, marked the end of the era when the United States was ruled by staid gentlemen of the Madison and Adams type. Palmerston could not love a bitter enemy of Britain who was the leader of a party which frankly called itself the Democratic Party; but he always respected a powerful opponent, and the references in his correspondence to 'General Jackson', as he called the President, show that he realized that here was a man who was not to be trifled with. Jackson, on his side, was too shrewd a man to provoke conflict with Britain, and Anglo-American relations did not become dangerous until after the expiry of his second term in 1837.

Palmerston's chief anxiety, as far as the Americans were concerned, was that they would invade and conquer Canada; and this remained a great source of anxiety to him all his life. Like other British statesmen, he had been alarmed at the doctrine proclaimed by President Monroe in 1823, which asserted that no European power could acquire fresh territory on the American continent. The British Government had always refused to recognize the Monroe Doctrine, and did not believe the assurances of the United States Government that it had no application to territory already held by European powers in North and South America. Apart from the main problem of Canada, Britain held a colony in Honduras and a protectorate over the neighbouring kingdom of Mosquito; she held British Guiana in South America, as well as the West Indian islands; and she hoped to develop trade with Mexico and some of the new South American republics. Palmerston therefore thought it advisable, not only to prepare to repel by force any attempt by the United States to expand to the north, but also to discourage her, as far as possible, from increasing her influence to the south.

When Palmerston first became Foreign Secretary, Britain was engaged in a dispute with the United States about the demarcation line of the American north-east frontier with Canada. The frontier was supposed to have been fixed by the Treaty of Versailles in 1783 which ended the American War of Independence; but there was a disparity between the various maps which had been drawn at the time, and forty-five years later the frontier became a major cause of dispute. In 1828, when Wellington was Prime Minister, the British and United States Governments agreed to refer the dispute to the arbitration of the King of Holland. All the time while Palmerston was supporting and opposing the Dutch claims in Belgium and Luxemburg, the King of Holland was determining what should be the frontier of the British Empire in North America. He eventually gave a decision which was more favourable to the United States than to Britain, as it gave most of the disputed territory to the Americans; but it did not give them all that they had claimed. Nevertheless it was Britain who accepted the award, and the United States who rejected it. Palmerston courteously thanked the King of Holland for the pains which he had taken in the matter, and reluctantly offered to accept the arbitration award, as Britain had agreed in advance to do so; but the people of Maine were very angry that they had not been awarded all that they claimed, and they succeeded in getting the United States Senate to reject the King of Holland's decision. This confirmed Palmerston's distrust of arbitration. He always refused to submit to arbitration any dispute in which Britain was involved, for he thought that British interests, being world-wide, conflicted at some point or other with those of every other nation, and that it was therefore impossible to find any other government which was impartial where Britain was concerned.

The dispute was therefore left to be settled by negotiation between the two governments, and very little progress was made. There were arguments about the boundary line across Lake Huron, and at the north end of Lake Champlain, where the American military authorities had built a fort in the disputed territory; but it was further east that the quarrel was most serious. Here both sides claimed a triangular tract of land about the size of Belgium, between the St. Lawrence and the St. John. Both Palmerston and the United States Government wished to settle the matter peaceably; but the provincial and state authorities, and the local inhabitants, were less reasonable. The sturdy, independent-minded farmers of Maine took the law into their own hands, and moved the boundary stones, and squatted across the Canadian border; while a Canadian company, with the consent of the Governor of New Brunswick, made plans to build a railway from Halifax to Quebec across the disputed territory, and were only stopped by directives from Palmerston. When Canadian lumbermen felled timber in the forests along the Aroostook, officials of the state of Maine arrived with an armed posse to prevent this trespass on the soil of the United States, and were surrounded and interned by British troops who had been hastily sent to relieve the lumbermen. The incident had to be smoothed out by Palmerston and the United States Secretary of State.

Palmerston did his best to cool down the passions on the American-Canadian border. In October 1839, he wrote to Lord John Russell that there were only two ways in which the frontier dispute could be settled – by war or by negotiation; and as war was quite out of the question, there was nothing to do except solve it by negotiation, however long this might take. But in these negotiations, Palmerston gave nothing away. According to Brougham, he discovered that there was a map in the British Museum which had been drawn at the time of the peace negotiations in 1783 and which proved that the American contention about the disputed land was correct; and he thereupon had the map removed from the British Museum to the Foreign Office, and suppressed all knowledge of its existence. Daniel Webster, the US Secretary of State, found a map in Washington which established the British case, and he, too, suppressed it.

The democratic United States was the most powerful slave nation in the world. In the states south of the Mason and Dixon line, four million negro slaves worked for powerful white slave-owning families, who had great political influence in Washington and played a prominent part in the Government there. The American Government had prohibited the slave trade as early as 1807, in the same year as the British; but no serious attempts were made to enforce the ban, and most of the slaves who were brought from Africa to Cuba and Brazil were carried in ships flying the American flag. The United States Government adopted much the same attitude towards the slave trade that Palmerston did towards opium-smuggling: they considered that the evils of the trade were less important than the need to protect the honour of the American flag. They refused to sign a treaty with Palmerston for the mutual right of search, for they had fought the War of 1812 to prevent the British Navy from searching American ships, and Britain still refused to relinquish the right to impress, for service in the Navy, British subjects who were found on American ships.

There was also trouble about fugitive slaves. Negro slaves sometimes escaped from the slave states of the USA, and made their way to Canada, though this only became a serious problem after 1850, when the American Fugitive Slave Law made it no longer safe for escaping slaves to remain in the Northern states of the Union. Occasionally, when slaves were being carried by sea from one Southern port to another, they mutinied, killed some of the crew, and brought the ship into a port in the British West Indies. The British authorities refused to surrender these runaway slaves; and when Palmerston negotiated an extradition treaty with the United States, he was very careful to exclude mutiny at sea, or other crimes that might be committed by slaves when escaping from slavery in the United States to freedom in British territory. Another source of friction was the law of South Carolina, which made it a criminal offence for any free negro who was not a slave to be at large in the state. This law, which was designed to make it easier to catch escaping slaves, was applied against negroes from the West Indies who served as members of the crew of British ships which docked at Charleston. If they went on shore, these British subjects were arrested and sentenced to sixty days' imprisonment. Palmerston sometimes ordered the British minister in Washington to raise this matter with the US Secretary of State, and with the Senators from South Carolina; but he obtained no redress, and as usual took the view that he could not protect British subjects who violated the criminal law of foreign states.

The United States was bounded on the south and west by the republic of Mexico, which included the provinces of Texas and California, and in the north bordered on the virtually uninhabited territory of Oregon, which was claimed by both the United States and Britain. Mexico had won its independence from Spain in 1821, and had immediately fallen into a state of chaos, with one President or Emperor succeeding another after a series of insurrections and coups d'état. The central government exercised only nominal control over most of the country; robbery, gang warfare, and attempted revolutions threatened the safety of foreign residents, and damaged their property. There were a number of British merchants, engineers and business men in Mexico, most of them being concerned with the silver mines on the Pacific coast; and they were involved in many disputes with the Mexican authorities about tax claims, forced loans to the various belligerents in the civil wars, and damage to their property in the fighting, or by pillage by revolutionaries or non-political brigands.

Palmerston did his best for these British subjects, but he was tied, as always, by his respect for international law. There were no treaties or trade agreements between Britain and Mexico which gave any privileges to British subjects in Mexico, so Palmerston refused to make any demands to the Mexican Government to exempt them from taxes or other burdens; and most of the British traders who appealed to him for help were told that he had no right to intervene, and were advised to seek redress through the Mexican law courts. Despite occasional friction, Palmerston established good relations with Mexico, and the Mexicans appreciated his attitude, which was much less high-handed than that of many other European powers. Some of the foreign diplomats in Mexico considered the possibility of overthrowing the chaotic republic and putting a Spanish Prince on the throne as Emperor of an independent Mexico. Palmerston thought that this would never be accepted by the Mexicans, and would have nothing to do with the scheme. After twelve years of turmoil, General Santa Anna seized power in 1833, and established a military dictatorship. Palmerston was pleased, and hoped that Santa Anna would restore law and order in Mexico.

In 1835, the people of Texas rose in revolt against the Government of Mexico, and proclaimed their independence. Nearly half the population of Texas were immigrants who had recently arrived from the United States, and they not only expected help from the United States Government, but also looked on independence as a temporary stage before being incorporated in the United States. The United States Government was reluctant to be directly involved, but gave moral support to the rebels. Volunteers from the United States hurried to their aid, including many new Scottish and Irish immigrants, who went with David Crockett to the Alamo to help the fight for Texan freedom. But the freedom for which the Texans were fighting included the freedom to own negro slaves, which had been abolished in Mexico; and when the fight was over, Houston and his fellow-Liberals found that the slaveowners were the chief beneficiaries of their heroism.

Palmerston pursued a policy of strict neutrality in the war between Mexico and Texas, though he was eager to prevent any increase in the power of the United States. As soon as the revolt broke out, he urged the Government of the United States to remain neutral, and not to help the Texans. He rejected the overtures of the Texan emissaries in Europe, who cunningly tried to persuade him that if Britain recognized the independence of Texas, it would prevent the Texans from falling under American influence. He rejected the demands of the anti-slavery MPs that he should help the Mexicans; but he had no objection to British adventurers joining the Mexican forces and operating as privateers against the Texan coast, or to British arms manufacturers selling weapons to both sides. When General Urrea massacred four hundred of his Texan prisoners in one day, Palmerston sent a protest; but he was not pleased when Houston defeated Santa Anna at San Jacinto, and took him prisoner, and Mexico, freed from the rule of the dictator, relapsed into anarchy.

By 1840, when it was clear that the Mexicans could not reconquer Texas, Palmerston recognized the new independent republic. Texas suppressed the slave trade, while retaining slavery within its territory, and signed a treaty with Britain for the mutual right of search. Palmerston encouraged Texas to enter into friendly relations with Mexico, hoping that this would counter the influence of the United States; but he was quite unsuccessful here.

In 1841, the Texans asked him to mediate in a dispute in which they had become involved with France. The French chargé d'affaires, Saligny, who was annoyed with the Texan Government because they had stopped his land speculations in Texas, had threatened to call in the French Navy to obtain satisfaction for an assault on his servant. As this was a case in which French, not British, honour was involved, Palmerston treated the matter as a great joke. In his despatch to Bulwer in Paris on 21 August 1841, he described how Saligny had not

kept the fences around his garden in good repair, and how the
garden had consequently been invaded by the pigs of his
Texan neighbour. 'Mr. Saligny ordered his Servant to put the
Pigs to death, the next time he found them on the French
side of the Boundary Line. The Pigs repeated the offence, and
the servant armed with a Pitch Fork, killed them accordingly.
The owner of the Pigs, enraged at his loss, vowed vengeance
against the Servant, and having the next day met him in the
street, took summary satisfaction by giving him a sound beating. Mr. Saligny thereupon addressed a note to the Secretary of
State demanding the severe and immediate punishment of the
person who had committed this outrage as M. Saligny termed
it, upon a member of the French Mission'. The Texan Secretary of State explained to Saligny that his servant must seek
redress through the law courts; so Saligny asked President
Lamar to dismiss his Secretary of State, and when Lamar refused, Saligny sent for gunboats from France.

The story did not seem so funny to General Hamilton, the
Texan representative in Britain, when he read in the newspaper that a fleet was leaving Toulon for Texas; and he asked
Palmerston's advice as to what to do. Palmerston was very
helpful. He advised him to write a friendly letter to Guizot,
who was, he told Hamilton, a most reasonable man; but when
Hamilton proposed telling Guizot that the Texans were thinking of inviting the United States to send a fleet to Galveston
to watch the French ships, Palmerston did not like this idea
at all. He told Hamilton that it would be inadvisable to mention this, because it would seem to Guizot to be a threat, and
if the United States did not in fact decide to send the fleet,
the threat would be an idle one. Palmerston told Bulwer to
put in a friendly word for Texas with Guizot; but he had
left the Foreign Office before he could do any more in the
matter.

The dispute between France and Mexico was more serious.
In 1838, the shops of some French traders in Mexico were
looted and destroyed in a riot. The French Government demanded an apology and compensation, and the punishment of
the responsible officials; but the Mexicans rejected their demands as exorbitant. The French Government sent Admiral

Baudin and a fleet to blockade the Mexican Atlantic ports. Palmerston offered to mediate, and both France and Mexico accepted his offer. The British Minister in Mexico, Ashburnham, arranged a meeting between Admiral Baudin and the Mexican representative at Jalápa, near the Atlantic coast and nearly five hundred miles from Mexico City. Baudin now demanded, in addition to the previous French claim for compensation, that Mexico should pay the whole cost of the French Naval expedition. Ashburnham strongly urged the Mexicans to accede to the French demands, even though he thought that they were unreasonable, and had almost persuaded them to do so when Baudin suddenly presented an ultimatum, demanding even higher compensation and requiring compliance within six days. There would hardly have been time for the Mexican delegate to report back to his Government and communicate their acceptance to Baudin; but the Mexican Government, incensed at the French attitude, refused their demands. Baudin then renewed the blockade of the Mexican east coast ports. Mexico quixotically declared war on France, and the French landed in Mexico, occupied several forts on the coast, and tightened the blockade. Eventually the Mexicans submitted, and paid the compensation demand, and a large war indemnity as well.

Palmerston told the French Government that they had behaved unreasonably throughout the dispute; but he was not going to wreck the Anglo-French alliance because of Mexico. He persuaded the French to make various concessions to British traders, and to allow British postal packets and specie through the blockade at Tampico and Vera Cruz; and he ordered the Navy in the West Indies to sail to the Mexican coast to watch the situation. But as the blockade was legal under international law, he told the British merchants and the Royal Navy to submit to it. When a British ship which contravened the blockade was seized by the French warships, he made no protest, but tried by friendly negotiations with France to get the ship released. The French action, and Palmerstons' inaction, were severely criticized in the House of Commons. Lord Sandon said that if Canning had been Foreign Secretary, he would never have tolerated this outrage against our commerce, and he accused Palmerston of being a minister of France, not a minister of England.

By this time, British relations with the United States had become very bad. In 1837, there was a rebellion in Canada under the joint leadership of the French Canadian separatist, Papineau, and the Scottish-born Radical republican, William Lyon Mackenzie. The Government sent Lord Durham to suppress the revolt by a mixture of repression and reform, and the rebels were soon driven across the American frontier; but from here they organized raids into Canada. They had a great deal of sympathy in the United States; but, to the anger of many Americans, President Van Buren, who had been the American minister in London for a few months in 1831 and had been on friendly terms with Palmerston, refused to quarrel with Britain, even when Palmerston suggested that British troops might pursue the rebels for a short distance across the American frontier. Papineau believed that 'the smallest success' by the Canadian rebels 'would have induced the American Government, in spite of its President, to support the movement'.

The rebels purchased a small steamboat, the *Caroline*, on the Niagara river, and ran small bodies of men and supplies in the steamship across the river from the state of New York into Canada. On the night of 29 December 1837 a band of the Canadian militia crossed the river and attacked the *Caroline* as she lay at anchor on the New York shore. They set the ship on fire, and one American citizen was killed in the action. This incident caused a furious outcry in the United States; but Van Buren only sent a mild protest. On the contrary, he sent General Scott with some army units to patrol the Canadian border in order to prevent any more inroads from the United States; and Mackenzie was prosecuted in the American courts, and sentenced to eighteen months' imprisonment for violating the American neutrality laws. Palmerston thanked the United States Government for their friendly attitude during the Canadian rebellion.

In November 1840, Alexander McLeod, a member of the Canadian militia, happened to pay a visit to New York city. He drank too much in the whisky bars, and began to boast

of the deeds of valour which he had performed when he and
his comrades had burned the *Caroline*, though in fact, on that
night three years before, he had been engaged in the dullest
of routine duties with his detachment of the militia. But his
American listeners believed him, and became so indignant that
some of them called the police, who arrested him, and removed him to the jail in Lockport, where he was charged with
the murder of the American citizen who was killed on the
Caroline.

When this news reached England, Palmerston sent a note
to the United States Government, demanding the release of
McLeod. He said that the attack on the *Caroline* had been carried out at the orders of the British authorities, and that the
Americans should demand redress from the British Government alone; and while he did not admit that McLeod had had
anything to do with the attack, he argued that even if he had,
the American courts were not entitled to punish him for it,
as it was an act which he had committed under the orders of
his Government. Palmerston was quite consistent on this
point, as he showed at this very time in connexion with a dispute in which he was involved with the Danish Government.
Seven negro slaves – two men, four women and a child – tried
to escape from the Danish colony of St. Thomas in the West
Indies by seizing a boat and rowing to the British territory
of Thatch Island, in the Virgin Isles. The Danish authorities
caught up with them at the moment when they landed on
Thatch Island. They fired at the negroes as they ran inland or
clambered out of the water. Four of them escaped, but one
woman was killed, and another woman was wounded, and
dragged back, with her child, to slavery. Palmerston demanded, and obtained, an apology for this violation of British territory, and the release of the wounded slave-woman
and her child, who were sent to freedom in the Virgin Isles.
He also, at first, asked the Danes to surrender the officer who
had killed the other escaping slave-woman, so that he could be
tried for murder in the British courts; but when he discovered
that the killer had been a Danish coastguard carrying out his
duties, he immediately abandoned this demand. On 18 March
1841, he told the Danish Government that as 'the act com-

mitted by Lieutenant Hederman on British Territory was done by the Lieutenant in obedience to orders of a superior authority, and as the Lieutenant conceived in the execution of a Public Duty, Her Majesty's Government cannot pretend to made [sic] the Lieutenant individually responsible for his conduct'. He therefore contented himself with telling the Danes that 'the Danish Government may, if it pleases, permit its Officers to shoot Women and children when come up with either within Danish Territory or upon the high Sea; but Her Majesty's Government cannot allow such revolting crimes to be committed with Impunity upon ground belonging to the British Crown'.

In the case of McLeod, Palmerston began by adopting a most truculent attitude. He used far harsher language than he normally used in his disputes with powerful states, which shows the intensity of his feeling and of public opinion in Britain. He might have acted differently if Andrew Jackson had been in office, and was perhaps encouraged to take a firm line by the conciliatory way in which Van Buren had behaved during the Canadian rebellion. On 9 February 1841 he wrote to Fox, the British minister in Washington, and congratulated him on the tough tone which he had adopted. 'There never was a matter upon which all parties – Tory, Whig, and Radical – more entirely agreed; and if any harm should be done to McLeod the indignation and resentment of all England will be extreme. Mr. Van Buren should understand this, and that the British nation will never permit a British subject to be dealt with as the people of New York propose to deal with McLeod, without taking a signal revenge upon the offenders. McLeod's execution would produce war, war immediate and frightful in its character, because it would be a war of retaliation and vengeance'. Despite the respect which he normally had for the rule of law, he brushed aside the legal and constitutional difficulties which faced the United States Government, and the conflict of powers between the Federal and State authorities. If the American Secretary of State wished to avoid war, he wrote, he could find the means of doing so. 'I presume that if we tell him that in the event of McLeod's execution we should make war upon the State of New York, he would reply that in such case we should *ipso facto* be at war with the rest of the Union. But if that is so, the rest of the Union must have the means of preventing the State of New York from doing a thing which would involve the whole Union in war with England'. He added that he had told Stevenson, the American minister in London, 'speaking not officially, but as a private friend, that if McLeod is executed there must be war. He said he quite felt it'. Palmerston ordered Fox to leave Washington, and the fleet to sail to the United States' coast, if McLeod were executed.

But he was, as usual, optimistic, and felt sure that his firm stand would persuade the Americans to give in rather than go to war. 'This affair of Mr. McLeod in America is awkward and unpleasant', he wrote to his brother William later on the same day, 'I cannot think, however, that the Americans will proceed to extremities with him, and I am the more inclined to think so in consequence of the violent speech of Mr. Grainger, a friend of the new President. Mr. Grainger said that if McLeod was proved to be guilty, he would be convicted; that if convicted, he would be condemned; and if condemned, he would most assuredly be executed. When a man connected with a government that is or is to be holds such language in Parliament, it seems clear to me that it is for the purpose of holding high a principle which he thinks will not be carried into practice. If they were to hang McLeod we could not stand it, and war would be the inevitable result'.

His attitude undoubtedly had its effect on the new President, Harrison, and his Secretary of State, Daniel Webster. After consulting his legal advisers, Webster told the British Government that he agreed with their argument; if the attack on the *Caroline* was an official act of the British Government, then, although the United States might seek redress from Britain or declare war, the individuals concerned in the attack could not be punished. Webster therefore asked the authorities of the state of New York to release McLeod. But feeling in New York ran very high, and William H. Seward, the Governor of New York, refused to comply with Webster's request. When McLeod appeared at the court house in Lockport for the preliminary hearing, he was nearly lynched. The United States Government applied to the Supreme Court of New York to quash the proceedings; but the court ruled that if McLeod had killed the man in the *Caroline*, he was guilty of murder by New York law, as war had not been declared at the time, and that his trial for murder must proceed.

In Britain, feeling was nearly as violent as in the United States. Palmerston was repeatedly urged by MPs to take steps to save McLeod. The Tories, who had always been more hostile than the Whigs to the United States, demanded strong action, and after the general election of July 1841, when it was clear that the Whig Government would soon be forced to resign, Stevenson thought that the situation would become much more dangerous if the Tories came to power. A few Radicals were sympathetic to the United States, but most of them were much too bellicose and nationalist not to clamour as loudly as anyone for a vindication of the national honour, and no MP pressed Palmerston in the House more energetically than Roebuck.

When Palmerston realized the seriousness of the situation, he tried to gain time and avoid war as long as possible. He told the American Government that he was grateful for their efforts to free McLeod, and appreciated the difficulties which confronted them; and when he heard that the New York Supreme Court had refused to stop McLeod's trial, he decided to take no further action until the trial was held. Stevenson was glad that Palmerston was in charge of affairs at this moment, and was satisfied with the cool way in which Palmerston dealt with the question in the heated atmosphere of the House of Commons.

Palmerston had left the Foreign Office before McLeod's trial took place. The United States Government paid for the most eminent lawyers to defend McLeod, and counsel for the defence took up their brief knowing that on their efforts depended not only the life of their client, but also the lives of many British and American soldiers and sailors, as the result of the trial would mean either peace or war. They succeeded in proving that McLeod had an alibi for the night of

29 December 1837, and the jury disagreed. McLeod was therefore acquitted, and was smuggled out of prison and to safety across the Canadian frontier.

The tension over McLeod – and also, perhaps, the successes which a tough policy had achieved in Naples, China and the Middle East – made Palmerston adopt a harder line on the boundary and slave-trading disputes with the United States. He urged the authorities in Canada to show no weakness along the St. John and the Aroostook; and in a despatch on 27 August 1841 – his last day at the Foreign Office – he demanded very firmly that the United States Government should grant the mutual right of search. He claimed that the right of search was essential in order to make sure that a ship which was flying the American flag was in fact entitled to do so; for the British Government could not admit 'that a merchant-man can exempt herself from search by merely hoisting a piece of bunting with the United States' emblems and colours upon it'; it was therefore 'absolutely essential' that British cruisers should be entitled to 'visit' ships flying the United States flag in order to inspect the ship's papers. Palmerston's logic was impeccable, but his language caused resentment, and the story spread, in Britain and in the United States, that he had called the American flag 'a piece of bunting'.

Palmerston believed that firmness was the only language which the Americans understood. 'With such cunning fellows as these Yankees', he wrote to Lord John Russell on 19 January 1841, 'it never answers to give way, because they always keep pushing on their encroachments as far as they are permitted to do so; and what we dignify by the names of moderation and conciliation, they naturally enough call fear; on the other hand as their system of encroachment is founded very much upon bully, they will give way when in the wrong, if they are firmly and perseveringly pressed'. Five years later, President Polk wrote in his diary: 'The only way to treat John Bull is to look him in the eye. . . . If Congress falters or hesitates in their course, John Bull will immediately become arrogant and more grasping in his demands'. Events tended to show that Palmerston and Polk were both right.

Chapter Twenty

In Opposition:
The Webster-Ashburton Treaty

In the summer of 1841, Palmerston's prestige stood very high throughout Britain. Eighteen months before, after nine years at the Foreign Office, very few people had a good opinion of him. His support for the British Legion in Spain had won him some Radical support, but they were still very dissatisfied with other aspects of his policy; and as he drew closer to the Radicals, the Tories hated him more than ever. Praed's mockery in 1832 of Palmerston who 'was 'not a Tory now' had developed by 1839 into more savage abuse:

> *Oh what a light will history shed*
> *Hereafter round your Lordship's head!*
> *How consecrate to deathless fame*
> *Your great forgetfulness of shame. . . .*
> *Sure none should better know how sweet*
> *The tenure of official seat,*
> *Than one who every session buys*
> *At such high rate the gaudy prize;*
> *One who for this so long has borne*
> *The scowl of universal scorn,*
> *Has seen distrust in every look,*
> *Has heard in every voice rebuke. . . .*
> *Exulting yet – as home he goes*
> *From sneering friends and pitying foes –*
> *That shun him, loathe him, if they will,*
> *He keeps the seals and salary still.*
> *And truth to say, it must be pleasant*
> *To be a minister at present. . . .*
> *And gossip here, and gossip there,*
> *With ladies dark and ladies fair;*

> *To sketch, when Fancy prompts exertion,*
> *A note for Metternich's diversion.* ....

But 1840 and 1841 had been years of triumph. Except for the pro-French Radicals, all the nation, and especially the Tories, applauded his handling of the Middle Eastern crisis. They felt that the defeat of Mehemet Ali, and the isolation and humiliation of France, had been achieved by Palmerston alone, who had pressed on with his policy when most of the Cabinet and the diplomatic corps were trembling at the prospect of a European war. Disraeli, who a few years before had been castigating Palmerston, in his articles in *The Times*, with his most merciless invective and sarcasm, had nothing but praise for his handling of the Middle Eastern crisis.

When we consider the position of the minister at home, not only deserted by Parliament, but abandoned by his party and even forsaken by his colleagues; the military occupation of Syria by the Egyptians; the rabid demonstrations of France; that an accident of time or space, the delay of a month, or the gathering of a storm, might alone have baffled all his combinations; it is difficult to fix upon a page in the history of this country which records a superior instance of moral intrepidity. The bold conception, and the brilliant performance, were worthy of Chatham; but the domestic difficulties with which Lord Palmerston had to struggle place the exploit far beyond the happiest achievement of the elder Pitt.

There were also a succession of smaller triumphs to add to the great victory over France and Mehemet Ali. By a use of force – the blockade of Naples – Palmerston had forced the Neapolitan Government to alter its internal laws and revoke a grant of a monopoly which injured the commercial rights of British subjects. By a victorious war against China, he had vindicated the honour of the British flag, and greatly improved the trading prospects of British merchants in illegal opium. He had saved the life of a British subject by threatening to go to war with the United States in the McLeod case. By 1841, the Palmerston legend was already firmly established.

Amid all his triumphs during his last two years in office, he met with one defeat: he was decisively repulsed by a lady whom he attempted to seduce at Windsor Castle. It was in

1839, when Palmerston was aged fifty-five and on the point of getting married, that he was involved in an incident with Mrs. Brand, the wife of Lord Dacre's son, who was one of the Queen's ladies-in-waiting. Eleven years later the incident was used by Prince Albert in an attempt to dismiss Palmerston from the Government. Charles Greville described it in his diary. 'Palmerston, always enterprising and audacious with women, took a fancy to Mrs. Brand (now Lady Dacre), and at Windsor Castle, where she was in waiting, and he was a guest, he marched into her room one night. His tender temerity met with an invincible resistance. The lady did not conceal the attempt, and it came to the Queen's ears. Her indignation was somehow pacified by Melbourne, then all-powerful, and who on every account would have abhorred an *escalandre* in which his colleague and brother-in-law would have so discreditably figured. Palmerston got out of the scrape with his usual luck, but the Queen has never forgotten and will never forgive it'. Prince Albert's secretary, George Anson, thought that Palmerston had entered Mrs. Brand's room by mistake, when he was looking for the room of another lady who was expecting him; but if so, he said or did enough to persuade Mrs. Brand that his entry was not merely accidental.

In the summer of 1841, the Tories succeeded in overthrowing the Government by a skilful Parliamentary manoeuvre. In 1840, they had managed to reduce the Government majority to nine by utilizing the moral indignation of many Whigs and Radicals at Palmerston's support of the opium-smugglers at Canton; and a year later, they achieved a greater success by fighting on another moral issue – slave sugar. In the Budget of April 1841, the Government abolished or lowered the tariff of a number of imports, including Brazilian sugar. The Tories united the protectionists and the anti-slavery forces by concentrating their attack on the Brazilian sugar, which was the product of slave labour. They were relying on a great new force in British politics – the humanitarian instinct and Nonconformist conscience which aroused passionate and disinterested sympathy for oppressed peoples and classes. This sympathy was often so intense that it became very selective. It was difficult to persuade Lord Dudley Stuart and his Polish

Committee to be interested in the sufferings of anyone except the Poles; but the members of the Anti-Slavery Society intervened in debates about Poland to assert that the miseries of the Poles were trivial compared to those endured by the negroes in the slave ships or on the plantations in the United States, Brazil and Cuba. Many Chartists and Socialists were disgusted at the attitude of the aristocratic and middle-class hypocrites who wept over the fate of negro slaves and cared nothing about English children who worked for fourteen hours a day in mines or factories; and some of them, like Thomas Carlyle and Charles Kingsley, were driven by this resentment into becoming violently anti-negro. John Bright and the middle-class manufacturers of the North indignantly opposed the campaign to improve the conditions of the factory workers on the grounds that conditions were much worse among the rural population on the lands of the nobles and gentlemen in the South of England who cared so much for the Lancashire weavers.

The only one of these good causes with which Palmerston had ever been associated was the anti-slavery movement. Although he had disappointed the abolitionists by his support for the apprenticeship system in the British colonies and for the flogging of negro apprentices, they could find no fault with his zealous efforts to suppress the international slave trade. British warships chased slave-ships, and when they caught them, freed the slaves. Palmerston's Chinese policy had to some extent had a detrimental effect on the suppression of the slave trade, for, as Palmerston himself admitted, there had been a great increase in the shipments of slaves from Africa to America when many of the British warships were withdrawn from the West African coast to assist in naval operations against China. But in the spring of 1841 Palmerston had delighted the abolitionists when he endorsed the action of Captain Denman, who burned down a barracoon in the Spanish West African territories where some negroes, who were British subjects, were being held as slaves while they awaited embarkation in the slave ships.

Yet it was the anti-slavery forces in Parliament which drove Palmerston from the Foreign Office; and in the debate on the

Brazilian sugar tariff, in which he was the main speaker for the Government, he played for the support of those who sympathized more with the hungry British workmen than with negro slaves. 'The party opposite', he said, 'stand upon principle against interest. The principle they stand upon is the principle of humanity; the interest they oppose is that of 25,000,000 of people who inhabit these islands.... They say humanity is their principle – an excellent principle it is – charity is said to begin at home; why should not humanity also be a domestic virtue? True it is there are millions of suffering negroes abroad; true also is that we have millions of suffering fellow-countrymen at home. Why should our humanity bestow itself exclusively on the former, instead of giving a share of its attention to the latter?' He also ridiculed the inconsistency of the Tories, who objected only to Brazilian sugar, because they did not dare to face the consequences of objecting equally to the slave-produced cotton, rice and tobacco which were imported from the Southern states of the USA. But Duncombe and the Chartist MPs were unimpressed by Palmerston's new interest in the misfortunes of the British working classes, and they and the Radicals voted with the Tories, who defeated the Government by 317 votes against 281.

When the Cabinet met to consider what to do, Palmerston urged Melbourne not to resign, but to dissolve Parliament. Melbourne decided to adopt neither course, and instead to ignore the adverse vote in the Commons as a merely incidental set-back. This action was not as unconstitutional in 1841 as it would be today; but it proved impracticable. Peel's motion of censure on the Government for failing to resign was carried by one vote, and in June Parliament was dissolved. Palmerston was quite confident that the Government would win the election, and went off to Tiverton in his usual optimistic mood. He had fought a fiercely-contested election there in 1837, when his Tory opponent had attacked him for his support of the new Poor Law, and for his immoral private life. His speeches had been constantly interrupted by hecklers shouting: 'Lord Cupid! Sly Cupid!'

In 1841, the new Poor Law was again the main issue at

Tiverton. This measure, which had been introduced by the Whig Government in 1834 in order to remedy the extravagances of the old Speenhamland system of poor relief, had caused bitter resentment throughout the country. It aimed to ban all 'outdoor' relief, by providing that no public assistance of any kind should be given outside the workhouses; while the workhouses were to be made as unpleasant as possible so as to deter everyone from applying for public assistance if there was any way of avoiding it. In order to achieve this object, the control of the workhouses was removed from the local squires, who in many cases had some sympathy for the poor of their parish, and entrusted to a centralized government bureaucracy under the supreme direction of three well-meaning progressive reformers who became popularly known as the three Pashas of Somerset House. These three gentlemen set about drafting a mass of regulations with the declared object of making the workhouse 'an uninviting place of wholesome restraint', in which the overseer would be 'the hardest taskmaster and the worst paymaster that the idle and the dissolute can apply to'. The paupers were forced to do hard manual labour, such as breaking stones, or oakum picking for women and children, which were chosen on the grounds that it would be more heartbreaking for the paupers if the work was known to be useless; the food ration was inadequate and unpleasant; beer and tobacco were forbidden; husbands, wives and children were segregated; no visitors or gifts were allowed; and the paupers were not allowed out. In many cases, they were not even allowed to go to church on Sundays, because this outing, by relieving the monotony of their existence, would weaken the deterrent effect of the workhouse. Once the regulations were promulgated, the rule of law, as well as the duty of saving the ratepayer's money, made it necessary to enforce them rigidly, and impelled the three Commissioners to dismiss a workhouse overseer who had been found giving an extra food ration to the children in his charge as a special Christmas treat.

The new Poor Law was opposed, not only by the Chartists and the working-class organizations and papers, but also by large numbers of Tories. Wellington and Peel had given official Tory support to the new Poor Law, but many Tory squires detested the centralized bureaucracy which had usurped their powers, and both Tories and Radicals repeatedly attacked the workhouses in Parliament. The Bishop of Exeter, Philpot, who usually spoke in the House of Lords in order to denounce Socialism and the atheistic doctrines of Robert Owen, spoke up against the new Poor Law, and quoted cases where doctors had certified that the food ration was not enough to maintain the inmates in good health; but Melbourne, in his most bland and unruffled manner, rejected this evidence on the grounds that doctors, being used to dealing with the sick, could have no knowledge as to what was a suitable diet for healthy people.

Palmerston was a keen supporter of the new Poor Law. If he had been merely the jovial Tory landowner that he seemed to be to so many of his contemporaries, and to future generations, he would have opposed the new workhouses; but under this genial exterior there was the other side of Palmerston – the cold, heartless bureaucrat, the doctrinaire progressive, with all those characteristics which made him as much Lord Pumicestone as Lord Cupid. He spoke in favour of the new Poor Law in Parliament in 1834, although at this time he rarely took part in any debates except on foreign affairs; and he made it the main plank in his election campaign in South Hampshire in 1835 and at Tiverton in 1837. In both cases he was fighting Tories who opposed the new law. The Poor Law was again the principal issue in the election of 1841. Palmerston and Heathcote, his fellow MP, faced one Tory opponent and one Chartist, who each contested separately for one of the two seats. The Tory candidate, Ross, who had formerly been an MP, made great play with the fact that he had voted against the new Poor Law when the bill was before Parliament; and the Chartist candidate, a local butcher named Rowcliffe, vigorously denounced the 'Poor Law Bastilles'.

Elections at Tiverton were colourful affairs. The candidates took up their residence in one of the local inns, and harangued the electors from the balcony; they hired a band to play at the start of their meetings and brought as many beautiful girls as possible to cheer them and wear their colours. In the

1837 election, the press reported that all the beauties of North Devon seemed to have come to Tiverton to support Palmerston. In 1841, Lady Palmerston came for the first time. Rowcliffe stood in the crowd and heckled Palmerston about the poor law. The Chartists were everywhere conducting a campaign against the regulation of the Poor Law Commissioners which forced the separation of even elderly husbands and wives in the workhouses, and Rowcliffe repeatedly asked Palmerston how he would like it if he and Lady Palmerston had to live in a workhouse separated from each other. The newspapers reported that when Palmerston was asked this question, there was 'laughter, in which the noble Lord joined heartily'.

Rowcliffe himself described it differently. He told an interviewer in 1872 that Palmerston usually had some answer 'ready for me; but one time I regularly shut him up. It was just upon the passing of the Poor Law Act which made legal the separation of man and wife after the age of sixty. I remember that day very well. There was Lady Palmerston there with a lot of ladies looking out of one window of the *Three Tuns*, all dressed out in ribbons and colours, cheering and laughing in high glee. His Lordship was at the other window speaking to the crowd and when he was going to get rid of this subject of the Poor Law, I ups and says: "You ought to have consulted Lady Palmerston before passing that there Act. How would you and her like to be separated after you was sixty years of age? Are your feelings any finer than those of the poor people you've been legislating for?' His Lordship pretended not to hear that, but I think he did, and so did Lady Palmerston too. That's what I call bringing it home to them.'

Nomination day at Tiverton was on 29 June. Palmerston had taken the unprecedented step of making special arrangements for the London press. He persuaded the Mayor to hold the election proceedings in front of the old Town Hall, and to provide a special cart on which the journalists could sit while Palmerston spoke from a window of the hall. The Mayor put a room in the hall at the disposal of the journalists, and Palmerston arranged with them that he would speak for exactly twenty minutes, and end in time for them to catch

the last train back to London, so that they could print their
reports in the morning papers next day. This was the only
time that he had to make this arrangement, because before the
next election in 1847 the electric telegraph had come to
Devonshire, and the journalists could telegraph their reports
to London.

It was perhaps in order to distract attention from his opponent's attack on the Poor Law and on his voting record
in connexion with negro apprenticeship that Palmerston used
the occasion to launch a violent attack on French policy in
Algeria. He contrasted the kind and lenient way in which
the British Army behaved in Asia with the cruel methods
which the French forces had used to suppress a revolt of
Arab tribesmen. Whereas in Asia, the British Army had
shown 'a scrupulous reference to justice, an inviolable respect
for property, an abstinence from anything which could tend
to wound the feelings and prejudices of the people', the
French Army in Africa had disgraced itself by its conduct.
'They sally forth unawares on the villagers of the country;
they put to death every man who cannot escape by flight,
and they carry off into captivity the women and children
(*shame, shame!*). They carry away every head of cattle, every
sheep, and every horse, and they burn what they cannot carry
off. The crop on the ground and the corn in the granaries
are consumed by the fire (*shame!*). What is the consequence?
While in India our officers ride about unarmed and alone
amidst the wildest tribes of the wilderness, there is not a
French man in Africa who shows his face above a given spot,
from the sentry at his post, who does not fall a victim to the
wild and justifiable retaliation of the Arabs (*hear, hear!*).'

In referring to the kindness and sense of security of the
British forces in India, Palmerston was expressing an opinion
which was widely held in Britain until the country was
roughly awakened to reality by the Indian Mutiny sixteen
years later. But it was much less usual in 1841 than it is today
for Foreign Ministers to make public attacks on foreign
governments, and Palmerston's speech caused great anger in
France. Guizot made a protest to Bulwer, who wrote to
Palmerston in some concern to tell him that the speech had

done a great deal of harm to Anglo-French relations. Palmerston replied that he felt so indignant at the French atrocities that it was impossible for him to keep silent, and that he thought that it would be less offensive to France if he made his comments in his constituency rather than in the House of Commons or in an official despatch. He wrote to Bulwer on 17 August 1841: 'If the public discussion which my speech produced shall have the effect of putting an end to a thousandth part of the human misery which I dwelt upon, I am sure M. Guizot will forgive me for saying that I should not think that result too dearly purchased by giving offence to the oldest and dearest friend I may have in the world. But I am quite sure that M. Guizot regrets these proceedings as much as I can do; though I well know that from the mechanism of government, a minister cannot always control departments over which he does not himself preside'.

It is not easy to believe that Palmerston, having for so long been unmoved by Russian atrocities in Poland, to say nothing of the repeated cases which had been brought to his attention of the brutalities committed by British forces in Ireland and against the rebel negro slaves in Demarara, should suddenly have become so affected by the cruelties of French troops towards Algerian rebels, as to be unable to contain his indignation, whatever the consequences in international relations might be. He had always been careful to avoid public criticism of foreign governments, and when Britain had been criticized by an official spokesman for the Portuguese Government, he had declared that so great an insult was a sufficient ground for war. But it is equally difficult to explain his speech in terms of his foreign policy. He had said, throughout the Middle Eastern crisis, that he had no wish to ostracize France from the concert of the Great Powers, and only a few months before had prevented the Northern Powers from doing this when he refused to agree to a Four Power alliance against France. Yet in June 1841, having invited the national press to come down to Tiverton to hear him, he launched this unprecedented attack on France in a prepared speech. The explanation is that a new Palmerston was beginning to emerge. At the age of fifty-six, he was becoming a demagogue. Finding himself confronted with Chartist butchers who heckled him about the sufferings of the poor in the workhouse, with Radicals who considered that Britain's destiny was to free the oppressed peoples of other countries, and with journalists who were becoming a more and more important influence in public affairs, Palmerston moved with the times. At Tiverton in June 1841 he took the first step towards becoming a popular nationalist leader. It was a role which entailed a complete break with his past traditions, but was well suited to his character and inclinations.

After all this effort, he won the election at Tiverton without a contest, for both Ross and Rowcliffe withdrew on the hustings. Palmerston and Heathcote were elected unopposed. In the rest of the country, the Government did badly, and the Tories won the election with a majority of nearly a hundred in the House of Commons. Melbourne did not resign at once, for until 1868 the Government always waited until it was defeated in the new House of Commons, and for another two months Palmerston stayed at the Foreign Office, knowing that he was on the way out. His chief ambition was to get the Five Power slave treaty signed. This treaty, which gave full rights of mutual search to the ships of the great powers, and was an important step forward in the suppression of the slave trade, had been finally agreed after many years of negotiation, and now awaited only the formal ceremony of signature. Guizot, knowing that the Whig Government was about to fall, delayed signing for France until Palmerston had left the Foreign Office and had been replaced by Lord Aberdeen, in order to spite Palmerston, and to prevent him from having the credit for concluding the treaty. Guizot had been on friendly terms with Palmerston when he was Ambassador in London in the previous year, and had taken office as Prime Minister and Foreign Minister in October 1840 with the chief aim of improving Anglo-French relations; but all this had been changed by Palmerston's speech at Tiverton.

Palmerston was annoyed when he realized what Guizot was up to, and wrote to Bulwer on 10 August 1841 that it was 'very shabby of Guizot' to delay signing the treaty, 'in order to sign with Aberdeen a treaty which I have been hammering at these four years'. But Guizot would not sign till Palmerston had left the Foreign Office, and took care that Bulwer should know that it was because of the Tiverton speech.

The Government resigned on 28 August. As soon as Parliament rose at the beginning of October, Palmerston went to Ireland for the first time for twelve years. Lady Palmerston went with him for the first time. They went to Dublin, and to Palmerston's estates in Sligo, and encountered the worst snowstorm that Palmerston had ever known. On their way home they visited North Wales, driving through the snow to Palmerston's slate quarries at Tan y Bwlch, near Caernarvon, and lamenting the absence of railways. They returned to Broadlands in time for the first full shooting season that Palmerston had enjoyed since 1829. He also hunted regularly with the Hursley Hunt and the New Forest Foxhounds, checked over his estate accounts, sacked a gamekeeper who had been seen drinking in the local inn with well-known poachers, and tried to discourage another gamekeeper, who had become a lay preacher, from spending quite so much time on his religious activities. He rode, and took as much exercise as possible, and walked with Lady Palmerston in his park, where they planted trees together. In the evening, he played billiards. He was moderately good at billiards, often playing risky shots, and tending to be lucky. He did not mind losing, but enjoyed winning, particularly when Lady Palmerston was watching.

Palmerston had owned racehorses ever since he was a young man, having won his first race at Winchester in 1815. His trainer was John Day, who kept his stables at Danebury, near Stockbridge. Palmerston used to ride over to Danebury from Broadlands, twelve miles away, with his groom. He would gallop at full speed, riding so fast that when he arrived at Danebury he had to go several times round the yard in order to slow down; and as his black dress-coat was unbuttoned, it blew open in the wind as he rode. He would walk briskly round the stables, chatting to Day about the horses; but though he occasionally accepted an invitation from Mrs. Day to come into the house for a glass of sherry, he usually declined, and hurried back to Broadlands at full gallop. When he was asked why he rode so fast, he said that it was because it was 'such capital exercise'. When he was in London, and was not too busy with Foreign Office despatches, he used to walk down to 'The Corner' at Covent Garden on Sunday afternoons, to inspect the horses that were to be sold there next day. Day's son William states that Palmerston never went to see his horses run, except at Tiverton, if the races there happened to be on when he was visiting his constituency. He used to say to John Day: 'Run them where you like, and when you think best. Only let me know when they are worth backing, or that you have backed them for me.' But William Day is not a wholly reliable authority, for the Days quarrelled with Palmerston when they insisted that one of Palmerston's horses was not fit to run in a big race, and Palmerston was persuaded to remove his horses from Danebury to another stables at Littleton near Winchester. Palmerston no doubt considered horseracing chiefly as a means of making money, of which he was so often in need; but he certainly went more often than Day suggests to see his horses run. His most successful racehorse was the mare Iliona – he insisted on pronouncing the name with the 'o' short – who won the Cesarevitch in 1841: but he also won the Ascot Stakes with Buckthorn in 1853. In October 1845 he was elected an honorary member of the Jockey Club because of his work, as an Opposition MP, to procure the repeal of some of the archaic laws which placed arbitrary restrictions on horseracing.

His married life was very happy, despite the fact that he was still interested in other women. Lady Palmerston, on her side, was still attractive, and even coquettish; and when she was over sixty, she asked her son-in-law, Lord Jocelyn, to travel in her coach, so that she would not be alone there with 'Poodle' Byng, as she thought that Palmerston would be jealous if she travelled unchaperoned with this famous roué. Palmerston never allowed their wedding anniversary to pass without making some gesture of appreciation and gratitude, and once wrote her a love poem on this occasion. Her greatest use to Palmerston was as a hostess, and her Saturday evening parties in London were famous. After his marriage, Palmerston moved from the house in Stanhope Street, where he had lived for thirty-three years, and took a larger house in Carlton Gardens, with a fine view overlooking St. James's Park. Lady Palmerston was delighted with the house, and the rooms were big enough for her balls and parties.

They were able to spend more time in the country now that Palmerston was out of office, and like other English society families were usually out of London during the Parliamentary recess and the shooting season from September to January. Apart from Broadlands, which Lady Palmerston loved, they also sometimes visited her son's house at Panshanger in Hertfordshire, where Palmerston had often stayed with her when her husband, Lord Cowper, was alive. It was very near Melbourne's house at Brocket, which passed to Lady Palmerston when Melbourne died in 1848. Lady Palmerston spent a good deal of time with Melbourne during his long illness, with Palmerston's full approval. Palmerston was less sympathetic about the ailments of his nephew, Stephen Sulivan, saying that the chief trouble with Sulivan was that he ate too much and took no exercise.

They all met quite often at family parties. Lady Palmerston's son, the new Earl Cowper, had married, as had both Lady Palmerston's daughters, Minnie marrying Lord Ashley, the future Lord Shaftesbury, and Fanny marrying Lord Jocelyn. Both Ashley and Jocelyn were Tory MPs, but political differences did not spoil the family friendships. Another addition to the family was Lady Palmerston's new sister-in-law, Lady Beauvale. Beauvale had retired from the diplomatic service, and returned from Vienna with a wife who was thirty-five years younger than he. She was the twenty-four-year-old Alexandrina von Maltzahn, the daughter of Count von Maltzahn, the former Prussian Ambassador in Vienna. There were some adverse comments about the marriage, but Lady Palmerston approved of it, because the pair were happy, and because Alexandrina was a Protestant, and had 'lived much with Prince Metternich, who is a great friend of hers and has much wished this match'. This was a great recommendation for any girl, whatever disagreements might exist between Palmerston and Metternich. Lady Beauvale exasperated some people by her timidity and over-eagerness to please; but Palmerston liked her. 'We are all charmed with Lady Beauvale', he wrote to his brother William on 1 September 1842, 'she is really a most amiable and pleasing person. Beauvale has made an excellent choice, and she speaks English so well that one almost forgets the only fault she has, which is the being a foreigner'.

For a few months after the Whig Government fell, Palmerston thoroughly enjoyed his new leisure; but before the winter was over he was feeling very angry and resentful over the fact that he was no longer at the Foreign Office. Visitors to Broadlands found him irritable and bitter. When Lady Palmerston's daughter-in-law, the young Lady Cowper, stayed at Broadlands in January 1842, she wrote to her mother: 'Lord Palmerston is bitter as usual, and evidently cannot get reconciled to not being longer Secretary, though he don't appear at all bored from having a great deal to do, but he abuses everything and everybody connected with the Tories. Thinks Lord Ashburton a rascal, Sir R. P. (Peel) ditto: Lord Aberdeen ditto: ditto: and so on. Whereas Lord Melbourne shines beside him by his candour. Thinking everybody means well and will do well'. Lady Palmerston was as disgusted with the Tories as Palmerston was, even though she was glad that Peel had tried to make up for his own 'lack of family' by giving office to young aristocrats like her son-in-law Lord Jocelyn.

Palmerston was in a better mood by next summer, being encouraged by the hot weather, which he always liked and which reminded him of his childhood days in Italy. The summer of 1842 was the warmest for many years, but though other people complained of the great heat, and said that the temperature was nearly 100 in the shade, Palmerston insisted that it was only in the upper eighties, and would hear no criticism of it. He was not worried about the disorders in the North of England, or by the general strike that the Chartists had called to support their demand for universal suffrage, the secret ballot and the other points of the People's Charter. 'The people are gradually returning to work', he wrote to William Temple on 1 September. 'They must do so or starve, and I presume that in the long run they would prefer labour to death'.

Being in Opposition had its political advantages, as he had

discovered fifteen years before. His prestige was much higher now than it had been in 1828, and he used his seat on the Opposition front bench to consolidate his position as a great national figure. The years in Opposition between 1828 and 1830 had turned Palmerston from a Tory into a Whig; the years between 1841 and 1846 almost turned him from a Whig into a Radical – but not quite. The old-style Whig politician was on the way out, and politics were taking on a new look. Four main groups were emerging in the Parliament of 1841 – the official Tory or Conservative Party, in which old-type Tories like Wellington and new-type Conservatives like Peel still worked together; young Tory progressives like Disraeli; 'Manchester' Radicals like Cobden and Bright and the Anti-Corn Law League; and the patriotic, bellicose Radicals, of whom Roebuck was perhaps the most typical example.

The official Tories stood for good order at home and abroad. They saw no reason to make any major change or introduce any substantial reforms at home, and in foreign affairs stood both for the maintenance of British interests and for friendship and co-operation with the governments of foreign states against the forces of revolution and disorder. The young Tories agreed with them on foreign policy, but in home affairs demanded a programme of reforms to help the hungry and oppressed working classes, and looked to the nobility and to the State to protect the people from the rapacity of the middle-class business man. The Cobdenites believed in political and economic freedom, opposed aristocratic government and extravagance, and were against war, partly because it was economically wasteful and interfered with free international trade, and partly out of a humanitarian horror of war. They wished to solve international disputes by arbitration and concessions on both sides. Most of them were Northern middle-class manufacturers, and some, like John Bright, were Quakers. The bellicose Radicals, on the other hand, though they agreed with the Cobdenites on political liberty, free trade, and hatred of aristocratic privilege, thought that it was Britain's mission to liberate oppressed foreign peoples from their tyrants, and were always ready, and even eager, to go to war with Russia and other autocratic states. They were as zealous as Palmerston in upholding British prestige and the honour of the flag, being convinced that this was essential to further the cause of freedom, and that, from the nature of things, Britain must always be morally in the right in any international quarrel.

Palmerston had at least one point in common with every one of these four groups. In the past he had been a typical old Tory, opposing disorder at home and collaborating with the Tsar and other foreign rulers in his foreign policy. To the end of his life he was really closer to this group than to any other; but for a number of reasons he drifted away from them. His quarrelsomeness made him fall out with nearly every foreign statesman; and as he tended, as Talleyrand said, to allow his personal antagonisms to affect his foreign policy, he found it difficult to pursue a policy of friendship with any foreign power. His invariable optimism made him much less anxious than most Tory statesmen to prevent revolutions abroad. They were worried when their neighbours' house caught fire; but Palmerston was so sure that his house was non-inflammable that he did not care, and would go to no trouble to help his neighbour to put out the fire. This drew him to some extent away from the Tories and nearer to the bellicose Radicals. When he was rude to Metternich they imagined that he must be a Radical.

Palmerston had never had any sympathy with the point of view of the young Tories. On his own lands he was a paternal landlord; but he never believed that paternalism should play any part in national politics, or should be practised by the State. He was, however, on friendly terms with Lord Ashley through their family connexion. Ashley was not a member of Disraeli's young Tory group, but he shared their concern about the conditions of the working classes, and he persuaded Palmerston, at the age of sixty, to take an interest in this question for the first time in his life. Palmerston had even less in common with the Cobdenites, but he did at least share their belief in free trade. On all other matters he absolutely disagreed with them. He disliked their pacifism and middle-class leadership, and for the last twenty years of his life Bright was his chief political enemy. He had much more in common with the bellicose Radicals. He never became one of them, for apart from the fact that he had no sympathy with their policy at home he was much too experienced a statesman to accept their unrealistic foreign policy. But he was often their spokesman, especially when he was in Opposition, and a number of circumstances led him, during his last term at the Foreign Office, to become their hero.

One of the first actions of Lord Aberdeen when he became Foreign Secretary in 1841 was to try to settle the differences with the United States. He sent Lord Ashburton to Washington to negotiate with Daniel Webster. Lord Ashburton, who had been born Alexander Baring, was the head of the Baring financial house, and had close business links with the United States. He had first visited the United States in the early years after the foundation of the republic, and in 1798 he had married an American wife. He had also had a long political career in Britain, having sat for many years as a Tory MP in the House of Commons before going to the Lords, and having held office in Peel's Government in 1834. He reached agreement with Webster on all the points of difference. The Webster-Ashburton Treaty of August 1842 gave the United States just over half of the disputed land on the American-Canadian frontier, which was less than the United States would have obtained under the King of Holland's arbitration award of 1831, which Palmerston had accepted and the Americans had refused, but was more than Palmerston had ever been prepared to offer in the subsequent negotiations. On the question of the slave trade, Ashburton agreed to relinquish the demand for the mutual right of search, in return for the Americans agreeing to send eighty ships to patrol the West coast of Africa to help catch the slave ships.

Palmerston vigorously denounced the Webster-Ashburton Treaty. 'We seem to have made a most disgraceful and disadvantageous arrangement with the Americans', he wrote to William Temple on 1 September 1842, 'but how could it be otherwise when we sent a half Yankee to conduct our negotiation? Lord Ashburton has, if possible, greater interests in America than in England. He thinks the most important thing to England, because it is the most important to himself, is peace between England and America; and to preserve that peace he would sacrifice anything and everything but his own private and personal interest.... It quite makes me sick to think of it'. As Parliament was in recess, he launched a campaign against the treaty in the *Morning Chronicle*. He had had the support of the *Chronicle* during his last years at the Foreign Office, and he continued to maintain friendly relations with it now that he was in Opposition, asking the proprietor, Sir John Easthope, to Broadlands, and prompting the general line of the paper on foreign affairs.

When Parliament met, Palmerston pursued his campaign on the floor of the House of Commons. On 21 March 1843 he spoke for three and a half hours against a motion congratulating Ashburton on having negotiated the treaty. His language was much more restrained than in his private correspondence; but he shocked many people by his personal criticisms of Ashburton, and by his indirect reference to the fact that Lady Ashburton was American by birth. He began by stating that he fully realized that if he criticized the Treaty of Washington, he would be accused of wanting a war with the United States; but he despised such insinuations, as the manner in which he had conducted British foreign policy for ten years 'would prove that he was not so rash or irrational as to underrate the value of being at peace with all nations', and that he looked on peace 'as the highest blessing which any nation could enjoy, and that he considered war the greatest possible affliction which could befall mankind'.

He then proceeded to attack the treaty on every point. He assured the House of his 'most perfect personal respect' for Lord Ashburton; but Ashburton was 'connected very deeply and in a binding manner with the United States. He did not find fault with Lord Ashburton for this. Quite the contrary – he thought men of that sort – men who had great interests at stake both in America and here, were not only an honour but an advantage to both countries, and he looked on them as bonds of union – ties which tended to common peace and friendship, and prevented small differences from assuming a grave aspect. But every man had his use. Were two countries to agree to choose a person as a mediator between them, they might very properly select a person who had almost an equal affection for each; but when a Government appointed a Minister to fight for them an adverse battle with another negotiator whose feelings were enlisted all on one side, then it was fit to choose some person who had no private connexion with the other party'.

He criticized Ashburton for referring, at a public dinner in Boston, to 'the hallowed spot which was the model of American freedom and independence'. He was astonished that any British subject should refer to our defeat in the American War of Independence 'among the men whose fathers had occasioned them, and who had gained a triumph over us. That language was dictated more by the feelings of the American citizen than by those of the British subject. It might be just and fair for the American citizen, but hardly becoming in a British subject holding an honourable and responsible situation under the British Crown'. Palmerston felt strongly about this. When he was Foreign Secretary he had told the British Minister in Washington not to attend the American independence celebrations on 4 July.

Many of the other Whigs were shocked at Palmerston's attack on Ashburton and the treaty. They were annoyed that he had not consulted them before making his speech in Parliament, and even more angry at the press campaign that he was waging in the *Morning Chronicle*. It was widely believed that he had written some of the offending articles himself, and he did not protest when his admirers reprinted one of them in a pamphlet in which Palmerston was named as the author. His critics feared that his speeches and articles would cause resentment in the United States; but Palmerston reassured them.

The fact indeed is [he wrote to Lord John Russell] that these articles will be looked upon in the United States as complimentary because they tended to show that Webster proved himself what according to Dickens the Americans call a *smarter* man by far than Ashburton; and no nation is much offended by its being shewn that they have concluded a negotiation with another and with a stronger power by a treaty in all respects greatly to their advantage.

He was a little more restrained in his criticism of Aberdeen's attempts to improve relations with France, perhaps because the Queen was closely involved in this. In 1843, she and Albert visited Louis Philippe at the Château d'Eu, near Le Tréport. It was the first time that a British sovereign had visited a foreign King since the days of Henry VIII; but after a lapse of three centuries the Russian Tsars had revived the practice of paying state visits to foreign monarchs. In 1844 Louis Philippe visited London, and Victoria went to the Château d'Eu again in 1845. Palmerston did not openly attack the visits, but disparaged them by faint praise. 'I do not depreciate the visits of sovereigns,' he said in the House of Commons on 4 February 1845, 'but however gratifying they may be, they do not impress me with such entire confidence with regard to the maintenance of our mutual peaceful relations' as to justify any reduction in British armaments. Some years later, he told the Queen that he was sure that when she was at the Château d'Eu, Louis Philippe had stolen the key of her despatch box from under her pillow and had read her secret state papers.

The Tsar also visited England in 1844. He made a very good impression with his charming manners, and was cheered by the people on the racecourse at Ascot. Palmerston did not share the anger of the Radicals about Nicholas's visit and at his popularity in England. 'I hope he will be pleased at his reception', wrote Palmerston to William Temple on 5 June. 'It is important that he should go away with a favourable impression of England. He is powerful, and can do us an ill turn or a good turn upon many occasions, according as he is ill or well-disposed towards us; and if we can purchase his good-will by civility, without any sacrifice of national interest, it would be folly not to do so'.

Aberdeen's policy led to a great improvement in British relations with France, Russia and the United States; but the Anglo-French rapprochement was threatened by difficulties in Tahiti, where the French had established a protectorate in 1843. There was a good deal of conflict in Tahiti between French Catholic and British Protestant missionaries, which had not been abated by Palmerston's efforts, when he was Foreign Secretary, to persuade the French Government

that Christian missionaries of all denominations had enough
work to do in converting heathens to Christianity without quarrelling amongst themselves. When Queen Pomare
resisted the French attempt to seize Tahiti, the French Admiral blamed the British Protestant missionaries and the British Consul, Mr. Pritchard. He arrested Pritchard and held
him under house arrest for a short while before deporting
him. Aberdeen sent a gunboat to Tahiti and a protest to Guizot, who apologized. Palmerston denounced Aberdeen in the
House of Commons for not taking a higher tone; he said that
the Government should have sent two gunboats, not one, to
Tahiti, and should have insisted on a more ample apology.

Palmerston was disgusted at the Government's policy of
conciliation and compromise in foreign policy. 'The motto of
the Government in foreign affairs seems to be "Give away" ',
he wrote in a private letter to Lord Minto. 'There is for this
course a plausible defence, that it preserves peace, but that
defence will not stand examination and discussion'. He wrote
to his brother William: 'We yield to every foreign state and
power all they ask, and then make it our boast that they are
all in good humour with us. This is an easy way of making
friends, but, in the end, a somewhat costly one'. He expressed
this view in a long denunciation of the Government's home
and foreign policy in the House of Commons on 28 July 1843.
'A wise Government in its home policy considers the reasonable wants of the people; in its foreign policy it is prepared
to resist the unjust demands and the unreasonable views of
foreign powers. The present Government inverts this method;
it is all resistance at home, all concession abroad.' Lord Stanley, the Colonial Secretary, replying for the Government, ridiculed Palmerston's anxieties, and particularly his fear of
France. 'France is, in fact, his bugbear, his *bête noire*; he is
always suspicious that France is interfering from jealousy of
England'.

Chapter Twenty-one

The Ten Hours Bill: Foreign Travels

It was during the five years that Palmerston was in Opposition that he emerged for the first time as a champion of the oppressed working man. This was certainly due to the influence of Lord Ashley. In 1830 Ashley had married Lady Palmerston's daughter, Lady Minnie Cowper, who was a great favourite with Palmerston and may well have been his illegitimate daughter. As Minnie was very much in love with Ashley, Lady Palmerston strongly approved of the marriage; but some members of the family found Ashley's humanitarian zeal a little boring. Beauvale wrote to Lady Palmerston about 'the inconvenience of Ashley', and Lady Palmerston herself, though she liked Ashley and admired his idealism, wished that he would pursue his worthy objects with less discomfort to himself and Minnie.

Ashley was a profoundly religious man, and belonged to the Low Church, Evangelical sect in the Church of England. He was inspired in his great humanitarian work by his religion, by his compassion, and by his fear of Socialism and atheism, which amounted almost to an obsession with him. When he married Minnie, he had just been elected as a Tory MP, and began at once to campaign in Parliament for the enactment of legislation to limit the hours of work in factories of persons under eighteen to fifteen hours a day; and he spent most of his life alleviating the conditions of women and children in mines, chimney sweeps, and factory workers. The Cobdenites denounced him as a hypocrite, and reminded him of the conditions of the agricultural labourers on the estates of his father, Lord Shaftesbury; but Ashley did not feel justified in stating publicly that he had had bitter quarrels with his father about this.

Ashley played a very important part in rousing the conscience of the rich. Seventy years later, old Lady Dorothy Nevill looked back in disgust at the attitude of the wealthy classes in her girlhood days in the eighteen-forties. 'Many enormously rich men of the present day are very kindly and good-natured', she wrote in 1910. 'In old days a good many of the wealthy had no more heart than a stone peach on a lodging-house chimney-piece'. Palmerston had been one of the stone-hearted men, because he belonged to a generation which had been brought up to believe that degrading poverty and suffering were inevitable, and that the British constitutional, political, legal, economic and social systems were as near to perfection as any merely human institution could ever be. Ashley changed their complacency. He would not allow himself the pleasure of self-satisfaction until after he had done something to relieve the wretchedness of the poor. Only then would he confide, in his diary, his belief that nothing that he had done that day was displeasing to God.

Like other profoundly religious men, Ashley was a wily politician. He was a master of Parliamentary procedure and at manipulation of the time-table of the House, and knew all the tricks of manoeuvre and compromise which it was necessary to adopt if his great humanitarian measures were to succeed. He knew the importance of winning over a prominent figure like Palmerston, and succeeded so well that many people thought that Palmerston would do anything that Ashley wanted. Ashley himself knew that this was far from being the case. He strongly disapproved of Palmerston's policy on several issues, particularly as regards China, for Ashley had denounced the Opium War in the House of Commons; and he knew that if Palmerston supported the cause of right and justice on any issue, it was for ulterior motives. On 1 August 1840, at the height of the Middle Eastern crisis, Ashley had dinner with Palmerston and persuaded him to urge the Turkish Government to allow the Jews to settle in Palestine after the province had been regained from Mehemet Ali. Ashley was President of the Society for the Propagation of the Gospel among the Jews, and believed that God's chosen people should return to the promised land. Palmerston thought that Jews could play a useful part in modernizing the Turkish Empire, and in developing opportunities for British commerce in the Middle East. That night Ashley wrote in his diary: 'Palmerston has already been chosen by God to be an instrument of good to His ancient people; to do homage, as it were, to their inheritance, and to recognise their rights without believing their destiny. And it seems he will yet do more. But though the motive be kind, it is not sound. I am forced to argue politically, financially, commercially; these considerations strike him home; he weeps not like his Master over Jerusalem, nor prays that now, at last, she may put on her beautiful garments'.

Palmerston gave Ashley his full support in pressing for improvements in working conditions. He supported a bill to prohibit the employment of women and young children in mines; in his speech in the House, he stressed particularly the fact that if children worked in mines, they would have no opportunities for the education which alone could raise the moral level of the working classes. The bill was passed, despite the fierce opposition of Lord Londonderry, one of the biggest mineowners in the country, who threatened to prosecute Ashley and his supporters for publishing obscene literature, because they had circulated distressing pictures of half-naked women toiling in the mines.

There was a harder struggle about the Ten Hours Bill, which Ashley first introduced in 1844. The bill prohibited the employment of women, and males under eighteen, for more than ten hours a day in any factory. It placed no restrictions at all on the hours of employment for men; but as work in most factories was so organized that essential jobs were performed by women and children, it was practically impossible for the men to work alone, and the effect of the measure would be to make the factories idle for fourteen hours out of every twenty-four, and in practice enforce a ten-hour day for men as well. For this reason, the bill was bitterly opposed by the Northern manufacturers, and by at least some working men, who wished that they and their wives and children should be free to earn more money by working longer hours; but the Chartists and the Trade Unions strongly supported it, and put all their efforts behind Ashley, who three years before had complained that 'the two great demons in morals and politics, Socialism and Chartism, are stalking through the land'.

The Trade Unions sent agents to London to lobby MPs. Two of them called at Palmerston's house in Carlton Gardens on the day before the debate was due to begin. One of them, Philip Grant, afterwards described their experiences in the somewhat pompous language in which working-class writers of the period more than equalled the style of upper- and middle-class authors and orators. When they arrived at the house at two o'clock in the afternoon, they saw Palmerston's carriage waiting at the door, and Lady Palmerston walking on the balcony as she waited for her afternoon drive. The footmen told them that his Lordship was not at home. 'Not at home to visitors?' they said. The footman smiled, and was about to leave, when they persisted, and urged him to take in their cards; but he refused, saying 'It is more than my place is worth'. But at this moment Palmerston happened to be passing across the hall, and inquired what the argument was all about; and when he was told, he ordered them to be admitted. 'They were at once ushered into the large dining-room', writes Grant, 'at that time so much famed for the evening parties of Lady Palmerston, and the munificent dinners given by his Lordship. They found the member for Tiverton in excellent temper, and as lively as a cricket'. They described to him some of the hardships suffered by children in factories: but Palmerston said: 'Oh, the work of the children cannot be so hard as you represent it, as I am led to understand that the machinery does all the work without the aid of the children, attention to the spindles only being required'. Grant says that 'to carry conviction to a mind so strongly impressed with the ease and comfort of factory labour for a moment staggered the deputation'; but he suddenly thought of a way of showing Palmerston what factory work was really like. He and his colleague Haworth took hold of two large lounging chairs on castors, and proceeded to push them around the room, and run around them, to illustrate the operation of the looms and the labour which the children had to perform. Palmerston quickly understood the process, and, calling in the footman to assist him, the two of them joined Grant and Haworth in pushing chairs around the room and going through the motions of factory labour.

The noise attracted the attention of Lady Palmerston, who had become impatient for her afternoon drive. She 'entered the room', wrote Grant, 'and appeared no little surprised to see her banqueting-room turned into a spinning-factory. Her Ladyship, however, appeared to enjoy the illustration, good-humouredly remarking "I am glad to see your Lordship has betaken yourself to work at last". The veteran statesman, who appeared a little fatigued by performing the duties of "Old Ned" (the engine), with a significant look and shrug of the shoulders, said, "Surely this must be an exaggeration of the labour of factory workers"'. But Haworth, who had come straight from the wheel-handle in Bolton, showed Palmerston the marks on his hands, and then, pulling up his trousers, other marks on his knees. This finally convinced Palmerston that Ashley was right when he said that children who worked in factories had to walk or trot twenty-five or thirty miles a day; and he promised them that if Ashley even half corroborated their evidence, he would support their cause in Parliament. 'A promise which that great man ever afterwards kept,' wrote Grant, 'and on all occasions when the subject was before Parliament, he diligently performed by speaking and voting in favour of the "poor factory child".'

Palmerston voted for the Ten Hours Bill, but it was defeated in the House of Commons. When the Government introduced a bill which limited the working time for women and males under eighteen to twelve hours a day, Ashley moved an amendment to reduce the period from twelve hours to ten hours, which Palmerston supported; but after being carried on one occasion it was eventually lost, though the Twelve Hours Bill became law. Peel opposed the Ten Hours Bill on the grounds that it would ruin the national economy; but the main opposition came from Cobden and Bright and the pacifist Radical MPs from Lancashire. Bright fought the bill all the way with great vigour, denouncing it as an attempt to interfere with freedom of contract and labour, and asserting that the Northern millowners, who were often self-made men sprung from the working classes, were on much better terms with their workpeople than Ashley and the stiffnecked Southern aristocrats and landowners were with their oppressed rural tenants and labourers.

In the summer of 1842, Palmerston took up a case of judicial victimization of a Chartist agitator. The Chartist, Mason, had insisted on addressing an open-air meeting in Sedgley, near Wolverhampton, despite the fact that a local JP had warned him 'that if a Chartist dared to show his face in the town, he should be immediately arrested'. Mason had only said a few words at the meeting about the laws of England being made by aristocrats to oppress the poor, when Police Constable Beman lifted up the bench on which Mason was standing and threw him to the ground. He then arrested Mason. Mason summoned PC Beman for assault before the local justices, where the case was tried by the magistrate who had said that any Chartist who came to Sedgley would be arrested. He acquitted Beman, but convicted Mason and seven of his colleagues of unlawful assembly on the evidence of Beman alone, and sentenced them to terms varying from two to six months' imprisonment in Stafford jail.

The Chartist MP, Duncombe, raised the case in the House of Commons. Sir James Graham, the Home Secretary, refused to intervene, on the grounds that it was improper for Parliament to inquire into the decisions of the judiciary; but Palmerston supported Duncombe, and said that though he detested Mason's opinions, he thought that he had been a victim of injustice and of a shameful attempt to suppress freedom of speech. This was certainly a new line for Palmerston to adopt. For nearly thirty years he had listened to pleas in the House for victims of oppression, from the case in 1822 of the woman who lost her baby in Ilchester jail because she was refused milk or water during the night for the crying child, to the debate in 1841, when the Radical MPs denounced the treatment of the Chartists in various prisons, where prisoners were flogged and put to work on the treadmill for ten and a half hours a day. In every case, Palmerston had voted against an inquiry or any attempt to expose or remedy the injustice. But his attitude changed after 1842. When he was Home Secretary ten years later, he introduced various measures of penal reform. As his biographer and admirer, the Radical Henry Bulwer, said of him: 'In the march of his epoch he was behind the eager but before the slow'.

His readiness to protest against the injustice to the Chartist agitator makes his silence in the case of the Mazzini letters particularly significant. In 1844 Sir James Graham ordered the Post Office to intercept and read the letters which passed between Mazzini, who was a refugee in London, and the members of his revolutionary underground organization in Italy. The letters revealed that the two Bandiera brothers were plotting a mutiny in the Austrian Navy and an insurrection in the Kingdom of Naples. Graham passed on this information to the Austrian Government, who told the Neapolitans; and the rising was foiled, and the two young Bandieras were captured and shot. When the truth leaked out, there was a great outcry among the Whigs and Radicals in Britain, and the Opposition moved a vote of censure on Graham and the Government. Palmerston did not attend the debate, and said nothing at all about the case, although it was a matter in which he, as the leading Opposition authority on foreign affairs, might have been expected to play a prominent part. He obviously had more sympathy with Graham than with the official line of his Opposition colleagues. He never wavered in his attitude that refugees who were granted asylum in Britain should not carry on any activities from British soil against any foreign government. Mazzini had violated this rule; and as Palmerston also condemned his Radical and republican opinions, he had no desire to enter into the contest on Mazzini's side, especially against Graham, who was a personal friend of his.

Palmerston spoke several times on Irish questions, which were becoming more dangerous than ever. O'Connell was leading a powerful campaign in favour of repeal of the Act of Union of 1801 and for Irish Home Rule, and was also demanding legislation to protect the Irish peasants from eviction by their landlords. Ireland was suffering from overpopulation; its population of eight million was nearly half the population of England and Scotland, and there was no industry to support it. As the number of tenants on the small agricultural holdings increased through the high birth rate among the tenants, the landlords evicted them in the interests of good agriculture; and in the comparatively rare cases where hard-working tenants improved their holdings, they, too, were evicted so that the landlord could re-let the land at a premium to a new tenant. The landlords could not do this in Ulster, where for several centuries the common law of tenant-right had protected tenants from eviction and prevented the landlord from increasing their rent; and the Irish MPs demanded legislation to extend the law of tenant-right to the other parts of Ireland.

In his speeches on Ireland, Palmerston supported all measures in favour of religious equality, such as the bill to permit Catholics to serve on juries, and opposed all demands for the repeal of the Union and for home rule. He supported some of the steps proposed for the suppression of sedition in Ireland, but not the most extreme measures of coercion; and he kept silent when O'Connell was arrested and convicted of sedition, and acquitted on a technicality by the House of Lords. On the question of tenant-right, Palmerston deplored the conduct of landlords who ejected their tenants without just cause, but thought that this was not a subject which should be dealt with by legislation. 'It would be unjust', he said in the House of Commons on 23 June 1843, 'for Parliament to interfere in the arrangements between the landlord and tenant. To do so would be to establish a principle of confiscation – to interfere with the rights of property, the foundation of all human society – property which the poorest man by his own industry and exertions might acquire, as well as the wealthy and powerful'. He said that in England, if an agricultural tenant was ejected, he could find work in the manufacturing towns; but in Ireland there was no industry where he could find work, and he could only starve in the bogs. He urged landlords not to act so inhumanly, and said that even if a landlord suffered some financial loss through allowing his poorer tenants to remain on his land, 'he would be amply repaid for the diminution in his profits by the cordial welcome with which he would be greeted on visiting those estates on which he had allowed the poorer tenants to remain'.

Three weeks later, he spoke again in the House, and called on the force of public opinion to prevent the landlords from acting so harshly. He said that 'if any measure can be proposed ... which shall apply any remedy to the existing evils without trenching on the rights of property in Ireland, a great source of discontent and dissatisfaction will be removed'. But he would not support any proposal for tenant-right. On 15 November 1843 he wrote to Lord Lansdowne: 'I, for one, have no particular fancy for being compelled to buy back my estate from time to time from my tenants'.

His greatest speech in Parliament during his five years in Opposition – perhaps the greatest speech of his life – was his denunciation of the slave trade on 16 July 1844. He opened a debate on the suppression of the trade with a three-hour speech which is worthy to rank with the greatest contributions of Wilberforce, Brougham and Buxton to the struggle against the slave trade, and was afterwards published as a pamphlet by the Anti-Slavery Society. In noble language, he described the raids at night on 'some peaceful African village, whose unsuspecting inhabitants are buried in that repose which nature has kindly bestowed upon man to fit him again for the useful occupations and for the innocent enjoyments of the succeeding day'; the seizure of the inhabitants, the murder of the useless infants, and the pursuit of those who had escaped into the hills, where they were smoked out of caves, and compelled, by the stopping-up of the wells, to 'barter their liberty for a few drops of water'. He described the horrors of the march to the coast, the hours of waiting in the barracoons, and the sufferings of the sea-voyage, with the slaves battened down below the hatches in the stench and excrement. He explained how the traders, like good business men, overloaded the ships in order to allow for loss of cargo through deaths on the voyage, and threw overboard any slave who fell ill, as the insurance money was higher on slaves who were jettisoned as ballast than on those who died from disease. He then proceeded to denounce the French Government for failing to ratify the slave trade treaty, the United States Government for refusing to concede the right of search, and Aberdeen for allowing France and the United States to behave in this manner. It may have occurred to some of those who heard and read Palmerston's speech that most of the horrifying details about the slave trade which he had so graphically described came from the evidence given to Parliament in 1791, fifteen years before Palmerston fought the Cambridge by-election as the anti-abolition candidate. But no one could deny that in more recent times he had been as zealous in deeds as in words in suppressing the slave trade, even if he had never been so eager to suppress slavery itself.

He justified this distinction in a debate next year. On 8 July 1845, in another speech against the slave trade, he regretted that many members of the Anti-Slavery Society were ceasing to agitate against the slave trade, and concentrated instead on working for the abolition of slavery. They argued that if slavery were abolished, the slave trade would automatically end; but Palmerston pointed out that it would be more difficult to abolish slavery than the slave trade, because this involved an interference with a species of private property. Slaveowners would fight bitterly to preserve their right to own slaves, whereas many of them would be prepared to suppress the slave trade, and might even favour this, as it would prevent new rivals from competing with them by acquiring a supply of slave labour.

At the end of the session of 1844, Palmerston and Lady Palmerston went on a holiday abroad. They went first to Belgium, where they dined with King Leopold and his Queen at their country palace at Lachen, and again next day in Brussels. Palmerston was very impressed by the speed of travel which the railways had made possible. They left London at 3.30 p.m. on 13 August on the Dover train, and were in Brussels next day; and they afterwards took only a day to go from Brussels to Cologne, and another day from Cologne to Ems, so that the actual travelling time from London to Ems was only three and a half days. At Ems Palmerston met a French Cabinet minister on holiday, who told him that the French Radicals wished to nationalize the railways, which convinced Palmerston that they were the disciples of Robespierre; and on the journey to Frankfort they shared a railway carriage with the French General Jacquinot. Palmerston dined with

Anselm Rothschild, the banker, in Frankfort, and reassured Rothschild's anxiety about the imminence of a war between Britain and France over Tahiti. They went on to Wiesbaden, where they found the Beauvales, the Lansdownes, the Clarendons and many other prominent English families. Here the weather turned very wet at the beginning of September, giving Palmerston a sudden attack of gout and holding up their journey for more than a fortnight. They travelled by road from Wiesbaden to Dresden – a six-day journey – and on by train to Berlin, where they dined with the King of Prussia and Palmerston learned a great deal about the economic and social developments in Prussia. Palmerston came to the conclusion that Prussia would be a more important power in future than she had been in the past. The German press published a sensational story about a secret meeting between Palmerston and the Turkish Ambassador in Berlin, at which they had discussed the defence of Constantinople against the Russians; but there was no truth in this, as Palmerston had merely met the Ambassador one evening at a dinner party.

They stayed longer than they had planned in Berlin, because Palmerston was so interested in all that he saw and heard about Prussia; and after ten days they went by train to Dresden, covering the hundred miles in twelve hours. They dined with the King of Saxony at Pillnitz, and then entered the Austrian Empire and stayed in Prague. Palmerston had hoped to visit Metternich, whom he had never met, at Metternich's country estate at Johannisberg on the Rhine; but Metternich had already returned to Vienna. Palmerston intended to go on to Vienna, and meet Metternich there, and then return by Munich, which he remembered well from his visit when he was a boy of nine; but the delay at Wiesbaden and Berlin had upset their programme, and at the end of October they travelled straight home from Prague. The weather was very cold, particularly between Lille and Calais, and the trains were uncomfortable and badly heated. When Palmerston reached the milder English climate, he wrote to his brother William: 'I am confirmed in a long-entertained opinion that there are few climates in Europe which, taken for the year round, are better than our own'.

On the last stage of their journey, they travelled in a private railway coach from Dover to London. At one of the stations where the train stopped, Palmerston looked out and saw that the train was being drawn by two locomotives, one at the front and one at the back of the train. He thought this was dangerous, and questioned one of the railwaymen about it, and was told that it was because the railway company was saving money by building engines which were not powerful enough to pull the train without the assistance of a second locomotive in the rear. Next summer there was a railway accident on the London–Dover line in which several persons were killed because the front locomotive stopped suddenly and the rear one crashed into the carriages. When the accident was debated in the House of Commons, Palmerston related his experiences on the same stretch of line in the previous November. He was promptly waited on at his house in Carlton Gardens by all the directors of the South-Eastern Railway Company, who assured him that it was not because of a desire to save money that they had put on two locomotives, but because they had not yet managed to make one that was powerful enough to pull a train up gradients unaided. They explained that the two engines were only used on hills, and that on these occasions the speed of the train was limited to 15 m.p.h. Palmerston promised to explain this to the House of Commons, but he added that this was not a sufficient excuse for their action. He said that if one engine was too weak to pull a train uphill, they should reduce the number of carriages; that if it were necessary to have two engines, they should both be in front; and that if ever a train was being drawn by one engine in front and one in the rear, it seemed to him, though he was no expert, that 15 m.p.h. was too fast, and that the maximum speed on these occasions should be 4 m.p.h.

It was during the Parliamentary session of 1845 that Palmerston first began to interest himself in the questions of national defence to which he devoted so much attention during the last twenty years of his life. He was still very adaptable, at the age of sixty, to modern developments, and was one of the first men to realize how changes in technology had affected Britain's military security. For forty years the people of Britain had felt safe from invasion; it was deeply ingrained in the national consciousness that the Navy was a sure protector. Another equally deeply established belief in Britain in 1845 was that the paramount duty of a government was to save the tax-payer's money by reducing all public expenditure to the absolute minimum.

Palmerston was therefore advocating a very unpopular line when he urged the Government to spend more money on national defence, and to fortify the naval dockyards against foreign invasion. He was also indirectly attacking Aberdeen's policy of friendship with France, for it was obvious that France was the only power which was in a position to invade Britain, and Palmerston made no secret of the fact that it was against France that he wished to rearm. He had been alarmed by French rearmament, and by the claims about military superiority which French ministers had made in their public speeches.

On 13 June 1845 he raised the matter in a long speech in the House of Commons. He said that times had changed since Talleyrand had told him, some twelve years before, that Britain was fortunate in not needing to spend any money on defence because she had no land frontier. Thanks to the railways and the steamships, the French could now assemble an army in their northern ports and carry them across the Channel much more quickly than in the old days, so Britain would have much less time to assemble a fleet to repel invasion. What he chiefly feared was not an attempt to conquer Britain, but damaging raids in which the French would burn Portsmouth and Plymouth and destroy the dockyards and the ships in port. As he could not hide the fact that his proposed defences would be directed against France, he went out of his way to praise the courage and patriotism of the French people. He said that if the French Government were to call for volunteers to take part in a raid to burn Portsmouth or Plymouth, the response would be overwhelming, even if it were known that none of the raiding party would survive the operation; and he urged Englishmen not to lag behind the French, who with admirable patriotism had not hesitated to vote taxes for the building of fortifications for the defence of Paris.

Peel's Government took no action. It was only when Palmerston himself was Prime Minister, fifteen years later, that anything was done; but this question was never out of Palmerston's mind. From henceforth he became keenly interested in all kinds of military matters, learning all the technical details about muskets, heavy guns and armour casing for forts and gun emplacements. He became the leading apostle of rearmament in Britain, advocating it in Parliament when in Opposition, and in Cabinet memoranda to his colleagues when in office.

In September 1845, Palmerston paid another visit to his Sligo estates. Lady Palmerston went with him, and found the Irish people untrustworthy, but delightful. She sat in the sun having picnics between the hills and the sea, and admiring the wonderful scenery, while Palmerston inspected the progress of the building works at the harbour and factories, and discussed all the problems with his land agents and nine hundred tenants.

They returned to a political crisis. In December Peel, faced with an imminent famine in Ireland, decided to repeal the Corn Laws – a policy which Palmerston had been advocating ever since he went into Opposition. As this proposal threatened to split the Cabinet and the Conservative Party, Peel resigned. The Queen asked Lord John Russell to form a Whig Government. Lord John chose Palmerston as Foreign Secretary; but Palmerston's old enemy, Ellice, intrigued against him and worked up the opposition to his appointment among the other leading Whigs. Lord Grey – the son of the former Prime Minister – thought that if Palmerston became Foreign Secretary, it would wreck the good relations which had been established with France, and he refused to join the Cabinet if Palmerston was a member of it. Lord John Russell, the tiny little aristocrat who, more than any other politician, represented the new kind of Whig who had emerged since the Reform Bill, was a very different character from Palmerston. He held far more Radical opinions about Parliamentary reform and the extension of the franchise, and was very shocked at

Palmerston's love affairs; but he had a great respect for
Palmerston's abilities, and was a little afraid of him. He insisted on having Palmerston as Foreign Secretary; but Grey
would not give way. Eventually Russell gave up his attempts
to form a government, and Peel came back. The effect of this
was to increase Palmerston's popularity among the Whigs, and
to silence his opponents in the party; for the majority of Whig
MPs blamed Ellice and Grey for their refusal to join a government which contained Palmerston, and they were held responsible for the fact that Peel remained in office.

But Peel's decision to repeal the Corn Laws lost him the
support of the Tory landowners. Disraeli's vitriolic attacks on
Peel made the split in the Tory Party irrevocable; and Palmerston and his colleagues on the Opposition front bench made
no attempt to hide their satisfaction while Disraeli was speaking. It was now clear that Peel could only last for a few weeks,
and that the Whigs would come to power with Palmerston as
Foreign Secretary, for Ellice and Grey would obviously not
dare to oppose him again. But Palmerston decided to scotch
the prevalent idea that his return to the Foreign Office would
ruin Anglo-French relations. During the Easter recess in 1846,
he went to Paris with Lady Palmerston in order to show the
British politicians and public how well he could get on with
the French. Before they left, Brougham told Lady Palmerston
that when she dined at the Tuileries she would see a large,
deep bowl with a ladle in it which would be of interest to her.
When they arrived, they found that the thing to which
Brougham referred was an enormous ornate silver soup
tureen. Brougham was thinking of the well-known saying in
London society that when the Palmerstons came to dinner,
they always missed the soup.

In Paris, Palmerston was charming to everyone. He dined
with the King, and with the Princess Lieven and Guizot, and
had several meetings with Thiers, his great antagonist in the
Middle Eastern crisis, and other members of the Opposition.
Hearing that Ibrahim was in Paris on a diplomatic mission
from Mehemet Ali, he immediately called on him, and was
not at all put out when Ibrahim roared with laughter when
Palmerston greeted him warmly. Soon after Palmerston ar-

rived in Paris, he was attacked in the Chamber of Deputies by Count Montalembert, the Liberal-Catholic politician and writer. A few days later, Palmerston was attending a party when Montalembert was announced. The hostess was most embarrassed, as were many of the guests; but Palmerston strode eagerly across the room with outstretched hand, and told Montalembert, in his perfect French, that he was delighted to meet him again. When he dined at the house of the Duke Decazes, the famous Liberal statesman, he met Victor Hugo and Alexandre Dumas the elder. Victor Hugo was disappointed with Palmerston. He felt that Lord Lansdowne, who was also present, was the perfect type of English gentleman, but that Palmerston's appearance was rather common. When Victor Hugo commiserated with Palmerston on the famine in Ireland, Palmerston said that it was the fault of the Irish soil and climate, and then proceeded to praise the good soil and the beautiful climate of France. Victor Hugo wrote in his diary that Palmerston belonged a little to history, but much more to fiction. He preferred talking to Lady Palmerston, and decided that she must have been a beautiful woman when she was young.

The French formed a mixed impression of Palmerston. Some of them were a little taken aback by his bounce, and felt that he lacked the gravity and reserve which they expected to find in an English nobleman. They were put out by his breaches of etiquette in writing to congratulate the King on having escaped from an attempted assassination, and in calling on Ibrahim before Ibrahim had been presented at Court. Madame de Lieven wrote to Aberdeen that Palmerston had behaved 'like an old dandy of second-rate society'; but most of the people whom he met were quite won over by his charm. Bulwer stated that by the time he left Paris, 'ce terrible Lord Palmerston' had become 'ce cher Lord Palmerston'; and Palmerston returned to London with the firm impression that he had succeeded in making the French forget all the injuries and insults of the past. Within three months he had discovered that it would take more than personal affability to make Louis Philippe and Guizot forget the Treaty of London of 1840 and the Tiverton speech of 1841.

Chapter Twenty-two

The Spanish Marriages

On 29 June 1846, Peel resigned. Next day Lord John Russell, after a meeting with Palmerston and a few of his senior colleagues, accepted the Queen's invitation to form a government. By becoming Premier, Russell had been promoted over Palmerston's head, for he was nearly eight years younger than Palmerston, and had been a junior minister outside the Cabinet in Lord Grey's Government in 1830, when Palmerston was Foreign Secretary. But if Palmerston had no chance of the Premiership, no one could keep him out of the Foreign Office. Ellice and Grey made no further attempt to do so. Ellice had no place in the new government, and Grey was lucky to get the Colonial Office.

Palmerston knew that the opposition to his becoming Foreign Secretary was due to a fear that he would wreck the friendly relations which Aberdeen had established with France and the United States; and he immediately set out to dispel these anxieties. Almost the last act of Peel's Government was to settle the Oregon frontier dispute with the United States. The wild territory of Oregon, which comprised the modern states of Oregon, Washington, Idaho and parts of Wyoming and Montana and the province of British Columbia, had been claimed by Russia, Britain and the United States. Russia abandoned her claim in 1824; but Britain and the United States persisted, and nearly went to war about it in 1845. Aberdeen settled the dispute by a compromise which fixed the frontier along the forty-ninth parallel, although the Americans had claimed the territory as far north as 54°40′, and had threatened to fight for it. When the Oregon settlement was debated in the House of Commons a few days before

Peel resigned, Palmerston did not repeat any of the strictures which he had pronounced in 1843 against Aberdeen's appeasement in compromising over the frontier in the East in the Webster-Ashburton Treaty. He welcomed the Oregon agreement as a reasonable settlement, and spoke hopefully of the prospect of improved relations with the United States. His imminent return to the Foreign Office had a great deal to do with this.

The United States was in an aggressive and expansionist mood. In 1845 Texas, after nine years' existence as an independent state, applied to be incorporated into the United States, and was admitted as the twenty-eighth state of the Union. This led to frontier disputes with Mexico, and in March 1846 American forces invaded Mexican territory. The pressure for war came chiefly from the Southern slave-owners, who had so much influence in Washington; it was opposed by many of the Whigs in the north, including Congressman Abraham Lincoln of Illinois, who did not wish to go to war with Mexico in order to acquire new territory which would be developed by slave labour, and would add to the voting strength and influence of the slave power in Congress. As it happened, the main territorial acquisition of the war was California, which, contrary to everyone's expectation, prohibited slavery and entered the Union as a free state.

When the war began, Aberdeen was Foreign Secretary; but Palmerston succeeded him within a few weeks of the news reaching England. Aberdeen had offered to mediate. The Mexicans would have been glad to accept, but the United States rejected it out of hand. Although the Mexican forces in the field outnumbered the Americans by five to one, their morale was very low, and they were decisively beaten in every battle of the war. They were convinced that they would lose from the very beginning and were especially doubtful of their chances of holding California, where there were many discontented immigrants who had recently arrived from the United States. Santa Anna therefore offered to cede California to Britain. The offer was made unconditionally; but he knew that if the British Government accepted it, this would inevitably bring Britain into the war on Mexico's side. The Mexican inhabitants of California were in favour of this solution, and the local authorities in San Francisco urged the British Vice-Consul, Forbes, to persuade Britain to accept the gift of the province. Rumours of the offer reached the United States, where fear of British designs on California encouraged the United States Government to order that military action should be immediately taken against California. Colonel Fré-mont – a passionate abolitionist fighting in a slaveowners' war – crossed the continent and entered California with a small band of soldiers, and incited the American settlers to begin a revolution against the Mexican government.

Forbes reported on the situation from San Francisco to his superior officer, the Consul at Tepic near the west coast of Mexico, 1,500 miles to the south. Not altogether surprisingly, in that age of appointment by patronage, the Consul was the Vice-Consul's father. Mr. Vice-Consul Forbes wrote to Mr. Consul Forbes that the Americans had seized California 'in a manner perfectly characteristic of the nation that has been suffered to obtain by base intrigue and subterfuge and the open violation of the laws of nations, a country whose native inhabitants sought in vain the protection of Great Britain, and who even after the communication of the views of the United States' Government upon California, still flatter them-selves that England will rescue them!'

The Vice-Consul wrote his letter on 14 July 1846, and sent it by sea from San Francisco to Tepic. The Consul imme-diately forwarded it on 1 August to Bankhead, the British Minister in Mexico City. On 13 August Bankhead sent it on with an accompanying letter to Aberdeen, as he had not yet heard that Aberdeen had resigned six weeks before. He sadly observed that Mexican misgovernment and internal strife had placed in the power of the United States 'one of the most valuable possessions in the habitable globe, and whose re-sources are as yet most imperfectly known'. Realizing the im-portance and urgency of the news, and knowing that he had just missed the monthly packet ship from Vera Cruz to Southampton, he sent the letters by a messenger to Vera Cruz, from Vera Cruz to New Orleans on a British warship which was specially despatched for the purpose, and on by railway to New York, where they caught the transatlantic ship to Liverpool. Palmerston received them on 7 October, nearly three months after Forbes's letter had left San Francisco.

This delay in communications was one of the factors which influenced Palmerston's assessment of the situation. He refused the Mexican gift of California. Writing to Bankhead on 15 August, he explained that Britain could not consider the offer, because, apart from all other objections, the situation was changing so rapidly that it was quite possible that California was already under American military occupation. He told Bankhead 'to impress upon the Mexican Government how important it is for them to lose no time in making the best possible arrangement with the United States. They must consider what sacrifices they can afford to make for the sake of Peace, and what chances of War are in their favour'. He warned them that they would have to give up the disputed territory on the borders of Texas, but might perhaps avoid any further cessions of territory if they made peace at once. 'We should prefer that the United States should not take California and divers other portions of Mexico which they mean to annex', he wrote to Normanby, the Ambassador in Paris, on 7 December 1846, 'but, unless we had been prepared to go to war to prevent them from doing so, I fear that any representation from us would only have exposed us to receive an unsatisfactory answer, such as we should give to any foreign power which should favour us with advice in regard to one of our own wars'.

Though Palmerston promised the Mexicans that he would use his influence with the United States to get them the best possible peace terms, there was little that he could do after Palo Alto and Buena Vista and the capture of Mexico City by General Scott's army. He confined himself to trying, not always successfully, to protect the lives and property of British subjects who were caught up in the war. He urged the Mexican Government not to impose forced loans on British subjects in Mexico, and made representations to Washington on behalf of Englishmen in Mexican territory occupied by the United States forces. The American military officers who were governing these localities behind the front line in Mexico did not always deal kindly with British subjects who argued with them about their rights as neutrals under international law, and Palmerston received a number of complaints from British residents who had been arrested by the United States forces, or who had had their property seized or destroyed. He did what he could for them, and in some cases obtained redress from the American Government after several years of negotiations. But he knew the weakness of his position. He always requested, and never threatened, and explained to the dissatisfied victims that they must not expect very much, as any army of occupation in war time had extensive powers under international law. The most serious issue which arose between Britain and the United States was when President Polk announced that any subjects of neutral states who were serving in the Mexican Navy as privateers would be shot, as pirates, if they were captured. Palmerston was on stronger ground here, both in international law and in international power. He sent the West Indies fleet to cruise off the Mexican coast, and made a vigorous protest against Polk's threat in so far as it applied to British subjects. The Americans did not execute any of the captured privateers.

In the same year, Britain took a more active part in hostilities further south on the American continent. For ten years the British Government had been inconvenienced by the difficulties which had arisen on the River Plate between France and General Rosas. Rosas was the son of a wealthy landowner; but he had been disinherited for an early marriage and for taking his father's money, and had been forced to earn his living as a cowboy on the pampas. He showed such skill and courage in defending his employer's cattle from the Indians that he decided to concentrate on this activity to the exclusion of the more humdrum aspects of a cowboy's life. He organized a band of riders who hired themselves out to protect the cattle of any rancher who engaged them. Soon Rosas's cowboys were the strongest force in the state, and within a few years Rosas was established in the presidential palace in Buenos Aires as President of the Republic and military dictator. He established a reign of terror throughout Argentina. He then interfered in a civil war in the neighbouring republic of Uruguay, where the Liberal and democratic leaders organized a people's war of national liberation against his puppet ruler, General Oribe, with the assistance, among others, of Giuseppe Garibaldi and other Italian Radical refugees.

Rosas seized the property of some French merchants in Argentina, and defaulted in his interest payments to French bondholders. This led to a dispute with France. In 1838, the French imposed a blockade of the River Plate, and toyed with the idea of assisting the people of Uruguay against Rosas. Palmerston, who was Foreign Secretary at the time, supported Rosas. Rosas had not interfered with the very few British merchants in Argentina, and Palmerston thought that in Argentina, as in Mexico, the rule of a dictator was most likely to provide the stable government under which foreign merchants could trade in peace. He was also suspicious of French designs in South America, and feared that they had territorial ambitions there, as well as in North Africa. But he was eager, at this time, not to injure the Anglo-French alliance; and as the French blockade was effective, and therefore legal under international law, he told British shipowners to submit to it. He urged the French Government to end it as soon as possible, to content themselves with obtaining redress from Rosas for the injury to French subjects, and not to attempt to overthrow his government or assist the Liberals in Uruguay. He offered to mediate between France and Argentina; but the French declined the offer. As Rosas refused to make any concessions to the French, the blockade was continued for many years, and was a recurring source of friction between Britain and France. The House of Commons became dissatisfied, and Palmerston was accused of weakness, and of appeasement towards France. Meanwhile the struggle for Uruguayan independence continued with increasing savagery, while Garibaldi's ships did extensive damage to the coastal areas in Rosas's territories.

It was not Palmerston, but Aberdeen, who brought Britain over to the side of Liberalism and the struggle for national freedom on the River Plate. Pursuing his policy of friendship with France, Aberdeen decided that the best way of ending the tensions caused by the French blockade was to help the French to overcome Rosas's resistance. Britain and France offered to mediate between Argentina and the Uruguayans; and when Rosas and Oribe refused, Aberdeen sent the Navy and an expeditionary force to the River Plate to collaborate with Garibaldi's Navy. Palmerston denounced Aberdeen in the House of Commons for collaborating with the French and helping the struggle of the Uruguayans against Rosas; but when he returned to the Foreign Office in 1846 he continued Aberdeen's policy. Rosas threatened to shoot any captured British soldiers, on the grounds that Britain had not declared war, and rejected Palmerston's protest against this degree; but Palmerston nevertheless abandoned the Uruguayan Liberals in July 1847, and left the French to carry on the struggle against Rosas without British support.

It was the beginning of the end for Rosas. In 1852 he was overthrown by one of his Generals, who was supported by the Uruguayan and Brazilian armies. He fled to England on a British warship; and the cowboy from the hut on the pampas, who had lived for twenty years in the presidential palace in Buenos Aires, ended his days in a mid-Victorian villa overlooking Southampton Water. Palmerston, as always, showed respect for a fallen opponent who turned to Britain for asylum in adversity. When Prince Albert died in December 1861, Rosas wrote a letter of condolence to Palmerston, who was then Prime Minister. Rosas mentioned, in the letter, that he was in splendid health because of the healthy English climate. Palmerston replied that the English climate could not claim the credit for Rosas's health, because his physical strength and his habit of taking daily exercise would have ensured his good health in almost every climate not positively injurious to man.

Britain's collaboration with France on the River Plate did not survive the deterioration in Anglo-French relations which followed immediately on Palmerston's return to the Foreign Office. When Palmerston became Foreign Secretary on 6 July 1846, it was his intention to continue Aberdeen's policy of friendship with France; but the first step which he took to achieve this had precisely the opposite effect, and resulted in a great diplomatic defeat for Palmerston. It arose in connexion with Spain. Espartero and the Radical Progresista Government had been overthrown in 1843 by a coup d'état instigated by the Queen Mother, Maria Cristina, in Paris, and by the French Government, and carried out by General Nar- váez. At the time, Palmerston had criticized Aberdeen for not supporting Espartero against the French; but the British Government had refused to act. Maria Cristina returned to Spain and became Regent in all but name, though Queen Isa- bella, who was now thirteen, was officially declared to be of age after the overthrow of Espartero's regency. Maria Cris- tina appointed Narváez as Prime Minister. Narváez, like Es- partero, had been a successful General on the Isabelinos' side in the civil war; but he attached himself to the Right-wing Conservatives. Though his party called themselves the Modera- tos, Narváez's actions were far from moderate. Within a few months of becoming Prime Minister he had suppressed all political freedom and constitutional rights in Spain, and had shot over two hundred prominent Radicals. He used to boast that he had no enemies, because they were all dead.

Queen Isabella and her younger sister, the Infanta Luisa, were approaching marriageable age. Metternich and the Northern Powers wished her to marry Don Carlos's son, the Count of Montemolin, who was regarded by the Carlists as King of Spain, for Carlos had abdicated in his favour. Monte- molin was absolutely unacceptable to Britain and France, and to the Queen Mother and Narváez. Louis Philippe had hoped that Isabella would marry his son, the Duke of Aumale, which Britain could not permit, as it violated the Treaty of Utrecht which had ended the War of the Spanish Succession in 1713. Britain, on the other hand, favoured Prince Leopold of Saxe- Coburg, who was a cousin of Queen Victoria and Prince Albert. The dispute was settled by a compromise reached in an informal and verbal agreement between Aberdeen and Guizot when Victoria visited Louis Philippe at the Château d'Eu in 1843. Guizot agreed to withdraw the Duke of Aumale as a candidate for Isabella's hand; in return, Aberdeen agreed not to support Prince Leopold, and to offer no objection to the marriage of Louis Philippe's youngest son, the Duke of Montpensier, to Isabella's younger sister, the Infanta. According to Guizot, they had agreed that Montpensier should not marry the Infanta until after Queen Isabella was married; according to Aberdeen, Montpensier's marriage was not to take place until after Isabella had had at least two children.

This left the question of Isabella's marriage open; and with Montemolin, Aumale and Leopold excluded, the choice seemed to be limited to Isabella's two Spanish cousins, Don Francisco, Duke of Cadiz, and his brother Don Enrique, Duke of Seville. Francisco was impotent, and Enrique was a Radical. The French Government, and the Queen Mother, objected to Enrique on political grounds; but Isabella, who was rapidly developing into a sensuous and passionate woman, objected to Francisco. Palmerston, in accordance with his policy of supporting the Radicals in Spain, favoured a match with Don Enrique; and in view of the fact that Francisco was his only rival, his prospects seemed excellent.

But Spain was to be the area where Guizot was to score his greatest diplomatic triumph, and gain his revenge over Palmerston for the affronts of 1840 and 1841. In the spring of 1846, Maria Cristina sounded Bulwer, the British Minister in Madrid, on the possibility of marrying Isabella to Leopold. There is good reason to believe that Maria Cristina suggested Leopold at Guizot's instigation, in order to set a trap for the British Government. Bulwer was in favour of pursuing the matter, as he realized that Maria Cristina would never allow Isabella to accept Don Enrique; but Aberdeen would not go back on his agreement with Guizot to exclude Leopold. Meanwhile Maria Cristina suggested that her own brother, the Count of Trapani, should marry her daughter Isabella; but apart from the fact that Trapani was Isabella's uncle, and a half-wit, he was a Neapolitan Bourbon, and was therefore as unacceptable as a French Bourbon to the British Government.

It fell to Palmerston to deal with the problem as soon as he returned to the Foreign Office. On 19 July 1846 he sent his first despatch to Bulwer, laying down British policy about the Queen of Spain's marriage. 'I have not at present any Instructions to give you in addition to those which you have received from my Predecessor in Office. The British Government is not prepared to give any active support to the pretensions of any of the Princes who are now Candidates for the Queen of Spain's hand, and does not feel itself called upon to make any objection to any of them. The choice of a Husband for the Queen of an Independent Country is obviously a matter with which the Governments of other countries are not intitled to interfere, unless there should be a probability that the choice would fall upon some Prince so directly belonging to the Reigning Family of some Powerful Foreign State, that he would be likely to connect the Policy of the Country of his adoption with the Policy of the Country of his birth, in a manner that would be injurious to the Balance of Power, and' dangerous to the interests of other States. But there is no Person of this description among those who are now named as Candidates for the Hand of the Queen of Spain, those Candidates being reduced to three, namely, the Prince Leopold of Saxe-Coburg, and the two Sons of Don Francisco de Paula [Francisco and Enrique]. I omit Count Trapani and Count Montemolin as there appears to be no chance of the choice falling upon either of them. As between the three candidates above mentioned, Her Majesty's Government have only to express their sincere wish that the choice may fall upon the one who may be most likely to secure the happiness of the Queen, and to promote the Welfare of the Spanish Nation'.

He then proceeded to discuss the political condition of Spain. 'That Political Condition must indeed be the subject of deep regret and concern to every well-wisher to the Spanish People. After a struggle of now thirty-four Years' duration for constitutional freedom, Spain finds herself under a system of Govt. almost as Arbitrary in practice, whatever it may be in theory, as any which ever existed in any former period of her history'. It is significant that Palmerston now regarded the promulgation of the Constitution of 1812, which he had so often condemned in the past, as the beginning of a thirty-four-years' struggle for 'constitutional freedom' in Spain. He told Bulwer that free Parliamentary debates, freedom of the press, and fair trials in Spain existed only in name, as no one dared criticize the Government, and many political oppositionists had been imprisoned, and even shot, without trial. He

threw the blame for this chiefly upon Narváez, who had resigned from the Government and retired to Paris as a result of
a disagreement with Maria Cristina; but the system still continued. 'This system of violence and of Arbitrary Power,
which was begun and carried on for several Years by a reckless Military Adventurer who was resolved to maintain at all
risks the Dictatorial Authority which he had acquired and
who is represented as having valued Power chiefly as a means
of amassing money seems in some degree to have survived
the fall of its Author.... It is greatly to be hoped that the
present Ministers in Spain, or those who may succeed them,
will lose no time in returning to the ways of the Constitution
and to obedience to the Law'.

But he warned Bulwer not to raise the matter directly with
the Spanish Government. 'Her Majesty's Government are so
sensible of the inconvenience of interfering, even by friendly
advice, in the internal Affairs of Independent States, that I
have to abstain from giving you Instructions to make any
Representations whatever to the Spanish Ministers on these
matters; but though you will of course take care to express
on no occasion on these subjects, sentiments different from
those which I have thus explained to you; and although you
will be careful not to express those sentiments in any manner
or upon any occasion so as to be likely to create, increase or
encourage discontent, yet you need not conceal from any of
those Persons who may have the power of remedying the existing evils, the fact that such opinions are entertained by the
British Government'.

Next day the French chargé d'affaires, Count Jarnac,
called on Palmerston at the Foreign Office and discussed with
him the policy which the new British Government would be
pursuing about the Queen of Spain's marriage. It was a fortnight after Palmerston had become Foreign Secretary, and
Palmerston seized the opportunity to show the French
Government that he intended to remain on friendly terms
with France. He assured Jarnac that he would not go back on
Aberdeen's policy about the marriage, and showed him the
despatch which he had written to Bulwer on the previous day.
He told Jarnac that he could, if he wished, take a copy of it

and show it to Guizot. Jarnac commented that there was stuff in the despatch which might cause a welter of trouble if the Spanish Government got to hear of it, and Palmerston cheerfully agreed.

When Guizot and Louis Philippe read the copy of Palmerston's despatch which Jarnac sent to them, they both independently had the same idea: this was a chance to score a diplomatic triumph at Palmerston's expense. They considered that the friendly talk and handshakes which had taken place when Palmerston visited Paris at Easter was just play-acting on both sides; for they were convinced that Palmerston had returned to the Foreign Office with the intention of wrecking Aberdeen's policy of friendship with France. For a few days, Guizot considered the possibility of collaborating with Palmerston, and of telling him that France would be prepared for Isabella to marry either Francisco or Enrique, and objected only to Leopold of Saxe-Coburg; but Princess Lieven persuaded him to abandon this idea. She became friendly with Lord William Hervey, the First Secretary at the British Embassy in Paris, who hated Palmerston; and, after talking to Hervey, she assured Guizot that Palmerston was secretly planning to marry Isabella to Leopold. She thought that even if Palmerston would be prepared to abandon Leopold's suit, Queen Victoria would insist on his supporting it. Louis Philippe and Guizot therefore determined on a policy of diplomatic hostilities with Palmerston from the start, and this was too good an opportunity to miss. They sent a copy of Palmerston's despatch to the French Minister in Madrid, who showed it to Maria Cristina and the Spanish Premier, Isturiz; and they also arranged for Narváez to see it. Before the Queen Mother and Isturiz had recovered from their anger at Palmerston's remarks about Narváez and the régime in Spain, the French Government proposed an immediate double marriage between Isabella and Don Francisco, and between the Duke of Montpensier and the Infanta.

But Palmerston had no idea of what was in the offing. On 22 August he wrote to Bulwer giving his views about Isabella's marriage in greater detail. He did not mention the possibility of Leopold. He rejected Montemolin as an impossible husband for the Queen. 'He pretends to be her Sovereign, instead of aspiring to be her husband; he offers to make her the consort of the King, instead of offering himself to be the consort of the Queen'. Then there was Francisco, the Duke of Cadiz. There were no political objections to him, as there were to Montemolin; but there were personal objections, because he was 'deficient in understanding, destitute of Instruction, devoid of Manly Habits, and ridiculous and Mean in Personal appearance. In all these Respects he is the Reverse of What the Husband of a Queen of a great Country ought to be'. He therefore advocated the suit of Enrique. It was true that Enrique was associated with the Radical Progresista Party; but Palmerston, with his usual shrewd appreciation of political realities, pointed out that if Enrique became the Queen's consort, he would not wish to weaken the Spanish monarchy. 'Such a fear seems to be wholly chimerical, and at variance with the principles of human nature. Don Henry, married to the Queen, would necessarily find his feelings and interests identified with those of the Sovereign to whom he was united; and his influence, whatever it might be, would of course be exerted to maintain and not to overthrow that branch of the Constitution with which his fate was irrevocably bound up'. If he married the Queen, the Radicals would either turn against him, or else would stop attacking the monarchy out of respect for him; so, in either case, there was nothing to fear. Palmerston discussed the matter again with Jarnac, and suggested that Isabella should marry Enrique. Jarnac appeared to agree, and said that he thought that if Britain backed Enrique, the French Government would also support him.

On 4 September, the official newspaper of the French Government, the *Journal des Débats,* announced that at the end of October Queen Isabella would marry Francisco and the Infanta would marry the Duke of Montpensier. The Spanish Government made the same announcement next day. It was a great coup for French diplomacy. Isabella was to marry a Prince who was reputed to be impotent instead of Palmerston's Radical nominee Enrique, and her sister was to marry the son of the King of the French. There was thus every probability that Louis Philippe's daughter-in-law and grandson would succeed to the throne of Spain. When the British press attacked France for breaking the Château d'Eu agreement with Aberdeen, Guizot had two answers. He denied that they had ever agreed at Château d'Eu that Montpensier's marriage to the Infanta should not take place until Isabella had a child; he claimed that the agreement was merely that Isabella should be married first, and this agreement would be kept, because, though both marriages were to take place on the same day, the Queen was to be married first and the Infanta a quarter of an hour later. Secondly, he argued that France had been released from the agreement with Aberdeen, because Palmerston had broken it by advocating the claims of Prince Leopold of Saxe-Coburg to the Queen's hand. Having read Palmerston's despatch to Bulwer of 19 July, he knew that Palmerston had done no such thing; but having been persuaded by Princess Lieven that Palmerston was secretly working for the Coburg match, he ingeniously interpreted a passage in the despatch to prove his argument. Palmerston had listed the names of all the five possible candidates – Aumale was ineligible, having already married a Neapolitan Princess – and had written Leopold's name first. He had then stated that Montemolin and Trapani were out of the question, but that Britain would neither advocate nor oppose the marriage of any of the other three to Isabella. Guizot argued that by including Leopold's name along with the names of Francisco and Enrique, Palmerston had shown 'that they are thus, for the first time, all three included by the English Government in one and the same approval. ... Admitting that Lord Palmerston did not intend to put forward or to recommend Prince Leopold of Coburg, he will certainly acknowledge that he said absolutely nothing which could tend to set him aside or to discourage the Spanish Government with regard to him'.

Palmerston sent a formal protest to the Spanish Government against the forthcoming marriage of the Infanta to Montpensier. He stated that it violated the Treaty of Utrecht, and threatened the national independence of Spain. Isturiz, in his reply, thanked Palmerston for his solicitude about Spanish independence, but told him that Spain would protect her independence unaided. 'The loss of her extensive dominions abroad and of Gibraltar in her own territory, the recent destruction of her fleets in war, and the loss of the greatest part of her colonies during peace, have left remembrances to Spain which are neither forgotten nor unprofitable, and which teach her to rely only upon her own strength and her own justice. Moreover, the spirit of the present times is contrary to the engagements of former times, and the political institutions with which the nation is now endowed render them impossible'. The loss of Gibraltar and the destruction of the Spanish fleet had been due to British action, and public opinion in Spain also held Britain responsible for the loss of the Spanish colonies in South America. Isturiz's meaning was unmistakeable.

The marriages of the Queen and the Infanta took place on 10 October – three weeks before the date which had been announced. It was Isabella's sixteenth birthday, and the Infanta was only fourteen. Palmerston tried to enlist Metternich's support against the Montpensier marriage, because Austria had always been vitally interested in upholding the Treaty of Utrecht and preventing the union of France and Spain. But Metternich was interested in Guizot's plans for a rapprochement with Austria and the Northern Powers, and he did not wish to embarrass Guizot's Conservative Government, which was under attack from the Liberal Opposition in France. He blandly told Palmerston that as Austria considered that the Count of Montemolin, as Don Carlos's heir, was the rightful King of Spain, he could not protest to Madrid against the fact that Montpensier had married a Princess who had no claims to the Spanish throne; and he persisted in this view despite all Palmerston's arguments to the contrary. Palmerston's only consolation was that no one could claim that he was responsible for forcing Isabella to marry the repulsive Francisco. 'Her Majesty's Government have good reason to believe', he wrote to the Marquis of Normanby, the Ambassador in Paris, on 22 September, 'and it appears, indeed, by the avowal of the French Government, that this marriage was brought about by French influence at Madrid. Her Majesty's Government rejoice to think that the British Government was no party to that arrangement'.

Isabella burst into tears when her mother told her that she must marry Francisco; but she soon consoled herself with lovers. Within a few years she was reputed to be having love affairs with many of the officers and sergeants of her Guard. This was the factor which caused most distress to Prince Albert. 'The Queen has her lovers,' he wrote, 'What will Louis Philippe have to answer for in Heaven!'

Palmerston's action in showing Jarnac his despatch of 19 July has usually been considered an enormous blunder, and as the one great error of a brilliant Foreign Secretary. But just as he has often been given the credit for successes which were merely lucky flukes, so, on this occasion, he has been unfairly blamed for an error of judgment which was almost forgivable, and which led to consequences for which he cannot really be blamed. He knew very well that there were risks involved in showing despatches to foreign governments. In 1833 he had severely reprimanded Bligh, the chargé d'affaires in St. Petersburg, because Bligh had shown the Prussian Minister there a copy of a despatch from the British Ambassador in Berlin which Palmerston had sent to Bligh for his information. Palmerston had laid down rules for the guidance of the diplomats abroad. They might, in exceptional circumstances, show the Governments to which they were accredited a despatch which they had received from Palmerston, even though he had not expressly authorized them to do so; but they must never, without Palmerston's permission, show anyone a copy of a despatch which had been sent to or from another Court. The decision whether to show a despatch to a foreign government was one which only the Foreign Secretary should take; and Palmerston, bearing all the relevant considerations in mind, sometimes directed his diplomats to show a despatch to foreign statesmen and to allow them to take a copy of it, sometimes told them to show them the despatch but not to allow them to take a copy, and on other occasions took care to keep the despatch secret. Palmerston fully realized that a foreign statesman might double-cross him in this connexion, for on one occasion he had himself tried to embarrass Metternich by telling the authorities in Frankfort about the criticisms which Metternich had made of them in a conversation with

Lamb. But it is impossible to conduct a nation's foreign policy without taking some risks in order to gain the confidence of a foreign government. Palmerston took the risk of trusting Guizot, knowing what the consequences might be if Guizot betrayed his confidence – Jarnac had actually pointed them out to Palmerston at the time – and the gamble failed. If Palmerston made a blunder, it was in failing to realize how bitterly he had offended Guizot in 1840 and 1841.

Palmerston never knew that his error of judgment did not in fact have the serious consequences which he believed it to have had; for the French would have known in any case what he had written to Bulwer. Princess Lieven, who did not know that he had shown the despatch to Jarnac, managed to intercept it while it passed through Paris on its way to Bulwer in Madrid, and sent an accurate summary of its contents to Guizot, who had received Jarnac's report shortly before Princess Lieven's successful but superfluous piece of espionage.

When it was known what Guizot and Louis Philippe had done, there was great indignation in Britain, from Victoria downwards. Aberdeen and the Tories denounced Louis Philippe, as did the pro-French sympathizers, who were more angry than anyone else. Palmerston, too, expressed himself forcibly in private, but took the set-back more philosophically than most other people. He took the attitude that it served the British Government right for having been so foolish as to try to reach an agreement with France about the Spanish marriages, instead of boldly going ahead, in the face of French opposition, and marrying Leopold of Saxe-Coburg to Isabella. 'Louis Philippe and Guizot had carried their point by boldness', he wrote to Lord John Russell on 10 September 1846, and added: 'Louis Philippe and Guizot, like practical and sagacious men, determined to knock us down at once, and make an apology afterwards if necessary to pacify us'.

In February 1846, a revolt broke out in Galicia and elsewhere in Austrian Poland in favour of an independent Polish republic. As the revolt was led by the Polish aristocracy, the Austrian Government armed the Polish peasants, and gave them free rein to kill their landlords and burn their castles. In the Republic of Cracow – the only Polish territory which still remained nominally independent – the people rose in sympathy with the nationalist rebels; and the Cracow Government was induced to ask Austria for assistance in suppressing the revolt. After sending Austrian troops into Cracow for the second time in ten years, Metternich called a conference of the Northern Powers in Vienna in November 1846, at which Russia and Prussia agreed that the Republic of Cracow should be incorporated into the Austrian Empire. This was a breach of the Treaty of Vienna against which Britain and France could be expected to protest. Guizot had no sympathy with the Poles. He was working for a rapprochement with the Northern Powers, and his mistress, Madame de Lieven, encouraged his anti-Polish sentiments. But French popular opinion was as pro-Polish as ever, and Guizot could not ignore it. He therefore proposed to Palmerston that Britain and France should send a joint protest to the Northern Powers about Cracow.

Palmerston had forestalled him. As soon as he heard of what Metternich was proposing to do, he warned the Austrian and Prussian Governments that it would be a violation of the Treaty of Vienna if the Republic of Cracow were extinguished without the consent of all the signatories of the Treaty. When Guizot proposed that a joint protest be sent, Palmerston declined on the grounds that he had already written his protest earlier that day, and wished to send it off the same evening. Guizot therefore sent a protest on his own.

It has often been said that the inability of Britain and France to do anything about Cracow was the unfortunate result of their quarrel about the Spanish marriages; that Palmerston refused to join in a joint démarche with Guizot in order to get his own back for being double-crossed over Spain; and that the Northern Powers were encouraged to proceed with the incorporation of Cracow by this proof that Britain and France were disunited. This is an over-simplification. Palmerston was no more prepared to go to war for Poland in 1846 than in 1831 and 1863; and in view of this, as he told Czartoryski, there was nothing that he could do to help the Poles. He therefore framed his protests to the Northern Powers with an eye on his duel with Guizot. In 1831 he had

THE SPANISH MARRIAGES 429

refused the French proposal for joint action over Poland because he wished to prevent a Left-wing French Government from launching a European war in order to save the Poles; in 1846 he refused to send a joint protest because he wished to snub a Conservative French Premier and to vie with him for Radical support. When his warnings to Austria and Prussia had no effect, and Cracow was annexed by Austria, he sent a protest to the three Northern Powers which was so mild that it pleasantly surprised Nesselrode, who deduced, with some justice, that the weakness of Palmerston's response was due to the resoluteness of the action of the Northern Powers; but Palmerston was no longer hoping to make any impression in St. Petersburg. He wanted to win the sympathy of the Liberals of Europe. In November 1846 he spoke at the Guildhall at the Lord Mayor's banquet, and condemned the seizure of Cracow. This was a different attitude from that which he had adopted fourteen years before, when he had more or less defended the Russian action in Poland in his public speeches in the House of Commons. The Polish Historical Society were so pleased with his speech at the Guildhall that they presented him with a medal bearing the head of Czartoryski.

However angry with Guizot Palmerston might be, he did not allow this to interfere with his policy about Cracow, and it was not for this reason that he ended his collaboration with France on the River Plate. Louis Philippe and Guizot might harbour personal resentments, but Palmerston did not allow his attitude to France to be influenced by such considerations. A few months later, Lord Normanby, the Ambassador in Paris, became involved in a bitter personal quarrel with Guizot. Palmerston insisted that he patch up the quarrel, and conduct business with Guizot in a friendly manner.

A more complicated situation arose in Portugal. In the general election in 1845, the Right-wing Chartist Government, who had ruled ever since they had seized power in their coup d'état in 1839, were heavily defeated, and the Radical Septembrists were returned with a large majority in the Cortes. As a result, Queen Maria da Gloria dissolved the Cortes, annulled the Constitution, and appointed Marshal Saldanha as

dictator. In October 1846 the Septembrist leaders seized power
in Oporto and set up a revolutionary junta in opposition to
the Queen's Government. The President of the Junta was
General das Antas, whose anti-British proclamation in 1837
had led Palmerston to threaten war against Portugal. Both
sides prepared for civil war.

The Queen's Government asked Britain, France and Spain
for help under the Quadruple Treaty of 1834. Lord Howard
de Walden, the British Minister in Lisbon, was as pro-Chartist
and anti-Septembrist as he had been ten years before. He sent
Palmerston copies of Septembrist leaflets which threatened the
Queen with the fate of Louis XVI, and which denounced
foreign nations, especially Britain, for interfering in the internal affairs of Portugal; and he urged Palmerston to help the
Queen and Saldanha suppress the revolt. Victoria and Albert
strongly agreed with him, being eager to go to the assistance
of Maria da Gloria and her German husband, who was their
cousin. But Palmerston was as reluctant to intervene as he
had been in 1836. He was never eager to be involved in civil
wars in foreign countries; and he realized that a strong body
of public opinion in Britain would not wish to see the British
forces allied with the Queen of Portugal against rebels who
demanded only the restoration of the Constitution, a free
Parliament, freedom of the press, and trial by jury. So he
pursued the same course which he had adopted in 1836. He
sent the Navy to the Tagus with orders to intervene in order
to save the Queen's life, but otherwise to preserve a strict
neutrality.

Palmerston also tried to mediate. He sent Colonel Wylde on
a special mission to the headquarters of the Junta at Oporto.
Palmerston told him to point out to Antas that the Septembrists had no chance of victory in the civil war, but that if
they would return to their allegiance to the Queen, the British
Government would use its influence to induce Maria da
Gloria to restore constitutional rights in Portugal. Antas assured Wylde of his friendship for Britain, but refused to submit to the Government.

The other Governments of the Quadruple Alliance were
more ready than Palmerston to assist the Portuguese Govern-

ment. The Right-wing Government of Spain was eager to help suppress the forces of Radicalism in Portugal; but Palmerston urged the Portuguese Government not to ask Spain for military aid, and argued that it would be very un-desirable for Portugal if Spanish troops were to occupy the country. He also claimed that the Quadruple Alliance was only intended to apply against a threat from Dom Miguel, and not to civil strife between the different factions who recog-nized Maria's title to the Crown. This argument was weak-ened by an unfortunate development. While the Portuguese politicians, and the politically conscious minorities, divided into Chartists and Septembrists, the great majority of the people, especially the peasants, were still devoted to Miguel. When they heard that a rebel administration had been set up at Oporto, they assumed that the revolutionaries were Miguelites. There were spontaneous risings all over the coun-try; and, to the great embarrassment of the Septembrists, the peasants marched to their support with the cry of 'Viva Dom Miguel!' But the British Consul in Portugal, Henry Southern, who was as sympathetic to the Septembrists as Howard was to the Queen and the Chartists, assured Palmerston that the Septembrists were not Miguelites; and Palmerston repeated this assurance to the governments of Spain and France, tell-ing them that Miguel was at present living incognito in Lon-don, and was not in contact with anyone in Portugal.

Although Victoria and Albert were very displeased with Palmerston's policy, he continued not merely to refuse to send help to Maria da Gloria, but also to show his sympathy for the Septembrists. When Marshal Saldanha re-issued a decree which Pedro had promulgated in the civil war against Miguel in 1833, under which all rebels taken in arms against the Queen's Government were to be summarily shot without trial, Palmerston protested against it. Saldanha refused to revoke the decree, but promised the British Government that it would not be enforced. Palmerston showed that it was not only the Queen whom he was prepared to rescue if she was in danger; he ordered the Navy to receive the Countess das Antas on board at Lisbon, and carry her safely to her husband in Oporto. He refused to recognize the blockade of Oporto by

the Portuguese Government's ships on the grounds laid down
by international law that a blockade was illegal unless it could
be adequately enforced. He also put strong pressure on the
Spanish Government through Bulwer in Madrid not to send
troops into Portugal in reply to Maria da Gloria's appeal for
help. Guizot, on the other hand, was urging the Spanish
Government to intervene, hoping thereby to crush Radical
revolution in Portugal and to annoy Palmerston.

In December 1846 Antas's army attacked Saldanha's at the
lines of Torres Vedras, and was repulsed. A number of Antas's
soldiers were taken prisoner in the battle. They were not shot,
but were sent as prisoners to the Portuguese colony of Angola
in Southern Africa. The Septembrists denounced this as an
outrage, and Palmerston protested to the Portuguese Government against it. Victoria and Albert strongly disapproved of
Palmerston's intervention on behalf of the prisoners. They
were not vindictive towards the Septembrists, and hoped that
Maria da Gloria would be as lenient as possible; but they felt
that Britain had no right to stand between foreign rebels and
the justice of their sovereign.

By the spring of 1847, Guizot and the Spanish Government
were becoming more insistent on intervention in support of
the Queen of Portugal. But Britain, with its old links with
Portugal and its navy in the Tagus, was still the strongest
piece on the board; and Palmerston persuaded Maria da
Gloria to agree to a joint mediation of Britain, France and
Spain between the belligerents in Portugal. He called a conference at the Foreign Office with the French and Spanish
Ministers, and proposed peace terms under which the Septembrists would disband their army, dissolve the Junta in Oporto,
and return to their allegiance; and the Queen would rescind
the emergency decrees, summon a new Cortes, and restore all
constitutional rights, with freedom of the press and trial by
jury. Maria da Gloria and Saldanha reluctantly accepted the
terms. The Junta in Oporto accepted them as a basis for negotiation, but put forward additional demands for the dismissal
of reactionary ministers from the Government, and for certain guarantees that free elections should be held.

When Palmerston received these replies, he called a con-

ference at the Foreign Office on 21 May at which he and the
French and Spanish Ministers decided to intervene by force
to assist the Queen of Portugal under the terms of the
Quadruple Alliance. Palmerston ordered the Navy to make
Saldanha's blockade of Oporto effective, and Admiral Parker
summoned the Junta to surrender to their sovereign. When the
Junta refused, a joint British and Spanish military force under
General Maitland marched on Oporto. Eventually the Sep-
tembrists surrendered to Maitland. Maria da Gloria annulled
the emergency decrees and restored the Constitution, and
Saldanha and the Right-wing Government remained in power.
Peace was restored in Portugal on the terms which Palmerston
had first proposed to the parties.

Palmerston was criticized, at first, by the Radicals inside and
outside the House of Commons for having sent British forces
to break the resistance of the Septembrists. He justified himself by claiming that he had forestalled intervention by Spain.
If the Septembrists had been defeated by the Spanish Army
alone, they would have been in a far worse plight; there would
have been no amnesty, and no return to constitutional government. There was a great deal of force in this argument. Short
of intervening on the side of the Septembrists – which would
have been very difficult in view of Victoria's attitude, apart
from any other reason – Palmerston could not have done
more to help the Portuguese Radicals. He might have adopted
the policy which he had pursued in 1833, and forced Spain to
refrain from helping the Portuguese Government by threatening to intervene on the side of the rebels if they did; but in
1847 France was supporting Spain, whereas in 1832 she had
supported Britain against Spain. In any case, this policy would
not have been of any help to the Septembrists, for their Generals were much less efficient than Saldanha, and there was
every reason to believe that they would get the worst of the
fighting if the civil war continued without any foreign intervention. Palmerston succeeded in persuading his Radical
critics that he had really been on their side; and the reactionary governments in Europe were convinced of it. Prince Albert
expressed his satisfaction that, for once, British forces had
intervened in Portugal on the side of the Crown; but both he

and Victoria, as well as King Leopold of Belgium – to say nothing of Guizot, the Spanish Government and the Northern Powers – were incensed at the way in which Palmerston had forced the Queen of Portugal to pardon her rebels and grant them concessions. So the events in Portugal in 1847, when Palmerston used force to defeat the Radicals, actually increased Palmerston's reputation throughout Europe of being the great champion of Radicalism.

Chapter Twenty-three

The Civil War in Switzerland

Eighteen-forty-seven was the worst year of the Irish famine. The potato blight of 1845 and 1846 hit a nation where the average wage of the labourer was only fivepence a day, as compared with 1s. 6d. in England, and where there was no poor relief of any kind. By the end of 1847, nearly 300,000 people had died of starvation. The Government at first refused to take any measures for public relief, believing that poverty should be relieved by private charity; but eventually they decided to contribute a sum equal to the amount that was raised in any district by private subscription, and to open workhouses where, as in England, relief would be granted under very disagreeable conditions. The Irish peasant avoided the workhouses for as long as possible, but as famine developed they soon filled up, and were quite insufficient to house more than a fraction of the destitute. The great-grandfathers of these Irish paupers had died, unnoticed, during the famines of the eighteenth century; but humanitarianism had begun to be an important factor in the world of 1847. The plight of the Irish aroused pity all over Europe, and in America both Congress and private organizations and individuals contributed funds to Irish relief. Palmerston, as Foreign Secretary, wrote and thanked the United States Government and people for their help; but he supported the reluctance of the British Government to give any relief to able-bodied persons in Ireland.

The famine, and the reaction of the British Government, caused great anger in Ireland. The people particularly resented the fact that food was exported from Ireland during the famine. Armed soldiers guarded convoys taking grain to the ports from attack by starving mobs along the route. This was an issue which had arisen, in a less acute form, in several countries of the world, and had involved Palmerston in arguments with foreign governments. These governments prohibited the export of corn during the period of food shortage in 1847, thus preventing British merchants from carrying out their contracts. Palmerston protested, and adopted the stern attitude which he always did when the legal rights of British subjects were interfered with; but he did not go to the lengths of actually threatening a blockade or other measures of coercion, and eventually contented himself with giving the foreign governments a lecture on the merits of free trade.

In a despatch to Lord Cowley, the Ambassador in Constantinople, on 3 November 1847, Palmerston explained to the Turkish Government how wrong they had been when they banned the export of corn from the island of Lemnos during the food shortage there in September. If there was a food shortage in a country, the price of corn there would rise. This in itself would prevent merchants from wishing to export the corn to other countries where the price of corn was lower; on the contrary, it would lead merchants to send corn from abroad to the hungry country where they could sell it at a high profit, which would cause the price of corn to fall there; and soon the scarcity would be replaced by such a glut of corn that some merchants would be unable to sell their corn. They would therefore wish to export it again and sell it in another market; but if the export of corn was banned, they would not be able to do so, and the shrewd merchants, realizing this, would not risk sending corn to the hungry country, and the famine would continue. Palmerston told the Turkish Government that it was for this reason that the British Government had always refused, at the height of the Irish famine, to ban the export of corn from Ireland, and he urged the Turkish Government to follow suit in Lemnos. But the Turks were not converted to a belief in laissez-faire economics by Palmerston's exposition of the infallible operation of the law of supply and demand.

The starving Irish sought relief in emigration to America on a scale which reduced the population of Ireland by twenty per cent in five years. Many voluntary societies were formed to encourage emigration. Palmerston was strongly in favour of sending the surplus Irish to America, where they could find work and food, where the enterprising could make their fortunes, and where the malcontented could attain their hearts' desire of living in a democracy. He contributed to the fare of any of his own tenants who wished to go to the United States or Canada, and paid for them to be provided with hot rum punch on the ship. But the priests and the temperance societies objected to this, and told Palmerston that it had led to drunkenness and other regrettable consequences. Palmerston therefore stopped the alcohol ration, and arranged for them to be given coffee and a biscuit instead.

During the summer and autumn of 1847 nine ships arrived at Quebec and St. John carrying a total of two thousand of Palmerston's tenants from Sligo. The Canadians were shocked at the conditions of the immigrants, who arrived in a state of complete destitution. The shipping agents and middlemen who had arranged the transport had sent them in very overcrowded conditions, and had not provided them with any clothing; and though Palmerston had announced that every family would be paid between £2 and £5 on arrival at Quebec, no representative of the agents was there to meet them, or provided them with any assistance, and they were left to beg in the snow, barefoot and in rags, during their first Canadian winter. One of the nine ships – which, ironically, was named the *Lord Ashburton* – arrived at Quebec on 30 October, which was too late in the year for the safety of the passengers. 107 of Palmerston's tenants had died of fever on the voyage; and of the 477 who had survived, 174 were almost naked. The local inhabitants of Quebec had to provide them with clothes before they could leave the ship. When another shipload of Palmerston's tenants arrived nine days later, one woman was completely naked, and had to be carried ashore wrapped in a blanket.

Palmerston was strongly criticized in the Canadian press. The town council of St. John wrote to him, expressing their deep regret that one of Her Majesty's ministers should have sent his tenants to endure the rigours of a New Brunswick winter without any means of support, in a dreadful state of health, and almost naked. One of the members of the Canadian Legislative Council wrote to Lord Grey, the Colonial Secretary, stating that Palmerston had sent his tenants to Canada 'without regard to humanity or even to common decency', in ships which were loaded to twice their proper capacity with passengers lying huddled between the decks with inadequate supplies of food and water, in conditions which were as bad as the slave trade. Palmerston immediately raised the matter with his agents in Ireland, and sent a copy of their rather unsatisfactory explanations to the Governor-General of Canada.

Lord John Russell's Government was supported by a minority of members of the House of Commons, but thanks to the split between the Peelites and Disraeli's Tories over the repeal of the Corn Laws, they had been able to carry on for a year with the Parliament elected in 1841. In the summer of 1847 a general election was held. The main issue was free trade, though in many places, where the Conservative candidates were Peelites, there were no important points of difference between the candidates. The result was that the Government gained a few seats from the Peelites, but still had only 330 seats in the House of Commons against 335 for their combined opponents. This was quite sufficient, because Disraeli and Peel would not unite on any issue, and Russell carried on as Prime Minister for another five years.

At Tiverton the election campaign was much more lively than in most places. No Conservative candidates stood against Palmerston and Heathcote; but the Chartists decided to fight him for propaganda purposes, though they knew that they had no chance of winning the seat on the restricted Parliamentary franchise which disqualified ninety-five per cent of adult males from voting. Palmerston's opponent, on this occasion, was not his usual adversary, the local Chartist butcher, Rowcliffe, but a far more formidable figure – Julian Harney, one of the national leaders of the Chartists, and their chief specialist on foreign affairs. The candidates met on election day, 31 July, in the presence of a large body of Chartist supporters, a smaller number of Palmerston's followers, and journalists from nearly every national newspaper.

Before proceeding to the hustings, the parties assembled in the Guildhall for the preliminaries and for refreshments. Harney found himself sitting next to a gentleman who greeted him by name, but whom Harney did not recognize. Harney was used to being treated with rudeness by arrogant gentlemen whom he had encountered during his election campaign, and was surprised to find that his neighbour was exceptionally courteous and friendly towards him. He was even more surprised when he discovered, on reaching the hustings, that he had been speaking to Palmerston. As the sitting member, Palmerston was entitled to speak first on the hustings; but he agreed with Harney that Harney should speak first, as he was intending to attack Palmerston and his foreign policy, and leave Palmerston to speak last in reply to Harney's criticisms.

Harney's chief object was to persuade the Radicals and the more progressive Whig supporters that Palmerston was not a Radical or a progressive, and did not deserve to have the support, which he was beginning to acquire, of the patriotic Radical groups. He attacked Palmerston's past record as a member of the governments of Perceval and Liverpool, when Palmerston had supported the suppression of political freedom at the time of the Six Acts and Peterloo. He denounced the new Poor Law, and criticized the Government's handling of the Irish famine, which he blamed on the profiteers in foodstuffs and on the Government's refusal to buy food abroad for the starving Irish. He attacked Palmerston's handling of the Belgian crisis of 1831, his appeasement of Russia and foreign despots, his support of the Sultan against Mehemet Ali, the Opium War in China, his failure to help the Poles in Cracow, his recent support for the Queen of Portugal against the rebels at Oporto, and his policy of assisting British bondholders to extort unearned profits from the people of Spain. Palmerston's reply lasted for three hours. It was reported almost verbatim in the London newspapers, and was later published as a pamphlet. It was a brilliant speech – well-reasoned, very persuasive, jocular, full of distortions, with a few deliberate untruths, and all carried through with bonhomie and great charm. Even his opponents were too amused to be really angry with him.

He twitted Harney with returning to the days of Perceval. He admitted 'that in those days laws were passed, and measures taken by the Executive Government, very different in principle to the measures and laws of the present times'; but though he had always favoured reforms, he believed that reforms should be pressed by reason and argument, or by peaceful agitation, and not by physical force; and the reason for the Six Acts and the repressive measures of the Castlereagh era was that in those days the reformers relied on physical force instead of argument to achieve their ends. He thus ignored the fact that the Six Acts, with their restrictions on public meetings and freedom of the press, had very largely prevented the reformers of 1819 from carrying on their agitation by peaceful means. With regard to the Irish famine, he said that Harney was going back even beyond the days of Perceval if he criticized those merchants who played so essential a part in the national economy by buying food and re-selling it at a profit; and Harney's suggestion that the Government should buy food abroad for the Irish showed his ignorance of political economy. 'If the Government had turned merchant (which no Government ever ought to do) it would have driven the private merchant out of trade'; and the Government alone could not have supplied all the wants of the Irish people without ruining the taxpayer. As for the Poor Law, he claimed the credit for the Government of having remedied the worst abuses by the Act of 1847, which had been passed just before the general election; and he reminded the electors of Tiverton that 'the Poor Law is a law by which the destitution of some is to be relieved out of the property of others, and that the property out of which that destitution is to be relieved is the property of all who possess property – of the farmer or of the tradesman, just as much as of any member of either House of Parliament'.

Turning to foreign policy, he said that it was amusing, 'after I have been accused all over Europe of being the great instigator of revolution, the friend and champion of all popular insurrections, the enemy of all constituted authorities – after I have been charged with disturbing the peace of Europe by giving encouragement to every revolutionary, anarchical set of men – it is somewhat amusing to hear charges the very reverse made against me by my present opponent'. He claimed the credit for establishing ·Belgian independence – this was not what he had told the Prussian Government in 1830 – and for defeating Carlos and Miguel. 'Did we set up Don Miguel? No, we put him down', he said, again ignoring his action in preventing the French from overthrowing Miguel in 1831, and his insistence on strict neutrality in the earlier stages of the civil war between Miguel and Pedro.

He made his audience laugh loudly by his references to the Middle Eastern crisis of 1840. 'Mr. Harney says we made a great mistake in Syria; he tells us that there was a most excellent worthy old gentleman called Mehemet Ali, who ruled in Egypt, and who had conquered Syria, and that we ought to have left him quietly there. Mr. Harney says we fought the battle for the rights of Kings by driving Mehemet Ali out of Syria, and restoring that country to the Sultan'. But if Mehemet Ali had retained Syria, he would have proclaimed his independence from the Sultan, and this would have so weakened the Turkish Empire that it would have become the vassal of some foreign power who was hostile to British interests. 'This was our reason for driving Mehemet Ali back to his country house at Alexandria. But it is said this worthy old gentleman was so much beloved in Syria that his rule formed a perfect paradise compared with the hell on earth which has existed there since he was driven out. Now how was it we did drive him out of Syria? Merely by giving a few muskets to the people of the country; by sending a few hundred marines on shore to aid them, and saying "Go it, my boys; if you want to get rid of Mehemet Ali, here we are to back you; if you intend to act, now's your time". They took us at our word; they kicked him out neck and crop, and his army too; they hailed us as their deliverers'. Palmerston had found his natural bent. This kind of stuff went down much better than the pompous evasions in his speeches in the House of Commons.

He dealt in the same vein with the Opium War. Harney had accused him of forcing the Chinese to buy opium; but that was as if a man were accused of forcing the people of England to drink beer. The Chinese people wanted nothing better than to buy our opium; and the mandarins who were supposed to suppress it connived at the smuggling, and smoked opium themselves. 'But these Chinese authorities suddenly turned round upon the men who had been their partners in this smuggling trade, and in order to extort money from them, required them to give up all the opium they had in their possession', and threatened to starve British merchants and the British Consul if the opium was not surrendered. Apart from the fact that Elliot had not been officially a Consul, Palmerston gave no indication that the Chinese Government was trying to suppress opium-smoking; and there was no truth at all in his statement that the Chinese had demanded the surrender of the opium in the receiving ships in order to extort money. 'We said "This won't do; this is no go, gentlemen of China. You have extorted valuable property from British subjects by threat of locking them up till they die of starvation".' So we used force against China. 'In this instance, at least, our policy was unattended with any expense. We said to the Chinese: "You have behaved very ill; we have had to teach you better manners; it has cost us something to do it, but we will send our bill in, and you must pay our charges". That was done, and they have certainly profited by the lesson. They have become free traders too'.

His greatest sleight-of-hand was when he dealt with Harney's criticisms of his recent intervention in Portugal. He said that the people of Portugal, deprived of their Parliament and constitutional rights, had risen to fight for their freedom, as Englishmen in former times had fought for their constitutional liberties. 'They took to arms, and said: "If you will not let us have a Parliament in which to state our grievances, we will state them in the field". I think the people of Portugal were justified in that conduct'. The electors of Tiverton cheered loudly at this. Palmerston claimed that Britain had prevented the Spanish Government from sending troops to crush the Portuguese people. Then, finding that the Queen of Portugal was prevented by her tyrannical ministers from granting the just demands of the Liberals, we had offered to intervene. 'Our offer was accepted by the Crown; it was for a time refused by the Junta; but at last it was accepted by them; and we have the satisfaction of thinking that, by our timely interference, we have saved the people of Portugal from the calamities of a desolating civil war, and have obtained for them the establishment of their constitutional liberties'. Many of Palmerston's audience can have had no idea that he had sent the British Army and Navy to fight against, not for, the Portuguese patriots whom he was praising so warmly.

When Palmerston had finished, his colleague, Heathcote, waived his right to speak, and the vote was taken by show of hands. The Chartists had turned out in great strength, and Harney and Heathcote were declared elected; but most of Harney's supporters were not qualified to vote, and Palmerston demanded a poll. Harney then announced that he would withdraw from the contest as a protest against the electoral system under which the mass of the people were disfranchised; and Palmerston and Heathcote were returned unopposed.

Before the end of the year, Palmerston achieved a great triumph in connexion with Switzerland. In 1798, when the French revolutionary armies invaded Switzerland, they had replaced the old confederation of independent cities and cantons by a centralized republic on more democratic lines; but in 1814 the Congress of Vienna established a constitution which was a compromise between the ancient and the Napoleonic systems. For the next thirty-three years there was continual conflict in Switzerland between the Liberal, centralizing faction, and the Catholic Party, who favoured cantonal independence; and there was also trouble about Neuchâtel, which, though a canton of the Swiss Confederation, was a hereditary possession of the King of Prussia. By the eighteen-forties, Switzerland was being transformed, economically, into a modern state. Steamships were carrying the local inhabitants and tourists on most of the lakes; excellent carriage-ways had been built across the high Alpine passes; the first railway was being constructed. But in the Catholic canton of Schwyz torture was still used as an official part of judicial proceedings; and, thanks to internal fiscal regulations, it was cheaper for a citizen of Geneva to send a letter to Constantinople than to Lucerne.

Faced with the increasing menace of Radicalism, seven of the Catholic cantons – Lucerne, Zug, Schwyz, Uri, Unterwalden, Valais and Fribourg – united in a Separate League – the Sonderbund – to protect their interests against the Radical majority in the Federal Parliament. But in 1847 the Radical leader, Ochsenbein, who was under sentence of death in Lucerne for taking part in an unsuccessful insurrection there, became President of the Federal Government in Berne. A few months later the Radicals seized power in Geneva by a revolution, and won an election in St. Gall. This gave them control of twelve cantons, which was the majority that they needed to change the Constitution of the Swiss Confederation. The central Government in Berne decided to expel the Jesuits from Switzerland, and decreed the dissolution of the Sonderbund; but the Sonderbund refused to acknowledge the authority of the Federal Government. Both sides prepared for civil war.

Metternich supported the Sonderbund. He had been suspicious for a long time of the Swiss Radicals, and on several occasions during the previous sixteen years would have taken action against them had it not been for his fear of provoking counter-measures in their support from the French Government. But now Guizot wished to reverse French policy towards Switzerland; he was eager to use this opportunity to take the first steps to build up an anti-British alliance with Austria. The Swiss Radicals, lying between Guizot and Metternich, were in an unenviable position. To the north, the states of the German Confederation were Austrian satellites. The King of Prussia was prepared to forget his Protestant prejudices in order to support Metternich, the Sonderbund, and the cause of absolutism. On the southern frontier of Switzerland were the territories of Charles Albert, King of Sardinia, whose kingdom included Piedmont and Savoy. Charles Albert could never make up his mind whether to support the cause of Liberalism or monarchical absolutism; but on this occasion he lined up at once with Austria and France. From further afield, the Tsar gave moral support to the Sonderbund. Only Britain supported the central government.

British public opinion was, of course, strongly on the side of the Swiss Liberals against the Jesuits and the Sonderbund, and the absolutist Courts. Ochsenbein was too extreme a Radical for Palmerston's liking, and had attacked Palmerston in the Swiss Parliament for helping the Queen of Portugal against the Septembrists; but Palmerston sent him a message of support. This was very welcome to the friendless Swiss Radicals, and their newspapers encouraged their supporters by proclaiming that Britain was on their side and would save them from the absolutist powers. But Palmerston was much too experienced a statesman to imagine that he could do anything effective to help the Government of Berne. If Austria, France and Sardinia marched in to help the Sonderbund, Palmerston could do no more for Switzerland than for Cracow. The Swiss Radicals, by proclaiming their absolute reliance on Palmerston, were placing him in a position which was likely to involve him in a serious loss of prestige, though he reminded them that the British Government had not given any undertaking as to what action they would take if Switzerland were to be invaded.

Metternich and Guizot were planning to take action against the Swiss Government. As early as November 1846, Metternich had proposed to Guizot that Austria and France should send troops into Switzerland to overthrow the Radical Government in Berne. Guizot did not dare to agree to this proposal. French Liberal opinion strongly supported the Swiss Radicals, and Guizot and Louis Philippe were becoming very unpopular in France owing to their internal policy and to a number of sensational scandals involving the Court and the nobility. Guizot therefore proposed a more devious plan. He suggested that Austrian troops should invade Switzerland to help the Sonderbund. The French Army would then enter Switzerland from the other side, ostensibly to resist Austrian aggression. With Europe apparently on the verge of war, the French and Austrian Governments would reach a compromise agreement at the last moment which would save peace and give internal independence to the cantons of the Sonderbund. Metternich was very suspicious. Guizot's reputation, and his behaviour about the Spanish marriages, were not calculated to inspire trust; and Metternich thought that he might be trying to double-cross him, and involve Austria in a war in which she would appear to be the aggressor and would unite the other powers against her. He insisted that there should be a joint Austro-French intervention on behalf of the Sonderbund.

Palmerston's only hope was to play for time and try to gain something by mediation and negotiation. He proposed that, as the Swiss Constitution had been established by the Treaty of Vienna, the present threat to the constitutional structure in Switzerland should be referred to an international conference of the great powers. Guizot, with an eye to French public opinion, accepted this proposal, while he carried on his secret negotiations with Metternich. The Swiss Radicals bitterly resented the idea of an international conference as a tyrannical interference of the great powers in the internal affairs of Switzerland; but just as Palmerston had intervened on the side of the Queen of Portugal in order to force her to restore the Constitution, he now took the lead in the move for a great power conference on Switzerland so that he could restrain the great powers, as far as possible, from interfering in Switzerland. He played for time, hoping that passions would cool. When Guizot drafted a note which was to be delivered to the Government of Berne on behalf of the five great powers, proposing that the conference be held, Palmerston objected to the draft, and prepared another draft. He proposed that the great powers should agree, before the conference met, to the expulsion of the Jesuits from Switzerland, on condition that they received fair compensation for their property; though he accepted Guizot's demand that the Federal Government should be required to acknowledge the existing rights of the Sonderbund cantons. He held up proceedings from July to November while he and Guizot argued about the preliminary conditions for the Conference and the wording of the note.

Palmerston also tried to take advantage of the accession of the new Pope, Pius IX, who immediately began to carry out a policy of reforms in the Papal states. In the spring of 1847 revolutionary demonstrations took place in Modena, Parma, Florence and the cities of Northern Italy, and Austrian troops again occupied Ferrara. Palmerston sent Gilbert Elliot, his old friend of Edinburgh University days, who had now suc-

Metternich, mezzotint by Sir Thomas Lawrence

Lord John Russell, engraved by D J Pound
from a photograph by Mayall

Mehemet Ali, by David Wilkie, in 1847

are the Bills to be allowed
to come in ... Feb
or previous Question to be , 61,
moved
For letters agt
therein
Granville   Grey
Lewis   Chancellor
Kinley   Cardwell
Torrens   Wood
Newcastle
Gibson   Herbert
Villiers
Gladstone   Palmerston
Argyll
Russell

Palmerston's handwriting

William Gladstone, by G F Watts, in 1858

Cambridge House in 1854

Palmerston in old age, from a photograph

been responsible for the decision of the Swiss Government to attack Fribourg and start the civil war. They said that he had planned every move of the Swiss Radicals, and that Ochsenbein and his colleagues were merely pawns and agents of Palmerston. The British Liberal press took up this theme, and gave Palmerston full credit for everything for which the foreign Conservatives blamed him. Palmerston denied in the House of Commons that he had urged the Swiss Government to attack, or had advised them in any way; but as he would obviously have had to say this in any case, neither his friends nor his enemies believed him, though it was in fact the truth, or almost the truth. It became generally accepted that Palmerston had saved the cause of freedom and Radicalism in Switzerland.

Ochsenbein and the Swiss Government knew how precarious their position was. At any time, France and Austria might invade Switzerland under some excuse or other, and Palmerston would be powerless to do anything to save Liberalism in Switzerland, or his own prestige from a heavy blow after the exaggerated hopes which had been raised by his apparent triumph over the Sonderbund, Guizot and Metternich. But the main danger came from Prussia. King Frederick William was seriously alarmed at the Radical victory in Switzerland, which he thought constituted a menace to his principality of Neuchâtel, and he demanded that the international Conference be held to settle the new Constitution of Switzerland and the safety of Neuchâtel. Palmerston sent Sir Stratford Canning to Switzerland to play for time once again, to urge restraint on the Swiss Government and to appease the Prussian fears.

At Christmas 1847, the Austrian and Prussian representatives in Paris proposed to Guizot that Austria, Prussia and France should invade Switzerland if the Government at Berne would not agree to refer the future Constitution of the Confederation to an international Conference to be held at Neuchâtel. Guizot accepted the proposal, and on 18 January the three powers sent a threatening note to Berne demanding that the Conference be held.   Ochsenbein would not give way, and denied the right of foreign powers to intervene in Swiss internal affairs. On 13 February Russia added to the pressure by withdrawing her undertaking to maintain the neutrality and independence of Switzerland. But on 12 January a revolution had broken out in Sicily. Before the end of the month it had spread to Naples, and the King capitulated and granted a Constitution. Four weeks later, on 24 February, the people of Paris revolted, Louis Philippe abdicated, and he and Guizot arrived in England as refugees. On 13 March the revolution reached Vienna, and Metternich, too, fled to England. On 18 March there was a revolution in Berlin, and Frederick William was forced to accept a Constitution and a Liberal Government. The Swiss Radicals were saved, but not by Palmerston; they, and Palmerston's reputation, were saved by the revolutions of 1848.

Chapter Twenty-four

1848: France and Spain

By the beginning of the year of revolutions, 1848, Palmerston was firmly established in popular imagination as the leader of the cause of freedom and Radicalism in Europe. The attacks of the Right wing Continental press convinced the Radicals that Palmerston was their champion; and Radical applause and Conservative abuse drove him to become what he was believed to be. The stories about him spread all over Europe. The German Conservatives made up a rhyme, '*Hat der Teufel einen Sohn, so ist er sicher Palmerston*'; and it was proudly translated by Palmerston's British admirers, 'If the devil has a son, his name is surely Palmerston'. They told the story about the Austrian frontier official who, when a British traveller showed him his passport, signed by Palmerston, struck through Palmerston's signature with his pen, saying 'It is a hateful name'; and there was the less credible story about another Austrian frontier official who refused to allow the importation of British cutlery marked 'PALMER&SON' because he had confused the manufacturer's name with Palmerston's, and therefore imagined that the knives were being sent to Austria for use by revolutionaries. Even in Russia, Turgeniev was once asked by a peasant whether Palmerston was still alive.

This state of affairs put an end to responsible Radical criticism of Palmerston. In July 1847 he had been attacked in the House of Commons by Hume and Lord Dudley Stuart and his old critics for his support of the Queen of Portugal; but the next attack, six months later, came only from the lunatic fringe of Radicalism. David Urquhart, who had been dismissed by Palmerston from the embassy in Constantinople in 1837 and had been attacking him in his paper ever since, was elected to Parliament in 1847. He proceeded, with the support of one or two colleagues, to draft a motion demanding the impeachment of Palmerston for having betrayed his country on twenty-three occasions. The first count accused him of having been employed as a Russian agent by the Lievens when he was Secretary at War in Wellington's Government in 1828. Other charges included his failure to go to war with China when Lord Napier was expelled from Canton in 1834, his failure to act when the Russians seized the *Vixen* off the Circassian coast in 1837, and his alliance with Russia against France and Mehemet Ali in 1840. The case was presented in the House of Commons by Urquhart; but the main argument was developed by his colleague Thomas Anstey, a slightly unbalanced Catholic barrister who was MP for Youghal in Ireland. On 8 February 1848 Anstey spoke on the subject in the House; but after he had been speaking for several hours, someone pointed out that there were only thirty-nine members present, and the House was counted out.

Anstey tried again a fortnight later. This time he spoke for nearly six hours; and on 1 March Palmerston replied at length. He dealt with every point of the indictment, and defended himself persuasively, and with dignity, without showing any sign of rancour against his accusers. He ended by enunciating the principles on which he had based his foreign policy. 'I hold with respect to alliances that England is a power sufficiently strong, sufficiently powerful, to steer her own course, and not to tie herself up as an unnecessary appendage to the policy of any other Government. I hold that the real policy of England – apart from questions which involve her own particular interests, political or commercial – is to be the champion of justice and right; pursuing that course with moderation and prudence, not becoming the Quixote of the world, but giving the weight of her moral sanction and support wherever she thinks that justice is, and wherever she thinks that wrong has been done'. If Britain pursued such a policy, she could be sure that she would always find some allies to support her. 'Therefore I say that it is a narrow policy to suppose that this country or that is to be marked out as the eternal ally or the perpetual enemy of England. We have no eternal allies, and we have no perpetual enemies. Our interests are eternal and perpetual, and those interests it is our duty to follow. ... It is our duty not to pass too harsh a judgment upon others, because they do not exactly see things in the same light as we see; and it is our duty not lightly to engage this country in the frightful responsibilities of war'. He closed his speech with the words: 'If I might be allowed to express in one sentence the principle which I think ought to guide an English minister, I would adopt the expression of Canning, and say that with every British minister the interests of England ought to be the shibboleth of his policy'. The combination of national interest and morality made a deep appeal, not only to the House of Commons, but also to the country.

The interests of England were undoubtedly the shibboleth of Palmerston's policy in dealing with the events of 1848. His reaction to the revolutions was mixed. He could not conceal his satisfaction that they got rid of his two greatest adversaries, Metternich and Guizot, and put an end to Guizot's plan of building an anti-British alliance of the great European powers; and they vindicated his belief in the superiority of the British constitution, which weathered the storm to which the Continental monarchies succumbed. But Palmerston had never liked revolutions, and the revolutions of 1848 had features which he found particularly detestable. The revolutionaries tried to establish republics, not constitutional monarchies; and in several countries Communism appeared as a factor for the first time in history. 'The Struggle now going on in many parts of Europe', wrote Palmerston to Milbanke, the British Minister in Munich on 20 April 1848, 'is one between those who have no property and those who have and wish to keep it'. Palmerston had no doubt on which side he stood in such a struggle; but his reaction to the revolutions, like his feelings, was varied. He supported the revolutionaries wholeheartedly in Spain, to a limited extent in France and Italy, was neutral in Hungary, and opposed them in Germany. He suffered defeat in both Spain and Italy; but he emerged from the events of 1848–9 more popular than ever with the British people and with the Radicals of Europe.

At 11.30 p.m. on 25 February 1848 the Macdonald

brothers – two Scotsmen who carried on business in France – arrived at the House of Commons with a letter written on the evening of the 23rd by Lord Normanby, the British Ambassador in Paris, who had rightly thought that the Macdonalds would reach London before the Queen's messenger. They told Palmerston that revolution had broken out in Paris two days before. The revolutionaries would have nothing to do with Thiers and the official Liberal Opposition, or with any of the professional politicians who had been active under the Orleanist monarchy. A Provisional Government was set up with the poet, Lamartine, as President, and including not only extreme Radicals and Democrats like Ledru-Rollin, but even Socialists like Louis Blanc.

Palmerston immediately decided to pursue a policy of friendship towards the revolutionary régime. He did not follow the example of the United States Minister in Paris, who at once gave full *de jure* recognition to the Provisional Government; but he told Lord Normanby to remain in Paris and to establish unofficial relations with Lamartine. Normanby was to explain to Lamartine that although Palmerston could not give *de jure* recognition at this stage, he would be eager to do so as soon as the new Government was firmly established on a permanent basis. The chief difficulty here was Queen Victoria, who strongly objected to the establishment of a republic in France, and for a long time refused to recognize it. Palmerston tried unsuccessfully to persuade her to receive at Buckingham Palace the French Government's representative in London, who, like Normanby, was carrying on all the duties of an Ambassador without being officially accredited.

Apart from her opposition to republicanism, Victoria had liked Louis Philippe personally. Palmerston agreed to her suggestion that the British Government should give financial help to Louis Philippe in his exile at Claremont near Esher. He gave him £1,000 out of the Secret Service money, but insisted that it should be kept secret even from Louis Philippe himself. It was given anonymously by a donor described as a well-wisher, for Palmerston did not think it right that Louis Philippe should feel under any obligation to the British Government, as this might embarrass him if he ever returned to the throne, or played any future part in politics. Palmerston also asked Lamartine not to confiscate Louis Philippe's property in France.

Louis Philippe was not the only opponent of Britain who turned to her for asylum. Guizot and Princess Lieven settled down in Pelham Crescent, South Kensington – or Brompton, as it was then called; and Metternich and his wife bought a house at Richmond. Palmerston now met Metternich for the first time. He was very friendly to him and to Guizot, inviting them both to a dinner at the Foreign Office, and keeping up social relations with them. But Metternich saw more of Disraeli, and helped to brief him for his attacks on Palmerston's policy in debates in the House of Commons.

On 29 February – when Metternich was still in power in Vienna – Palmerston wrote to the three Northern Powers to urge them to accept the new régime in France, and to take no hostile measures against it. He stated that he had every confidence in the sincerity of Lamartine's declaration of his peaceable intentions, but that any hostile actions by foreign powers could easily produce a revolutionary war in Europe. Karl Marx denounced Lamartine, Ledru-Rollin and Louis Blanc because he thought that they alone were restraining the Paris proletariat from making a Communist revolution; and Palmerston supported them for the same reason. 'It appears to be at present the unanimous opinion of everything that is respectable in France', he wrote to the Northern Powers, 'including men of all political parties, that the only hope for the maintenance of internal tranquillity, and for the permanent restoration of order in France, lies in the continuance, for the present at least, of M. Lamartine and his Colleagues in Power'. He expressed his views more forcibly in his private correspondence. 'I grieve at the prospect of a republic in France', he wrote to Normanby on 28 February. 'Large republics seem to be essentially and inherently aggressive, and the aggressions of the French will be resisted by the rest of Europe, and that is war; while, on the other hand, the example of universal suffrage in France will set our non-voting population agog, and will create a demand for an inconvenient extension of the suffrage, ballot, and other mischievous things. However, for the present, *vive Lamartine*!'

On 7 March Lamartine issued a manifesto on foreign policy which did not make Palmerston's position any easier. It declared that France would not recognize the frontiers, or any of the other provisions, of the Treaty of Vienna because old treaties could not check the national aspirations of peoples; but it also announced that the French Government wished to live in peace with all nations, unless France were subjected to intolerable wrongs. The manifesto caused alarm in Vienna, Berlin, and St. Petersburg; but Palmerston took it very calmly. He realized that Lamartine had issued the manifesto in order to appease the Radical extremists and the Socialists in France. In a private letter to Lord Clarendon, he expressed his disgust at the spectacle of 'a nation of 33 millions ... despotically governed by eight or nine men who are the mere subordinates of 40, or 50,000 of the scum of the faubourgs of Paris'; but he assured the Northern Powers that they need not worry about Lamartine's manifesto.

The French Provisional Government was the most Left-wing government that had ever been established in Palmerston's lifetime. The Portuguese Septembrist government of Count das Antas and Baron Sa de Bandeira were moderate Liberals as compared with men like Ledru-Rollin and Louis Blanc, who introduced universal suffrage and set up National Workshops at the demand of the industrial proletariat. But Palmerston gave this régime his full support, and treated it with a tolerance which he had never shown to any other foreign government. As soon as news of the revolution reached London the British Chartist leaders went to Paris to congratulate Lamartine and his colleagues. They were received by Garnier-Pagès, one of the ministers in the Provisional Government, who warmly welcomed them in a public speech, praised the British Chartists, and told them that the French Government felt a closer link with them, the true representatives of the British people, than with the British Government. Palmerston sent the mildest of protests to Lamartine. He said that such statements, from a member of the French Government, were irregular, and must do harm to

France's international relations; and he asked how Lamartine would like it if the British Government declared that it felt closer solidarity with the counter-revolutionary forces in France than with Lamartine's Government. He protested more vigorously a few days later when he heard that Lamartine himself was intending to receive Mitchel and O'Brien and the delegates of the Irish nationalists who were wanted by the police in Ireland on a charge of sedition. He said that it would be improper for Lamartine to meet the Irish leaders, and could only harm Anglo-French relations. Despite Palmerston's protests, Lamartine insisted on receiving them, but told them that France could not interfere in British internal affairs. Normanby and Palmerston were perfectly satisfied with this.

One of the first actions of Lamartine's Government was to announce their intention of nationalizing the French railways. Normanby was approached by British shareholders in the Orleans and Bordeaux Railway and in the Havre and Rouen Railway, who asked him to prevent the nationalization of these enterprises in which British shareholders held more than half the total capital of 35,000,000 Francs. Normanby warned Lamartine that such 'spoilation ... would excite such an outcry amongst the English capitalists as must affect the intimacy of the relations between the two countries'. But he told the shareholders that he could do nothing more, as they must take the risks of foreign investment, and the British Government could not interfere officially in a matter of French internal national policy. Palmerston approved of Normanby's attitude.

At the beginning of March, an angry crowd at Granville, where there was a food shortage, refused to permit a British merchant to export the corn which he had bought in France; while at Rouen, a number of English artisans were expelled from the town. Palmerston handled the situation in a way which showed unusual consideration for Lamartine. 'You will say', he wrote to Normanby on 7 March, 'that Her Majesty's Government are quite aware that in the present State of Things in France the Provisional Government cannot entirely prevent Occurrences of this Kind, and that all that can be expected is that they should do what M. Lamartine has so readily and so handsomely undertaken to do in the case of the People expelled from Rouen, namely repair the Injury and endeavour to prevent its Recurrence'.

In the summer, the Provisional Government broke up. Ledru-Rollin and the Socialists resigned, and the Government, under pressure from the Conservative politicians and the business interests, suppressed the National Workshops and ordered that the unemployed should be taken into the army or sent to work in the provinces. The Paris working class took up arms and erected barricades, and Lamartine resigned after appointing General Cavaignac as Dictator. Cavaignac overcame the resistance of the artisans after four days' street fighting, which cost the lives of 10,000 men and of more army officers than fell in any of Napoleon's victories. Palmerston had acquired such a reputation as an instigator of revolution that he was accused by the French Conservative press of having organized the rising of the Paris Communists in the June days. He told Normanby to take steps to rebut this slander, and approved of Normanby's action in congratulating Cavaignac on his victory. He was very pleased that the revolution in France, after the uncertainties of the first four months, had culminated in Cavaignac.

Cavaignac dealt very harshly with the defeated rebels. 3,000 were shot without trial immediately after the fighting, and 4,500 were sentenced by courts-martial to long terms of imprisonment in the penal settlements overseas. Palmerston made no attempt to persuade Cavaignac to deal leniently with the rebels: he did not send him any of those appeals for moderation which he had issued after the Isabelinos' victory over the Carlists in Spain, after Maria da Gloria's victory in Portugal, or in 1831 after the defeat of the risings in Italy and Poland. He did, however, protest when some of the Communist prisoners were sent to prison camps in Tahiti. He argued that as Tahiti was only a French protectorate, France ought not to exercise rights of sovereignty there by establishing a prison camp. He thought that the island of Réunion, near Madagascar, would be a more suitable place for the prisoners, as it seemed unfair to the inhabitants of Tahiti that desperate criminals should be sent among them. The French Government tried to reassure him by pointing out that all the deportees were political prisoners, and not ordinary convicts; but Palmerston replied that 'some of the most active Leaders of Insurrection in Paris during the last twelve Months have been men of the worst Moral Character'. But when Louis Blanc fled to England, and was sentenced in his absence by the French Courts to transportation to the prison camps for having organized the June rising, Palmerston not only assured him that he would have the right to publish his vindication in Britain, but allowed him access to the state papers in the British Museum which he needed to write his *History of the French Revolution*.

Cavaignac's severity to the defeated rebels, and his policy as Dictator, made him popular with the French middle classes; but he was hated by the working classes, and at the election which was held to choose a President of the Republic by universal suffrage on 10 December 1848, he was heavily defeated by Louis Napoleon Bonaparte. Louis Napoleon was elected by the votes of 5,000,000 Bonapartists, Socialists and peasants against the 1,500,000 votes for Cavaignac, and a mere handful cast for Lamartine and Ledru-Rollin, the official Socialist candidate. Once again a Bonaparte was ruler of France, and the other great powers accepted, without a protest, this situation which they had pledged themselves never to permit at the Congress of Vienna. Before long, Louis Napoleon turned on the Socialists; but it was some time before the Conservatives ceased to think of the Bonapartes as dangerous Socialist Democrats. Princess Metternich told Disraeli, at a party at her house in August 1849, that Louis Napoleon's cousin, Charles Lucien, Prince of Canino, was a 'Red Republican'. The conversation then turned to Palmerston. 'Worse than Canino', said Princess Metternich. Just at that moment Palmerston was announced, and the Princess hastened to greet him at the door with the most gracious of smiles.

The revolution also came to England, but here it fizzled out. The Chartists called a great demonstration on 10 April 1848 at Kennington Green, and proclaimed their intention of marching on the Houses of Parliament. The Government banned the demonstration, and made careful preparations to meet it. They put Wellington in command of the army in London, and called on the middle classes, and the loyal sections of the working classes, to protect London against the Chartists. 175,000 men were enrolled as special constables, and the public buildings and government offices were barricaded against attack. Palmerston was placed in command of the detachment defending the Foreign Office, and thoroughly enjoyed himself. Word had gone around that foreign agitators were leading the Chartists; but there was no sign of them. 'The foreigners did not show', wrote Palmerston to Normanby next day, 'but the constables, regular and special, had sworn to make an example of any whiskered and bearded rioter whom they might meet with, and I am convinced would have mashed them to jelly'. Lady Palmerston strolled down to the Foreign Office from Carlton Gardens with her daughter Lady Ashley, although she had been warned to stay indoors. She was impressed at the sight of men of all classes – gentlemen, middle class and workmen – talking together on terms of friendship and equality as they waited for action. It was an extraordinary sight to see, but she thought it was an excellent thing for all classes, and wished that it could occur more often.

The Chartists halted on Westminster Bridge when faced with Wellington's troops, and the movement rapidly disintegrated. The Government could congratulate itself that revolution could succeed in Palermo, Paris, Vienna, and Berlin, but not in London. There was more serious trouble in Ireland, where a state of disorder had existed for some time. Palmerston had hoped that the famine would make revolution less likely, 'as men must eat to be able to fight'; but he had nevertheless been urging Lord John Russell to introduce legislation to give the Lord Lieutenant emergency powers to suppress violence by drastic means. On 10 April – the day of the Chartist demonstration – O'Brien made a defiant speech in the House of Commons and walked out to organize a revolution in Munster, having, in Palmerston's words, 'surpassed himself last night in dulness, bad taste and treason'. The revolution failed, and O'Brien, Mitchel and the other leaders were sentenced to transportation for life to Van Diemen's Land. Mitchel was treated with great consideration by the captain of the ship which transported him, and was regularly invited to drink sherry in the captain's cabin. The Irish in America had planned to rescue him when his ship reached Bermuda; but the British embassy in Washington discovered the plot, and Palmerston passed on the information to the authorities in Bermuda.

On 26 March 1848 the revolution reached Madrid; but Narváez's dictatorship resisted it as successfully as the British constitutional government. The rising was suppressed with great severity, the Cortes was dissolved, and Narváez ruled by emergency decree. Bulwer's sympathies were entirely with the revolutionaries, and he was disgusted at the unnecessary brutality of the soldiers, who opened fire at the least excuse, and killed and wounded several British subjects. This placed a further strain on Bulwer's relations with Narváez and the Spanish Government. Bulwer was a more colourful and romantic figure than the ordinary British career diplomat. He had formerly been a Radical MP, and was strongly in sympathy with the Spanish Progresistas, and with Palmerston's policy of friendship towards them. He ate Spanish food, kept a siesta, and often visited the Progresista leaders in their homes. His despatches made life at the Spanish Court and the British Legation in Madrid sound as romantic as one of the historical novels of his brother, Bulwer-Lytton. Unfortunately, his zest sometimes led him to pursue risky policies. He was sure that the Queen's life was in danger, because if she died childless, her sister the Infanta, Duchess of Montpensier, and her French husband, would obtain the throne; and he believed that French interest in Montpensier and the throne of Spain had not ceased with the fall of Louis Philippe in France. He also believed that the Queen was a virtual prisoner in the hands of her mother and Narváez. He had several secret meetings with Isabella, but he realized, from her signs and hints, that an agent of Narváez was listening to their conversation from behind a curtain. One day a lady-in-waiting brought him a message from the Queen, asking him to meet her in her chamber at midnight. Bulwer did not go, for he was sure that it was a trap to involve him and the Queen in a scandal. He later discovered that the lady-in-waiting was in Narváez's pay.

Ten days before the insurrection broke out in Madrid, Palmerston had offered advice to the Spanish Government as to how to deal with the situation.

Sir, [he wrote to Bulwer on 16 March] I have to instruct you to recommend earnestly to the Spanish Government and to the Queen Mother, if you have an opportunity of doing so, the adoption of a legal and constitutional course of government in Spain. The recent fall of the King of the French and of his whole family, and the expulsion of his ministers, ought to teach the Spanish Court and Government how great is the danger of an attempt to govern a country in a manner at variance with the feelings and opinions of the nation; and the catastrophe which has happened in France must serve to show that even a large and well-disciplined army becomes an ineffectual defence for the Crown, when the course pursued by the Crown is at variance with the general sentiments of the country. It would then be wise for the Queen of Spain, in the present critical state of affairs, to strengthen the Executive Government by enlarging the basis upon which the administration is founded, and by calling to her councils some of those men who possess the confidence of the Liberal party. I am, etc., Palmerston.

This despatch was couched in less tactful language than Palmerston usually employed on such occasions; but Bulwer, on his own responsibility, showed the despatch to the Spanish Foreign Minister, the Duke of Sotomayor; and Palmerston subsequently approved his action. Sotomayor refused to accept the note, and returned it to Bulwer. He stated that the Spanish people would not permit any foreign power to meddle in its internal affairs, and asked the British Government how they would like it if he gave them advice on how to govern Ireland. Palmerston replied that if Queen Victoria had had to fight for her throne in a civil war, and had only been victorious because of the help which she had received from the Spanish Government and Spanish volunteers, Sotomayor would be fully entitled to give him advice as to how to rule Ireland. 'I think I may confidently affirm that under such circumstances any Statesmen who might be Ministers of the British Crown, instead of sending back the note in which such representations were conveyed, and instead of replying to it in discourteous terms, would have accepted the communication in the same spirit of friendship in which it was made; and whether they adopted or not the advice which it contained, would at least have considered it as a proof of the continued existence of that friendship on the part of Spain, to which in such case would have been owing the circumstance that those British Ministers had the honour of being advisers of the Crown, instead of being prescribed exiles in a foreign land'. Sotomayor answered that the Spaniards were grateful for British help in the Carlist wars, but they knew that on this occasion, and whenever British soldiers had fought in the Peninsula, they had only acted 'as nations act on similar occasions, always consulting their own glory, their policy, and their interest'.

This was the signal for a violent attack on Bulwer in the Spanish press. He was accused of having organized the revolutionary outbreak of 26 March, and of having tried to assassinate Narváez. Then, on 17 May, the Spanish Government asked Bulwer to leave Spain; and when he refused he was handed his passports and ordered to leave the country within twenty-four hours. A rupture of diplomatic relations was a much rarer, and more serious, step in the nineteenth century than it is today, and summary expulsion in such a manner was often regarded as a provocation to war. There were violent protests in the House of Commons when the news reached London. Palmerston proposed in the Cabinet that the Navy should be sent to blockade Seville, and that Britain should threaten to seize the Spanish colony of Cuba as reparation for the insult; for he was sure that Maria Cristina would sacrifice Narváez to save Cuba. But the Cabinet would not agree. Bulwer later attributed their pusillanimous attitude to the panic which had been caused in Britain by the Chartist demonstration in London, which had produced a Conservative reaction in British political circles and made everyone disinclined to do anything that might appear to be helping the Spanish Radicals to weaken the authority of established governments. The Spanish Minister was ordered to leave London; but no further action was taken.

The Spanish press acclaimed this as a great victory over Palmerston, and Narváez became the hero, not only of the

Conservatives throughout Europe, but of the whole Spanish people. The Progresistas were submerged by the outburst of patriotic enthusiasm, and suffered a big set-back as a result of this slap in the face that Narváez had given to Palmerston. Relations between Britain and Spain were confined to consular level until diplomatic relations were resumed, through the mediation of King Leopold, in a friendly spirit on both sides in the summer of 1850.

Chapter Twenty-five

1848-9: Italy, Hungary, Schleswig-Holstein

The revolutions of 1848 had begun in Italy, which was already seething with discontent by the beginning of 1847. The new Pope, Pius IX, was in favour of introducing some liberal reforms; but Metternich was strongly opposed to any concession, and in July 1847 sent Austrian troops to occupy Ferrara in the Papal territories. Palmerston at first adopted the same attitude about Italy as in 1831: he urged the people not to revolt, and the rulers to avoid revolution by giving timely concessions and at least some measure of constitutional government. Again, as in 1831, the British diplomats in Italy were more afraid of the revolutionaries than Palmerston was. In March 1847 Scarlett, the British Minister to the Grand Duke of Tuscany at Florence, warned Palmerston that 'the doctrines of the Communists have undoubtedly taken some hold of the minds of the peasantry'; and a fortnight later Abercromby reported from the King of Sardinia's Court at Turin that the Government had seized pamphlets which 'advocated principles of an ultra-revolutionary and Communist tendency'. But Palmerston was confident that all serious trouble would be avoided if the Grand Duke of Tuscany and King Charles Albert would introduce constitutional reforms. He tried unsuccessfully to persuade Metternich to encourage such a policy, and ridiculed Metternich's fears that the dissatisfaction was about to erupt into a formidable movement for a united Italy. On 13 August 1847 he wrote to Lord Ponsonby, the Ambassador in Vienna: 'Excepting in the minds of some enthusiasts nothing has occurred that can be called a revolution, or that indicates a probability of an attempt to unite Italy under one head. The reforms contemplated would counteract any such designs by making the people contented'. He tried to persuade Metternich not to provoke the Italians by sending reinforcements into Lombardy.

The situation was transformed by the revolution in Vienna and the fall of Metternich in March 1848. The moderate Conservative Government which succeeded Metternich managed to restore some kind of order in Vienna; but it was quite unable to cope with the insurrection which spread throughout the Austrian provinces of Lombardy and Venetia and the whole of Northern Italy. King Charles Albert of Sardinia now joined the Liberal and patriotic movement, and put himself at the head of the demand for a united Italy. He declared war on the tottering Austrian Empire, and invaded Lombardy and Venetia. By May 1848 these provinces seemed lost to Austria, even if the new French Republic did not march to Sardinia's assistance; for the Austrian Army was penned up in the area around Mantua and Verona, between the Adige and the Mincio, which was known as the Quadrilateral. Meanwhile the Magyars of Hungary, under the leadership of the young Radical member of Parliament, Kossuth, declared their independence from Austria. The Czechs in Bohemia took tentative steps in the same direction. Successful revolutions broke out in most of the German kingdoms. Austrian influence in Germany collapsed, and the Diet of the German Confederation at Frankfort was replaced by a democratic and Liberal Parliament, which claimed to speak for a united Germany.

These events forced Palmerston to revise his policy, for he realized that the situation had gone too far to be dealt with by a grant of concessions. Although he had always advocated constitutional reforms in Germany, he did not welcome the German revolutions and the movement for a united German republic; and he was cool from the beginning towards the struggle for Hungarian independence. On 30 June 1848 he wrote to Ponsonby that with regard to 'the danger which in your opinion the Monarchical Power in Austria is exposed to by the machinations of the Ultra Democratic Party at Vienna. ... I have to say that Her Majesty's Government fully concur in the opinions which your Excellency expresses as to the importance of maintaining the Austrian Empire as united and as strong as possible, and your Excellency will on all occasions consider that object as one of the ends the attainment of which you should by all proper means in your power contribute to accomplish'. It would have surprised Palmerston's Radical admirers if they could have read this passage in the despatch of the statesman who was now regarded on all sides as the champion of Radicalism in Europe, and was thought by many to be the mastermind directing the revolution in every country except England and Ireland.

In Italy, circumstances led Palmerston to pursue a more Radical policy. As in 1831, his object was to prevent a clash between France and Austria which might lead to a European war, and a growth of French influence which would upset the balance of power in Europe. In April 1848 he first suggested to the new Austrian Government of Count Ficquelmonte that Austria would be well advised to cede Lombardy to Sardinia, and to grant some kind of home rule to Venetia; and he continued to press this suggestion throughout the year. Ficquelmonte proposed to introduce a series of Liberal reforms in Lombardy and Venetia, and to sever them officially from Austria, but to retain them in fact through the personal rule of the Emperor of Austria as Grand Duke of Lombardy and Venetia. Palmerston told Ficquelmonte that this proposal would be suitable for Venetia, but had come too late for Lombardy. He insisted that it was essential, in Austria's interests, to cede Lombardy to Sardinia; otherwise Charles Albert would conquer it by force, probably with French assistance; and in this case the French might keep Lombardy for themselves. He told Ficquelmonte that it would be better for Austria to have Lombardy as a province of Sardinia rather than as a province of France. He certainly thought that it would be better for England.

Ficquelmonte was not enthusiastic about this suggestion; but as the Austrian armies were being hard-pressed in the Quadrilateral, and Austrian authority was collapsing in Hungary and Germany, he sent Baron Hummelauer to London to discuss the possibility of Britain mediating between Austria and Sardinia. Palmerston told Hummelauer that he would only agree to mediate if Austria would agree to the cession of Lombardy to Sardinia and home rule for Venetia with the

Emperor of Austria as Grand Duke. Hummelauer, after first refusing, and repeating the offer of home rule for both provinces, agreed to Palmerston's terms. But Lord John Russell had always been a more enthusiastic supporter than Palmerston of Italian unity; and the Cabinet was not satisfied with the Austrian concession. Despite Palmerston's opposition, they insisted that he reject Hummelauer's offer; and Palmerston informed Hummelauer that Britain would only mediate if Austria agreed to cede not only Lombardy, but also those parts of Venetia which demanded union with Sardinia. Hummelauer had no authority to go as far as this, and had to refer to Vienna for further instructions. Palmerston meanwhile used all his influence at Turin to prevent Sardinia from asking France for assistance in the war against Austria. He also urged Lamartine, and later Cavaignac, not to interfere in the war in Italy.

But Palmerston had reckoned without another old man with as much energy as he possessed himself. Field Marshal Radetzky, who had fought in his first battle when Palmerston was eighteen months old, had been appointed to command the Austrian armies in Italy at the age of eighty-two. After suffering a number of defeats at the hands of Charles Albert in the first stage of the fighting, Radetzky began to win victories during the summer of 1848, and on 25 July decisively defeated the Sardinian Army at Custozza. After Custozza, Charles Albert was very happy to agree to the armistice which Radetzky granted him. Radetzky's victories had a great effect in raising Austrian morale, and his army in Italy was the training-ground for the men, from the Archduke Francis Joseph downwards, who were soon to restore the Austrian Empire for a brief period to its former greatness. It also made Ficquelmonte much more reluctant to surrender either Lombardy or Venetia.

Palmerston now proposed that the conflict between Austria and Sardinia should be settled by a joint mediation by Britain and France, hoping that by involving France in this diplomatic action he would prevent her military intervention in Northern Italy. But he rejected the suggestion that the affairs of Italy should be decided at an international Congress. Hav-

ing all his life been a man of international Conferences, he
now argued like a Radical against the Congress system.

> The Congress of Vienna [he wrote to Normanby in Paris on 10
> October], which is the Example to which those Persons look who
> incline to a renewed Congress now, was assembled under Circum-
> stances very different from those which at present exist. The Tide
> of War had swept over the whole Surface of Europe from the
> Rhine to Moscow, and from Moscow back to the Seine; all the
> smaller States of Europe had been conquered and reconquered,
> and were considered almost at the arbitrary Disposal of the Great
> Powers whose Armies had decided the Fate of the war. The States-
> men who sat in Congress therefore considered themselves at liberty
> to parcel out with great Freedom the Several Territories of Europe
> with as much Freedom as if they had been Commissioners under
> an Inclosure Act allotting the waste and Common Lands of a
> Parish. The smaller Sovereigns Princes and States had no Repre-
> sentatives in the deciding Congress and no voice in the Decisions
> by which their future Destiny was determined; but they were all
> obliged to yield to overruling Power, and to submit to Decisions
> which were the result as the case might be of Justice or of Expe-
> diency, of Generosity or of Partiality, of Regard to the Welfare of
> Nations, or of Concession to personal Solicitations. But England
> France Austria Prussia and Russia have not at present any similar
> Pretence to dispose of the Affairs of any of the smaller States of
> Europe either in Italy or elsewhere, and a Congress assembled for
> the Purpose of dealing with those Affairs, ought perhaps to consist,
> not only of the Representatives of the greater Powers, but also of
> Envoys from all the smaller States whose Interests were therein
> to be treated. But the Representatives of the greater Powers would
> of course assume and exercise a preponderating Influence in the
> Proceedings of such a Congress, and if they should happen to be
> agreed, those Proceedings would gradually assume the Character
> of a Dictation, not perhaps quite in Harmony with Public Feeling
> in England and in France;*

while, if the great powers did not agree, nothing at all would
be achieved at the Congress.

Eventually, Palmerston reluctantly agreed to submit the
issue to a Conference of the great powers in Brussels. His
position, as in Portugal in the previous year, was weakened by
the attitude of the Queen. Victoria and Albert had no sym-

---

*From Palmerston's draft in the Broadlands Papers. Some of
these passages were omitted in the final text of the despatch.

pathy with the Italian Liberal and nationalist movement, and were annoyed at Palmerston's proposal to dismember the Austrian Empire by transferring Lombardy to Sardinia. 'Why Charles Albert ought to get any additional territory the Queen cannot in the least see', wrote Victoria. She has been criticized for seeing the situation in these purely personal terms; but Palmerston's viewpoint was not much wider. He still did not take the question of Italian unity seriously, and went no further than to suggest, as a tentative possibility, that some form of customs union might be established between the Italian states. He wanted Lombardy to be given to Charles Albert so that there should be no danger of the French getting it. If Palmerston's attitude was governed by broader anxieties about the balance of power and the danger of war, Victoria, too, saw the problem in terms of a great principle. 'It will be a calamity for ages to come', she wrote to Lord John Russell on 14 October, 'if this principle is to become part of the international law, viz. that a people can at any time transfer their allegiance from the Sovereign of one State to that of another by universal suffrage'.

Neither Radetzky nor Victoria could induce Palmerston to alter his attitude. Under pressure from Lord John Russell he stuck to his proposal that Lombardy, if not Venetia, should be ceded to Sardinia. In view of the fact that he genuinely wished to preserve the Austrian Empire, and that he had no real interest in Italian unity, his determination must be attributed solely to obstinacy and to his failure to appreciate the realities of the military situation in Northern Italy. Egged on by pique and Radical applause, he became more and more anti-Austrian; and with his wonderful ability to identify himself completely with a cause that he had temporarily taken up, he became converted to a belief in Italian national freedom. 'My dear Ponsonby', he wrote on 31 August 1848, 'The real fact is that the Austrians have no business in Italy at all, and have no real right to be there. The right they claim is founded upon force of arms and the Treaty of Vienna. The Treaty of Vienna they themselves set at nought when they took possession of Cracow. . . . Providence meant mankind to be divided into separate nations. . . . We do not wish to threaten; but it is the part of a friend to tell the truth, and the truth is that Austria *cannot*, and *must not*, retain Lombardy; and she ought to think herself well enough off by keeping Venetia, if, indeed, that province is really advantageous to her. They will twit you at Vienna with Ireland, and say what should we reply if they were to ask us to give up Ireland; but the cases are wholly different'. In Ireland, the races were mixed, and all the people spoke English; 'and the land, and wealth, and intelligence of the country is for the connection' with England. 'North of the Alps', he wrote, we wish Austria 'all the prosperity and success in the world. Events have rendered it unavoidable that she should remain, in some shape or other, South of the Alps, and as far West as the Adige. Beyond that line, depend upon it, she cannot stay'.

This was written a month after Radetzky's victory at Custozza. Palmerston apparently thought that Ficquelmonte and the Austrian civil government would be weak enough to let slip the benefits of Radetzky's military achievements. On 26 September Palmerston wrote to Ponsonby that with regard to 'the objection of the Austrian Army to the cession of Lombardy, I have to observe that if the policy of the Austrian Government is to be determined according to the dictation of the Army, the Austrians had better at once follow the example of the Roman Empire in the period of decay and degeneration, and make General Radetzky Emperor'. Meanwhile Austria played for time in connexion with Italy as effectively as Palmerston had done a year before about Switzerland. They delayed appointing their delegates to the Brussels Conference, although Palmerston repeatedly asked them to do so.

The armistice had left Radetzky in occupation of Milan and nearly all the cities of Lombardy and Venetia except Venice. The Italians in the occupied towns resisted the Austrians by hostile gestures, insults, and attacks on the soldiers; and Radetzky, and his military Governor, General Haynau, retaliated in the usual way by seizing hostages, imposing collective fines, and billeting troops on the householders in streets where the offences had occurred. In some cases Haynau ordered men, and also women, to be flogged. The Italian press denounced the Austrian atrocities, and their campaign was taken up in the British press. Palmerston became very indignant about the atrocities. When he drew the Queen's attention to them, she said that they had probably been grossly exaggerated.

Radetzky and the Austrian Government began to toy with the idea of pursuing in Italy the same policy which they had adopted with such success in Poland, and posing as the champions of the peasants and the lower classes against the native nobility. On 11 November Radetzky issued a proclamation in which he announced that he would not punish the ignorant people who had been misled into revolting against Austria, but only those ringleaders who had been responsible for inciting these innocent dupes. These leaders would be required to pay large fines. He published a list, which included many members of the aristocratic and wealthy classes, giving the names of those selected and the amounts which they had each to pay. These sums were large enough to amount to a confiscation of a substantial part of their property. Palmerston received advance notice of the terms of the proclamation, and wrote to Ponsonby on 14 November telling him to urge the Austrian Government not 'to imitate the most universally condemned excesses of the most desperate and unprincipled Revolutionists'. After he had received the text of Radetzy's proclamation, he wrote to Ponsonby again on 20 November.

'You will represent to the Austrian Government that if Marshal Radetzky had been bound and restrained by no engagements and had been perfectly free to resort to such manoeuvres as those announced in his proclamation, yet the moral feeling of mankind, and every sentiment of generosity and justice, would have revolted against a proceeding conceived in the spirit of the most odious oppression, and enunciated by doctrines which belong only to the disciples of Communism, and which are subversive of the very foundations of social order, and it would have been impossible even in that case to suppose that the Austrian Government, when it became acquainted with this proclamation, would have delayed for a single hour to send to Marshal Radetzky the most peremptory orders to cancel an announcement so utterly at variance with the principles upon which the acts of the Gov-

ernment of a great European country ought to be founded.
But the Austrian Government cannot have forgotten, though
Marshal Radetzky appears to have done so, the solemn and
public engagements, into which Radetzky had entered in the
armistice with the Sardinian commander. 'I should find that
I was wanting in due respect for the Imperial Government if
I was to instruct your Excellency to enter into any argument
to prove that the proclamation of Marshal Radetzky is a
'flagrant an palpable violation' of the armistice. Ponsonby
was therefore to read this despatch to the Austrian Chancellor, and 'earnestly to conjure him by his regard for the high
character of his country, and for the honour of the Imperial
Crown, to lose no time in taking the necessary steps to prevent Marshal Radetzky from carrying his iniquitous intentions
into execution.'

By the time that Ponsonby received this despatch, a decisive
change had taken place in Austria. On 16 June, Windischgrätz
had bombarded Prague and crushed the Czech resistance
without much difficulty. At the end of October he marched
against Vienna. A few weeks earlier, the extremists had made
another revolution in Vienna. The Emperor and his Court,
with the foreign Ambassadors, had retired to Olmütz in Bohemia, leaving Vienna in the control of a revolutionary
council under the Radical journalist and politician, Robert
Blum, with the Polish General Bem – a hero of the Polish
revolution of 1830 – in command of the revolutionary defence
force. Windischgrätz bombarded Vienna and captured it by
storm after four days' street fighting, and Robert Blum and
twenty-three other revolutionary leaders were shot after a
summary trial by court-martial. One of them was Robert
Becher, another Radical journalist. The day before Becher's
execution, one of his friends called at the British embassy and
asked Ponsonby to intervene to save Becher, because Becher,
having been born in London, was a British subject. Ponsonby
refused. Palmerston, who received Ponsonby's report of the
incident after Becher had been shot, told Ponsonby that he
had acted correctly. Palmerston wrote that he had received
documents which indicated that Dr. Becher had been born in
Manchester, not in London as Ponsonby had been told; so it

was possible that the whole story was an invention, and that Becher had not been born in Britain at all. Even if he had, his parents had not been British, and he had never made use of his British nationality, and had never before contacted the British embassy in Vienna. In any case, wrote Palmerston, the British Government would not intervene to save a British subject who had been justly punished under Austrian law for taking part in a revolution in Vienna.

On 2 December the Emperor abdicated, and was succeeded by his nephew, Francis Joseph, who thus began a reign which was to last till 1916. Prince Schwarzenberg, coming straight from Radetzky's headquarters in Italy, became Chancellor and Foreign Minister. Schwarzenberg's first action was to reply to Palmerston's despatch about Radetzky's proclamation of 11 November. It was in the form of a private letter to the Austrian Under-Secretary for Foreign Affairs, who was told to show it to Ponsonby. After pointing out that all Palmerston's forecasts about events in Italy had been proved wrong, Schwarzenberg proceeded: 'In truth, my dear Baron, Lord Palmerston is a little too much inclined to consider himself the arbiter of the destinies of Europe. For our part, we are not in the least disposed to allow him to play, in our own affairs, the role of Providence. We never pressed on him our advice concerning the affairs of Ireland. . . . I must frankly confess that we are tired of his eternal insinuations, of his tone now protective and pedantic, now insulting, but always unbecoming, and we have decided that we shall no longer tolerate it. Lord Palmerston remarked one day to Baron Koller that if we wanted war, we should have it; and I told him that if he wants it he shall have it. I do not know whether Lord Palmerston applies to himself the phrase of Louis XIV, and thinks that *l'Angleterre c'est lui*'. Schwarzenberg went on to say that though an Austrian Archduke would be sent to every other Court to announce Francis Joseph's accession to the foreign sovereigns, they would not be sending one to England, as Schwarzenberg was not prepared to expose a Prince to contact 'with the devoted protector of the Emperor's rebellious subjects, in short with such a man as Lord Palmerston'.

Ponsonby forwarded a copy of the letter to Palmerston.

Palmerston declared that it resembled 'the outpourings of an enraged woman of the town when arrested by a Policeman in the act of picking a Pocket'. His chief concern was to stop people hearing about the letter. In 1860, Prince Albert's equerry, General Grey, told Albert that Palmerston had ordered that every copy of the letter should be removed from the embassy files, and destroyed. Palmerston was no doubt anxious not to be subjected to another public rebuff like that which he had received from Narváez; he was just the man to adopt the attitude that a defeat does not matter very much if no one knows about it. He must also have been particularly eager to prevent the Queen from seeing the letter, for everything in it was calculated to enrage her against her Foreign Secretary who believed that 'he was England'. But General Grey and the Prince Consort may have made too much of this. The document was a private letter from Schwarzenberg to his Under-Secretary. Private letters were not normally placed on the Foreign Office or embassy files. If Schwarzenberg had wished to put his feelings in a more permanent form, he could have written it in a despatch to his Ambassador in London, and given Palmerston a copy; and he could have published it, like Palmerston published his despatch to Ponsonby about Radetzky's proclamation of 11 November. As it was, Schwarzenberg saw to it that Metternich and his friends in England received copies of the letter, and eventually a copy was sent to Prince Albert; but he did not wish to engage in a public propaganda duel with Palmerston. He knew that when members of absolutist governments engage in such contests with champions of Radicalism, they are apt to get the worst of it. His object in writing the letter was, on the contrary, to dissuade Palmerston from carrying on a public slanging match with the Austrian Government; and in this he very largely succeeded.

In November 1848 a revolution broke out in Rome against the Papal Government. Pius IX was already beginning to regret that he had embarked on a course of progressive reforms, and the revolution completed his conversion to the side of reaction, and his return to the old policy of his predecessors. A republic was proclaimed in Rome, which soon passed under the control of Mazzini and Garibaldi. Pius fled to Gaeta, in the Kingdom of Naples, and appealed to all the Catholic powers of Europe – except one – to restore him to his temporal authority. The only Catholic sovereign who was not invited to assist was Charles Albert of Sardinia. Austria immediately prepared to answer the Pope's call. Narváez declared that Spain would help. All the Italian rulers who had been restored to their thrones followed suit. The great question was how France would react. The French Government, as the government of a Catholic state, had received the Pope's call for help; but all precedents suggested that the French Republic would be more likely to intervene in favour of the Roman Republic rather than help Austria to crush it. The Government of Louis Napoleon decided to join the side of Catholic reaction. Louis Napoleon carried out the manoeuvre which Guizot had hoped to carry out in Switzerland in 1847. By agreement with Austria, he sent the French fleet to Civita Vecchia on the pretence of watching the situation and restraining Austria. Then suddenly, while the Austrian troops halted more than a hundred miles from Rome, the French landed troops at Civita Vecchia and attacked the Roman Republic in the back, despite the violent protests of the Socialists and Radicals in France who had voted Louis Napoleon into power.

Palmerston was not happy about the events in Rome. He had no sympathy with Mazzini and Garibaldi, and did not wish to see Papal rule replaced by a revolutionary republic; but the idea of a joint military intervention in Italy by France and Austria, in order to settle Italian problems without consulting Britain, was not at all to his liking. On 9 March 1849 he wrote to Normanby that although Britain was not as interested in the welfare of the Pope as a Catholic state like France, Queen Victoria had none the less many Catholic subjects. 'The British Government must therefore be desirous, with a view to British interests, that the Pope should be placed in such a temporal position as to be able to act with entire independence in the exercise of his spiritual functions'. But Britain did not like the idea of armed intervention. 'It seems to Her Majesty's Government that a strong and unanimous manifestation of the opinion of those Powers in support of order on the one hand, and of constitutional rights on the other, would bring to reason the minority who now exercise paramount authority at Rome; and would give courage and confidence to the majority who have been hitherto intimidated and overborne; and if Great Britain had been invited to be a party to these negotiations', we would have advised this. If intervention was unavoidable, Britain would have liked Sardinia to be invited to join in; and if it should become necessary to resort to armed force, it would be much better to send Charles Albert's Piedmontese troops rather than those of Austria or any other non-Italian state. Palmerston stated that Britain thought 'that it would be desirable that every endeavour should be made to bring about a settlement between the Pope and his subjects by negotiation and moral influence before resorting to the employment of force', and that the Pope should only be reinstated on condition that he promised to maintain the Constitution which he had granted the year before.

As Radetzky's troops marched on Rome, with Haynau's military police following in his rear, hanging men and flogging women, public opinion in Piedmont demanded that Charles Albert should go to the help of the Roman Republic. Palmerston warned him that it would be a fatal error to re-open the war against Austria; but in March 1849 he heard from Abercromby in Turin that Charles Albert had announced in Parliament that he would terminate the armistice and renew the war. Palmerston sent immediate instructions to Abercromby to do all he could to prevent this disastrous step; and when he heard that Charles Albert had given notice to Austria that he had ended the armistice, he still urged the Sardinian Government to refrain from actually starting hostilities. His arguments were in vain, and all he could do was to tell the Austrian Government that Sardinia would not have denounced the armistice if Austria had been less dilatory in appointing its delegates to the Conference in Brussels.

When Charles Albert resumed the war, the Austrians announced that they would not send delegates to Brussels, and the Conference was never held. Radetzky shattered the Sardinian Army at Novara, and Charles Albert abdicated and fled to Portugal. His son, Victor Emmanuel, succeeded to the

throne; and his first act as King was to go to Radetzky's headquarters to sue for an armistice. Radetzky treated him with
great courtesy, but his terms were hard. Palmerston tried to
persuade the Austrian Government to modify the harshness
of the terms; but his pleas, made from a position of weakness,
were not likely to have much weight with Schwarzenberg.
Palmerston did not conceal his annoyance at the course
which events had taken. When the news of Novara reached
London, Victoria congratulated the Austrian Ambassador,
Colloredo, at a reception at Buckingham Palace, and all the
other guests did the same, except for Palmerston. His action
attracted much attention, though he chatted pleasantly to
Colloredo about other things. The Conservative Clerk of the
Privy Council, Charles Greville, was shocked. 'I do not think
anything Palmerston had done has excited so great a sensation, and exposed him to so much animadversion, as his behaviour to Colloredo at the Drawing-room. . . . The impolicy
of this unmistakable display of *animus* is the more striking,
because we are now (through Ponsonby) entreating the Austrian Government to show moderation, and not to exact large
contributions' from Sardinia. Lord John Russell pointed out
to Palmerston the inadvisability of antagonizing the Austrian
Government if they hoped to persuade them to soften their
peace terms; and he altered the wording of Palmerston's despatches to Vienna so as to make them more conciliatory.

In the end, the Austrians were satisfied with a lower indemnity from Sardinia than they had at first demanded. This
was probably because they hoped to win the goodwill of the
new King, Victor Emmanuel; and having originally imposed
terms which were so harsh, they could modify them without
losing very much. But Palmerston got the credit for having
gained this concession for Sardinia among Radicals in Britain
and all over Europe, and in Turin itself.

The Roman Republic held out for another three months.
Garibaldi defeated the French, who were glad to grant him
an armistice; but later they violated the armistice without
notice and captured Rome. Mazzini fled to Switzerland, and
Garibaldi, after a hazardous retreat through the forests with
his dying wife, reached the coast and took ship for America.

Many of the Republican leaders only escaped from the vengeance of the French because Freeborn, the British Consul in
Rome, issued British passports to them. This did not please
Palmerston, who showed less sympathy with the revolutionary Italian refugees than he had shown for the French residents in Rome in the days of the Republic. In April he had
ordered Freeborn to take the French citizens under his protection during the siege, despite the fact that Freeborn
thought that this would seriously discredit the British Government in the eyes of the people of Rome; but now, in July, he
objected that Freeborn, by issuing the passports, had 'without any Necessity (as it would appear) encouraged and aided
Five Hundred Foreigners to come to England Who will probably be destitute of any Means of subsistence when they arrive
here'. He was, however, satisfied when Freeborn assured him
that he had granted the passports only to 'men of respectable
families' whose lives would otherwise have been in danger,
and that only five hundred passports had been granted, whereas the United States, Swiss, Bavarian and Sardinian Consuls
had given passports to three thousand of the Roman rebels.

The revolution was also defeated in the Kingdom of Naples,
and again Palmerston suffered a diplomatic set-back which
increased his popularity with the Radicals. King Ferdinand,
having appeased the revolutionaries in Naples by granting a
Constitution in January 1848, proceeded to try to suppress the
resistance of his Sicilian subjects, who managed for more than
a year to hold the island against him. Palmerston tried to mediate. At first he hoped to persuade the Sicilians to be satisfied
with the grant of constitutional government; but when he
realized that they would never agree to be ruled by Ferdinand,
he proposed that Sicily should be granted semi-independence
under Ferdinand's son, who would nominally rule as Viceroy for his father. Neither side was prepared to accept this
suggestion.

In November 1848, the Sicilian rebels approached a British
arms manufacturer, and asked him to sell them arms. The
manufacturer had recently supplied some arms to the War
Office, but owing to a mistake he had delivered a larger quantity than the War Office had ordered. When he received the

urgent Sicilian order for arms, he approached the War Office and asked them whether they would release from Woolwich Arsenal the surplus quantity which they did not require so that he could send them to Sicily. The War Office, realizing that international political questions might be involved, consulted the Foreign Office. Palmerston, without referring the matter to the Prime Minister or the Cabinet, directed that the arms should be sent back to the supplier, who sent them to Sicily. A few weeks later, the arms manufacturer happened to go hunting with a party which included Delane, the editor of *The Times*. He chatted to Delane at the meet, and casually mentioned that Lord Palmerston had arranged for him to send arms to the Sicilians. Delane made further inquiries, and in January 1848 published the story in *The Times*.

This was the evidence for which the European Conservatives had been waiting; here was the proof that Palmerston was instigating the revolutions which were shaking Europe. Palmerston was unrepentant, but Victoria was very angry, and Lord John Russell was embarrassed. The Cabinet decided that Palmerston must explain the circumstances to the House of Commons, and say that an error of judgment had been made. When his colleagues suggested that Britain should apologize to the King of Naples, Palmerston objected on the grounds that the Neapolitan Government had not asked for an apology; but as the Cabinet insisted that an apology should be sent, he gave way, and drafted a suitable despatch. In the summer of 1849 Ferdinand bombarded Palermo – thus earning the nickname of 'King Bomba' – and suppressed the revolution in Sicily. He also rescinded the Constitution which he had granted to his subjects in Naples. His firing squads became busy, and his underground prisons were rapidly filled with Liberals and Democrats.

As soon as the revolution had been suppressed in Prague and Vienna, the Austrians turned on Hungary. The nationalist movement in Hungary aroused the enthusiasm of the European Radicals; but the Hungarian Liberals, having gained their independence from Austria, made it clear that they would not permit the nine million Germans, Slavs and Rumanians in Hungary to free themselves from the rule of

five million Magyars. This enabled the Croat Count Jellacic
– a General in the Austrian Army who was posing as a Croat
nationalist – to raise a large force of Slavs to suppress the
Hungarian revolutionaries. For six months Kossuth and the
Hungarians, helped by large numbers of Polish refugees under
General Bem, held back and defeated the Austrian Army
and Jellacic's men, while the European Liberals applauded
the greatest struggle against despotism which had been seen
since the Polish revolt of 1830–1. But Palmerston did not think
that it would be in Britain's interest if the Austrian Empire
were to fall, and he refused to give any help or encouragement to the Hungarians. When Kossuth's envoy, Szalai, came
to England, Palmerston refused to receive him, and stated
that it would be improper for him to have any communication
with rebels against a friendly sovereign. He told Szalai that if
he wished to communicate with him, he should do so through
the Austrian Ambassador in London. Palmerston did agree
to have a private meeting with Pulzsky, who had been sent
to England by Kossuth to make propaganda for the Hungarian cause; but he gave Pulzsky no comfort, and told him
that the maintenance of the Austrian Empire was essential to
Britain, as Austria was the natural ally of Britain in the Balkans and the Middle East.

The Austrians, after being repeatedly defeated in Hungary
by Bem, asked the Tsar for assistance, and on 30 April 1849
Russian forces invaded Transylvania. No action of the Tsarist
régime caused so much anger in Liberal circles, and it played
an important part in arousing the passionate hatred of Russia
in Britain which, five years later, was the chief cause of the
Crimean War. After a desperate resistance, the Hungarian
patriots and their Polish comrades were defeated and retreated
across the Turkish frontier, where they were interned and
granted asylum, leaving the Austrian and Russian forces in
Hungary free to carry out hangings and floggings on a large
scale.

Palmerston did not make any formal protest against the
Russian invasion of Hungary. When Buchanan, the chargé
d'affaires in St. Petersburg, heard that the Russian troops had
entered Hungary, he merely commented to Nesselrode that
it was unfortunate that the Austrian Government had been

unable to suppress the Hungarian revolt without invoking Russian aid. Nesselrode coolly remarked that it was indeed regrettable. When Palmerston received Buchanan's report, he approved of his conduct. On 17 May, he wrote to Buchanan: 'Much as Her Majesty's Government regret this interference of Russia, the causes which have led to it and the Effects which it may produce, they nevertheless have not considered the occasion to be one which at present calls for any formal expression of the opinions of Great Britain on the matter'. It was only in August, when the fighting was nearly over and the punishment of the rebels was in full swing, that Palmerston, in response to British public opinion, began protesting against Haynau's cruelties in Hungary.

The revolutionary movement was also defeated in Germany. Here Palmerston had been involved in a conflict with the revolutionary forces over Schleswig-Holstein. Since 1721 the King of Denmark had been the ruler of Schleswig-Holstein as hereditary Grand Duke; but in Holstein, unlike Denmark, the Salic Law applied. King Christian VIII of Denmark, realizing that his son Frederick was unlikely to have children, and that there would be difficulties in Schleswig-Holstein about the succession passing through the female line, took steps in 1845 to simplify the position by officially incorporating Schleswig-Holstein into Denmark. This sparked off the resistance of the German-speaking population of Schleswig-Holstein. The Duke of Augustenburg, who was a Prince of the Danish royal house, but also a German-speaking Liberal, claimed the Dukedom of Schleswig-Holstein under the Salic Law; but in Denmark the constitutional Liberal movement had also taken on a nationalist form. It demanded 'Denmark to the Eider', and insisted that Schleswig, if not Holstein, should be incorporated into a constitutional Denmark, and not ruled arbitrarily by the King as Grand Duke. The situation was building up when the revolution of 1848 broke out in Germany; and the Frankfort Parliament took up the cause of Schleswig-Holstein, and demanded that it be included in a democratic German republic. The revolution in Berlin had taken Prussia into the Liberal and anti-absolutist camp. When Danish troops entered Schleswig-Holstein, the Prussian Government, to the disgust of King Frederick William but with the support of all Liberal Germany, declared war on Denmark and invaded Schleswig-Holstein. Russia supported Denmark, and threatened war on Prussia in defence of the rights of Princes.

Palmerston offered to mediate. He had no more sympathy with revolutionary nationalism in Schleswig-Holstein than in Lombardy, and his chief object in both cases was to prevent a European war; but in other respects the two situations were different. He did not think that it would decrease the chances of war, or further British interests, if Schleswig-Holstein were ceded to Prussia or Germany; and his policy in the dispute was to preserve the status quo. He therefore lined up with Russia and the absolutist powers against Liberal and Radical opinion. This did not, as might have been expected, win him the support of Queen Victoria and Prince Albert. Their pro-German sympathies made them support the Prussians over Schleswig-Holstein, even though this meant being on the Liberal and revolutionary side. Count Otto von Bismarck, a Right-wing member of the Prussian Parliament, was more far-seeing, and opposed the German nationalist movement as long as it was under Liberal leadership.

Palmerston's arguments, combined with Russian threats and the strength of the Danish Navy, which was capable of destroying Prussia's Baltic trade, induced the Prussian Government to agree to an armistice with Denmark. Palmerston then persuaded both sides to submit the dispute to an international Conference in London in October 1848. He presided at the Conference, and as usual mastered every detail of the problem with which he had to deal – the Salic Law and the claims of each branch of the Danish royal family, the Letters Patent of 1721, the Fundamental Law of Denmark, and the conflicting demands of the Danish monarchy, the Germans in Schleswig, and the Danes in the Eider region. Palmerston put forward a compromise proposal to unite Schleswig with Denmark, while leaving Holstein under the personal sovereignty of the King of Denmark but a member of the German Confederation. This novel solution, which involved a dissolution of the unity of Schleswig and Holstein which had existed since 1460, seemed at one time to be acceptable, in some form or other, to both sides; but they were quite unable to agree about the details of the plan, and eventually the Danes rejected it completely.

In March 1849 the Danish Government sent an ultimatum to Prussia, which they asked Palmerston, as the chairman of the Conference, to transmit. Palmerston, who as usual was overworked, forgot to deliver the ultimatum, and only remembered two days later to give it to Bunsen. For the second time in his career as Foreign Secretary, he was denounced in Parliament for forgetting to pass on an urgent document during a grave international crisis; but though he admitted the oversight, he insisted that the delay had made no difference whatever, as Bunsen had no authority to accept the ultimatum. The Danes then denounced the armistice and the war began again.

Austria intervened in support of Danish absolutism, and threatened to attack Prussia in the rear; but Palmerston and the Russians again persuaded the belligerents to stop before any decisive result was achieved. The London Conference then accepted Palmerston's proposal that Schleswig should be governed temporarily by three Governors – one Danish, one German, and one British. In July 1850 Denmark and Prussia made peace, and the parties in Schleswig-Holstein were eventually forced to accept the peace terms. Nothing was formally said about incorporating Schleswig-Holstein into Denmark; but it was to continue, as before, united with Denmark through the personal link of the King as Grand Duke. The London Conference settled the question of the succession. The Duke of Augustenburg and the other claimants were bought off, and Prince Christian of Glücksburg was declared to be the heir to all the territories that were ruled by the King of Denmark.

Schleswig-Holstein was Palmerston's only real success out of all the problems which he handled in connexion with the revolutions of 1848. But the Queen and Prince Albert were not pleased with him. They were opposed to his German policy, and to his failure to support Prussia against the attempts of Austria to re-establish its hegemony over the German Confederation. On 18 November 1850 Victoria wrote to Palmerston complaining that while he had always encouraged Liberal demands for a constitution 'in the Queen's opinion, unwisely, in such countries which from their state of civilization were not fit for constitutional government, like Greece, Portugal, Spain, Sicily, and Naples, etc. etc.' he had not been prepared to resist Austria's threat to constitutional liberty in North Germany. Palmerston replied that he did not believe that Austria would try to 're-establish despotic government in a nation so enlightened and so attached to free institutions as the German people now is. The danger for Germany seems to be rather in the opposite direction, arising from the rash and weak precipitation with which in 1848 and 49 those governments, which before had refused everything, resolved in a moment of alarm to grant everything, and, passing from one extreme to the other, threw universal suffrage among people who had been some wholly and others very much unaccustomed to the working of representative government. The French have found universal suffrage incompatible with good order even in a republic; what must it be for a monarchy?'

Palmerston's attitude caused great disappointment to the German Liberals. Baron Christian von Bunsen, the great Liberal scholar who had been appointed as the Prussian Minister to London, soon realized that the hero of the European Radicals would give no assistance to the German Liberals. On one occasion Palmerston took him down to Osborne to see the Queen, and travelled back to London with him. The sea crossing was very rough, but Palmerston took over the steering of the ferry boat, so that the helmsman could assist with the oars, explaining to the astonished Bunsen that a man learns boating at Cambridge, if nothing else. On reaching Southampton, they found that they had missed the train, and would have to wait many hours for the next one; and as Palmerston had urgent business at the Foreign Office, he asked the station-master to put on a special train. The station-master said that this would be against the regulations, that it might endanger the safety of passengers in other trains on the line, and that he was not authorized to provide a special train on his own responsibility. 'Do it on my responsibility, then', said Palmerston. He got his special train and gave Bunsen a place in it; but he did nothing to help German Liberalism.

Chapter Twenty-six

Don Pacifico

Nothing that Palmerston did so impressed the British public as his handling of the case of Don Pacifico in 1850. In diplomatic circles, Palmerston was respected for his skill in managing a conference and in mastering the complex details of intricate international problems. The Continental Radicals admired him as a champion of the cause of freedom against absolutism. But the ordinary Englishman loved Palmerston because he sent gunboats to protect the rights of any British subject who was injured or insulted in any part of the world. The English tourist and the Scottish engineer could live among Mexican bandits or Asiatic tribesmen, and know that while the natives of the district were being robbed and tortured, he would be safe; for no one would dare to touch a hair of his head as long as Palmerston and the British Navy were behind him.

Not everyone in Britain approved of Palmerston's methods of enforcing British rights by gunboat diplomacy. Many members of the cosmopolitan aristocracy – the class to which Palmerston himself belonged – deplored his habit of violating the rights of other nations. Queen Victoria thought it absurd of Palmerston to pick a quarrel with a foreign government because some English rascal had been flogged somewhere abroad; and Wellington condemned his bullying tactics in international affairs. The strong moral sense of Victorian Britain, and especially the Nonconformist conscience, was often thrown into the scales against Palmerston. Many of the most virtuous of the British middle class managed to reconcile their strict moral code with ardent approval of Palmerstonian foreign policy; but others could not. The new traditions springing up in the public schools about not fighting smaller boys, and the popularity of romantic historical novels in which the hero refuses to engage even the most villainous of caitiffs if he has him at a disadvantage, made people feel that there was something unsporting in Palmerston's policy of bullying smaller states. Although old men who had been at Harrow in 1797 told stories of how young Harry Temple had always fought bullies who were twice his size, many Englishmen noticed that, as Foreign Secretary, Viscount Palmerston nearly always chose to take on nations less than half his size.

Bulwer, in his biography of Palmerston, described how Palmerston reacted to the argument that it was beneath the dignity of Britain to use its overwhelming power to enforce its demands on a weaker nation. 'Lord Palmerston had none of these scruples', wrote Bulwer. 'Right, in his eyes, was right; and if he insisted upon it when a formidable enemy might be provoked, he treated with becoming scorn the argument that we should deal more gently with an inferior delinquent. "What?" he used to say, "we are to tax our people for the purpose of giving them a strong government, and then we are not to maintain the rights of our people because their government is strong. The weaker a government is, the more inexcusable becomes its insolence or injustice" '.

From the nature of things, the British subjects who benefited most from Palmerston's vigorous protection were merchants and business men. Most of the cases which Palmerston took up with foreign governments were those in which British traders resident abroad had had their property seized, had been forced to contribute to a forced loan by some authority during a civil war in the place where they were living, or whose commercial privileges, as guaranteed by treaty, had been interfered with. But Palmerston was just as zealous in protecting the rights of other British subjects when the occasion arose. He pestered and threatened foreign governments on behalf of Wellington and Beresford if some damage had been done to their great estates in Spain and Portugal, on behalf of Maltese labourers in Constantinople, and of Ionian peasants in Greece. He always impressed on British Ambassadors and Consuls the duty of protecting every British subject who was in difficulties.

In 1840, an English traveller named Miller was arrested in Ostend and taken to the police station on a charge of assaulting a Belgian in the town. He appealed for help to Mr. Fauche, the British Consul in Ostend. Fauche contacted the authorities there, who told him about the offence with which Miller had been charged, whereupon Fauche went home and did nothing more except give Miller the name of a Belgian lawyer whom he could employ if he wished. The British Vice-Consul in Bruges was not satisfied with what had been done, and reported the case to the embassy in Brussels. Palmerston heard about it at the most critical moment of the Middle Eastern crisis, when war with France seemed imminent at the beginning of October 1840; but he found time to give the case his personal attention. He told Sir Henry Seymour, the Ambassador, to congratulate the Vice-Consul in Bruges, but to reprimand the Consul in Ostend for his failure to help a British subject in distress. Fauche wrote to Palmerston and tried to exonerate himself by saying that he did not see what more he could have done, as it would have been impossible for him to influence the Belgian courts who were dealing with the case.

This did not placate Palmerston. He instructed Seymour to tell Fauche 'that I never supposed or expected that he was to have influenced the decision of the Tribunal by which Mr. Miller was to be tried, which on the contrary it would have been very improper for Mr. Fauche to have attempted to do; but that it was his duty, as British Consul, when he found a British Traveller who was friendless and a stranger in the place involved suddenly in distressing difficulties to have afforded that Traveller assistance in finding the proper means for making his defence, and it seems to me that Mr. Fauche even by his own account neglected his duty in this instance'. He added, in another despatch to Seymour three weeks later, that 'it is the duty of a Consular officer to go immediately to any British Subject who from having been arrested or for any other difficulty in which he may find himself with the local Authorities, may request his aid; and such Consular Officer is not performing his duty when he rests satisfied with the statements made to him by Authorities who have arrested a

British Subject as to the grounds on which they have done so; and who neglects to go and hear from the accused himself what he may have to say on his own behalf. A British Subject may be unjustly accused by the Officers of the Police. And a British Consular officer would very imperfectly perform his duty by sending him the name of a lawyer to be employed, instead of enquiring into the case and giving such assistance as might appear expedient and proper'.

Palmerston's insistence on the rights of British subjects sometimes aroused great resentment in foreign countries. There were the difficulties which arose when he insisted that British merchants should be permitted to perform their contracts to export food from countries where there was a famine or a food shortage. There were far more frequent conflicts about quarantine regulations. Soon after Palmerston first became Foreign Secretary, a great cholera epidemic spread from Turkestan through European Russia into Poland, where it played havoc in the ranks of both armies during the fighting in 1831, and then reached Western Europe and Britain. It caused very high mortality and great panic everywhere, killing the Russian Commander-in-Chief in Poland, the French Prime Minister Casimir Périer, and more than 50,000 people in England and Wales alone. The worst areas in Britain were Sunderland and the ports of north-east England. All ships coming from Britain were then subjected to a period of quarantine in Naples and Spain and other Mediterranean countries. Palmerston protested against the quarantine regulations, which he said interfered with British rights of free trade that were guaranteed by treaty. As always, he referred to British expert opinion, and accepted its decision as final. He accepted the necessity of submitting to a reasonable period of quarantine; but if countries imposed a longer period than that which Britain herself imposed, and which British medical authorities considered necessary, Palmerston insisted that the foreign government was imposing the additional restriction in order to discriminate against British trade; and he would not accept the evidence of foreign doctors that the British quarantine regulations were not stringent enough. The problem became less serious after the cholera epidemic had passed; but it did not disappear, and revived every time that there was a new outbreak of cholera or other serious disease.

Palmerston also became involved in a controversy with the Belgian Government about British passports. At this time, a British passport was a large sheet of parchment, signed by the Foreign Secretary, stating that the holder was a British subject, giving his name, and asking all concerned to give him assistance and protection. In 1835 the Belgian Government became alarmed at the number of foreign revolutionaries who were seeking refuge in Belgium with passports in false names, and they devised a plan by which the operations of the revolutionaries would be made more difficult. Photography was still in too primitive a stage for it to be possible to have photographs on the passports; but the Belgians asked all foreign governments to give particulars, on their passports, of the age, the height, and the colour of the eyes and hair, of the passport-holder. All other governments agreed to the Belgian request; but Palmerston refused. He said that no Englishman could be subjected to the humiliation of having to give such personal details to government officials.

The Belgians had some reason for anxiety about the British practice with regard to passports, as was shown when a German revolutionary obtained a British passport with a false name from the British embassy in Brussels. Palmerston made inquiries as to how this had come about. He was told that the applicant had called at the embassy and had asked for a passport, and as he was 'evidently an Englishman and apparently a gentleman', he had been granted it without further inquiries. Palmerston told British embassies and consulates that they must be more careful about issuing passports in future; but he refused to issue particulars, on passports, of the passport-holder's physical appearance and gave strict instructions to the embassies and consulates that they were not to do so. 'The whole System of Passports', he wrote to Brussels on 10 November 1835, 'is so repugnant to English usages that the Secretary of State could not propose to British Subjects to submit additionally to the degrading and offensive Practice' of giving particulars as to their personal appearance. A number of British travellers, including Lord Londonderry, were turned back at the Belgian frontier because they had not got the kind of passport which the Belgians required; and Palmerston protested to the Belgians about this. Eventually the Belgians gave way after Palmerston had told them that if they wished to injure their tourist trade by excluding all British subjects from Belgium they were perfectly entitled to do so, but that no British passport would contain any particulars except the holder's name.

Palmerston would not accept the argument that Britain had no right to intervene if British subjects who resided in a foreign country were punished according to the law of that country. 'As to the laws of Venezuela', he wrote to the British Minister at Caracas on 3 September 1859, 'the people of Venezuela must of course submit to them but the British Government have shewn that England will not permit gross injustice to be done or gross oppression to be inflicted upon British subjects under the Pretence of Venezuelan law'. But this is an oversimplification of Palmerston's attitude. Palmerston respected international law, and always believed that Britons abroad should obey the laws of the foreign states wherever they happened to be. He insisted, however, that international law and treaty rights were above the law of the foreign state, and he would therefore not permit a foreign government to enforce a law which violated these treaty rights.

He also took the line that, where British subjects were concerned, the British Government was the supreme court of appeal from the courts of foreign states. When a British subject abroad complained that he had suffered some legal wrong, Palmerston usually told him to seek redress in the courts of the foreign country; but if he lost his case in the courts, Palmerston would ask the British Consul for a report about the trial. If the Consul reported that the trial had been fair, Palmerston would do nothing more; but if the Consul said that the court had been prejudiced against the Briton, Palmerston would take up the case with the foreign government, even if no question of international law or treaty rights were involved. He would insist that justice be done, as required by the foreign state's own law, to the British subject; and if necessary he would send the Navy to see that it was. It was different if the case occurred in France. Then Palmerston would adopt the attitude that as the French courts were independent of the government, and of a high standard of integrity and judicial reputation, he would hear no suggestion from anyone that they had been unfair to the British subject.

In 1838, difficulties arose with Turkey about a wave of crime in Constantinople, which the Turkish Government blamed on the immigrants from Malta and the Ionian Isles, who were British subjects. The Turks asked Britain to relinquish their treaty rights which entitled an official representative of the British Government to be present at the trial of any British subject in Turkey, and complained that these British representatives were impeding the administration of justice. Ponsonby wrote to Palmerston and told him that he was anxious to cooperate with the Turkish authorities in preventing crime, but hesitated to take any step which might lead Palmerston to think that he was not zealous in defending the rights of British subjects. Palmerston replied on 8 June. 'I feel equally with Your Excellency the importance of endeavouring without delay to remedy a state of things, which cannot continue to exist without reflecting serious discredit on the British name. . . . No such apprehension as that mentioned by Your Excellency of being blamed for not affording sufficient protection to British subjects ought in future to deter Your Excellency from taking the most active steps consistent with the line of your duty and within the limits of your authority for preventing offences and for bringing offenders to punishment. Her Majesty's Government can never sanction the principle that British subjects are to be protected whether right or wrong'.

He then stated that Britain would not relinquish the right to have observers at the trials of these Maltese and Ionians, because it was essential to ensure that they should have a fair trial; for 'though the punishment of real offenders tends to repress crime, no such effect is produced by unjustly sacrificing men who are innocent. On the contrary to do so is to afford an encouragement to the real criminals, who finding that others have suffered for them, and that investigation has ceased, when a Punishment has been inflicted are stimulated to persevere in their career of crime by the prospect of continued impunity'. But he reminded Ponsonby that the British observers were not entitled to intervene in the proceedings, to act as advocates for the British defendants, or to attempt to prevent their punishment if they were rightly convicted. They were merely entitled to be present as observers, and must not exceed the powers which Britain had been granted by treaty.

The question of legal proceedings against British subjects also arose in Egypt in 1847, where Palmerston's respect for law caused great exasperation to the British Consul and the British community in Alexandria, and placed them in considerable difficulties. The British residents felt that the Egyptian courts were oppressive, and that they could obtain no justice there. The British Consul, Murray, therefore informed the Egyptian authorities that British subjects would not submit to the jurisdiction of the Egyptian courts, and he set up his own court where he tried criminal offences committed by British subjects against Egyptian law. All the other foreign Consuls in Alexandria did the same. The Egyptian authorities accepted the position; but when Palmerston heard about it, he insisted that Murray close down his court at once, as he had no legal authority to hold one. Such a court could only have jurisdiction if it was authorized by a British Act of Parliament, and if a treaty granting the right were negotiated with the Turkish Government in Constantinople.

Murray protested to Palmerston against this order, and took the responsibility of disregarding it until Palmerston had considered the matter further. He told Palmerston that if his court were closed down, it would mean that British subjects could commit crimes in Egypt with impunity, as it was out of the question to surrender them to the mercy – and the bastinado – of the Egyptian courts; and the Egyptian authorities, who were perfectly happy to have Murray's court keeping the British in order, would deeply resent it if British subjects could commit crime without restraint. Palmerston would not accept this argument, and told Murray that the British subjects must submit to the jurisdiction of the Egyptian courts, and rely on the power of Britain to compel the Egyptian authorities to see that no injustice was done to them. The most that he would allow Murray to do was to ask the Egyptian authorities not to bastinado British subjects. He persisted in his attitude when Murray told him that his action would cause great anger among the British in Egypt, who would be the only European residents who were liable to be tried in the Egyptian courts and not by their own Consul. To all Murray's arguments, Palmerston repeated that the law must be observed and that no British court could function without valid authority from Parliament and international law.

Whenever Britain, or a British subject, became involved in a dispute with a foreign government which involved a question of international law, Palmerston referred it to the Queen's Advocate, whose decision was final. If he said that the British subject had no claim, Palmerston would do no more; if he said that the claim was justified, Palmerston would hear no arguments to the contrary, either from the foreign government or from critics in Britain. Nor would he consider refering the dispute to the arbitration of a third power. He pressed the claim until the foreign government gave way. If other arguments failed, Palmerston used the ultimate one – the blockade.

But there was another factor which played an important part in Palmerston's calculations. He only enforced the claims of a British subject against powers which were unable to resist. If the other power could not be coerced, because it was either militarily too powerful or geographically too inaccessible, there was nothing to be done, and Palmerston did not try to do anything. When a British subject was assaulted and arrested in Frankfort for having accidentally kicked a lump of snow towards an Austrian sentry, Palmerston was very satisfied when he obtained his release by gentle persuasion, and told the British Minister not to make any demand for compensation. When two Ionians were arbitrarily imprisoned by the Russian military authorities in Bucharest, Palmerston did nothing except protest. There were only two occasions when he came near to using force against a great power to uphold the rights of a British subject or the honour of the British flag. Both times it was against the United States. The first occasion was when McLeod was put on trial in New York for murdering the man on the *Caroline*, and the pressure of British public opinion drove Palmerston to the brink of war. The other was the case of the *Trent*, during the peculiar circumstances of the American Civil War.

Once – but only once – political considerations drove Palmerston to sacrifice the rights of a British subject. In 1834, when relations with Turkey were very delicate after the Treaty of Unkiar Skelessi, and British influence at Constantinople was weak, an Ionian Jew was grossly ill-treated by the Captain Pasha. Ponsonby thought that it would be unwise to raise the matter, as the Captain Pasha was a great favourite with the Sultan; and Palmerston agreed. If the circumstances had arisen fifteen years later, Palmerston would probably have adopted a different attitude.

The Emir of Bokhara discovered that remoteness was as good a protection as military might against Palmerston's determination to uphold British rights. In 1838 Colonel Stoddart was sent by the British Minister in Persia on a diplomatic mission to Bokhara. He angered the Emir by riding his horse into the courtyard of the palace, and was thrown into prison. When rumours of his imprisonment reached the East India Company, they sent Captain Conolly to negotiate for his release; but Conolly did not return. After many months, letters arrived from Stoddart and Conolly, revealing that they were together in a dungeon of the Emir. Their relatives in England stirred up public opinion, and a society was formed to obtain their release; but nothing more was heard of them.

When Palmerston returned to the Foreign Office in 1846, he considered what to do. Bokhara was 1,200 miles from the Persian Gulf, which was the nearest that the British Navy could get to it. If a British army had marched to Bokhara from India, it would have had to travel nearly a thousand miles through mountainous country; and Russia would not have remained passive when faced with a British invasion of Bokhara. Palmerston reluctantly decided that, however ignominious this course might be, there was nothing to be done except to offer to pay a ransom to the Emir of Bokhara for the two British subjects. He felt that the Government was morally bound to do this, as it was the only way to save the men; and in October 1846 he ordered Sheil, the British Minister in

Persia, to get in touch with the Emir. But Sheil was not at all clear how to set about doing this. The Jews of Teheran had contacts in Bokhara; but they warned Sheil that if an envoy was sent with money, the Emir would simply seize the money and throw the envoy into a dungeon. Palmerston decided to ask the Russian Government for assistance, and asked Nesselrode to transmit a personal letter from Queen Victoria to the Emir; but the Russians had broken off diplomatic relations with Bokhara, and did not venture to send an envoy there. Eventually, in March 1850, Palmerston received a report from Sheil of news which he had heard from a man who was travelling from Bokhara to Constantinople. The man said that both Stoddart and Conolly had been publicly beheaded in Bokhara in 1842. Palmerston decided to take no further action.

Greece was geographically in a very different position from Bokhara; but Palmerston waited for many years before taking drastic action against a Government with whom his relations had been strained from the first. When Palmerston, after resigning from Wellington's Government in 1828, began speaking in Parliament about foreign policy, one of the first problems to which he devoted his attention was Greece. With Princess Lieven's approval he supported the Greek struggle for independence against Turkey. When he became Foreign Secretary in 1830, the Conference of the great powers on Greece was in session in London, and he presided at its meetings. In September 1831 the Northern frontiers of Greece were fixed along the line between the Gulfs of Arta and Volo, which Russia had always demanded, and which Palmerston had advocated when in Opposition, as opposed to the line along the Isthmus of Corinth on which Wellington's Government had insisted.

The great powers had also to settle the form of government of the new state. During the War of Independence the Greeks proclaimed a republic under the presidency of John Kapodistrias, the Greek who for many years had been the Russian Minister for Foreign Affairs, but had returned to his native country to lead the struggle for independence. The idea of a republic was not acceptable to any of the great powers, and neither Britain nor France wished to see a former Russian

Foreign Minister at the head of the Greek state. In any case, Kapodistrias was assassinated in 1831. It was therefore necessary to find a King for Greece. The great powers agreed to have Prince Otho, the seventeen-year-old son of the King of Bavaria, after Palmerston had persuaded the Left-wing French Government to abandon their objection to Otho. Otho sailed for Greece in a British warship in 1833, accompanied by a Bavarian adviser, Count Armansperg, and a bodyguard of Bavarian soldiers. Greece was helped to pay for the Turkish assets which she acquired, and for putting the country on its feet, by a loan from the Rothschilds which was guaranteed jointly by Britain, France and Russia. These three powers were declared to be the protectors of Greece.

Otho became King of Greece as an absolute monarch. The protocol of the London Conference of May 1832 had contained some vague provision about the liberties of the Greek people; but Palmerston was not particularly eager, before August 1832, to secure constitutional government for foreign peoples; Tsar Nicholas would never have agreed to such a stipulation; and in the state of anarchy and banditry which prevailed in Greece, it hardly seemed possible to arrange to have an elected National Assembly. King Otho, however, and Armansperg, who was appointed Prime Minister, promised to set up local Councils which would be elected by the inhabitants of the area; and Palmerston repeatedly pressed them to implement their promise. There were frequent reports of arbitrary arrests and tortures inflicted on Greek peasants who would not pay their taxes, or were recalcitrant in other ways. King Otho and his Bavarian guard and retinue became very unpopular in Greece, and soon Radical MPs in the House of Commons were criticizing Palmerston for having foisted Otho on the Greek people, and for doing nothing to prevent him from misgoverning the country. Palmerston defended Otho in debates in the House, but at the same time wrote increasingly impatient despatches to Athens, urging Otho and Armansperg to mend their ways. He wrote similar despatches to Munich, because the King of Bavaria was known to exercise a powerful influence over his son.

Palmerston was very alarmed at the financial situation in

Greece. He had imagined that the Greek Government, by efficient administration, would restore order and put an end to the chaotic conditions in which Greece had been left by the nine years' War of Independence, that they would collect the taxes, and achieve financial stability. They would then begin to repay the loan which Britain, France and Russia had persuaded Rothschild to grant them, and which the three powers had guaranteed. But no progress was made in this direction. The Greek Government failed to pay the interest due on the loan in March and September each year, and the three powers had to pay it to Rothschild. At the same time, King Otho was maintaining one of the most extravagant courts in Europe, building great new palaces for himself, granting lands and gifts to favourite Bavarians, and appointing them to well-paid sinecure offices. Palmerston urged the Greek and Bavarian Governments to put a stop to this extravagance and to try to pay the Greek debt.

He was hindered by the fact that his co-creditor, Russia, refused to join him in pressing the debtor. The Tsar was anxious to establish Russian political hegemony in Greece. He achieved this by making use of the gratitude of the Greeks for Russian assistance during the War of Independence, by the powerful links between the Greek and Russian Orthodox Churches, and by encouraging King Otho to reign as an absolute monarch. With the Greek Government under Russian influence, the Opposition party tended to look to France, and their leader, Kolettes, developed very close links with the French embassy. His party became known as the French Party. Palmerston did not wish to get involved in Greek politics, and at first pinned his hopes on the unpopular Armansperg, hoping that his despotic methods would at least succeed in restoring order and financial prosperity in Greece, and hoping, too, that things would improve when Otho was old enough to play an independent role in the Government. But Palmerston was disappointed. The older Otho grew, the worse things became. In 1837 Otho dismissed Armansperg and appointed another Bavarian, Rudhart, as Prime Minister, who was even more autocratic and unpopular than Armansperg. Finding the Government of Greece under Russian influence, and the Opposition looking to France, Palmerston encouraged another Opposition party under Mavrocordatos, though he was not pleased when Mavrocordatos's group became known as the English Party. Things were made worse by the bad personal relations between the Greek Government and the British Minister in Athens. Palmerston had given the post to Captain Lyons of the Royal Navy. Lyons was able and honest, but was too outspoken, and lacked some of the finesse of the professional diplomat. His relations with King Otho became very strained. There was an unpleasant incident, in which Palmerston became involved, when the Court officials refused to provide Lyons with a chair when he took his place with the King in the royal box at a gala performance at the Athens Opera House.

Palmerston's policy of winning Turkish goodwill after the Treaty of Unkiar Skelessi, and his failure to obtain any influence for Britain in Athens, led him to support Turkey against Greece in the disputes between the two countries. When quarrels arose as to the interpretation of the financial clauses in the peace treaty which had ended the War of Independence, Palmerston supported the Turkish interpretation. He supported Turkey when there was trouble about bandits and border violations on the Northern frontier of Greece, and when Greece and Turkey nearly went to war about an insult to the Turkish Minister in Athens. During the Middle Eastern crisis of 1840, the Greeks looked to France and Mehemet Ali to help them against the Turks; but King Otho, after playing with the idea of invading Thessaly, was deterred by Palmerston's threats.

Palmerston also discouraged the nationalist movement in Crete, which was trying to free the island from Turkish rule and unite it with Greece. When he was in Opposition before 1830, he had demanded that Crete should be included in the new Greek state; and he sympathized with the Cretans who were living under the military dictatorship and planned economy of Mehemet Ali. He tentatively suggested in 1833 that Mehemet Ali should free himself from the burden of governing Crete by restoring it to the direct rule of the Sultan; but he rapidly abandoned the idea when Mehemet Ali turned

rather than united with Greece and detached from the nominal suzerainty of the Sultan. Under the final settlement of the
Middle Eastern crisis in 1841, Mehemet Ali evacuated Crete,
which passed under the direct rule of the Sultan. Henceforth
Palmerston used all his influence to keep it in the Turkish Empire. He urged the Sultan to grant reforms, and to deal
leniently with revolutionary outbreaks among the Greek population; but he rejected all appeals from the Cretan exiles in
Athens, who asked him to intervene in favour of Cretan freedom, and he ordered Lyons to refuse to have anything to do
with them. He censured the British Consul in Crete for encouraging the Greek nationalists, and threatened to recall
him; and in 1841 he ordered the Navy to assist in the transport
of Turkish troops to Crete to suppress a rebellion there. At
the same time, disturbances broke out among the Greek population at Salonika. Here, too, Palmerston sent the Navy to
transport Turkish troops to suppress the troubles.

In 1843 a revolution broke out in Greece, and forced the
King to grant a constitution. Palmerston, from the Opposition
benches, welcomed the revolution, which he compared to the
Revolution of 1688 and the French Revolution of 1830; but
the hopes of the revolutionaries were soon disappointed. Although Greece now had a Parliament, the King appointed
ministers who had no Parliamentary support; and he and the
pro-French Kolettes, who became Prime Minister, rigged the
elections by fraud and terror. After the Greek general election of 1847, Palmerston sent a strong protest to the Greek
and Bavarian Governments against the way in which the election had been conducted, and drew their attention to several
cases where Opposition candidates had been assaulted, and
their supporters prevented by threats and violence from going
to the polls. His attitude to Greece was therefore very hostile
when, on returning to the Foreign Office in 1846, he took
over from Aberdeen the handling of the cases of British subjects who had been wronged by the Greek Government.

In 1830 George Finlay, a Scottish historian, bought a house
in Athens and settled down to write a seven-volume history
of Greece from the time of the Roman conquest to the present day. Property was going cheap in Greece in the last stages

of the War of Independence, and Finlay bought the house at a low price from a Turk who had hastily left Greece after the overthrow of Turkish rule. The price of land in the centre of Athens rose very rapidly in the first few years of peace, after the capital was transferred from Nauplia to Athens, and speculators bought land for development; but in 1836 the Greek Government passed a law which authorized the King to acquire, without paying compensation, any land which he needed to build a royal palace in Athens. Finlay's garden was taken, along with the land of several Greeks, and he was not paid anything for it. He protested to the Greek Government, and Lyons and Aberdeen took up his case; but ten years after the garden had been seized, he had not obtained a single drachma's compensation.

On 7 August 1846, Palmerston wrote his first despatch about the case. He told the Greek Government that he realized that in certain circumstances a government could legitimately acquire land by compulsory acquisition, but that this interference with the rights of property owners should not be resorted to merely in order to provide a King with a palace garden. He realized that the people of Greece had insisted that their King should have an impressive palace; but he was sure that this could have been erected without violating the rights of individuals. He reminded the Greek Government that when Frederick the Great of Prussia had built his palace of Sans-Souci, a cottager had refused to sell his plot of land to the King; and the cottage still stood today in the royal grounds as proof that great Kings respected the property of their most humble subjects. If King Otho was not prepared to equal the generosity of the great Frederick, he should at least have paid Mr Finlay for the value of his garden. Kolettes denied that the land had anywhere near the value which Finlay claimed. In 1847, eleven years after the gardens had been seized, the Greek Government offered all the dispossessed property-owners a sum of money as compensation which Finlay claimed was only a fraction of what the land had been worth in 1836. The Greek property-owners accepted the offer; but Finlay refused, and demanded the market value of the land in 1836 plus interest since that date at the rate of

15 per cent per annum, which was the usual rate of interest in Greece. Kolettes then proposed that they should pay Finlay a sum to be fixed as fair compensation by the Greek courts; but Finlay refused, on the grounds that it was notorious that the Greek Courts gave any verdict that the Government required. Eventually the Greek Government proposed that the dispute be referred to arbitration. This offer was accepted by Finlay; but as the Greek Government did not produce the necessary documents, the arbitration lapsed.

Palmerston was involved in further conflicts with the Greek Government about the inhabitants of the Ionian Isles, which had been ceded by Turkey to Russia in 1800 and after being held by Napoleon were granted by the great powers to Britain in 1815. They were administered from Corfu by the British High Commissioner under the directions of the Colonial Office in London, and the 230,000 inhabitants were British subjects. In July 1846 an Ionian blacksmith was arrested in the Greek port of Patras and charged with committing robbery with violence in a dwelling house. As he refused to confess he was flogged and tortured in the police station; policemen stamped on his chest, and twisted cord around his testicles. Two other Ionians were flogged by the Greek authorities a few months later. After Lyons had protested, the Greek Government conducted an investigation, and announced that they were satisfied that the men had not been flogged or tortured; but the doctors and other witnesses secretly told the British Vice-Consul at Patras that they had been compelled to give false evidence in order to exonerate the police. Lyons asked the Greek Government to hold another inquiry in public at which the Ionians could be represented by the British Consul; and when this was refused, he demanded £20 compensation for each of the men. He also demanded compensation from the Greek Government when half a dozen bandits captured a Greek frontier post on the north-west coast of Greece, and proceeded to seize some boats belonging to some Ionian fishermen. Lyons believed that the Greek authorities in the district had connived at the action of the bandits. Palmerston endorsed Lyons's action on all points, and pressed all these claims on Kolettes.

There was also trouble about the sovereignty of two tiny islets off the west coast of the Peloponnesus. Sapienza was 4½ miles long by 4 miles wide, and Cervi was 3 miles long by 1 mile wide. They had always been considered part of Greece. Cervi was separated from the Greek mainland by 220 yards of shallow water, which was usually fordable, though Palmerston managed to prove that at certain times of the day the water, for a short distance, was between 9 and 12 foot deep. Greek shepherds walked over every day with their herds, and returned to the mainland at night; and a Greek Government official sometimes went there, and built himself the only hut on the island. In 1839, Lyons suddenly claimed the two islands as part of the Ionian Isles; but the Greek Government refused to admit this, and said that they were not included in the territory which Turkey had granted to Russia in 1800, and that the Turks had continued to occupy them till 1830, since when they had been part of Greece. Palmerston tried to argue the British case in his most able fashion, after thoroughly mastering the documents and maps of the treaty of 1800; but his case was so weak that he ultimately fell back on the strange argument that it was not for Greece, a state which had only come into existence in 1831, to argue about frontiers that had been drawn up in 1800.

In 1847, Palmerston took up his complaints against Greece with the Bavarian Government. He urged the Government in Munich to persuade King Otho to grant compensation to Finlay and the Ionians and combined it with an unprecedented denunciation of the unconstitutional actions of the Greek Government. His language about Kolettes and King Otho was such as no other Foreign Minister of the time would have used; and Palmerston himself would never have used it during his earlier terms at the Foreign Office. On 20 May 1847 he wrote a despatch to Milbanke, the Minister in Munich, and told him to read it to the Bavarian Prime Minister.

That M. Coletti [Kolettes] should hate a constitutional form of Government is not surprising. He was brought up as a boy in the Palace of Ali Pacha of Iannina, one of the most cruel and ferocious tyrants that have appeared in late times even in a Turkish Province, and inferior in that respect perhaps to none but to Djezzar Pacha of Acre; his youth was spent in irregular War, Part of his manhood in the amusements of Paris, and now at a more advanced Time of Life he finds himself destitute of the acquirements, the knowledge of the parliamentary faculties which are necessary for a Constitutional Minister. It can be no wonder that M. Coletti should think that it would be more convenient and agreeable to be the Minister of a despotic Sovereign and to govern by making or breaking laws as it might suit his purpose of the moment. But it was certainly not to be expected that King Otho should imbibe a fixed aversion of Constitutional Government. He was chosen to be King of Greece specifically because it was hoped that a son of the wise and enlightened Sovereign of Constitutional Bavaria would have been early imbued with suitable notions in Principles of Government and would have had instilled into his mind just feelings of respect for the rights of his Grecian Subjects. It might also have been expected that King Otho would have been duly impressed with the consciousness that Greece was not detached from Turkey and erected into a separate and independent State, merely for the personal Benefit and Advantage of a Younger Prince of the house of Bavaria.

A few months later, Kolettes died; but this did not lead to any improvement in Anglo-Greek relations. Lyons told Palmerston that King Otho had appointed his new Prime Minister, General Zavellos, after a long and private talk with the French Minister in Athens, Piscatory; and Palmerston protested about this in Munich, and told the Bavarian Government that Mavrocordatos should have been chosen as Prime Minister of Greece. But when the Bavarian Foreign Minister, Prince Wallenstein, made an attempt to bring about a rapprochement between Britain and Greece, Palmerston administered a very sharp rebuff. Wallenstein told Milbanke that he was worried at the growth of Russian influence in Greece, and that he thought that Palmerston would prefer to have a government in power there which would be more favourable to Britain. He suggested that this might be achieved by making a fresh start. As Kolettes had died, and Piscatory had been transferred to the French embassy in Madrid, Wallenstein suggested that Lyon, too, hould be removed from Athens. Palmerston replied that if Wallenstein was worried about the growth of Russian influence in Greece, the British Government was not, and that it was completely immaterial to Britain whether or not the Greek Government was pro-British. All that Britain required of King Otho was that he should restore constitutional government to Greece. Palmerston would not consider removing Lyons from Athens, and on 22 January 1848 wrote to Milbanke: 'I do not see that the death of M. Colletti who misgoverned Greece, or the promotion of M. Piscatory to the Post of Ambassador at Madrid apparently as a reward for the course which he has pursued at Athens can afford any reason why Sir E. Lyons should be removed from his present post; and I have upon that latter topic only to request that you will never in future allow yourself to be made the Channel for any application of a similar nature in regard to any of your Colleagues abroad. Any foreign Government which has any such communication to make to Her Majesty's Government should be left to employ its own diplomatic Agents for such a purpose'.

The bad relations between Britain and Greece were made worse by the trouble in the Ionian Isles. When Britain first took over the islands in 1815, the British High Commissioner ruled autocratically, and a press censorship was established; but in 1848 the High Commissioner, General Lord Seaton, removed the censorship and began consultations with the local leaders about drafting a constitution for the islands. The result was almost immediately an outburst of revolutionary violence, particularly in Cephalonia, where the peasants were angry about the policy of agricultural development and enclosures which the British Government had pursued and which deprived them of their customary right to collect firewood. Lord Seaton dealt with the trouble on the best Palmerstonian principles: he granted the constitution, promised reforms, and after suppressing the disorders granted an amnesty to the rebels. But this was 1848, the year of revolutions. The people demanded an end to British rule and union with Greece. The movement came under the leadership of Cephalonian intellectuals who practised as barristers in Athens, and of men who were described by Sir Henry Ward, the new High Commissioner who replaced Lord Seaton, as not having a shilling in the world and being 'fed upon the histories of Lamartine and

Thiers'. In the summer of 1849 a peasant revolt broke out in Cephalonia. Sir Henry Ward sent troops who suppressed the revolt, and many peasants and priests were tried by court-martial and sentenced to be hanged or flogged. Aberdeen stated that the Government, in appointing Ward to succeed Seaton, had decided 'that the mild rule of a military Conservative might be advantageously succeeded by the stern rule of a Whig civilian'.

Apart from hanging and flogging the peasants, Ward arrested a number of the intellectual leaders. Some of them were being transported in a small boat to another island when they were thrown ashore, in adverse weather, on the Island of Cervi. The Greek shepherds on the island rescued the prisoners from the British and took them across to the mainland, claiming that they had reached Greek soil when they landed on Cervi; and they were granted political asylum. Palmerston thereupon ordered the authorities in the Ionian Isles to assert British sovereignty over Sapienza and Cervi; but they did not, for the time being, proceed to throw the Greek shepherds off the islands.

The presence of British warships in the Ionian Isles, and the feeling aroused in Greece by the disturbances there, led to another incident. A midshipman of the British ship *Fantome* was detained by the Greek police when his ship called at Patras and he went ashore in civilian dress. The Nomarch of Achaia, who administered Patras, stated that the midshipman had falsely said that he belonged to a ship called the *Spitfire*, not the *Fantome*, and the police had therefore thought that he was lying and had come on shore for illegal purposes; and this accusation was published in the official newspapers of the Greek Government. Lyons then complained that the Nomarch had insulted a British officer by accusing him of lying, and said that the British Government would either have to dismiss the midshipman from the service in disgrace or take steps to avenge the insult to his honour by the servant of the Government of Greece.

Palmerston had also taken up the case of David Pacifico. The Chevalier Pacifico, as he called himself, was a Spanish Jew who, like his father, was born in Gibraltar, and was therefore a British subject by birth. He had lived all his early life in Portugal, and had become a naturalized Portuguese subject; and in 1839 he had been appointed Portuguese Consul in Athens. On arriving in Athens, he had taken the precaution of applying to the British legation for a British passport, apparently without mentioning the fact that he had been naturalized Portuguese. Some years later, he made a claim for money against the Portuguese Government, and tried to strengthen his case by forging a document; but the forgery was discovered, his claim was rejected, and he was dismissed from his post as Consul. He nevertheless remained in Athens, where his misconduct towards the Portuguese Government was not generally known, and became a prominent figure as a leading member of the Jewish community.

It was the custom in Athens, every Easter, to burn an effigy of Judas, and this was always the occasion for anti-Semitic outbursts, as there was strong feeling against Jews throughout Greece. At Easter 1847 Rothschild came to Athens to discuss the repayment of the loan by the Greek Government; and in view of the presence of their Jewish creditor, the Government thought that it would be tactful to ban the Judas-burning festivities. This caused great anger among certain sections of the people, and the rumour spread that it was Pacifico who had induced the Government to impose the ban. An angry crowd assembled in the evening in front of his house, broke in the door, manhandled his wife and children, stole his wife's jewellery and set fire to the house. Several aristocratic youths were among the crowd, including young Zavellos, the fourteen-year-old son of the Minister of War. Pacifico sent for the police, but they stood and watched, and for three hours made no attempt to control the mob.

As Pacifico was born in Gibraltar, and still held a British passport, he asked Lyons to take up his case. He claimed £5,000 for the damage to his property destroyed in the fire; but he also claimed that he had a lawsuit pending against the Portuguese Government for nearly £27,000 due to him under various transactions, and that the documents which were necessary for him to prove his case in the Portuguese courts had been in his house in Athens, and had been burned in the fire. He would now be unable to recover the money from the Portuguese Government, and claimed the loss of this £27,000 as damage resulting from the riot. Palmerston endorsed Lyons's action in taking up Pacifico's case. He told Lyons that as far as the claim for the loss of the documents was concerned, Pacifico might not be able to substantiate his claim for the £27,000; but he told him to claim it, as it was for the Greek Government to challenge Pacifico's assertions about this. He then told Lyons to claim another £500 over and above the total which Pacifico had demanded, as compensation for the insult and suffering to which this British subject and his family had been subjected.

The Greek Government expressed its great regret for what had occurred, and assured Palmerston that there was no religious or racial persecution in Greece; but they said that a Government was not responsible for wrongs committed by a disorderly mob of private individuals, and that Pacifico's remedy was to claim damages from the persons responsible and sue them in the Greek courts. They refused his demand that they should bring a criminal prosecution against the offenders, on the grounds that Pacifico, by complaining to the British legation instead of to the police, had made it impossible for them to trace the offenders; and when Pacifico contemplated bringing a civil action against young Zavellos and his associates, no lawyer was prepared to act in a case against a member of General Zavellos's family, especially as the General had now left the War Office to become Prime Minister. So Pacifico turned again to the British Government, and his appeals to Lyons and Palmerston were well calculated to meet with a response. 'Allow me, in my capacity of English subject, to implore your powerful protection', he wrote to Lyons on 20 September 1847, '. . . to obtain satisfaction for my just rights by means of that influence with which Her Majesty the Queen, our beloved Sovereign, has invested you'. On 8 October he addressed himself directly to Palmerston: 'I am an English subject and of the Jewish religion; I have seen my wife, my children, insulted; my house rifled, my furniture, my goods pillaged, my money stolen. . . . A strong hand, a firm will, are necessary to compel the Greek Government to perform a duty of equity and of justice. That strong hand can only be yours, my Lord; that firm will my just rights lead me to hope will be yours likewise.

On 11 May 1847 Palmerston sent a note to the Greek and Bavarian Governments warning them that if compensation were not paid to Pacifico, to Finlay, and to the injured Ionians, the British Government would be reluctantly compelled to use force to obtain their demands. But Palmerston took no action against Greece for another two years; and when he finally acted, it was as a result of a completely different incident which arose out of the defeat of the Hungarian struggle for independence.

Chapter Twenty-seven

'Civis Romanus Sum'

In August 1849, Kossuth and Bem and their soldiers retreated across the Turkish frontier and surrendered to the Turkish authorities. The Russian and Austrian Governments demanded that the rebels should be extradited and handed over to them, the Austrians demanding Kossuth and the Hungarians, and the Russians asking for Bem and the Poles. The British Ambassador, Sir Stratford Canning, persuaded the Sultan to refuse these demands. But the Tsar persisted. He had intervened in Hungary in order to show all revolutionaries that a revolution could never succeed in any country, because of the international solidarity of rulers; and now he wished to teach them a still more terrible lesson, and prove that rebels would never be able to escape punishment. Russia was on stronger grounds than Austria in international law, because in 1774 the Sultan and Catherine the Great had signed the Treaty of Kainardji, under which they agreed to extradite each other's rebels.

On 4 September Prince Radzivil arrived in Constantinople from St. Petersburg to demand the surrender of the Poles, while the Russians let the Turks know, unofficially, that a refusal would be considered by Russia and Austria as an act of war. Canning urged the Turks to stand firm; but they told him that Turkey could not go to war with Russia and Austria without the support of powerful allies, and that they would have to give way to the Russian and Austrian demands unless the British Government would give an undertaking to declare war on Russia and Austria if they attacked Turkey. Canning had no authority from the British Government to give such an undertaking, and it might have taken two months to write to London for instructions and to receive a reply; but he decided to give the guarantee on his own responsibility. He ordered Admiral Parker, the Commander-in-Chief of the Mediterranean fleet at Malta, to bring the fleet to the Dardanelles as a gesture in support of Turkey; and he persuaded the French Ambassador in Constantinople to summon the French fleet to the Dardanelles for the same purpose. He then wrote to Palmerston and asked him to ratify what he had done, while Russia and Austria broke off diplomatic relations with Turkey.

Palmerston supported Canning. He had always sympathized with the Hungarians, even though he did not think that it was in Britain's interests to help them against Austria; and he objected, as he had done in 1833, to the Tsar's attempts to pursue the Polish refugees who had escaped abroad. Apart from this, he believed that the Russian and Austrian demand was a threat to the independence of Turkey; and, as always, he was determined to uphold the policy of a British representative abroad. He persuaded the Cabinet to endorse Canning's action, and sent the news to Canning by the Queen's Messenger, Townley, who reached Constantinople after riding across Europe in twenty-four days – a remarkable feat which was duly commemorated in the poem 'Townley's Ride'. Palmerston told the Russian Ambassador, Brunnow, that Britain would back Turkey to the limit in resisting the Russian demand for the surrender of the refugees. At the same time, he ordered the fleet to stay just outside the Dardanelles, and told Canning to be very careful to see that they did not violate the Convention of 1841 by entering the Straits; and he ordered the ships to withdraw from the outer waters of the Dardanelles, where some of them had taken shelter, in case this might be said to be a breach of the Convention. The Russian and Austrian press attacked Turkey, France and Britain, and especially Palmerston; but Russia and Austria did not go to war with Turkey, and on 17 October the Russian and Austrian Governments withdrew their demand for the extradition of the refugees.

On 6 October Palmerston sent a note to Nesselrode, in which he ingeniously argued that the Treaty of Kainardji gave Turkey the option either to extradite the Poles to Russia or simply to expel them from Turkey. But Russia and Austria were not at all satisfied with this. On the contrary, they told the Turks that if they would not extradite the refugees, they should intern them in Turkey and not allow them to go to Western Europe. They were particularly eager to prevent Kossuth from making propaganda in Britain and France. This seemed absurd to Palmerston. 'What a childish, silly fear this is of Kossuth', he wrote to Ponsonby in Vienna on 30 November. 'What great harm could he do to Austria while in France or England? He would be the hero of half a dozen dinners in England, at which would be made speeches not more violent than those which have been made on platforms here within the last four months, and he would soon sink into comparative obscurity; while, on the other hand, so long as he is a state *dêtenu* in Turkey, he is a martyr and the object of never-ceasing interest'.

Queen Victoria did not approve of Palmerston's policy. 'What business have we to interfere with the Polish and Hungarian Refugees in Turkey?' she wrote to Lord John Russell. But Palmerston's action was very popular in Britain; and in the eyes of the Hungarian nationalists and the Radicals in Europe, he had fully atoned for his failure to help the Hungarian national movement. He also sent protests to Austria against the severe repression in Hungary, which had shocked even the Tsar by its savagery. As usual, he went completely with the tide of public opinion, and indeed did his best to increase the anti-Austrian feeling in Britain. When the Austrians imprisoned Kossuth's old mother, he asked his friend Borthwick, the editor of the *Morning Post*, to publish the news in his paper, and added: 'You might make such observations as may suggest themselves upon this unmanly war waged against Hungarian women and children by those Austrians who were unable to stand up against the Hungarian men until they had called in to their assistance an army of 150,000 Russians'. He felt strongly about the Austrian atrocities, and expressed himself forcibly in his private letters. On 9 September 1849 he wrote to Ponsonby: 'The Austrians are really the greatest brutes that ever called themselves by the undeserved name of civilized men. Their atrocities in Galicia, in Italy, in Hungary, in Transylvania are only to be equalled by the proceedings of the negro race in Africa and Haiti. Their late exploit of flogging forty odd people, including two women at Milan, some of the victims being gentlemen, is really too blackguard and disgusting a proceeding'. But Austria was not the only power that flogged rebels. At this very time, the Admiralty ordered that one of the ships which was protecting the refugees at the Dardanelles should sail to Cephalonia to take an extra supply of cat-o'-nine-tails for the punishment of the rebellious peasants.

Palmerston thought that as the fleet was in the Eastern Mediterranean, this would be a good opportunity to settle accounts counts with Greece. On 30 November he ordered Admiral Parker to sail with the fleet to Athens and place himself under the orders of Mr. Wyse, who, earlier in the year, had succeeded Lyons as Minister to Greece. Wyse was no more of a professional diplomat than Lyons, but was one of those Radical politicians, like Bulwer, whom Palmerston employed as an Ambassador when he wished to adopt a tough and provocative policy towards absolutist governments. He was an Irish Roman Catholic, a champion of Catholic Emancipation and Irish freedom, a former Liberal MP, and the husband of Louis Napoleon's cousin, Laetitia Bonaparte of Canino, though he had quarrelled violently with her and had lived apart from her for more than twenty years.

On 3 December Palmerston wrote to Wyse to tell him that the fleet was coming to Athens, and directing him to use it, to the extent that he deemed necessary, to obtain satisfaction of the British claims against Greece. 'You will of course', he wrote to Wyse, 'persevere in the *suaviter in modo* as long as is consistent with our dignity and honour, and I measure that time by days – perhaps by some very small number of hours. If, however, the Greek Government does not strike, Parker must do so'. Wyse was to demand payment for Pacifico, Finlay and the Ionians in full, and an apology for the insult to the midshipman of the *Fantome*; but he was to make it clear that Britain was not demanding repayment of the loan to Greece of 1832, or taking any action in support of the British claims to the two off-shore islets. It was undesirable to introduce the question of the loan, as this would involve Russia and

France, the two other co-guarantors; and the claim to Sapienza and Cervi was too bogus to be seriously pressed. While leaving Wyse a completely free hand as to how to act, Palmerston suggested the possibility of landing a force from Parker's ships to find and seize some of the Greek Government's gold up to the amount of the sums claimed; but Wyse never took this step, which would have meant war.

The fleet arrived off the Piraeus on 15 January 1850. Admiral Parker paid the usual courtesy call on King Otho; but next day Wyse presented a note to the astonished Greek Foreign Minister, Londos, in which he demanded payment of £31,000 to Pacifico, with interest at 12 per cent since 1847; £750 for Finlay, with interest at 12 per cent since 1836; and £20 for each Ionian who had been tortured, with interest at 12 per cent since 1846 and 1847. He told Londos that unless the Greek Government agreed to pay the whole sum demanded within twenty-four hours, the British Navy would act against Greek shipping. Londos suggested that the dispute be referred to the arbitration of a third power, and also asked for more time to consider the ultimatum; but Wyse refused both requests. Next day Parker seized one of the ships of the Greek Royal Navy. As this brought no result, Wyse decided to blockade the Piraeus, and a few days later extended the blockade to Patras and the other Greek ports. Foreign ships were allowed to pass, but no Greek vessel was allowed in or out. Wyse proceeded slowly to tighten the screw step by step, and at the end of January ordered Parker to seize Greek merchant vessels and remove them to Salamis.

Wyse's action caused difficulties from the very beginning with other nations, especially with France and Russia. Londos appealed to all the foreign diplomats in Athens for assistance, and asked them to mediate; but Wyse refused both the French and the Russian offer of mediation. Soon the French, Russian, Austrian and Swedish Ministers in Athens, and even the Turkish Minister, were signing protests to Wyse against the high-handed attitude which he was adopting towards Greece, and the damage caused to their nationals who had chartered Greek ships, or who had shipped, or insured, goods which were being carried in them. Wyse, who never resorted to the hectoring language which Lyons and Palmerston sometimes used, replied with the greatest courtesy that he deeply regretted any inconvenience caused to foreign traders; but he did not yield an inch. Several Greek vessels were then transferred to Russian owners. Wyse refused to acknowledge any transfer of ownership which had taken place after the date when the blockade started, and Russian ships were stopped by Parker's fleet and required to produce their papers. Some of the Russian ships were detained, and tension rose. On the other hand, in Greece itself, there was no strong feeling against Britain, and the British blockade was actually welcomed by large numbers of the political opponents of King Otho.

In London, Palmerston was being subjected to a good deal of criticism. The French and Russian Ambassadors protested against the British action on the grounds that unilateral debt-collecting prejudiced the position of France and Russia as co-guarantors of the Greek loan and joint protectors, with Britain, of the Greek state under the Treaty of 1832. On 19 February Nesselrode sent a strong protest to Palmerston, complaining that Britain had given no notice to Russia of the steps which she was intending to take, and, since the threatening despatch of May 1847, had sent no prior warning to Greece until the twenty-four hours' ultimatum was suddenly given. 'It remains, indeed, to be seen', wrote Nesselrode, 'whether Great Britain, abusing the advantages which are afforded her by her immense maritime superiority, intends henceforward to pursue an isolated policy without caring for those engagements which bind her to the other Cabinets ... and to authorize all great powers, on every fitting opportunity, to recognise towards the weak no other rule but their own will, no other right but their own physical strength'. Palmerston rejected the protest, and said that he had not given Russia any notice of the action which he proposed to take because it was no business of Russia's. The French Government used more restrained language, but showed very clearly that they disapproved of Palmerston's policy. Victoria and the Conservatives also disapproved, and Lord John Russell and the Cabinet were uncomfortable about it. In the face of all this opposition, Palmerston was less obdurate than Wyse. On 12 Feb-

ruary he agreed to the French Government's offer of
mediation, and ordered the blockade, and all other action
against Greece, to be suspended for an indefinite period while
he and the French Ambassador in London, Drouyn de
Lhuys, and the Greek Ambassador, tried to reach a peaceful
solution of the dispute. He also sent instructions to Wyse to
enter into negotiations with the French Minister in Athens,
Baron Gros, who would attempt to mediate between Wyse
and the Greek Government.

On 19 April, an agreement was reached between Palmerston, Drouyn de Lhuys and the Greek Ambassador. Greece
was to pay in full the claims of Finlay and the Ionians, and
apologize in vague and perfunctory terms for the insult to the
officer of the *Fantome*. With regard to Pacifico's claim the
Greeks agreed to pay £8,500 – which was a little less than Palmerston had originally demanded – to cover all damages except the loss of the documents relating to Pacifico's lawsuit
against the Portuguese Government. Pacifico's claim for
£27,000 under this last head was to be referred to three arbitrators who were to meet in Lisbon to investigate it. One arbitrator was to be appointed by the British Government, one
by the Greek Government and the third by the French Government. Drouyn de Lhuys immediately sent news of the
agreement to Gros in Athens; but Palmerston did not write
to Wyse for several days. After telling Wyse the terms that
had been agreed in London, he added that if, before this despatch arrived, Wyse had made any other arrangement with
Gros and the Greek Government, 'such other arrangement
of course stands good', and the London agreement would fall
to the ground.

The mediation in Athens had not been going so smoothly.
Gros succeeded with great difficulty in persuading Wyse to reduce some of his demands, and to accept £6,400 for the damage to Pacifico's furniture and valuables; but Gros still thought
that Wyse's claims were exorbitant. Wyse insisted that the
Greek Government should pay all the claims in cash at once,
except in the case of Pacifico's claim with respect to the loss of
his documents. On this point, he demanded that the Greek
Government should deposit shares worth £5,000 with Wyse

while the British Government investigated the genuineness of this claim. If the British Government decided that more than £5,000 was owing, the balance would be paid by the Greeks; if less was owing, Wyse would repay the excess to the Greek Government. The Greeks must agree to accept the British decision as final. He also insisted that the Greek Government should agree to compensate the Greek shipowners for any loss that they had suffered from the British blockade, and not to make any claim against Britain for this. The greatest difficulty arose about the apology for the insult to the officer of the *Fantome*. Wyse at first insisted that the Greek Government should promise, in the apology, that they would never employ, in any public office, the Nomarch of Achaia who had called the British midshipman a liar. He eventually withdrew this demand, but he rejected as unsatisfactory the apology which Gros persuaded Londos to write, though this was a good deal more abject than the one that Palmerston had accepted in London. Gros then gave up his attempt to mediate, telling Wyse that he was not prepared to give Londos a slap in the face on Wyse's behalf. Wyse thereupon ordered Parker to reimpose the blockade.

On the morning of 24 April, a few hours before the time fixed by Wyse for the resumption of the blockade, Gros received news from Drouyn de Lhuys that he was on the point of reaching agreement with Palmerston on the settlement of the British claims against Greece. Gros immediately told Wyse, and asked him not to resume the blockade until he received his next instructions from Palmerston. Wyse refused, telling Gros that Palmerston had not sent him any information about the London negotiations. Two days later, after a secret all-night session of the Greek Parliament, in which the Opposition strongly denounced the Government for their obstinacy and mishandling of the situation, Londos informed Wyse that Greece would agree to all the British demands. The decisive factor had been the advice of the Russian Government; they urged the Greeks to submit and to proclaim to all Europe that they had been compelled by superior force to yield to an unjust claim. The full amount claimed, and the shares to be deposited in respect of the loss of Pacifico's documents, were delivered to Wyse that same day. On receiving the money, Pacifico paid out 5,000 drachmas to individual Greeks who had suffered loss through the British action. The blockade was immediately called off.

The news of the events in Athens reached Paris while Normanby was attending a banquet at the Ministry of the Interior at which the President was present. Louis Napoleon was very angry at the action which his Irish cousin had taken, and made this very clear to Normanby at the banquet. The French Government made a formal protest against Palmerston's proceedings. They accused him of double-crossing them, and of deliberately holding back the news of the London agreement from Wyse by waiting for the packet boat. The French Foreign Minister, General Lahitte, declared that at a moment when the news of the London agreement was already known in Athens, 'Greece, attacked afresh by the naval forces of Great Britain, in spite of the energetic remonstrances made by the French envoy, was obliged, in order to escape complete ruin, to accept without discussion the clauses of an ultimatum infinitely more rigorous'. He demanded that the British Government repudiate the agreement between Wyse and the Greeks, and agree to substitute the London agreement. Palmerston refused, and pointed out that the agreement reached in Athens was in some ways more favourable to the Greek Government than the London agreement, as it provided that only £6,400 was to be paid to Pacifico for the loss of his furniture and valuables, for which he had been awarded £8,500 under the London agreement.

On 14 May, Louis Napoleon ordered Drouyn de Lhuys to leave London in protest against Palmerston's action. Public opinion in France became so enraged that there was talk of war with England; but Palmerston believed that Louis Napoleon was merely indulging in some Napoleonic sabre-rattling because this would be politically useful at home. Palmerston adopted a conciliatory attitude towards France. When he was asked in the House of Commons why Drouyn de Lhuys had left London, he replied that he had gone to Paris 'in order personally to be the medium of communication between the two governments'. Palmerston knew very well that this state-

ment was quite untrue, for next day he wrote a despatch to
Lord Bloomfield in St. Petersburg in which he gave the real
reason for Drouyn de Lhuys's departure; and when the truth
was known, Palmerston was strongly criticized by the Opposition for this crude attempt to mislead the House. His chief
motive was probably to prevent an exacerbation of the ill-
feeling between Britain and France. He told the French Government how much he regretted that the French mediation,
which he had hoped would strengthen the friendship between
Britain and France, had in fact had the opposite result; and
he did not withdraw Lord Normanby from the embassy in
Paris in reprisal for the departure of Drouyn de Lhuys. He
told Bloomfield, in a private letter, that he had kept Normanby in Paris in order to annoy the Russian Government and
Princess Lieven, whom he called 'the Tambour-Major of
Paris', as they had hoped to see a diplomatic breach between
Britain and France; but his action was everywhere interpreted
as a conciliatory gesture to appease the French anger.

On 17 June the Conservative leader, Lord Stanley – soon to
inherit his father's title of Earl of Derby in addition to the
peerage which had been granted to him – moved a vote of
censure on the Government in the House of Lords for their
conduct towards Greece. His motion stated that the House,
while agreeing that it was the duty of the Government to protect British subjects abroad, regretted that on this occasion
they had made unjust demands. The House, and the Strangers'
Gallery, were packed, and peeresses sat on the floor to hear
the debate. Stanley stated the case for Greece with great eloquence. Britain ought always, he said, to behave in the same
way towards a weak state as she would do, in the same circumstances, towards a powerful state. Yet Palmerston had
bullied Greece into paying a false claim by Pacifico, who had
lost his British nationality when he became a naturalized Portuguese; and he had relied on Pacifico's uncorroborated
word as to the damages which he had suffered, although Pacifico had been guilty of forgery on a previous occasion. Finlay's claim was preposterous, for he was asking £1,500 for land
which he had bought for £10 or £20. All the evidence showed
that the Ionians had not been tortured, and Palmerston was

asking the Greek Government to pay damages for having arrested some thieves. It seemed very likely that the midshipman of the *Fantome* had in fact been lying, but even if he had not, Palmerston had made a mountain out of a molehill of the whole affair. Stanley thought that Londos's despatches to the British Government had been models of restraint, whereas Palmerston had sent notes to the Greek Government in language which, if any Ambassador in London had dared to use to us, would have been followed by his immediate expulsion from Britain. Stanley was supported by Lord Cardigan, who denounced all Palmerston's foreign policy. Cardigan was notorious for having flogged more men than any other officer in the Army; and he declared that in view of the fact that we frequently flogged rebels in India and in Cephalonia, he saw no reason why we should object if the Austrians and Neapolitans did the same in Italy and Hungary. The vote of censure was carried by 169 to 132, and Palmerston's only consolation was that he had obtained the support of the great majority of the Bishops.

Two days after the debate in the House of Lords, Palmerston informed the French Government that Britain would hand back to the Greeks the shares which had been deposited with Wyse, and would refer Pacifico's claim for compensation for the loss of the documents to the British, Greek and French arbitrators in Lisbon, as had been agreed in the London agreement. In all other respects, the Athens agreement would remain in force, so that Pacifico would receive £6,400, not £8,500, in respect of the other heads of damage. From Pacifico's point of view, this was worse than either the London or the Athens agreement. In due course, the three arbitrators mét in Lisbon and next year decided that Pacifico was entitled to £150, not £27,000, for the loss of his documents.

The affair of Don Pacifico had thus ended with a loss of prestige for Britain, a loss of prestige for Greece, some loss of prestige for Russia, and a considerable gain in prestige for Louis Napoleon. General Lahitte did not spare British feelings on this point; for he declared in the French Chamber, using more provocative language than Palmerston would ever have used about another great power in the House of Commons, that Palmerston had completely capitulated to the French demands. But if British international prestige had undoubtedly suffered by this surrender to France, as Palmerston had warned Lord John Russell that it would, the Government could still do something to save its prestige in Britain. Here the role of Lord John was decisive. He was the most vacillating and unpredictable politician in the country; but on this occasion his political intuition served him well. When Palmerston offered to resign, he refused to accept his resignation. Pressed by the Queen, the House of Lords, and most of responsible political opinion, to throw over Palmerston, he decided to back him to the full, and to appeal to the Commons against the Lords, and to the people of Britain against the Establishment. He really had little alternative, for after his Government had been defeated in the House of Lords he was confronted with the simple decision – to resign or not to resign. When Disraeli asked him in the House of Commons on 20 June whether the Government would resign, he announced that he would ask the House of Commons for a vote of confidence, and warmly praised Palmerston, declaring that Palmerston 'will act not as the Minister of Austria, or as the Minister of Russia, or of France, or of any other country, but as the Minister of England'.

On 24 June, Roebuck moved a resolution declaring that Palmerston's foreign policy was calculated to preserve the honour of England and to maintain peace and friendly relations with other countries. The debate lasted for four nights, and resulted in the greatest victory of Palmerston's career. He won by relying on the support of the patriotic Radicals, and by appealing to national pride and chauvinism, and to hatred of King Otho and all other Continental monarchies. It was a victory of emotionalism over reason, and of all the forces and instincts which Palmerston had always opposed. Roebuck opened the debate by attacking the House of Lords which had dared to vote against Palmerston, and urged the people's government not to resign merely because the peers were against it. He then proceeded to denounce King Otho, the Tsar, and the Austrians, and – last but not least – the French. In order to show how impudent it was of the French to criticize Palmerston for blockading Greece, he reminded the House, with superb lack of logic, how in 1831 the French had not merely blockaded but bombarded Lisbon, in order to bully 'poor little Portugal' – the Portugal of Miguel! He praised Palmerston for vindicating the honour of a British midshipman and for protecting the oppressed Jew, Pacifico; quoted 'our immortal bard', who had written 'Hath not a Jew eyes?'; sneered at 'our dear Aberdeen' – this was a gibe at the Queen – and at Cobden's Peace Society; and referred to 'the immeasurable superiority, the stern serenity, of the people of England ... soaring in our inapproachable greatness'.

Palmerston spoke on the second night of the debate. He rose to speak at a quarter to ten on the evening of 25 June, and spoke for nearly the whole of the short summer night, sitting down just as dawn was breaking at twenty past two, after speaking for more than four and a half hours. He had prepared his speech very carefully, but he held no notes except a half-sheet of paper with a few notes on it. He had two oranges and a glass of water beside him, but he did not touch them during his speech. The House was packed, and the tension was great. Palmerston said that the issue involved was a simple one: ought the British Government to protect British subjects and enforce their claims against foreign governments if the British subjects could not get redress through the foreign law courts? He insisted that Britain was entitled to do this in all countries where there was no constitutional government, and also in constitutional states where the courts were not independent of the government. He talked about all the misdeeds of the Greek Government, and claimed that Pacifico's previous misconduct should not debar him from receiving justice; if a man has done wrong, 'Punish him if you will – punish him if he is guilty, but don't pursue him as a Pariah through life'. Nor would he accept that 'because a man is of the Jewish persuasion, he is fair game for any outrage'.

He then passed to a review and a defence of the whole of his foreign policy, moving from 'the sunny plains of Castille and the gay vineyards of France' to 'the mountains of Switzerland'. He had been criticized earlier in the debate by Sir James Graham, who pointed out that he had utterly failed in his object of establishing constitutional government in Spain and Portugal. Palmerston dealt with this criticism by blandly assuring the House that Narváez's Government was a constitutional one, although he had just read out his despatch to Bulwer of 16 March 1848 in which he denounced Narváez for his tyranny; and he tried hard to make out that the Spanish Government's note, in which they had suggested that diplomatic relations with Britain should be resumed, was an apology for their conduct in expelling Bulwer. He denied that he had instigated revolution in Europe, and that he had incited the Swiss Government to attack the Sonderbund in 1847; and he defended himself against most of the accusations of the Conservatives, one of whom called him a 'Red' in the course of the debate. In repudiating the Conservative attacks, Palmerston said many things which ought to have displeased the Radicals; but they did not notice. Palmerston said one thing and they heard him say something else.

He ended with a passage which made a deep appeal, which expressed the fundamental philosophy of early Victorian England, and was probably largely responsible for the success of his speech and the immortality which it achieved. Unlike the rest of the speech, he had learned it by heart. He said that he could not blame the Opposition for trying to defeat the Government and gain power for themselves, for

the government of a great country like this is undoubtedly an object of fair and legitimate ambition to men of all shades of opinion. ...For while we have seen ... the political earthquake rocking Europe from side to side; while we have seen thrones shaken, shattered, levelled, institutions overthrown and destroyed; while in almost every country of Europe the conflict of civil war has deluged the land with blood, from the Adriatic to the Black Sea, from the Baltic to the Mediterranean; this country has presented a spectacle honourable to the people of England, and worthy of the admiration of mankind. We have shown that liberty is compatible with order; that individual freedom is reconcilable with obedience to the law. We have shown the example of a nation in which every class of society accepts with cheerfulness the lot which Providence has assigned to it; while at the same time every individual of each class is constantly striving to raise himself in the social scale – not by injustice and wrong, not by violence and illegality – but by persevering good conduct, and by the steady and energetic exertion of the moral and intellectual faculties with which his Creator has endowed him. To govern such a people as this, is indeed an object worthy of the ambition of the noblest man who lives in the land.

But he did not think that the Government had done anything to forfeit the confidence of the country; and he therefore asked the House, 'as representing a political, a commercial, a constitutional country', to decide

whether, as the Roman, in days of old, held himself free from indignity when he could say *Civis Romanus sum*; so also a British subject, in whatever land he may be, shall feel confident that the watchful eye and the strong arm of England will protect him against injustice and wrong.

When he sat down, they cheered and cheered, and it seemed that the cheering would never stop.

The speech was a tremendous success, not only among the MPs who heard it in the House, but also among all the middle-class Englishmen who read it in their newspapers. The debate continued for another two days, but no one could say anything to counter its effect. It was useless for Gladstone to talk for over three hours on the duty to respect the rights of others and the need for observing a code of morality in international affairs. It was useless for Cobden to point out that Palmerston had not intervened in Greece in order to liberate the Greek people from the tyranny of King Otho, and had given no support to the Hungarians during their struggle against Austria and Russia. It was useless for Peel and Disraeli to refer to the fact that the French had forced Britain to climb down with regard to the claim for the loss of Pacifico's documents, and to quote the jubilant speeches of French politicians boasting of their victory over Palmerston. It was useless for any of them to show that the Romans who said *Civis Romanus sum* ruled over all the known world as a privileged race oppressing other peoples. The members would not listen, and Palmerston's opponents were constantly interrupted. They were all receiving letters from their constituents in support of Palmerston; and the House responded to the country. 310 MPs voted for the Government and 264 against – a majority of 46. All the Radicals, except Hume, voted for Palmerston; so did the old Chartist MPs like Wakley; and so did Anstey, who had moved Palmerston's impeachment two years before, but who now spoke in support of Palmerston and expressed himself as fully satisfied with everything that Palmerston had done since the impeachment debate of February 1848. Against him were Cobden and Bright and the great majority of the Conservatives.

Charles Greville, riding with Lord Grey in the park next day, agreed with him that the middle classes were solidly behind Palmerston. Bright and Cobden were expecting to lose their seats in Manchester and the West Riding because they had voted against Palmerston in the debate. Palmerston's admirers commissioned Partridge to paint a portrait of him, and presented it to Lady Palmerston; but Palmerston persuaded his friend Borthwick of the *Morning Post* not to report the highly provocative speech which Lady Palmerston made in accepting the portrait. Lady Palmerston was the most enthusiastic of all her husband's supporters. When she heard that Greville had been criticizing Palmerston, she wrote him an indignant letter, which was much talked of in society. Her friends said that Lady Palmerston had been so nasty to Greville on this occasion because she had been much too nice to him in the past.

Palmerston was invited to a celebration dinner by two hundred and fifty members of the Reform Club. He told William Temple that if they had wished they could have held the dinner at Covent Garden and had over a thousand people present. It was a thoroughly patriotic, Radical and middle-class affair. Lord John Russell and all the Cabinet ministers, except Palmerston, refused an invitation to attend, and no one who was known in society was there. The guests greeted Palmerston enthusiastically, sang *God save the Queen* at the top of their voices, cheered loudly at the line 'Confound their politics, frustrate their knavish tricks', and thoroughly enjoyed their nine-course dinner with eighty-one different dishes. Palmerston himself was quite restrained in his speech. He stated that Britain would always support the cause of freedom throughout the world, and that no nation was any more eager to go to war with Britain than Britain was to go to war with it. The chairman, Bernal Osborne, spoke in Palmerston's praise, and applying the words of 'one of the greatest and most favoured of modern writers', said that if foreign Governments hated Palmerston, 'This proved his worth; hereafter be our boast: Who hated Britons hated him the most'. Bulwer-Lytton was not altogether pleased at this misquotation from his poem. He himself described Palmerston as 'mamma England's spoilt child'; when he went wild and broke all the crockery, the proud mother told everyone how high-spirited he was.

Palmerston's critics were limited to a small number of educated people, most of them members of his own class, and many of them his personal friends; his supporters were the country squires and country parsons, the solicitors and doctors in the towns, the City of London, nearly all the Jews, the business men – even those in Manchester – and the great mass of the working class who talked about Palmerston in the inns. They were all firmly convinced that the vote against Palmerston in the House of Lords, and all criticism of him, was part of a foreign conspiracy to get rid of the Minister of England. Palmerston himself accepted this far-fetched theory, and wrote to his brother William about 'a foreign conspiracy, aided and abetted by a domestic intrigue'; but as usual he bore no personal ill-will against his opponents, and praised the speeches of Gladstone, Peel and Disraeli in the debate. Among his own side, he was most impressed, not by the emotionalism of any of the enthusiastic Radicals who had supported him, but by the coolly-reasoned speech of Sir Alexander Cockburn, the Attorney-General, who made the only speech in favour of Palmerston's policy which was purely rational in its approach. Palmerston thought that it was the best speech that he had ever heard. He was delighted at his great victory, and his great popularity in the country. He thought that there would have been demonstrations in his support all over Britain if the Government had been defeated in the Commons, and had resigned.

The British people were sure that Palmerston would protect them wherever they might be. In the debate Roebuck had declared that though the Tsar could send any of his own subjects to Siberia at his whim, Palmerston would never permit him to do the same to a British subject. The public looked for action in April 1850 when they heard how a West Indian negro, who was a British subject, had been dragged off a British ship in Charleston harbour and sentenced to two months' imprisonment under the law of South Carolina which made it an offence for a free negro to be at large in the state. The negro, who was named Bowers, was the steward on the ship which was sailing from Liverpool to Havana. The ship's master, Mr. Waddington, who knew the law of South Carolina, advised all his negro crew to leave the ship at Boston, because she was due to call at Charleston on the voyage to Havana; but, though all the other negroes followed his advice, Bowers insisted on staying with the ship. When they reached Charleston he was arrested on board ship by the South Carolina authorities, and sentenced to sixty days' imprisonment. When the ship returned to Charleston on the return journey from Havana, Bowers was released and put on board, after Waddington had paid the costs of his trial and imprisonment. Bowers claimed his wages from the shipowners for the time when he had been in jail at Charleston, as it was during the period covered by his contract of service; but the shipowners, who had already been involved in expense through what they considered was Bowers's stupidity in not leaving the ship at Boston, refused to pay. Bowers then sued the shipowners for the wages in the Thames Police Court in London.

The sympathies of Mr. Yardley, the magistrate, were entirely with the seaman, and he gave judgment in his favour. During the hearing, both the magistrate and Bowers's solicitor, Mr. Pelham, expressed themselves freely about what had occurred, and their remarks were reported in the *Morning Post*:

'*Mr. Yardley.* What was the steward sent to prison for?

'*Mr. Waddington.* To prevent his contaminating the slaves. No free person of colour is allowed to be at large either at New Orleans or at Charleston, and if any man of colour is found on board ship of any country, the sheriff takes him out and charges the ship with the expense.

'*Mr. Pelham.* This is free America – the boasted land of

liberty, where a man is imprisoned for his complexion. What crime had this man committed?

'*Mr. Waddington.* A very great one. He is a black man; that is a crime in the slaveholding states of America.

'*Mr. Pelham.* I think this is a case for Lord Palmerston'.

The case was reported in the press under the headline: 'A case for Lord Palmerston', and the editorials declared that the nation was looking to Palmerston to prevent such treatment of a British subject. But Palmerston knew that the United States was not Greece, and he refused to take any action, even though he had justification under international law. When MPs pointed out that the Anglo-American treaty of 1815 guaranteed freedom of movement to each other's nationals in Britain and the United States, and that this treaty-right was violated when peaceful British subjects were punished for entering South Carolina, Palmerston told the House that the United States Government took the view that this clause must be interpreted as permitting freedom of movement only in so far as this was not forbidden by local law; and that if Britain would not accept this interpretation, the United States would give twelve months' notice of their intention to rescind the treaty. Palmerston argued that, in view of this, nothing would be gained by raising the matter with the United States. Bowers discovered that it was as pointless to say *Civis Britannicus sum* in South Carolina as in Bokhara; but this did not shake the belief of the British public that Palmerston would protect them throughout the world. Even if he could sometimes do nothing, he always gave the impression that he was trying to do something; and his compatriots remained convinced that any injustice to an Englishman abroad was 'a case for Lord Palmerston'.

Chapter Twenty-eight

The Dismissal from the Foreign Office

When Queen Victoria came to the throne, Palmerston had every reason to believe that his relations with his new Sovereign would be very satisfactory. He had had difficulties with William IV, because, though the old King liked Palmerston personally, he had disapproved of his policy of friendship with France and his support of constitutional government in Germany. The young girl of eighteen seemed likely to be more amenable. The Prime Minister, Lord Melbourne, was her greatest friend and support, and Lady Cowper was one of her favourite ladies-in-waiting; so Palmerston had good friends in the closest proximity to the Queen. He himself saw a great deal of Victoria. During the first two years of her reign he was very often in attendance at Windsor Castle and at the Brighton Pavilion. He went riding with her, and, with Melbourne and Hobhouse, gave her contradictory and bad advice when she played chess. She considered that Lord Palmerston, like Lord Melbourne, was a charming man. These were the days before the Queen married Prince Albert, when she sometimes danced all night, and Wellington described her as being very gay.

Victoria's opinion of Palmerston was shaken when she discovered that the avuncular statesman whose manners were so gentlemanlike had been caught in the bedroom of one of her ladies-in-waiting in the middle of the night at Windsor Castle. She considered that, in the circumstances, this attempt on the virtue of Mrs. Brand was an affront to herself. It was just about the time when Victoria and Albert were married in February 1840. Albert implanted a new seriousness in Victoria, who was completely devoted to him and adopted his strict moral code. He completely replaced Melbourne as the

Queen's confidant. He acted as her private secretary and made her interested in politics. Within a year of her marriage, she had her first disagreement with Palmerston on foreign policy, when she criticized his reluctance to facilitate a rapprochement with France in the winter of 1840-1, after the Mehemet Ali crisis. In this she was encouraged by her uncle, King Leopold of Belgium, who warned Albert that 'Palmerston, rex and autocrat', was 'far too irritable and violent'. When Melbourne's Government fell, the Queen and Albert found the foreign policy of Peel and Aberdeen more to their liking than Palmerston's, and strongly supported Aberdeen's policy of friendship with Louis Philippe.

Victoria and Albert were sorry when Aberdeen left the Foreign Office and Palmerston returned in 1846; and the trouble about the Spanish marriages within a few weeks confirmed their worst fears. Although they blamed the conduct of Guizot and Louis Philippe in revealing Palmerston's despatch of 19 July to the Spanish Government, they felt that the difficulty would never have arisen but for Palmerston's foolish action in criticizing Narváez and the Spanish Government in his despatch, and his unjustifiable interference in Spanish internal affairs in order to support the Spanish Radicals. They disapproved still more of his policy towards Portugal, and his determination to prevent Maria da Gloria from punishing her rebellious subjects. Prince Albert paid a grudging tribute to the success of Palmerston's policy in Switzerland in 1847; but he and the Queen opposed Palmerston's friendly attitude towards the new French Republic in 1848, and Palmerston's support of Sardinia against Austria during the war in Italy in 1848-9. They also disapproved of his policy in resisting the attempts of Russia and Austria to obtain the extradition of the Poles and Hungarians from Turkey, and his bullying behaviour towards King Otho in the case of Don Pacifico.

The Queen and Prince had another complaint against Palmerston. As long as William IV was alive, Palmerston always submitted to the King the drafts of his despatches to foreign governments before he sent them off to the British embassies abroad; and William often insisted on making alterations in Palmerston's draft. When Victoria came to the throne, Palmerston began to acquire the habit of sending off the despatches without submitting them to the Queen. In June 1838 he told his Under-Secretary that he was sure that the Queen would not wish to be troubled with despatches during Ascot week, and that she should therefore be sent as few of them as possible. It was only after Victoria married Albert that she realized what Palmerston was doing. In October 1840 Albert wrote a letter to Palmerston, telling him that the Queen wished to see the drafts of all despatches before they were sent. Palmerston promised to see that this was done.

During the civil war in Portugal in 1846-7, Victoria and Albert discovered that Palmerston was sending despatches to Southern and Seymour in Lisbon without having shown the drafts to the Queen. They reprimanded Palmerston, who expressed his deep regret and blamed his staff at the Foreign Office for having carelessly failed to send the despatches to the palace; but as the Queen insisted on altering many of his drafts in order to tone down his expressions of friendship for the French Republic and for Sardinia, and his criticism of Austria and King Otho of Greece, Palmerston continued to send despatches from time to time without having obtained the Queen's prior approval. The Queen's reprimands became sharper. Eventually, in September 1848, both Victoria and Albert asked Lord John Russell to remove Palmerston from the Foreign Office. Lord John was embarrassed by the conflict between the Queen and Palmerston. He did not entirely approve of Palmerston's conduct, and he was eager to please the Queen; but he did not wish to anger the Radical and Liberal MPs who admired Palmerston and on whose support the Government relied. He suggested that when an appropriate opportunity presented itself, Palmerston should leave the Foreign Office and become Leader of the House of Commons, while he himself should become Foreign Secretary and go to the House of Lords. The Queen did not like the idea of having Palmerston as Leader of the House, but she agreed to Russell's suggestion as being the best way of getting rid of Palmerston as Foreign Secretary. Palmerston rejected the proposal. When the House of Lords censured his policy about Don Pacifico, Victoria and Albert thought that he would at last be forced to resign; but after his triumph in the House of Commons, this was out of the question. Palmerston's popularity had never been higher than on the morning after 25 June 1850. Russell now supported him wholeheartedly, and was convinced that the Queen and Prince would make no further attempt against Palmerston for some time.

But Prince Albert returned to the attack within little more than a fortnight, and raised a new issue. On 11 July he had an interview with Russell and told him, as the Prince noted in his diary, that 'I felt it necessary that he should know the full extent of the Queen's objections to Lord Palmerston, which were connected with her knowledge of Lord Palmerston's worthless private character. How could the Queen consent to take a man as her chief adviser and confidential counsellor in all matters of State, religion, society, Court, etc., he who, as her Secretary of State, and while under her roof at Windsor Castle, had committed a brutal attack upon one of her ladies? Had at night, by stealth, introduced himself into her apartment, barricaded the door, and would have consummated his fiendish scheme by violence had not the miraculous efforts of his victim and such assistance attracted by her screams, saved her'. Russell admitted that Palmerston's conduct had been very bad, and made it impossible for him ever to become Prime Minister; and he told Albert that unfortunately he knew another lady in society with whom Palmerston had tried the same thing. But he reminded Albert that Palmerston was now sixty-five, and he thought that he was too old to cause much trouble in future.

In August, Albert drafted a memorandum which the Queen sent to the Prime Minister. In it, she demanded that Palmerston should give an undertaking not to send off any despatches without first submitting them to her, and to give an accurate summary of his conversations with all foreign Ambassadors. Russell thought that the memorandum was so humiliating that no minister would ever accept it, and that Palmerston would be certain to resign; but Palmerston agreed without protest to do as the Queen required. A few days later, Palmerston had an interview with the Prince, at which he behaved in a very different manner from the way in which his Radical supporters would have imagined that the patriotic Minister for England would handle a royal German meddler. He was very humble, and said how deeply he regretted having offended the Queen. Political disagreements were one thing, but to accuse him of having offended a Princess whom he admired so greatly both as his Sovereign and as a woman was an aspersion on his conduct as a gentleman, and he deeply regretted that he had given cause for such complaints to be made. Albert noted that Palmerston had tears in his eyes as he spoke. Albert allowed him to finish without interrupting him, and then told him somewhat sternly, but not unkindly, that he hoped he would mend his ways in future.

In September 1850, General Haynau visited England. Haynau had been singled out in the British press as the man primarily responsible for the flogging of women and all the other atrocities which the Austrians had committed in Italy and Hungary. Under the nickname of 'General Hyena', he was bitterly hated throughout Britain. When the General visited Barclay's brewery in Southwark, he was set upon by the workers in the brewery and given a sound thrashing. He fled through the streets to a public house, where he was rescued by the river police. The Queen immediately demanded that the Government should send an apology to the Austrian Government for this outrage against 'one of the Emperor's distinguished Generals', as she called Haynau. Palmerston entirely agreed that an apology must be sent, though he was personally as delighted as any man in England at what had occurred, and said so very plainly in his private letters to Sir George Grey, the Home Secretary. He duly wrote an official despatch for Ponsonby to present to Schwarzenberg, in which he expressed his regret for the attack on Haynau, but added that it was most ill-advised for Haynau to have come to England, in view of the indignation which was felt against him throughout the country. He told the Austrian Ambassador that it would be foolish for the Austrian Government to press for a prosecution to be brought against the workers at the brewery, because if they were put on trial, the defence counsel would obviously bring up all the atrocities which Haynau had committed in Italy and Hungary.

When Palmerston showed the Queen the draft of the despatch which he had sent to Vienna, she was indignant at his language. She insisted that Palmerston should send an unreserved and very ample apology, and that all criticisms of Haynau's visit should be deleted. Palmerston then told her that it was too late to make the alterations, as the despatch had already been sent to Vienna. The Queen had never been so angry with Palmerston. She insisted that he take the unprecedented step of writing another despatch to Ponsonby, instructing him to tell Schwarzenberg that the previous despatch was cancelled, and to substitute a new despatch expressing an unqualified apology. Palmerston told Russell that such a despatch would have to be signed by another Foreign Secretary, and that he would resign rather than comply; and Russell thought that Palmerston would never stomach such a humiliation. But Palmerston did everything that the Queen had commanded, and did not resign.

In the summer of 1851, the Turkish Government at last summoned up its courage, and, despite Russian and Austrian protests, agreed to permit the Hungarian and Polish refugees to leave Turkey. This was partly due to the pressure which Palmerston had put on them to do so, and his promise to support them against any measures which the Russians and Austrians might take; but the chief credit was due to the United States Government, who offered to take all the refugees and to send the American Navy to transport them from Turkey to the United States. A few of the refugees chose to come to Britain, including Kossuth himself. There were reports that the Russians and Austrians were intending to send their fleet to intercept Kossuth at sea, and remove him to an Austrian prison; so the United States sent a frigate to fetch him from Constantinople. When Kossuth arrived at Southampton, he was given a great reception; he was entertained at a banquet by the Mayor and Corporation, and thousands of people turned out to cheer him at the Guildhall. The English Radicals who organized his visit brought him to London by road in short stages, and he was entertained at banquets by the local authorities all along the route. The Queen was angry, and the Cabinet were a little anxious about the effect on relations with

Austria; but the *Morning Post* announced that when Kossuth reached London, he was going to call on Palmerston to express his thanks for everything that Palmerston had done for the refugees in Turkey.

As soon as this announcement appeared, Lord John Russell was approached by numerous colleagues, and urged to prevent Palmerston from receiving Kossuth; and the Queen was even more insistent about this. Russell spoke to Palmerston about it; but Palmerston refused to give any undertaking not to receive Kossuth. He made it clear to Russell that he did not wholly approve of Kossuth, and said that if Kossuth went on making the extreme statements which he was reported to have made on the American frigate, he would soon lose all influence in Britain; but he said that Lord Dudley Stuart and many local authorities had asked him to receive Kossuth, and he intended to do so, for 'even if he is mad as you say, and which is not unlikely, I am not afraid of his biting me.' Russell then asked the Queen to send a direct order to Palmerston forbidding him to meet Kossuth; but when Russell transmitted the order to him, Palmerston merely replied that he would not be dictated to as to whom he should receive in his own house.

On 3 November, Russell raised the matter in the Cabinet. After all the ministers had stated that it would be unwise and improper for Palmerston to meet Kossuth, Palmerston agreed not to do so. Greville wrote in his diary: 'The end was that Palmerston (as he has invariably done on all other occasions when tackled and driven to submit or resign) knocked under, and agreed not to receive Kossuth'. But two days later, Palmerston received a deputation from the boroughs of Islington and Finsbury, who came to present him with a memorial thanking him for what he had done for the Hungarians in Turkey. Finsbury was one of the most Radical areas in the country. It had been sending a Radical to Parliament when Palmerston first entered the House, and afterwards had been one of the very few constituencies in Britain to return a Chartist MP. In the address, the deputation thanked Palmerston for having saved the Poles and Hungarians from those despots, tyrants and odious assassins, the Emperors of Austria and

Russia. Palmerston replied in a short speech in which, after stating that they could not expect him to endorse the language which they had used about the Tsar and the Emperor of Austria, he thanked them for the honour which they had done to him in making the presentation. The ceremony was a private one, but a journalist was present, and the speeches were reported in the press. The Queen, Prince Albert, and all Palmerston's critics thought, like Greville, that this was even worse than if Palmerston had received Kossuth. But Russell knew that in view of the public enthusiasm for Kossuth, it was impossible to throw out Palmerston on this issue.

A more suitable issue arose within a month. In France, Louis Napoleon had been consolidating his position and playing off all his opponents against each other. In 1848 he had become President with the support of the Socialists who hated the bourgeois Republicans; in 1851 he could become dictator with the support of all who feared the Socialists. In case fear of Communism and democracy was not enough, he spread a wholly unfounded rumour of a plot to restore Louis Philippe to the throne. The feeling grew, on all sides, that only Louis Napoleon could restore security to France; and this feeling took root abroad, and in the most unlikely places. 'France needs a Napoleon', wrote the Duke of Wellington. The arch-Tory, Lord Londonderry, believed that they could trust Louis Napoleon to save France from Socialism. 'I feel every confidence in his pluck, firmness and prudence', he wrote to Lord John Russell. Palmerston felt the same way, and was alarmed, not only at the danger of Socialism, but also at the story of the plot to restore Louis Philippe. On this issue, Palmerston was quite isolated from his Radical supporters. The Radicals had mistrusted Louis Napoleon ever since he crushed the Roman Republic. Palmerston thought that Louis Napoleon alone could save France from anarchy.

On 2 December 1851 – the anniversary of the coronation of Napoleon I and of the battle of Austerlitz – Louis Napoleon dissolved the National Assembly, arrested Thiers, Cavaignac and the leaders of the Republicans, and carried through a coup d'état. The British Radicals were indignant, and so were most of the Liberals and many Conservatives. 'That one man', wrote the Duke of Argyll, 'without the shadow of a legal right, should arrest in their beds some dozens of the most distinguished citizens of France, and should march them off to prison under the guard of a file of soldiers, seemed simply an act of coarse and brutal violence'. That sure weathercock of public opinion, Alfred Tennyson, wrote a poem denouncing Louis Napoleon. If Palmerston had realized that the people would react so violently, he might have acted differently; but on the day after the coup d'état, he had discussed the coup with the French Ambassador in London, Count Walewski, who was the illegitimate son of Napoleon I and Marie Walewska. He told Walewski that he congratulated Louis Napoleon on the coup d'état. On the same day, he wrote a private letter to Lord Normanby, the Ambassador in Paris. He told Normanby that it was one thing to admire constitutional government in a country like England, where the constitution was rooted in antiquity, but quite another to respect the constitution of a country like France, which had had five revolutions since 1789. He referred to the French Constitution of 1850 as 'the day-before-yesterday tomfoolery which the scatterbrain heads of Marrast and Tocqueville invented for the torment and perplexity of the French nation', and added: 'It was high time to get rid of such childish nonsense; and as the Assembly seemed to be resolved that it should not be got rid of quietly and by deliberate alteration and amendment, I do not wonder that the President determined to get rid of them as obstacles to all rational arrangement. If, indeed, as we suppose, they meant to strike a sudden blow at him, he was quite right on that ground also to knock them down first'.

Queen Victoria was suspicious of the Bonapartists, and would have preferred to see a restoration of Louis Philippe. Many of the Whigs in the Government also disapproved of the coup d'état; and when the matter was discussed in the Cabinet on 5 December, it was decided to adopt a strictly neutral attitude towards the recent events in France. Palmerston therefore sent a despatch to Normanby instructing him to adopt an attitude of strict neutrality. When Normanby told Turgot, Louis Napoleon's Foreign Minister, that British policy was to be neutral about the coup, Turgot replied that he was surprised to hear this, as Walewski had reported that Palmerston warmly approved of it.

Normanby was sympathetic to the French Republicans. He was also, like most other British diplomats, on rather bad terms with Palmerston. He wrote to Palmerston and complained that Palmerston had placed him in a very embarrassing position by giving him instructions to say one thing in Paris, and then saying something else to the French Ambassador in London. Queen Victoria had been annoyed at Normanby's sympathies with the French Republicans, and had criticized him to Palmerston for this reason in 1848; but Normanby's brother, General Phipps, was Prince Albert's equerry, and was in favour at Court. While Normanby wrote and protested in his despatches to Palmerston, Lady Normanby wrote in stronger terms to General Phipps, who passed on the information to Prince Albert.

Palmerston wrote to Normanby explaining why he had acted as he did, and stating that when he spoke to Walewski, he was merely expressing his personal opinion. There was nothing very provocative in the despatch; but when the Queen wished to make a correction in the draft, she was told that Palmerston had already sent it off. She then demanded that Russell dismiss Palmerston. Here was an issue on which Palmerston would have no sympathy from the Radicals. Russell wrote him a very short note on 19 December demanding his resignation from the Foreign Office, and offering him the post of Lord Lieutenant of Ireland and a peerage of the United Kingdom.

Palmerston was very angry. He refused the offer of Ireland and the peerage, and withdrew to Broadlands. Russell told him to deliver the seals of office to the Queen at Windsor at 2.30 p.m. on 26 December; but he did not go, apparently because of a misunderstanding for which he later apologized to the Queen. After the Queen and Prince had waited till four o'clock for him, they accepted the surrender of the seals from Russell. Lady Palmerston complained bitterly to all her friends about Lord John's disgraceful behaviour in throwing over Palmerston. The *Morning Post* and the *Morning Chronicle* worked up a protest campaign against Palmerston's dismissal, and the Radicals denounced it as a foreign royalist plot to get rid of the people's minister. *The Times*, which, as always, was anti-Palmerston, pointed out to the Radicals that Palmerston had been dismissed for supporting the setting-up of the dictatorship of Louis Napoleon; but the Radicals continued to denounce both Louis Napoleon and Palmerston's dismissal from the Foreign Office. The Chartist paper, *Reynolds' Weekly*, published a poem denouncing 'small Lord John' for having 'turned adrift Lord Palmerston . . . for he's the people's darling'. The Radicals accused Albert, the foreign Prince, of having been responsible for the dismissal of the 'Minister of England'.

According to Delane, the editor of *The Times*, who was biassed but was usually well-informed, Palmerston himself thought of secretly adopting this line. Delane said that Palmerston engaged the services of a scurrilous journalist named Phillips, invited him to Broadlands, gave him the relevant information and documents, and paid him £100 to write a pamphlet attacking Prince Albert. But Lord Lansdowne pointed out to Palmerston that if the pamphlet were published, it would do no harm to Prince Albert, but would do a very great deal of harm to Palmerston; and Palmerston therefore suppressed the pamphlet, paid off the journalist, and tried to destroy every copy that had been printed. When Delane succeeded, with great difficulty, in gettng hold of a copy, he found that it was much less scurrilous than he had been led to believe.

On 3 February 1852, the House of Commons re-assembled after the autumn recess, and the Radicals raised the question of Palmerston's dismissal. Everyone was expecting a great fighting speech from Palmerston in the spirit of his Don Pacifico speech. But Russell explained that Palmerston had been dismissed because he had supported Louis Napoleon's coup d'état, and because he had sent off despatches without submitting them to the Queen; and he read out the Queen's memorandum to Palmerston of August 1850. This shook the Radicals, and it shook Palmerston; for the Radicals were quite taken aback to hear how Palmerston had submitted to the humiliating memorandum in order to remain in office. Palmerston said afterwards that he was not expecting Russell to make the memorandum public, and he complained to his friends that by doing so, Russell had acted unfairly, because it introduced the Queen's name into the controversy, and made it impossible for Palmerston to defend himself without attacking a lady whom he respected as a Sovereign and a woman; but Russell had in fact informed him three days before that he would read out the memorandum to the House. Palmerston sat in the House with his head in his hands – feeling, according to Disraeli, like a beaten fox – and when he spoke it was a halting and most unconvincing performance. Political observers felt that he had discredited himself, and Disraeli said to Bulwer: 'There *was* a Palmerston'.

Palmerston was soon to show that there was still a Palmerston; but the Palmerston of the last few years was indeed no more. His dismissal from the Foreign Office ended his Radical phase. He did not immediately lose all his Radical support overnight, and he never completely lost it; but events had made it impossible for him to continue his performance in the strange role of a Radical leader. It was one thing to attend banquets at the Reform Club with middle-class Liberals when no other member of society was present; but it was another to lead a Radical assault on the monarchy. Palmerston had gone as far as he could go in alliance with the Radicals; but there were other possibilities open to an elder statesman out of office at a time when there were four parties in the House of Commons, and none of them could survive without the support of one of the others. The Whigs, under Lord John Russell, had about 330 MPs, or just under half the total members of the House; the Tories – or, as they now called themselves, the Conservatives – under Lord Derby, had about 200; the Peelites had about 100; and the Irish Nationalists had about 35. Peel had died after falling from his horse a few days after his speech in the Don Pacifico debate, and the Peelites were now led by Lord Aberdeen, Sir James Graham, Sidney Herbert and Gladstone. They supported the Whigs against the Conservatives on free trade, but opposed them on other issues, especially on Palmerston's bellicose foreign policy.

Louis Napoleon's coup d'état had aroused great fears in Britain, where the people began to think that a second

Napoleon was on the point of preparing another Grand Army for the invasion of England. The Government decided to strengthen the national defences, and put the Army into training at a camp on Chobham Heath in Surrey; and the people sang: 'If Boney comes to Chobham Camp we'll show him English power'. For the first time for twenty years, Palmerston was completely out of sympathy with public opinion in favouring a policy of friendship with the Government of France – the same policy which had caused his unpopularity in 1832. He therefore kept quiet about Louis Napoleon, but took the opportunity of advocating the cause which he had so much at heart – the need for more armaments, coastal fortifications, and greater military preparedness. He said that having powerful military forces was like taking an umbrella on a fine day: if you took it you were sure not to need it, but if you did not take it you would regret it.

On 16 February 1852, Lord John Russell's Government introduced the Militia Bill in the House of Commons. It provided for setting up local militia in the counties, and for their equipment and military training. Palmerston moved an amendment urging that a national militia should be established, and argued that a centralized organization was necessary, as an invader could not be repulsed by local bodies that were not organized on a national basis. The Government opposed the amendment, but the Conservatives supported it, and on 20 February it was carried by a majority of thirteen votes. Lord John Russell resigned. The Palmerstons were jubilant: this was their revenge for Palmerston's dismissal from the Foreign Office. Two months after Palmerston's fall, and seventeen days after his humiliation in the House of Commons, he had shown that the Government could not survive without him. Lady Palmerston, who had been in the Ladies' Gallery during the debate, rushed home to give a victory party; and on 24 February Palmerston wrote to his brother: 'My dear William, I have had my tit-for-tat with John Russell, and I turned him out on Friday last'.

The Queen asked Lord Derby to form a Government. In view of the weakness of the Conservatives in the House, Derby searched for allies, and turned to Palmerston. He invited

Palmerston to be Chancellor of the Exchequer and Leader of the House of Commons. The Exchequer was no longer the job for young men that it had been when Palmerston was offered it at the age of twenty-five; it was now considered to be the second office in the Cabinet. But Palmerston, despite his bitterness against Lord John Russell, had no wish to precipitate himself into the arms of the Conservatives without very careful consideration; and he refused the Exchequer in 1852, as he had done in 1809 and 1827. Derby formed a purely Conservative Government, with Disraeli as Chancellor of the Exchequer and Leader of the House. Lord John Russell became Leader of the Opposition, and Palmerston, sitting on the Opposition benches but a little apart from the Whigs in the House, adopted a sympathetic attitude towards the Conservatives whom he had put in power. In view of Palmerston's deep-rooted Toryism, and his past career, the political observers began to wonder if he would join the Conservatives. For some years past, he had been on friendly personal terms with Disraeli, and now their contacts increased. He was also friendly with the Conservative Foreign Secretary, Lord Malmesbury who was the grandson of the old Lord Malmesbury who had been Palmerston's guardian forty years before, and had obtained for him his first political office as a Junior Lord of the Admiralty in 1807. Palmerston was glad to have the opportunity of repaying Malmesbury for the political assistance and training in diplomacy which he himself had received from Malmesbury's grandfather, and he gave the new Foreign Secretary disinterested and patriotic advice as to how to run the nation's foreign policy. He told him that the most important thing to remember was that England's prestige was very high abroad, and that a British Foreign Secretary must take care not to lower it by any act of weakness; and he reminded him that though it was advisable 'to keep well with France', the relationship of Britain and France in the Middle East was like that of two men who were in love with the same woman.

Derby and Disraeli continued to make unofficial approaches to Palmerston about the possibility of his joining the Government. Palmerston gave an equivocal answer but gave them to understand that he would like to accept. He was still in debt, and though he was making good progress in paying off the mortgages on Broadlands and his Irish estates, the loss of his ministerial salary was a worry to him, as it always was when he went into Opposition. The only real obstacle to his joining the Conservatives was free trade. Palmerston's political doctrines were flexible, and he had always been opportunistic in his attitude to political parties; but he had his principles, and there were none which he held more sincerely than his devotion to free trade. He flirted with the Conservatives, and enjoyed being wooed by them; but he hesitated to join them. He was hoping that, by holding out, he would be able to get them to agree to abandon their protectionist policy as a condition of his joining the Cabinet; and he had good grounds for this hope. There was a widespread feeling in the country that protection was out of date, and electorally a loser. Disraeli, who had risen to eminence in the Conservative Party by his vicious attacks on Peel for betraying protection by repealing the Corn Laws, was the first to advise Derby that the Government should declare themselves in favour of free trade. In the summer of 1852, Palmerston was invited to speak at a banquet of the Royal Agricultural Society in Lewes. The Sussex farmers were stoutly Tory and protectionist; but Palmerston, in his speech, made jokes, and talked about the use of chemical substances in agriculture and air pollution in the cities. He was loudly cheered when he condemned the importation of artificial manures from abroad at a time when manure was available on Sussex farms; but he did not commit himself politically.

In July 1852 a general election was held, and Palmerston went to Tiverton, where he and Heathcote were re-elected by a large majority after the usual conflict with Rowcliffe. In his speech at the hustings, he avoided talking about free trade, and Lady Palmerston pointed out to all her Conservative friends that he was not committed on the subject. His speech was calculated to appeal to Conservatives rather than to Radicals or Whigs; and when Rowcliffe accused him of being ready to join any government, whatever its political complexion, Palmerston said nothing to deny the possibility that he might take office in a Conservative Government. He merely replied gaily that he had at any rate never contemplated joining a Rowcliffe administration. He praised the British respect for past traditions, and stated that although in France and other Continental countries an innkeeper who wished to attract custom would call his inn 'The New White Horse', or 'The New Golden Cross', in England inns were called 'Old' – 'The Old Hats', or at most 'The Old Plough New Revived'; and there was an inn in the City which was not only called 'The Old King's Head', but also boasted that it was the oldest turtle house in London. He advocated increased expenditure on national defence, argued that because England had not been invaded since 1066 this did not mean that she would not be invaded in the future, and told the story of the silly old woman who lived in Henley when he was young, and who believed that there was no danger of Napoleon coming to Henley because the Young Pretender had never arrived.

Palmerston criticized the Chartist programme in his speech, and stated, amid laughter, that he was too old to become a Chartist. He particularly criticized the Chartist demand for voting by secret ballot. A resolution to introduce the ballot at Parliamentary elections had been regularly moved in the House of Commons at frequent intervals during the previous twenty years, and always defeated by large majorities. The chief argument against it was that it was shameful for free-born Englishmen to cast their vote secretly, and not openly; but a case which arose during the General Election of 1852 showed why the demand for the ballot was gaining ground. When some of Sir Roger Palmer's tenants voted against his candidate in County Mayo, they were evicted from their holdings by Sir Roger's land agent. They wrote to Sir Roger to inform him of what had occurred, only to be told that the land agent had acted on Sir Roger's authority, because they had been so ungrateful as to vote against his wishes at a Parliamentary election, and 'such conduct deserves punishment'.

Palmerston strongly disapproved of this kind of political victimization, but he remained unconvinced by the arguments in favour of the ballot. 'With regard to vote by ballot', he said at Tiverton, 'secret voting, I object to it, because I think it at variance with the national character, and with the principle of our constitution. I think a true Englishman hates doing a thing in secret or in the dark. I do not believe that a majority of Englishmen would consent to give their votes in secret, even if the law permitted them to do so; and I think if the law compelled them to do so, it would be a debasement of the national character. But I have a higher objection. I hold that the right of voting is a trust reposed in the elector for the public good. ... I say that any trust reposed in a man for the public good he ought to perform in public. I say, that for men who are charged with the high and important duty of choosing the best men to represent the country in Parliament to go sneaking to the ballot-box, and, poking in a piece of paper, looking round to see that no one could read it, is a course which is unconstitutional and unworthy of the character of straightforward and honest Englishmen'. But on another occasion when he was asked at Tiverton why he opposed the ballot and Parliamentary reform, he answered more briefly, and perhaps more honestly, that it was 'because we are not geese'.

The Conservatives gained over 100 seats in the General Election of 1852, while the Whigs and the Peelites each lost about 60 seats; but the Conservatives were still a minority in the House, having 310 members against 270 Whigs, 40 Peelites and 40 Irish Nationalists. The Conservatives now definitely decided to abandon protection, and declared themselves in favour of free trade. The Whigs moved a vote of censure on the Government, accusing them of insincerity in supporting free trade for purely opportunistic reasons. It was the first trial of strength in the new Parliament. No one knew which way Palmerston would vote. In fact, he moved an amendment, welcoming the Government's adoption of free trade, and deleting the criticisms in the Opposition motion. In his speech, he appealed to the Whigs not to rake up old animosities, but to accept the Conservative change of heart in a friendly spirit. 'We are here an assembly of gentlemen', he said, 'and we who are gentlemen on this side of the House should remember that we are dealing with gentlemen on the other side'. The Conservatives voted for Palmerston's amendment and it was carried against Lord John Russell and the Whigs.

Palmerston had saved Derby's Government; but not for long. In December, Disraeli introduced a supplementary budget which increased taxation in order to offset the loss of revenue from the repeal of customs duties on several classes of imports under the new free trade policy. The Whigs moved a vote of censure, and the Peelites supported them. Again everyone wondered what Palmerston would do. He stayed away from the House on the grounds of ill-health. Hardly anyone believed that his illness was genuine; but it may well have been, for he had suddenly grown very old at the age of sixty-eight. He had suffered his first attack of gout some years before; but these had become much worse during 1852. His friends noticed that now, for the first time, he walked like an old man.

The Government was defeated in the vote on the budget, and Derby resigned. Lord Aberdeen formed a coalition government of Whigs and Peelites, and offered Palmerston the post of First Lord of the Admiralty. After some hesitation, Palmerston declined. He would have liked, had it been possible, to return to the Foreign Office; but he knew that the Queen had decided that he should never again be Foreign Secretary. He had no particular desire for any other office; so he could not make up his mind whether to join a Whig-Peelite Government or to join Disraeli and the Conservatives in Opposition. But Lady Palmerston was very anxious that he should join the Government, as he had been out of office for a year, and they were beginning to feel the pinch without a ministerial salary. She dropped hints in the right places, and Aberdeen came back, offering Palmerston his pick of any department that he fancied except the Foreign Office. He chose the Home Office. On 23 December 1852, a year almost to the day after he resigned from Russell's Government, he became Home Secretary under Aberdeen. Lord John Russell was Foreign Secretary, but a few months later became Leader of the House of Commons, without portfolio, and was succeeded at the Foreign Office by Lord Clarendon, who as George Villiers had served so ably as Minister at Madrid during Palmerston's first term as Foreign Secretary. Gladstone was Chancellor of the Exchequer.

On 31 December, Palmerston wrote to his brother-in-law, Sulivan, and explained why he had taken office under Aberdeen. 'I have for the last twelve months been acting the part of a very distinguished tight-rope dancer and much astonishing the public by my individual performances and feats.... So far, so well; but even Madame Sacqui, when she had mounted her rope and flourished among her rockets, never thought of making the rope her perch, but prudently came down again to avoid a dangerous fall'. Palmerston had come down on the side of the Whigs and Peelites. His flirtation with the Conservatives was over.

Chapter Twenty-nine

Home Secretary: The Eastern Question

On 29 December 1852, Aberdeen and his ministers had their first Cabinet dinner. They got on well together from the first, and the young Duke of Argyll, who was a Peelite and joined the Cabinet as Lord Privy Seal, found Palmerston particularly affable to everyone. This general satisfaction did not extend to the Queen, who was not pleased to have Palmerston back in the Government, even though she was relieved that he was not at the Foreign Office. In September 1853, Aberdeen persuaded her to let Palmerston take his place as minister in attendance at Balmoral; but a few weeks later, she had a fresh cause of complaint against him. Palmerston suggested that Princess Mary of Cambridge, the Queen's cousin, should marry Napoleon III's cousin, Prince Napoleon Jerome, whom Napoleon III had nominated as heir to the French Imperial throne. Victoria did not like the Bonapartes, and Prince Napoleon, apart from being a Roman Catholic, was alleged to be a lascivious rake. She was indignant at Palmerston's suggestion. Palmerston explained to Aberdeen that though the Queen and the Duchess of Cambridge might be prejudiced against the marriage, this should not prevent a match which would be politically beneficial; and he had reason to believe that Princess Mary herself was favourable to the idea. At any rate, Prince Napoleon was good-looking and intelligent, 'and would be likely to make a better Husband than some petty Member of a petty German Prince's House'. When the Queen heard about Palmerston's letter, she was more angry than ever, and said that Palmerston had no reason whatever to say that Princess Mary was in favour of the proposal, as no one had ever mentioned it to her.

Palmerston set out to run the Home Office efficiently, and to master the details of his department as thoroughly as he had learned the details of the Belgian treaty or the Schleswig-Holstein problem. With the encouragement of Ashley – now Lord Shaftesbury – he introduced a number of measures to improve the conditions of the factory workers; but he listened to the objections of the factory owners, and took note of the practical difficulties which the civil servants and experts pointed out. He disappointed Shaftesbury and the ardent reformers by refusing to reduce the working hours of women and males under eighteen from 60 to $57\frac{1}{2}$ hours a week in the Factory Act of 1853; but the Act, which Palmerston introduced, removed many of the loopholes in the earlier Acts, and prohibited all labour by young persons between 6 p.m. and 6 a.m. He introduced a bill which confirmed the rights which had been granted to Trade Unions in the Act of 1825 to combine for lawful purposes; but he resisted the demands of the Unions, and of many MPs, to make peaceful picketing legal, for which the Unions had to wait till 1859; and in any case, Palmerston's bill was withdrawn in the House of Lords. Palmerston introduced the Truck Act, which prohibited employers from paying their workmen in goods instead of money, or from compelling them to buy supplies from shops owned by the employers. This removed a grievance which had been particularly resented by the mineworkers.

He dealt with the serious problem of smoke from coal fires, which had existed in London ever since the seventeenth century, but which had been made very much worse by the industrial revolution. London fogs were famous all over Europe, and the smoke of the murky industrial cities of the North was a characteristic feature of Victorian Britain. In August 1853 Palmerston moved the first Smoke Abatement Bill, which did a little good, though much too little to check an increasing evil. Some of his measures were opposed by interested parties, and theorists who did not believe that government interference with private liberty was ever justified; but Palmerston's belief in freedom of trade did not extend to tolerating practices which interfered with public health, and he entirely accepted the doctrine, which developed during this decade, that public health should be administered by Boards staffed by government officials with compulsory powers. He was responsible for the adoption in Britain of the system of compulsory vaccination, in which his father had always believed. When a private member's bill to make vaccination compulsory was introduced in 1853, Palmerston gave it cautious support, and persuaded the Government to adopt the bill, which became law.

His most controversial measure was the bill which prohibited the practice of burying the dead in churches, and which provided that, on grounds of public health, the corpses must be buried outside in the churchyard, or in a public cemetery. The right to be buried within the church itself was held by influential and wealthy parishioners whose families had purchased it in the past. Palmerston's bill violated ecclesiastical tradition, class privilege, vested interests and a profitable source of income for the Church. But Palmerston insisted that the bill was necessary for public health, and it became law. When the Mayor and corporation of Romsey approached Palmerston, as Lord High Steward of Romsey – a sinecure post, to which he had been appointed like his father before him – and asked him to prevent the closure of the burial place in Romsey Abbey, he refused to intervene.

Palmerston was receptive to the views of the Temperance societies, which were gaining ground rapidly in Victorian England. He had always been alive to the dangers of alcohol, if not of opium. Whatever his excesses in other respects, he had never been a heavy drinker, and drank almost as little now as when he was a student in Dugald Stewart's household in Edinburgh. When he was Secretary at War, in the days before Waterloo, he was eager to stop the soldiers from spending their bounties on drink; forty years later, as Home Secretary, he tried to discourage drinking in public houses. He did not mind if people drank at home, but he thought that beer-shops should only be granted an off-licence. 'The Beer Shops licensed to have the Beer drunk on the Premises', he wrote to Gladstone on 20 October 1853, 'are a Pest to the Community. They are Haunts of Thieves and Schools for Prostitutes. They demoralize the lower Classes. . . . The words "licensed to be drunk on the Premises" are by the common People interpreted as applicable to the Customers as well as to the Liquor'. But he would not agree to suppress betting. When he was urged to do so by a private member, Palmerston would neither support nor oppose it.

As Home Secretary, Palmerston became involved in the controversial question of prison reform. He was under constant pressure both from the experts, with their modern theories of penology, and the press and MPs who demanded in Parliament that prisoners should be treated more severely. Most of the prisons in England were county jails, over which Palmerston had no control; but by 1850, two great penitentiaries had been opened at Millbank and Pentonville, and the Home Office had purchased jails at Wakefield and Leicester. These Home Office prisons were run on the modern principle of solitary confinement, which had been introduced in many foreign countries, especially in the New England states of the USA. By the end of the nineteenth century, solitary confinement would be condemned as inhuman by prison reformers; in 1853 it was considered as a great advance which prevented young convicts and first offenders from being contaminated or terrorized by the hardened criminals in the prison with them. It was, however, only considered suitable for short-term prisoners, and no one was imprisoned in solitary confinement for more than eighteen months. Palmerston reduced this period to nine months. Long-term prisoners were transported to Van Diemen's Land – as Tasmania was then called – for seven or fourteen years, or for life. In Van Diemen's Land the well-behaved prisoners were put to work with local farmers, or even granted land of their own to farm, and allowed to roam freely in the district on ticket-of-leave. The worst offenders were sent to the penal settlements at Port Arthur, either as a punishment for misbehaviour in Van Diemen's Land, or as part of the original sentence. Here conditions were very severe, and discipline was enforced by savage floggings.

In 1853, the inhabitants of Van Diemen's Land and other British colonies objected so strongly to the presence of convicts in their midst that the British Government agreed to end the system of transportation. This raised the problem of how to punish the long-term prisoners. If a sentence of transportation was simply transposed into an equal sentence of imprisonment in an English penitentiary or county jail, the result would be greatly to increase the severity of the punishment; and though this would have satisfied many of the MPs and the public who for many years had been denouncing transportation as too soft a punishment, Palmerston and the Home Office experts and the penologists thought that this would be harsh and unjust. 'Men who were held out promise of ticket of leave in Van Diemen's Land *must* be set free now', wrote Palmerston to Aberdeen on 20 May 1853. Palmerston therefore introduced the Penal Servitude Bill in August 1853, which abolished transportation and substituted penal servitude in prisons in Britain, but which reduced the maximum sentence which could be imposed for most offences, and also provided that the Home Secretary could release prisoners in Britain on ticket-of-leave, as had been done in Van Diemen's Land.

This proposal aroused a great deal of opposition in Parliament and in the country, and was strenuously resisted in the House of Lords by Lord St. Leonards, who had been Lord Chancellor in Derby's Conservative Government. But Palmerston got the bill through. After it became law, he was confronted with repeated demands that it should be modified, and that the prisoners released on ticket-of-leave should be compelled to report to the police, and otherwise placed under observation; and he was also urged to make conditions in prison harsher, and the food less palatable. He ordered that prisoners should be compelled to undertake the strenuous labour on the crank, as well as on the existing system of the treadmill; but for the moment he resisted the attacks on the ticket-of-leave system. Ten years later, when he was Prime Minister, he surrendered completely to popular pressure on this point, though it was not until after his death that the Government imposed those harsher conditions for prisoners which led, in turn, to the reaction in favour of milder treatment which began in 1895, and has continued to the present day.

Palmerston was particularly interested in the modern ideas of treatment of juvenile prisoners, which had arisen largely as a result of the publication of Dickens's *Oliver Twist* in 1838. Melbourne had thought that *Oliver Twist* was a subversive book, and was distressed to find Queen Victoria reading it; but Shaftesbury was prominent in the campaign to reform, rather than punish, juvenile delinquents, and stirred the conscience of the public by disclosing that there were nearly twelve thousand children under seventeen in prison. As a result of this campaign, a separate prison for young offenders was opened at Parkhurst in the Isle of Wight; but Palmerston, whose interest in this problem had been aroused by Shaftesbury, introduced a new principle with the Reformatory Schools Bill of 1854. This provided that the Home Secretary could order that boys who had been sentenced to imprisonment could be transferred to a reformatory school, though Palmerston was obliged to accept an amendment to the bill which stipulated that no boy should be sent to a reformatory school until he had first served at least three months in prison.

In October 1854, Palmerston visited Parkhurst, inspected the cells and spoke to three of the boys, who seemed to him to be very well behaved. He suggested that these boys, and many others, ought to be transferred, as soon as possible, to a reformatory school. He found that the ventilation in the cells was unsatisfactory, and ordered that steps should be taken to improve it. He also ordered an improvement in the living quarters of the prison warders.

In 1854, Shaftesbury formed the first Prisoners' Aid Society, with the approval of the Queen, in order to help released prisoners to find work and lead an honest life on their release from prison. Palmerston was very interested in these schemes, particularly in the case of the young offenders. He put forward a plan for sending the youths from the reformatory schools to the colonies, where they could start life afresh in a land of opportunity; but the Colonial Office objected, fearing that the Government would be accused of secretly reviving transportation.

Although the abolition of transportation as a punishment had prevented any more convicts being sent to Van Diemen's Land, those who had been sentenced in earlier years were still there, and were the Home Secretary's responsibility. When Palmerston became Home Secretary, the convicts in Van Diemen's Land included the Chartists who had taken part in the rising at Newport in South Wales in 1839, and the leaders of the Irish rebellion of 1848. They had been condemned to death, and their sentences commuted to transportation for life. From time to time, Radical MPs had tried unsuccessfully to persuade the Government to pardon the Newport Chartists; and Palmerston had always voted against the motions asking for a pardon whenever the question was debated in the House of Commons. The Irish nationalists had been even less successful in arousing sympathy for Mitchel and O'Brien and the Irish leaders in Van Diemen's Land; and any suggestion that they might be pardoned led to protests, not only from Conservative MPs, but also from patriotic Radicals like Roebuck. MPs periodically protested that the political prisoners were being too well treated in Van Diemen's Land, especially after the press had published accounts of how they were cheered and feasted by sympathetic Australians, and how the Governor and officers of the colony were granting them all kinds of favours. Palmerston refused to pardon them, but also resisted all demands to make their treatment harsher, or to censure the officials who had granted them indulgences. Many MPs objected that Mitchel should be allowed to wander freely in Van Diemen's Land after he had given his word of honour not to try to escape. O'Brien refused ticket-of-leave, and was confined in Port Arthur.

In July 1853 Mitchel walked into the office of the local police chief at Bothwell, withdrew his promise not to escape, and before the police chief could react, ran out of the office, jumped on his horse, and rode away. In due course he was smuggled on to a ship which carried him to Sydney, from where he took another ship to safety in San Francisco. When the news reached England, there was an outcry in the House of Commons, and MPs denounced Mitchel for having in effect broken his parole. Palmerston did not directly comment on Mitchel's conduct, but he praised O'Brien for having refused to accept ticket-of-leave, and said that though he was a rebel and a traitor, he had behaved like a gentleman. O'Brien did not welcome the compliment. He saw it as an attempt to make it appear as if he had condemned Mitchel's conduct in escaping, and said that he would not accept 'a compliment from my Lord Palmerston accompanied by an insult to my friend Mr. Mitchel'. In 1854 Palmerston persuaded the Cabinet and the Queen to pardon O'Brien and all the Irish nationalists and Chartists in Van Diemen's Land, on condition that they did not return to the United Kingdom. They sailed to America or to France. Two years later, they were permitted to return to Ireland and to Britain.

As Home Secretary, Palmerston had control of the Metropolitan Police. The force had been set up by Peel in 1829, but it was still strongly resented by large sections of the public, who felt that a police force under the control of the central government had more in common with the *gendarmerie* of the Continental despotisms than with the traditional constables and vergers of the English shires and boroughs. In April 1853 the Chief Commissioner of the Metropolitan Police, Sir Richard Mayne, who, because of his office, was a far from popular figure, told Palmerston that the police had discovered that Kossuth was plotting to manufacture arms and export them to Hungary, where his followers would use them to start a revolution against the Austrian Government. Kossuth, who had settled in Manchester, was a friend of Mr. Hain, an English arms manufacturer of Radical sympathies; and Hain was making the arms for Kossuth in his factory in Rotherhithe. With Palmerston's authority, Mayne applied for a warrant to search the premises, and the police found, and seized, a large stock of gunpowder, rockets and other weapons. The stock of gunpowder exceeded the quantity which an arms manufacturer was permitted, under the Explosives Act, to store without a licence, and Hain was charged with an offence under the Act. The story was leaked to the press, and *The Times* revealed Kossuth's plot, and worked up a campaign against the refugees and the foreign revolutionaries in Britain.

The first reports which appeared in the newspapers were misleading. There was no mention of a factory owned by a British arms manufacturer, and the public had the impression that Kossuth was secretly making arms in a house in Rother-hithe. The Radicals came to Kossuth's rescue. They attacked *The Times* for its campaign against Kossuth, claimed that Kossuth had nothing to do with the arms, and suggested that the police were harassing the refugees at the instigation of Austrian agents. The police were not able to find any evidence incriminating Kossuth, so the only charge brought was a prosecution against Hain under the Explosives Act for holding a quantity of gunpowder in excess of the amount allowed in his licence.

The Radical MPs, especially John Bright, raised the matter at question time in the House, and asked Palmerston to state that Kossuth had nothing to do with the gunpowder. This Palmerston refused to do, to the great chagrin of his Radical admirers. The Radicals at first preferred to believe that Sir Richard Mayne had acted without Palmerston's knowledge; but Palmerston assumed full responsibility for the police action. The Radicals' dissatisfaction increased when Palmerston, after originally stating that 500 lb. of gunpowder had been discovered in Hain's factory, afterwards admitted that the quantity was only 260 lb. Palmerston treated the matter somewhat jocularly, but nevertheless in such a manner as to confirm the rumours of a revolutionary plot by Kossuth. He said that the rockets found in the factory were of a type more suitable for use on the battlefield than at Vauxhall's, and stated that if the Austrian authorities had been alarmed at the importation of knives marked PALMER&SON, it would not be right to alarm them even more by allowing arms to be sent from Rotherhithe to Hungary. He was asked whether he was accusing Kossuth of being connected with the arms, and replied that no one except Hain had been charged; but when he was pressed to exonerate Kossuth, he refused on the grounds that he could not comment on a case which was *sub judice*.

He was then asked how the police had discovered about the factory. Without giving a clear answer, he said enough to show that it was because plain-clothes policemen had been trailing Kossuth and the Hungarian refugees. This caused great protests among the Radical MPs, many of whom were shocked when Palmerston disclosed that for many years past the

Government had employed plain-clothes policemen to follow political refugees and other persons, and that this practice was still continuing. He insisted that the police must adopt such measures if they were to prevent crime. But he strongly denied that he had acted at the request of the Austrian Government, and said that no foreign government had ever made any approach to Britain about the refugees here.

The Kossuth incident went a long way towards shaking the Radicals' faith in Palmerston. But he was no longer relying on the Radicals' support. He looked now to the middle-class readers of the *Morning Post* and the people whom they influenced. The *Morning Post*, after continuing as a moderately successful newspaper for seventy-five years, had fallen into great difficulties, and in 1847 had been acquired by its creditors, the paper manufacturers, the Cromptons. They appointed Peter Borthwick as editor, with Borthwick's son Algernon as foreign correspondent in Paris. The Borthwicks made friends with Palmerston, and often went to Broadlands. They also, like Palmerston, strongly supported Louis Napoleon, who in December 1852 proclaimed himself as the Emperor Napoleon III. Palmerston still had the support of the *Globe* and the *Morning Chronicle*, but after 1850 the *Morning Post* was his chief mouthpiece. The circulation of the *Morning Post* was under 3,000 in 1853, as compared with the 50,000 daily readers of *The Times*; but it was an influential paper.

A few days after his coup d'état in December 1851, Louis Napoleon put forward for the first time a claim to be the protector of the Roman Catholics in Turkey, just as the Tsar had for many years claimed the right to protect the Orthodox Christians there. One of Palmerston's last actions before leaving the Foreign Office was to write to Normanby to urge him to prevent Louis Napoleon from putting forward this claim, which was likely to lead to difficulties with Russia in the Middle East. But Louis Napoleon continued to press this claim, and the war party in St. Petersburg seized the excuse to pursue an aggressive policy towards Turkey. The Tsar told the British Ambassador that Turkey was the sick man of Europe, and sent Prince Menshikov to Constantinople to demand that the Tsar should be granted the right to protect the

Orthodox Christians throughout the Turkish Empire with certain powers sufficient to enable him to exercise an effective control over the Turkish administration. The Turks considered that this would destroy the independence of Turkey. They refused to comply.

During 1853, Europe drifted slowly into the first war between the great powers which had been fought for forty years. Napoleon III, who was annoyed with the Tsar for addressing him as 'My dear friend' instead of 'My brother', pursued a very anti-Russian policy, and the French press wrote about revenging 1812. The British Government was divided. The Ambassador in Constantinople, Sir Stratford Canning – now Lord Stratford de Redcliffe – was eager to stand firmly by Turkey, and so was Palmerston; but Lord Aberdeen, who virtually took over the direction of British foreign policy from his Foreign Secretary, Lord Clarendon, had publicly declared that the Turks had no business to be in Europe, and, like his Chancellor of the Exchequer, Gladstone, was uncomfortable about supporting the Turkish Government against their Christian subjects and Russia, the protector of the Christians. Aberdeen was eager to avoid war and reduce the international temperature.

The British press, especially the *Morning Post*, denounced Aberdeen for what today would be called appeasement. They wrote that Palmerston ought to be in charge of British foreign policy; and thousands of Britons were thinking the same. The idea of Palmerston at the Home Office had always struck the public as rather absurd, for he was so closely associated in everyone's mind with foreign affairs. This gave rise to many stories about him. It was said that his first action on becoming Home Secretary was to send the Home Office clerks to the Foreign Office to learn the correct way of folding despatches and papers, and to obtain a supply of blue tape with which to tie them up, instead of the green tape which was used at the Home Office. The story was told that when the great wave of strikes broke out in the North of England, and there was a certain amount of rioting, the Queen summoned Palmerston to the palace to discuss the alarming situation caused by the strikes. When she asked him what was the latest news, he replied: 'There is no definite news, Madam, but it seems certain that the Turks have crossed the Danube'. Even men who did not wholly approve of Palmerston's policy felt that he ought to be at the Foreign Office at such a moment.

The public may have been right. Whatever criticisms may be made of Palmerston, there are good grounds to believe that if Palmerson had been Foreign Secretary in February 1853, the Crimean War would have been avoided. The mixture of firmness and moderation which he displayed when dealing with great powers would have been invaluable. He would have warned the Tsar and restrained Napoleon III. His presence at the Foreign Office would have been enough in itself to make the Russians pause. Nicholas and Nesselrode knew how Palmerston felt about Wallachia and Moldavia, for when the Russians, with the consent of Turkey, sent troops to suppress a rising in Bucharest in 1848, Palmerston had repeatedly asked them to withdraw, and they had eventually done so after he had made it clear to them that even if Turkey had no objection, Britain would never agree to Russian troops remaining permanently in the principalities. But the Tsar had reason to hope that Aberdeen would not object as strongly as Palmerston to the Russian demands against Turkey; for when Nicholas had visited England in 1844, he had discussed the question with Aberdeen, and had found him vague and conciliatory.

But to have Palmerston in the Cabinet and not at the Foreign Office had the worst possible result. Palmerston forced Aberdeen to pursue a policy which antagonized Russia without being able to direct and control this policy. In order to counter Aberdeen's appeasement, he urged Aberdeen to take stronger action than he himself might have taken if he had been in charge of affairs; and he certainly made more provocative speeches about Russia in the House of Commons than he usually did when he was handling a critical international situation. Instead of writing despatches to St. Petersburg, he wrote directives to the *Morning Post*. This whipped up anti-Russian feeling in Britain, without making Nicholas realize that Britain would go to war to prevent him from dominating Turkey.

When Prince Menshikov presented his demands to the Turkish Government in February 1853, Lord Stratford de Redcliffe realized at once that a very serious situation was about to develop. With Menshikov being wildly cheered by crowds of Christians in Constantinople, and Russian troops assembling in the Black Sea ports and along the Pruth on the Wallachian border, it became clear that Russia was threatening to go to war with Turkey if her demands for control over the Orthodox Christians were refused. Stratford and the French Ambassador decided to summon the British and French fleets to the Dardanelles in reply to the Russian troop concentrations, and as a warning to Russia. But Aberdeen countermanded the order, and the French fleet sailed alone. Palmerston strongly objected to this decision in the Cabinet, and Lord John Russell supported him; but they were over-ruled.

In May, the Russians threatened to invade the principalities of Wallachia and Moldavia unless the Sultan complied with their demands – demands which alarmed Austria, for the Austrians, to the indignation of the Tsar, showed less gratitude for the Russian assistance in Hungary in 1849 than anxiety at the prospect of Russian penetration of the Balkans. Palmerston urged the Cabinet to take decisive action at once. He proposed that the fleet be sent to the Dardanelles, and that Stratford should be given authority to order it to enter the Straits and the Sea of Marmora and to sail into the Bosphorus and into the Black Sea, where the British ships could assist the Turkish Navy in protecting the Turkish coast. He also proposed that a note should be sent to Russia warning the Tsar that Britain would go to war if Russian troops invaded the principalities. Aberdeen objected to all these proposals. After a discussion in the Cabinet, in which Lord John Russell supported Palmerston, Aberdeen gave way and agreed to send the fleet to the Dardanelles; but he refused to agree to Palmerston's other proposals. Britain therefore did enough to annoy the Tsar, but not enough to deter him. The fleet anchored just outside the Dardanelles; but unfortunately the weather turned very rough, and the ships took shelter in the outer waters of the Straits. Russia claimed that this was a violation of the

Straits Convention of 1841, and in reply invaded the principalities, announcing that they did not intend to take any further military action, but would hold the principalities as a guarantee that Turkey complied with their demands.

Palmerston thought that it was all the result of British weakness. On 12 July he wrote to Aberdeen that the Russian invasion of Wallachia and Moldavia

shews how imperfectly we have understood the character of the Russian Government, and how entirely thrown away upon that Government has been the excessive forbearance with which England and France have acted. But the result might have been foreseen; it is the nature of men whose influence over events and whose Power over others are founded on intimidation, and kept up by arrogant assumptions and pretensions, to mistake forbearance for irresolution, and to look upon inaction and hesitation as symptoms of fear, and forerunners of Submission.

He was sure that the Russians would not have invaded the principalities if they had been clearly told that if they did so, the British and French fleets would enter the Bosphorus or the Black Sea; but he still favoured negotiations with Russia.

The Austrian Government tried to mediate, and invited the powers to enter into talks in Vienna. Palmerston and Russell were opposed to the idea of talks in Vienna, though in Palmerston's case he was eager to conduct negotiations in London. But Aberdeen and the Cabinet overruled these objections, and the British, French and Russian Ambassadors in Vienna set to work with the Austrian Foreign Minister, Count Buol, to find a solution to the dangerous situation. They agreed on a formula which provided that Turkey should grant Russia certain rights of protection over the Orthodox Christians, though these would fall far short of the original Russian demands. Stratford thought that this formula was very dangerous, and gave Russia a foothold in Turkey which would threaten Turkish independence; and Lord John Russell supported this view in the Cabinet. The situation was made worse by the disclosure of a secret Russian memorandum which showed the full extent of Russia's real designs against Turkey. Palmerston was prepared to accept the Vienna formula, and Aberdeen asked him to assist Clarendon in drafting the final form of the agreement. The Tsar and Napoleon III accepted the agreement; but the Turks refused. They said that it violated the independence of Turkey, and called on the Russians to withdraw from the principalities.

The press in Britain was arousing public opinion against Russia. They reminded Englishmen of the horrors of Siberian prisons, of the Polish women who had been publicly flogged for sending Christmas greetings to their husbands who were refugees abroad, of the Russian intervention in Hungary in 1849 and their attempt to bully Turkey into surrendering the Hungarian and Polish refugees. Kossuth and the Polish leaders addressed large meetings all over Britain; and experts on foreign affairs stressed the danger to Britain if the Russians took Constantinople. The people felt that only Palmerston could save the situation. The Radical MP, Whitty, who had been very disappointed about Palmerston's conduct three months before in the case of Kossuth and the arms in Rotherhithe, wrote in his diary on 6 August: 'What can the despotic system apprehend, when it sees its favourite aversion, Palmerston, placidly engaged in contesting whether he should go on with a Truck Act, or withdraw a Smoke Nuisance Abatement Bill?'

But it was now that Palmerston's influence had the worst possible effect. If he had been at the Foreign Office, it would have been much better. Assuming – which is unlikely – that he would have allowed the situation to reach such a stage, he would have kept a firm control over both Stratford and the Turks. As it was, he frustrated Aberdeen's attempts to do this. He had been partly responsible for working up public opinion into a war mood, through his speeches in Parliament and his directives to the *Morning Post*; and now, as usual, he was carried along by public opinion. Bright accused him of having formed a 'war party' in the Cabinet; and after October 1853 – though not before – there is some truth in this. He was, however, much less bellicose than the ordinary Englishman, and less bellicose than Lord John Russell, who was more vocal in the Cabinet than Palmerston in expressing his disagreement with the Premier's appeasement policy. The Duke of Argyll states in his memoirs that Palmerston 'was singularly silent, and when he did discuss, it was always frankly, always with perfect temper, and always acquiescing without any show of irritation in the general sense of the Cabinet'. When he wished to state his objections to Government policy, he did so in a letter to Aberdeen rather than at a Cabinet meeting. He could sometimes be very cunning and tactful. On 31 July he wrote to Clarendon, warmly approving of the draft of a despatch to Russia which Clarendon had read out to the Cabinet, and explained: 'I did not like to say too much in its praise at the Cabinet, for fear that by doing so I might lead others to think it was too strong'.

At the Cabinet meeting on 7 October, Palmerston proposed that the Navy should be sent into the Black Sea with orders to seize every Russian ship that they could find, and bring them to Turkish ports, while Russia should be informed that the ships would be restored when the Russian troops withdrew from the principalities. The Cabinet rejected this proposal. But the Turkish Government decided that, as in 1839, they could force Britain to follow them if they acted alone. On 11 October they declared war on Russia and sent their troops across the Danube into Wallachia to expel the Russians from the principalities.

The news was welcomed enthusiastically in Britain, where there was a great clamour for war which was cheered on by such diverse characters as Roebuck, the Reverend Charles Kingsley, and Karl Marx. Though the Tsar proclaimed a crusade in support of the oppressed Christians against the Mohammedan Turks, Kingsley declared that the Turks were 'fighting on God's side'; and Marx pronounced that the British and the French ruling class were being driven by the inexorable force of history to take sides with the enemies of the Tsar. Only Cobden and Bright and their Peace Society opposed the popular feeling. They sent envoys to Russia to ask the Tsar to use his influence for peace. Nicholas received them with great courtesy, and assured them that he wished to avoid war; but he did not withdraw his troops from the principalities. The Peace Society achieved nothing by their visit except a high degree of unpopularity in Britain.

Tennyson inserted into his poem, 'Maud', fifty-nine lines in praise of war, and denouncing peace; and many less gifted poets followed suit. One of them harangued the Peace Society:

Go home, you idle teachers! You miserable creatures!
The cannons are God's preachers when the time is ripe for war.

Palmerston suggested that the British fleet should give full support to Turkey, and that British volunteers should be allowed to join the Turkish armed forces. Aberdeen refused, and sent Palmerston a memorandum from Prince Albert, which proposed a plan by which Turkey would be compelled to withdraw from Europe, and that the territories evacuated by the Turks should be formed into a new Greek Empire. Palmerston had gone to Broadlands for a week's shooting, and on 1 November wrote from there to Aberdeen. He rejected Prince Albert's proposal, and said that if we wished to establish a Greek Empire in place of the Turkish Empire in Europe, we should change sides and help Russia against Turkey, instead of Turkey against Russia. He argued that the fact that Turkey had declared war on Russia should not lead us to cease supporting Turkey. 'The Turkish Government Seeing no apparent Prospect of better Results from Negotiation and aware that Lapse of Time was running to the Disadvantage of Turkey at Length after having for some considerable Time yielded to our advice to remain passive, came to a Determination not unnatural and not unwise, and issued that Declaration of war, which we had officially & publicly Said that the Sultan would have been justified in issuing the moment the Russians invaded his Territory. This Declaration of war makes no Change in the Position of England and France in Relation to Turkey we may still try to persuade Russia to do what she ought to do, but we are still bound by a Regard from our own Interests to defend Turkey. Peace is an Excellent Thing, & war a great Misfortune. But there are many Things More valuable than Peace, and many Things Much worse than war. The maintenance of the Ottoman Empire belongs to the First Class, The occupation of Turkey by Russia belongs to the Second. But we passed the Rubicon when we first took Part with Turkey and sent our Squadrons to Support her, and when England and France have once taken a Third Power by the Hand, that

Third Power *Must* be carried in safety through the Difficulties in Which it may be involved. England & France cannot afford to be baffled, and Whatever Measures may be necessary on their Part to baffle their opponent, those Measures Must be adopted; and the Governments of the Two most powerful Countries on the Face of the Earth must not be frightened either by words or Things Either by the name or by the Reality of war. . . . But it is said the Turks seem to wish for war, while we wish for Peace. I apprehend that both Parties wish for one and the same thing, namely the Relinquishment by Russia of inadmissible Pretensions and her Retirement from the Turkish Territory, both Parties would rather gain their ends by the Pen than by the Sword. We only differ in our Belief as to the efficacy of these Two Methods'.*

But Aberdeen would make no move against Russia. 'Peace is still our object', he wrote to Palmerston on 4 November, 'and we have surely a right to expect that the Turks should do nothing to counteract the endeavour we are making on their behalf'. The Prime Minister was becoming more and more unpopular. Lord Dudley Stuart noticed that 'wherever I go, I have heard but one opinion on the subject, and that one opinion has been pronounced in a single word, or in a single name – Palmerston'.

Lord John Russell was strongly opposed to Aberdeen's policy, and threatened to resign; but he had another interest which kept him in the Cabinet. He had developed a plan for introducing an important measure of electoral reform, the effect of which would be to give the vote to a small section of the working class in the towns. He had first proposed such a plan when he was Prime Minister in 1849, and had again proposed it in 1851; but he had not proceeded with it owing to the opposition in his Cabinet, where Palmerston in particular had strongly opposed it. In the summer of 1853, he raised it again in Aberdeen's Cabinet. His colleagues were divided, some being for, and some against. The strongest opponent of

*Ashley, in his *Life of Palmerston*, published the full text of this letter, but altered the wording in several passages so as to hide the fact that the memorandum which Palmerston criticized had been written by Prince Albert.

the plan was Palmerston. He was prepared to consider some of the measures which Russell proposed, such as redistribution and disfranchisement of certain constituencies which had not been disfranchised under the compromise which had been reached in 1832, and the removal of some anomalies by which a few groups of educated people were ineligible to vote; but he was determined to prevent Russell from giving the vote to the urban working class. It was principally due to Palmerston that this extension of the franchise was held up for fourteen years, and not enacted until 1867, after Palmerston's death.

Aberdeen appointed a sub-committee of the Cabinet to consider Russell's proposals for electoral reform. It consisted of Russell, Lord Granville, the Duke of Newcastle, Lord Lansdowne, and Palmerston. The sub-committee was divided, but Russell and Graham won over Aberdeen and the Cabinet, and the Government agreed to introduce a bill in the next session of Parliament along the lines which Russell had proposed. Palmerston objected very strongly to this, and on 8 December wrote a letter to his old friend Lord Lansdowne, who as Henry Petty had defeated him in his first election at Cambridge in 1806. 'I have told Aberdeen', he wrote, 'that I am persuaded that the measure proposed by John Russell and Graham will not pass through the two Houses of Parliament without material modifications, and that I do not chuse to be a party to a contest between the two Houses, or to an appeal to the country for a measure of which I decidedly disapprove; and that I cannot enter into a career which would lead me to such a position; that, in short I do not chuse to be dragged through the dirt by John Russell. ... I have thought a good deal on this matter. I should be very sorry to give up my present office at this moment; I have taken a great interest in it; and I have matters in hand which I should much wish to bring to a conclusion. Moreover I think that the presence in the Cabinet of a person holding the opinions which I entertain as to the principles on which our foreign affairs ought to be conducted, is useful in modifying the contrary system of policy, which, as I think, injuriously to the interests and dignity of the country, there is a disposition in other quarters to pursue; but notwithstanding all this, I cannot consent to stand forward as one of the authors and supporters of John Russell's sweeping alterations'.

Two days later, he wrote to Aberdeen, and sent him a copy of his letter to Lansdowne, which he asked Aberdeen to return. He told the Premier that although it was sometimes wise and inevitable for a politician to surrender to overwhelming popular pressure and introduce a measure of which he personally disapproved, this did not apply in the present case. 'The great Mass of the Intelligent Portion of the Nation deprecate any Material Change in the organic arrangements of the House of Commons'. After these introductory remarks, he went on to a lengthy criticism of the Government's policy in the Eastern crisis, and their failure to give resolute help to Turkey.

Aberdeen informed the Queen about Palmerston's letter, and she consulted the Prince. Albert urged Aberdeen to seize this opportunity of getting rid of Palmerston, and to make sure that Palmerston resigned over reform and not over the policy towards Turkey. Aberdeen had some doubt as to whether it would be honourable to make use of Palmerston's letter to Lansdowne, in view of the fact that Palmerston had asked him to return it; but Graham thought that this was being over-scrupulous. He had been a personal friend of Palmerston's for many years, but he told Aberdeen that Palmerston was a 'crafty foe', and advised Aberdeen to make a copy of Palmerston's letter to Lansdowne before returning it to Palmerston. Then, on 11 December, came the news from Sinope. The Turks had sent their fleet into the Black Sea, relying apparently on the Tsar's undertaking that he would confine his military operations during the winter to defensive measures. The Russians seized their chance, and on 30 November attacked the Turkish fleet at Sinope, and annihilated it, drowning four thousand Turkish sailors. The news caused great indignation in Britain. The press wrote about the 'massacre of Sinope', and, overlooking the detail that Turkey had previously declared war on Russia, denounced Russian treachery in attacking the unsuspecting Turks. But their strongest criticism was reserved for Aberdeen and his Government, who were accused of betraying Turkey by failing to send the

British Navy into the Black Sea to protect the Turkish ships. The press and public spoke of 'England's shame', and said that it would never have occurred if Palmerston had had his way.

On 14 December – three days after the news of Sinope reached London – Aberdeen wrote to Palmerston. He returned the copy of Palmerston's letter to Lansdowne, and, after telling Palmerston that he had made another copy of the letter, which he was keeping, he dealt at length with the proposals for Parliamentary reform, and ended by saying that as there was no prospect of the Government changing its policy on reform, he regretted that he could not dissuade Palmerston from resigning from the Government. Palmerston replied in a very short note: 'My dear Aberdeen, I have received your note of this Morning and in Consequence I have to request you to lay before Her Majesty the Resignation of my Office. I shall be ready to give up the Seals at any Time that may best Suit your Convenience. Yours sincerely, Palmerston'. His letter of resignation was published in the newspapers next day; but the *Morning Post* added the information that, although the reform proposals were the ostensible grounds for Palmerston's resignation, the real reason was his disgust with Aberdeen's refusal to help the gallant Turks and his anger at the shame of Sinope.

Palmerston's resignation increased the popular indignation with Aberdeen. It also caused strong criticism of Prince Albert, for the Court was thought to have been responsible once again for the dismissal of Palmerston, and the press and public hesitated to attack the Queen herself. It made Palmerston more popular than ever, and everyone felt that the Government would be compelled to resign. No one doubted the statement in the *Morning Post* that Palmerston had resigned because of Sinope and Aberdeen's foreign policy. *The Times*, which almost alone of the press was still supporting Aberdeen and was as hostile to Palmerston as ever, tried to remind the public that Palmerston had not resigned over foreign policy, but because he was a determined enemy of all proposals for Parliamentary reform. Palmerston then issued a brief statement, denying that he had resigned because he was opposed to all measures of reform, and stating that he objected merely to the proposals which Lord John Russell had brought forward. This statement made no mention of foreign policy; but, by denying *The Times*'s statement as to the cause of his resignation, confirmed the public belief that he had resigned because of Sinope. Meanwhile the Government sent a strong protest to Russia about Sinope, and informed the Russian Government that Britain considered that the Russian attack on the Turkish fleet was an attack on Britain herself. The British and French fleets sailed into the Black Sea and right up to the entrance to the harbour of Sevastopol.

On 22 December, Aberdeen wrote to Palmerston and asked him to withdraw his resignation. He explained that Russell's plans for reform had only been tentatively accepted, and that although the Cabinet were determined to introduce some measure of Parliamentary reform, they had not finally decided on the details. Palmerston then wrote to Aberdeen, stating that he had not realized that nothing had been definitely settled about reform, and that in view of this he agreed to withdraw his resignation. Aberdeen replied, in a letter intended for publication, that he failed to see how Palmerston could possibly have imagined that the question of reform had already been settled by the Cabinet, and went out of his way to inform Palmerston about the decisive steps which the Government had taken against Russia during Palmerston's absence; but in view of the popular feeling he was glad to have Palmerston back on any terms. On Christmas Eve, Palmerston returned to the Cabinet and the Home Office; and the Government agreed not to introduce a Reform Bill in the 1854 session of Parliament, but to defer it for a year while Russell and Palmerston went into the matter more closely to see if they could agree on some compromise.

There was much speculation among political commentators at the time as to the real reason for Palmerston's resignation; and the controversy has continued ever since. One theory, which was afterwards confirmed by no less a witness than Aberdeen's son, was that the Queen, Prince Albert and Aberdeen wished to get rid of Palmerston, and that Aberdeen adopted Russell's reform proposals in order to provoke Palmerston into resigning. Another theory is that Palmerston and Borthwick contrived the whole thing with the object of making Palmerston the hero of the nation. They knew that if he resigned over Sinope, he would win great popularity; but if he left the Government on these grounds, Lord John Russell would certainly have resigned with him, and as he was even more pro-Turk than Palmerston, he would have shared the popularity with Palmerston, or even have eclipsed Palmerston. By resigning in protest against Russell's reform proposals, Palmerston made it impossible for Russell to resign too; so he resigned officially for this reason, while Borthwick explained in the *Morning Post* that he had resigned over Sinope. But it is very unlikely that either Aberdeen or Palmerston was so far-seeing. Palmerston handled political intrigue at home in the same way as he handled British foreign policy – not by long-term Machiavellian strategy, but by brilliant tactical improvisations in difficult situations. He wrote his letter to Lansdowne, in which he only hinted at the possibility of his resigning, because he sincerely objected to Parliamentary reform, and wished to persuade the Government to abandon it by raising the possibility that he might resign. Aberdeen, taking the opportunity to throw out Palmerston, made it very difficult for Palmerston not to resign; and by telling Palmerston that he had kept a copy of Palmerston's letter to Lansdowne, he made it impossible for Palmerston to make out that he was resigning on any other issue. Then came the news of Sinope; and Palmerston, by resigning without giving any official reason in his letter, made it possible for Borthwick to write in the *Morning Post* that it was because of Sinope. This statement rallied overwhelming public support to Palmerston, and also had the merit of being true – at least in one sense.

By resigning over reform, Palmerston had risked antagonizing the Radicals; but he was no longer relying mainly on Radical support. He was relying on the ordinary member of the middle class who wished to uphold British prestige and interests, and to keep the Russians out of Constantinople, and who disapproved of Continental despots, but who, having the vote already, did not care greatly about reform. Some of them actively opposed the grant of the vote to the working classes;

but most of them were just not interested. Yet Palmerston did not, in fact, lose the support of the Radicals. They forgot his support for Napoleon III, his treatment of Kossuth, and his opposition to reform, and thought of him only as the enemy of Tsarism. Marx was disgusted at the Radicals' admiration for Palmerston, which struck him as yet another example of the gullibility of petty bourgeois democrats. As the London correspondent of the *New York Herald Tribune*, he wrote a series of articles attacking Palmerston. He argued very convincingly against the widely accepted view that Palmerston was a Conservative at home and a Radical abroad, and claimed that Palmerston had repeatedly opposed the cause of freedom and progress abroad, ever since his first speech on foreign policy in 1808, when he had defended the shameful attack on Copenhagen during the counter-revolutionary war against France. Marx at one time collaborated with Urquhart in his campaign against Palmerston, though he was too shrewd to repeat in public the ridiculous assertions of Urquhart that Palmerston had been in the pay of the Russian Government since 1828. Palmerston himself was just as wide of the mark in thinking that Urquhart was a Russian agent. 'As to Urquhart', he wrote to John MacGregor, MP, on 29 October 1855, 'I have no doubt whatever that he is hired by the Russian Government to abuse and calumniate me. . . . He is more than half mad, and wholly bad'.

The Radicals combined their enthusiasm for Palmerston and for war with Russia with a campaign against the monarchy which was masked under the form of an attack on Prince Albert. He was denounced as an agent of an international conspiracy fomented by the crowned heads of Europe with the object of helping Russia to crush constitutional freedom and to destroy Palmerston. He was even accused of being a Russian spy. Libellous ballads about him were printed and sung. Some Radical newspapers demanded that he should be arrested and sent to the Tower, and the rumour spread in London that he had actually been imprisoned there. *The Times* and all the respectable newspapers condemned the scandalous campaign against the Prince – except for the *Morning Post*. For nearly a month, the *Morning Post* made no statement, either one way or the other, about the attacks on Albert; and the story went around that the attacks had been instigated by Palmerston. In society and in political circles, people began to criticize Palmerston for this. But on 25 January 1854 Palmerston wrote to Borthwick: 'I think it would be useful if you were to put into the *Post* the following paragraph: We have observed that some of our contemporaries have endeavoured to connect the resignation of the Home Secretary with some proceedings on the part of the Court. Now we believe we may confidently affirm, without the slightest fear of contradiction, that the resignation of the noble Lord was the result of some misunderstanding between himself and some of his colleagues, and had not the remotest connection with anything on the part of the Court'. This was putting it too strongly, for Albert had certainly had at least some part in the affair of Palmerston's resignation; but whatever Palmerston's private feelings might be, he would never join a Radical campaign against the monarchy.

The declaration of war was still delayed while notes passed between London, Paris and St. Petersburg, taking a week over the journey each way; but everyone knew that war was inevitable. Aberdeen was sure that he could no longer prevent it. He made up his mind that if war came, he would remain in office in order to reduce military operations to a minimum, and to make peace as soon as possible. On 27 February Britain and France sent an ultimatum to Russia to withdraw from the principalities within one month. The Tsar did not reply; he had already recalled Brunnow from London. On 28 March 1854 Britain and France declared war.

Chapter Thirty

The Crimean War

Aberdeen's Government and the British people prepared to fight the Crimean War with the methods of 1815. Tocqueville described the British as being a warlike, but not a military, nation; and the middle-class Londoner and the Radical Lancashire artisan who cheered on the war against Russian despotism intended to carry on business as usual while the war was fought by aristocratic officers and men whom they despised as the scum of the earth. But in the course of the war a great change took place in public opinion; they came to despise the aristocratic officers as incompetent bunglers, and to regard the common soldier as a hero.

At the outbreak of the war, neither the Government nor the high command had any idea as to where they were to fight. When the matter was first discussed in the Cabinet, Aberdeen had no clear plan, and seemed very happy to do nothing at all. Palmerston suggested that a British army should be sent to the Crimea: as the British Navy had command of the Black Sea, they could land the men near Sevastopol, and the army could then invest the town, which would soon be forced to surrender. He also suggested an invasion of Russia through the Caucasus from Turkey, and inciting the Circassians to rise against their Russian conquerors. Other possible plans were to send British troops to support the Turks who were fighting the Russians in Wallachia, or to sail up the Baltic and attack St. Petersburg. But in May the Russians withdrew from Wallachia and Moldavia in order to please the Austrians; if they had done so two months earlier it might have prevented the war. It was decided to leave the invasion of the Caucasus to the Turks with the help of British military advisers, to send the main Anglo-French force to the Crimea, and to send a fleet to attack the naval fortress of Kronstadt. If Kronstadt could be captured, and held, it could be used as a base for a direct assault on St. Petersburg at some future time.

The command of the Baltic fleet was given to Admiral Sir Charles Napier. Napier's exploits in the Portuguese civil war and in the Syrian campaign against Mehemet Ali had made him a very popular figure, and his popularity was enhanced by his imposing presence, his wild black whiskers, and his gallant nonchalance and charm. On 7 March – after the British ultimatum had been sent to Russia, but before it expired – Napier was entertained at a banquet at the Reform Club to celebrate his appointment and his imminent departure for the Baltic. Sir James Graham, the First Lord of the Admiralty, was invited to make a speech at the dinner; but it was typical of public feeling that it was the Home Secretary who was asked to preside and propose Napier's health.

Graham, like everyone else, assumed that Britain was already at war, and made an appropriately aggressive speech. Palmerston was in his most rumbustious form. He described how Napier, his gallant friend, had distinguished himself in Portugal, where, on one occasion, when he had boarded an enemy ship, 'a Portuguese officer ran at him full dart with his drawn sword to run him through. My gallant friend quietly parried the thrust, and, not giving himself the trouble to deal in any other way with his Portuguese assailant, merely gave him a hearty kick, and sent him down the hatchway. (*Roars of laughter*.) Well, gentlemen, that victory was a great event (*much laughter*) – I don't mean the victory over the officer who went down (*renewed laughter*), but the victory over the fleet, which my gallant friend took into port; for that victory decided a great cause then pending. It decided the liberties of Portugal'. Palmerston also told how on one occasion during the Portuguese civil war, Lord William Russell and a colleague had visited Napier's headquarters before Valenza. 'Lord William Russell told me that they met a man dressed in a very easy way (*great laughter*), followed by a fellow with two muskets on his shoulders. (*Renewed laughter*.) They took him at first for Robinson Crusoe (*roars of laughter*); but who should these men prove to be but the gallant Admiral on my right and a marine behind him. (*Laughter.*) "Well, Napier", said Lord W. Russell, "what are you doing here?" "Why", said my gallant friend, "I am waiting to take Valenza". "But", said Lord William, "Valenza is a fortified town, and you must know that we soldiers understand how fortified towns are taken. You must open trenches; you must make approaches; you must establish a battery in breach; and all this takes a good deal of time, and must be done according to rule". "Oh", said my gallant friend, "I have no time for all that. (*Cheers and laughter.*) I have got some of my blue-jackets up here and a few of my ship's guns, and I mean to take the town with a letter". (*Laughter.*) And so he did. He sent the Governor a letter to tell him that he had much better surrender at discretion. The Governor was a very sensible man (*cheers and laughter*); and so surrender he did'.

The evening ended in noise and laughter, and loud cheers for Napier and Palmerston. But John Bright was shocked when he read the reports in the press, and raised the matter in the House of Commons. He said that he had no criticism to make of Napier's modest speech at the dinner; but he thought that it was improper for Graham to talk as if Russia was our enemy when we were not yet at war, and Palmerston's speech appeared to him to be in very poor taste. Palmerston had treated war as a joke, at a time when in 25,000 English homes a family was anxiously waiting to hear the fate of their loved ones, which depended on the question of whether it was to be peace or war.

Palmerston rose to reply. 'Sir', he began. 'If the honourable and reverend gentleman' – and he was interrupted by Cobden, who rose on a point of order to say that the epithet 'reverend', though no doubt not intended to be offensive, was flippant and undeserved. At this point the House was still in a good temper; but Palmerston proceeded: 'I will not quarrel, Sir, with the honourable Member for the West Riding [Cobden] about words; but as the honourable gentleman [Bright] has been pleased to advert to the circumstance of my being chairman at the dinner to which allusion has been made, and as he has been kind enough to express an opinion as to my conduct

on that occasion, I deem it right to inform the honourable
gentleman that any opinion he may entertain either of me
personally, or of my conduct, private or political, is to me a
matter of the most perfect indifference. I am further convinced that the opinion of this country with regard to me and to
my conduct will in no way whatever be influenced by anything
which the honourable gentleman may say. I therefore treat
the censure of the honourable gentleman with the most
perfect indifference and contempt. (*"Order!"*). That may be
Parliamentary or not. If it is not, I do not insist upon the expression'. Later, when Palmerston was sarcastically discussing
the possibility of Bright's joining the Reform Club, someone
interrupted to say that Bright was a member of the Reform
Club. 'Oh, he is a member, is he?' said Palmerston. 'A most
unworthy member, I must say'.

Palmerston was going with the full tide of public opinion,
which was indulging in a hate-campaign against Bright and
the Peace Society; but, though such remarks would have gone
down well outside the House, they shocked many MPs. It was
not unknown for an MP to make a personal attack on another member in speeches in the House; but these were much
less common than they later became when Palmerston's worst
fears had been realized, and democracy had triumphed in
Britain. In 1854, Palmerston's behaviour was considered to
be in bad form, even by many of his supporters. The arch-
Palmerstonian, Macaulay, who hated Bright as well as being
a great admirer of Palmerston, was very embarrassed. 'Palmerston's want of temper, judgment and good breeding was
almost incredible', he wrote.

A few weeks later, Palmerston made another powerful attack on Bright in the House. He said that Bright 'reduces
everything to the question of pounds, shillings and pence', and
that if he were confronted with the threat of immediate invasion, Bright 'would sit down, take a piece of paper, and
would put on one side of the account the contributions
which his Government would require from him for the defence of the liberty and independence of the country, and he
would put on the other the probable contributions which the
General of the invading army might levy upon Manchester',

and that if he found that it would be cheaper to be conquered than to pay for defence, 'he would give his vote against going to war for the liberties and independence of the country rather than bear his share in the expenditure which it would entail'.

Palmerston had meanwhile succeeded in preventing the Cabinet from introducing any measure of Parliamentary reform. He first of all set to work to convince Russell that it was both undesirable and politically inexpedient to give the vote to the urban working classes. The lower classes were unfit to have the vote, for they would be open to bribery and to intimidation by their Trade Union leaders; and one could see 'daily in the United States the lowering effect of this dependence of members upon the lower orders of the community'. He assured Lord John that it would harm his political prospects if he continued to press for reform, as it was very unpopular, not only with the great majority of MPs, but in the country. 'Your measure may possibly give you some small and fleeting popularity among the lower classes, though there seems good reason to doubt whether the balance of feeling would not be against you for not giving to all that which you would grant to a few. But your intended course is openly disapproved by all the intelligent and respectable classes whose good opinion is most to be valued, and you can hardly be aware of the feelings of personal hostility towards you which are daily spreading through all the party which has hitherto acknowledged you as their leader'.

As he could not convince Russell, he turned to the Prime Minister. On 12 February he wrote to Aberdeen and stated his objections to Russell's proposals. He stated that he would be prepared to agree to some scheme by which about twenty seats in the smallest constituencies might be disfranchised, and some new constituencies created, and a seat in Parliament granted to the Inns of Court. He would favour reducing the property qualification for the vote in the counties, and granting it to 'large Classes of the Intelligent Men of Sufficient Means', and to persons who had deposited £100 – he did not think £60 was enough – for a specified time in a savings bank. But he was resolutely opposed to any proposal to reduce the qualification in the boroughs from £10 to £6. The result of such a measure would be to increase the total electorate in Britain from 600,000 to 750,000; and the additional 150,000 would 'be inferior to the £10 voters, in Intelligence and in Independence. They will be Ignorant, poor and dependent. Their Ignorance will prevent them from exercising a Sound Judgment, their Poverty will make them accessible to Bribes, their Dependence will make them the victims of Intimidation. . . . Everybody who knows anything about the working Classes will tell you that they are not free agents. The System of organization which universally prevails among them by means of the Trade Unions, gives to their agitating Leaders an absolute Despotism over the Masses. This has been abundantly proved by the recent Strikes. The Strikers are compelled to refuse to work at a certain Rate of wages on the Pretence that these wages are not enough to support them with the present Prices of Things and yet other Men at work at those very Rates are compelled to contribute a Portion of those wages towards the Support of those who have Struck, and are earning nothing. These £6 voters will on the one Hand be coerced by their Leaders to vote for Chartist or ultra Radical Candidates, and on the other Hand will be urged by their Employers to vote for Some other Person; They will be between the Hammer and anvil like the Irish Peasant, and will cry loudly for Ballot as their only Protection, or where this struggle may not arise they will sell themselves to the highest Bidder; Can it be expected that men who murder their children to get £9 to be Spent on Drink will not sell their vote for whatever they can get for it. You may depend upon it that this lowering of the Borough Franchise is particularly distasteful to the great Body of our Friends and Supporters and is looked to with great and general disapprobation'. A few weeks after he wrote this letter, Britain was at war, and Palmerston persuaded the Cabinet to shelve all proposals for reform for the duration.

The majority of Englishmen were certainly more interested in the war than reform in the spring of 1854, and were confident that it would end in a quick and easy victory. In June the Cabinet were persuaded by the Army command to adopt the plan, which Palmerston had first suggested some months earlier, to send an army to the Crimea. At a meeting held after a Cabinet dinner at Lord John Russell's house, Pembroke Lodge in Richmond Park, on a beautiful summer's evening on midsummer day, it was decided to propose to the French Government that some 60,000 men – 30,000 British and 30,000 French – should be landed near Sevastopol, in order to attack the town from the north while the Navy attacked it from the sea. The Duke of Argyll, who was a prudent young Scotsman, was a little anxious about the plan. A few nights later, he was walking down from the Athenaeum Club to Downing Street for a Cabinet meeting, when he recognized 'the square form and sturdy step of Palmerston approaching the top of the steps leading to the Duke of York's column'. He overtook Palmerston just as he had crossed the Mall and was walking down the Esplanade. Taking him by the arm, he told Palmerston that though he felt sure that they had done the right thing in ordering an attack upon Sevastopol, he could not help feeling a little nervous about it. 'On which', wrote Argyll in his memoirs, 'Palmerston replied in his most cheery and jaunty tones: "Oh, you need not be in the least anxious. With our combined fleets and our combined armies we are certain to succeed" '; and he went on to explain to Argyll that it was an axiom of military science that an invested fortress was sure to fall in time. 'We shall have one battle to fight outside the walls', said Palmerston, 'and then the siege. The end is certain'. He continued in this strain till they reached 10 Downing Street. 'I wondered at the sanguine nature of the man', wrote Argyll, and added: 'I felt as if I were the elder of the two, although Palmerston was then seventy and I was just thirty years of age'.

Lord Raglan and Marshal St. Arnaud, the British and French Commanders-in-Chief, had been assured by their spies that Sevastopol could not be defended from the north. They were therefore sure that the town would fall at the first attack, and that the campaign would be very short; and the British Generals issued orders that the troops were not to be encumbered with winter equipment in the Crimea, though the first landing did not take place until 14 September. A few days later, the invading armies met the Russians at the Alma, and had to climb the ridge in the face of heavy fire and fierce resistance. Over three thousand Allied soldiers fell in the battle. A false report reached England that Sevastopol had surrendered, and church bells were rung and windows illuminated; but in fact, Raglan and St. Arnaud did nothing for three weeks, while the Russians blocked the harbour at Sevastopol by scuttling their own fleet and by a great feat of skill and energy put the defenceless northern side of the town into an excellent state of defence. The joy of the British public at the great Allied victories at Balaclava and Inkerman, where attacks by superior Russian forces were repulsed with heavy loss, was clouded by the anger at the bungling of the charge of Lord Cardigan's Light Brigade, and at the outbreak of cholera among the army in the Crimea. Bad news also came from the Baltic, where Admiral Napier, after enabling a French force to capture the Russian naval base on the island of Bomarsund, decided that Kronstadt was impregnable with the forces at his disposal. When the Admiralty sent him orders to assault Kronstadt, he disobeyed them, and brought the fleet home for the winter. Palmerston's gallant friend had shown that he possessed wisdom as well as dash, but he had bitterly disappointed the hopes that had been placed in him in England, and was so savagely attacked in the British press that he retired from the Navy in disgust.

The Times had sent William Howard Russell to the Crimea. He was the first journalist ever to accompany an army as a war correspondent, and his reports made the people of Britain aware of what was happening in the Crimea. His account of the incompetence and horror in the military hospitals at the front line and at the base of Scutari in Turkey, which he contrasted with the efficient way in which the French military hospitals there were run by the French Sisters of Mercy, caused Florence Nightingale to pester Sidney Herbert, the Secretary at War, into allowing young women of good families to go as nurses to Scutari. Florence Nightingale was the daughter of William Nightingale of Embley Park in Hampshire, who had seconded Palmerston's nomination when he stood as a candidate in South Hampshire twenty years before. The Nightingales were social acquaintances of the Palmerstons in the country. Palmerston encouraged Florence Nightingale's enterprise. Lady Palmerston was at first a little taken aback at the idea. When she was young, during the Peninsular War, the women who accompanied the Army were women of the lowest class, if not outright prostitutes; but, like other people of her age and position, she reconciled herself surprisingly easily to the idea that young ladies of quality would be as safe with British soldiers as the high-class young Frenchwomen of the Sisters of Mercy were with the French troops.

On 15 November, the Government received Lord Raglan's despatch giving the news of the victory at Inkerman, but asking for reinforcements to be sent from England. The Cabinet now learned that of the 30,000 troops who had landed in the Crimea, 6,000 had fallen in action in seven weeks, and 8,000 were on the sick list suffering from wounds or cholera. They decided to summon a special session of Parliament in December to vote the money for the reinforcements; but they did not know how to transport the troops, for all the ships of the Royal Navy were in the Black Sea and could not be made available in time. The Queen offered to lend the royal yacht if this would help at all; and Cunard offered to place enough merchant ships at the Government's disposal to carry 14,000 men. When Graham announced this at the Cabinet meeting, Palmerston, who as usual was not talking much, raised his head, and asked: 'What is Mr. Cunard's Christian name?' 'Samuel', replied Graham. 'Sir Samuel', said Palmerston. But Cunard had to wait five years for his knighthood.

The cold winter of 1854–5 brought increased suffering to the troops at Sevastopol, and caused rising anger in Britain. The Government was becoming very unpopular, the General Staff was derided, and the Duke of Newcastle, the Secretary of State for War, was held responsible for all disasters. A new feeling, which had never been known in Britain before, swept through the country: for the first time war was seen, not only as something glorious, but as something tragic and terrible. Palmerston was infected by the general depression. At the end of November, he was sent to Paris for talks with the French Government. The French made him aware of facts which had not been fully brought to the attention of the Cabinet at home, and his colleagues, knowing Palmerston's usual optimism, were alarmed when they received his letters from Paris, which showed that he was deeply disturbed about the state of the army in the Crimea. Soon after he returned to England, he was at a Cabinet meeting when a despatch from Lord Raglan was read out. It stated that the army at Sevastopol was losing men at the rate of a regiment a day. Palmerston half rose to his feet, saying angrily: 'But why should this be?' By now he had come to share the general belief that Raglan was incompetent; but he said that it was impossible to remove him.

Of all the disasters which had befallen the army, it was the charge of the Light Brigade which had most affronted the public. The press and the nation demanded an inquiry. They agreed with Tennyson that 'someone had blundered'; and it was widely assumed, without any justification, that the person responsible was the Duke of Newcastle. On 13 December, Lord John Russell raised the matter in the Cabinet. He demanded that Newcastle should resign, and that Palmerston should succeed him as Secretary for War. The other ministers rallied to Newcastle's support, especially his fellow-Peelites. Aberdeen, Graham, Gladstone and Argyll defended him from Russell's attacks; for though many of them felt that Newcastle had been too slow and easy-going, he was certainly not responsible for the charge of the Light Brigade, and they wished to be loyal to an old colleague. Palmerston strongly opposed Russell's suggestion that he should replace Newcastle, and won the admiration of all the rest of the Cabinet for his loyalty. He said that if anyone were to resign, it should be he himself, for he had not succeeded in getting any of his Public Health and Smoke Abatement bills through the House during the last session. Aberdeen commented that this was perhaps due to Palmerston's lack of energy – a joke which was thoroughly enjoyed by the Cabinet. Russell was not amused, and gave notice that he might resign when Parliament re-assembled in January; and the public clamour for Newcastle's resignation continued. But Lady Palmerston could not conceal from her friends her delight at the way things were going. Everyone was saying that only Palmerston could save the country.

On 23 January 1855, the MPs returned to Westminster in the middle of one of the coldest spells of weather that had been known for many years. While a freezing fog hung over London, and the ice on the railway tracks impeded communications between London and Windsor, a serious political crisis developed. On the day that Parliament re-assembled, Roebuck gave notice that he would move a resolution demanding that a Parliamentary Committee of Inquiry be set up to investigate the conduct of the war. Aberdeen was shocked; he considered that this was not merely a vote of censure on his Government, but an unconstitutional attempt of the House of Commons to interfere with the executive government and the royal prerogative. Next day, the Duke of Argyll arrived early at 10 Downing Street for a meeting of the Cabinet, and found, to his surprise, that Palmerston, who was usually late, had arrived before him, though no one else was there. Palmerston, with a very grave face, handed him a letter which he was holding in his hand. It was a letter from Lord John Russell to Aberdeen, resigning from the Government in protest against the incompetent administration of the War Office and the failure to appoint Palmerston as Secretary for War. Palmerston wrote to Russell, and stated that he considered that Russell had injured the national interest by resigning at such a time.

On 25 January, Roebuck moved his resolution in the House. The Conservatives united with the patriotic Radicals to attack Newcastle, and also Aberdeen. Lord John Russell spoke in favour of the motion, explaining why he had resigned from the Government, and demanding that Palmerston be appointed Secretary for War. Palmerston, who had succeeded Russell as Leader of the House, replied for the Government. He defended Newcastle and the Government's conduct of the war, and appealed to members not to endanger national unity in wartime; but Argyll felt that he had made a very weak speech, and many MPs found him half-hearted and unconvincing. Roebuck's motion was carried by 305 votes to 157 – a much larger majority than anyone expected; and the Government resigned. Palmerston was in the same position as Churchill was in during the debate on Norway in May 1940: the House, by voting against his arguments, was voting to make him Prime Minister.

But the Queen was not eager to invite Palmerston to form a Government. She first of all, quite properly, asked Lord Derby, as leader of the Opposition, to take office. Derby offered Palmerston the post of Secretary for War in a coalition government, with the leadership of the House of Commons. Palmerston could not refuse this appeal to his patriotism. He agreed to serve under Derby on condition that Clarendon remained Foreign Secretary. As everyone knew, Clarendon detested Derby. Palmerston saw Clarendon the same day. Clarendon told him that he would make any sacrifice, at this juncture, to serve the country, provided that it was not contrary to his honour, but that he felt it would be dishonourable to join the Government of such a man as Derby. Palmerston wrote to Derby in the evening, expressing his deep regret that, owing to Clarendon's attitude, he could not join Derby's Government. Derby then gave up the attempt.

Everyone thought that the Queen would now send for Palmerston; but she summoned Lansdowne. As he told her that he was too old, she turned next to Clarendon; but he also declined. The Queen then invited Lord John Russell to form a Government, When Russell asked his former colleagues if they would serve in his Cabinet, he met with a sharp refusal. There was a strong feeling of resentment against him for having attacked Newcastle and deserted his colleagues in Aberdeen's Government. The only person who was willing to serve under Russell was Palmerston, to whom Russell offered the leadership of the House of Commons; he was willing to serve the country under anyone in this hour of danger, provided that Clarendon was Foreign Secretary. But Clarendon refused to join Russell's Government, even though the Queen asked him to do so as a personal favour. The Queen was very upset. 'Lord John Russell may resign', she said to Clarendon, 'and Lord Aberdeen may resign, but I *can't* resign. I sometimes wish I could'. Clarendon told her that all she could do was to send for Lord Palmerston.

At the Queen's request, Russell made one more attempt to get Clarendon. He invited Clarendon and Palmerston to call on him together that same evening. Clarendon gave Russell a piece of his mind, telling him that he had brought on a Cabinet crisis and endangered national unity at a critical time. When Russell asked him if he would accept the Foreign Office, he replied curtly: 'Certainly not'. Palmerston said nothing, but sat near the fire, holding up a newspaper to keep the heat off his face. Clarendon told Russell that he would never succeed in forming a Government, and asked Palmerston if he did not agree with him. Palmerston, according to Clarendon, 'hummed and haw'd in his usual way', and then said sadly to Russell: 'I told you that you would meet with some trouble'. The two guests left their disconsolate host, and later that night, Palmerston wrote a note to Russell saying that as it was impossible to persuade Clarendon to accept the Foreign Office, he himself could not serve under Russell.

Next day, 4 February 1855, Palmerston was summoned to Buckingham Palace and invited to form a Government. He accepted the task, but found it was not easy. The Peelites refused to join his Government out of loyalty to Aberdeen, though Argyll at least felt that Palmerston ought to be Prime Minister. 'Of course,' wrote Argyll in his memoirs, 'I had no sympathy with the absurd popular superstition that he was the only man who could conduct the war, or that he could have prevented it. I knew that he had been quite as unforeseeing as any of us as regards all the unexpected contingencies which had led to our difficulties; I knew that he had proposed nothing which could have had any effect either in meeting them or in preventing them. But ... the popular impression of Palmerston's powers as a War Minister, even although it was largely a delusion, was in itself a qualification for the moment. I was therefore clearly and strongly in favour of his forming a Cabinet'. He nevertheless felt that he could not betray Aberdeen. 'I could disregard the prevalent nonsense about Lord Palmerston, but I could not stoop to any, even seeming, acquiescence in the prevalent nonsense about Aberdeen'. So Argyll, Gladstone and Herbert each told Palmerston that they would only join his Government if the other two did; and when Palmerston walked into Clarendon's house in Grosvenor Crescent at half-past eleven that night, he told Clarendon and Lady Clarendon that he had not found anyone who would serve under him. But Clarendon, of course, agreed to do so;

and next day Palmerston tried again with Argyll, Gladstone and Herbert. He told them that they ought to join his Government out of consideration for Aberdeen, because if they did not, the public would think that Aberdeen had persuaded them not to, and that Aberdeen had put his personal resentment before his duty to the country. This did not quite convince the three Peelites; but Palmerston told them that if they refused to join, he would have to form a purely Whig ministry with Lord John Russell. Aberdeen himself, who had decided to retire from public life with the Garter that the Queen offered him, used all his influence to persuade his loyal followers to join Palmerston so that the Queen's Government could be carried on; and the Peelites, with some reluctance, agreed to join.

That evening, 5 February, Palmerston formed his Government and took office as Premier. Clarendon remained as Foreign Secretary, Gladstone as Chancellor of the Exchequer, Graham as First Lord of the Admiralty, and Lord Cranworth as Lord Chancellor. Lord Panmure, a Whig who had been Secretary for War in Lord John Russell's Government in 1846–52, was given the same post now, and the War Office was placed in his charge, the office of Secretary at War being abolished. Herbert, who had held it under Aberdeen, was made Secretary for the Colonies, Sir George Grey became Home Secretary, and Argyll Postmaster-General. Palmerston wanted to appoint Lord Shaftesbury as Chancellor of the Duchy of Lancaster – the solitary Conservative in his Government. He succeeded, with great difficulty, in persuading Shaftesbury to accept, though Shaftesbury thought that he could do more to achieve social and humanitarian reforms outside the Government than in it. But Lansdowne and all the Whigs objected so strongly to having Shaftesbury that Palmerston gave way, and, to Shaftesbury's great relief, did not include him in the Government.

There remained Lord John Russell, who had at one time seemed to be Palmerston's great rival for the role of saviour of the nation, but was now pushed right out into the cold after clearing the way for Palmerston. This was a position which Russell might one day turn to advantage, for, as the only Whig leader of eminence outside the Government, he might well become a rallying point for the opposition which would arise if there were any more disasters in the Crimea. But Palmerston had other plans for Russell. The Austrian Government had invited the belligerents to send envoys to Vienna to open peace negotiations. Palmerston did not believe that the moment was ripe for peace talks to succeed; but he was anxious to remain on friendly terms with Austria, for he knew that Austria was very suspicious of Russia's designs in the Balkans, and he was hoping to draw Austria into the war on the Allied side. He therefore decided to accept the Austrian invitation, and asked Lord John Russell to go to Vienna as the British plenipotentiary to the peace talks. Russell, who was very conscious of his political isolation, was pleased to accept.

On 16 February, Palmerston faced the House of Commons as Prime Minister. He was confronted with Roebuck's motion for the appointment of the committee of inquiry, which had been passed before Aberdeen resigned. He appealed to the House to rescind the resolution, which created constitutional difficulties, and to trust him to put matters right. He appealed to them, he said, as Richard II had appealed to the peasants in revolt when he faced them at Blackheath after Wat Tyler's death, and said to them: 'I will be your leader'. He himself, as Premier, would investigate the conduct of the war. But this appeal did not go down as well as Palmerston had hoped. The MPs in 1855 proved less gullible than the peasants in 1381; they demanded to have the committee, and for the first time directed their criticism against Palmerston personally. Palmerston then made a rapid, but graceful, retreat. Next day he told his Cabinet that he had decided to accept the House's demand for a committee of inquiry.

He had some difficulty in persuading even his Whig ministers to agree to this; and the Peelites absolutely refused to do so. They said that a serious breach of constitutional practice was involved; and on 21 February Gladstone, Herbert and Graham resigned from the Government. Argyll, alone among the Peelites, decided to remain. Palmerston thought that Gladstone, Herbert and Graham were really resigning because they were secretly against the war; but he did not care, for he

did not need them now. If they had refused to join him a fortnight earlier, he could not have formed a Government. Now
their resignation could not bring his Government down. He
appointed Sir George Cornewall Lewis and Sir Charles Wood
to replace Gladstone and Graham at the Exchequer and the
Admiralty. Herbert's post of Secretary for the Colonies he
gave to Lord John Russell, on the understanding that he himself would run the Colonial Office till Russell returned from
Vienna.

Aberdeen and Newcastle had lost the confidence of the
House of Commons and the nation because of the way in
which the war had been conducted. Lord John Russell had
lost the confidence of the Whig and Peelite leaders because he
had denounced Aberdeen and Newcastle. Derby had lost the
confidence of the Conservatives because he had not succeeded
in forming a Government. Now Gladstone, Herbert and Graham had lost the confidence of everybody because they had
abandoned Palmerston. Only Palmerston had emerged from
every incident with an enhanced reputation. John Bright commented bitterly that fifty thousand Englishmen had died to
make Palmerston Prime Minister; but Palmerston knew that
in the present mood of the country, he was the only man who
could form a Government. As he wrote to his brother William
on 15 February: 'I am, for the moment, *l'inévitable*'.

Chapter Thirty-one

Prime Minister: The Peace Negotiations

The news that Palmerston had become Prime Minister came as a great relief to the British people. They felt that, at last, the conduct of the war and the honour of Britain was in safe hands. There was much less enthusiasm in Parliament and in political circles. 'Palmerston Prime Minister! What a hoax!' wrote Bright. 'The aged charlatan has at length attained the great object of his long and unscrupulous ambition'. Many MPs who were less hostile than Bright were unenthusiastic. 'I fear he is not popular', wrote the young Lady Cowper, 'except out of doors among the people, who say he is a true English-man'. But everyone, as Palmerston himself said, considered him to be inevitable; and even those who believed that the public had exaggerated his abilities thought him a gentleman and an honest man. Palmerston was respected among the governing hierarchy as well as popular with the middle classes. The political leaders were favourably impressed with the gentlemanly way in which he had stood by Newcastle and Aberdeen; and they felt that he should be given his chance, and the public its desire.

Thirteen years later, Peter Bayne, a journalist, writing in the *St. Paul's Magazine*, described the feeling of the ordinary middle-class Englishman in February 1855 when Palmerston took office. 'When we were at war with Russia and when the nation, after trying statesman after statesman, continued in the distressing consciousness that the administration lacked vigour, the man who, for a quarter of a century, had been checkmating the policy of Russia was naturally called for. In no spirit of confidence or enthusiasm – feeling clearly that was yet discovered – England said: "Try Palmerston". It was others had failed, but by no means certain that the right man on 8th February 1855 that the Earl of Derby withdrew, and that he took the helm. On the 16th he explained his position to the House. Already all the machinery of an energetic administration was at work, and, as the new Prime Minister glanced at department after department, detailing what had been done and what was planned, members felt that a new spirit of energy was already penetrating the framework of government. The country looked on in hope, beginning to breathe more freely. Month after month went by; month after month the public watched. Troubles came at first in threatening battalions upon the ministry; but the practical instinct of the nation gradually decided that Palmerston was the man to whom the business of war could be committed, and in whose hands the name of England was safe'. Older men with longer memories, who remembered the controversies of 1831 and 1840, might not have agreed that Palmerston had been checkmating Russia for the last twenty-five years; and Bayne was not only wrong in his dates, but inaccurate in other matters. But he expressed the feeling of the public about Palmerston; this was the Palmerston myth.

Th MPs had in fact been more critical of Palmerston on his first appearance before them as Prime Minister, as they showed when they rejected his appeal to them to forego their demand for a committee of inquiry into the conduct of the war. Apart from anything else, they were worried about his health. Both party spite and artistic licence made Disraeli overstate this problem in a letter which he wrote to the Dowager Lady Londonderry on 2 February, three days before Palmerston took office. Palmerston, he wrote, 'seems now the inevitable man; and though he is really an imposter, utterly exhausted, and at the best only ginger-beer and not champagne, and now an old painted pantaloon, very deaf, very blind, and with false teeth which would fall out of his mouth when speaking if he did not hesitate and halt so in his talk, here is a man which the country resolves to associate with energy, wisdom, and eloquence, and will until he has tried and failed'. This was certainly an exaggeration, as everyone realized after Palmerston had tried and had not failed. His eyesight was going, and he was often involved in difficulties through his reluctance to wear spectacles; his gout was a more serious trouble than formerly, and occasionally prevented him from attending to his public duties; and he sometimes fell asleep in the House of Commons and at Cabinet meetings. But he combined this with periods of health and energy which were extraordinary for a man of seventy, outlasting everyone else on the Treasury Bench during long all-night sittings, and riding to hounds and taking long walks in the country when he found time to spend a few days at Broadlands.

The main outlet for his energy was in the direction of the war. When the terrible winter in the Crimea ended at last, the Allied forces were still encamped before Sevastopol, which showed no signs of surrendering. By the summer of 1855, the Allies had nearly 250,000 troops in the Crimea, of which only 45,000 were British, the rest being French and Sardinian soldiers, and foreign mercenaries hired by the British Government. Cavour had persuaded King Victor Emmanuel to declare war on Russia, and to send Sardinian troops to fight for Italian freedom at Sevastopol, as being the best way of gaining the sympathy of Britain and France. The employment of mercenaries by Britain had been strongly criticized in the House of Commons, but Palmerston had defended it, because it had proved to be satisfactory during the Napoleonic Wars, and was the only way in which the Government could meet Lord Raglan's demand for more men. The British Government scoured the world for soldiers. Palmerston was particularly eager to enrol some Swiss mercenaries.

Palmerston busied himself with all sorts of details about the war and the Army administration. He showed his usual interest in the various types of cannon, shells and rifles, and was also active concerning the health of the soldiers, in which so much public interest had been aroused by William Howard Russell and Florence Nightingale. As the summer advanced, and the troops at Sevastopol complained, no longer of cold, but of the heat, Palmerston suggested to the military authorities that white cloths should be issued to the soldiers for them to hang over their caps and helmets to protect them from the sun. The cholera was killing between twenty and thirty British soldiers every day in the Crimea, though Palmerston assured the House of Commons that the Russians had lost far more men from the disease, which indeed was true. He sent orders that health inspections should be carried out twice a day in the front line, and directed that measures should be taken to ensure the cleanliness of the camps. He instructed Clarendon to urge the French Government to see that the same precautions were taken in the French camps.

But energy and initiative about details were not enough to introduce efficiency into the administration of the army in the Crimea. For this, able administrators and leaders were necessary, and here Palmerston did nothing to improve the situation. His high-level appointments turned out to be unfortunate. Lord Panmure, whom he appointed as Secretary for War, was even slower, more unimaginative, and more obstructionist than the Duke of Newcastle. But Palmerston, who liked Panmure personally, supported him throughout, and would not consider sacrificing him to the public clamour for his removal. He refused to remove Lord Raglan from the supreme command because Raglan got on well with the French; but in June 1855 Raglan died. Palmerston appointed General Simpson in his place. Simpson turned out to be a good deal more incompetent than Lord Raglan, and after a few months he was persuaded to resign. The press and public had been demanding that General Sir Colin Campbell, the Scottish crofter's son, should be appointed Commander-in-Chief in the Crimea; but Palmerston turned down this suggestion when it was put forward in the Cabinet, and appointed General Codrington to succeed Simpson. Public opinion was appeased to some extent when Sir Colin Campbell was sent out to Sevastopol, though in a subordinate capacity.

In April 1855, Lord Ellenborough gave notice that he would move a resolution in the House of Lords censuring the Government for their failure to remove incompetent administrators in the Crimea. Palmerston then gave way to public feeling, and agreed to remove some inefficient leaders of the second rank. On 1 May, he wrote to Panmure, and told him to appoint Mr. Watkins, the manager of the Manchester and Sheffield Railway, as head of the commissariat in the Crimea instead of Filder, for 'we cannot consign our Troops to the tender mercies of Filder'. He also demanded the removal of Sir John MacNeill, the head of the investigating commission in the Crimea, and of General Airey, the Quarter-Master-General, and of General Estcourt, the Adjutant-General. If these changes were made, 'we should be able to make a good defence in Parliament against the attacks which are coming upon us for want of Energy and resolution in regard to our Military arrangements, but I, for one, cannot undertake to stand up in my place in Parliament and defend an inactivity which would leave our army to be in the ensuing Campaign the victims of that knot of Incapables, who in the last eight months have been the direct cause of the disability and deaths of thousands of our brave men'. On 8 May he wrote again to Panmure: 'I clearly foresee that unless you should be able to say that more efficient men than Andrew Smith, Filder, Airey and Estcourt are appointed, or about immediately to be appointed ... the Debate will be as damaging to yourself and to the Government, as the continuance of those men in their several places is detrimental of the welfare of the Army and the best interests of the Country. ... It will be in vain to say that MacNeill has made good arrangements for the Commissariat. The answer will be what business has a Scotch Poor Law Commissioner to be buying Bullocks and Hay in Asia Minor for the use of an Army in the Crimea? Let him come home and do his own business, and let a proper man be sent out to the Crimea to take charge of the Business to be done there'.

But although he was prepared to remove individuals, he resolutely refused to change the military system and the aristocratic leadership of the Army. On this issue, he was confronted with a new challenge from Henry Layard. Layard, the son of a middle-class member of the Ceylon Civil Service, had become an archaeologist, and achieved fame by his excavations at Nineveh. As a result of his extensive travels through the Middle East, he had become the greatest expert in Britain on the Turkish Empire, and during Palmerston's last term as Foreign Secretary, it was suggested to Palmerston that Layard should be given a post at the embassy in Constantinople. There was considerable opposition at the embassy and the Foreign Office to having this middle-class outsider, and Palmerston had at first rejected the suggestion; but after he had had an interview with Layard, who impressed him favourably, and had been subjected to more canvassing on Layard's behalf, he appointed Layard to the embassy. Layard returned to England after a few years, and was elected as a Radical MP. He became a passionate advocate of resistance to Russia during the crisis of 1853, and when war broke out he went himself as an observer to the Crimea. After witnessing the charge of the Light Brigade, he returned to the House of Commons to denounce the incompetence of the Army leadership at Sevastopol and of the Duke of Newcastle at the War Office. Not content with this, he criticized the aristocratic monopoly of the Army, and demanded that military promotion should be open to men of all classes who possessed ability. The press, especially *The Times*, wrote that Layard was the only man in the House of Commons who knew what he was talking about when the Crimea was debated, and suggested that he should be appointed Secretary for War.

Palmerston's first idea was to appease public opinion and keep Layard quiet by giving him a place in his Government. When he formed his administration, he proposed that Layard should be Under-Secretary for War under Lord Panmure. But the Queen objected because of the attacks which Layard had made on the aristocracy; and Layard himself refused to join Palmerston's Government unless a number of other Radical middle-class MPs who had criticized the conduct of the war were also included in it. Palmerston had therefore to leave Layard out, and face him as a critic in the House.

When Palmerston's new Government asked the House of Commons for a vote of confidence on 19 February 1855, Layard was one of the foremost speakers in the debate. He denounced aristocratic inefficiency, as exemplified in the Duke of Newcastle, and urged that the House should send MPs to the Crimea who should have power to overrule and dismiss incompetent commanders, like the Commissioners that the French Convention of 1793 had sent to their revolutionary armies. 'I have no doubt', he said, 'that a Cavendish in the Cabinet is a very important thing, but the public think more of 20,000 lives than they do of a Cavendish.' Such talk, which became a commonplace in the wars of the twentieth century, caused a sensation in 1855. Palmerston vigorously repudiated this attack on the aristocracy. 'Talk to me of the aristocracy of England! Why, look to that glorious charge of the cavalry at Balaclava – look to that charge where the noblest and wealthiest of the land rode foremost, followed by heroic men from the lowest classes of the community, each rivalling the other in bravery, neither the peer who led nor the trooper who followed being distinguished the one from the other. In that glorious band there were the sons of the gentry of England; leading were the noblest of the land, and following were the representatives of the people of this country'.

Layard continued his campaign, and carried it outside the House of Commons. Using the slogan 'The right man in the right place', he formed the Administrative Reform Association, whose object was to secure an end to aristocratic monopoly of military and civilian government, and addressed public meetings all over the country, as well as speaking repeatedly on the topic in the House of Commons. Having got rid of the Duke of Newcastle, he directed his fire at General Lord Hardinge, the Commander-in-Chief. After addressing a mass rally in Liverpool which caused a great deal of controversy, he wrote an open letter to Lord Hardinge, in which he invited him to resign, on the grounds that although Hardinge had been a competent subordinate commander in the Peninsular War nearly fifty years before, he was now too old and old-fashioned to perform the duties of his present office. He received a very testy reply from Hardinge, which, like Layard's letter, was published in the press; and on 27 April Layard found himself assailed by a bevy of army officers in the House of Commons, of whom Colonel Knox, the MP for Marlow, was the most vociferous.

The debate was conducted in an unusually heated atmosphere, and Layard was interrupted and shouted down by the infuriated military MPs. Palmerston spoke more in sorrow than in anger, regretting that Layard should have used his great abilities to attack the distinguished leaders of the Army; but he was criticized by the Radicals for not reprimanding or restraining the MPs who created the uproar. *Punch,* which usually supported Palmerston, not only supported Layard but came near to attacking Palmerston personally in a verse which they published about the debate. After referring to the conduct of the Army MPs, with their 'groans, hootings, shrieks and howls' which made Westminster 'resound with cries more dire and dread than you ever heard in the Regent's Park when the animals are fed', it described Colonel Knox calling on Palmerston to stamp on Layard, for here was a mouth which must be choked: 'Down, down upon him, Palmerston. . . . Kick him, and kick him hard; he has among ourselves no friends'; but to this, Layard's thirty million friends outside the House would reply:

Hit Layard? Hit him if ye dare! Avert, dishonest crew!
Humbugs, get out and make room for a better man than you!

Palmerston was determined to defend the aristocratic control of the Army; but he realized the strength of the campaign behind Layard, and he trod warily. He adopted the line of injured innocence rather than the aggressive arrogance of the Army officers; and Layard lost some sympathy when he attacked Palmerston personally at a great public meeting at the Drury Lane Theatre in May, where, in a reference to one of Palmerston's jocular speeches, he said that Palmerston had jested at the sufferings of the people. On 15 June Layard moved a motion censuring the Government for maintaining aristocratic privilege in the Army, and the system of the sale and purchase of officers' commissions. Palmerston opposed the resolution, denied that he had ever jested at the sufferings of the people, and said that Layard's appointment to the embassy in Constantinople and his subsequent rise to prominence showed that it was possible for men without family connexions to rise by ability alone. Bulwer-Lytton moved an amendment deleting the criticism of the Government, and calling for the appointment of a Committee of Inquiry into aristocratic influence in the Army and the purchase of commissions. Palmerston as usual sensed the mood of the House, and accepted the amendment, and this saved his Government from almost certain defeat.

When the Committee met next year, Palmerston gave evidence before it. He admitted that the purchase of commissions was unsatisfactory in theory, and that there were some abuses in practice; but on the whole the system had worked very well. It had produced some excellent officers, and by causing the army leadership to be in the hands of the landed aristocracy, it prevented the rise of a professional military caste which might threaten the Constitution and civilian government. He 'thought it was very desirable to connect the higher classes of society with the Army; and he did not know any more effective method of connecting them than by allowing members of high families who held commissions to get on with more rapidity than they would by seniority.... If the connexion between the Army and the higher class of society were dissolved, then the Army would present a dangerous and unconstitutional appearance. It was only when the Army was unconnected with those whose property gave them an interest in the country, and was commanded by unprincipled military adventurers, that it ever became formidable to the liberties of the nation'. The abolition of the purchase of commissions, like other reforms, had to wait till Palmerston died. It was abolished by Gladstone's Government in 1870.

Palmerston was prepared to move with the times on questions such as public health and prison reform; but he would not change the discipline and composition of the Army. He believed as strongly as he had done fifty years before in the necessity of retaining flogging. He felt that though it was possible to dispense with flogging in an army like the French, which was selected by conscription from men of all classes and was a cross-section of the nation, including its most respectable elements, it must be retained in the British Army, where the rank and file was composed largely of criminals. He did not wish to change this state of affairs. He explained this to William Howard Russell. When the famous journalist returned to England from the Crimea in 1856, and was showered with invitations from London society as well as from Radical lecture groups, Palmerston asked him to breakfast. Russell awaited the interview with some trepidation, fearing that Palmerston might have resented his attacks on the Army establishment in his articles in *The Times*; but when Palmerston, who was in good health that day, bounced into the room and advanced to greet Russell like a young man might have done, Russell found him charming, and immediately felt at ease. Palmerston listened attentively to Russell's criticisms of the army in the Crimea, but then praised the qualities of the British Army, and the fact that it was raised by voluntary recruitment and not by conscription. The village constable, he said, was the best recruiting officer which the Army had, for he persuaded young men to join the Army who would otherwise be prosecuted for poaching, or sued for the maintenance of their bastard children. He said that he knew that some people thought that this was as much compulsion as the conscription used to fill the ranks of the Continental armies; but he did not agree, and believed that the British system was much better.

In April 1855, Napoleon III and his Empress, Eugénie, came to London. Queen Victoria, who had regarded Napoleon III as an adventurer and Eugénie as an adventuress, was delighted with both of them, and was completely won over, by their personal charm, to Palmerston's policy of friendship with Bonapartist France. The British public was equally captivated, and the hated Boney became a gallant ally. Between the state occasions and his meetings *en famille* with Victoria, Napoleon found time for political discussions with Palmerston. Palmerston was worried over Napoleon's declared intention of going to the Crimea and taking personal command of his army, because Palmerston realized that if the Emperor made use of this advantage which his sex gave him over Victoria, he would completely eclipse Raglan. He managed to persuade Napoleon to give up this plan.

He had a more serious disagreement with Napoleon III over the question of making peace. Soon after the outbreak of war, in August 1854, Britain and France had put forward four points that Russia would have to accept before the Allies made peace. These were the withdrawal of Russian troops from Wallachia and Moldavia – which had already taken place; free navigation of the Danube; the security of Turkey against Russian aggression; and the abandonment by the Tsar of his claim to protect the Orthodox Christians in Turkey. In December 1854, the Austrian Government, faced with a threat from Britain and France to break off diplomatic relations unless Austria took some action against Russia, agreed with Turkey to send 200,000 Austrian soldiers to occupy Wallachia and Moldavia, thus freeing the Turkish forces there for operations in the Crimea and the Caucasus. This was a more serious reverse for Russia than anything that had happened in the Crimea, and Tsar Nicholas offered to make peace on the basis of the Four Points. The Allies were no longer prepared to make peace on these terms, but agreed, in order to please Austria, to open peace negotiations with Russia in Vienna. On 2 March 1855, Nicholas I died, and was succeeded by Alexander II. The new Tsar, who had Liberal opinions, wished to abolish serfdom and introduce other internal reforms, and he was eager to make peace as soon as possible. Palmerston found that Napoleon III was inclined to make friendly overtures to Alexander II, and that both Napoleon and Lord John Russell in Vienna were prepared to make peace on terms which Palmerston considered were too soft.

In the negotiations in Vienna, the Russian delegate, Prince Gorchakov, accepted three of the Four Points without any difficulty. But Palmerston and Clarendon, who were in complete agreement about the peace terms, put forward a new demand under the third head – the protection of the Turkish Empire. They insisted that neither Russia, Turkey nor any other country should maintain warships in the Black Sea. This meant that Russia was to give up having a Black Sea fleet. Gorchakov rejected the proposal, and put forward alternative proposals for freedom of navigation in the Black Sea, which were rejected by Lord John Russell and Drouyn de Lhuys, the French plenipotentiary in Vienna. The Austrian Foreign Minister, Count Buol, then put forward a compromise plan, by which Turkey and Russia would reduce their fleets in the Black Sea and not exceed the agreed limits; and Buol offered to make an alliance with Britain and France under which the three powers would guarantee the independence of Turkey against Russian aggression. Lord John Russell and Drouyn de Lhuys wished to accept, but felt it necessary to refer the matter to their Governments. Napoleon III was prepared to agree; but Palmerston was not.

Palmerston now formulated his own terms of peace. Russia

was to cede the Crimea to Turkey. The Crimea had been part of the Turkish Empire within living memory, for it was only in 1774 that Catherine the Great had seized it from the Turks. Palmerston also demanded that Russia should restore independence to the Circassians and evacuate the territories which she had conquered in the Caucasus during the last twenty-five years. The province of Bessarabia, between the Pruth and the Dniester, which Russia had taken from Turkey in 1812, was to be ceded to Moldavia, which Palmerston proposed should be granted, along with Wallachia, self-government within the Turkish Empire and placed under the protection of Britain, France, Austria and Turkey. He knew that Russia would not accept these terms at present, and therefore proposed breaking off the peace talks in Vienna and continuing the war, while increasing diplomatic pressure on Austria to come into the war on the Allied side. He was sure that the Allies could win some victories in the Crimea and capture Sevastopol during the 1855 campaign, and that Austria would then declare war on Russia. This would compel the Russians to accept his terms.

But Palmerston was not in favour of including in the peace terms any demand for the independence of Poland. When the war broke out, Prince Adam Czartoryski approached Palmerston with more optimism than at any time since 1831, and offered him the services of the Polish refugees in the war against Russia. Czartoryski hoped that the Allies would include the liberation of Poland among their war aims, and this demand was supported by the patriotic Radicals in Britain. Napoleon III was prepared to consider it, for public opinion in France had always been strongly in favour of the Poles. But Palmerston was against the plan, and persuaded the French Government to reject it. Whatever the Radicals might hope, he had no intention of turning a war to prevent Russian expansion southwards into a war for the overthrow of Tsarism. He told Czartoryski that his aim was not to cripple Russia, but merely to compel her to abandon her designs on Turkey and in the Black Sea. Apart from this, any demand by the Allies for the liberation of Poland would have antagonized Austria; and Palmerston thought that the Austrian Empire was a far more valuable ally than the Polish nationalists. He listened in silence to Czartoryski's arguments, with a wooden expression on his face; he made no attempt to argue, but would not budge an inch. He also rejected the proposal to form a Polish Legion fighting under the Polish national colours, even at the time when the British Government was looking everywhere for foreign mercenaries. The Poles, like all other foreigners, would be welcome if they joined the British forces as individuals, but not as a unified body with their national colours and aspirations. He also, of course, ignored the demand which Kossuth and his Radical supporters were putting forward at mass meetings throughout Britain, that the war for the liberation of Europe from despotism must be waged against Austrian, as well as Russian, tyranny.

Palmerston persuaded Napoleon III to reject the Austrian compromise proposal, and to break off the peace talks in Vienna. 'We should thank Austria for her offer', he wrote to Clarendon on 20 May 1855, 'but her proposals to Russia are too harsh if we decide we want peace at any price, and not harsh enough if we think we can win the war. Austria does not hold out the inducement that she will enter the war on our side if Russia refuses, so what motive have we for accepting her intervention? ... We do not want the Conference to meet again until there shall be some fairer prospect of a satisfactory issue of negotiating'. Lord John Russell and Drouyn de Lhuys were recalled from Vienna. Drouyn de Lhuys resigned from the French Government; Russell, after considering resignation, remained in the British Government as Colonial Secretary. On 9 June Palmerston obtained a vote of confidence in the House of Commons after a debate in which the Peelites joined with Cobden and Bright in attacking the Government for having rejected this opportunity to end the war. Palmerston spoke vigorously in the debate. He attacked Gladstone and Herbert for their attitude, and revealed that when they were ministers in Aberdeen's Government they had agreed to put forward the demand for the neutralization of the Black Sea which they now condemned as excessive. The public had lost some of their passionate enthusiasm for the war, but they were still solidly behind Palmerston's war policy; and so was the Queen. For the first time for many years she approved of everything that Palmerston was doing. She favoured the French alliance, which was strengthened by a return visit which Victoria and Albert paid to Napoleon III and Eugénie in Paris in August 1855; and, though she and Albert had been reluctant to go to war with Russia in 1853, she felt strongly that once war had been declared, Britain should insist upon peace terms which were sufficiently harsh to make it clear that Britain had won the victory.

Six weeks later, Buol revealed that Lord John Russell, as well as Drouyn de Lhuys, had provisionally accepted his compromise peace plan at the Vienna Conference. When called upon to explain his conduct in the House of Commons, Russell at first refused to resign, and then changed his mind, and resigned. He had utterly discredited himself with everyone. Palmerston appointed Sir William Molesworth to succeed Russell as Colonial Secretary. With the warm approval of the Queen, he persuaded Napoleon III to recall the British and French Ambassadors in Vienna as a protest against Buol's pro-Russian attitude at the Peace Conference. He was convinced that Austria would wish to join the winning side, and would be more inclined to do so, the tougher the Allies became. He was right. Sweden, too, climbed on the bandwagon, and signed a treaty of friendship with Britain and France. But Prussia stayed strictly neutral, thanks to the advice given to King Frederick William by Bismarck, who was the Prussian Minister to the German Confederation at Frankfort. He thought that Prussia would gain nothing by joining the Allies, but would win Russian friendship for the future by being the only neighbour who did not stab her in the back during her time of trouble.

In the Crimea, operations were proceeding with mixed success. In May the British troops captured Kertch in the east, and looted the town and ill-treated the civilians; when reports reached England, Palmerston ordered Panmure to investigate and ascertain what steps had been taken to prevent such outrages. On 18 June, General Simpson celebrated Waterloo Day by an attack on the Redan fortress at Sevastopol, which was repulsed with heavy loss. In September, the assault on Sevastopol was resumed, the British again attacking the Redan while the French attacked the neighbouring Malakov fortress. The British were driven back from the Redan with many casualties, but the French captured the Malakov; and as a result, Sevastopol surrendered. Palmerston asked the Archbishop of Canterbury to order a day of thanksgiving on a Sunday; but he refused the suggestion that there should be a special Thanksgiving Day on a weekday, as had been done after Waterloo. He argued that the capture of Sevastopol was not, like Waterloo, a decisive victory which would end the war; its importance was more comparable to the victories at Salamanca and Vitoria during the Peninsular War, which had been celebrated by a Sunday thanksgiving. The joy at the fall of Sevastopol was soured for Palmerston, as it was for many other Englishmen, by the fact that the French had done much better at the Malakov than the British at the Redan; this was a shock to a nation which had been convinced for forty years of its military superiority over the French. There was also bad news from the Caucasus, where the Russians captured the Turkish town and fortress of Kars, along with a British General and a Turkish army.

In September, Buol invited Britain, France and Russia to resume the peace talks in Vienna, after warning the Russians that they would be forced to accept worse terms than those which he had put forward in his proposal in the spring. Palmerston's first reaction was not enthusiastic. 'My dear Clarendon', he wrote on 9 October, 'It is of course to be foreseen that between this time and the Spring the Russian Government will make as vigorous efforts to escape the further Pressure and defeats which another Campaign is sure to bring on, as they have made to maintain themselves in Sebastopol, and it must be our business to baffle them. With Nesselrode's two Daughters, one at Paris, the other at Brussels, with money and all the other Russian Agents acting on the French Government, and with Vienna and Berlin co-operating we shall find all our steadiness and skill required to avoid being drawn into a Peace which would disappoint the just expectations of the Country, and leave unaccomplished the real objects of the War.... The fact is, as you said the other day,

Russia has not yet been beat enough to make Peace possible at the present moment'.

But by 23 November he had changed his attitude. He believed that Russia now realized the weakness of her position, for her Baltic fleet was bottled up, her Black Sea fleet destroyed, and she knew that in the next campaign in 1856 the Allies would invade Finland, capture Kronstadt, and threaten St. Petersburg, while in the south they would capture the ports of Kherson and Nikolayev. 'The French Government', he wrote to Clarendon, 'affect to consider this Austrian Proposal as a mere blind under which Austria is to break off her diplomatic relations with Russia. I may be mistaken, but I am much inclined to think its character much more real and serious; I think it highly probable that Austria has privately ascertained that Russia will accept the terms specified, and that we are therefore on the eve of a practical negotiation'. He therefore agreed to resume peace talks in Vienna, and sent Sir Hamilton Seymour, who had served Palmerston well in the past as British Minister in Rome and Lisbon, to be the plenipotentiary at the Peace Conference. On 15 December Buol presented Russia with an ultimatum: Austria would declare war unless Russia agreed to negotiate on the basis of the Allied demands for the cession of Bessarabia and the neutralization of the Black Sea. Palmerston was not satisfied with this. He wanted the Crimea for Turkey, and an independent Circassia. 'My dear Seymour', he wrote on 24 January 1856, 'I am sorry to perceive by your recent communication and especially by your telegram of yesterday that the relaxing atmosphere of Vienna has begun to take effect upon you. Pray put a little more starch into your neckcloth, and while you observe the "suaviter in modo", do not forget the "fortiter in re" '. But Palmerston was prepared to accept Buol's terms as the basis for negotiation on which a definite Peace Congress could be held; and, faced with the Austrian ultimatum, Russia accepted.

Palmerston suggested that the Peace Congress be held in Brussels; but Napoleon III insisted that it be held in Paris, where the delegate of a victorious France, presiding at the Congress of Paris, could efface the memory of the French humiliation at the Congress of Vienna. Palmerston was perfectly willing to agree to this, which had certain advantages for him. As it was a Congress, and not merely a Conference, Britain would be represented by the Foreign Secretary, Lord Clarendon, who had been a close personal friend of Napoleon III's when Napoleon was a refugee in England. In Paris, Clarendon would be able to talk to the Emperor personally, and to try, with the assistance of the French High Command, to counter the influence of Napoleon's pro-Russian Foreign Minister, Walewski. It would also be possible for the Ambassador in Paris, Lord Cowley, to assist in the negotiations. Cowley, like Clarendon, fully shared Palmerston's views on the need to prevent too soft a peace.

On 25 February 1856 the Congress opened in Paris, and an armistice was signed next day. Palmerston had instructed Clarendon to press for the independence of Circassia. But he received alarming reports from Paris which showed that the French Government was not merely unwilling to support the British demands on this point, but was prepared to abandon the conditions about the cession of Bessarabia and the neutralization of the Black Sea which Russia had already accepted in Vienna as the preliminary conditions for the Peace Congress. Palmerston learnt that Napoleon III was considering pursuing a new and forward policy in Italy, by which he would ally himself with Sardinia and wage war against Austria with the object of liberating Italy from Austrian rule and establishing French influence there. Napoleon therefore contemplated an anti-Austrian alliance with Russia, and wished to pave the way for this by making friends with the new Tsar and granting him an honourable peace. This ran completely counter to Palmerston's policy of building up an alliance with Austria against Russia. Palmerston had always regarded Austria as a useful bulwark against Russian expansion in the Balkans, and a Franco-Russian alliance as the greatest threat to British influence in Europe. He therefore told Clarendon to see Napoleon III personally, and to tell him that Britain insisted that Russia adhere to the conditions which had been agreed in Vienna, and that, rather than sign a peace treaty which did not contain them, Britain would continue the war alone.

But Palmerston did not have the support of all his own

Cabinet in his insistence on a tough peace. When the Congress opened, Palmerston informed the Cabinet of the line which Clarendon would put forward, and said, briefly and confidently, that of course we would never agree to relinquish any of our demands. Everyone seemed to concur with him, so he passed on without more ado to a discussion of other matters. After the meeting, as the ministers discussed the problem among themselves, they discovered that a majority of them thought that Palmerston's demands were unreasonable. At the next Cabinet meeting, the Duke of Argyll and other ministers raised the question again, and the majority opinion was that, while Clarendon must insist on the demilitarization of the Black Sea, he should not hold out unreasonably for the other demands. This time it was Palmerston who made no attempt to argue, and seemed willing to agree with the majority opinion; but he alone was in telegraphic communication with Clarendon, and he sent him a succession of coded telegrams urging him to stand firm for the original British demands.

'If the Russians had not accepted purely and simply the Austrian conditions', he wrote to Clarendon on 25 February, 'there would have been no conferences or negotiations for Peace, and it is an instance of flagrant bad faith on their part to pretend now to insist upon a modification of a condition, the pure and simple acceptance of which recorded in a protocol forms part of the Grounds upon which they appear at Paris to negotiate. I think we ought to hold them fast bound to all that they have formally and deliberately accepted. If this condition is allowed to be a debatable matter, the whole arrangement is at sea, and the accepted Ultimatum goes for nothing. . . . It seems to me that a show of weakness on our part in the outset would be fatal to the whole negotiation, and throw discredit upon us all'. He specifically warned Clarendon against the machinations of the chief Russian delegate, Count Orlov, to whom Palmerston had had a special aversion ever since Orlov negotiated the Treaty of Unkiar Skelessi in 1833; and he became indignant when Orlov put forward, as a bargaining point, the demand that if Russia was to demilitarize her Black Sea ports, Britain should demilitarize Heligoland. 'As to Orloff's proposal that we should engage not to fortify

Heligoland, it required Russian Impudence to put forward such a pretension. It is not to be for a moment talked of. He might as well ask us to withdraw our Fleet from the Mediterranean'. He added that Orlov 'might be made civilly to understand' that Britain had been very moderate in not demanding that Russia pay an indemnity for the cost of the war, as the Russians themselves had always demanded after their victories over Turkey, Persia and France; but if the Russians failed to make peace now, and the war was resumed, a demand for an indemnity might be made. 'As to Orloff, I know him well – he is civil and courteous externally, but his inward mind is deeply impregnated with Russian Insolence, arrogance and pride. He will do his best to bully without appearing to do so. He will stand out for every point which he thinks he has a chance of carrying, and he has all the cunning of a half-civilized savage. But like bullying and cunning men, he will give way before a stout and steady Resistance'. Apart from the reference to 'a half-civilized savage', the description was very similar to what hostile observers said about Palmerston himself.

In order to encourage Clarendon to hold out for tougher terms, Palmerston drew his attention to suitable proverbs. 'Faint Heart never won fair Lady', he wrote on 28 February; and next day he sent him a Leap Year's message: *'Chateau qui parle est a moitié rendue'* [sic]. He wrote letters in fluent French to his old friend Flahaut and to the pro-Russian Walewski, in the hopes of stiffening the French attitude. 'Rely upon it', he wrote to Clarendon on 29 February, 'that Russia *must* have Peace, and will consent sooner or later to all the conditions which I have sketched out in my former letters provided only that England and France hold together – and the Emperor will hold with us if he sees no wavering or hesitation on our part'. He was sure that Napoleon's position in France would be strengthened if he broke up the Congress and resumed the war. 'Some of the Gamblers about the Court and Government are for peace', as were the 'Lieven salons' and Orleanist and Legitimist circles; but 'the bourgeoisie felt like the English nation', and only wanted peace if it could be obtained on honourable terms. Occasionally he put forward tentatively some new proposal for Clarendon's consideration

– for example, that Wallachia and Moldavia should be granted to Austria, or that Sardinia should be rewarded for her part in the war by being granted the Crimea as a colony, in return for her abandoning her claims to Lombardy and Venetia.

But now a new factor entered in. Napoleon III, in one of his informal talks with Clarendon, said that if the French people were to be induced to continue the war, it would have to be a war fought for wider and nobler aims than to obtain territorial gains for Turkey at Russia's expense. If the Congress of Paris proclaimed an end to the system initiated by the Congress of Vienna, the French nation would be ready to fight for the rights of small nations, for the liberation of Italy and Poland, and for the break-up of the old absolutist Empires of Russia and Austria. This was not a prospect which appealed to Palmerston; he preferred even a soft peace to a revolutionary war. He also knew that his threat that Britain would refuse to sign the peace treaty, and would continue the war alone, was bluff. British troops now numbered less than twenty per cent of the total Allied forces in the Crimea, and the war was becoming expensive to the British taxpayer. Clarendon was holding out firmly in Paris for the demilitarization of the Black Sea, which he thought the most important point; but he realized that if he was to gain this, he must give way on other matters. Clarendon and Cowley, who had both agreed with Palmerston on the need for a hard peace, were in a good position to convince him that he would have to be satisfied with a compromise.

After a month's hard bargaining, the terms were agreed. Instead of ceding the whole of Bessarabia up to the Dniester, the Russians ceded only a small area in the south which they had seized in 1828, though this had the important result that they no longer controlled the mouths of the Danube. They escaped without making any other territorial concessions, for they retained the Crimea and Circassia. They agreed to evacuate Kars, and to demilitarize the Black Sea, as well as the Åland Islands in the Baltic. The agreement about the Black Sea was the greatest British gain and the greatest Russian setback. Sevastopol, Odessa, Kherson and Nikolayev were to be demolished as naval bases, and Russia agreed not to keep any warships in the Black Sea except for a small number of light vessels permitted by the treaty. Fourteen years later, when Palmerston was dead, when Britain, under Gladstone, had withdrawn into isolationism from European politics, and when France was engaged in the war of 1870, Russia denounced the treaty and built up a new Black Sea fleet; but during Palmerston's lifetime the Russian threat to Turkey no longer existed.

Palmerston was not happy about the solution of the problem of the principalities. It was decided to unite Wallachia and Moldavia in one autonomous state to be known as Rumania, which remained under the nominal suzerainty of the Sultan, but was independent in all but name. Palmerston did not object to the autonomy, but thought that Wallachia and Moldavia should remain separate, because he feared that if they were united, they would constitute a powerful threat to the integrity of the Turkish Empire. His fears proved to be well-founded, for Rumania became a passionately Christian state, with an equal hatred for Moslems and Jews, and in 1878 became an independent Kingdom after the Congress of Berlin, when Russia regained the territory in Bessarabia which she had ceded in 1856.

Apart from relinquishing the demand – to which Russia had agreed in Vienna – that the whole of Bessarabia should be ceded to Moldavia, Britain made another important concession in Paris. The Congress, following the precedent set by the Congress of Vienna, settled a number of questions of international concern which had nothing to do with the war and the peace treaty. Palmerston and Clarendon prevented Napoleon III from doing anything to help Italy at the Congress; but the laws of naval warfare were changed. It was agreed that privateering, and the grant of letters of marque to private citizens authorizing them to plunder enemy vessels in wartime, should be prohibited; and the rights of neutral shipping were safeguarded. The powers agreed that, with certain exceptions, cargoes carried in neutral ships should not be seized by the belligerents. Thus Britain, who had gone to war with the United States in 1812 in order to preserve this right of seizure, now relinquished it. There was no doubt that this clause in the treaty would operate to the disadvantage of Britain, who, with her naval superiority, had been in the best position to make use of this right.

The Treaty of Paris was signed on 30 March 1856. Palmerston held a Cabinet meeting and informed his ministers, in his most cheerful tones, that the peace would be signed, and that, though some points of it might be criticized in England, he thought that, in the main, it was very satisfactory. The Cabinet was very pleased; but Argyll felt that Palmerston's cheerfulness was put on. Palmerston then went off to the wedding of Lady Elizabeth Hay, and told the wedding guests about the peace as if it were very welcome news. But, as Palmerston expected, the treaty was criticized in Britain. The heralds were hissed when they proclaimed the peace in the City; and MPs denounced it as too soft. The chief points of criticism as the provisions about naval warfare; but Palmerston gained a vote of confidence in the Commons and the Lords, and his popularity in the country was undiminished. The Queen was disappointed that the war had ended with a British defeat at the Redan, and would have wished it to continue for another campaign so that the British Army could win a victory to efface this memory; but though Palmerston shared her feelings about the Redan, he persuaded her that it was impossible to continue the war for this reason alone. His relations with the Queen were better now than anyone would have thought possible a few years before: and in April 1856 she gave him the Order of the Garter.

Palmerston became involved in some violent altercations with the Russians over the implementation of the peace treaty. The Russians blew up the fortress of Kars before evacuating it, and did the same with the border fortresses in the strip which they ceded to Moldavia. Palmerston denounced this as a breach of faith by the Russians. He was also indignant when they tried to retain a part of the territory in Bessarabia which they had agreed to cede through making use of a confusion about two towns of the same name. Palmerston also complained about the Russian delay in demolishing the fortresses in the Black Sea coast towns. He kept the Navy in the Black Sea, though even the Turks had asked them to leave, until the Russians had given way and carried out the peace treaty. When diplomatic relations were resumed, and the new Russian Ambassador, Count Chreptovitch, arrived in London, there was more unpleasantness. Palmerston complained that a long time had elapsed between Chreptovitch's appointment and his arrival in London, and said that this showed a lack of respect to the Queen. He therefore told Chreptovitch that normally, if a new Ambassador arrived in London while the Queen was at Osborne, the Foreign Secretary immediately took the Ambassador to the Isle of Wight to present his credentials, but that in this case this would not be done, and Chreptovitch would have to wait until the Queen returned to London; for as he had delayed so long in coming to Britain, he could now wait a little longer. Whatever Chreptovitch may have felt about the interview, Palmerston treated it all with his usual good temper. 'We parted with much mutual cordiality', he wrote, 'and tender inquiries about mutual friends, English and Russian'.

Chapter Thirty-two

The Lorcha *Arrow*

Despite the unpopularity of some of the terms of the Treaty of Paris, the British people welcomed the peace. It was celebrated, as usual, with firing of cannon in the parks and illumination of windows; and Palmerston told Shaftesbury that it was estimated that 500,000 people had come into London for the celebrations, and that 2,000,000 Londoners were in the streets. The first summer of peace was marked by an unusually gay society season, and both society and the masses were stimulated by one of those famous murder trials which so impressed Victorian England. The majesty of English law in action, the excitement of the prisoner's struggle for his life, and the moral lesson to be derived from his final expiation of his crime on the scaffold, were all present in the trial of William Palmer, the Rugeley poisoner. Local prejudice against Palmer was so strong in Staffordshire that his trial had to be held in London, and, if the Marquis of Lorne is to be believed, a deputation from Rugeley called on Palmerston after Palmer had been executed, and asked him to authorize a change in the name of their town, as it had become so notorious through its association with Palmer. Palmerston mischievously suggested that they might do him the honour of renaming Rugeley after him – a suggestion which the delegation eagerly accepted until they realized that the name 'Palmerston' could easily be mistaken for 'Palmer's town'.

The First Commissioner of Works, Sir Benjamin Hall, thought that in this victory summer it would contribute to the gay and military mood of the people if military bands were to play in the London parks on Sunday afternoons. Palmerston approved of the idea, and so did the Queen; and the concerts began in May 1856, and were well attended and very popular with the Sunday afternoon crowds. But the believers in Sunday observance were deeply shocked, and Palmerston received many protests about the concerts. Some of the working-class organizations opposed it, as they thought that it was the thin end of the wedge which would introduce Sunday labour in factories; and many people objected to the bands as a German innovation which had been introduced by Prince Albert. When the matter was raised in the House of Commons, Palmerston defended Hall's decision, and refused to stop the Sunday concerts; and the opposition grew more vociferous. No one was more indignant than Lord Shaftesbury, who was a fervent believer in Lord's Day Observance. 'Violent and fearful struggles on Sabbath question', he wrote in his diary on 17 May, 'Palmerston suffered himself to be dragged through the dirt by Sir B. Hall, and endorsed all the follies, insolences, outrages of that perilous fellow. Mighty feeling against him in House of Commons – his Government endangered. I had forewarned him heartily, earnestly, but he rejected my advice'. Shaftesbury persuaded the Archbishop of Canterbury to write a strong letter of protest to Palmerston; and after a long late-night argument with Shaftesbury, Palmerston gave way. He cheerfully told the Cabinet that though he personally believed that the bands were harmless, the Government faced defeat in the House of Commons on this issue, so there was no alternative but to give way; and the concerts were stopped. On the next two Sundays, Shaftesbury's house was besieged by angry crowds; but he was happy, as he was sure that God's cause had prevailed.

Though Palmerston suffered this minor set-back at home, his attention in 1856 was mainly directed to international affairs. Of the three powers which Palmerston believed could alone constitute a challenge to British power – Russia, France and the United States – Russia had been engaged and defeated, and had temporarily withdrawn into isolation; France was still a friend and ally, though there were signs of possible friction developing in future; and the United States continued, as always, to irritate Palmerston. A new and serious cause of conflict between Britain and the United States had arisen in

Central America. For two hundred years, Britain had exercised a protectorate over the Indian kingdom of Mosquito on the Atlantic coast of Nicaragua. Nicaragua, after becoming an independent republic when the Spanish Empire collapsed in 1821, had developed close links with the United States. The Americans were eager to build a canal between the Atlantic and Pacific, in order to shorten the long route to California around Cape Horn. The experts had advised that the shortest way – across the Isthmus of Panama – presented serious difficulties; so the United States Government had decided to go across Nicaragua. This increased the importance of Nicaragua to the United States.

The people of Mosquito – a dark-skinned race, interbred from the original Red Indian inhabitants and negro slaves – were on bad terms with the white inhabitants of Nicaragua, and their quarrels involved their respective protectors, Britain and the United States. In 1848, when Palmerston was Foreign Secretary, fighting broke out for possession of the port which the British called Greytown and the Nicaraguans San Juan del Norte, and the British and American navies became involved. Palmerston was determined not to give way over Greytown, in order to make it clear that Britain did not recognize the Monroe Doctrine. The United States Government then offered to make a treaty with Britain by which both powers would undertake not to acquire territory in Central America. The proposed treaty also provided for co-operation between Britain and the United States in building the canal which was to link the two oceans. Palmerston did not reject the proposal, but he was a little suspicious, and as usual tended to raise difficulties. Bulwer, who had been sent as Minister to Washington after his expulsion from Spain, accepted the American offer, and practically confronted Palmerston with a *fait accompli*. Palmerston tolerated things from Bulwer which he would never have endured from other British diplomats, and he persuaded the Cabinet and Parliament to ratify the Clayton-Bulwer Treaty of 1850. It seemed as if all the disputes between Britain and the United States in Central America had been settled, in a satisfactory manner for both sides.

Everything was upset by a journalist from San Francisco. William Walker of Tennessee, after roaming over Europe and trying his hand at law, medicine and journalism, found himself at the age of twenty-nine a bored and frustrated reporter on a San Francisco newspaper. He therefore sailed with a few friends to the Mexican territory of Lower California, seized it, and made himself dictator of the area. He was soon thrown out by the Mexican and United States authorities; but his activity had attracted the attention of the Liberals of Nicaragua, who were revolting against their Conservative Government, and they offered him the command of their forces. Walker accepted, and became dictator of Nicaragua, being supported and financed by the American rivals of Cornelius Vanderbilt, whose ships Walker seized and confiscated. He also won the sympathy of the Southern states of the USA, and of the influential slaveowners' lobby in Washington, by reintroducing slavery in Nicaragua; and his régime was recognized by the United States Government, who decided to give him full support. In 1856, with the help of American privateers, he seized Greytown from Mosquito.

This came at a time when relations between Britain and the United States were already strained as a result of the Crimean War. The United States was neutral in the war, but Russia was confronted with so many enemies that she considered a neutral almost as a friend, and links between the two countries increased during the war. Several United States citizens served as experts and doctors with the Russian forces in Sevastopol. This in itself caused only a minor strain on relations with Britain; but things got worse when the British Government, in its desperate search for more mercenaries to serve in the British forces in the Crimea, tried secretly to recruit volunteers in the United States in breach of the United States Neutrality Laws. In July 1855 the United States Ambassador in London, James Buchanan, protested to Clarendon, who expressed his regret, and said that he knew nothing of the matter. A few months later, the United States Government discovered – what Palmerston and Clarendon may not have known – that the British Minister in Washington, Crampton, had been personally connected with the illegal recruiting campaign. There was a great outcry in the United States, and the United States Government insisted that Crampton should be replaced. As Palmerston refused to agree to this, Crampton was eventually handed his passport.

Palmerston was very angry. A new United States Minister, Dallas, had just arrived in London to replace Buchanan, who returned home to stand as a candidate for the Presidency in 1856. Palmerston wished to expel Dallas immediately. He was overruled by the Cabinet, who did not wish to be involved in too much trouble with the United States, and felt that, in any case, Britain was in the wrong in the dispute. Palmerston reluctantly agreed to do nothing, and contented himself with sarcastic references to the fact that the United States, the so-called land of the free, had refused to join with the other nations who had fought for the rights of free peoples against Russian despotism.

On top of all this came the news that Walker had seized Greytown. Palmerston summoned the Cabinet, and told them that the Navy must sail at once to the Mosquito Coast and blockade the Nicaraguans in Greytown. The other members of the Cabinet objected to a policy which they thought would precipitate a clash, perhaps even a war, with the United States. They won over Clarendon, who was always a key figure in the disagreements in the Cabinet over foreign policy, for, apart from the fact that he was Foreign Secretary, Palmerston had a high respect for his opinion. Clarendon urged that the Navy should be sent to Greytown in strength, but that no blockade should be established until they had conducted negotiations with the United States; and Palmerston agreed. The Duke of Argyll wrote in his memoirs that the incident was 'typical of what I have often observed in Palmerston. His first impulse was always to move fleets and to threaten our opponents, sometimes on trivial occasions, on the details of which he had not fully informed himself by careful reading. Then, on finding his proposals combatted, he was candid in listening and in inquiring and if he found the objections reasonable, he could give way to them with the most perfect good humour. This was a great quality in a man so impulsive and so strong-headed as he was, and so prone to violent action.

It made him a much less dangerous man than he was supposed to be. But it made it an all-important matter that he should have colleagues who understood him, and were not afraid of him'.

Clarendon wrote a strong despatch to the United States, who decided not to support Walker; and the Nicaraguans withdrew from Greytown. Next year, the United States Government grew tired of Walker, and Vanderbilt persuaded them to send a naval expedition to expel him from Nicaragua. In 1860, Walker returned to Central America to assist a revolt in Honduras. He was intercepted by a British naval vessel, which handed him over to the Honduran authorities, who shot him.

The friction between Britain and the United States was not limited to the American continent, for the United States Navy now sailed all over the world. In 1850 the United States made a claim against Portugal for compensation for the seizure of American ships nearly forty years before by the Portuguese Navy during the Napoleonic Wars. When the Portuguese refused to pay, an American warship sailed for Lisbon. Palmerston felt that he had the exclusive right to bully the Portuguese, and owed them the duty, in return for their complying with British demands, to protect them against outsiders. He asked the United States to modify their claims, informed them that Britain could not remain indifferent to American action against Portugal, and offered to mediate. The United States Government virtuously told Palmerston that the United States did not bully small nations like Portugal – it was at the time of the case of Don Pacifico; and Palmerston persuaded the Portuguese Government to satisfy most of the American demands.

In 1856 there was a possibility of an Anglo-American confrontation as far away as Persia. British relations with Persia were always difficult, because of Persia's position as a buffer state between Russia and British India. The Persians disliked the Russians, the Turks and the British in almost equal measure. They had not forgiven Russia for seizing their Northern provinces in the war of 1828; they had frequent trouble with Turkey along their Western frontier; and the British prevented them from capturing Herat from Afghanistan in the south-east. Palmerston demanded nothing from Persia except neutrality between Britain and Russia and passivity towards Afghanistan. When he was Foreign Secretary in 1846 he prevented a war between Persia and Turkey by mediating in their disputes. He tried, with varying success, to induce the Persian Government to refuse the Russian demands for hospital facilities for their naval forces, and for other privileges, on the southern shore of the Caspian.

During the Crimean War, the Persians rejected secret overtures from Russia, who offered them territorial gains at Turkey's expense if they entered the war on Russia's side, and followed the advice of the British Government to stay neutral. But no sooner was the war over than Anglo-Persian relations became very bad. The Persian Prime Minister, the Sadr Azim, objected to the employment of a certain Persian as a British diplomatic agent by Murray, the British Minister in Teheran. When Murray made difficulties about dismissing the Persian, the Sadr Azim said that this was because the Persian's wife was Murray's mistress; and when Murray indignantly demanded an apology for the insult, and threatened to leave Teheran, the Sadr Azim said that if Murray did so, he would publicly reveal the details of Murray's love affair. Murray refused to be blackmailed, and left the country. Soon afterwards Persian troops entered Herat on the pretence of assisting one of the factions in an unusually complicated civil war. Palmerston waited for some time in the hopes that the Persians would withdraw, or would be expelled by local revolutionaries; but eventually Britain declared war, and landed an Indian army at the Persian port of Bushire.

As Palmerston had realized, Russia was in no position to intervene, which she would certainly have done in the days of Nicholas I before the Crimean War; but at this moment, to Palmerston's great annoyance, the United States signed a commercial treaty with Persia. In his private letters to Clarendon, Palmerston expressed himself very forcibly about the 'impudent intermeddling' of the United States in Persia, and hoped that the United States Government would refuse all proposals from Persia for a military alliance. 'If therefore the Government of the United States wish for secure relations of Peace with England', he wrote to Clarendon on 27 May

1856, 'they will refuse the engagement proposed by Persia. If, on the other hand, they wish for War with England, it can hardly be necessary for them to go so far Eastward to lay the ground for a Quarrel'.

The Persian forces were decisively defeated and Persia sued for peace. To their surprise and relief, Britain did not insist on any annexation of territory or any indemnity for the cost of the war, and merely required that the Persians withdraw from Herat, apologize for the insult to Murray, and suppress the slave trade in the Persian Gulf. The peace treaty was signed in Paris in March 1857. After peace had been restored, Palmerston received a letter from the Sadr Azim who had been the chief advocate in Persia of the policy which had led to war. The Sadr Azim made out that he, alone of all the Persian politicians, had always been in favour of friendship with Britain, and expressed the hope that Anglo-Persian relations would prosper in future. Palmerston replied on 8 September 1857, and stated that the war 'was occasioned solely and entirely by your Excellency's own unfriendly conduct, and by the violent hostility which your Excellency displayed towards England, both in word and deed; and, therefore, so far from your Excellency having been alone in endeavours to preserve friendship between the two Governments, your Excellency was the main and principal cause of the cessation of that friendship. I have no doubt that your Excellency, in seeking a quarrel with England, believed that you were promoting the interests of Persia, and I am bound to suppose that your Excellency considered yourself as performing on that occasion the part of a true patriot; and this belief on my part strengthens my confidence in the future maintenance of friendship between the two Governments and countries, because the events of the war, and the decisive victories obtained by the British troops over superior numbers of Persian troops, must have shown and proved to the sagacious mind and powerful understanding of your Excellency that the true interests of Persia are best promoted by peace and friendship with England, and that the sure results to Persia of war with England must be defeat and disaster. . . . With every wish for the health and happiness of your Excellency, and with a fervent hope that the reign of your illustrious master and Sovereign the Shah of Persia may be long and prosperous, I have the honour to remain, Your Excellency's most obedient and faithful Servant, Palmerston'.

But Palmerston's difficulties with the Peacock Throne of Persia were less prolonged than his conflicts with the Chinese Empire of the Son of Heaven. By the Treaty of Nanking of 1842 the Chinese Government had conceded every British demand except the legalization of opium. Palmerston did not believe that it would be proper for Britain to insist that this alteration in the internal laws of China should be included as a condition of a peace treaty; but before he resigned from the Foreign Office in 1841, he had urged the Chinese Government to give up their hopeless attempt to prohibit opium-smoking, and to legalize and tax the trade. This would have the double advantage of opening a source of revenue for the Chinese Government, and removing a perpetual cause of conflict with British merchants.

But one of the unforeseen results of the Treaty of Nanking was to create a new body of opinion which was opposed to opium. The terms of the treaty made it possible for Christian missionaries from Britain and the United States to settle in China. Many went in the years after 1842, and had more success than they had dared to hope for. Christianity, with its egalitarian doctrines, made a great appeal to many of the lowest classes in China, and was adopted as the creed of the revolutionary peasant movement of the Taipings which sprang up after 1850, and worried the European merchants in Shanghai and Canton as well as the Emperor of China and the mandarins.

The British missionaries, like the Taipings themselves, opposed opium-smoking; and as the missionaries had powerful supporters in Britain, including Lord Shaftesbury, Palmerston was continually receiving memorials and petitions from the Missionary Societies asking him to collaborate with the Chinese authorities in suppressing the opium trade. The British merchants organized counter-propaganda, and sent Palmerston a large number of statements from English and Scottish doctors who had practised for many years in the Far East.

These doctors explained that the evils of opium-smoking had been much exaggerated, and that opium, like alcohol, was harmful if taken in excess, but not if used only in moderation. It was therefore no more necessary or justifiable to prohibit opium than to ban all alcoholic beverages; and the doctors did not hesitate to say that alcohol was worse than opium, because the opium-addict harmed no one but himself, whereas the drunkard often caused injury to others. With the arguments for and against banning opium lying equal in the balance, the doctrine of free trade easily tipped the scales, in Palmerston's view, in favour of the merchants and against Shaftesbury and the missionaries. He continued to urge the Chinese Government to legalize the opium trade, though he would not give any support to the British smugglers who tried to evade the laws of China.

The ill-feeling between the British merchants and the Chinese led to numerous incidents. The Chinese authorities violated the provisions of the Treaty of Nanking by prohibiting British subjects from entering certain places, such as the walled city of Canton. Englishmen who ventured to go for walks in the country were sometimes hooted at and stoned by the villagers; and on a number of occasions resentment was aroused when Chinese children were accidentally shot and wounded by British subjects who were out shooting game. Relations were worst at the seat of the original trouble – Canton – where there was a serious incident between British and Chinese in July 1846, a few days after Palmerston returned to the Foreign Office. Mr. Charles Compton, an English merchant, was trying to enjoy his afternoon sleep in his house in the English residence when he was disturbed by the raucous cries of a Chinese street-vendor selling his fruit outside the house. As the fruit-seller ignored Compton's exhortations to him to keep quiet, Compton rushed out of the English residence, kicked over the fruit-stall, and drove the fruit-seller out of the street. The fruit-seller did not venture to return; but another Chinese fruit-seller appeared in the same street four days later, and the sleep of the English in their residence was again disturbed. Compton and a colleague then came out of the house, dragged the fruit-seller into the English residence, tied him up, and flogged him. That evening an infuriated crowd of Chinese assembled, and attacked the English residence. After they had done a great deal of damage, the British opened fire on the mob and killed three of them. Eventually Chinese troops arrived and drove off the crowd.

Sir John Davis, the Governor of Hongkong, ordered the British Consul to impose the maximum fine of 200 dollars on Compton for his assault on the Chinese fruit-seller, and demanded that the Chinese rioters who had attacked the English residence should be severely punished by the Chinese authorities. The Consul fined Compton 200 dollars; but Compton appealed to the Court of Appeal in Hongkong, and his appeal was allowed on the grounds that he had been charged under the wrong regulation. There was strong sympathy for him among the British residents in Canton and Hongkong, and the Chief Justice of Hongkong, in allowing his appeal, criticized the Consul for having taken proceedings against Compton. Palmerston was very angry that Compton had been acquitted. 'It cannot be tolerated', he wrote to Sir John Davis on 25 January 1847, 'that British subjects should indulge towards the people of China in acts of violence or contumely which they would not venture to practise towards the humblest and meanest individual in their own country'. He told Davis not to offer any apology to Compton when he returned his fine; and when Compton wrote to Palmerston to complain of Davis's conduct in initiating proceedings against him, Palmerston directed his Under-Secretary to reply that Palmerston thoroughly approved of the fine, and much regretted that Compton's appeal had succeeded. The merchants' organizations in Manchester and Liverpool sent protests to Palmerston about the attitude that he had adopted towards Compton; but Palmerston rejected them, and told the merchants that Compton's conduct had been inexcusable.

At the same time, Palmerston insisted that the Chinese should punish the rioters. 'We shall lose all the vantage ground we have gained by our victories in China if we take a low tone', he wrote to Davis on 9 January 1847. 'Of course we ought – and by we I mean all the English in China – to abstain from giving the Chinese any ground of complaint, and much more from anything like provocation or affront; but we must stop on the very threshold any attempt on their part to treat us otherwise than as their equals, and we must make them all clearly understand, though in the civilest terms, that our treaty rights must be respected. The Chinese must learn and be convinced that if they attack our people and our factories, they will be shot; and that if they ill-treat innocent Englishmen who are quietly exercising their treaty right of walking about the streets of Canton, they will be punished.' He approved of the action of the British merchants in forming armed associations for their defence against the Chinese. 'Depend upon it that the best way of keeping any men quiet, is to let them see that you are able and determined to repel force by force; and the Chinese are not in the least different, in this respect, from the rest of mankind'.

The Chinese Commissioner at Canton was Kiying, who had always been in favour of friendship with Britain and had negotiated the Treaty of Nanking which ended the Opium War. Whenever any British subject was murdered, assaulted or insulted, Kiying had the criminals and their associates beheaded, tortured, flogged with the bamboo, or cangued; and Palmerston had to instruct the British agents in China not to press for the infliction of the excessive punishments which Chinese law prescribed for such offences. But Palmerston always insisted that the Chinese authorities should take action against any Chinese who had affronted a British subject; and his attitude inspired the British authorities in Hongkong to take a more vigorous line than they had done when Lord Aberdeen was Foreign Secretary. Aberdeen had urged them not to cause unnecessary offence to the Chinese, and to do nothing which might embarrass the pro-British Kiying at a time when he was confronting an increasingly threatening movement of the rebellious peasantry in the country around Canton. Palmerston was no more concerned to help Kiying out of his difficulties with the peasants than he had been to save the Chartist Government in Portugal from embarrassment when he pressed them to pay their British creditors as relentlessly as he had pressed the Septembrists.

When two British sailors were beaten up by a crowd of

Chinese in Canton in October 1846, Palmerston directed Davis to inform Kiying that if the Chinese did not punish the guilty individuals, 'the British Government will be obliged to take the matter into their own hands, and it will not be their fault if in such a case the innocent are involved in the punishment which may be sought to be inflicted on the guilty'. On receiving Palmerston's despatch, Davis sent in the Navy, who demolished the defences of Canton; and Palmerston subsequently endorsed his action. Palmerston took the occasion to remind the Chinese 'that, if occasion required it, a British military force would be able to destroy the town of Canton not leaving one single house standing'. He also encouraged subordinate officials to take action on their own initiative. When three English missionaries were assaulted at Tsingpu by Chinese junkmen in March 1848, the British Consul at Shanghai, without consulting his superiors in Hongkong, seized the ships in the harbour which contained food supplies for the Emperor's Court and refused to release them until the Chinese authorities had produced ten of the guilty men; and ten men were promptly found, and sentenced to wear the cangue for a month in the British settlement. The Governor of Hongkong reprimanded the Consul for acting without authority; but Palmerston told the Governor that the Consul had been justified on this occasion, though it was not a precedent which should be generally followed.

Kiying's policy of collaboration with the British authorities led him into great difficulties. When he called in Chinese and British soldiers to surround a village where six Englishmen and two Chinese had been killed in an affray, and decapitated four of the villagers in the presence of British officials in order to level the score between the two nations, his countrymen regarded him as a traitor; but when he refused some British demand, and British troops occupied part of Canton, it weakened his authority and prestige, and encouraged the peasant revolts. In 1848 Kiying was dismissed by the Emperor, and replaced as Commissioner for Canton by a more intractable successor, who in 1852 was in turn replaced by his still more intractable deputy, Yeh Ming-chin. Yeh adopted a more hostile attitude to the British than any of his predecessors had done, and was even more ruthless in suppressing the peasant revolts. He ordered large-scale massacres, and at one time nearly a thousand rebels were beheaded every day in Canton.

The British authorities in Hongkong were so far away from England that they had often to act on their own initiative without referring to the Foreign Office for orders. It no longer took between five and seven months for despatches from London to reach them, as it had at the time of the Opium War; but, though a regular steamship service had been established between London and Hongkong, the mail from London still took seventy-eight days to arrive. It was therefore impossible for the Government in London to exercise day by day control over events; but the general line of policy of the officials on the spot depended very largely on who was Foreign Secretary. When Palmerston left the Foreign Office in 1851, the Governor of Hongkong immediately received despatches from the new Foreign Secretary, Lord Granville, reminiscent of those which his predecessor had received from Aberdeen before Palmerston took office in 1846. Granville urged them to show restraint, and to avoid embarrassing the Chinese authorities in Canton. After 1855, the knowledge that Palmerston was Prime Minister encouraged the British officials to adopt a tougher line; and as the two men in the key positions in 1856 were both men of vigorous and aggressive temperament, the tension mounted. The Governor of Hongkong was Sir John Bowring, a former Radical MP; and the Consul at Canton was a very able and forceful young man, Harry Parkes, who, like Bowring, was of middle-class origin. He had gone to China at an early age, spoke Chinese perfectly, and thought that he knew how to handle the Chinese officials, as well as the Chinese people, for whom he had a real affection. He was imbued with patriotic and slightly Radical ideals, believing in Britain's greatness and in her destiny to bring civilization to China. He wished to use her power, as far as he justifiably could, to remedy the backwardness and social injustices in China, as well as in upholding British commerce, honour and prestige, and demanding redress for every injury or insult to a Briton or to the British flag. His attitude was shared by his chief, Sir John Bowring.

The British merchants had been inconvenienced by the fact that the Chinese authorities, and the Chinese people, often victimized those Chinese who collaborated or traded with the British. In order to protect these people, the Government of Hongkong adopted the practice of granting British registration to ships belonging to Chinese subjects who traded with Hongkong, as the Chinese authorities were prevented, by the terms of the Treaty of Nanking, from interfering with British ships flying the British flag in Chinese territorial waters. Soon Chinese pirates began to register their ships in Hongkong, and many pirate vessels off Canton operated under the British flag. The British Navy assisted the Chinese authorities in their operations against the pirates; but piracy increased rapidly, and Commissioner Yeh considered that the British practice of granting registration to Chinese ships was largely responsible for this.

In October 1856 a small vessel of the type which the Portuguese at Macao called a lorcha was engaged in piracy in the Canton river. It had been registered at Hongkong two years before as a British ship under the name of the *Arrow*, though it was owned by a notorious Chinese pirate. The pirate found a twenty-four-year-old Ulsterman who had never been a seaman, and made him the nominal captain of the *Arrow*; and the *Arrow* set out with the Ulsterman and twelve Chinese on board, and the British flag at the mast, to rob the ships trading in the Canton river. It was intercepted in Chinese territorial waters and boarded by Chinese coastguards, who hauled down the British flag and arrested the thirteen members of the crew. The Ulsterman was immediately released, but the twelve Chinese were imprisoned in Canton. Parkes accused the Chinese coastguards of insulting the British flag, and demanded an apology and the immediate release of the twelve pirates, offering to investigate the charges against them if they were handed over to him at the British consulate. Yeh offered to release nine of them, but not the pirate leader and two of his most notorious followers. Parkes refused to accept the nine unless all twelve were released, and again demanded an apology, pointing out that under the terms of the treaty the prisoners should have been immediately handed over to the British consulate. At this juncture, the authorities in Hongkong discovered that the registration of the *Arrow* as a British ship had expired three weeks before the Chinese had seized her, and that at the time she was no longer a British vessel and had no right to fly the British flag. But Bowring and Parkes decided that they could not now withdraw from the position which they had taken up, and that, as the Chinese coastguards were not aware at the time that the *Arrow*'s registration had expired, they could not rely on this fact to excuse their action.

Parkes therefore again demanded that Yeh release all the pirates and apologize for the insult to the British flag. Yeh released all the twelve prisoners under protest, but refused to send an apology. Bowring then ordered the Navy to bombard Canton. Yeh's palace was destroyed, a large part of the city was set on fire, and there was considerable loss of life, though it was a matter of dispute as to whether the worst damage was caused by the British bombardment or by the large-scale looting by the Chinese criminal population which followed it. Yeh replied by a proclamation which called on the people to exterminate the British barbarians, and offered 30 dollars for the head of every Englishman. The people of Canton launched a partisan war against the British, in which no rules of warfare were observed. All the British factories in Canton were destroyed. Saboteurs tried to blow up British ships, Chinese cooks in Hongkong put ground glass and arsenic into the food of their British employers, and Englishmen who strayed abroad were murdered. The British Navy sank Chinese boats, and summarily shot the saboteurs whom they captured. By the end of 1856 war was being waged in the vicinity of Canton; but the Emperor and his Government in Peking made no move, and all was quiet between British and Chinese in the four other treaty ports.

When the news reached London, the Cabinet was disturbed. Most of them felt that Bowring had acted unwisely; but while some thought that it was impossible to endorse an action which was both legally and morally wrong, the majority believed that the rules of international law could not be applied to a barbarous country like China, and that it would be fatal to British prestige in China, and throughout the Far East, if the act of a high-ranking British official were repudiated by his Government. Palmerston told the Cabinet that he had invited the Attorney-General to be present, and suggested, if they had no objection, that the Attorney-General be asked in, so that he could explain the legal position to them. This was an innovation, for no junior minister outside the Cabinet had ever before been invited to attend a Cabinet meeting: the law officers had previously submitted opinions in writing to the Cabinet. The ministers agreed to hear the Attorney-General. He was Sir Richard Bethell, later Lord Westbury, one of the most brilliant and successful advocates at the Chancery Bar. The little man with the enormous bald head and the slow, mincing utterance, gave a masterly exposition of the legal issues in the case. Although it could be argued that the *Arrow* remained a British ship until the end of the voyage during which her registration expired, he had very little doubt that Bowring had been wrong in international law, because even if the *Arrow* was a British ship when the Chinese captured her – and this was doubtful – Bowring should not have bombarded a city in the territory of the Emperor of China until the British Government had raised its complaint with the Chinese Government in Peking. When Bethell had finished, Palmerston thanked him most courteously for his assistance, and, as soon as he had withdrawn, told the Cabinet that they would of course have to support Bowring, as they had no choice in the matter. All his ministers agreed with him.

The Government's policy was strongly attacked in Parliament, where they faced a coalition of both the Nonconformist and the High Church Tory conscience, and the political interest of the Conservative Party. In the Lords, Lord Derby's motion of censure was defeated by 146 votes to 110. In the Commons Cobden moved the vote of censure on high moral grounds, and was followed in this vein by Gladstone and Lord Robert Cecil, who, at the age of twenty-seven, was already well embarked on the political career which led him, twenty-eight years later, when he was Marquis of Salisbury, to become Prime Minister. Sir James Graham, Lord John Russell, Bulwer-Lytton, Milner-Gibson and Disraeli supported the motion of censure, as did several eminent lawyers. All these speakers condemned Bowring's action in the strongest terms as illegal and outrageous, and praised the restraint which had been shown by Yeh and the Chinese authorities. The only speakers of note who supported the Government were a number of junior ministers, the witty and cynical Bernal Osborne, and Admiral Napier, who regaled the House with a description of what he would do to anyone, particularly to any Frenchman, who insulted the British flag. Even Roebuck, who had moved the resolution congratulating Palmerston in the Don Pacifico debate, spoke against him on this occasion. He said that he was reluctantly compelled to support the censure motion, for on this occasion Britain was clearly in the wrong. Disraeli challenged Palmerston to fight a general election on the issue. After saying that during the last half-century Palmerston had 'professed almost every principle, and connected himself with almost every party', Disraeli concluded: 'Let the noble Lord not only complain to the country, but let him appeal to the country. . . . I should like to see the programme of the proud leader of the Liberal party – "No Reform! New Taxes! Canton Blazing! Persia Invaded!"'

On the fourth night of the debate, 3 March 1857, Palmerston rose to speak. The issue, he said, was between Sir John Bowring and Yeh. 'Who is Sir John Bowring? . . . Was he a member of that aristocracy which some people wish to banish from public employment? Sir John Bowring is essentially a man of the people'; and he had at one time been a member of the Peace Society. 'What is this other man who has been made the subject of panegyric, and whose productions have been praised at the expense of those of our own officers? What is the character of this Yeh? He is one of the most savage barbarians that ever disgraced a nation. He has been guilty of every crime which can degrade and debase human nature. In the contest between these two men, it is most extraordinary that partiality should turn rather towards this barbarian than towards the British representative'. He pointed out that Yeh had decapitated 70,000 Chinese in a few months; and though speakers in the debate had praised Yeh for his forbearance, the only forbearance which he had shown was a forbearance in speaking the truth. He then made a strong attack on Cobden. Cobden had said that Bowring was an old personal friend of his; then how came it that Cobden now attacked an old friend in his hour of need? And Cobden had said that British merchants in China sometimes behaved in an overbearing manner. Where had Cobden learnt to form such an opinion of his fellow-countrymen? Was it in his travels on the Continent? The whole of Cobden's speech had been pervaded with 'an anti-English feeling, an abnegation of all those ties which bind men to their country and to their fellow-countrymen, which I should hardly have expected from the lips of any member of this House. Everything that was English was wrong, and everything that was hostile to England was right'. As for Cobden's gibe that the Government behaved very differently towards a strong power like the United States than towards a weak nation like China, and had taken no action when coloured British subjects were ill-treated in South Carolina, this only showed that Cobden and the Peace Society wanted to go to war with that progressive republic, the United States. Gladstone had condemned Bowring's action; but then Gladstone had cheered in 1840 when the Chinese poisoned the wells. If this censure motion were carried, it would mean that the House had voted to 'abandon a large community of British subjects at the extreme end of the globe to a set of barbarians – a set of kidnapping, murdering, poisoning barbarians'.

The vote of censure was carried by 263 votes to 247. This was much closer than had seemed likely from the course of the debate, and Palmerston had done well to lose by only sixteen votes. He had rallied the support of many silent backbenchers who never spoke in the House. Next day, Palmerston told his ministers at a Cabinet meeting that he had decided to ask the Queen for a dissolution of Parliament. The reports which he received from all over the country convinced him that he could safely take up Disraeli's challenge. The Queen, who warmly approved of Bowring's action and Palmerston's attitude, granted him the dissolution, and Palmerston prepared to fight the general election on his China policy and on his achievement in leading the nation to victory in the Crimean War.

Some of his ministers suggested that it might be advisable to give some pledge about electoral reform. Reform had been shelved, by general consent, for the duration of the Crimean War; but twelve months had elapsed since the conclusion of peace, and the Government had done nothing further about reform. Palmerston said that he did not think that it was necessary to say anything about reform at the election. The ministers then asked Lord Lansdowne, the father of the Cabinet, to intervene with Palmerston. At Lansdowne's insistence, Palmerston agreed to include a reference to reform in his address to the electors of Tiverton; but he drafted a passage which was so ambiguously worded that it was not clear whether he was referring to a major reform of the franchise or to some minor administrative reforms.

But it was not the references to reform that people noticed when they read Palmerston's election address to his constituents. They noticed only one sentence – a sentence which summarized the policy upon which Palmerston's candidates were fighting the election, and which was quoted by them in every constituency: 'An insolent barbarian wielding authority at Canton had violated the British flag'. Thousands of copies of Palmerston's election address were printed and distributed all over Britain, and for the first time in British political history the Prime Minister was making a personal appeal to the whole nation as well as to the electors in his own constituency. The Conservatives and Cobdenites realized almost immediately that they would lose the election, and complained that Palmerston had acted unfairly in forcing a general election on this issue. They also resented his imputations on their patriotism. For the first time for many years, personal friendships were affected by the bitterness of the political controversy, and Lady Palmerston ceased, for the time being, to invite Palmerston's opponents – 'the Chinese', as she called them – to her Saturday evening parties.

The middle classes, particularly the business community in the great commercial centres, were solidly behind Palmerston. The associations of merchants trading in the Far East sent him messages of support from Manchester, Glasgow, Dundee and other cities; and Palmerston told them how encouraging it was to know that those persons with expert knowledge and experience of China approved of the Government's policy. The City of London was most enthusiastic of all. He declined the offer from the members of Lloyd's to nominate him as a candidate for the City at the general election, for he was safe enough at Tiverton; but he accepted an invitation to speak at a dinner at the Mansion House during the election campaign. His speech enraged the Conservatives. Speaking in the presence of the Lord Mayor and the diplomatic corps, he said that the Conservatives were so pro-Chinese that, if they had been logical, they would have offered to provide the money which Yeh had offered as a reward for the heads of Englishmen. The guests at the Mansion House cheered him loudly, but Lord Malmesbury wrote him an indignant letter, which he published in the press. He said that it was unpardonable of Palmerston to make such allegations against men on whose political support he had relied in the past, including Lord John Russell, who, until recently, had been a member of his own Cabinet. He asserted that it was unworthy of a Prime Minister to descend to such depths of political controversy; this kind of 'electioneering claptrap' might be excusable if uttered on the hustings at Tiverton, but it was unforgiveable in the staid and responsible atmosphere of a dinner at the Mansion House. He then expounded, at some length, his criticism of Bowring's action and of Palmerston's policy towards China.

Malmesbury's letter ran to fourteen pages. Palmerston's reply, which was also published in the press, covered less than one page: 'My dear Lord Malmesbury, I have received this Evening your letter of this day. I have neither Time nor Inclination to renew the China debate. I have used a Right which I do not deem myself deprived of by my Official Position to express publicly my opinion of the Conduct of public Men on an occasion of no small public Importance, and I have nothing to retract or to qualify. Yours faithfully, Palmerston'.

Palmerston won a resounding victory at the General Election. Bright and Milner-Gibson lost their seats in Manchester. Cobden was thrown out at Huddersfield, and Layard at Aylesbury. Roebuck just managed to hold Sheffield, and, to everyone's surprise, Lord John Russell achieved a great personal triumph by retaining his seat in the City of London by a very small majority after a bitter contest. Palmerston was returned unopposed at Tiverton; for though Bronterre O'Brien, the Chartist leader, had announced that he would stand against Palmerston, he withdrew before the election. In the country as a whole, Palmerston won a clear majority of 85 seats over all his opponents in the House of Commons. It was the greatest electoral victory that a party leader had won since Lord Grey's victory in the first election after the passing of the Reform Bill in 1832; and by increasing his majority in the House of Commons after having held office as Prime Minister for a substantial time, Palmerston achieved a feat which he repeated in 1865, but has subsequently only been equalled in 1918, 1959 and 1966. Disraeli and Lord Robert Cecil learned the lesson that, from an electoral point of view, it does not pay to support international morality against patriotic fervour. Shaftesbury, who, despite opium, supported Palmerston on the China issue in 1857 because he believed that Palmerston was the instrument chosen by God to carry out Shaftesbury's social and religious aims, wrote in his diary: 'P's popularity is wonderful – strange to say, the whole turns on his name. There seems to be no measure, no principle, no cry, to influence men's minds and determine elections; it is simply, "Were you, or were you not? are you, or are you not, for Palmerston?"'

Chapter Thirty-three

The Indian Mutiny:
The Orsini Plot

After winning the verdict of the electorate in the general election, Palmerston decided to pursue the conflict in China to a successful conclusion. Though he had defended Bowring's action in the case of the *Arrow*, he agreed with the rest of the Cabinet that Bowring had mishandled the situation; so he sent Lord Elgin to supersede him. As the Queen's Plenipotentiary Extraordinary, Elgin had powers to make war or peace with China. The despatch of the reinforcements was held up for six months by the outbreak of the Indian Mutiny; but by Christmas they had arrived, and Elgin was able to send an ultimatum to Yeh, demanding an indemnity for the cost of the British operations and compensation for the destruction of the British factories in Canton. Yeh sent a conciliatory reply, but as he still claimed that he had been justified in the case of the *Arrow*, and stated that Chinese subjects had suffered far greater losses than the British merchants through the British bombardment of Canton, Elgin declared war, thereby achieving his aim of carrying operations beyond the Canton area and involving the Emperor at Peking in negotiations. By the beginning of February 1858 Palmerston was able to announce in the House of Commons that Canton had been taken by storm and that Yeh had been captured disguised as a coolie in a poor quarter of the city. He was sent to India as a prisoner of state, being treated with the greatest deference by his captors, and confined in a luxurious villa near Calcutta, where he died a year later.

Palmerston had meanwhile turned his attention to a controversial domestic issue. In 1857 he introduced the Matrimonial Causes Bill, which for the first time made it possible in England to obtain a divorce by an action in a court of law.

The divorce law of England was substantially the same as it had been before the Reformation. The ecclesiastical courts would grant a decree of nullity for non-consummation and other reasons, after which the parties were free to re-marry; but for adultery and other matrimonial offences the ecclesiastical courts granted only a decree of judicial separation, which entitled the parties to live apart, but not to re-marry. During the seventeenth century the practice began by which a spouse who had obtained a decree of judicial separation in the ecclesiastical courts could, if he could afford it, procure a private Act of Parliament by which the marriage was ended and both spouses were free to re-marry; but those who were not wealthy enough to pay the large sums involved in obtaining the Act of Parliament had to rest content with a separation, and were not free to marry again. There had been complaints for some years about the injustice of this law, and in the spring of 1857 a bill was introduced in the House of Lords to make it possible to obtain a divorce by proceedings in a court of law, which had been the practice in Scotland since the Reformation of 1560.

The bill abolished the matrimonial jurisdiction of the ecclesiastical courts, and transferred it to a new court to be known as the Divorce Court, which was replaced in 1875 by the Probate, Divorce and Admiralty Division of the High Court of Justice. A husband was to be entitled to a divorce if he could prove that his wife had committed adultery; when a wife petitioned for a divorce she was required to prove that, in addition to committing adultery, the husband had aggravated it by some other matrimonial offence, such as desertion or cruelty. The Court was to have a discretionary power to grant a divorce to a petitioner who had himself committed a matrimonial offence; but it was understood that the Court would only exercise this discretion in very rare cases, and until 1919 the courts nearly always refused to grant a divorce to a petitioner who had committed adultery.

The bill was strongly opposed by the High Church party, and six thousand clergymen petitioned against it. But Palmerston showed more determination than usual in resisting public pressure, and after the bill had passed the House of Lords he made up his mind to get it through the Commons, where Gladstone opposed it vigorously. Apart from objecting on principle to the whole bill, the opponents criticized the distinction made between husband and wife, by which a single act of adultery by the wife was sufficient to enable the husband to get a divorce, whereas repeated adultery by the husband was not sufficient unless accompanied by cruelty or desertion; but Palmerston argued that although morally the offence might be as grave whether committed by a husband or a wife, from a social point of view adultery by the wife was much more serious. The critics also objected to the fact that, after being divorced for adultery, the guilty spouse could marry the lover, and wished to introduce a clause like that which had hitherto existed in Scotland, prohibiting the guilty party from remarrying after a divorce; but the Government rejected this on the grounds of humanity, and because the result of it would be to perpetuate an immoral relationship.

But Gladstone and the opponents of the bill in the House of Commons did not rely mainly on argument. They embarked, for the first time in Parliamentary history, on a new tactic, and determined to prevent the passage of the bill by wasting time. Palmerston stated in the House 'that one prominent opposer of the bill said to me on one occasion, "You never shall pass this bill". I replied: "Won't we!"' He never used the 'guillotine' procedure, which was not adopted in the House of Commons until thirty years later; and Gladstone and his friends, in this first attempt in history to kill a bill by talking it out, did not go to the lengths which were later adopted by the Irish members and which made it necessary to introduce the guillotine in 1887. Palmerston got the bill through by the simple process of keeping Parliament sitting, through one of the longest and hottest summers of the century, until the bill was passed. Parliament usually rose for the recess about the middle of August, and did not meet again until the end of January; but on 24 July Palmerston announced that he was prepared to sit until the middle of September, if necessary, to get the bill through. On one occasion Palmerston tried to argue that the twenty-fifth of the Thirty-nine Articles proved that the Church of England did not consider that the indissolubility of marriage was part of the law of God; but generally speaking, he left all the theological and legal arguments to Bethell, the Attorney-General, who hammered them out with Gladstone, while Palmerston sat, silent and alert, ready to intervene to thwart any procedural trick by which the opponents of the bill tried to hold up proceedings. Both sides accused the other of un-Parliamentary procedure, and tempers sometimes rose; but Palmerston remained unruffled, and less tired than most of the younger members at 2 a.m. 'I certainly congratulate the opponents of this bill', he said on 13 August, 'on the success with which they have, for ten hours, contrived to exercise their ingenuity upon three lines of a clause. If they will allow me, however, I beg to inform them that we shall return and sit here day by day, and night by night, until this bill be concluded'. Gladstone, like Palmerston, was largely immune to physical fatigue; but though he was only forty-seven, and Palmerston was nearly seventy-three, he could not wear Palmerston down. Eventually Palmerston won without having to go into September. The bill passed the Commons on 25 August.

By now public interest was much more concerned with the news from India. On 8 May 1857 some sepoy troops at Meerut refused to accept the cartridges which had been issued to them because they believed that they were smeared with pork and cow fat, which it would offend their religious principles to lick. They were court-martialled, and sentenced to ten years' imprisonment. Two days later the other sepoys shot their British officers, released their imprisoned comrades, and marched on Delhi. The mutiny spread to the sepoy troops throughout the North-Western Provinces. It was not a national rising, and was confined to a small area round Delhi, Lucknow and Cawnpore. It was instigated by a few Hindoo Princes who believed, with good reason, that their kingdoms and principalities were threatened with annexation by the Governor-General of India; and the rebel soldiers were the Moslems and high-caste Hindoos who constituted the privileged army corps of sepoys, in whom the East India Company and their British officers had placed their fullest confidence.

Palmerston and his Cabinet did not hear of the outbreak of

the mutiny until the middle of June, for it took five weeks for news from India to reach England; but during the rest of the summer, as the reports from India came in, the people of Britain read with increasing anxiety of the danger not only to their Empire but to the lives of their countrymen and country-women in India. As they heard how the sepoys had killed their British officers, and also civilians and in some cases women and children, there was widespread fear for the safety of the British families besieged in the residencies at Delhi and Luck-now. At the end of August came the news from Cawnpore, where the local Hindoo ruler, the Nana Sahib, after granting the British civilians a safe-conduct to leave the besieged resi-dency, had fired on them as they went down the Ganges on the barges, and then, after imprisoning the surviving women and children in a house, had sent in bands of murderers to kill them all in cold blood two days before the relieving British army captured the town. All England was shocked at the savageries of those whom Shaftesbury called the 'incarnate fiends of Hindostan'.

But the Prime Minister preserved his usual cheerful opti-mism, and for once his mood did not impress the public favourably. There was a general feeling, at least in political circles, that Palmerston was not taking the crisis sufficiently seriously, and the Queen became angry, and told him that if she had been an MP she would have denounced him in the House of Commons for his incompetence. He did, however, send Sir Colin Campbell to India, and took steps to send re-inforcements from Britain. Both the King of Prussia and King Leopold wished to stand by their fellow-Europeans in their fight against the Asian rebels, and offered to send Prussian and Belgian troops to help suppress the mutiny; but Palmerston rejected the offer. He thought it essential for British prestige that Britain should beat the rebels 'off her own bat', and save her Indian Empire without outside assistance; for he did not wish to see a repetition of what had happened at the Redan and the Malakov, when the British troops had been rescued by the French. Nor would he avail himself of Napoleon III's offer to allow the British reinforcements for India to travel by train through France to Marseilles, though this would have saved several days when time was running out for the defenders of Lucknow. Clarendon was perturbed by Palmerston's attitude. 'Confidence and courage are fine things and contain in them elements of success,' he wrote in his diary on 5 September, 'but they are bad when, as with Palmerston, they lead to neglect of the means of which success can be attained'. Three weeks later he wrote: 'Palmerston opposes everything that is out of the beaten track, and I own that his want of energy, and his system of hoping and believing, instead of acting, have disappointed me woefully'. But Palmerston was quite confident that, when the reinforcements reached India, they would reconquer the country in five or six months; then, as he wrote to Lord Fitzwilliam on 9 September, 'I trust we shall have a satisfactory account of those dark coloured Miscreants'.

But the fate of the British residents, if not of the British Empire, in India was certain to be decided, one way or the other, in a matter of a few months, before any reinforcements from Britain could arrive. Under the command of middle-class Generals, who had little in common with the officers of the army in Britain, the British soldiers took the offensive against enemies who outnumbered them by more than five to one, and defeated them by courage, audacity and ruthlessness. By the end of the summer they had recaptured Delhi, Lucknow and Cawnpore, and virtually crushed the revolt.

Among the British inhabitants in India, and also in Britain, there was a cry for vengeance against the Indians. All sepoys who were taken prisoner were executed by being blown from the guns. General Nicholson officially asked permission to torture his sepoy prisoners, and to burn them alive. At the capture of Delhi, where Nicholson was killed, there was a massacre of the Indian civil population. As the British army marched through the countryside in a temperature of 115°F., any Indian who, as a gesture of contempt, turned his back on the marching column was hanged, and whole villages were systematically burned. When General Havelock and Colonel Neill recaptured Cawnpore, they found remains of the corpses of the British women and children, and their congealed blood lying two foot deep in the house. Neill ordered that the sepoy prisoners should be forced to clean up a portion of the room, 'in a manner as revolting to their feelings as possible', so as to make them lose caste, and directed that the Provost-Marshal, after enforcing this order 'if necessary with the lash', was to hang the prisoner immediately. A leading Indian lawyer, who was captured at Cawnpore, was compelled to lick up the blood with his tongue before being flogged and hanged.

These actions led to a controversy in Britain which caused some embarrassment to Palmerston. During September and October the press, with *The Times* leading the way, called nearly every day for a racial and religious war of extermination against the Hindoo and the Moslem in India; for public opinion was inflamed, not only by the all too true reports of the massacre of Cawnpore, but by wholly false reports of the violation of British women by the sepoys. The press published letters from British officers in India describing how they had tortured their sepoy prisoners, and congratulated these officers in their editorials. At this moment news reached London that the Governor-General of India, Lord Canning, had issued an order to the Army to refrain from indiscriminate execution of captured sepoys, who were not to be executed unless they had committed crimes, or had engaged in armed mutiny, though all who had belonged to units which had revolted might be hanged unless they could prove that they had taken no part in the mutiny.

This proclamation was enough to cause a public outcry in Britain. Unfounded reports reached Britain that Canning had granted an amnesty to all the mutineers who had not committed murder, and had ordered Neill to stop his blood-cleaning activities at Cawnpore. *The Times* denounced Canning and his Minister of Justice, Grant, and called for death for every mutineer, the destruction of all Moslem mosques, and the razing of Delhi and its utter obliteration as a city. 'Every tree and gable-end in the place should have its burden in the shape of a mutineer's carcass', wrote *The Times* on 29 October, 'but between justice and these wretches steps in a prim philanthropist from Calcutta'. It dubbed the Governor-General as 'Clemency Canning', and Grant as 'an Indo-maniac'. His Royal Highness the Duke of Cambridge, the Commander-in-Chief, joined in. 'I trust that no undue leniency will be adopted', he said at Sheffield on 21 October, 'I am sure that the country will support all who have the manliness to inflict the punishment'.

But Palmerston said nothing. During the Carlist wars in Spain, he had hastened to urge the Isabelinos to refrain from all acts of revenge, and to grant a full amnesty to the Carlists, although the Carlist bands had killed more women than the sepoys, and the vengeance of the Isabelinos had fallen far short of that of the British commanders in India. But now he kept silent, neither upholding the vilified Governor-General nor joining the hue-and-cry against him. He had every excuse for keeping quiet, because since Parliament had risen for the recess he had had no occasion to make a public speech, and would not have to do so until he spoke at the Lord Mayor's banquet on 9 November; but Canning greatly resented the fact that the Prime Minister had not sent him any word of approval since the mutiny began, though Canning believed that he deserved the credit for the prompt action which he had taken to crush the mutiny. Canning's friends in England, who were receiving indignant letters from Lady Canning, took what action they could on Canning's behalf. Lord Granville, the Lord President of the Council, lobbied in his favour, and won the keen support of the Queen and Prince Albert. But he could not persuade Palmerston to declare himself in favour of Canning. Palmerston told Vernon Smith, the President of the Indian Board of Control, that he strongly disapproved of Canning's clemency order, and thought that it was 'ill-timed'. Vernon Smith thereupon proposed in the Cabinet that the Government should publicly annul Canning's order; but when Granville and Clarendon strongly opposed this, Palmerston swung round, and decided that Canning should be informed that the Government approved in principle of the clemency order, but could not say so publicly until they knew more of the facts.

At the beginning of November, public opinion began to change, as the newspapers were filled with accounts of the recapture of Delhi and other victories instead of details of the Cawnpore massacre. A few clergymen who preached on the

National Fast Day suggested that revenge should not be indiscriminate. On 3 November *The Times*, in a very different tone from that which it had adopted every day throughout October, denied that it had ever called for the execution of innocent Indians. On 4 November the Duke of Cambridge and Lord Granville spoke at a function at the Mansion House. The Duke stated that he had never suggested that all Indian villages should be burned. Granville defended Canning, denying that Canning had tried to restrain Neill's revenge at Cawnpore or wished to pardon the mutineers; and though he apologized to Canning, in a private letter, for having shown so little humanity in his speech at the Mansion House, he said enough in defence of Canning to anger his audience, which he stated, thirty years later, was the most hostile that he had ever faced. Granville, Argyll and Clarendon now set to work on Palmerston, urging him to support Canning when he spoke at the Guildhall on the Lord Mayor's Day. Granville found that Palmerston had no sympathy for Canning, and was almost as much opposed to clemency as Shaftesbury; but he was impressed, as always, by the argument that it was necessary to defend a servant of the Crown from public criticism. Palmerston wrote a somewhat ambiguous letter to Clarendon, saying that he had read Granville's speech at the Mansion House with interest, and thought that Canning had been unfairly blamed for the 'twaddling order' against indiscriminate executions, as he was 'sure he never wrote a word of it, but only adopted the rigmarole of other people'.

On 9 November Palmerston arrived at the Guildhall with Lady Palmerston, being greeted with loud cheers from the diners. He spoke about the events in India, praising the courage not only of the troops, but of the civilian men and women. 'In the ordinary course of life the functions of woman are to cheer the days of adversity, to soothe the hours of suffering, and to give additional brilliancy to the sunshine of prosperity; but our countrywomen in India have had occasion to show qualities of a higher and nobler kind. . . . Henceforth the bravest soldier may think it no disparagement to be told that his courage and his power of endurance are equal to those of an Englishwoman'. He then spoke about the Governor-

General. 'Lord Canning has shown throughout the greatest courage, the greatest ability, and the greatest resources'. He said that Canning would have the difficult task of punishing the guilty and sparing the innocent. 'To punish the guilty adequately exceeds the power of any civilized man; for the atrocities which have been committed are such as to be imagined and perpetrated only by demons sallying forth from the lowest depths of hell. But punishment must be inflicted' – at this point he was interrupted by loud cheers; but he continued: 'not only in a spirit of vengeance, but in a spirit of security, in order that the example of punished crime may deter from a repetition of the offence, and in order to assure the safety of our countrymen and countrywomen in India for the future. (*Cheers*.) He will have to spare the innocent, and it is most gratifying to know that while the guilty may be counted by thousands, the innocent must be reckoned by millions'.

The audience accepted Palmerston's remarks more readily than they would have done a fortnight earlier, or than they would have done even now from any other speaker. In December, when Palmerston spoke in the House of Commons on the motion of thanks to the Army in India, he paid a longer and more outspoken tribute to Canning. Canning and Lady Canning were most grateful to Palmerston, and told Granville that, since Palmerston's speech at the Guildhall, the British press in India had ceased to attack Canning. The speech had the same effect in Britain. Public opinion had in fact already begun to change in Canning's favour before Palmerston made his speech; but his intervention came at just the right moment to complete the process effectively. While Canning gave Palmerston the credit for abating the indignation against him, the public gave him the credit for the suppression of the mutiny. Malmesbury wrote in his diary on 27 November that 'people talk of our victories in India as being proofs of Lord Palmerston's glorious administration', though Malmesbury himself believed that Palmerston's delay in sending reinforcements to India had been responsible for the massacre at Cawnpore.

There was, however, one passage in Palmerston's speech at the Lord Mayor's banquet which had unfortunate repercussions. He said that if any European power, at the height of the mutiny, had contemplated taking advantage of the difficulties in which Britain was involved in India by adopting a different tone towards Britain from that which they would have adopted at other times, they soon thought better of it when they realized that it would not be safe for them to do so. Napoleon III thought that the remark referred to France, and was offended in view of the fact that, far from wishing to take advantage of Britain's difficulties, he had offered to assist her to suppress the mutiny. Clarendon deplored Palmerston's tactlessness; but Palmerston thought that Napoleon III was being unnecessarily touchy, as the words might have referred to half-a-dozen other European countries as well as France. He noted in his pocket-book that the speech 'Gave much offence at Compiègne [Napoleon's palace] – can't be helped – *il n'y a que la verité qui blesse*'.

In looking for a scapegoat, public opinion turned from Canning to the East India Company. The dual control over the Governor-General and his Council in Calcutta, which was exercised by the directors of the Company and by the Government in London, had not been responsible for the mutiny, for policy had in fact always been controlled by the Government, and not by the Company; but the system was obviously an anachronism, and there was a general feeling that it should be changed, and India brought under the direct control of the Crown. Palmerston wrote to Clarendon about this early in September, when Clarendon was staying with the Queen at Balmoral. Clarendon wrote to Lady Clarendon that Palmerston 'seems to have made up his mind to throw over the East India Company, and asks me while *I am shaving or walking* to think what sort of government should be established in place of it! He has a jolly way of looking at disasters'. When a bill was drafted, Palmerston mastered all the details. There was considerable opposition from the East India Company and its nominees and friends in Parliament. The official Conservative Opposition criticized the detailed provisions of the bill, though they supported, in principle, the transfer of authority to the Crown; but Palmerston persisted, and carried the bill through the House.

On 14 January 1858 a bomb was thrown at the carriage of Napoleon III as he and Eugénie drove to the Opéra in Paris. Neither the Emperor nor the Empress was hurt, but several of the bystanders were killed. The assassin was an Italian republican follower of Mazzini named Orsini; and after he was arrested, the police discovered that he had links with some Italian refugees in London, and that the explosives in the bomb had been made in England. This caused a violent outburst of anti-British feeling in France; and while the French police rounded up hundreds of innocent republicans throughout France, a number of French officers published a petition to the Emperor, asking permission to seize London and destroy for ever the haunt of the assassins. Napoleon III apologized to the British Ambassador for this outburst, but directed Walewski to send an indignant protest to the British Government against the activity of the refugees in England, and demanding that steps should be taken to stop their conspiracies.

Palmerston had always been consistent in his attitude about political refugees. Britain was entitled to give them asylum, but must not permit them to engage, on British soil, in any activity against the government of their own, or any other, country. As he had adopted this attitude towards Italian and Hungarian refugees from Austrian rule, even at a time when his relations with Austria were unfriendly, he had all the more reason to adopt it in the case of refugees from Napoleon III with whom he was on friendly terms. He had for some time been viewing with suspicion the activities of the refugees in the Channel Islands, where French Republicans, among them Victor Hugo, had taken refuge after Napoleon III's coup d'état. Soon after he became Prime Minister, Palmerston took the opportunity, when he was writing to the Home Secretary, Sir George Grey, about Florence Nightingale, to add a few lines about the refugees in the Channel Islands.

'My dear Grey', he wrote on 12 October 1855, 'Mankind are governed by a Judicious Administration of Rewards and Punishments. I wish to propose to you a dose of each.' The reward ought to go to Miss Nightingale. He was afraid that it would be impossible to give her the Order of the Bath; but was there not some kind of honorary distinction, or personal titular denomination, which it would be possible for the Queen to give to a woman? 'The reverse of the Medal is the conduct of the French Refugees, who are meeting, and in Speeches and Newspapers openly recommending assassination not only of the Emperor of the French, but of Sovereigns in general. I have little doubt that they are pushed on by Russian Agency'. He therefore proposed that all the refugees should be deported from the Channel Islands, and brought to Britain, where they could do less harm than in the Channel Islands. 'Some of them may be apparently quiet and well conducted, so much the worse for them that their associate Fellow Countrymen render measures of severity necessary. But we are not doing Justice by our faithful and zealous Ally the Emperor of the French, by allowing a knot of his mortal Enemies to be plotting within an hour's sail or row of his Shore. ... I think they ought all and every one without any exception to be sent out, and that the misconduct of their Fellow Refugees should be assigned as the reason'. He told Grey to inquire into the possibility of prosecuting the refugee paper, *L'Homme*, and to set agents to watch the refugees in the hopes of being able to find evidence of other offences which they had committed.

Palmerston was therefore perfectly ready to appease the indignation of the French about the presence of refugees in Britain who were planning to assassinate the Emperor, and after receiving Walewski's protest he instructed Bethell to introduce a Conspiracy to Murder Bill, which made it a felony, instead of merely a misdemeanour, to plot in England to murder someone abroad. He had no idea what a storm of criticism his action would arouse. The Radicals attacked him for interfering with the freedom of refugees in Britain at the behest of a foreign despot, and asked why he had not indignantly rejected Walewski's insolent demand. But when the Conspiracy to Murder Bill was introduced in the House of Commons, Disraeli and the Conservatives supported Palmerston against the indignant Radicals; and the bill was carried on the first reading by 299 votes against 99.

On 18 February 1858 the Government of India Bill passed the House of Commons on the third reading by 318 votes to

173. This was a much larger majority than anyone had expected, and was regarded as a triumph for Palmerston. After the debate, Palmerston walked home from Westminster to his house in Piccadilly with Bethell. The little Attorney-General had exasperated his ministerial colleagues by his sycophantic attitude towards Palmerston; and Greville noted in his diary how, when Palmerston addressed his ministers, Bethell would sit gazing admiringly at him, from time to time interrupting to say, in his mincing voice: 'Oh, my dear Lord!' As he walked home with Palmerston in the early hours on the night of 18 February, he told him the story of the Consul in ancient Rome who employed a slave to remind him, in his hour of triumph, that he would die one day, for he was only a mortal man. Bethell said that Palmerston, too, needed such a slave to remind him that he was not immortal. Bethell's remarks were untimely, for Palmerston received a sharper reminder of the fact within less than twenty-four hours.

Next day, the House of Commons debated the second reading of the Conspiracy to Murder Bill. An amendment was moved by Milner-Gibson and John Bright, who, having lost their seats at Manchester at the general election, had been returned at by-elections for Ashton-under-Lyme and Birmingham. The amendment expressed abhorrence at the attempted assassination of Napoleon III, but regretted that Palmerston had not rejected Walewski's note. Bright had some qualms of conscience about this attempt to whip up nationalist and anti-French feeling; and Palmerston was indignant that the pacifist Radicals should accuse him of cringing to the foreigner. His usual suavity deserted him, and he lost his temper. He stated that the Conspiracy to Murder Bill would not interfere with the right of asylum of peaceful refugees in Britain, and was in any case in no way a threat to the liberties of Englishmen, as it affected no one except foreign immigrants. Then he hit back hard at Milner-Gibson.

When the right honourable gentleman stands forth as the champion of the honour of England and the vindicator of the rights of this country against foreign nations, it is the first time in my life that I have seen him in that character. During the period that he and I have sat in Parliament together, upon every occasion that I can recollect, when the rights of England have been called in question by a foreign country, the right honourable gentleman has been the advocate of the foreign country against our own, and has turned that eloquence and power of language, with which he always conducts his argument, to prove his own country to be in the wrong and the foreign country in the right. Sir, the policy which the right honourable gentleman has invariably advocated is a policy of submission – of crouching to every foreign power with which we have had any difference to discuss; and even when occasion has arisen when this House has been called upon to furnish the means of national defence, the right honourable gentleman's voice was sure to be raised to paralyse the arm of the country and deny it those means of defence which were necessary.

Palmerston even asserted that Milner-Gibson had once said that he did not care if Britain were conquered by a foreign power provided that the conquerors allowed us to continue to work our mills – a statement which brought strong denials from the Radical benches. Palmerston became so angry that he shook his fist at Milner-Gibson and Bright.

Disraeli seized his chance. He made a complete volte-face from the position which he had adopted ten days before, and led all the Conservative MPs into the lobby in support of the Radical amendment. The Government was defeated by 19 votes, the amendment being carried by 234 votes against 215. Palmerston had for once completely misjudged the feeling of the House. If he had gauged it with his usual skill, he could have made another of his graceful retreats and withdrawn the bill in response to the wishes of MPs; but he had been led up the garden path by Disraeli, and left stranded. Next day, he was hooted by the people as he rode in the park; and two days later, he resigned – less than ten months after his triumph at the general election. Lord Derby became Prime Minister, with Lord Malmesbury as Foreign Secretary and Disraeli as Chancellor of the Exchequer. The Conservatives did not have a complete majority in the Commons; but Bright and the pacifist Radicals, Lord John Russell and his Whigs, and Gladstone and the Peelites, were prepared to put the Conservatives in to get Palmerston out.

Chapter-Thirty-four

The Return to Power: The Italian Crisis

Palmerston resigned himself to a prolonged spell in Opposition. When Argyll told him that he was sure that they would soon be back in power, he replied that he did not think so, because the House had not thrown him out in order to put him back immediately, and if all his opponents could unite to turn him out, they could remain united to keep him out. Meanwhile he staked his claim to be regarded as the Leader of the Opposition, in a House where the Conservative Government was confronted by Palmerstonian Liberals, Cobdenite Liberals, Lord John Russell's Liberals, and Gladstone's Peelites, by attending regularly at Parliamentary debates and offering responsible and constructive opposition to the Government's measures. Derby withdrew Palmerston's Government of India Bill, though it had already passed the House of Commons, and substituted his own bill, which also transferred power from the East India Company to the Crown, but differed in its details from Palmerston's bill. Palmerston unsuccessfully opposed the alterations at every stage in the House. He also served on a Parliamentary committee to inquire into the pressing subject of the pollution of the Thames.

In April 1858, Palmerston presided at a public dinner in London to raise money for the Royal Literary Fund, which had been established to give assistance to impecunious authors. It was a great literary occasion. One of the guests was Turgeniev, who afterwards wrote an account of the dinner in a St. Petersburg journal. He was very interested to see Palmerston, having heard so much about him during the Crimean War as the great enemy of Russia. He admired Palmerston's dignified aristocratic bearing, but was less impressed as he watched his face, which struck him as wooden, hard and insensitive – a criticism similar to that which had been made some years before by both Victor Hugo and Prince Czartoryski. Palmerston proposed the Queen's health, which was received with nine rousing cheers – three times three – and great banging of plates and cutlery; and he then made a speech which Turgeniev thought was very commonplace. He paid a tribute to literature, and mentioned that the Queen enjoyed reading books – a statement which was greeted with loud cheers; but when Palmerston referred to Prince Albert, and said that no one could converse with him without having his mind improved as a result, the statement was received in complete silence. Turgeniev deduced that, though the Queen was very popular, Albert was not.

As usual when he was in Opposition, Palmerston made use of the opportunity to travel and spend more time in the country. He often entertained guests at house parties at Broadlands. When Chichester Fortescue, who had been Under-Secretary for the Colonies in Palmerston's Government, spent a few days at Broadlands in October 1858, he found it most enjoyable, with the atmosphere very relaxed, no attempt at any kind of punctuality about meals, and old 'Poodle' Byng, who in his youth had been an intimate friend of the Prince Regent, telling scandalous stories about the love affairs in which his host and hostess had been involved many years ago. Breakfast was served late, though Fortescue saw Palmerston riding off in his pink coat to the hunt before any of his guests were up; and in the evening, they did not sit down to dinner before half-past eight, or even later. Palmerston invited the United States Minister to London, Dallas, to come shooting with him at Broadlands, and Dallas was impressed to see Palmerston, who was nearly seventy-four, tramp for five hours through the covers in pursuit of pheasants, though Dallas, to his delight, managed to beat Palmerston at billiards.

After Parliament rose in August, Palmerston went to Ireland with Lady Palmerston to inspect his estates at Sligo, and then paid a visit to Paris, where he dined with Napoleon III and went shooting at St. Germain. But in Britain, feeling about France had undergone another violent change. The Conspiracy to Murder Bill had aroused strong anti-French feeling, and this was followed by a panic when it was discovered that Napoleon III had built a new harbour at Cherbourg for his steam-propelled warships, and the fear was only heightened when he invited Queen Victoria and Prince Albert to inspect it in August 1858. In the autumn Napoleon III made himself even more unpopular in Britain by authorizing the prosecution of Montalembert on a charge of sedition for having published an article in which he praised the British system of government and argued that it was superior to the régime in France. The Emperor also enraged British public opinion by conniving at the renewal of the slave trade by certain French seamen, and by bullying the Portuguese Government into paying compensation to a French slave-trader whom they had arrested for slave-trading in the Portuguese colonies.

It was therefore a considerable embarrassment to Palmerston when Napoleon III invited him and Clarendon to stay with him at his palace of Compiègne, where Napoleon went hunting in November every year. Palmerston realized that, in view of the anti-French feeling in Britain, and the fact that he had been accused of cringing to Napoleon III about the Conspiracy to Murder Bill, it might do him a great deal of harm, politically, if he stayed with the Emperor as his guest; but he thought it would be inadvisable to offend Napoleon by refusing, particularly as he might one day become Premier again, though this seemed increasingly unlikely to Clarendon and to most political observers. After he and Clarendon had discussed the matter, they decided to go.

They were lavishly entertained at Compiègne. During the day they hunted stags in the forest, and Palmerston surprised his French hosts by turning out in the pouring rain wearing nothing over his pink coat of the New Forest Foxhounds, though all the other members of the party were well wrapped up in raincoats; but he assured them that his coat was waterproof, for *'rien ne perce un habit rouge'*. In the evenings there were dinners, balls, charades and entertainments at the palace, with the Empress and other ladies being present. Palmerston was deeply impressed with the beauty of Eugénie; but, according to Clarendon, he was quite unresponsive to the thirty-five-year-old Princess Mathilde Bonaparte, the Emperor's cousin, who sat next to him at dinner, and concentrated all his attention on the food. The party at Compiègne broke up prematurely because Eugénie and the Emperor's mistress, the Countess Walewski, objected to his flirtation with Clarendon's sister-in-law, Lady Craven. After Palmerston returned to England, he was attacked in the press for having visited Napoleon III at such a time. Many people thought that he had committed political suicide, and that he had wrecked any chances which he might have had of ever becoming Prime Minister again.

Palmerston's political recovery was almost as sudden as his fall. His opponents, who had united to bring him down, were divided by the greatest controversy of the day – electoral reform. The Conservatives were resolutely against reform; but Lord John Russell and John Bright were determined to give the vote to the higher-paid artisans by reducing the property qualification in the towns. It was an issue on which both Russell and Bright preferred Palmerston to Derby and Disraeli; for Palmerston had at least pledged himself, however vaguely, to favour some kind of reform, while the Conservatives were openly against it. Reform was an issue on which all the Liberals could unite against the Conservatives. They did so in March 1859, when Russell moved a resolution in the House of Commons in favour of a reduction of the £10 property qualification in the boroughs. Russell favoured a £6 qualification, which Palmerston had opposed when Russell had first proposed it in Aberdeen's Cabinet in 1853; but as Russell's resolution did not mention any figure beyond demanding a reduction below the £10 level, Palmerston voted in favour of it, and it was carried by 330 votes to 291. Instead of resigning, Derby decided to fight a general election, and three weeks later Parliament was dissolved.

As the parties prepared to fight the election on the question of reform, a controversial issue of foreign policy also arose. Napoleon III made an alliance with Victor Emmanuel of Sardinia, and prepared to go to war with Austria to liberate Italy. Cavour skilfully provoked the Austrian Government into sending an ultimatum to Sardinia requiring her to disarm, and when Sardinia refused, Austria declared war. This was what Cavour wanted. Napoleon III, to the distress of Eugénie and the pro-clerical party in France, declared war on Austria and led his armies into Italy. Queen Victoria and the Conservatives supported Austria. Derby's Government declared that the French invasion of Lombardy constituted a threat to the peace of Europe, and it seemed as though Britain, in its anti-French fervour, might intervene on Austria's side. But Lord John Russell had always been a fervent supporter of Italian unity and freedom. Gladstone had espoused the cause when he visited Naples in 1851, and saw for himself the horrors of King Bomba's prisons. He was now a more ardent champion of the Italians even than Russell. The Cobdenites were pacifist as usual. There were therefore powerful forces in Britain which were opposed to British involvement on Austria's side, and the question became an issue, second only to reform, in the general election of April 1859.

This was the situation which Palmerston had been trying for thirty years to avoid. In 1831, he had opposed the revolutions against the absolutist governments of the Italian states in order to prevent a war between France and Austria which would lead to French domination of Northern Italy. In 1848 he had supported Sardinia against Austria, once again with the primary motive of preventing Sardinia from turning to France and bringing French troops into Lombardy. How Palmerston would have handled the situation if he had been in power in the spring of 1859 is a matter for speculation; but in Opposition he backed the Franco-Italian side against the Austrians. He could never persuade the Radicals that he believed in reform as sincerely as Lord John Russell; but he could outbid Russell for Radical support on the Italian question.

Palmerston and Heathcote were returned unopposed at Tiverton, as Rowcliffe contented himself with heckling from the audience when Palmerston made his speech on the hustings. The national press was there, and Palmerston had provided the journalists with a hand-out of his speech in advance. After making a vague declaration in favour of reform, he dealt with the international crisis. His theme was that Britain must remain neutral in the war in Italy, and that the Conservative Government must not draw Britain in on the side of

Austria. He had written this in the hand-out that he had given to the journalists; but when he spoke on the hustings he went further, and added that he hoped that Austria would be driven north of the Alps. Lord John Russell, in his election speech in the City of London, also called for neutrality in the war; but he was not as pro-Italian as Palmerston.

The Conservatives lost a few seats at the general election, but the balance of forces in the House of Commons was basically unchanged. The Conservatives had about 300 MPs, and their combined opponents numbered 350. Everything depended upon whether the Opposition forces could unite. Apart from the Peelites, all the Opposition groups in Parliament – the Cobdenite Radicals, Lord John Russell's Liberals and Palmerston's followers – were nominally members of the Liberal Party, but they were divided by deep political and personal differences. One of the points at issue was who should be the leader of a united party, and who would become Prime Minister if they defeated the Tories. There were two contenders for the post – the two ex-Premiers, Palmerston and Russell. Whichever of them became Prime Minister could only survive with the help of the other; but their past relations made it difficult for them to collaborate. In 1851 Russell had dismissed Palmerston from the Foreign Office in circumstances which Palmerston had never forgiven; in 1852 Palmerston had brought down Russell's Government; in 1855 Palmerston had used Russell as his pacemaker and had become Prime Minister and war leader while Russell was sent off to discredit himself in Vienna; in 1858 Russell had played a prominent part in forcing Palmerston's resignation over the Conspiracy to Murder Bill. But unless they could unite, the Conservatives would remain in office.

Disraeli, seeing the danger of a union between Palmerston and Russell, tried to steal a march on Russell. Immediately after the general election, he wrote to Palmerston and invited him to join a Conservative Government. He said that even if Palmerston thought it inexpedient to take the Foreign Office, 'the foreign policy of every Government of which you are a member must be yours'; and with Conservative support, Palmerston could introduce as moderate a Reform Bill as he liked. Disraeli even hinted that Derby was about to retire, and that Palmerston could then become Prime Minister and Leader of the Conservative Party. But though Palmerston had often changed sides, he never did so in a hurry; and he was too cautious to rush into the arms of the man who had placed him in such difficulties just over a year before in connexion with the Conspiracy to Murder Bill, particularly at a time when there was so much talk of the possibility of uniting the Liberal factions. Lady Palmerston and Lady John Russell were meeting each other in the most friendly way, and Palmerston and Lord John went out for a drive together in Lord John's carriage.

On 6 June 1859, the 274 members who comprised the Parliamentary Liberal Party met at Willis's Rooms in St. James's Street. Palmerston was very opposed to the idea of deciding political issues at a party meeting, but he was persuaded to agree to it. The meeting had been called to demonstrate the unity of all the Liberal factions, and it has been said that it marked the birth of the modern Liberal Party. Palmerston, who was the first to mount the platform, was greeted with loud cheers; and the cheers redoubled when Palmerston stretched out his hand to help Lord John Russell up on to the platform. There they were joined by John Bright. Palmerston spoke first, and called for unity, and offered to serve in any Government which was headed by Russell. The next speaker was Russell, who offered to serve in any Government which was headed by Palmerston. Bright spoke third; he called for reform, and pledged his solidarity with Palmerston and Russell. A number of other speakers followed, all of whom praised the unity of the party and thanked Palmerston and Russell for their attitude. The only discordant voice was Roebuck's. The man who had championed Palmerston in the Don Pacifico debate had now turned resolutely against him, and declared that he would never support a Palmerston Government because Palmerston had bowed to Napoleon III over the Conspiracy to Murder Bill; but Roebuck was not well received by the audience.

As Palmerston sat on the platform on that June afternoon and watched the splendid display of Liberal unity, he was in surroundings which were very familiar to him. Fifty years be-

fore, Willis's Rooms had been known as Almack's – the club
that they called the 'despair of the middle classes'. In 1809,
as a young man of twenty-five who was already a minister in
a Tory Government through rank and influence, he had come
here in the evenings in bright-coloured coat and pantaloons,
passing the watchful doorkeeper, to dance the quadrille and
the waltz with Lady Cowper and the Princess Lieven; in 1859, -
he came here in the afternoon, dressed in a black frock-coat,
to shake hands with John Bright and form the modern Liberal
Party. Many things had changed since those days, apart from
the change of name from Almack's to Willis's Rooms. Captain Gronow had also been a member of Almack's in the days
before steamships, railways and the battle of Waterloo. He
remembered how, in 1810, the young women had been de-
mure and haughty, and difficult to win – not like the girls of
the eighteen-sixties, who walked out with their petticoats girt
up to their knees, and addressed men as Jack, Tom or Harry.
In 1810, all Gronow's acquaintances tried to make out that
they were related to a peer; but now he found that anyone
who was related to a peer tried to keep it dark. But though
much had changed, Lord Palmerston was still there, and so
was Lady Palmerston, though she was no longer the flirtatious
Lady Cowper, but a majestic and vivacious old lady of
seventy-two who would be remembered many years later, in
the twentieth century, by the young girls of 1859 as 'one of
the last of those great ladies of England which the modern
world does not know how to produce'.

One question had not been settled at the meeting at Willis's
Rooms. Was it to be a Palmerston Government with Russell in
it, or a Russell Government with Palmerston in it? During the
next few days, the opinion among Liberal MPs came round to
the view that Palmerston, not Russell, should be Prime Minister. They considered that Palmerston was more reliable than
Russell. They realized that he was an opportunist in politics,
and might at any time desert them and join the Conservatives;
but they knew that he would never lose his head, and indulge
in the quixotic behaviour in which Russell sometimes indulged. Palmerston was more likely than Russell to hold the
support of the Right-wing Liberals, and he might attract the

Peelites and a number of Conservative votes. Another factor in his favour was Lady Palmerston. It was felt that her Saturday evening parties would be very useful to the Liberal Party, whereas Lady John Russell was modest, and something of a recluse, and could never entertain in Lady Palmerston's style.

On 11 June the Government was defeated on a vote of confidence in the House of Commons by nine votes, and Derby resigned. To everyone's surprise, the Queen sent for Lord Granville, and explained to him that since it would be invidious to choose between Palmerston and Lord John, she was inviting him to form a Government. Granville asked both Palmerston and Russell if they would serve in his Government. Palmerston agreed, but Russell refused, saying that he was prepared to be the second man in a Palmerston Government, but not the third man in a Granville Government. The fact that Palmerston was more willing than Russell to serve under another Prime Minister swung opinion in his favour, as it had done in 1855; and when Russell's refusal made it impossible for Granville to form a Government, the Queen turned next to Palmerston.

Palmerston succeeded in forming a Government, though it was not the Government that he wanted to form. He realized that it would have to be based, not only on all sections of the Liberal Party, but on a coalition of all anti-Conservatives. He wrote to some of his friends, and to the colleagues who had served under him in his previous Government, and told them that he regretted that he could not give them office, but that he was not free to choose the ministers whom he would have liked to have. He was as eager as ever to have Clarendon at the Foreign Office; but Lord John Russell insisted on having the Foreign Office for himself. If Palmerston had again beaten Russell in the contest for the Premiership, Russell knew that Palmerston could not survive without him, and that he was in a good position to dictate his terms. Palmerston reluctantly agreed to have Lord John as Foreign Secretary. He tried hard to persuade Clarendon to join his Government in some other office, or without portfolio; but to his great regret, Clarendon refused.

It had been unofficially agreed, in the talks which had preceded the meeting at Willis's Rooms, that the Cobdenites should be given office, though it had also been made clear that Bright himself could not be chosen. Bright had toured the country during the previous winter, and had made a series of speeches in which, as well as calling for electoral reform, he had attacked the House of Lords and the aristocracy. His speeches had outraged the Conservatives and the upper classes, and had particularly angered the Queen; and it was generally agreed that this had disqualified him from holding office. Palmerston was ready to offer posts in his Government to any of the other Cobdenite leaders. On the other hand, he wished to balance them by including representatives of the extreme Right wing of the Liberals, and also some Peelites, in his Cabinet, though the Peelites had voted for Derby's Government in the vote of censure which had brought Palmerston and the Liberals into power.

He offered Gladstone the Exchequer. Gladstone had strongly opposed Palmerston's policy in China and his Matrimonial Causes Act, and believed that his aggressive foreign policy was immoral and dangerous. Less than a year before, Gladstone had declared that it was essential to prevent Palmerston from ever returning to power. But Gladstone was always liable to take up a particular cause, and fight for it to the exclusion of all other considerations. In 1859 his cause was the liberation of Italy. Palmerston's election address at Tiverton had made a deep impression on Gladstone, and was the chief reason why he joined Palmerston's Government. His fellow-Peelites, Herbert and the Duke of Newcastle, joined the Government as Secretary for War and Secretary for the Colonies. Sir George Lewis, who had been Chancellor of the Exchequer in Palmerston's previous Government, became Home Secretary, and Sir George Grey, his former Home Secretary, became Chancellor of the Duchy of Lancaster. Granville and Argyll held their old posts of Lord President of the Council and Lord Privy Seal. The aged Lord Campbell, the Lord Chief Justice, was brought back into politics at the age of eighty as Lord Chancellor.

These Right-wing ministers were diluted with a sprinkling of Radicals. It was less than eighteen months since Palmerston had denounced Milner-Gibson, in the bitter debate on the

Conspiracy to Murder Bill, for always supporting foreign nations against his own; now he appointed him President of the Board of Trade. Charles Villiers, who was another Cobdenite Radical despite the fact that he was Clarendon's brother, was given the Poor Law Board. Palmerston had wished to give the Board of Trade to Cobden, though he had attacked Cobden as violently as Milner-Gibson, having roundly abused him as unpatriotic in the debate on the lorcha *Arrow*. On 27 June he wrote to Cobden and told him that it was essential to form a Government based on all sections of the Liberal Party. 'Mr. Milner Gibson has most handsomely consented to waive all former Differences and to become a Member of the New Cabinet. I am most exceedingly anxious that you should consent to adopt the same line and I have kept open for you the office of President of the Board of Trade which appeared to me to be the one best suited to your views and to the distinguished Part which you have taken in Public Life'.

Cobden went to see Palmerston, though he had definitely decided, after discussing the matter with Bright, that it was impossible for him to take office under a man of whose internal and foreign policy he disapproved so deeply. Palmerston coaxed Cobden, laughed about their political battles of the past, and was so persuasive and charming that Cobden nearly changed his mind. But he said that he would not join unless Bright were also included. Palmerston said that he feared that Bright's attack on the House of Lords had made this impossible; and when Cobden pointed out that Bright had spoken in general terms, and had not attacked any individual nobleman personally, Palmerston said: 'It is not personalities that are complained of. A public man is right in attacking persons, But it is his attacks on classes that have given offence to powerful bodies, who can make their resentment felt'. He nevertheless made indirect approaches to Bright about the possibility of his joining the Government; but Bright refused, and in any case the Queen would not have him at any cost, and refused to agree to Palmerston's proposal that Bright should at least be made a Privy Councillor as an honorific distinction. It was not until after Palmerston's death that the Queen met Bright, and formed a favourable opinion of him.

Cobden, to Palmerston's regret, did not join the Government; but he accepted Palmerston's invitation to go to Paris to negotiate a trade agreement with the French Government, and returned early in 1860 with a commercial treaty which virtually abolished tariffs between Britain and France. Both Cobden and Bright agreed to support Palmerston in Parliament.

Twelve days after Palmerston became Prime Minister, the armies of Napoleon III and Francis Joseph met in battle at Solferino, and the Austrians had the worst of a very bloody engagement. A Swiss tourist, Henri Dunant, wandered on to the battlefield, and was so shocked at the horrible conditions of the wounded that he began his campaign which resulted, five years later, in the foundation of the International Red Cross. All the great powers eventually agreed to Dunant's proposal for an international organization which would care impartially for the wounded on both sides, though Dunant encountered more opposition from Palmerston than from most other Governments. The British authorities believed that the medical services of the respective armies could deal adequately with the situation; but they eventually agreed that Britain should adhere to the Geneva Convention of 1864.

The horrors of Solferino were one of the factors which caused Napoleon III to make peace. After a personal meeting with Francis Joseph in a peasant's hut near the battlefield, the peace of Villafranca was signed on 12 July. It was a great disappointment to Victor Emmanuel and Cavour. They had gone to war to gain Lombardy and Venetia; but instead of gaining two provinces, they gained one and lost one. Austria, who retained Venetia, ceded Lombardy to Sardinia; but a few months later Sardinia was required to cede Savoy and Nice to France.

Palmerston, like the majority of the British people, condemned the peace settlement. In a way, it was a blessing in disguise for Palmerston. If Napoleon III had pursued his anti-Austrian and pro-Sardinian policy to its conclusion in Italy, Palmerston would have had to deal with the situation that he had been trying to avoid since 1831, and prevent French control of Northern Italy without supporting the Austrians in

suppressing Italian freedom; and he might have found it difficult to reconcile his policy when in power with the speeches
which he had made in Opposition during the general election.
But after the peace settlement he could be anti-French without being anti-Italian. He could continue to support the
liberation of Italy while denouncing France for annexing
Savoy, for her aggressive imperialist ambitions, and for betraying the cause of Sardinia and Italian freedom. Everyone
from the Queen to Gladstone supported his anti-French
policy, and the British press incited anti-French feelings in
Britain. There was talk of war and of the danger of French
invasion, and Palmerston played it up and seized the opportunity to implement his plans for increased arms expenditure and the erection of a system of fortifications along the
south coast. At the same time, he expressed his sympathy with
Sardinia, and tried to win over Victor Emmanuel and Cavour
by persuading them that Britain was a far more reliable and
disinterested friend of Italian unity than France was.

But Victor Emmanuel and Cavour were cautious in choosing between France and Britain, and continued to remain
friendly with both powers. They agreed that Palmerston's
interest in Italy was more disinterested than Napoleon III's,
but thought that for this very reason Palmerston was less
likely to give them practical aid. Napoleon III might have
made them pay the price of Savoy, but he had at least gone to
war to win Lombardy for them, which Palmerston had never
shown any sign of doing. Palmerston, finding that Cavour was
still intriguing with Napoleon III, became suspicious of Cavour.

In May 1860 Garibaldi landed in Sicily with a thousand of
his Redshirts, and proclaimed his object of conquering the
whole of the Kingdom of Naples for King Victor Emmanuel
of Sardinia. The people of Sicily rose in his support, and within a few weeks he was master of the island and prepared to
cross the Straits of Messina to invade the Neapolitan territory
on the mainland. Victor Emmanuel and Cavour encouraged
him secretly, but publicly dissociated themselves from his
activities, being afraid of antagonizing Napoleon III and becoming involved in a war with Naples, the Papal states and

Austria without French support; for Garibaldi had been considered to be a revolutionary firebrand and a follower of Mazzini ever since he had commanded the troops of the Roman Republic in 1849.

Garibaldi's expedition was cheered on by the Radicals all over Europe, and by a strong body of opinion in Britain. But Palmerston was very suspicious about it. He believed that Napoleon III had made a secret agreement with Cavour, under which France would permit Garibaldi to seize Sicily and the Kingdom of Naples for Sardinia, in return for Sardinia ceding Genoa and the island of Sardinia to France. Palmerston did not wish to see either Genoa or the island of Sardinia turned into a French naval base. Cavour assured him that there was no truth at all in the rumour; but as Cavour had previously denied that Sardinia would cede Savoy and Nice to France until shortly before the cession took place, Palmerston refused to believe Cavour's assurances unless Sardinia would make a treaty with Britain by which Sardinia would agree not to cede any territory to any foreign power without the consent of Britain.

Palmerston, after considering the position of the three protagonists – the King of Naples, Cavour and Garibaldi – toyed in turn with the idea of supporting every one of them. His first idea was to support Neapolitan Bourbon absolutism. He did not wish to see the Kingdom of Naples conquered by a pro-French Sardinia; and it was easier than it would have been a year before to support the King of Naples, because King Bomba had died, and the new King, Francis II, had always been more Liberal than his father. On 17 May 1860, Palmerston proposed to Lord John Russell that the British fleet should be sent to the Straits of Messina. If Cavour would sign a treaty by which Sardinia agreed not to cede any territory without Britain's consent, the British Navy would stay neutral; if Cavour refused, the Navy would prevent Garibaldi from invading the mainland, and Britain would guarantee the independence of the Kingdom of Naples, on condition that King Francis agreed to introduce constitutional and Liberal reforms throughout his realm. But Lord John Russell objected, and Palmerston soon realized that his Government could never survive if he pursued this policy. On 10 July, he proposed an entirely different policy to Russell. He now suggested that they should approach Garibaldi, and point out to him that it would not be to the advantage of the Italian cause if the Kingdom of Naples should fall into the power of a Sardinian Government that was dominated by France. Garibaldi should be asked to delay for three weeks before proclaiming the annexation of Sicily by Sardinia. If during those three weeks Cavour signed the treaty which Palmerston proposed, Garibaldi would be permitted to go ahead: if Cavour refused, then Britain would propose to Garibaldi that he should be satisfied if Sicily were granted complete autonomy within the Kingdom of Naples, and that the British Navy would assist Garibaldi's operations against Naples in order to compel the King of Naples to agree.

But this plan was also abandoned; and a fortnight later, the French Ambassador, Persigny, approached Russell with a proposal that the British and French fleets should combine to prevent Garibaldi from crossing the Straits of Messina. Russell gave Persigny the impression that he was in favour of accepting the offer, apparently under the mistaken idea that the Sardinian Government was sincere when it dissociated itself from Garibaldi's expedition. Persigny also saw Palmerston, and put the idea to him. Palmerston must have been a little perplexed at this proposal, as he had hitherto acted on the assumption that Garibaldi's expedition against Naples was instigated by Cavour and Napoleon III. This had been the chief reason why he had wished to stop Garibaldi from crossing the Straits; if Napoleon III also wished to stop him, there was much less reason for Palmerston to do so. Palmerston nevertheless viewed Persigny's proposal favourably. He had always been reluctant to upset the status quo in Central and Southern Italy; and in view of Cavour's continuing tendency to remain on good terms with France, it would be better if Sardinia did not conquer Naples. Persigny reported to Paris that both Palmerston and Russell were in favour of the French proposal.

At this moment, Eugénie was indiscreet enough to reveal the French plan to the Sardinian Minister in Paris. He contacted d'Azeglio, the Sardinian Minister in London, who immediately sent Sir James Lacaita, an Italian-born examiner in the British civil service, to see Lord John Russell. Lacaita, who was an intimate friend of the Russells, found that Lord John was closeted with Persigny, and could not be disturbed, and that Lady John was ill in bed. He persuaded Lady John to send a note to Russell to come to her at once. Russell hurried upstairs in the belief that his wife's health had taken a turn for the worse, whereupon Lacaita appealed to him, as a Liberal and a friend of Italian freedom, not to hold back the Sicilian revolt against the King of Naples, as Palmerston had done in 1848, but to allow Garibaldi to cross the Straits. If Lacaita's account is correct – and there is no reason to doubt it – the Foreign Secretary of the strongest power in the world reversed his policy, at a critical moment in the history of Italy, because of an emotional appeal to him at his wife's bedside. When the matter was discussed in the Cabinet, Lord John proposed that the French proposal be rejected, and was strongly supported by Gladstone. They argued that if the people of Naples were loyal to their King, they would resist and defeat Garibaldi; if they welcomed Garibaldi, it would be wrong and unwise for Britain to become involved in a war against powerful popular forces in Southern Italy. Palmerston was won over, and the rest of the Cabinet, who were not very interested, offered no objection. Palmerston proposed that they should notify the French Government that they would not assist in stopping Garibaldi, but would have no objection if the French did this by themselves. As he now realized that Garibaldi was not an instrument of Napoleon III, Palmerston was prepared to be strictly neutral.

Napoleon III decided not to stop Garibaldi. He thought that Palmerston was hoping that France would act alone, so that Victor Emmanuel and Cavour would break with France and ally themselves with Britain. Garibaldi's Redshirts crossed the Straits without interference and conquered Naples for Victor Emmanuel. By abandoning, at the last moment, his plan to stop Garibaldi, Palmerston achieved the reputation among his contemporaries and future historians of being one of the architects of Italian unity.

During the autumn and winter of 1859, the anti-French agitation in Britain continued. It was useful to Palmerston, as it not only enabled him to put through at last the programme of rearmament which he had so long advocated, but also provided another excuse for postponing any action about Parliamentary reform. A new volunteer defence organization was formed, and all over Britain volunteers enrolled, drilled, and engaged in rifle practice. Tennyson exhorted his readers to stop arguing about reform for the moment, and to practise at the butts instead, for it was better to have a few rotten boroughs than to see English boroughs burning after a French invasion. Palmerston only partly endorsed these sentiments. He was opposed to forming rifle associations in the industrial towns, where they might be infiltrated by Chartists and Socialists; and during the Crimean War he had discouraged the formation of such associations so effectively that the commanders of certain units had protested to him that he was deterring volunteers from enrolling. Palmerston had to explain that his words had referred only to the Northern and Midland towns, and that he had no wish to discourage recruitment in the country districts, where the volunteers would be under the command and observation of the country gentry. He himself was invited in 1860 to attend the presentation of the colours to the 11th Hampshire Volunteers at Romsey. The ceremony was postponed to enable him to be present, but was held on 28 December, when a large crowd assembled in the snow in the little square before the Town Hall. It was one of the coldest days for many years. Palmerston and Lady Palmerston sat on the platform, well wrapped up against the cold, while the commander's wife presented the flag, and said that it was unnecessary to remind them that it was their duty, as soldiers, to rally round it and defend it to the death; and the Rector of Romsey offered a prayer that the flag would never be unfurled in an unrighteous cause. But Palmerston directed the Government of Ireland not to form militia units there.

The defence programme involved Palmerston in a controversy with his Chancellor of the Exchequer. Gladstone not only believe¹ i ɪ the Victorian ideal of sound finance, economy and low taxation, but to some extent sympathized with the pacifist view of the Cobdenites. He grudged every penny that had to be spent on national defence. He was particularly insistent that the whole defence expenditure in each financial year should be paid for from the budget surplus of that year, whereas Palmerston considered it justifiable to incur expenditure on defence which would be paid for out of the next three or four years' surplus. Gladstone felt so strongly about this matter that he threatened to resign; but Palmerston told the Queen that it would be better to lose Mr. Gladstone than Portsmouth or Plymouth.

But defence was only one of the issues involved in a serious clash which arose between Palmerston and Gladstone in connexion with the budget of 1860. When Gladstone came to introduce his first budget as Palmerston's Chancellor of the Exchequer, he found that he had a surplus of £5,000,000 to distribute. It was generally assumed that he would use it to abolish income tax. The idea of a tax on income had first been introduced by Pitt in 1798 as a wartime measure, and had been abolished after Waterloo; but in 1842 Peel's Government introduced it for the first time in peace time. In 1853 Gladstone, as Chancellor of the Exchequer in Aberdeen's Government, had given an undertaking that income tax would be abolished by 1860, if not before; but the tax was still imposed, and under Palmerston's Government in 1856–7 it rose to 1s. 4d. in the £ – the highest level which it had ever reached – though it was later reduced to 9d. in the £. Now that 1860 had arrived, people expected the tax to be abolished; but Gladstone had other ideas. He proposed increasing it from 9d. to 10d., and using the money raised to abolish the paper duties.

This proposal was much more than a mere fiscal measure. It raised deep political passions which went back to an earlier generation – to the days when Palmerston was Secretary at War in a Tory Government. In 1819 that Government had sharply increased the stamp duty on newspapers with the intention of preventing the circulation of seditious literature among working-class readers. Richard Carlile spent nearly ten years in prison for defying the law by selling books and newspapers without paying the stamp duty, and had earned a reputation as a martyr for free speech by his struggle against the 'tax on knowledge'. In 1836 the Whig Government reduced the stamp duties to a penny, thereby ending the practical grievance under which Radical journalists had suffered, and the stamp duty was finally abolished in 1855; but the paper duties still kept up the price of books and newspapers, and were disliked, not only by Radical politicians, but by the numerous workers' educational colleges and mechanics' institutes which were springing up on all sides as the second half of the nineteenth century got under way.

The budget of 1860 caused the first split in the discordant Cabinet. The Radicals supported Gladstone's proposal to abolish the paper duties. The Right-wing ministers opposed it, and urged that the income tax should be abolished instead, thus fulfilling the undertaking that had been given in 1853. A third body of opinion believed that both taxes should be retained, but that the duty on tea should be abolished, which would be more popular than either of the other two proposals. Palmerston favoured a fourth course: he wished to retain both income tax and the tea and paper duties, and spend the money on armaments.

The majority of the Cabinet decided in favour of Gladstone's proposal, and to Palmerston's great dissatisfaction it was included in the budget which Gladstone presented to the House of Commons. It was then the usual practice to draft separate bills containing the different financial proposals; and the bill to abolish the paper duties was criticized by the Conservatives and some Right-wing Liberals, and only passed the Commons by a small majority. Palmerston rejected a suggestion from a Liberal MP that he should secretly organize opposition to the bill among the Government supporters in the House; but it was an open secret that the Prime Minister was against the proposal of his Chancellor of the Exchequer. This encouraged the Conservatives to fight it vigorously. When it passed the House of Commons, the question arose as to whether the House of Lords would reject it. They were legally entitled to do so; but the Lords had not rejected a finance bill for more than two hundred years, and there was a widespread feeling in political circles – and not only among Radicals – that finance was the exclusive business of the House of Commons, as it would be wrong for the Lords to tax the people. While the Radicals warned the Conservatives that there would be a serious constitutional crisis if the House of Lords rejected the bill, the rumour spread that Palmerston had secretly told Derby that he hoped that they would do so. He certainly wrote to the Queen, who shared his dislike for the bill, that 'he felt bound in Duty to Say' that the Lords would 'perform a good public Service' if they threw out the bill. On 21 May the House of Lords defeated it by 193 votes against 104. When the result was announced, Lady Palmerston, who was in the Ladies' Gallery, applauded vigorously. This public expression of her delight at the defeat of one of the budget proposals of her husband's Government did not pass unnoticed.

The Radicals launched a strong attack on the House of Lords. They demanded that the bill be sent back a second time to the House of Lords, and that the action of the Lords in rejecting the bill should be treated as a breach of the privileges of the House of Commons and referred to the Committee of Privileges. Palmerston was of course opposed to both proposals. He told Gladstone that he could sympathize with his disappointment at the defeat of the bill, because he himself felt very disappointed that his horse had failed to win the Derby; but he urged Gladstone not to 'pitch into the House of Lords'. He realized, however, that the strength of feeling among the Radicals was so strong that his Government could not survive unless some concession were made. He therefore opposed the proposal to send the bill back to the Lords, but agreed that the Government should propose that the conduct of the Lords should be referred to the Committee of Privileges. He obtained the support of the Cabinet for his compromise proposal. Only Gladstone, Milner-Gibson and the Duke of Argyll were in favour of sending the bill to the House of Lords for a second time; only Campbell opposed the proposal to refer the matter to the Committee of Privileges.

Palmerston himself moved the resolution in the Commons referring the issue to the Committee of Privileges. He spoke strongly in favour of the privileges of the House of Commons, but angered the Radicals by his failure to make any attack on the House of Lords. His speech increased the resentment which had been caused by Lady Palmerston's demonstration in the House of Lords; and Sir Robert Phillimore commented on the strange spectacle of 'Palmerston moving a resolution condemnatory of the Lords, and yet speaking in defence of their conduct'. But Palmerston had only postponed the conflict. The House of Commons accepted the report of the Committee of Privileges that the action of the House of Lords had violated the privileges of the Commons; and when Gladstone prepared his budget next year, the question arose again. On 12 April 1861 the Cabinet discussed which taxes should be repealed. Only Gladstone and Milner-Gibson wished to abolish the paper duty. Lord John Russell, Granville, Herbert and Villiers wished to abolish the duty on tea. Palmerston, Lord Campbell, Argyll, the Duke of Somerset, Cardwell, Stanley, Wood, Grey and Lewis wished to reduce the income tax from tenpence to ninepence. But a few days later, Gladstone announced that he would be able to reduce the income tax to ninepence, and also abolish the paper duty. He told the Cabinet that he proposed to introduce both proposals in the same Finance Bill, so that the Lords would have to accept or reject them together. This novel idea won the support of the majority of the Cabinet. Palmerston became very angry, and for the first time lost his temper with Gladstone; but only Lord Campbell spoke out in Palmerston's support, though Gladstone felt that many of the other ministers did not like his proposal. It was agreed that Gladstone should introduce both proposals in his budget; but next day Palmerston wrote to Gladstone and told his indignant Chancellor of the Exchequer that he did not propose to treat the budget as a question of confidence when it was introduced in the House.

But Gladstone went ahead, and introduced his budget. 'The battle in Parliament was hard', he wrote, 'but was as nothing to the internal fighting'. The House of Lords gave in, and the bill passed in both Houses. The paper duties had been repealed at last, and the clash between Lords and Commons was postponed for forty-eight years.

Chapter Thirty-five

The Last Premiership: Internal Affairs

In the opening chapter of Anthony Trollope's *Barchester Towers* the upper-class and worldly Archdeacon Grantley is anxiously waiting, 'in July 185–', to see whether his uncle, the Bishop of Barchester, will die before the political crisis compels the Government to resign. The Archdeacon recently stayed with the head of his Oxford college when the Prime Minister spent the night there, and it was arranged that the Archdeacon should be the next Bishop. But his hopes are disappointed. The Government falls before the Bishop dies; and the new Prime Minister, who is the champion of the Low Church party, appoints the unctuous middle-class Dr. Proudie as Bishop, with his odious chaplain, Mr. Slope. All Trollope's readers knew the political controversies and leaders to whom he was referring. The out-going Prime Minister, appointing High Church gentlemen over the port at Oxford, was Lord Derby; the in-coming Prime Minister, who brought in with him the Low Church, middle-class Proudies and Slopes, was Palmerston.*

This is another of the anomalies in Palmerston's political career. He championed the Low Churchmen in the great controversy which divided the Church in the middle of the nineteenth century. This was largely due to the influence of Shaftesbury, who was an ardent Evangelical, and a great opponent of Popery and the Oxford Movement, which was drawing a small, but influential, intellectual élite in the Church

---

*Barchester Towers was written in 1857. It portrayed an imaginary situation, in which a Conservative Government under Lord Derby was replaced by a Liberal Government under Palmerston. This situation in fact occurred two years later, in June 1859.

of England towards Roman Catholicism. When Palmerston first became Prime Minister, Shaftesbury had feared the worst. 'I much fear that Palmerston's ecclesiastical appointments will be detestable', he wrote to his son Evelyn Ashley on 28 February 1855. 'He does not know, in theology, Moses from Sydney Smith. The Vicar of Romsey, where he goes to church, is the only clergyman he ever spoke to; and, as for the wants, the feelings, the views, the hopes and fears, of the country, and particularly the religious part of it, they are as strange to him as the interior of Japan. Why, it was only a short time ago that he heard, for the first time, of the grand heresy of Puseyites and Tractarians!' But Shaftesbury soon changed his mind. Palmerston relied almost entirely on Shaftesbury in making his ecclesiastical appointments. He consulted Shaftesbury about all the five Archbishops and the twenty Bishops whom he appointed or translated in England and Ireland, and only once – in choosing a Canon of Canterbury – did he make even a minor ecclesiastical appointment without taking Shaftesbury's advice. Shaftesbury was persuaded that God, in His wisdom, had chosen Palmerston to be the instrument, under Shaftesbury's guidance, by which the Church of England would be preserved from Popery and the Oxford Movement. The Low Church Bishops who were appointed by Palmerston were popularly known as 'Shaftesbury Bishops'.

Palmerston's Secretary of State for India, Charles Wood, like Gladstone and other members of Palmerston's Cabinet, was High Church, and objected to the Shaftesbury Bishops. Palmerston explained his policy in a letter to Wood in very different terms from those which Shaftesbury would have used. 'The population of England and Wales', he wrote on 20 November 1856, 'may be said to be divided, two thirds Church of England, one third Dissenters. The Dissenters pretend equality; I do not believe it. The two thirds of Churchmen are split into High Church and Low Church. The High Church are few in number and are found chiefly in the higher classes, the different degrees of Low Church or at least of those who are against High Church are numerous, among the higher classes and one may say universal among the middle and Lower Classes of churchmen. The Dignitaries of the Church who are of the High Church Party are verging towards Papacy, and are in constant antagonism with their Low Church Brethren and with all the Dissenters. The Dignitaries who are of the Low Church school are more forebearing towards their High Church Brethren, and are at peace with the Dissenters. In this state of things it seemed to me that if one is to err on either side (and able men and energetic are not easily found among those who are neither one thing nor the other) the safest course is to lean towards the Low Church by which means a greater Degree of religious Harmony is obtained than by the other course'.

Palmerston's hostility towards High Churchmen was certainly influenced by his attitude to Roman Catholics. Gladstone, whom Palmerston wrongly suspected of being almost a Roman Catholic himself, wrote that Palmerston was absurdly suspicious of Roman Catholics; and Shaftesbury wrote approvingly that Palmerston 'regarded any approximation to Popery, Popish doctrines, and Popish practices, with special dislike and even fear'. This is not surprising, in view of Palmerston's background as an Anglo-Irish Protestant landlord. It is much more surprising that even in his younger days, when in all other respects he was a loyal Tory, he was in favour of Catholic Emancipation; but this, as he explained in his first public speech on the topic of 1813, was because he thought that it was politically expedient to employ upper-class Roman Catholics in the Army and in the political service of the State; and after 1825 he supported it as the only means of preventing civil war in Ireland. He never changed his attitude of 1813 that Roman Catholics had no right to hold any political or other positions in a Protestant country, and were entitled to do this only as a privilege granted to them at the discretion of the State.

His respect for Roman Catholic landowners and Army officers did not extend to Roman Catholic priests. 'These Catholic Priests are no less cunning than encroaching', he wrote to Cardwell, the Secretary for Ireland, on 15 September 1859. He was, of course, speaking more than half jokingly when he wrote to Minto in 1847, at the time of the famine and of great unrest in Ireland, that if it were possible to hang a dozen Catholic priests in Ireland, this would be the best way of putting an end to the troubles there; but he thought that he was fully justified in victimizing them in less dramatic ways. When he was Home Secretary in 1853, he wished to prosecute a monk in Worcestershire under a sixteenth-century statute, for showing himself in public in monastic dress, but was dissuaded by the Prime Minister, Lord Aberdeen; and when the Viceroy of Ireland proposed, in July 1865, to grant the Catholic College in Ireland the power to acquire land, Palmerston overruled him, because 'the example of the London University is not a case in Point and there is an admissible Difference between a Catholic and a Protestant Institution'. His anti-Catholic prejudice, however, was always subordinated to political exigencies. Even as a young man of twenty-four, on his first visit to Ireland in 1808, he had realized that he would have to appoint Roman Catholic teachers in the schools on his estates in Sligo if he wanted his tenants to send their children there; and in the last year of his life he ordered the portrait of William III to be removed from the Court room in Sligo, which he owned, in order to avoid offending the Roman Catholics. He also insisted that Lord O'Hagan, who was a Roman Catholic, should be appointed Chief Justice of Ireland, despite the fact that many Protestant barristers objected that there was already a majority of Roman Catholics on the Irish bench.

When Palmerston was Home Secretary in 1853, he had to deal with the Six Mile Bridge affair. There was a riot at Six Mile Bridge, in Ulster, and the troops fired on Catholic demonstrators. A Catholic priest was charged with inciting the disturbances. Lord Aberdeen told the indignant peers in the House of Lords that the priest would be prosecuted; but the authorities in Dublin thought that this would be very inadvisable, and that it would be difficult to find any jury which would convict him. Meanwhile a grand jury in Ulster had brought in a bill for murder against the soldiers who had fired on the crowd. Palmerston advised the Government of Ireland to proceed with the trial of the soldiers, for there was a good chance that they would be acquitted, and if they were convicted the Crown could always pardon them; and he agreed that the charge against the priest should be dropped if the Irish law officers considered this advisable, though Aberdeen was very reluctant to do this after the statement which he had made in the House of Lords. But when the Catholic Archdeacon Mc-Carren urged Catholic soldiers to refuse to fire on their fellow-Catholics, Palmerston insisted that he should be prosecuted because even if he were acquitted it would 'put these Revd. malefactors to shame'.

Though it might sometimes be politically inadvisable to prosecute Roman Catholic priests in Ireland, it was politically very rewarding in England to denounce them in the House of Commons. In 1850 Pope Pius IX decided to appoint Roman Catholic Bishops for English sees. There was a great outcry in England at the prospect of a Papist Bishop setting foot on English soil for the first time since Cardinal Pole in 1558; and Palmerston, though he was not as active as Lord John Russell himself in the campaign against 'Papal aggression', made a strong anti-Catholic speech in the House of Commons. But Cardinal Wiseman, though he was violently abused in the press at the time, and for many years afterwards, was not arrested and prosecuted, as the extreme Protestant organizations demanded, under the sixteenth-century statutes against those who acknowledged the authority of the Bishop of Rome in England; and Palmerston would never have advocated such a course. He was content to gain the applause of the Protestants and Radicals by his denunciation of Wiseman and Popery in the House of Commons.

Palmerston showed both his anti-Catholic prejudices, and his tendency to give way to public pressure, in connexion with William Turnbull's work on the State Papers of Edward VI. In 1859 the Government authorized Sir John Romilly, the Master of the Rolls, to begin the colossal venture, which has still not been completed after a hundred years, of publishing summaries of all letters and documents relating to public affairs in the sixteenth century. Romilly appointed Turnbull as editor and directed him to begin work on the documents at the Public Record Office. Turnbull was a barrister who had written several historical books; but he was also a Roman Catholic. The Protestant Truth Society protested strongly against his appointment: they said that he would be prejudiced, and would destroy documents which he found in the Record Office if they discredited the Catholics of the sixteenth century. Shaftesbury was particularly active in the campaign against Turnbull. Romilly backed Turnbull, and rejected the public clamour for his dismissal. Palmerston was anxious about the matter, and raised it several times with Romilly; but Romilly insisted that Turnbull was a conscientious and able historian, and that this was simply a case of religious prejudice; and Palmerston assured Shaftesbury and his friends that there was no substance in their criticism.

In 1861, the first two volumes were published. They summarized the documents dealing with foreign affairs in the reigns of Edward VI and Mary, and contained an introduction by Turnbull, which was an essay on the subject matter covered in the volumes. The two volumes are not as complete and satisfactory as those which were published in later years, but they were the beginning of a project which has transformed the study of sixteenth-century history and may be said, along with the work of the Protestant J. A. Froude which was also being published at this time, to have started the scientific approach to the history of the Reformation. But British Protestants, who had been used to reading only Protestant propaganda books like Foxe, Strype and Burnet, strongly objected to this new approach, and to Turnbull's introduction, though it was completely objective, and much less anti-Protestant than those of his Protestant successors forty years later.

After talking to Shaftesbury, Palmerston wrote a strong letter to Romilly, complaining that Turnbull's introduction was biassed and wrong, and insisted that Turnbull be dismissed from his post. Romilly persuaded Palmerston to read the introduction before making up his mind about it. When Palmerston eventually found time to do this, he admitted that it contained no trace of Catholic bias, though he objected to the fact that Turnbull was pro-Scottish in his account of the English invasion of Scotland in 1547, and disliked Turnbull's style of writing. But though Romilly sturdily refused to sacrifice Turnbull, Shaftesbury and his supporters redoubled their pressure; and in January 1861 Palmerston, who had become seriously worried at the possible repercussions in Parliament, ordered Romilly to dismiss Turnbull, because Turnbull's zeal as a 'bigotted pervert' of the Roman Catholic Church made him an unsuitable person to deal with this period of our history. Romilly was reluctantly compelled to comply; but fortunately Turnbull's successor, the Protestant clergyman, Brewer, turned out to be a better historian than Turnbull, and was more outspoken in his criticism of many of the actions of the Protestant authorities in the reign of Henry VIII.

Palmerston had no religious enthusiasm. He was irregular in his church attendance on Sundays, and from time to time made statements which offended religious susceptibilities. When he was Home Secretary in 1853, he told the ministers of the Church of Scotland, who had asked him to appoint a Fast Day for prayer against a cholera epidemic, that it was more important to improve the sanitation in Edinburgh. On another occasion, when he was asked to order a day of prayer on account of the threat to the harvest from the rainy weather, he said that he thought that it was too late, as the harvest was 'past praying for'. A statement which he made in a public speech in 1854 to the effect that all children were born good, and were led into crime by bad education and bad associations, was criticized by churchmen, and made it necessary for Palmerston to assure them that he had not intended to challenge the doctrine of original sin. Some churchmen complained that he treated Heaven like a foreign power.

He disappointed the Archbishop of Canterbury by refusing to sanction the appointment of a Bishop in Southern Africa, who would live among the native tribes. 'It may greatly be doubted', he wrote to Archbishop Sumner on 15 July 1860, 'whether any real advantage could be gained by sending a British Functionary of such a character to reside in Places where he would be liable to insults and injuries which would excite the just indignation of the British Nation, but which we should be unable to avenge and which our evident inability to punish would encourage the Nations [sic] to perpetrate'.

But Palmerston always supported the Church of England as an institution. In his Tory days in 1824 he spoke in the House of Commons on the importance of preventing the falling off in the congregations of the Church of England, in view of the role which the established Church performed in upholding the social structure of England; and he was always suspicious of 'Dissenters', as he called the Nonconformists. In 1860 he angered them by insisting that everyone should be required to state his religion on the census form. When he was told that many people nowadays did not profess to have any religion at all, he said that if this was so, it was important to have statistical information as a preliminary to taking measures to remedy such a deplorable state of affairs. The Radicals succeeded in defeating the proposal in the House of Commons. Palmerston refused to abolish the exclusive right of the Queen's Printer to publish the Bible and the Prayer Book, on the grounds that this was a necessary safeguard against unorthodox innovations in religion. In September 1860, at the request of the Mayor of Romsey, he wrote to the Lord Chancellor and directed him not to appoint two Nonconformists who had been recommended as Justices of the Peace at Romsey, but told him not to make his reasons known to the Romsey Borough Council.

Palmerston was less troubled about ecclesiastical appointments than by applications for honours. He was always being pestered by acquaintances asking him to make them peers. When he gave house-parties at Broadlands, he would sometimes ask his more intimate friends not to leave him alone with some of the guests who he knew had come in order to ask him for a peerage. Once, when one of the guests invited him to play billiards in the evening, he arranged for other people to come and watch the match, saying that he was willing to give his challenger a good game of billiards, but not a peerage. The worst offender was Lord Oranmore, who was an Irish peer, but was so eager to be created a peer of the United Kingdom that he wrote about this to Palmerston four times in one year, though Palmerston refused him unequivocally on every occasion.

Palmerston's objection to Oranmore was that he was not rich enough, for Oranmore had an income of only £3,000 a year. He pointed out to Oranmore the difference between an

Irish peer and a peer of the United Kingdom, which it was easier for him to do, being an Irish peer himself. 'There is a great and manifest difference between the position of an Irish Peer and a British Peer', he wrote on 13 August 1856, 'The first may live as he likes, and is a private Gentleman; the second is a member of the Legislature, and is exposed to expenses' if he is to perform 'his public and social duties'. Palmerston believed that, except in the special case of Generals and politicians who had rendered outstanding service to the State, no one should be created a peer unless he had a much higher income than £3,000 a year. He would not always make an exception even for leading Generals. He refused a peerage to General Sir Harry Smith, who is commemorated by the town of Harrismith in South Africa, because his income was too low, explaining to Smith that 'your title ... to the respect of your countrymen depends not upon what you are called but upon what you have done'. When General Cavendish's father disinherited him, and left his money to his younger son, Palmerston made the younger son a peer, instead of the General. 'These things do not go according to seniority in families', he wrote to General Cavendish on 3 September 1857, 'and much in regard to them depends on the amount of fortune possessed by those who may be thought of for advancement to the Upper House. You will say no doubt that it is a double Hardship on you that your younger brother should be chosen instead of yourself, because he is in possession of a fortune which you think ought to have been yours but those who have to advise the Crown in regard to these matters can only take things as they find them without enquiring into the Causes which may have produced that state of things'.

Palmerston took political affiliations into account in offering peerages and other honours. In appointing the Lords Lieutenants of the counties, he insisted that they should be 'men of rank, influence and large property' who were Liberals, not Conservatives. Personal friendship was also a factor, for in February 1856 he offered a peerage to Pemberton Milnes, reminding him that 'We began Public Life together, and it was to your declining the office of Secretary at War that I owe my appointment to that post'. In 1863 he made Milnes's nephew, Monckton Milnes, a peer. Monckton Milnes was a poet and essayist of distinction, but Palmerston would not have given him a peerage if he had not also been a Liberal MP. On another occasion, Palmerston rejected the suggestion that peerages should be conferred on eminent authors or doctors. He was not at all impressed by the arguments of men who wrote asking for a peerage on the grounds that some ancestor of theirs in the thirteenth or fourteenth century had been a peer. This did not seem to Palmerston to be any valid reason for granting a peerage to the descendant in the nineteenth century. Money, not ancestry, was the criterion. Palmerston did not have the romantic view of aristocracy which was held by Lord John Manners and Disraeli. For Palmerston, the peerage served the very practical modern function of being a constitutional bulwark against democratic government. It is significant that in his many letters about creating titles, he hardly ever used the term 'a peerage', but usually wrote about 'a seat in the Peers' House'. The important point was that one of the two Houses of the Legislature should consist of the wealthiest landowners in Britain.

One class of persons who had sometimes to be given peerages, whatever the amount of their income, were eminent Judges who were needed in the House of Lords when the House sat as the highest court of appeal in judicial cases. These Judges were often middle class in origin and had not always made a large enough fortune at the bar to be able to maintain a peerage. In 1856 Lord Cranworth, the Lord Chancellor, suggested to Palmerston that the solution to this difficulty would be to give them a life peerage which would expire at their death. Sir James Parke, a Judge of the Court of Exchequer, was therefore created a life peer with the title of Lord Wensleydale; but this aroused great opposition in the House of Lords, especially among the Judges, who thought that if the precedent was followed, lawyers would not be granted hereditary peerages in future. To the Queen's great annoyance, the House of Lords ruled that the Crown had no power to create peerages which were not hereditary, and that Lord Wensleydale's title therefore took effect as a hereditary one. Palmerston was fortunate to escape a vote of censure in the

House of Lords, and at one time it seemed that his Government would fall on this issue. His idea of creating life peerages for the law lords had to wait until 1876, when it was implemented by Act of Parliament.

Where law reform was concerned, Palmerston was no more conservative or obstructionist than he was in his implementation of measures of public health. In an age when there were far fewer statutes passed each year than at present, and when lawyers were much more reluctant than now to change the common law, Palmerston was responsible for introducing some very important and far-reaching measures of law reform. Apart from the controversial Divorce Act of 1857, his Government passed the Joint Stock Companies Act of 1856, which for the first time made it possible to form a limited liability company without obtaining a private Act of Parliament. Six years later, during his second administration, the Companies Act of 1862 laid the basis of modern company law. The main responsibility for introducing both these Acts rested with his departmental ministers and the Lord Chancellor and the law officers; but Palmerston mastered all the details of the bills, was present in the House throughout most of the Committee stage, and helped to smooth over the difficulties by his mastery of Parliamentary procedure, and his skill in handling the MPs with charm and humour. In 1861 the Offences against the Person Act codified and reformed the criminal law. Palmerston had some excuse for saying to Goschen in January 1864 that 'we cannot go on adding to the statute book ad infinitum', and that all they need do in the coming session of Parliament was to introduce 'a little law reform'; for he had already introduced, by the standards of the time, a large number of reforms.

So far was Palmerston from closing his mind to any idea of change that he gave very sympathetic consideration to a proposal made by several MPs that a decimal currency should be introduced. The idea had already been accepted in principle, and in 1849 the Government, as a first step, had introduced a new coin, the florin, valued at two shillings, or one-tenth of a £; but the full introduction of the scheme was postponed on the grounds of expense, and had to wait for over a hundred years. Palmerston strongly objected, however, to adopting the litre and French units of measurement, as he told Milner-Gibson, the President of the Board of Trade, in May 1864, when Milner-Gibson, Cobden and Ewart put forward proposals along these lines.

Nothing is so difficult to change as the traditional habits of a free People in regard to such Things. Such changes may be easily made in Despotic countries like Russia, or in countries where notwithstanding theoretical freedom the Government and the Police are all powerful as in France.... Can you expect that the People of the United Kingdom will cast aside all the names of Space and weight and capacity which they learnt from their infancy and all of a sudden adopt an unmeaning jargon of barbarous words representing Ideas and Things new to their minds. It seems to me to be a Dream of pedantic Theorists.... I see no use however in attempting to Frenchify the English Nation, and you may be quite sure that the English Nation will not consent to be Frenchified. There are many conceited men who think that they have given an unanswerable argument in favour of any measure they may propose by merely saying that it has been adopted by the French. I own that I am not of that school, and I think the French have much more to gain by imitating us than we have to gain by imitating them. The fact is there are a certain set of very vain men like Ewart and Cobden who not finding in things as they are here, the Prominence of Position to which they aspire, think that they gain a step by oversetting any of our arrangements great or small and by holding up some foreign country as an object of Imitation.

Palmerston did not hesitate, if necessary, to abolish the most ancient institutions. In 1860, the office of Lord Warden of the Cinque Ports fell vacant at the death of Lord Dalhousie. The office, which dated back to the early Middle Ages, had become a sinecure, but was conferred, along with the Lord Warden's residence at Walmer Castle, on the most eminent servants of the State. During Palmerston's lifetime, it had been held by Pitt and Wellington. When Palmerston had to fill the vacancy in 1860, he suggested that the office be abolished in order to save the public the cost of the upkeep of Walmer Castle. There was so much opposition to this plan that he abandoned it, and decided instead to become Lord Warden himself. In January 1861 he abolished the sinecure office of Lord Clerk Register in Scotland which had also fallen vacant on Dalhousie's death; but he withdrew his proposal to abolish the office of Viceroy of Ireland when Lord Carlisle died in 1864, because of the widespread opposition which it had aroused.

Palmerston was installed as Lord Warden of the Cinque Ports with the traditional ceremony at Dover on 27 August 1861. In his speech at the banquet in the evening, he spoke about the need to improve the national defences. He said that there were only two ways in which a nation could be secure — either by perfect insignificance, or by being in a state of perfect defence. 'England will never, I think, enjoy the former'; but he hoped that she would long continue to enjoy the latter. From Dover he went to Walmer Castle, where he spent three weeks in September. The weather was as hot as it had been sixty-two years before, when he toured the area on horseback with his father in the first week of September 1799. He described it enthusiastically as 'weather truly Italian'.

Palmerston might have held more progressive views on education had it not been for the fact that he thought it much more important to spend money on armaments than on schools. He had always believed, like so many other well-meaning men of his generation, that the spread of education among the lower classes would be the cure for many social evils; and he had spent his own money in providing schools for the people in Sligo and Romsey. But when proposals for free compulsory education were put forward during his last administration, he was far from enthusiastic. He agreed that the Government should provide financial assistance to those local authorities who opened schools for the poorer classes; but he thought that it was out of the question for the Government to pay to establish schools in those areas where the local authority refused to contribute. He was interested in schemes for the education of the middle classes, and in 1855 suggested that it would be desirable to establish some more public schools to do for the middle classes what Eton and Harrow did for the upper classes. He strongly supported the proposal to introduce drill and rifle practice, as well as cricket and football, in the great public schools.

He took great interest in events at his own school, Harrow. When he was Home Secretary in 1853, there was a public outcry because the system of appointing the older boys as monitors, which had just been introduced by the new headmaster, Dr. Vaughan, had resulted in a case where two of the monitors had seriously ill-treated a junior boy. Palmerston wrote to Vaughan in some indignation about the case, but was satisfied with Vaughan's explanation, and not only upheld the monitorial system, but twice tried unsuccessfully to persuade Vaughan to accept a bishopric. When he was Prime Minister he often visited Harrow. In June 1858 he was present when Vaughan dedicated a chapel in honour of the old Harrovians who had been killed in the Crimea, and made a speech. John Addington Symonds, who had left Harrow the previous year, but came from Oxford for the ceremony, was as disappointed with Palmerston as Turgeniev and other literary men had been on other occasions; he thought that Palmerston's speech 'consisted of a series of commonplaces, disposed of in short barks'. But less intellectual Harrovians loved him, and cheered him loudly when he laid the foundation stone of the Vaughan Library, in pouring rain, on 4 July 1861.

Palmerston was not enthusiastic about the system, which was introduced in the eighteen-fifties, of selecting clerks for the civil service by competitive examination instead of by the old system of patronage. He thought that there were certain advantages in the system, but that no general rule should be laid down, because 'success at an examination is certainly not a decisive proof of Fitness for official employment, because after all, examination is chiefly a test of memory acting upon previous Study, and there are other qualities besides Memory and Studious Habits required to make a Good official Man, but this Test though imperfect is better than none at all'. As usual, he was reluctant to interfere in the internal running of a department, and thought that it should be left to each minister to decide about examinations. 'My dear Clarendon', he wrote on 16 December 1855, 'do as you like about the examination of your Clerks'; but he recommended that they should be required to pass an examination in mathematics, especially in Euclid, which he thought was excellent training for a diplomat. What he objected to was 'letting any Lad have by asking for it a Ticket in the Lottery of Examination for an appointment under Government, a Lottery in which the tickets would be unlimited while the Prizes would be comparatively few, I fear the Disappointments would create much Discontent though possibly they might tend to diminish the Demand for Reduction of Establishments'. If there were examinations, he thought it essential that the questions should be suitable for the type of person who sat for the examination; and he considered it ridiculous, and even improper, that candidates for subordinate posts in the Public Department should be asked, in their written examinations, to discuss the effect which the accession of the new Tsar was likely to have on Russian policy in the Balkans.

On the punishment of crime and the treatment of poverty, he never really freed himself from the ideas which had prevailed in his youth. Although he introduced his penal reforms when he was Home Secretary, he was ready to throw them over when public pressure demanded severer measures. In 1862 there was a wave of violent crime in London, with many cases of strangling of victims by robbers. There was a clamour in the press and Parliament for harsher sentences, and for the abolition of the ticket-of-leave system. On 4 December 1862 Palmerston wrote to the Home Secretary, Sir George Grey, and urged him to introduce flogging as a punishment for robbery with violence; and ten days later he wrote again to demand the abolition of ticket-of-leave. He stated that he had introduced the ticket-of-leave system in 1853 when transportation was abolished, as otherwise it would have been too severe to substitute a sentence of imprisonment for transportation; but now that transportation had been abolished for ten years, this no longer applied, and he proposed that the ticket-of-leave system should be abolished. He even went so far as to urge Grey to use his powers under the Act of 1853 to arrest all prisoners who had been released on ticket-of-leave and whose sentences had not expired, and to send them back to prison. The ticket-of-leave system was not abolished, but more restrictions were placed on the released prisoners; and a statute passed in 1863, which was generally known as the Garrotters Act, added flogging as an additional punishment for robbery with violence.

Palmerston was firmly in favour of the death penalty for murder, though he no longer maintained that a poacher should be hanged for wounding a gamekeeper, and capital punishment for attempted murder was abolished by the Offences against the Person Act which his Government passed in 1861. In 1864 there was great public excitement about the case of Victor Townley, who had murdered his sweetheart because she broke off her engagement to him. Townley was convicted and sentenced to death, but his sentence was commuted to imprisonment as a criminal lunatic because three Home Office doctors had certified that he was insane. There was widespread indignation that Townley had not been hanged, and Palmerston wrote to the Home Secretary, Sir George Grey, to protest. After denouncing the 'benevolence-mongers' who had sympathy for murderers, Palmerston suggested that if a man were sane enough not to commit suicide, he was sane enough to refrain from killing others. In any case, the object of capital punishment was not vengeance but deterrence, and the value of the death penalty as a deterrent to men who were contemplating murder would be seriously weakened if they saw that an atrocious murderer like Townley was not hanged.

Palmerston opposed the campaign which Charles Dickens had initiated to abolish public executions in the street and to have them carried out in private within the prison. In this, as in other matters, Palmerston was only as far advanced as the majority of Englishmen of his generation. When he was Foreign Secretary in 1849, he ordered the British Minister in Teheran to join with his Russian colleague in telling the Shah of Persia that his habit of being present when criminals were strangled was barbarous, as no civilized ruler assisted personally at executions. But whenever a motion for the abolition of public hangings in Britain was discussed in the House of Commons, Palmerston voted against it, believing, like the majority of MPs, that it had a deterrent effect on the spectators, and that it would be a threat to the liberty of the subject if the Government could have people secretly executed in prisons.

Palmerston never abandoned the Malthusian theories of the

eighteen-thirties about the relief of poverty. Though he eventually supported the successive amendments to the new Poor Law which abolished some of the worst hardships of the workhouses, he did so for tactical, electoral reasons, rather than from any idea that life should be made more bearable for the pauper. When the cotton famine during the American Civil War caused mass unemployment and great distress in Lancashire, the local gentry and various philanthropic bodies organized a system of voluntary relief, in which Lord Derby, the Conservative leader, who was the greatest landowner in Lancashire, played a leading part. Palmerston was not happy about this. He was afraid that the voluntary committees, by paying out relief in circumstances where it would be refused by the Poor Law Guardians, would tend to break down the strict limitations which had hitherto been placed on public relief. When he heard that the committees were paying 3s. 6d. a week to a single man, and 2s. per head to a married man with a wife and child, he asked them to reduce these rates, because this meant that a man with a wife and four children was receiving 12s. per week, whereas agricultural labourers in employment in the southern counties, who might have equally large families, were being paid only 10s. per week.

He was not interested in the movement, which began towards the end of his life, to redeem prostitutes – or 'unfortunates', as they were significantly called. He surprised William Day, the son of his trainer, by saying that it would be regrettable if prostitution was suppressed, because its existence was a protection for respectable women. William Day, who was used to hearing people in public life talk of the need to save unfortunates, and suppress vice, thought that Palmerston's opinion was unusual and daring; but Palmerston was being less frank than Day supposed when he expressed his anxiety to safeguard the virtue of respectable ladies.

Though Palmerston was by no means opposed to all reforms, he always resisted those which he thought would change the class structure of British society, for he considered that the supremacy of the landed aristocracy was essential for the wellbeing of the country. This was why he opposed the proposals to reform the complicated and archaic law of real property. The reforms which were being advocated at this time all tended not only to simplify the law, but to make it easier to disentail and to transfer property, and to enable younger children and the next-of-kin to share the inheritance with the eldest son. These reforms were not achieved until 1882 and 1925, though no less than eight statutes introducing piecemeal reforms along these lines were enacted while Palmerston was Prime Minister. Palmerston opposed any reform which tended to break up landed estates, and to separate the property of the aristocracy from the family title. For the same reason he was opposed to any kind of death duties on land. He reluctantly agreed to maintain the succession duty which had been imposed in 1853 on land as well as on other property, and which, in the case of a son inheriting his father's land, was no higher than 1 per cent; but he told Lord Cranworth and Bethell that he would not consent to extend the probate duty to real property. 'I consider hereditary Succession to unbroken Masses of landed property to be absolutely Necessary for the maintenance of the British Constitution', he wrote to them on 10 December 1856.

He would not consent to change the law so as to permit aliens to own land in England in their own name, and refused to make an exception even for the Belgian diplomat, Van de Weyer, whom he liked and respected. On 20 February 1864 he wrote to Bethell – who was now Lord Westbury, the Lord Chancellor: 'I do not think that we ought to alter the long established law of our land to suit the private purposes of a Foreigner however respectable or entitled to consideration. ... According to our social habits and political organization the possession of Land in this Country is directly or indirectly the source of political Influence and Power and that Influence and Power ought to be exercised exclusively by British subjects and not to pass in any degree into the Hands of Foreigners. It may be said that the possession of landed Property by a few Foreigners would produce no sensible effect on the working of our constitution, but this is a question of Principle and not of Degree and you might on the same ground propose a law to allow Foreigners to vote at elections, as well as to allow them to purchase the means of swaying the votes of other Persons at elections'. After Palmerston's death, an Act of 1870 allowed all aliens to own land in Britain.

In Ireland, the agitation for granting tenants security against eviction and the right to compensation for improvements continued with increased vigour after the troubles of 1848. Palmerston was absolutely opposed to this on principle. When the Irish MPs demanded that this security against eviction, which had existed for many centuries in Ulster, and was known as 'tenant right', should be extended to the whole of Ireland, Palmerston refused, and stated that 'tenant right is landlord's wrong'. During his first term as Premier, he refused all such demands; but after 1859 he could not disregard the Radicals in his Cabinet and on the Government benches in the House of Commons. In 1860 an Act was passed which provided that a tenant should be entitled to compensation for any improvement made at his expense with the consent of the landlord. The Act was largely a dead-letter, as many landlords automatically refused their consent to improvements, thereby often driving the tenant to carry out the improvements without their consent, so that he lost the right to compensation. But Palmerston resisted all demands from the Irish and Radical MPs that tenants should be entitled to the compensation even if the landlord had refused his consent to the improvements, provided that an impartial tribunal decided that the improvements were necessary or desirable. He considered that all these proposals were part of a Roman Catholic plot to win power in Ireland. He told Queen Victoria that the Catholics' 'object is, by Tenant Right or by sale and purchase, to transfer the lands in Ireland from Protestant landlords to Catholic middle-class men, and thus to lay the ground-work for abolishing the Protestant Church and setting up the Catholic Church in its stead'. It was not only Popery, but also Communism. 'Gentlemen talk in the easiest way possible', he said in the House of Commons on 23 June 1863, 'of the manner in which owners of land should be compelled to make such and such arrangements with their tenants, and should receive only such rent as other people adjudge them entitled to. I say these doctrines are Communistic doctrines'.

The same issue arose in the little colony of Prince Edward

Island off the coast of Nova Scotia in the Gulf of St. Lawrence. At the end of the eighteenth century the British Government, in a transaction which was bitterly criticized at the time, and subsequently, as a particularly flagrant example of political corruption, granted the freehold of the land in Prince Edward Island for a nominal sum to a small number of English speculators who had never set foot there; and the inhabitants of the island, most of whom were Scottish immigrants, cultivated their holdings as tenants of the absentee landlords in Britain. The resentment in the colony against the landlords was very strong. After a long agitation, the Legislature of Prince Edward Island passed an Act which imposed a tax on the income which the absentee landlords derived from their rents, and provided that if the tax were not paid, the land should be sold to the tenant in order to raise the tax required by the Colonial Government. A second Act provided that if any tenant were ejected by the landlord for any reason – including non-payment of rent – he was to be entitled to compensation from the landlord on the basis of twenty times the increased value which his improvements had added to the annual value of the land. The Acts of colonial legislatures were liable to be vetoed by the Government in London; and unfortunately for the islanders these two bills were referred to the Colonial Office at the time when it was being administered by Palmerston during the illness of Sir William Molesworth, the Colonial Secretary, in 1855. Palmerston told Molesworth to veto both the bills.

Two months later, Molesworth died, and Palmerston appointed Labouchere to succeed him as Colonial Secretary. Labouchere was not unsympathetic to the tenants of Prince Edward Island, and some of his officials in the Colonial Office were even more in sympathy with their grievances. Labouchere therefore drafted an amended, compromise bill which compelled the landlords to compensate the tenants for improvements, but not if the tenants were ejected for non-payment of rent, and at a lower rate of compensation than that in the original bill. But Palmerston found this proposal equally objectionable. On 19 December 1855 he wrote to Labouchere and directed him to abandon the bill. The fact that the landlords had acquired their lands from the Crown under very favourable conditions was irrelevant: 'The Crown had full power to grant them ... and the people of the Island who were no parties to the transaction between the Crown and the Grantees had no right whatever to object' to the favours granted by the Crown. 'The present state of the matter then is that the owners have as good a right to their Property as you or I, or any other of us have to our Estates; and it would be as unjust and of as bad example to *extinguish* the Rights of these owners, as it would be to *extinguish* our Rights and to fix the conditions on which we should be compelled to make over our Farms to the Tenants to whom we have let them. The legitimate and only honest way in which one man can become possessed of what belongs to another is by Bargain and Purchase, giving him the value which the owner is willing to take for it'. After commenting on 'the total want of honesty and just principles which these Islanders have displayed', and a reference to the adverse 'Habits and Prejudices of our Race on the North American Continent', Palmerston said that he was sure that the agitation in Prince Edward Island, 'if met by a firm and steady adherence to the fundamental Principles of Justice on which human Society reposes, it will gradually settle down and be *extinguished*'.

The rights of the absentee landlords in Prince Edward Island continued unimpaired for the next eight years; but in 1863 the inhabitants raised it again. This ime, instead of passing a bill in their Legislature, they lobbied the Colonial Office; but Palmerston got to hear of it, and told the Colonial Secretary, the Duke of Newcastle, that in 1855 'I had to deal with a flagitious attempt on the part of a clique of Tenants in Prince Edward's Island to do what has been attempted but frustrated in Ireland, namely to transfer property from the lawful owner to the dishonest Tenant. I decidedly repelled this attempt at spoliation.... I believe you have had much trouble with these Gentry who, having rented lands on the condition of paying rent, discover that there is something in the atmosphere of the American Continent which is incompatible with the payment of rent but which does not preclude compulsion upon landowners to sell their Lands to their Tenants for a very small portion of the real value'. He told Newcastle that he was determined to prevent this expropriation of the landlords because, apart from the justice of the case, he had 'a near connexion who has lands in the island and is much interested in the Matter'. Next year the Legislature of Prince Edward Island again passed the bill granting tenant right: but at Palmerston's insistence it was again vetoed by Newcastle. In 1873, after Prince Edward Island had been incorporated into the Dominion of Canada and Palmerston was dead, Gladstone's Liberal Government consented to legislation which enabled the Government of Canada to buy out all the absentee landlords in Prince Edward Island by compulsory purchase.

Chapter Thirty-six

Old Pam

Disraeli described Palmerston as 'the Tory chief of a Radical Cabinet'. Lord Salisbury put the position more accurately: he said that Palmerston wanted Radical votes, Whig placemen, and Tory policy. There were never more than a handful of Radicals in Palmerston's Government; but in June 1861 he decided to strengthen the Radical element by appointing Layard as Under-Secretary for Foreign Affairs. The Queen objected very strongly to this for the same reason that she had refused to have Layard at the War Office in 1855 – because of his attacks on the aristocracy. She said that Layard was not a gentleman, and thought it particularly important that he should not be appointed to the Foreign Office. Palmerston told her that, without Layard, his Government might lose the support of the Radicals, and not survive; but she answered that the honour of the country was more important than the stability of the Government. After Palmerston had unsuccessfully tried to persuade Prince Albert to urge the Queen to change her mind, she eventually agreed to accept Layard if Palmerston assured her that this was essential in the national interest, though she begged him not to place her in this 'cruel dilemma'. But Palmerston did so, and Layard became Under-Secretary to Russell at the Foreign Office.

Apart from his unsatisfactory relations with Gladstone, Palmerston was on the best of terms with all his ministers, including the Radical ones. He interfered with them very little in the running of their departments, but gave them general directives on policy, leaving the implementation of the policy to them. This was true, to some extent, even of the Foreign Office, where he might have been tempted to act as if he were

himself the Foreign Secretary. He wrote frequent letters
to his two Foreign Secretaries, Clarendon and Lord John Russell; but he left them to handle the negotiations themselves,
and to draft their own despatches, though he read, and often
corrected, the despatches, and occasionally drafted them himself. He amplified the official despatches to foreign Governments by personal letters in French or Italian to foreign
Ambassadors or Foreign Ministers. He refused to intervene
in any way in the appointments to the Foreign Office or the
diplomatic service; even when he was asked by his most intimate friends to obtain an appointment for their sons or
nephews, he always refused, and told them that they must
write to the Foreign Secretary about it. He also left the administration of the Foreign Office entirely to the Foreign
Secretary, to the delight of the Foreign Office clerks, who
were much happier under Clarendon and Russell than they had
been in Palmerston's time. When Clarendon first became
Foreign Secretary, they brought him the day's despatches
at eleven o'clock at night, which Palmerston had required
them to do when he was Foreign Secretary; but they found
that Clarendon had gone to bed, and were told to bring them
at seven o'clock next morning. Clarendon even allowed the
clerks to smoke in the Foreign Office, for, like his friend Napoleon III, he had acquired the habit of smoking cigarettes,
which were now becoming popular.

In 1862 Russell, as Foreign Secretary, asked Palmerston to
intervene in an internal departmental matter, but more in a
personal than in an official capacity. In 1858 Bulwer was appointed Ambassador to Turkey. Before long, rumours were
circulating in Constantinople that Bulwer was having a love
affair with a Turkish woman, and eventually the matter became
so notorious that it was reported to Russell. Russell felt that
this was a matter which Palmerston could handle better than
he could; and though Palmerston did nothing about it for a
long time, he was eventually prompted into action when Bulwer wrote to ask him for a peerage. 'The Public abroad and
the Government at home', he wrote to Bulwer on 9 December
1862, 'have no Right to pry into the Gallantries of Diploma-
tists provided that they are covered with a decorous veil of

Privacy, but when such Things are thrust too prominently into view and are brought too glaringly into public notice they damage character by, at all events, and to put it on no higher ground, impugning soundness of judgement, and by implying a want of proper Respect for public opinion; and Things of this kind are the more remarked and commented upon when they apply to the Representatives of the Queen'. He also referred to the rumours about Bulwer's extravagance, and told Bulwer that 'one great method of maintaining personal Respect is the Habit of living within the means which a fixed income affords. Financial embarrassments and increasing Debts are as detrimental to an Individual as to a State'. This was a maxim which Palmerston himself had not observed.

Apart from the Foreign Office, the department with which Palmerston interfered most was the War Office. He continued to show great interest in the details of new types of rifles, cannon, fortifications and warships and in the possibilities of developing the submarine; and he followed closely all preparations for improving the defences against invasion. In April 1862 he tried unsuccessfully to persuade the War Office to move Woolwich Arsenal to Cannock Chase in Staffordshire, where it could not be so easily captured by the French.

He also interested himself in the detailed administration of the Board of Works in connexion with the parks, where he often walked. Soon after he first became Prime Minister, in the midst of the anxieties about events in the Crimea in the summer of 1855, he worked out a plan for building a road through St. James's Park. He pointed out to Sir William Molesworth, the President of the Board of Works, that 'From the Horse Guards up to Hyde Park Corner there is by reason of the Parks, and the Palace and its Garden, an almost impassable Barrier as regards Carriages, separating from each other the vast aggregations of Houses that lie on the opposite sides of that Barrier, and the progressive increase of the town in the neighbourhood of Belgravia makes this inconvenience felt more and more every year'. It would be undesirable to have a public road running immediately in front of Buckingham Palace, as this would intrude on the Queen's privacy; but a road should be built from St. James's Street to Victoria Street.

passing between St. James's Palace and Marlborough House, and running on high arches across the water in St. James's Park so as not to break up the continuity of the grass.

Molesworth's successor at the Board of Works, Sir Benjamin Hall, got into difficulties with Palmerston when he tried to erect hurdles around the grass in the parks, and to confine the public to the gravel paths.

My dear Hall, [wrote Palmerston on 29 October 1857], you have been greatly infringing in the Green Park upon the Liberty of the Subject and have carefully shut out all Her Majesty's subjects from that grass which by it's colour has given the Name to the Park. I presume that it is only a temporary Measure, for the purpose of enabling you to feed sheep on the grass so as to make it greener still and that in a short time the Iron Hurdles will be removed, for to keep them there permanently would be to deprive the Public of the greater part of the enjoyment derivable from the Park. People ask whether Sir Benjamin Hall is under the impression that grass is in this country so rare and precious a plant that it ought not to be trodden under foot by the vulgar crowd.

As Hall nevertheless continued with his preparations to erect the hurdles, he received two more caustic letters from Palmerston during the next five days. Eventually Palmerston wrote on 12 November:

Your Iron Hurdles are an intolerable nuisance, and I trust that you mean shortly to remove them. . . . I must positively forbid the prosecution of any such Scheme – as Head of the Government I should be held by the Public to have authorized these Arrangements and I do not chuse to be responsible for Things which I disapprove.

Palmerston interfered decisively with the plans of the Board of Works for the new Foreign Office building in Whitehall. The old Foreign Office, at the corner of Downing Street, was unsatisfactory. Palmerston had been complaining for many years that it was too small, and had no large rooms suitable for banquets and receptions. The Government commissioned Sir Gilbert Scott, the most fashionable architect of the day, to design the new building; and by the time that Palmerston returned to power in 1859, Scott's plans were far advanced. But Palmerston strongly objected to Scott's design. Scott was the leading exponent of the modern neo-Gothic style, which, under the patronage of Prince Albert, had become very popular; but Palmerston remained firmly old-fashioned in his architectural tastes. He insisted that the new Foreign Office should be in the classical style of the buildings of the Regency period, because he thought that Scott's Gothic design would make the Foreign Office look like a Continental cathedral, and it would be too dark for the clerks to see to work. He described Scott's project in the House of Commons as a 'hideous Gothic structure' and a 'frightful' building. Scott was very angry at Palmerston's attitude; but he eventually gave way, and built the present Foreign Office building in the style that Palmerston liked. He took his original design for the Foreign Office to the directors of the Midland Railway, who admired it, and it was erected as St. Pancras Railway Station.

Palmerston's devotion to the architectural style of his youth sometimes had less fortunate results. He not only disliked the modern architectural developments, but, like so many other members of his generation, had no respect for the buildings of earlier times. When he purchased an area of land which adjoined his property at Romsey, he pulled down a number of old houses and cottages, and replaced them with modern houses, though the local antiquarians felt that he was destroying buildings of historic interest. In 1852 his neighbour, the owner of Lee Manor House, died. Palmerston bought the property, and pulled down the sixteenth-century manor house which had for so long been a landmark for travellers on the Romsey-Southampton road.

Though Palmerston defeated Scott about the new Foreign Office building, he had to give way to Lord Panmure about Netley Hospital. When Florence Nightingale spent Christmas at Broadlands in 1856 she interested Palmerston in her efforts to persuade Panmure and the War Office to cancel the plans for the erection of this military hospital on Southampton Water, because she believed that its design made it not only very inconvenient for the nurses, but likely to spread disease by concentrating the patients together without proper provision for fresh air in the wards. Unfortunately, Florence Nightingale had not been consulted until building had already started, and Panmure assured Palmerston that £70,000 would be wasted if the work was discontinued; and though Palmerston at first insisted that the building be pulled down and thrown into the Southampton River, and the work begun again, he eventually gave way to Panmure, who refused to take the responsibility of defending the wastage of public money in Parliament. After a few minor alterations had been made to meet Florence Nightingale's objections, Palmerston declared that he was very satisfied with the hospital, though Florence Nightingale herself was convinced that it would be thoroughly unsatisfactory. For a hundred years, most of the people connected with Netley have agreed that she was right.

Despite these occasional disagreements with his ministers, Palmerston's relations with the Cabinet were excellent. Even in his younger days, when foreign diplomats and the Foreign Office staff were complaining about his behaviour, he had been amenable at Cabinet meetings. As Prime Minister, he pleased his colleagues by never attempting to dictate to them, but consulting them, or appearing to consult them, at every point. He even took the very unusual course of consulting them on his Cabinet and ministerial appointments; when he wished to appoint a new minister, he would sometimes submit three or four names to the Cabinet, and ask them to choose the one that they would like to have as their new colleague.

He handled the House of Commons just as tactfully. As Foreign Secretary, he had not always handled MPs wisely, and often annoyed them by taking the attitude that they must trust him and the Government, and not expect him to make public statements in Parliament on foreign affairs, as these might cause international embarrassments. But when he became Prime Minister and Leader of the House of Commons, he learnt to be much more tactful with MPs. He kept them sitting very late – much later than Disraeli or Lord John Russell, who liked to go to bed early – and often kept them up till 2 or 3 a.m. But he could always ease difficulties with a joke, and was particularly skilful at arranging things in the luncheon or smoking room.

His relations with the Queen continued, on the whole, to be satisfactory. She and Albert had very largely revised their

opinion of the man whom they had formerly referred to as
'the immoral one'. Victoria had been much more in sympathy
with Palmerston's policy during his first Premiership than during his last term at the Foreign Office; and though she had
more grounds for criticism after he returned to power in 1859,
this did not seriously damage their relationship. The Queen,
who supported Austria during the war of 1859, disapproved
of Palmerston's support of France and Sardinia; but the subsequent developments in Italy soon removed this cause of
disagreement. She was distressed that he insisted on her accepting Layard and Radical ministers in his Government; but
she could not question the skill with which he opposed the
attack on the House of Lords at the time of the paper duties
dispute, and the demands for Parliamentary reform. More
important than political considerations was the fact that Palmerston had at last learned to follow the advice which Lady
Palmerston had given him at the height of his controversy
with the Queen in 1848 – to handle Victoria more tactfully,
and to flatter her a little. Palmerston now showed her every
consideration. His letters to her were models of their kind –
solemn and formal, with a touch of respectful intimacy. He
always saw to it that the Foreign Office despatches were shown
to her before they were sent off; and when Lord John Russell
offended her by criticizing her opinions on foreign policy too
sharply in one of his letters to her, Palmerston stepped in to
smooth the Queen's feelings, and obtained an apology from
Lord John. Palmerston sat up late at night, when he had finished his other work, writing long reports to the Queen on the
proceedings in Cabinet and Parliament, and made a pretence, at
least, of consulting her closely on all important matters of state.

Victoria was particularly pleased at Palmerston's attitude
towards Prince Albert. Palmerston went out of his way to
praise, and even flatter, Albert in his letters to the Queen and
in his public speeches. It was easier for him to do this because, since the bitter campaign against Albert in the weeks
before the outbreak of the Crimean War, the Prince had
played a much less prominent part in politics; if he still sometimes influenced the Queen's policy, or suggested alterations
in despatches, he did it so discreetly that it went unnoticed.

In 1857 Palmerston gratified the Queen's desire that Albert should be given some official title. He achieved what every previous Prime Minister had declared would be impossible, and persuaded Parliament to pass an Act conferring the title of Prince Consort on Albert.

When Albert died in December 1861, at the age of forty-two, the Queen was deeply touched at Palmerston's conduct. Palmerston was at Windsor when the Prince fell ill with what was thought to be an attack of influenza, but which turned out to be typhoid fever; and while the doctors were cheerfully assuring the Queen that there was nothing to worry about, Palmerston was the first person to express serious anxiety over the Prince's symptoms. After Albert's death, when the Queen was in a state of the greatest distress which exceeded even what was considered proper in a bereaved widow of the period, she was very grateful for Palmerston's respectful sympathy. He showed great interest in her proposal to build a memorial to Albert, and suggested that an open Grecian temple should be erected, between Rotten Row and the carriage drive, on a raised platform with steps to ascend it; in the centre there was to be 'a statue of the Prince Consort of heroic size' on a pedestal, and the platform was to be surrounded with subordinate ornaments. Many politicians made or marred their reputation in the Queen's eyes by their reaction to Albert's death, and Palmerston passed the test most satisfactorily. Those who saw him with tears in his eyes when he talked about the late Prince, or when he watched the sorrow-stricken Queen two years later at the Prince of Wales's wedding – one of the few official functions which she attended – had no doubt of his sincerity; and in many of his letters to his friends he expressed his shock and grief at Albert's death. He had always possessed the ability to change his feelings when his politics or his interests changed, and unconsciously to adapt his emotions to the needs of the moment; he would not only act, but also feel, as a Liberal one day and as a Tory the next.

Whatever his personal antagonisms to Albert may have been at one time, his respect for the institutions of monarchy was sincere and permanent. He was eager to safeguard the reputation of the royal family, and for this reason wished to buy up and burn any letters in private hands which revealed the love affairs of George IV and the other sons of George III in the eighteenth century, more than eighty years before, though he was worried as to which section of the public funds could properly be used for this purpose. He always caused general satisfaction when he moved loyal addresses in the House, or proposed the Queen's health at public dinners, even if Turgeniev and other intellectuals thought that his speeches on such occasions were unoriginal. Opinions differed as to whether he looked impressive or ridiculous when he carried the sword of state at the wedding of Princess Victoria to Crown Prince Frederick of Prussia; but there was unanimous praise for his speech in the House of Commons on the occasion of the marriage of Princess Alexandra of Denmark to the Prince of Wales, when he declared that the bride possessed the four requirements which were necessary in a Princess of Wales – she was young, she was handsome, she was amiable, and she was a Protestant.

As far as human relations were concerned, Palmerston was a much greater success as a Prime Minister than as a Foreign Secretary. In 1856 he appointed a young relative of Lord Durham's, Charles Barrington, to be his private secretary. More than fifty years later, Barrington, shortly before his death, wrote a private account, for the members of his family, of his recollections of Palmerston. The kind, considerate master whom he describes is the same person as the arrogant chief about whom all the Foreign Office clerks were complaining fifteen years before. The Prime Minister who told Barrington to be always sure to offer a seat to every visitor to his office, because it always paid to be courteous, and because it was then possible to end the conversation gracefully by rising and shaking hands at the right moment, was the same man as the Foreign Secretary who kept as eminent a statesman as Prince Talleyrand waiting for two hours. At the Foreign Office he had unmercifully nagged his staff for using the wrong coloured ink, or using the same words of French origin which he used himself; but as Prime Minister he came into Barrington's room, and finding Barrington's desk in utter confusion said with a friendly smile: 'Every man understands his own chaos best'. No doubt old Barrington, in 1908, looked at the past with rose-coloured spectacles, and had forgotten any irritation that he might have felt before 1865 with the great Lord Palmerston; but no one could have written about an old employer in the way that Barrington did unless he had felt a deep affection for him; and there are many other witnesses who suggest that 'dear old Pam' was a very different person from 'Lord Pumicestone'.

Clarendon believed that Palmerston had become wiser and more patient with age, and less assertive after he had achieved the summit of his ambition. The old bull had perhaps lost some of his aggression with his sexual appetite; but the difference can also be accounted for by Palmerston's remarkable flair for knowing whom he could, and whom he could not, bully. It was more a question of personality than of social position, for Barrington was as much an underling as the clerks at the Foreign Office, who were socially as upper-class as Barrington. But there had always been those exceptional individuals, like Ponsonby, Bulwer, and of course Beauvale, who could get away with things which Palmerston would never have tolerated from any other subordinate; and young Barrington must have impressed Palmerston in the same way, and convinced him that he had ability and character. The important thing, as both Greville and Argyll noticed, was to have the courage to stand up to him. As far as the House of Commons was concerned, Palmerston realized the folly of trying to browbeat MPs, and after he became Leader of the House he nearly always handled them with the softest of velvet gloves. On the rare occasions when he slipped up, and lost his temper in the House, he paid the penalty.

Palmerston's skill in managing the House of Commons was the chief reason why he did not accept a seat in the House of Lords. After he became Prime Minister again in 1859, there was a rumour that he would be created a peer of the United Kingdom; but though Lady Palmerston was in favour, he preferred to stay in the Commons, where he thought he could handle matters better than Lord John Russell. Then, in 1861, Lord John asked for a peerage, as he had inherited enough money, on his brother's death, to be able to maintain his position as a peer. Palmerston obviously could not refuse it, and Lord John went to the House of Lords as Earl Russell. This removed any possibility that Palmerston might go to the Lords, because, had he done so, he would have had no choice but to appoint Gladstone to succeed him as Leader of the House of Commons; and he was becoming increasingly suspicious of Gladstone's new Radical tendencies.

A great deal of Palmerston's popularity in political and social circles was due to Lady Palmerston's parties. In 1855, Palmerston sold his house in Carlton Gardens, and bought the house in Piccadilly where the Duke of Cambridge had lived for the previous four years. It was a relatively small house for a royal Duke or a peer, but was an attractive and impressive building in the classical style of Palmerston's youth. It overlooked the Green Park across the other side of the street. The house* was usually referred to as Cambridge House, though Palmerston himself always used the address '94 Piccadilly'. Soon after the Palmerstons moved in, the hotel that was afterwards called the Berkeley was built nearby, to the annoyance of Lady Palmerston, who thought that it lowered the tone of the district. Palmerston continued to live at Cambridge House after he became Prime Minister, and only used 10, Downing Street as an office.

The Saturday evening parties were an outstanding event. Invitations were highly prized, and great intrigues were set on foot to obtain them; but Lady Palmerston went outside the ranks of London society, which at this time consisted of less than five hundred people. Middle-class MPs were invited, as well as Polish and Italian refugees, provided that their social position was moderately respectable and their political opinions were not too extreme. In 1849, an article in the *Morning Chronicle* complained that Lady Palmerston had invited a Neapolitan revolutionary, and that no Conservative refugee was ever asked; but Palmerston asked the *Globe* to publish a denial, pointing out that the Metternichs and the Guizots had attended, and stating that Lady Palmerston wished to provide an opportunity for distinguished people of the most differing views to meet for friendly social intercourse. His guests in-

*Now occupied by the Naval and Military Club.

cluded, as well as the revolutionaries, Neapolitan royal Princes, and even Narváez. In 1855 Queen Victoria tried to persuade Palmerston to refuse to invite journalists who had attacked the royal family and advocated extreme Radical opinions, so that these writers should be made to feel the social ostracism which their conduct had provoked; but Palmerston told her that it would be quite impossible to exclude journalists whose social position entitled them to an invitation, and in fact many journalists were invited, though the profession was not yet considered to be quite respectable.

As the guests arrived, they were received by the Palmerstons at the top of the great flight of stairs, Lady Palmerston looking regal in her diamonds and wearing the latest fashion in crinolines, though Sir William Fraser thought that not even the Garter could make Palmerston look aristocratic. Palmerston greeted every guest as if he were an old friend, though he often confessed that he had no idea to whom he had been speaking. The parties were always a great success, for Lady Palmerston personally supervised every detail of the arrangements; and politically they were very important to Palmerston, as MPs would do what Palmerston wanted so as to be sure of receiving an invitation to the parties. Sometimes political calculations were upset by Lady Palmerston's inclinations, as her old friend Abraham Hayward explained. 'She *would* have "those two pretty girls", and she would *not* have "that fat woman with her ugly daughters", although the fat woman was the wife of a county member, and the two pretty girls had neither father nor brother in either House'. Hayward thought that Lady Palmerston had not changed much since the days when he had seen her, as a young woman, rowing on the lake at Brocket, and offering to jump over a billiard table at Petworth.

Palmerston's generous temperament usually made it possible for him to forget old resentments and to overlook political differences. When it became necessary for him to make an alliance with Cobden and the Radicals, he was able to win over many of them by his personal charm, despite the strong political objections which they had to all his policies and his attitude to life. When Holyoake, who had suffered imprisonment and many years of poverty and victimization as a Chartist, a Socialist and a freethinker, was organizing a movement among the working class in favour of a reform of the franchise, Palmerston sent his friend Thornton Hunt, the consulting editor of the *Daily Telegraph*, to offer to find Holyoake a seat in the House of Commons. Holyoake thought that Palmerston's object was to prove that able men from the working classes could enter Parliament, even if they held extreme opinions, without the need for a new Reform Bill. Holyoake declined the offer; but he always had a sneaking affection for Palmerston. Thornton Hunt was no doubt right, in one sense, when he told Holyoake that Palmerston knew nothing of life below his carriage steps; but though Palmerston never really understood the point of view of the lower classes, he could talk to them with an easy informality.

Julian Harney, who opposed Palmerston at Tiverton in the general election of 1847, and was surprised to find him so friendly when they met on the hustings, became a great admirer of Palmerston in his old age. This was chiefly because Harney, after emigrating to America, abandoned most of his Chartist views and became a kind of patriotic Radical; but Palmerston's charm was partly responsible. Harney quotes examples, which are confirmed by Holyoake, of Palmerston's personal generosity to his political opponents. Holyoake organized a petition to ask Palmerston to provide some kind of pension from the public funds for the sister of Fergus O'Connor, the Chartist leader, who was in great poverty, largely on account of the victimization to which O'Connor had been subjected. Palmerston refused to give her a pension, regretting that it was not possible to place her case within any of the recognized categories which could qualify for a pension; but he offered to give her £100 from his own pocket, if she would be prepared to accept it, writing a very courteous and tactful letter on the subject. On another occasion, very shortly before his death, some Chartists organized a collection among the Radical MPs for a testimonial to some Chartist leader. While they were approaching the Radical MPs in the lobby of the House of Commons, Palmerston came by; and the Chartists, out of sheer devilment, approached him and asked him to subscribe. To their great surprise, Palmerston put his hand in his pocket and gave them something. After turning to leave, he came back to them, and asked them: 'Can you tell me what has become of an old Chartist acquaintance of mine, Mr. George Julian Harney?' When he was told that Harney was in America, he said: 'Well, I wish him good fortune; he gave me a dressing down at Tiverton some years ago, and I have not heard of him since; but I hope he is doing well'.

One of the men whom he won over by his friendliness was Anstey, the erratic barrister who in 1848 had moved the impeachment of Palmerston in the House of Commons for having been a Russian agent since 1828. Palmerston bore him no personal ill-will. Anstey was a garrulous and bombastic man, not devoid of ability, but so irresponsible that no one took him seriously. One day in the summer of 1859 Palmerston, who had just become Prime Minister, was sitting drinking a cup of tea by himself in the refreshment room in the House when Anstey came in. Anstey sat down at a table next to another MP and began talking to him; but this MP, after replying very curtly once or twice, buried his head in his papers and ignored Anstey's conversation. Anstey moved to another table and sat down next to another MP; but when Anstey tried to engage him in conversation, exactly the same thing happened. Palmerston then called out to Anstey to come over and sit at his table. He told Anstey that he was trying to make up his mind what to do about the Franco-Austrian war in Northern Italy; had Anstey any ideas on the subject? Anstey promptly launched forth and spoke for five minutes without pausing for breath, as he outlined his views about the Italian problem. Palmerston then rose and said that he unfortunately had to leave now, and thanked Anstey for his assistance, which had been most useful. From that day forward, Anstey was an ardent Palmerstonian. He was invited to Lady Palmerston's parties, and made Attorney-General of Hongkong. His former colleague, Urquhart, was disgusted; he said that Anstey had betrayed him for an iced lemon at Cambridge House.

Although Palmerston's jovial temperament made it natural for him to be friendly, there was also some political calculation involved. When Cobden went to Paris to negotiate the commercial treaty with France, Palmerston told Lord Cowley, the Ambassador in Paris, to introduce Cobden to Napoleon III, and to be particularly attentive to him. 'My dear Cowley', he wrote on 16 October 1859, 'Cobden is going to Paris and will probably stay there some Time – pray be civil to him. He is a good Fellow, but extremely sensitive to attentions, being like all Middle Class men who have raised themselves either by money making or by Talent very vain, under the semblance of not being so'. When Thornton Hunt went to Ireland for the *Daily Telegraph*, Palmerston gave him an introduction to the Earl of Carlisle, the Viceroy, and wrote to Carlisle on 27 February 1861 that Hunt 'is not insensible to Civility and attention from his superiors in Rank and Condition'.

Palmerston could sometimes be less generous when he found that these attentions to the middle classes were not appreciated as much as he expected. When Cobden returned to London after signing the trade agreement with France, Palmerston urged him to accept either a baronetcy or the rank of Privy Councillor; but Cobden refused, and until his death in the same year as Palmerston's he pursued his old activity of attacking Palmerston's policy in Parliament. He also angered Palmerston, and most of the journalists, by starting the practice of publishing signed articles, under the writer's real name, in his paper the *Morning Star*.

While Cobden was devoting his attention to politics, his business affairs went badly, and after returning from Paris he found himself in a state of real poverty. Lord John Russell proposed to Palmerston that Parliament should be asked to vote him a pension as a reward for his services to the State. Palmerston was against the idea, and though he said that he was ready to support it, he was obviously pleased when Brand, his Chief Whip, told him that there was no chance of it being accepted by the majority of the Liberal MPs. On 4 December 1863 he wrote to Russell that Cobden, 'having sadly mismanaged his own affairs just as he would, if he could, the affairs of the nation', would no doubt 'gladly accept a House of Commons Pension and I for my part should have no objection to propose it to Parliament if the Cabinet should think fit'. But he had offered Cobden the choice of being made a

Privy Councillor or a baronet, and 'in the true spirit of a Republican Radical he refused any Honor that was to come from that hated Being: a Sovereign'. Palmerston was sure that MPs would not support Russell's proposal, for 'Nothing can well be worse, with the single exception of Bright, than the Line which Cobden has taken and the Language he has held both in and out of Parliament during the last two years, and he has set against him the vast majority of honest men in the Country; and many men in the House of Commons would find it very difficult to vote him anything but a Censure'.

Russell persisted with his proposal; but Palmerston remained adamant. On 18 February 1864 he told Russell that Bright and Cobden – 'and in Public opinion they are inseparably linked together ... have run a muck against everything that the British Nation respects and values – Crown, Aristocracy, Established Church, Nobility, Gentry, Landowners. They have laboured incessantly to set class against class, and the Poor against the rich, those who have nothing against those who have something; and not content with arranging against them the Three Estates of the Realm they have lately and Cobden especially attacked what is called the Fourth Estate, and have invaded the liberty of the Press, by dashing through that anonymous character which is the great Protection of Newspaper writers, and have thus brought down, not *The Times* only as you seem to suppose, but the whole Newspaper Press of the country, except their own Paper, in condemnation of their Proceeding'. Cobden was granted no financial help during his lifetime, and though after his death Palmerston offered Mrs. Cobden a pension, in a tactful and charming letter, she refused it.

Palmerston had always attached more importance than most politicians of his time to cultivating good relations with the press, and as journalists became increasingly influential in political life, Palmerston paid more and more attention to them. When Peter Borthwick died, his son Algernon became editor of the *Morning Post*. Algernon Borthwick visited Broadlands even more often than his father had done, though he had to wait until thirty years after Palmerston's death, and the advent of a more democratic age, before he was created

Lord Glenesk, the first newspaper proprietor ever to be given
a peerage. While the *Morning Post* continued to be Palmerston's mouthpiece, he became almost as friendly with Delane,
the editor of *The Times*, as with Borthwick. In the past, *The
Times* had nearly always attacked Palmerston. During the first
twenty years of Palmerston's political career, when he was a
Tory, *The Times* was almost a Radical paper. When Palmerston changed sides and became a Whig Foreign Secretary, he
was for a few years very popular with *The Times*; but in 1834
The Times, too, changed sides, and henceforth attacked Palmerston from a Tory standpoint. Delane, as editor, had very
strongly criticized Palmerston's foreign policy during Palmerston's third term as Foreign Secretary, when he was encouraging Radical movements on the Continent. Delane had
caused Palmerston serious embarrassment in 1849, when he
revealed that Palmerston had allowed arms to be sent from
Government stores to Sicily. Even as late as 1854 *The Times*
was anti-Palmerston, being one of the last papers to continue
supporting Aberdeen during the Crimean War.

When Palmerston became the successful wartime Premier,
Delane changed his line, and Palmerston went more than half-
way to meet him. Delane was not only invited to Lady Palmerston's parties, and to come shooting at Broadlands, but
was confided in by the Prime Minister to a remarkable degree.
Palmerston often gave Delane important information before
he told the members of his Cabinet. On 24 July 1861 he wrote
to Delane to tell him of the Cabinet changes which he would
submit to the Queen at Osborne next day; and when, in April
1864, he again told Delane of further Cabinet changes which
he was about to make, Delane wrote to one of his assistant
editors: 'I don't believe half the Cabinet know it as I write'.
When the *Daily Telegraph* was first published in 1855, Palmerston immediately established good relations with it, and
became friendly with Thornton Hunt, its consulting editor.

Palmerston not only invited newspaper proprietors and
editors to come shooting with him, but also found time to be
friendly to reporters. The lobby correspondent, James Grant,
who, as a young reporter in 1836, had written such an unfavourable account of Palmerston's stuttering utterances and

lazy conduct in Parliament, wrote in a very different vein forty years later in his book *The Newspaper Press*. 'In the House of Commons there was one who, for the full period of half a century, was a special favourite' with the journalists. 'Need I name him?' Grant described how on one occasion during Palmerston's last Premiership, when Disraeli had moved a vote of censure on his Government, Palmerston came out of the debating chamber for a short rest while the debate was in progress. The division was expected to be close, and Grant thought that Palmerston would be anxious about the result; but he appeared to be quite unconcerned, and chatted to Grant for half an hour, telling him amusing anecdotes, and talking mostly about the days when he had been a student in Dugald Stewart's household in Edinburgh. Grant wrote that he had never known anyone who could tell a story better than Palmerston. Palmerston's lack of concern about the division was justified, because Disraeli withdrew his motion of censure without going to the vote.

Among the masses in the country, who had never met him personally, Palmerston was tremendously popular during the last years of his life. When he visited the Great Exhibition in Hyde Park in May 1862 with Denison, the Speaker of the House of Commons, he was loudly cheered; on all sides people were saying 'Lord Palmerston! Here is Lord Palmerston! Bravo! Hurrah! Lord Palmerston for ever!'; and one voice called out: 'I wish you may be minister for the next twenty years'. The drivers of the horse-drawn omnibuses would point him out to their passengers as they went down Piccadilly; for he was clearly visible to the passers-by as he stood at his first-floor window, writing – standing up – at his special desk. Barrington writes that the bus drivers used to say: ' 'E earns 'is wages; I never come by without seeing 'im 'ard at it'. This is not the only evidence that it was not only the middle classes who liked Palmerston. To the indignation of the Chartist and Radical leaders, many of the working classes admired him. When he visited Yorkshire in the summer of 1860 they greeted him warmly. He courteously declined an invitation from the Sheffield Mechanics' Institute to address them; but in Leeds the working classes were as enthusiastic as the middle classes.

Bright commented bitterly to Cobden that 'they rush to do honor to the man who despises and insults them'.

This popularity had originally been based on his aggressive and successful foreign policy – above all on his Don Pacifico speech and his ideal of *Civis Britannicus*. While this remained in the forefront of the people's minds, he was also admired during his last Premiership as a father-figure, an enduring institution. The cartoonists had usually portrayed him, even during the Crimean War when he was seventy, as a saucy tradesman's boy, cheeking the old man Aberdeen – who in fact was the same age as Palmerston – or being scolded by a prim, middle-aged lady whose features resembled those of the Queen; but in the cartoons of 1860 he was 'the old sentinel', standing wizened and erect beside a cannon on the turret of a fortress, and telling Gladstone and Cobden, with the accumulated wisdom of the ages, that the gun must always be kept in a state of readiness. One of the reasons for his popularity was his remarkable vitality. The people were delighted when they heard that he had bought himself a new pink hunting coat at the age of seventy-eight, and that he had ridden from his house in Piccadilly to Harrow in June 1864 for the annual speech day, covering the twelve miles in fifty-five minutes, shortly before his eightieth birthday. A year later, Holyoake saw him nimbly dodging the hansom cabs as he crossed Parliament Square. Speaker Denison urged him to take more care of his health, and feared that he would catch cold if he walked home so late at night. Palmerston replied: 'Oh, I do indeed. I very often take a cab at night, and if you have both windows open it is almost as good as walking home'. The Speaker was taken aback. 'Almost as good!' he commented. 'A thorough draught and a North-East wind! and in a hack cab! What a combination for health!'

The Speaker was equally impressed by Palmerston's healthy appetite. When Palmerston entertained him to the traditional Speaker's Dinner at the start of the Parliamentary session in February 1865, he noted that Palmerston 'ate for dinner two plates of turtle soup; he was then served very amply to a plate of cod and oyster sauce; he then took a paté; afterwards he was helped to two very greasy-looking entrées; he then des-patched a plate of roast mutton; there then appeared before him the largest, and to my mind the hardest, slice of ham that ever figured on the table of a nobleman, yet it disappeared, just in time to answer the inquiry of his butler: "Snipe, my Lord, or pheasant?" He instantly replied "Pheasant", this completing his ninth dish of meat at that meal'. He then pro-ceeded to eat a pudding, followed by a jelly, and ended the meal with some dressed oranges and half a large pear. He drank nothing all this time except selzer water, with one glass of sweet champagne with the jelly and a glass of sherry with the fruit. The French author, Prosper Mérimée, who at this time was the London correspondent of *Le Temps*, was equally impressed by Palmerston's great appetite and wrote that he 'ate like a vulture'.

But when necessary he was prepared to go without food for hours at a time. 'Some people wonder when he eats and sleeps', wrote William White, the doorkeeper at the House of Com-mons, who had closely watched him in the House. 'The ans-wer is, he eats and sleeps on the premises – eats at the restaurant, sleeps on the benches'. When he was engaged on the Committee stage of a bill, he would stay on the Treasury bench for the whole evening and more than half the night, with his frock coat buttoned across him, his neat trousers strapped down to his boots, and his gloves always on his hands, following the debate and taking the opportunity, while dull and long-winded speakers were talking, to doze off for a few minutes or write letters on international affairs and other sub-jects as he sat in his place. While the other MPs left for an hour or two to go to dinner, Palmerston would merely take a quarter of an hour's break for a cup of tea in the refreshment room of the House. He did much of his political business over these cups of tea.

Palmerston's sporting interests added to his popularity, though to some extent, like so many other elements in Pal-merston's public image, this was a myth. Palmerston had very little interest in any sport except hunting and shooting. He never himself played any outdoor game. The only national sport which interested him was horseracing, and even here, according to William Day, the son of Palmerston's trainer, Palmerston hardly ever went to the races except those in his constituency at Tiverton. But he also sometimes went to the Derby. The House of Commons always adjourned on Derby Day to enable MPs to go to Epsom; and every year, on the day before the race, some member moved that the House should not sit next day. In 1848 Bright and some of the Radicals, for the first time, opposed the motion for the adjournment on the grounds that Parliament had urgent work to do, and they divided the House on the motion; but they were defeated, and the practice of adjourning on Derby Day continued till the end of the century. When Palmerston was Prime Minister, he himself moved the adjournment for Derby Day, and added to the reputation which he had already established as an owner of racehorses. In 1860 his Mainstone was third in the betting to win the Derby, and he rode from Piccadilly to Epsom to see the race. He was loudly cheered on the racecourse; but Mainstone was beaten by the famous Thormanby. Palmerston was very disappointed at the result, and had to be content with winning the divisions in the House of Commons. Soon after Palmerston became Prime Minister in 1859, his trainer, Day, came to the House of Commons to discuss some urgent question about the horses with Palmerston. He managed to get a message to Palmerston, despite all the efforts of the policemen to stop him, and Palmerston left the Irish debate to talk to Day in the lobby. When Day congratulated him on becoming Prime Minister, Palmerston replied: 'Oh, thanks, John; I have won my Derby'.

Palmerston was also associated in people's minds with prizefighting, though this was largely an invention of the cartoonists. He was often portrayed in *Punch* cartoons standing in the ring preparing to fight big bullies, or 'the great Chinese warriors Dah-Bee and Cob-den'. In these cartoons, Palmerston was always drawn with a straw in his mouth. Many years later, the cartoonist, Tenniel, was asked why he always gave Palmerston the straw. He said that there was no particular reason, but that it was essential to think of something that Palmerston could wear or hold so that he would always be recognizable by the readers of *Punch*; and as Palmerston had no particularly prominent feature in his appearance or dress, Tenniel quite arbitrarily invented the straw.

In April 1860, a prize-fight was arranged between the British champion, Tom Sayers, and the American champion J. C. Heenan. It aroused very great excitement, for there was everything calculated to stir the feelings of Englishmen. Sayers was not only British, but much smaller and older than his young American opponent. Prize-fighting was illegal, but the championship fight was held at a secret venue in a field near Farnborough, and hundreds of society people were present, including several members of the Government. Though Sayers was knocked down again and again, he always continued the fight; and after he had nearly blinded Heenan, and Heenan had tried to strangle him, the referee declared the fight a draw after it had gone to thirty-six rounds and lasted for over two hours. The British public, who were convinced that Heenan had cheated, treated Sayers as a national hero; but some MPs were indignant that the illegal prize-fight had been winked at, and raised the matter in Parliament. The Home Secretary, Sir George Lewis, said that everyone who had been present at the fight could be prosecuted for taking part in an unlawful assembly; but Palmerston made light of the whole matter, and this made him more popular than ever in the country. It was widely believed that he himself had watched the fight, though this was not true. He was too cautious to take the risk of attending an illegal prize-fight, but benefited from the fact that his admirers thought that he had done so. Even his Chartist adversary, Rowcliffe, the Tiverton butcher, thought better of Palmerston when he heard that Palmerston had contributed the first guinea to the collection for Sayers in the House of Commons.

Even when Palmerston became involved in what might have been a discreditable incident, it often redounded to his advantage. On 16 June 1863, when he was nearly seventy-nine, he was visited at Cambridge House by Mrs. O'Kane, the wife of an Irish Radical journalist. Mrs. O'Kane was aged about thirty, and was short and plump, with dark hair and very beautiful eyes. O'Kane had sent her to see Palmerston on some

political matter; but, according to O'Kane, Palmerston immediately began to make love to her, and before she left the
house they had committed adultery. O'Kane alleged that they
subsequently committed adultery on a number of other occasions, and claimed £20,000 damages from Palmerston; and
when Palmerston denied the allegation, and refused to pay, he
petitioned for divorce in October 1863, citing Palmerston as
the co-respondent.

'In town and country, nothing was talked of for days than
the Palmerston case', wrote Clarendon to Cowley in Paris.
'The lady has been a governess and an actress, and is good-
looking, and said not to make unnecessary difficulties. An unscrupulous attorney was of course the manager' of it; but
party spirit hoped to arouse British hypocrisy 'to protect its
widowed Sovereign from the approach of her licentious minister'. Lady Palmerston talked gaily about the case to her
acquaintances, including those who had tactfully taken care
to avoid the subject; she treated the allegation as ridiculous,
and as a bare-faced attempt at extortion. Gladstone was deeply distressed, and both he and the Liberal Party Whips were
very worried about the effect which it would have on the
Nonconformist Liberal MPs and the voters in the constituencies; but Disraeli told Derby that he feared that it would
make Palmerston more popular than ever, and playfully suggested that Palmerston had deliberately spread the story
abroad because he was intending to hold a general election.
People said that though the lady was certainly Kane, the question was, Was Palmerston Abel?

Palmerston managed to extricate himself from the scandal.
Mrs. O'Kane not only denied committing adultery, but
claimed that she had never been legally married to O'Kane;
and Palmerston obtained an order in chambers, requiring
O'Kane to state the place and date of his marriage, and to give
further particulars of the alleged adultery. O'Kane did not
comply with the order, and Palmerston filed an affidavit stating that he believed that the petition had been presented for
motives of extortion, and that O'Kane had no case on the
merits. The case was then dismissed. Palmerston thus gained
both ways. While he stood vindicated and innocent in the eyes

of the Nonconformist Liberal voter, the naughtier elements of the population who laughed about the case on the racecourses and in the gin-palaces believed the worst about Lord Palmerston and loved him all the more for it.

Six months later, Palmerston encountered a more subtle attempt at blackmail. He received a letter from William Webb, the son of the brickmaker at Toothill, on the edge of the Broadlands estate, whose dog Palmerston had shot many years before. William Webb had made and lost a fortune as a coal-owner in South Wales, and in 1850 had emigrated to France, after accosting Palmerston at a party in London and obtaining a letter of introduction from Palmerston to the British Ambassador in Paris. He tried unsuccessfully to ingratiate himself with Napoleon III by revealing an imaginary revolutionary plot to murder the Emperor; but as this brought him no rewards, he moved to Belgium. In May 1864 he wrote to Palmerston from Brussels, and asked Palmerston to appoint him to some post in the British Embassy in Vienna, because his sister lived in Vienna, and he wished to live near her. He thought that Palmerston owed him this, because Palmerston had made a substantial profit by reselling to the railway company some land at Romsey which he had bought from Webb, and because Webb had never told anyone about three discreditable incidents in Palmerston's past. He had never revealed how Palmerston had shot his dear dog Lion, who had not even barked at him, and what Webb's schoolmaster had said about the young lord who 'rivalled Nero in the cruelty of his nature'. Nor had he supplied Cobbett with any details about the case of the headstrong, but lovable, young poacher, Charles Smith, who had been executed for wounding Palmerston's gamekeeper because of the vindictiveness of Palmerston and a 'game-preserving Judge'. He had also kept silent about another poacher called Jeffers, who had been sent to jail in Winchester prison for poaching in Palmerston's woods, and whose wife had died of shame, and the children sent to the workhouse, during Jeffers's imprisonment. When Jeffers discovered this, on his release, he had decided to shoot Palmerston, and was only dissuaded from doing so by Webb. Webb enclosed an account of these incidents on a separate sheet, with Palmerston's name left blank, but inserted very faintly in pencil, and told Palmerston that if he had disclosed these facts, 'it would never have been said in the House of Commons, as it was said a few weeks ago ... "that Lord Palmerston had won for himself not only the confidence of the country, but it's affectionate regards" '.

Palmerston wrote a draft for his secretary to use in his reply to Webb. He said that it was true that he had made a profit out of selling to the railway company the land which he had bought from Webb; but he had paid Webb more than the value of the land at the time when he bought it from him. As for Webb's 'Sentimental Story about a Bull Dog', he remembered the incident as clearly as if it were yesterday, though it had occurred more than half a century ago. The dog, who ought to have been chained up, would have killed him a moment later if he had not shot it in self-defence. As for Charles Smith, Palmerston wrote that he was a 'bloodthirsty ruffian', who had been rightly punished under the law as it then stood; and he had considered it his duty to his gamekeepers to exert all his efforts to catch Smith. As the end of Palmerston's note has been lost, we do not know his side of the story in Jeffers's case.

Webb had mistaken his man. 'Say I have received his Letter', wrote Palmerston, 'and the Libellous Extract from some intended publication Which he offers to suppress if I will procure for him a fresh employment under the Government. My first answer is that I can procure no Situation whatever for him'. Palmerston would not submit to blackmail.

Chapter Thirty-seven

The Last Premiership: Foreign Affairs

When Palmerston was invited by Napoleon III to go hunting with him at Compiègne in 1858, he hesitated to accept because he feared that it would prejudice his chances to become Prime Minister, but eventually decided to go in the hopes that it would ease Anglo-French relations if he did return to power. Neither his fears nor his hopes were realized. He became Prime Minister within seven months of the visit, but no sooner had he done so than his relations with Napoleon III became worse than they had ever been. Never again after the Treaty of Villafranca were they really friendly.

'My dear John Russell', wrote Palmerston on 4 November 1859, 'Till lately I had Strong Confidence in the fair intentions of Napoleon towards England, but of late I have begun to feel great Distrust and to suspect that his formerly declared Intention of avenging Waterloo has only lain dormant and has not died away. He seems to have thought that he ought to lay his Foundation by beating with our aid or with our concurrence, or our neutrality first Russia and then Austria: and by dealing with them generously to make them his Friends in any subsequent quarrel with us'. Four months later, his old friend Count Flahaut came to London, and called on Palmerston at Cambridge House. As Palmerston was just leaving for the House of Commons, he invited Flahaut to travel down to the House in his brougham, and they discussed Anglo-French relations on the way. When Flahaut protested against an anti-French speech which Russell had recently made, Palmerston gave him short shrift, and pointed out that, though perhaps he ought not to say so to a Frenchman, the English had not often had the worst of it in their wars with France. Flahaut said that he had fought at the battle of Waterloo, and knew that the French Army was much stronger today than in 1815. Palmerston replied that no doubt this was so, but the British Army was also stronger; and he reminded Flahaut of the conversation between Tallard and Marlborough after Blenheim, when Tallard congratulated Marlborough on having beaten the best soldiers in the world; 'The best', said Marlborough, 'except for those who have beaten them'. Flahaut said that his love for England made him reluctant to think of England being invaded by the French; but Palmerston replied that 'as for invasion, though it would no doubt be a temporary evil, we were under no apprehension as to the results'. They parted at the House of Commons, after Flahaut had told Palmerston that he would not exacerbate the international tension by reporting to Napoleon III what Palmerston had said. 'The conversation', wrote Palmerston, 'was carried on in the most friendly manner, as between two private friends who had known each other for a long course of years'. At this time there were children living who survived to the age of the hydrogen bomb.

British relations with France were as bad as they had been in the days of Louis Philippe; but Palmerston now had to deal not with Orleanist France in the aftermath of Waterloo and the Congress of Vienna, but with the Second Empire in the aftermath of the Crimean War and the Congress of Paris. Palmerston had been unable to prevent France from seizing Savoy and establishing her influence in Northern Italy. He also found it difficult to contain France in the Balkans and the Middle East. In the negotiations which followed the Treaty of Paris in 1856, Palmerston wanted Moldavia and Wallachia to remain separate principalities, and Napoleon III wished to see them united in one state of Rumania. It was Napoleon III who got his way.

In 1860, news reached the West that the Maronites of the Lebanon – an ancient tribe which had been Christian for sixteen centuries – were being massacred in their mountain villages by the Moslem tribe of the Druses. The Maronites were Roman Catholics, and Napoleon III, who, before the Crimean War, had asserted his claim to be the Protector of Roman

Catholics in the Turkish Empire, demanded that action should be taken to protect them. But the Druses, who had played the leading part in the rebellion against Mehemet Ali and Ibrahim in Syria in 1840, were favourites of the British Government, and Britain had always relied on their friendship as a factor in the Middle Eastern situation. While public opinion in Britain, as well as in France, was horrified at the news of the massacres that were taking place, Palmerston was in the awkward position of believing that British interests required him to support the Moslem murderers against the Christian victims.

Napoleon III suggested that the great powers should send an expeditionary force to Syria to protect the Maronites. Palmerston objected. He took the line that though the massacres must be prevented and the murderers punished, the Turkish Government could be relied upon to do this without the need of foreign interference. While he urged the Sultan to send troops to Syria without delay to restrain the Druses, he played for time in Paris in order to stop the French troops from going to Syria; for he firmly believed that if the French landed in Syria, they would remain there, as 'Partant pour la Syrie' really meant 'Restant dans la Syrie'. While he was stalling in the negotiations with Napoleon III, news arrived of the worst outrage yet – a hideous massacre in Damascus, in which three thousand Christians, including many foreign residents, had been murdered by fanatical Moslems. Napoleon III immediately prepared a naval expedition; and Palmerston could only make the best of a bad job by agreeing to an international Convention under which French troops were to be sent to Syria to restore order, but were to stay there only for six months, and were to be accompanied by an international Control Commission of representatives of the great powers, who woud advise the Sultan about the future government of Syria.

With French troops in possession of Damascus and the coastal towns, the Turkish Pasha arrived from Constantinople with Turkish troops to punish the guilty and take measures to protect the Maronites in future. Lord Dufferin, the British representative on the Control Commission, tried to prevent the Turkish authorities from punishing the Druse chiefs who had organized the massacres. He claimed that the Maronites had started the trouble and provoked the Druses, and that it was the Turkish officials in Syria, who had connived at the massacres, rather than the Druse chiefs, who should be punished. He also opposed the French proposal to nominate a Christian Maronite as Governor of the Maronites in the Lebanon, instead of the Druse chief who had been in charge at the time of the massacres. The Control Commission were still arguing about the future government of the Lebanon and the steps to be taken to safeguard the security of the Christians when the six months' period stipulated in the Convention expired at the beginning of February 1861, and the French were required to withdraw from Syria; but Russell had already demanded a month before that the French leave Syria immediately. All the other powers objected, and said that this would mean more massacres of Christians. Once again, Palmerston and Russell gave way, and agreed that the French troops could prolong their stay till June. When they left, on the agreed date in June 1861, they had established a Christian Maronite in charge of the Lebanon, and had greatly increased French influence in Syria. British influence with the Druses and the other tribes in Syria had sharply declined and the Christians henceforth regarded Britain as their greatest enemy.

Palmerston had another source of worry in the Middle East. In 1855 Ferdinand de Lesseps proposed to the Turkish Government that a canal should be constructed across the Isthmus of Suez, linking the Mediterranean with the Red Sea. This idea had been discussed for many years; but Lesseps, a former French Foreign Office official, had formed an association of French and foreign capitalists, and was ready to begin work as soon as the Sultan's permission was obtained. Palmerston was very suspicious of the scheme. He thought that it was a French plot to gain control of the Mediterranean and the route to India. When passengers and goods travelled from Western Europe to India, they went by sea to Port Said, and then travelled by camel for ninety miles to Suez, where they took another ship for Bombay; but warships sailed round the Cape of Good Hope. As long as they had to go round the Cape, the French, sailing from their Channel or Atlantic ports, did not have any great advantage over the British Navy; but if the Suez Canal were built, the French could get to India from their Mediterranean ports in a much shorter time than a fleet sailing from Portsmouth or Plymouth. Palmerston also feared that the Canal would tend to accentuate the separation between Egypt and the rest of the Turkish Empire, and would make it more difficult for the Sultan's armies to invade Egypt if it became necessary to suppress a revolt by one of Mehemet Ali's descendants.

Palmerston therefore directed Lord Stratford de Redcliffe to use all his influence at Constantinople to prevent the construction of the Suez Canal. As Stratford entirely agreed with Palmerston's appreciation of the situation, he carried out his instructions with his usual skill and energy, and persuaded the Sultan to refuse his consent. Lesseps and the French Ambassador tried in vain for three years to persuade the Turkish Government to change their minds; but Palmerston and Stratford thwarted all their efforts. Then in 1859 Napoleon III made a direct approach to the Khedive of Egypt, and work on the Canal began without the Sultan's consent. If this had occurred in 1840, Palmerston would have arranged with the Sultan to send the British Navy to restore the Sultan's authority in Egypt, to stop the work on the canal, and send the French engineers packing; but now Napoleon III, not Louis Philippe, was in power in France, the French had a powerful fleet of steamships at Cherbourg, and there were Cobdenite Radicals in Palmerston's Cabinet. So Palmerston made no move, and work on the canal continued. Palmerston directed the *Morning Post* to make insinuations about Lesseps' financial dishonesty; and when he discovered that the canal was being built by forced labour, he succeeded in working up some indignation in Britain over the sufferings of the Egyptian fellaheen and the conditions of slavery under which they worked. In 1863 Bulwer, Stratford's successor in Constantinople, persuaded the Sultan to order the Khedive to stop the forced labour, and threatened to intervene by force if work on the canal continued; but Napoleon III stepped in and insisted that he should be appointed as arbitrator in the dispute. Lesseps agreed to remedy the worst abuses, and to substitute labour which, in theory at least, was voluntary. Palmerston did not live to see the opening of the canal in 1869, or the establishment of British control over it by Disraeli's purchase of the Khedive's shares in 1875.

In China, however, Britain found herself collaborating with the French. When Palmerston went out of office in February 1858, the Conservative Government quickly carried his war against China to a successful conclusion. Derby, Malmesbury and Disraeli abandoned the high moral tone which they had adopted in the debates on the case of the lorcha *Arrow*, and dictated a peace by which China was compelled to pay an indemnity, to enter into diplomatic relations with Britain, and to receive a British Minister in Peking. They also took the step which Palmerston had refrained from taking in 1841, and made the Chinese agree, as a term of the peace treaty, that opium-smoking and the opium trade be legalized throughout China. As a result there was an enormous increase in the consumption of opium until it was banned by China, by international agreement, in 1906.

The term in the treaty to which the Emperor of China most objected was the provision for the admission of foreign diplomats to Peking. He and his envoys fawned and flattered, evaded and obstructed, and resorted to every artifice to avoid having to comply on this point; but Lord Elgin insisted on ratifying the treaty in Peking and establishing a British Minister there. Eventually the Chinese gave way, and a British delegation set out for Peking; but as they passed up the Peiho River they were halted at the Taku Forts and fired upon by Chinese troops. Palmerston then decided to send an army to capture Peking; and though Gladstone and other members of the Cabinet had some misgivings about this, Palmerston insisted that the humiliation of the Taku Forts must be avenged, in order to 'bring John Chinaman to his bearings'. At about the same time a French missionary was murdered in Shanghai, and Napoleon III proposed to Palmerston that a joint Anglo-French expedition be sent. Palmerston accepted the proposal, but gave orders that none of the new Enfield rifles should be sent to China in case the French got to know the design and capabilities of the weapon. He was sure that old rifles would be good enough to beat the Chinese.

The Anglo-French expeditionary force marched on Peking. On their march they sent Parkes and other envoys under a flag of truce to negotiate with the Chinese, who seized them and carried them to Peking, where they were imprisoned in very harsh conditions in the dungeons of the Emperor's Summer Palace. Several of them were tortured, and a few died under the treatment, though Parkes and the rest of the prisoners were released as the Allied army approached. Lord Elgin ordered that, as a punishment, the ancient Summer Palace should be burned; it had already been looted of its art treasures, and badly damaged by fire, by the French troops who captured it. The French commander protested against the burning of the most beautiful of the Emperor's palaces; but Elgin could think of no other suitable punishment which would hit the Emperor personally, and not the innocent people of China, and his action was endorsed by Russell and Palmerston. The French officers and journalists were as shocked at this act of vandalism as the British officers and journalists were at the disgraceful looting of the palace by the French.

Palmerston was very pleased about the burning of the Summer Palace. 'I am heartily glad that Elgin and Grant determined to burn down the Summer Palace,' he wrote to Sidney Herbert on 20 December 1860, 'and that "the blackness of ashes shall mark where it stood" ... It was absolutely necessary to stamp by some such permanent record our indignation at the treachery and brutality of these Tartars, for Chinese they are not'. He added that he would have been even happier if Elgin had burned another palace in Peking as well as the Summer Palace. He was pleased that in this, as in all the operations in China, it was the British, and not the French, who had taken the initiative; but he was worried when he heard that in Shanghai the French garrison outnumbered the British, and gave orders that the strength of the British forces there should be raised to the level of the French forces.

The repeated military expeditions against China, and the humiliations to which the Emperor's Government was exposed, encouraged the growth of the peasant revolts of the Christian Taipings. Palmerston, as usual, rejected the arguments of some of the experts on China who advised him not to embarrass the Chinese Government, as this would help the rebel peasants; but before long the British Government was sending Major Gordon – afterwards Gordon of Khartoum – and other military advisers to help the Emperor's Government against the Taipings. When news of these operations against the Christian rebels reached Britain, there was a great outcry, especially when the Imperial Chinese officials executed large batches of prisoners in breach of the surrender terms to which Gordon had agreed. But Palmerston defended his policy in the House, going out of his way on several occasions to praise the Chinese Government. He said that we had quarrelled with them in the past, but now we were on the most friendly terms, and our trade with China had greatly increased during the last four years. We were assisting the Chinese Government against the Taipings, because 'it cannot be for the advantage of those who trade with China that the country should be in a state of civil war'; and as the Taipings were not strong enough to capture power, the only way of ending the civil war was to assist the Emperor of China to suppress them. As for the execution of the Taiping prisoners after they had surrendered to Gordon, this was certainly regrettable; but 'I am afraid we must admit that all nations have their faults, and there are two faults which must be a matter of reproach to the Chinese – one is cruelty, and the other is perfidy'.

Palmerston had only one aim in China during the thirty years that he dominated Anglo-Chinese relations. He wished to increase the opportunities for British trade. He always emphasized that Britain had no territorial or exclusive ambitions in China. Whenever the British Government dictated peace terms to China, they never demanded special privileges for Englishmen, but asked for trading rights in opium and other goods, and access to Peking and Canton, for the subjects of all Western nations. As usual, Palmerston asked only for free trade, knowing that the excellence of British goods and the reliability of British exporters would always enable Britain to win in any fair and equal economic competition.

For this reason, Palmerston did not normally wish to acquire new territorial possessions for Britain, though it is an over-simplification to say that he was opposed to colonialism

and imperialism. The only territories which he was responsible
for acquiring during his thirty years in power were Hongkong
and Aden. He was not eager to take the 'desert island' of
Hongkong, and only accepted it as a second best, after the
Opium War, because the Chinese Government refused to grant
his first demand for the opening of the ports in North China
to British trade. In 1839 he accepted a cession of Aden from
the Turkish Government, chiefly to make sure that Mehemet
Ali did not get it. New Zealand was formally annexed by the
Crown in 1840, when Palmerston was Foreign Secretary, because British settlers feared that a French expedition was
coming to seize it for France; and in 1832 Palmerston sent a
naval force to re-occupy the Falkland Islands, which had
nominally belonged to Britain since 1771. In 1847 he accepted
the cession of the island of Labuan from Sir James Brooke,
the British Rajah of Sarawak; but he refused repeated requests from Brooke to annex Sarawak and Borneo for the
Crown; for though he admired Brooke's initiative, he did not
think that the British Government should involve itself, as
Brooke had done, in the rights and wrongs of the tribal wars
and massacres in the East Indies. He rejected all suggestions
that Britain should embark on an imperialist policy in Africa.
He ridiculed the idea that Dahomey should be annexed in order to suppress the slave trade at its source; and he did not
altogether rule out the possibility of ceding British territory in
Africa to the new negro state of Liberia.

But Palmerston supported the annexationist policy of Lord
Ellenborough and Lord Dalhousie in India. He was not
directly responsible for this policy, which concerned the President of the Indian Board of Control, not the Foreign Secretary; but he supported the seizure of Sind and Oudh from the
native Princes, and their incorporation in British India, and
defended the Governor-General's policy in the debates in the
House of Commons in the forties and fifties, where it was
strongly criticized. He also defended the Kaffir War, and the
military operations against the Maoris in New Zealand. He was
quite determined to defend the British Empire. Throughout
his life he feared an attack by the United States on Canada,
and though he appreciated the difficulties of defending

Canada against an invasion from the United States, he was determined to retain Canada, and stated that, irrespective of whether there were any practical advantages in doing this, it was essential for reasons of prestige. He resisted any moves towards separatism in the United Kingdom, and not only opposed all demands for Home Rule for Ireland, but discouraged attempts to adopt the Welsh language in Wales, and to appoint a Secretary of State for Scotland to whom the duties of the Home Secretary in Scotland could be entrusted. The office of Secretary for Scotland, which was abolished in 1746, was not revived until 1885.

It was, however, during Palmerston's Premiership that Britain surrendered two of her protectorates. In 1860, the Kingdom of Mosquito was handed over to Nicaragua; and in 1863 the Ionian Isles were ceded to Greece after having been a British possession for forty-eight years. When the movement for union with Greece developed during the revolutionary outbreak of 1849, Palmerston's reaction was that though it would serve the islanders right if they were handed over to King Otho's Government, this could not in fact be done, because if the British evacuated Corfu, the Russians would seize it, and Britain could not permit the Russians to have a naval base in the Mediterranean. When Otho's Government adopted a pro-Russian, anti-Turkish policy during the Crimean War, and British and French troops occupied the Piraeus, relations between Britain and the Ionian Isles became worse than ever, and Palmerston showed even less inclination to give up the islands to Greece. Then in 1862 a revolution broke out in Greece, and Otho fled to Munich. Palmerston welcomed the revolution, and compared it to 1688.

The great powers had now to find a new King for the Greeks. At Russell's suggestion, Palmerston agreed to tell the provisional revolutionary Government of Greece that Britain would give them the Ionian Isles if they accepted a King of whom Britain approved. The Greeks thereupon offered the throne to Queen Victoria's son, Prince Alfred, Duke of Edinburgh; but Palmerston had agreed with France and Russia to choose a King who was not directly connected with any of their royal houses, and one that was acceptable to all of them.

After a considerable number of European royal Princes had been considered, Prince William, the grandson of the King of Denmark, was selected. This was very satisfactory to Palmerston, because Prince William's sister, Princess Alexandra, had just married the Prince of Wales. Prince William became King of Greece under the name of George I, and the Ionian Isles were transferred to Greece, with the consent of its National Assembly, and despite the strong opposition of Derby and Disraeli in the British Parliament.

Palmerston had not been very enthusiastic about ceding the Ionian Isles to Greece; but the fact that he was prepared to agree to the proposal shows how little importance he had attached to territorial acquisitions in themselves. He made this clear in 1857 when Napoleon III made tentative proposals for a deal with Britain under which both powers would annex a part of Egypt. Palmerston rejected the proposal, because he thought that it would be immoral for Britain to be a party to a new partition of Poland in Africa; and although the Egyptians would no doubt be much better off if they came under British rule, this was not Britain's business, and Britain did not want the trouble of governing Egypt. Two years later, he repeated these arguments in a letter to Lord Cowley. 'Our interests,' he wrote on 25 November 1859, 'require that Egypt should remain what it is, an integral part of the Turkish empire. We do not want it or wish it for ourselves, any more than any rational Man with an estate in the North of England and a Residence in the South would have wished to possess the Inns on the North Road, all he could want would have been that the Inn should be well kept always accessible and furnishing him when he came, with Mutton chops and Post Horses.' Palmerston in fact required something more than this from the innkeepers; he wanted the right to enter any of the inns, armed with a gun, and force the innkeeper, at gunpoint, to agree to all his demands whenever there was any dispute about the quality or price of the mutton chops; and though, on these occasions, he made no attempt to seize the inn for himself, and always departed as soon as his demands were satisfied, he often took a large part of the contents of the till with him when he left to reimburse himself for the expenses of his visit. He showed no sign, as he grew older, of abating his tendency to indulge in these activities; for though he was becoming less aggressive and more considerate in his relations with his underlings and acquaintances, he was becoming more impatient with foreign governments who affronted British subjects. When the French fleet bombarded Lisbon in 1831, because the Portuguese Government had refused to give satisfaction for the flogging of a Frenchman by the Portuguese police, he had condemned the French for endangering the lives and property of innocent people; and in his own disputes with Portugal in the thirties, with Naples in 1840 and even in the Don Pacifico affair, he had merely imposed a blockade, and this only after several years of negotiations, warnings and threats. But he was less patient in Japan, which had been opened up to Western penetration by the American Navy in 1858.

In 1863, four British travellers became involved in an affray with a local Japanese chieftain near Yokohama, apparently because of a misunderstanding about the Japanese rule of the road, as a result of which one Englishman was killed and two others seriously wounded. At about the same time, two sentries who were guarding the British residents' quarters in Yedo were killed by Japanese police. Palmerston told Russell to demand £35,000 compensation for the relatives of the victims, and that the Japanese Government should in addition pay a fine of £100,000 to Britain, as well as sending an apology and executing the murderers. The Japanese Government at first refused, and claimed that in both cases the British had been to blame; but when the British Navy approached, they agreed to pay the compensation and the fine, and to make the required apology. They stated, however, that they were unable to find the murderers; whereupon the British Admiral seized three Japanese ships, and when the Japanese resisted, he bombarded the town of Kagoshima, killing more than 1,400 Japanese civilians. There were protests in Britain, and Buxton raised the matter in Parliament, where the bombardment of Kagoshima was compared to bombarding Bristol because a man had been killed on the road between London and Brentford; but Palmerston defended the Admiral's action in the debate on 9 February

THE LAST PREMIERSHIP: FOREIGN AFFAIRS 729

1864. He stated that the Admiral 'performed his duty as a British officer ought to perform it'. He claimed that the bombardment of towns was fully justified by the practice of civilized nations in time of war – this was not what he had told the Dutch Government when they had threatened to bombard Antwerp in 1831 – but that in fact Britain had refrained from bombarding Odessa during the Crimean War, and that at Kagoshima the Admiral had intended only to bombard the Japanese ships, and the shells had accidentally set fire to the town.

Palmerston stated his view of relations with Japan in a letter to Russell on 5 October 1864. 'I am inclined to think that our Relations with Japan are going through the usual and unavoidable stages of the Intercourse of strong and Civilized nations with weaker and less civilized ones. First – agreement for Trade, next Breach of Engagement, Injustice and outrage – The Redress demanded and refused – Then Reparation enforced by Hostility. Then temporary acquiescence – then renewed endeavours to break engagements – Then successful display of superior strength and then at last peaceful and settled commercial Intercourse advantageous to both Parties. We have gone through all these Stages with China – we have only got Halfway with Japan'. Palmerston stopped the story at this point. He was happily unaware of any subsequent stages in Britain's relations with China and Japan.

On the other side of the world, Palmerston became involved in friction with Brazil. The Brazilian economy depended on slavery; and when Palmerston began his campaign against the slave trade in the eighteen-thirties, he encountered the usual difficulties in persuading the Brazilian Government to cooperate in suppressing the trade. In 1845, when Aberdeen was Foreign Secretary, Peel's Government passed an Act which authorized the British Navy to stop and search any Brazilian ship, and to seize it as prize if it was found to be engaging in the slave trade. This had greatly angered the Brazilian Government, but had been effectively enforced.

By 1863 the international slave trade was at last on the point of being suppressed. After the election of Abraham Lincoln as President of the United States and the outbreak of the

American Civil War, the legislation against slave-trading was at last enforced in the United States, and despite strong public protests a young slave-trading captain was executed. By this time, a strong movement in favour of the abolition of the slave trade had developed in Brazil. This was encouraged by the Liberal policy of the Emperor Pedro II and the growth of Radical influence; but its success was largely due to the fact that in 1849 the slave traders had landed a cargo of slaves who had yellow fever, and started a serious epidemic in Brazil.

In 1863 the Brazilian Government suggested that in view of the fact that they themselves were now taking vigorous measures to suppress the slave trade, Britain should repeal the Aberdeen Act of 1845, which affronted the national dignity of Brazil. A considerable body of opinion in the British Parliament was in favour of complying with the Brazilian request; Cobden and Bright strongly supported it, and Russell was not unsympathetic. But Palmerston would not agree, and on 5 October 1864 he gave his reasons in a letter to Russell. He did not believe in the sincerity of the Brazilian Government. 'As to the notion that the Brazilian nation see the criminality of Slave Trade and have for ever abjured it; such a notion is too childish for a grown man really to entertain, however it may suit the Brazilians to endeavour to make it accepted. The plain truth is that the Portuguese are of all European nations the lowest in the moral state and the Brazilians are degenerate Portuguese, demoralized by Slavery and Slave Trade, and all the degrading and corrupting influences connected with both'.

He argued cogently that even if the Brazilian authorities were sincere in their attempts to suppress the slave trade, they could not succeed in a country which depended entirely on slave labour. 'Will any reasoning man believe that if a Landowner were offered 2 or 3 hundred additional negroes to increase the Produce of his estate he would refuse them for the sake of an Abstract Principle of Humanity? The Slave Importer would say – here they are in Brazil – the evil of tearing them from their Homes is done – They cannot go back to Africa – If you will not buy them some other Landowner will and his Estate will reap the advantages you are refusing for your own. The scruples of the most humane Brazilian – if there be such a man – would thus be overcome and the Slave Traders knowing that he would be sure of a good market would go on bringing in his Cargoes'. Palmerston was determined that the slave trade should not be given a new lease of life now that it had almost been stamped out. 'I have laboured indefatigably all the Time I was at the Foreign Office to put an end to the Slave Trade, and though not with entire at all events with some considerable success and nothing shall induce me to load my conscience with the guilt of having been a Party to promoting its revival. I am afraid Bright has been at you upon these Brazilian matters. He has always professed great Horror of Slave Trade and has invariably opposed the employment of any and every means by which it could be made to cease'.

The presence of the British ships which were patrolling the Brazilian coast led to a breach with Brazil in 1863. A British naval officer was arrested in a Brazilian port and charged with being drunk and disorderly. The British Admiral retaliated by seizing three Brazilian trading ships; and though both the British officer and the Brazilian ships were released after two days, the Brazilian Government indignantly demanded an apology and compensation for the losses which their shipowners had sustained. Russell wished to comply, but Palmerston objected, and persisted in his attitude despite criticism from his colleagues in the Cabinet. Brazil broke off diplomatic relations with Britain. Russell then suggested that the British Government, while publicly maintaining their refusal of the Brazilian demands in order to uphold their prestige, should privately agree to compensate the individual Brazilian shipowners. Palmerston rejected this suggestion. He wrote to Russell on 5 October 1864 that if this were done, 'Do it as you will the Brazilians would make it public and boast of it as a Russell capitulation'. It would destroy the effect of such reprisals in future if it were thought that the injured shipowners would ultimately receive compensation. 'Reprisals are an act of modified war. Now it sometimes happens that the Party which is successful in a war undertaken to redress a grievance imposes upon its enemy the Payment of the expences incurred by the Conqueror, but it would be new that the Conqueror in such a Case should pay the expences of the vanquished in its Resistance and yet that is what you propose to do'. Eventually Palmerston agreed, under pressure in the Cabinet and in Parliament, to ask King Leopold of Belgium to mediate. To Palmerston's great annoyance, Leopold gave an opinion which was substantially in favour of Brazil. Palmerston was convinced that the Belgian Ministers had been bribed.

Palmerston also intervened in Mexico, and not in favour of the constitutional and Liberal cause which he had so often supported in Europe. In 1859, after thirty years of national and civil wars, the Chief Justice of Mexico, Benito Juarez, took over the Government. Juarez, who had formerly been a Liberal politician, wished to restore law and order in Mexico, and reorganize the country on Liberal lines. A clerical and Conservative counter-revolution broke out against his Government; and though, after two years of civil war, Juarez had almost suppressed the revolt, the Mexican Government's debt to foreign bondholders had increased, and foreign residents in Mexico had been murdered, and their property damaged, in the fighting. Palmerston and Russell demanded that Juarez's Government should compensate British subjects for their losses; but Juarez refused to pay for the damage which had been done by the counter-revolutionaries who had been fighting against him. This was a point of principle on which he and Palmerston could not agree; for Palmerston always maintained that the Government of a country was responsible to foreign Governments for all the acts of their predecessors in office and of their rebels, whatever their differences with their fellow-countrymen about political opinions or régimes.

In the autumn of 1861, the Spanish Government proposed to Britain and France that the three powers should send a joint military force to occupy Vera Cruz in order to compel Juarez to pay the Mexican debts to Spanish, French and British subjects. Napoleon III and Palmerston, who knew that the reaction of the United States could be disregarded because of the American Civil War, agreed to the Spanish proposal; but Palmerston rejected the Spanish suggestion that the British marines should be placed under the command of a Spanish General, because 'we never allow any British Force

Military or naval to be placed under the command of any foreign Officer'. The United States Government, who were friendly to Juarez, tried to prevent this action by offering to pay the Mexican debt; but Palmerston would not accept this solution, which would have increased American influence in Mexico. He told Russell that the American plan 'lays the ground for foreclosure by the new creditor', and did not provide for the imposition of what he called 'strong government' in Mexico. He suggested instead that the United States should be invited to join the three European powers in a joint occupation of Mexico; but this, as he knew, was an offer that the United States could not accept, because of their friendship with Juarez and their involvement in the American Civil War.

Vera Cruz was seized by the British, French and Spanish forces. The three governments announced that they had no intention of acquiring territory or changing the government of Mexico, but would appropriate the customs revenues of Vera Cruz to the payment of the debts due to their nationals, and would then go home. Palmerston then discovered that Napoleon III had more far-reaching schemes in mind; he was planning to march to Mexico City, to overthrow Juarez's Government, and install the Archduke Maximilian of Austria as Emperor of Mexico and a French puppet ruler. Twenty years before, when Palmerston was dealing with the Government of Louis Philippe, he would have reacted as vigorously against the French plan as he did when he suspected, with much less reason, that France was using the excuse of a financial dispute with Rosas to establish a puppet state in Uruguay; but now, though Russell was shocked at the French action, Palmerston approved of it. He thought that it was desirable from two points of view. If Maximilian became Emperor of Mexico, he would establish law and order there much more effectively than a Mexican Liberal government; and if Napoleon III were occupied in Mexico, he would be too busy to cause trouble in Europe.

Palmerston therefore gave cautious support to Napoleon and Maximilian against Juarez. He prevented Russell from protesting to Paris against the French violation of the undertaking which the three powers had given when they occupied Vera Cruz. Nor would he allow Russell to exert influence in Vienna to dissuade Maximilian from becoming involved in Napoleon's schemes. In 1863, the French entered Mexico City, installed Maximilian as Emperor, and remained in permanent occupation of the country, while Juarez organized a national guerrilla war against them. The British troops withdrew from Vera Cruz; but Palmerston continued to give moral support to Napoleon III and Maximilian. Whenever he was questioned in the House of Commons about the events in Mexico, he always stated that Britain welcomed the efforts of France and the Emperor Maximilian to bring order and civilization to Mexico.

On 17 July 1865 – three months before his death – Palmerston wrote a letter in French to Maximilian. Juarez's fortunes were at their lowest point, and he had retreated to a small area in the north near the American frontier; but the American Civil War had just ended, and there was talk of United States military action to drive the French out of Mexico. Palmerston assured Maximilian 'of the interest that all of us in this country take in the success of the great task which your Majesty has undertaken, a success which would be beneficial for all Europe and would ensure the happiness of Mexico. As for the United States, they will be so busy reorganizing their vast territories and repairing the calamities following the disastrous war that it is more than likely that they will refrain from disturbing your Majesty and that you will be granted the time firmly to establish the Mexican Empire.' Next year the United States sent an army to the Mexican border, and Napoleon III withdrew his troops from Mexico; and in June 1867 Maximilian was captured by the victorious Juarez and shot at Queretaro.

Chapter Thirty-eight

The American Civil War

On 6 November 1860 Abraham Lincoln was elected President of the United States. Four days later, South Carolina decided to secede from the Union, and by the beginning of February 1861 all but three of the slave-owning states had joined together to form the Southern Confederacy. Ever since 1854, when the slaveowners broke the Missouri Compromise of 1820 and extended slavery into Kansas, the United States had been moving towards civil war. This had caused Palmerston to comment, in a letter to Sir George Lewis on 25 September 1856, that 'the State of things in the *Dis*united States ... affords an instructive illustration of the Blessings of a Republican Form of Government for anything larger than a Swiss Canton or a Hanse Town District'.

In the years before the outbreak of the civil war, there had been an improvement in Anglo-American relations. In the spring of 1860, Queen Victoria and Palmerston had agreed, with some misgivings, that the Prince of Wales, who was aged eighteen, should pay a visit to the United States after a tour of Canada; and the Prince had attended a ball and reception at the White House, and had delighted the Americans by placing a wreath on George Washington's grave. But Palmerston, like most of the British aristocracy, had not got rid of his deep-seated hostility to the United States, and awaited with unconcealed satisfaction the imminent destruction of the Union. On 1 January 1861, in a letter of New Year's greetings to Queen Victoria, he said that the concluding months of 1860 had seen events of decisive importance for the future taking place 'in three of the four quarters of the Globe. ... The capture of Pekin in Asia by British and French troops;

the Union in Europe of nearly the whole of Italy into one
Monarchy; and the approaching and virtually accomplished
Dissolution in America of the great Northern Confederation'.

On 12 April 1861 the Confederate artillery fired on the
Union garrison in Fort Sumter in Charleston Harbour, and
the civil war began. In Britain, opinion was sharply divided
on fundamental political and social lines. Bright and the
Cobdenites were ardent supporters of the North, and so were
the Socialist and Chartist groups who usually disagreed with
them. Even Marx and Engels, who were usually the odd men
out in the Left wing and Radical movement on questions of
foreign policy, agreed with all the others in supporting the
North; and Marx organized public meetings at which Bright,
whom he detested, was the main speaker. The war to end
slavery aroused a great flood of disinterested enthusiasm
among many sections of the lower and middle classes in the
North of England, despite the fact that their interests were
seriously injured by the Union blockade of the Confederate
ports, which prevented the export of cotton to Lancashire,
and caused loss of profits to Bright and his friends and unemployment and distress among the working classes. Among
the aristocracy and in London society there was great sympathy with the South, and a small group, which consisted
chiefly of Conservatives but included a few Liberals like Roebuck, were active propagandists for the Confederacy. They
had the support of about twenty members in the House of
Commons and a newspaper, the *Index*. In the Cabinet, the
Duke of Argyll, Charles Villiers and Milner-Gibson supported
the North, while Russell and Gladstone supported the South.
Palmerston, too, supported the South, though he was more
careful than Russell and Gladstone not to commit himself too
deeply, especially when it seemed as if the North were going to
win. The Conservatives in general supported the South, but
some, like Disraeli, adopted a neutral position. The Queen and
Prince Albert were also much more neutral than Palmerston,
Russell and Gladstone.

The civil war had broken out because of the conflict over
slavery. For thirty years the British aristocracy, especially the
Whigs, had favoured the abolition of slavery. Palmerston had

played a very active part in the suppression of the international slave trade, and had been one of the most prominent of
the social figures who had been invited to meet Mrs. Harriet
Beecher Stowe when she visited England in 1853 after the
publication of her *Uncle Tom's Cabin*. He attended the
Duchess of Sutherland's reception for Mrs. Stowe at Stafford
House, when the passionate little Abolitionist with the laughing eyes, whose life was in danger in her own country, had
gazed in some bewilderment at the eminent statesmen, authors
and noblemen who had come to pay her tribute. But though
Palmerston was delighted when slaves on the intercepted slave-
ships were liberated by the officers and gentlemen of the Royal
Navy, he was not so pleased at the prospect of the slaves on
the cotton plantations in the Confederate states being freed
by large armies of native-born and immigrant Americans commanded by cigar-smoking Generals in ill-fitting uniforms; and
he was as conscious as Bright and the Radicals that the Union
armies were the most powerful force of militant democracy
since the French revolutionary armies of 1793. Besides this, it
was one of Palmerston's chief maxims of foreign policy to
take advantage of the weakness of his opponents; and the
United States was greatly weakened by being involved in a
civil war. Palmerston therefore adopted a much more hostile
attitude to Lincoln's Government, which was the first Government of the United States to suppress the slave trade, than he
had shown to any of the earlier Governments in the United
States which had consistently obstructed his efforts to suppress
the slave trade, and had been so largely under the influence of
the Southern slave-power.

The position was complicated by the fact that Lincoln, who
was anxious not to alienate the three slave states who had remained loyal to the Union – Maryland, Kentucky and Missouri – not only refused, during the first eighteen months of
the war, to abolish slavery, but repeatedly declared that the
war was not being fought on the slavery issue, but only to prevent the secession of the Southern states. He continued to
enforce the Fugitive Slave Law, which had so deeply outraged
the feelings of Mrs. Stowe's readers, and to return runaway
slaves who had escaped from the loyal slave-states to the

North; and his Secretary of State, Seward, even demanded that the British authorities should return slaves who had escaped to Canada. In the days immediately before the outbreak of the civil war, Lincoln, in an attempt to prevent secession, had gone so far as to offer to amend the Constitution of the United States, to safeguard the existence of slavery in the Southern states; and Seward sent a note to all foreign Governments asking them to refuse to grant asylum to escaping slaves. It was therefore easy for the Confederate sympathizers in Britain to argue that there was nothing to choose between the North and the South on the slavery question, though no one who had any knowledge of the powerful Abolitionist forces in the North, and the pressure which they were applying to Lincoln, could have believed this for a moment. Many of the Northern Generals were releasing slaves in the rebel territories which they occupied, in defiance of Lincoln's order prohibiting them from doing so; and if Palmerston and Russell had really believed that slavery was not an issue in the American Civil War, their old acquaintance, Mrs. Stowe, could have disillusioned them. But it was Argyll and Bright, not Palmerston and Russell, who corresponded with Mrs. Stowe and the Abolitionists during the civil war.

Though Palmerston's sympathies were with the South, he did not wish to go to war with the North. But Seward did his best to provoke a conflict. Seward, who was generally considered to be Lincoln's intellectual superior and the strong man of his Government, had been secretly negotiating with the Confederate leaders until a few days before the start of the war. He may have been deliberately trying to involve the United States in a war with foreign powers, so that North and South could make peace and unite against a foreign enemy. He had always hated the British, who had not forgotten that he had been Governor of the state of New York at the time of McLeod's trial in 1841; and when the Duke of Newcastle visited Washington with the Prince of Wales in 1860, Seward got drunk at a dinner party and was offensive to the Duke. As for Lincoln, he had never been outside the United States, and had never shown any interest in questions of foreign policy; and he made no attempt to control Seward. But the United

States had the advantage of being represented in London by Charles Francis Adams, who replaced Dallas as Minister early in 1861. As an Abolitionist, Radical and democrat, Adams could enlist the maximum sympathy for the Northern cause among the Liberals and Radicals in Britain, while as a member of the élite of Boston society, he could hold his own in the hostile atmosphere which he encountered in Government and aristocratic circles in London.

As soon as the civil war began Palmerston and Russell decided to recognize the Southern Confederacy as a belligerent, and to receive their unofficial representatives in London. This did not mean, of course, that they were recognizing the Confederacy as a sovereign state; but Seward threatened to treat any power which recognized the South as belligerents, and received their unofficial envoys, as an enemy of the United States. Palmerston nevertheless recognized the state of belligerency, and sent military reinforcements to Canada, though he took care that no Irish regiments were sent, as he would not trust them to fight against the Irish immigrants in the United States Army. He was convinced that the North was planning to make peace with the South and then invade Canada; and Seward, unlike Lincoln, may really have toyed with this idea. Palmerston sent a stream of letters to the Duke of Somerset, the First Lord of the Admiralty, to the Duke of Newcastle, the Colonial Secretary, and to other ministers, denouncing the misdeeds of Seward and Lincoln, and warning them to be prepared. On 23 June 1861 he told Somerset that 'the Yankees will be violent and threatening in Proportion to our local weakness and civil and pacific in Proportion to our increasing local strength'. On 1 September he wrote to Newcastle that 'there can be no doubt that our having sent the small force which last went to Canada, has had a wholesome effect upon the Tone and Temper of Lincoln and Seward; but .... the only security for continued Peace with men who have no sense of Honor and who are swayed by the Passions of irresponsible Masses, and by a reckless Desire to hold their Positions by all and any means consists in being Strong by sea on their coasts and respectable in our Military Force in our Provinces'.

In July 1861 the first major battle of the war was fought at Bull Run in Virginia. The untrained Northern volunteers, who had expected to win an easy victory, were routed by the Confederates under their trained and skilful officers, who had formed the core of the United States officer establishment before the South seceded; and the Northerners fled in panic to Washington. It was a heavy blow to the morale of the North, and a great encouragement to Southern sympathizers abroad. When the news reached London, Palmerston was very pleased, and made jokes about the battle 'at Bull's Run, or rather at Yankees' Run'; and he hoped that Seward and Lincoln would become more reasonable as a result of 'the Bull's Run Races'. But he thought it was premature to recognize the Confederacy. On 20 October 1861 – his seventy-seventh birthday – he sent a note to Layard at the Foreign Office: 'It is in the highest Degree likely that the North will not be able to subdue the South, and it is no doubt certain that if the Southern union is established as an independent State it would afford a valuable and extensive Market for British Manufactures but the operations of the war have as yet been too indecisive to warrant an acknowledgement of the southern union. P. 20/10-61'.

As both sides in America settled down to a long war, Jefferson Davis decided to send two envoys to Europe to persuade Palmerston and Napoleon III to recognize his Government. He chose James Murray Mason and John Slidell, two leading Southern politicians who before the war had been prominent champions of slavery in the United States Congress, where Mason had been chiefly responsible for enacting the Fugitive Slave Law. Mason and Slidell evaded the Northern warships which were blockading the Southern coast, and reached Havana, where they embarked for Southampton on a British passenger ship, the *Trent*.

At the beginning of November 1861, Palmerston learnt that an American warship, the *James Adger*, had put into Southampton. He believed that she was intending to intercept the *Trent* in the Channel just outside the three-mile limit, and remove Mason and Slidell as prisoners of war. On 11 November Palmerston held a meeting with Lord Westbury, the Lord Chancellor; Lushington, the President of the Court of Admiralty; Sir George Grey, the Home Secretary; the Duke of Somerset; and the three law officers. He asked the lawyers what would be the position in international law if the *James Adger* stopped the *Trent* in the Channel and removed Mason and Slidell. To his great annoyance they told him that, if the arguments which the British Government had always put forward were correct, the *James Adger* would be justified in doing this; for the British Government had fought the War of 1812 in order to uphold their right to stop American ships and remove British deserters, and though the United States had denied their right to do so, the matter had been left unsettled by the Peace Treaty of 1814. The removal of Mason and Slidell from a British ship would therefore be legal according to the British contention, though illegal according to the American view. On the same day, Palmerston wrote to Delane, the editor of *The Times*, and told him that as the law officers, 'much to my regret', had advised that the seizure of Mason and Slidell would not be illegal, the Government had decided to do nothing except prevent any action by the *James Adger* within British territorial waters. He took comfort from the fact that the captain of the *James Adger*, 'having got very drunk this morning at Southampton with some excellent brandy, and finding it blow heavily at sea', had decided to remain for the time being in the Southampton river.

Palmerston decided, however, to speak to Adams on the matter. In his report to Seward, Adams described how Palmerston had received him in the library at Cambridge House, and told him that there was a rumour that the *James Adger* was intending to intercept the *Trent*, and that 'it would be regarded here very unpleasantly if the captain, after enjoying the hospitality of this country, filling his ship with coals and with other supplies, and filling his own stomach with brandy (and here he laughed in his characteristic way), should, within sight of the shore, commit an act which would be felt as offensive to the national flag'. Adams assured him that he knew nothing of any attempt to stop the *Trent*. But six days before, unknown to both Palmerston and Adams, the *Trent* had been stopped four thousand miles away off the coast of Cuba by Captain Wilkes of the US ship *San Jacinto*, who was returning from the coast of Africa and had decided, without receiving any orders, to intercept the *Trent* and remove the Confederate envoys whom he had heard were on board.

The Southern sympathizers in Britain raised a storm of protest over this insult to the British flag. The British press violently attacked the Americans and the authorities in Washington. In the United States, Captain Wilkes was greeted with great enthusiasm when he arrived at Fortress Monroe with his prisoners. He was cheered to the echo when he went to the theatre in Washington, the whole audience rising to their feet; and a resolution was passed in Congress congratulating him. Palmerston referred the question to the law officers again, and this time had a more satisfactory answer. The law officers now said that, though it would have been legal for Wilkes to seize the *Trent* and take her to a United States port as prize if she was carrying the Confederate envoys, he was not entitled to remove them from the *Trent* while allowing the *Trent* to proceed. Russell then sent a despatch to Washington demanding an apology and the release of Mason and Slidell. Palmerston ordered Lewis, the Secretary for War, to send an additional three thousand troops to Canada, and the press whipped up the bitterest feelings against the North. Adams and other political observers did not fail to notice that the most bitter of all the anti-American papers was the *Morning Post*, though it was nearly equalled by Delane in *The Times*.

Adams's son wrote in later years that if the Atlantic cable had already been in operation in December 1861, Britain would have gone to war with the North. But as it took five weeks for letters to cross the Atlantic and return, there was time for tempers in London and Washington to cool. When Russell's despatch was submitted to the Queen, Prince Albert, who was dying, dragged himself from his bed and altered the wording of the despatch. He suggested that it should state that the British Government had no doubt that Captain Wilkes had acted without the authority of the United States Government, so as to provide Seward with a loophole through which to retreat. Palmerston agreed that the Prince's amendment was very desirable, and the despatch was sent in this form. Meanwhile Bright had written to his friend Charles Sumner, the most prominent of the Abolitionist leaders in the United States Senate, and urged him to persuade the United States Government to free Mason and Slidell if they wished to prevent Britain from entering the war on the side of the South and dooming the Union and the Abolitionist cause. Sumner had already urged Lincoln to adopt this course. Lincoln and Seward decided to release Mason and Slidell, with a declaration that Wilkes had acted without authority, and that the attitude of the British Government showed that they now recognized the correctness of the United States contention about the right of search during the disputes which led to the War of 1812.

Thus Palmerston, in the great battle between freedom and slavery, threw all his weight into the scales on the side of slavery. If he did not actually seek a war with the North, he was not reluctant to be drawn into war, and did all he could, short of war, to injure the Northern cause. If his sympathies had been on the other side, he could have accepted the first opinion of the law officers, that the seizure of Mason and Slidell was legal; or he could have failed to take advantage of the somewhat technical point in the law officers' second opinion, that the United States had broken international law because they allowed the *Trent* to proceed instead of taking her, as well as Mason and Slidell, to a United States port. Instead, he called Wilkes's action 'a declared and gross insult', demanded the release of the author of the Fugitive Slave Law, and personally instigated an anti-Northern hate campaign in the British press. He himself expected that war would be the result. 'It is difficult', he wrote to Russell on 6 December, 'not to come to the conclusion that the rabid hatred of England which animates the exiled Irishmen who direct almost all the Northern newspapers, will so excite the masses as to make it impossible for Lincoln and Seward to grant our demands; and we must therefore look forward to war as the probable result'. There was sure to be war, because 'nations and especially republican nations or nations in which the masses influence or direct the destinies of the country are swayed much more by passion than by interest'. On 5 December he wrote happily to the Queen that 'Your Majesty's position is anyhow a good one'.

If Lincoln's Government granted Britain's demands for the release of Mason and Slidell, 'it will be honourable for England and humiliating for the United States'. If the demands were refused, 'Great Britain is in a better state than at any former time to inflict a severe blow upon and to read a lesson to the United States which will not soon be forgotten'. He agreed with Russell's suggestion that an embargo should be placed on the supply of arms from Britain to the North, though not to the South.

On 19 December Russell received a conciliatory reply from Seward, which gave every indication that Mason and Slidell would be released. But the Government refused to let the people know this. They suppressed the news of the despatch until Mason and Slidell had actually sailed for Britain. Meanwhile, on 30 December – eleven days after Russell had received Seward's note – the *Morning Post* published a violently anti-Northern article, which everyone assumed had been inspired by Palmerston, threatening war if Mason and Slidell were not released. Only when Mason and Slidell reached Southampton did Palmerston say that the crisis had been settled satisfactorily. On 17 February 1862 he wrote to the Queen congratulating her on the 'humiliation' of Bright's 'favourite North American Republic'.

But Palmerston was more tactful in his public statements. Parliament had not been in session during the crisis; but when it reassembled in February, Bright criticized the Government for its anti-Northern policy and its 'ferocious gestures' in sending the Guards to Canada. Bright maintained that Lincoln would have released the Confederate envoys if the British Government had asked him to do so in a friendly fashion. Palmerston replied that Bright spoke only for himself, as the entire nation had supported the Government's attitude. The only 'ferocious gestures' which had been made were when the troops stamped their feet and waved their arms as they went aboard at Liverpool, and they had done this in order to keep warm in the cold weather; but he was sure that the United States would not have released Mason and Slidell if the troops had not been sent to Canada. The United States would have adopted a much more aggressive attitude if Britain had not made it clear that she would not tamely submit to this 'insult and outrage'; for 'there is no doubt that all nations are aggressive; it is the nature of man'.

In February 1862, the North won its first major success by capturing New Orleans in an attack from the sea. The greatest port of the Confederacy was thus held by the North as an isolated pocket deep in the rear of the Southern territory. The army of occupation was commanded by General Benjamin Butler, a forceful Massachusetts lawyer who was one of the political Generals appointed at the beginning of the civil war, and had been the first of the Northern commanders to liberate the slaves in the territory which he occupied. In New Orleans the women of all classes were incensed at the presence of Butler's forces, and insulted the Northern troops in the street. They turned their backs on them, and spat at them, threw slops from the windows as Butler passed, and cheered and mocked at the funeral of a Northern soldier. Butler thereupon issued a proclamation that any woman insulting an officer or soldier of the United States Army would be treated as 'a woman of the town plying her avocation', and imprisoned in the house of correction with common prostitutes. There was no further trouble from the ladies of New Orleans, and none of them were therefore incarcerated with the prostitutes; but Butler shot a man who hauled down the Union flag, and annoyed the foreign Consuls in New Orleans by seizing money which had been deposited with the Dutch Consul.

Butler's order raised a howl of protest throughout the Confederate states, and Jefferson Davis announced that if he were captured he would be executed as a war criminal. The Southern supporters in Britain made great propaganda from the incident. Making use of the unfortunate wording of Butler's proclamation they interpreted it as meaning that women insulting the Northern soldiers were to be used, like prostitutes, for sexual intercourse, and that Butler was calling on his men to rape the women of New Orleans. Palmerston hastened to adopt this far-fetched interpretation, which could only have occurred to a man who had a profound hatred of the forces represented by Butler and the North. Without consulting Russell, he wrote a private letter to Adams on 11 June from Lady Palmerston's house at Brocket in Hertfordshire. 'My dear Sir, I cannot refrain from taking the liberty of saying to you that it is difficult if not impossible to express adequately the Disgust which must be excited in the Mind of every honourable man by the general order of General Butler given in the inclosed extract from yesterday's Times. Even when a Town is taken by assault it is the practice of the Commander of the conquering army to protect to his utmost the Inhabitants and especially the female part of them; and I will venture to say that no example can be found in the History of Civilized Nations till the publication of this order of a General guilty in cold Blood of so infamous an act, as deliberately to hand over the female inhabitants of a conquered city to the unbridled license of an unrestrained soldiery. If the Federal Government chooses to be served by men capable of such revolting outrages they must submit to abide by the deserved opinion which mankind will form of their conduct. My dear Sir, Yrs faithfully, Palmerston'.

When Adams received this letter, his first reaction was that Palmerston had decided to declare war on the North, and was deliberately trying to work up a quarrel. He considered that his first duty was to prevent this from happening. He therefore refrained from telling Palmerston, what he told his friends, that the fate of the women in New Orleans was preferable to those in Badajoz in 1812 after its capture by Wellington's troops, or in Delhi in 1857 after it fell to Nicholson's men. He merely wrote to Palmerston asking whether his note was meant to be a private letter or an official communication, and raised it with Russell, who was obviously annoyed that Palmerston had written to Adams without telling him anything about it. But Palmerston refused to retract his letter. He criticized Butler in the strongest language in the House of Commons, and urged Russell to send an official despatch to Seward protesting against Butler's order. The real meaning of the order had now been pointed out to Palmerston; but he thought that Seward should be told 'that construed in its literal sense it authorizes proceedings revolting to every manly feeling and without example in the history of the nations, and that taken in its narrowest and most restricted interpretation it is an outrage upon the feelings and practices of Christian nations, by rendering ladies and respectable women of every class liable to be sent to be imprisoned with the most abandoned and profligate and degraded of their sex'. Meanwhile the news reached London that Lincoln had replaced Butler at New Orleans, and though Butler's order was not officially repudiated, Palmerston chose to interpret Lincoln's action as a censure of Butler. Palmerston wrote to Adams that his letter was meant to be an official communication, but that he was now pleased to note that Butler had been repudiated by his Government. Adams and Mrs. Adams ceased to attend Lady Palmerston's parties.

A few days later, Adams heard that a ship was being built in Mr. Laird's shipyards at Birkenhead for use by the Confederate Navy against Northern shipping. As this was a breach of Britain's policy of neutrality, he asked Russell to stop the ship from sailing. But the Confederate agents who had commissioned the ship had carefully covered their tracks; and when Russell referred the matter to the law officers, they advised him that as there was no evidence, other than suspicion, that the ship was destined for use by the Confederate Navy, it would be improper to detain it. Russell then consulted Palmerston, who advised Russell that, in view of the law officers' report, no action should be taken. Three weeks later, on 22 July, Adams received clear evidence of the destination of the ship, and saw Russell again. Palmerston and Russell again referred the matter to the law officers, who studied the new evidence for a week, and then advised, on 29 July, that the ship should be detained. Next day, the Foreign Office referred the matter to the Treasury, and on 31 July orders were sent to Birkenhead to stop the ship. But the ship had sailed on the morning of the 29th – a few hours before the law officers had sent their report to Russell. As soon as the ship was outside the three-mile limit, she hoisted the Confederate flag and took the name *Alabama*; and for two years she did extensive damage to Northern shipping before being sunk off Cherbourg in the summer of 1864.

The United States Government protested to Britain, and

accused the British Government of connivance at the construction of the *Alabama* and its escape from Birkenhead. They demanded that Britain should compensate the United States for all the damage sustained by the *Alabama*'s depredations. Palmerston and Russell denied that the British Government had been culpable in any way, and rejected the claims for damages. They refused any suggestion that the dispute should be referred to arbitration. Adams complained to Russell that when he spoke to Palmerston about the damage caused by the crew of the *Alabama*, Palmerston replied: 'Catch them if you can'; but Palmerston told Russell that he had never said this, and added that in view of the way in which Adams had distorted their conversation, he would take care not to speak to him again. It was not until Gladstone became Prime Minister, after Palmerston's death, that Britain agreed to refer the dispute to arbitration and in 1872, in pursuance of the arbitrator's award, Britain paid $15,500,000 in gold as damages to the United States.

During the days when Palmerston had been failing to stop the *Alabama* from sailing, a series of battles were being fought in Virginia. When the news reached London that the Northern attack on Richmond had been repulsed with heavy losses, and that the Southern armies, under General Robert E. Lee, were preparing to invade the North and perhaps capture Washington, the agents of the Confederate Government redoubled their efforts to obtain recognition and assistance from the Governments of Europe. In Paris, Slidell persuaded Napoleon III, who was even more pro-South than Palmerston, to suggest to the British Government that Britain and France should offer to mediate in the American Civil War, and that if the North refused the mediation – as everyone knew they would – Britain and France should then recognize the Confederate Government and offer them all assistance short of war. The British Cabinet was divided on this proposal. Argyll and Milner-Gibson opposed it, but Russell and Gladstone were in favour. Palmerston was sympathetic, but more cautious than Russell and Gladstone. When the matter was first raised in the Cabinet, Palmerston supported the proposal, but began to hesitate when faced with the strenuous opposition of

Argyll and the Northern sympathizers. He then said that the moment was not yet ripe for such a move, because the North would certainly reject any offer of mediation, or any settlement based on the recognition of secession, and to propose it would be like offering to make it up between Sayers and Heenan after the third round; but the position might be different if Lee won a victory in Maryland. He therefore proposed that they should wait and see the result of Lee's invasion of the North. He also suggested that while they were waiting, Russia should be asked to join in the offer of mediation.

Gladstone would not wait. He made a speech at Newcastle on 7 October 1862, in which he praised the South and declared that Jefferson Davis had 'made a nation'. Everyone thought that the Government had decided to recognize the Confederate Government, and that Gladstone was expressing Palmerston's policy; but Palmerston made no move one way or the other. A week later Sir George Lewis, the Secretary for War, made a speech at Hereford in which he said that the Government had not decided to recognize the Confederacy. It was generally believed at the time, and ever since, that Palmerston had told Lewis to make the speech; but this was in fact not true, for Lewis had acted purely on his own initiative. Palmerston told Clarendon that he thought that Gladstone and Lewis had both been unwise to refer to the question in public speeches. Granville thought that Palmerston was as eager as Gladstone and Russell to recognize the South. Palmerston certainly had no sympathy whatever with the Northern cause. 'As to the American War', he wrote to Clarendon on 20 October 1862, 'it has manifestly ceased to have any attainable object as far as the Northerns are concerned, except to get rid of some more thousand troublesome Irish and Germans. It must be owned, however, that the Anglo-Saxon race on both sides have shown courage and endurance highly honourable to their stock'.

A week later the news came that Lee had been beaten in the battle of Antietam and was in full retreat. News also came of Lincoln's Emancipation Proclamation, which was issued five days after Antietam. It proclaimed that the slaves in any territory which was in rebellion against the Union Government on 1 January 1863 would be freed on that day by Lincoln as Commander-in-Chief. Russell thought that Lincoln was trying to incite a slave rebellion in the South, and condemned him for this; but though the Emancipation Proclamation was violently denounced in the *Morning Post* and most other British newspapers, it swung opinion in Britain in favour of the North, while Lee's defeat made Palmerston reject Napoleon III's proposal for mediation and recognition of the South. Lady Palmerston now engaged in complicated manoeuvres to persuade Adams and his wife to come to her parties again. He eventually came, but not until he had been asked more than once.

In January 1863 a great rally of trade unions was held in London in favour of the North. 'They met', wrote Henry Adams to his brother on 27 January, 'to notify Government that "they would not tolerate" interference against us. I can assure you that this sort of movement is as alarming here as a slave insurrection would be in the South. ... I never quite appreciated the "moral influence" of American democracy, nor the cause that the privileged classes in Europe have to fear us.' He felt proud to represent 'that great republic which, though wounded itself almost desperately, can yet threaten to tear down the rulers of the civilized world by merely assuming her place at the head of the march of democracy', and wrote confidently that 'with such a curb on the upper classes, I think they will do little more harm to us'. Adams's optimism soon gave way to a fear that this close association of the Northern cause with the forces of democracy in Britain would throw Palmerston and the Government on to the side of the South; but when, in March 1863, Seward informed the British Government of the North's intention to resort to more determined measures against neutral shipping, and demanded that steps should be taken to prevent a repetition of the case of the *Alabama*, Russell reacted with a speech in Parliament which Adams considered was the most satisfactory which he had yet heard; and Russell assured Adams that Palmerston had approved of the speech.

As soon as Parliament rose for the Easter recess, Palmerston went to Glasgow to be installed as Lord Rector of the University. He was cheered by great crowds, and sailed down the Clyde in a new steamer while the people packed the river banks on both sides. After addressing public meetings in Glasgow and Greenock, he went to Edinburgh. It was the first time that he had been in Edinburgh since he left the University there in the summer of 1803 to travel to Cambridge, on that journey which was interrupted at Doncaster by a report that the first Napoleon had landed. He found time to visit old Peggy Forbes in Edinburgh. He had known her sixty years before when he was a student and she was a servant in Professor Stewart's household; and she handed him a box of his tools, which she had kept all these years because they had belonged to him. Palmerston, who had more energy at seventy-eight than at eighteen, delighted the people by climbing to the top of Arthur's Seat.

In his speech in Glasgow, Palmerston referred to the American Civil War. He said nothing to commit the Government, and merely stated that he hoped that the American people would soon be freed from the dreadful evils of civil war. Next day, on 1 April, he attended a banquet in Edinburgh. After Palmerston had made a non-political speech, he was followed by Argyll, who had accompanied him on his tour. Argyll said that Palmerston's remarks at Glasgow yesterday about the evils of civil war must not be interpreted as a censure of Lincoln's Government for the measures which they were taking to suppress the rebellion of the South. He said that no Scotsman who had studied the history of Edinburgh in the sixteenth and seventeenth centuries could deny that great good could result from the evils of civil war, and that this would be the case in America if the civil war resulted in a victory for the North. Argyll's speech was widely reported in America, where it caused great satisfaction in the North; but Palmerston made no comment on it in his speech at Leith next day. He had remained equally silent six months before, when Gladstone had said precisely the opposite of what Argyll now said. In Palmerston's Cabinet, the tail was beginning to wag the dog.

In May 1863, Lee defeated an attack by the Northern armies at Chancellorsville, and again prepared to invade the

North. The Confederate supporters in Britain and France thought that this would be a suitable moment to press for the recognition of Jefferson Davis's Government. Roebuck went to Paris and met Napoleon III, and returned to tell the House of Commons that the Emperor believed that the South should be recognized. In the debate on 30 June, he made a strong attack on the North, declaring that free negroes were treated worse in the North than the slaves in the South, and that 'the men of the South were Englishmen, but that the army of the North was composed of the scum of Europe'. He said that it was vital for Britain that the South should be established as an independent state, because if the North and South were re-united in one nation, it would soon be the most powerful nation on earth. He was supported by a number of Conservative MPs, including Lord Robert Cecil, who said that it was only a question of days before Lee captured Washington, and that Britain should hasten to recognize the South before they finally won the war. Palmerston was prevented by an attack of gout from taking part in the debate; but when he returned to the House a few days later, he made a statement deprecating Roebuck's attempt to speak on behalf of the French Government, because communications from Napoleon III should be made through the proper diplomatic channels; and he refused to give any encouragement to the idea that Britain might recognize the South. He had judged the situation correctly, for a week before – though he did not know it – Lee had been decisively defeated at Gettysburg, and Grant, by capturing Vicksburg, had won the West for the North.

Gettysburg had a decisive effect, not only on the fighting in America, but also on the attitude of Palmerston. In September Adams drew Russell's attention to the fact that some rams were being fitted out in Laird's yard at Birkenhead, and that it was suspected that they were intended for the Confederate Navy. He asked Russell to seize the ships at once; but the law officers advised that there was no legal justification for doing so. On 5 September, Adams presented a note to Russell, warning him that if the rams were allowed to sail, 'it would be superfluous in me to point out to your Lordship that this is war'. It was the first time that Palmerston had ever received a note in these terms from a foreign government. He sent a directive to Russell on the same day, telling him to inform Adams that the Government would seize the rams at their own risk, despite the advice of the law officers. Three weeks later, he wrote to Russell complaining about Adams's 'somewhat insolent threats of war', and suggested: 'We ought I think to say to him in civil terms, You be damned'. But the rams were safe in Government custody, and did not sail.

The Government's action was strongly criticized in the House of Commons by Laird, who was a Conservative MP, and by other Conservative members. In the course of the next winter, the Northern Navy seized several British ships which they accused of breaking the neutrality laws; and in the case of the British ship the *Saxon*, which was boarded by the Northern Navy off the coast of South Africa, a British seaman was killed in resisting the boarding party. But the British Government took no action. When the matter was debated in the House of Commons on 12 February 1864, Palmerston argued that the Americans had been fully justified under international law. His speech caused great indignation among Conservative MPs. Lord John Manners said that they were 'assisting at the funeral rites and final interment of that celebrated historical personage, the *Civis Romanus*'.

In the summer of 1864 Grant launched his great offensive against Lee in Virginia. In a series of bloody engagements he advanced a few miles, but suffered such heavy losses that his victory was virtually a defeat. Morale in the North was affected, and many people believed that Lincoln would fail to be re-elected in the presidential election in November. There were rumours that the North might, after all, be forced to agree to some kind of compromise peace with the South; and Slidell in Paris and Mason in London became more hopeful that the Confederate Government would be recognized by France and Britain. Palmerston was approached by the Confederate supporters in the House of Commons and asked once again if he would meet Mason; and for the first time he agreed to do so. He was very anxious to win the support of as many MPs as possible for the forthcoming vote in the House of Commons on his Schleswig-Holstein policy; and either for this reason, or because of the stalemate in America, he threw out hints that he might perhaps recognize the Confederacy. But in September Sherman captured Atlanta, thus ensuring Lincoln's victory in the election; and by Christmas he had marched through Georgia to the sea, and the Confederacy was on its last legs.

In March 1865, as Grant and Sherman enclosed the Southern armies in a giant pincer movement, the Confederate Government, who had been outraged two years before when the North enrolled negro soldiers in their armies, proclaimed that any negro slave who volunteered for the Confederate Army would be given his freedom. Mason in London took his cue from the new policy of his Government. Without instructions from Richmond, he visited Palmerston, and asked him whether Britain would recognize the Confederacy if the Confederate Government abolished slavery. Palmerston would not even consider the suggestion, and told Mason that the existence of slavery in the South had never been a factor in preventing the British Government from recognizing the Confederacy. Three weeks later Lee surrendered at Appomatox, and the civil war was over; and five days after the surrender, Lincoln was assassinated. Palmerston was too ill to be present in the House to join in the glowing tributes that were paid by all the political leaders to Lincoln's memory.

Chapter Thirty-nine

The Struggle with Bismarck

The Liberal Party had won the election of 1859 on a programme of electoral reform; but after six years in office, no Reform Bill had been presented to Parliament when Palmerston died in 1865. Palmerston succeeded in holding up reform for fourteen years. He stopped it when it was proposed in Lord John Russell's Government in 1851 and in Lord Aberdeen's in 1853. In 1854 he had it postponed for the duration of the Crimean War. He reluctantly agreed, under pressure from his Cabinet, to include a promise about it in his election manifesto, in March 1857; but when he was urged to implement his promise in the autumn, he evaded taking any action, and nothing had been done when his Government fell in 1858. It was a much more difficult task to stall on reform for six years in a Cabinet which included Russell, Gladstone and Argyll; but Palmerston achieved the feat, and proved himself to be, in Disraeli's words, 'a gay old Tory of the older school, disguising himself as a Liberal, and hoaxing the Reform Club'.

Gladstone was not in favour of reform when he first joined Palmerston's Government in 1859. Even at the end of his life, he thought that there was something to be said for rotten boroughs, because since their abolition it had been much more difficult for able young men to get into Parliament at an early age. But during the lifetime of Palmerston's last Government, Gladstone moved sharply towards the Left, and before it ended he was strongly in favour of giving the vote to the working classes in the towns. This became another source of conflict between the Prime Minister and the Chancellor of the Exchequer, in addition to the paper duties and armaments expenditure.

Palmerston's greatest problem during his last Premiership

was how to handle Gladstone. Sir William Gregory was told by a member of the Cabinet that 'at the beginning of each session and after each holiday, Mr. Gladstone used to come in charged to the muzzle with all sorts of schemes of all sorts of reforms which were absolutely necessary in his opinion to be immediately undertaken. Lord Palmerston used to look fixedly at the paper before him, saying nothing until there was a lull in Gladstone's outpouring. He then rapped the table and said cheerfully: "Now, my Lords and gentlemen, let us go to business" '. Sometimes Palmerston considered it necessary, as he gaily told Granville, to bully Gladstone a little. Gladstone repeatedly threatened to resign, but he always withdrew his resignation, believing that he could do more good in the Cabinet than out of it. Palmerston said that he had received so many letters of resignation from Gladstone that he feared that they would set fire to the chimney at Broadlands.

Sometimes the majority of the Cabinet agreed with Gladstone against Palmerston. On these occasions, it was the Prime Minister who had to give way, and though he sometimes flared up, or sulked for a little, he usually surrendered with a good grace. He would sit in the Cabinet listening to the discussion, and drawing up two lists on little scraps of paper – a list of those for, and those against, the motion under discussion. Sometimes the majority were in favour of a progressive reform, and sometimes only a minority favoured it. But Palmerston always wrote 'Gladstone' and 'Gibson' in the list, however long or short, of those supporting the reform; and he always added, at the foot of the list of those opposing the reform, the name 'Palmerston'.

Palmerston was able to hold up electoral reform for six years only because there was much less support for it among the Parliamentary Liberal Party, and among the middle-class electors who already had the vote, than among the Liberal political leaders. He repeated his usual arguments against reform, writing to Russell on 26 December 1859 that he would never agree to 'giving up the representation of the great towns to the trades unions', and 'practically disfranchising ... the wealthy and intelligent men'; but chiefly he relied on the argument that a Reform Bill would split the Parliamentary Liberal

Party. He was fortified in his arguments by a memorandum on this subject which he received in February 1861 from Brand, his Chief Whip. Armed with Brand's memorandum, Palmerston again blocked the proposed Reform Bill, and promised to introduce, at some future date, another measure which would be more likely to win the support of the MPs.

In May 1864 Gladstone made a speech in the House of Commons on reform, in the course of which he said that he saw no reason, in principle, why every man who was not mentally incapacitated should not have the vote. He made it clear that he was not advocating the introduction of universal suffrage in the near future, and said that this would not come about until the working classes themselves showed more interest in obtaining the vote. Palmerston was as alarmed as the Queen at such a declaration from the Chancellor of the Exchequer, and thought that Gladstone's statement was an incitement to the working classes to begin an agitation for reform. He told Gladstone that he realized that many working men were as intelligent and as capable of exercising a vote as many men of the middle classes, but that if the working class as a whole were granted the vote, the country would pass into the power of the trades unions. But to Palmerston's great annoyance, the *Observer* published an editorial supporting Gladstone's statement.

On 15 May Palmerston scribbled a note to his secretary, Barrington, in a hand which was as illegible as any of those about which he had complained in the past – probably because of gout in his hand. 'I wish you would Send for Behan of the Observer and say I much wish he would not write Such articles as his leading one today calculated to rouse agitation which upon every account it is most desirable not to excite. He should be made aware that Mr. Gladstone Spoke for himself alone, and not by any means as the organ of the Government and he and Mr. Behan must surely be aware that Mr. Gladstone's Speech has produced an unfavourable Impression upon a large Section of the Liberal Party. P. 15/5–64. Mr. Gladstone's Doctrine which the Observer praised that every sane man has a moral Right to vote goes straight to universal Suffrage which not even the most vehement Reformer has hitherto advocated. Moreover if every sane Man has that Right why does it not also belong to every sane woman Who is equally affected by Legislation and Taxation. The Truth is that a vote is not a *Right* but a *Trust*. All the Nation cannot by Possibility be brought together to vote and therefore a Selected few are appointed by Law to perform this Function for the Rest and the Publicity attached to the Performance of this Trust is a Security that it will be responsibly performed. P.' This reference to publicity was a swipe at the idea of secret ballot.

Palmerston bitterly resented Gladstone's attitude. Shaftesbury, commenting on the affability which Palmerston normally showed towards all his political opponents, stated that there were only two men whom Palmerston hated — Gladstone and Bright. Bright had made himself very unpopular in the House of Commons. While Cobden, with his cool reasoning and courteous manner in debate, was respected and liked by men who disapproved strongly of his policies, Bright's violent language and boorish manners exasperated them and gave scope for their political prejudices. No one could accuse Gladstone of boorishness, but neither his opinions nor his character were likely to commend him to Palmerston. Gladstone and Palmerston had nothing in common except that they both behaved like gentlemen, and had enormous physical energy and capacity for hard work. They occasionally agreed over temporary political issues, as they did in supporting Sardinia against Austria and the South against the North in the American Civil War; but they disagreed fundamentally about more permanent questions, such as Church policy, international morality in foreign affairs, defence, and reform; and Gladstone was shocked at Palmerston's private life. When Palmerston quoted a medieval Latin poem, which he falsely ascribed to Martial, in the House of Commons:

> *Wine, women, baths our bodies undermine;*
> *But what were life without baths, women, wine?*

Gladstone was disgusted at its coarseness, though Palmerston had taken care to quote the poem in its original Latin, and not to give the English translation.

Palmerston usually managed to hide his feelings towards Gladstone, and even Gladstone was not immune to Palmerston's charm and good manners. Towards the end of Gladstone's life, when someone criticized Palmerston, Gladstone hastened to say that though Palmerston had had his faults, he had sound principles and genuine Liberal convictions, as opposed to Disraeli, who had debased political life. But Palmerston did not reciprocate the respect which Gladstone felt for him. His dislike of Gladstone went deep. He once said to Shaftesbury: 'Gladstone has never behaved to me as a colleague, in such a way as to demand from me any consideration'. Gladstone, like Bright, was too dangerous an adversary for Palmerston to show the same magnanimity which he did towards minority leaders like Harney and Holyoake. He could joke with the Chartist butcher at Tiverton in 1852 – fourteen years before the birth of Ramsay MacDonald – that he was not thinking of joining a Rowcliffe administration; but a Gladstone administration was not a joke. 'Gladstone will soon have it all his own way', he said to Shaftesbury, 'and whenever he gets my place we shall have strange doings'. He told another friend that he thought that Gladstone would wreck the Liberal Party and end up in a madhouse.

In 1863, another revolt broke out in Poland against the Russian authorities. The Liberal Tsar, Alexander II, had begun his reign by granting concessions to the Poles; but as this only encouraged Polish resistance, he reversed his policy, and when he encountered trouble from the students, he had a large number of them arrested in their beds and marched off to undergo military service in the Russian Army. This provoked a revolution which the Tsar claimed was a Socialist rising, but in fact was supported by most of the population. Again, as in 1830 and 1846, the events in Poland aroused strong feelings in France, and among the Polish sympathizers in Britain; and again Palmerston did nothing effectual, and restrained the French from doing anything. But this time, though he was dealing with a Russia that had still not fully recovered from the Crimean War, and was not the Russia of Nicholas I, he suffered a diplomatic defeat which he had skilfully avoided in 1831 and 1846.

A new factor in the situation was Prussia, where Bismarck had become Chancellor in September 1862. Prussia, throughout Palmerston's lifetime, had always been the weakest of the five great powers, and one from which Britain had nothing to fear. Yet Palmerston's relations with the Prussian Chancellors had always been stormy, perhaps because the attitude of the Prussian Junkers was so like his own. When Palmerston blustered and threatened the statesmen of other countries, they tended to resort to evasion and deceit; but the Prussian Chancellors replied in the same tone, and this resulted in a storm which often cleared the air. In 1832 Palmerston sent a copy of his protest against the action of the Diet at Frankfort to Vienna and Berlin. Metternich replied with a subtle and cutting answer; but the Prussian Chancellor, Ancillon, exploded, and refused to accept Palmerston's despatch, though he eventually felt obliged to do so. Five years later, there was another outburst from Ancillon's successor, Count Werther, who was so angered by one of Palmerston's despatches that he treated the British Ambassador to an exhibition of rage comparable to those which Ambassadors in London had sometimes to endure from Palmerston.

In 1860 Palmerston became involved in a controversy with Count Schleinitz, the Prussian Chancellor, when Captain Macdonald of the Queen's Bodyguard, who was travelling in Prussia, became involved in an angry altercation with a railway official about the reservation of a seat on a train, which resulted in Macdonald being marched off to jail and fined for misconduct. When Schleinitz refused Russell's demand for an apology and compensation, Palmerston weighed in with a strong denunciation in the House of Commons of Prussian police tyranny. Schleinitz replied with an attack in the Prussian Parliament on British arrogance. At the trial, the counsel for the prosecution stated that Englishmen travelling on the Continent were 'notorious for the rudeness, impudence and blackguardism of their conduct'. Palmerston then insisted on taking the unusual course of himself drafting a despatch to Berlin which was openly stated to have been written by the Prime Minister, in which he roundly denounced Schleinitz for his remarks. Schleinitz replied with an even stronger rejoinder, which he read out aloud in the Prussian Parliament.

After September 1862, Palmerston had to deal with Bismarck; and the most brilliant statesman of the nineteenth century, who combined all Palmerston's energy and tactical skill with a greater strategical vision and historical perspective, proved more than a match for a very old Pam. In February 1863 he concluded a Convention with Russia by which he permitted Russian troops to cross the Prussian frontier to pursue escaping Polish rebels, and offered material and moral support to the Tsar in his suppression of the Polish revolt. He thus ensured the defeat of a rebellion which might have led to trouble in the Polish territories of Prussia, and he also gained the friendship of Russia in his coming struggles with Austria and France. Napoleon III proposed to the British Government that they should send a joint note to Bismarck insisting on his repudiating the agreement with Russia: but Palmerston and Russell, who were now very suspicious of collaborating with Napoleon III except in distant regions such as China and Mexico, insisted that Austria should be invited to join in the démarche, and that the protest should be based, like Palmerston's despatches in 1831 and 1846, on the provisions of the Treaty of Vienna. This was perhaps juridically sound, but was calculated, as Palmerston and Russell well knew, to irritate Napoleon III. The British Government also insisted that the protest should be sent to St. Petersburg, not to Berlin, on the grounds that it was invidious to blame Prussia, the lesser culprit, instead of Russia, the main offender. Napoleon III argued that Prussia, on geographical grounds, would be more amenable to pressure than Russia; but Palmerston did not wish to do anything to encourage France to act against Prussia, as he did not want French troops to cross the Rhine. On the other hand, he was as eager as ever to aggravate relations between France and Russia. He therefore rejected all the French proposals, and wrote to King Leopold describing how he had avoided the 'trap' that Napoleon III had set for him.

After five months, the British and French Governments

had been unable to agree on what to do. Then, as the fighting was still continuing in Poland, Palmerston decided to act on his own. On 25 July he drafted a note, which he suggested that Russell should send to St. Petersburg; it protested against Russian tyranny in Poland in much stronger language than the tactful despatches, framed as friendly advice, which Palmerston had sent to Russia in 1831. The majority of the Cabinet thought that Palmerston's language was too strong, and Russell was directed to draft another note; but Russell's note was itself very strong. It was sharply rejected by the Russian Government. Napoleon III then proposed that Britain and France should invite Austria, Russia and Prussia to attend an international Congress to settle the future of Poland and other European problems; but Palmerston rejected this proposal, which would certainly not have been accepted by the Tsar and Bismarck. By this time, the Poles had been crushed and subjected to the most savage repression that they had hitherto encountered.

Palmerston was criticized in 1863, as he had been in 1831 and 1846, for doing nothing to help the Poles; but on all three occasions there was nothing that he could do, except go to war, and this he would not do. His real chance to help Poland was during the Crimean War and at the Congress of Paris, when he clearly refused to take the opportunity. But it is not so easy to see what he was aiming at in 1863 as in 1831 and 1846. In 1831 he wished to remain on friendly terms with Russia, and hoped to influence her, by his friendship, to show restraint in Poland; in 1846 he wished to vie with Guizot for Radical support. In 1863 he seems to have had no clear aim, except to give vent to the moral indignation that was felt in Britain, and to oppose every proposal put forward by Napoleon III.

The House of Commons debated Poland on several occasions. Palmerston was criticized by the Radicals for taking his stand on the Treaty of Vienna, and for refusing the French proposal for an international Congress, while the Conservatives blamed him for having sent a threatening note to Russia when he was unable to implement his threats. In reply he said that the best that the Poles could hope for would be to return to the status which they had been granted by the Treaty of Vienna and had lost in 1831, and that if the Russians paid no attention to the British and French protests they would react in the same way to the resolutions of a Congress. He rejected the argument that because Britain would not go to war for Poland, or give any practical assistance to the Poles, she ought not to express her moral indignation at the Russian actions.

He also used the Polish insurrection, like the American Civil War, as an argument in favour of British constitutional monarchy, when he asked the House of Commons to increase the Prince of Wales's income on the occasion of his marriage. 'We see in the East some of the evils which are incident to arbitrary Government. We witness in the West the widespread misery and desolation which are sometimes created by democratic and Republican institutions. We enjoy a happy medium between the extremes of these two forms of Government ... uncontrolled either by the edicts of despotic authority or by the lynch law of an ungovernable mob'. He hoped that the British people would turn their hearts to the 'Almighty Dispenser of events ... with reverential thankfulness for the lot which has thus been assigned to them', and that 'their bosoms will be full of the most affectionate attachment towards that Sovereign and family under whose mild and beneficent sway, humanly speaking, those blessings have been conferred'.

Bismarck now made an alliance with Austria with the object of seizing Schleswig-Holstein, which he coveted chiefly because he wanted the port of Kiel. The old legal arguments of 1848 were revived, but Bismarck was not interested in the conflicting claims of the Danish and German populations nor in the inclusion of the duchies in a Liberal German Republic. His plan was for Prussia to grab Schleswig and Austria to grab Holstein, and then to go to war with Austria to get Holstein too, and to replace Austria as the dominating power in the German Confederacy. Palmerston supported Denmark, as he had done in 1848, and public opinion in Britain was behind him.

Most people in Britain disapproved of Bismarck, as Palmerston did. Bismarck's action in upholding King William's right to govern without the consent of the Prussian Parliament by relying on the Army had displeased Palmerston; and he had been shocked when Bismarck told the Liberals in the Parliament that the great questions of the day were not decided by speeches and resolutions but by iron and blood; for although Palmerston himself often acted on this principle, it was not in the Whig tradition to say so. On 15 November 1863 Palmerston wrote to King Leopold: 'The King of Prussia seems to have made his models of action Charles the first of England and Charles the Tenth of France and Bismarck is an humble Imitator of the Ministers of those Two unfortunate Sovereigns. I hope the King's fate will not be like theirs. The King ... is quite wrong in attempting unconstitutionally to force his opinions upon his Parliament. He ought to give way and he will be compelled to give way'.

Bismarck's support of Russia against the Polish rebels had further antagonized the British people; and in the Schleswig-Holstein dispute they regarded the Danes, not as the champions of royal absolutism as the German Liberals had seen them in 1848, but as a small nation fighting for its independence against Prussian and Austrian tyranny. The sympathy for Denmark was increased by the popularity of Princess Alexandra, who arrived in London to marry the Prince of Wales, at the height of the diplomatic crisis over Schleswig-Holstein. The Queen, unlike her son and daughter-in-law and most of her subjects, was on the side of Prussia and Austria, and this led to a renewal of ill-feeling between her and Palmerston. Palmerston found it necessary to write to her on 4 January 1864: 'Viscount Palmerston can quite understand Your Majesty's reluctance to take any active part in measures in any conflict against Germany, but he is sure that Your Majesty will never forget that you are Sovereign of Great Britain'; and she wrote to her uncle Leopold of Belgium complaining of Palmerston and Russell, 'those two dreadful old men'.

Bismarck pursued his preparations against Denmark fully conscious of the strength of his position. His army possessed the Dreyse needle-gun, which, unlike the rifles of the British Army, was loaded at the breach, not at the muzzle, so that it could fire six times as quickly; and he had a brilliant Chief of the General Staff, the Danish-born General von Moltke. In

1848, when Prussia had acted without Austrian assistance, Russia had been the chief support of Denmark; now Russia was Bismarck's friend. France had never been interested in Schleswig-Holstein, and was not disposed, at the moment, to act in concert with Britain. Britain was the only power which would be likely to stand by Denmark; and Britain had a pro-German Queen and some pacifist elements in the Cabinet. Having carefully weighed the odds in his favour, Bismarck was ready to take on Palmerston.

Palmerston completely failed to understand the situation. Twenty-six years earlier, when Moltke, as a Prussian Captain, was training the Turkish Army, Palmerston had wanted the Turkish Government to dismiss him, because he feared that a Prussian officer would be too pro-Russian; but he had been reassured when Lord William Russell, the British Minister in Berlin, assured him that Moltke was too incompetent to be a danger to anyone. In 1863 Palmerston still did not appreciate Moltke's ability, or the efficiency of his Army. On 27 June 1863 he told Layard that 'the crazy minister at Berlin' should be made to realize that if, as a result of his policy in Schleswig-Holstein, the Prussian Army was involved in a war with France, 'the first Serious Encounter between it and the French would be little less disastrous to Prussia than the Battle of Jena'.

On 23 July he spoke in the House of Commons about the situation. He declared that the British Government, like France and Russia, wished that 'the independence, the integrity, and the rights of Denmark may be maintained. We are convinced – I am convinced at least – that if any violent attempt were made to overthrow those rights and interfere with that independence, those who made the attempt would find in the result that it would not be Denmark alone with which they would have to contend'. He said that he was sure that the German Diet would not act on the ultimatum which they had sent to Denmark and that he thought that there was not even a remote danger of war over Schleswig-Holstein.

For five months Palmerston was convinced that his optimism had been justified, for Bismarck was anxious to achieve his aims without war if possible, and took no action to implement the ultimatum of the German Diet. But in November the Danish Government proclaimed a new Constitution for Schleswig-Holstein which linked it closer to Denmark, and Prussia and Austria announced that they would act on the Diet's resolution. During the last days of the year, the German armies were massing on the Eider, and the British Ambassador in Berlin reported to Russell that war was now inevitable. Palmerston believed, or pretended to believe, that Rechberg, the Austrian Foreign Minister, and Bismarck, far from wishing to defeat Denmark in war, were anxiously seeking for a way to extricate themselves from a dangerous position. 'Rechberg and Bismarck are both struggling in the torrent and crying out for help from some friendly hand', he wrote to Russell on 7 January 1864. 'Let us give it to them'. This extraordinary appreciation of the situation, like the whole of his policy in the Schleswig-Holstein crisis, resulted from his conviction that France was much stronger than Austria and Prussia, and a much greater threat to British interests.

On 1 February the Prussian and Austrian troops invaded Schleswig-Holstein. Ten days later, the Danish Government made a formal appeal to Britain for aid. They relied partly on a far-fetched interpretation of the treaty of 1720, but chiefly on Palmerston's declaration of 23 July that Denmark would not fight alone. But when Russell urged Palmerston to take action, he found, to his astonishment, that Palmerston was proposing to do nothing, and to allow the Danes to fight alone. Russell suggested that they should send a fleet to Copenhagen to assist the Danes, and proposed to Napoleon III that he should mobilize his troops on the borders of the Prussian Rhineland provinces; but Palmerston replied that the Navy could not achieve much at Copenhagen, and that nothing should be done to encourage Napoleon III to cross the Rhine.

Palmerston had resigned himself to the fact that there was nothing that he could do to help Denmark. For four hundred years, Britain had not fought a war in Europe except as an ally of a major European power; and there was now no such ally available to help her in a war against Austria and Prussia. Russia had reason to be grateful to Bismarck, and none to be grateful to Palmerston; and Napoleon III was as irked at Palmerston's recent attitude as Palmerston was suspicious of him. But while Palmerston coolly replied to the indignant letters of Russell by telling him that there was nothing that he could do against 200,000 soldiers, he was still alert to seize an opportunity to score a point. His chance came at the end of April, when an Austrian fleet sailed for the Baltic with the intention of attacking Copenhagen. On his own initiative, without consulting the Cabinet, Palmerston saw the Austrian Ambassador, Apponyi, on 1 May, and told him that Britain could not permit an Austrian Navy to sail up the English Channel in order to enable Austria and Prussia to dictate peace and the dismemberment of Denmark in Copenhagen. He told Apponyi that if the Austrian fleet sailed into the Baltic, the Royal Navy would follow them, and that the result would probably be a war between Britain and Austria and Prussia. Apponyi assured Palmerston that the Austrian fleet would not enter the Baltic, and it stopped off Deal. Palmerston then told Russell, again without consulting the Cabinet, to send an official despatch to Vienna asking the Austrian Government to confirm the undertaking which Apponyi had given. But the Queen got to hear of it, and asked Lord Granville to raise the matter in the Cabinet. The majority of the Cabinet insisted that the despatch should not be sent to Vienna, and Palmerston and Russell gave way. But the Austrian fleet did not enter the Baltic.

Bismarck was perfectly happy about the situation. As the German troops were in occupation of Schleswig-Holstein, he offered to make an armistice on the basis of the status quo, and accepted Russell's proposal that the problem of Schleswig-Holstein should be referred to a Conference in London. It was the Danes who made difficulties about accepting the armistice and attending the Conference as long as the Prussians and Austrians were in possession of Schleswig-Holstein; and when the Conference met in May, they refused to make any concession. They were encouraged by Russell's attitude of support, and hoped, by their determination, to draw the British Government after them, like the Turks had so often done. On 19 June the situation was discussed in the British Cabinet, and Russell got the impression that his colleagues were prepared to help the Danes. He therefore gave a virtual pledge of support to the Danish Minister in London; and three days later, the Danish delegates to the London Conference announced that they would not extend the armistice when it expired on 26 June. This suited Bismarck. The Austrian and Prussian troops swept into Jutland and rapidly advanced on Copenhagen.

The British people, and all Europe, now waited for Palmerston's reaction, and received a profound shock. On 25 June the Cabinet discussed what to do, and Russell found that the majority of his colleagues were determined not to go to war to save Denmark. His proposal to send the fleet to help defend Copenhagen was carried by Palmerston's casting vote; but Palmerston then said that in view of the strength of the opposition in the Cabinet, it was impossible to send the fleet, and it was decided to take no action at all. Two days later, Palmerston and Russell made their eagerly-awaited statements in Parliament. Malmesbury, who was present in the House of Lords when Russell spoke, wrote in his diary: 'Lord Russell got up and spoke for nearly two hours; for the first half-hour he was almost inaudible, but after that I heard enough to know that the Government were for peace at any price, and meant to desert the Danes'.

In the House of Commons, the MPs heard Palmerston's speech with mounting indignation. 'We believed', he said, 'that, from the commencement to the end of these last events, Denmark had been ill-used (cheers); that might had overridden right (renewed cheers); and we knew also that the sympathies of almost the whole of the British people were on her side'. But he then made it clear that Britain would do nothing, though he tried to convey the impression, in a long, rambling statement, that he would act if the Prussians and Austrians advanced to Copenhagen and threatened the existence of Denmark as an independent state. 'I do not mean to say therefore – I think it right, indeed, to put in this reservation – that if the war should assume a different character; if the existence of Denmark as an independent power in Europe should be at stake; if we had reason to expect to see at Copenhagen the horrors of a town taken by assault, the destruction of property, the sacrifice of the lives, not only of its defenders, but of its peaceful inhabitants, the confiscation which would ensue, the capture of the Sovereign as a prisoner of war, and other humiliation of that kind – I do not mean to say that if any of those events were likely to happen, the position of this country might not be a subject for reconsideration'. At this point, uproar broke out, and his words were drowned in mocking laughter from the Conservative benches. Eventually he was able to add: 'We might then think it our duty to adopt another course'; but he had seriously shaken the confidence of the House.

The Conservatives attacked Palmerston and the Government for having betrayed the Danes, and carried a vote of censure in the House of Lords by a majority of nine. Palmerston was thought to be also in danger of defeat in the House of Commons, and looked everywhere for every vote he could find. He agreed, for the first time, to meet Mason, Jefferson Davis's envoy, in order to win the support of the small group of Confederate supporters in the House of Commons; and he made approaches to the Roman Catholics in an unsuccessful attempt to gain the Irish MPs. But he relied mainly on the support of the Cobdenite pacifists. In the four-day debate in the Commons at the beginning of July, Cobden criticized Palmerston's foreign policy, but said that he would vote for him as this would be a vote for peace; and Bright had the tact to say nothing. The debate was bitter, and Palmerston and other Government speakers intervened to protest against the un-Parliamentary language of their critics. 'Is it come to this', asked General Peel, 'that the words of the Prime Minister of England, uttered in the Parliament of England, are to be regarded as mere idle menaces to be laughed at and despised by foreign powers?'

Palmerston replied on the last night of the debate. 'I say that England stands as high as she ever did', he declared, 'and those who say she has fallen in the estimation of the world are not the men to whom the honour and dignity of England should be confided'. He said that the whole Government stood firmly behind Russell's policy, and that it was unfair of the Opposition to throw the blame on Russell personally – thus blandly ignoring the fact that most of the criticism had been directed, not against Russell, but against Palmerston himself. Then he referred to his declaration a year ago that the Danes would not fight alone, and explained that he had meant that they would not fight alone because France and Russia might help them. This brought a rejoinder from Disraeli that no one in Denmark was blaming France or Russia for having betrayed them, but they were all blaming Palmerston. Palmerston devoted the rest of his speech to reminding members of the Government's great achievements in domestic legislation, referring proudly to many of the reforms which he himself had opposed in the Cabinet. The Opposition vote of censure was defeated by 313 votes to 295 – a Government majority of 18. Bright and Cobden hailed it as a great victory. After fighting for years against Palmerston's foreign policy, they had won at last – under the leadership of Palmerston.

Palmerston had won, even if the Danes had lost. When the result was announced at half-past two in the morning, Palmerston ran up the stairs to the Ladies' Gallery and embraced Lady Palmerston. Such actions won the admiration even of opponents. 'What pluck', wrote Disraeli, 'to mount those dreadful stairs at three o'clock in the morning, and eighty years of age!' As long as he could run up a steep flight of stairs in his eightieth year, it did not matter to the public that he could not save the Danes.

But the summer of 1864 was a bad time for Palmerston. Apart from the humiliation of Schleswig-Holstein, there was the spectre of universal suffrage which had been conjured up by Gladstone's speech in May; and Palmerston was not happy about Garibaldi's visit in April. When Garibaldi arrived at Nine Elms Station, 500,000 people turned out to welcome him; and it took five hours for his carriage to travel the three miles from Nine Elms to the Duke of Sutherland's residence at Stafford House. A few days later, he addressed an enormous demonstration at the Crystal Palace. He was also welcomed by London society, including the Prince of Wales, though the Queen did not approve. Both the young Duchess of Sutherland and her mother-in-law, the Dowager Duchess, fell in love with Garibaldi. They invited the Palmerstons to meet him at a dinner party at Stafford House. After dinner the guests were shown over the house, being admitted even to that most private place, the Dowager Duchess's exquisitely furnished boudoir. The other guests thought that the Dowager Duchess would never forgive Garibaldi when he lit a cigar in the boudoir; but she wrote to him next day to tell him that though she could not expect so great a hero to look at a woman of fifty, she was at his disposal if he wanted her.

Palmerston invited Garibaldi to a more private dinner, and had a very friendly talk with him; but he was disturbed at the popular demonstrations, both because they angered the Austrian Government and Napoleon III, and because he dreaded any manifestation of democratic fervour. When he heard that an organizing committee of Radicals and Socialists had arranged for Garibaldi to tour the provinces and address large rallies at Bristol and Birmingham, he tried to prevent Garibaldi from going. He suggested, perhaps not wholly in jest, that they should marry Garibaldi to one of the rich ladies who doted on him, as this would be the best way of keeping him quiet. The round of social engagements and public demonstrations had tired Garibaldi, and affected his health; and he was annoyed that, while he himself had been fêted by society, his comrades-at-arms who had come with him had been neglected and left to fend for themselves in cheap hotels. Garibaldi suddenly cut short his stay in England, and went home to Italy in a bad temper without going to the Midlands. The Radicals raised the matter in Parliament, and suggested that Palmerston had forced Garibaldi to go because Napoleon III had protested against his reception in England; but Palmerston denied this, and stated that it was because Garibaldi, whose health was still affected by a wound which he had received in 1862, had been too ill to continue his tour.

In August, after Parliament had risen for the recess, Palmerston made a series of public speeches at various places in the country. Brougham was astonished, for when he was Lord Chancellor thirty years before, he had been told that he should not even be seen at a public dinner; but by 1860 the idea of addressing large public meetings, which five years before had been considered to be a Radical practice, was being adopted not only by the unorthodox Chancellor of the Exchequer, but by the old Premier himself. Palmerston had started doing this when he spoke at the Radical banquet after his Don Pacifico speech. He addressed a number of public meetings and dinners during his visit to the North of England in the autumn of 1856 when he astounded his contemporaries by making three speeches in one day; but he spoke at many more public functions during his last Premiership, sometimes making half-a-dozen speeches a year outside Parliament. He often spoke at public functions at Romsey and Southampton, but also went all over the country to speak at dinners given by the Chamber of Commerce, at reviews of the Volunteers, or at the opening of new railway lines, when Lady Palmerston laid the first sod, and Palmerston made a short, amusing speech.

His visit to Bradford in August 1864 was less satisfactory than other such occasions. He went to speak at a banquet for four thousand diners, and the visit was organized by a committee of local business men. The Chartist and Socialist organizations wished to present a petition to him, asking him to give the vote to the working man; but the chairman of the organizing committee refused to let them do so. Holyoake, who was one of the organizers of the petition, thought that 'the worst enemy of Lord Palmerston could not have done him a worse service. Nothing would have pleased him better than to have met a working-class deputation. His personal heartiness, his invincible temper, his humour and ready wit would have captivated the working men, and sent them away enthusiastic, although without anything to be enthusiastic about'. Palmerston was always happy to meet a deputation. He once defined a deputation as 'a noun of multitude signifying many but not much'.

As Holyoake and his friends were prevented from presenting the petition, they decided to organize a silent protest demonstration. They packed the square in front of the Town Hall with 30,000 working men, and when Palmerston appeared at the top of the steps, surrounded by the reception committee, they stood in stony silence, while a few business men tried to raise a cheer. Palmerston looked surprised and pained, but had recovered his usual bounce by the time he addressed the banquet that evening, when he thanked the people of

Bradford for the wonderful welcome that they had given him. He was followed by Forster, the Radical MP for Bradford, and by Crossley, another Radical MP. Forster and Crossley shocked the reception committee by attacking Palmerston in outspoken language for not introducing a Reform Bill, and demanded the vote for the working man in the towns.

From Bradford, Palmerston proceeded to more friendly territory. He went to Tiverton, where he reviewed the local Volunteers and made a speech in which he mentioned briefly how deeply everyone must regret that they had been unable to help Denmark, and then praised the legislative achievements of the Government. He also went to the races at Tiverton. 'Many will remember his appearance on that occasion', wrote a local inhabitant thirty years later, 'an old man with a genial cheery smile playing over his furrowed features. His dress was very plain and peculiar, consisting of a somewhat rusty green swallow-tail coat, a check neckerchief tied stiffly and in ample folds round his neck, coarse striped trousers, and a white hat, very much the worse for wear – all that was left of the once gay Pam'. He talked in his usual friendly way with Rowcliffe, and commiserated with him that he, too, suffered from gout; and he attended the twenty-first birthday party of his election agent's daughter, where he chatted gaily to the local tradesmen who comprised the other guests, poured out the whisky, and made a speech full of compliments to everyone, and especially to the young lady.

After leaving Tiverton, he went to Herefordshire, where he dedicated a monument to Sir George Lewis, and then went to Wilton. He reviewed the local Volunteers in Wilton Park and made a speech. From Wilton he went to Broadlands. He had been able to spend much more time at Broadlands since the railway came to Romsey in 1847, which made it possible for him to travel from Broadlands to the Foreign Office – a distance of seventy-five miles – in three and a half hours. He had at first disliked the railways; but in this, as in other matters, he adapted himself to modern changes, and became an enthusiastic supporter of railway development. In 1856 he laid the first sod of the Andover-Southampton railway. He sold some land to the railway company at a substantial profit, and arranged with the company, as part of the transaction, that they should pay the cost of building the red brick wall round the park at Broadlands.

He spent the autumn of 1864 at Broadlands with Lady Palmerston, being visited by Lady Palmerston's son, William Cowper, the future Lord Mount Temple, and his wife, and by Lady Palmerston's daughter Minnie, Lady Shaftesbury, who was probably Palmerston's illegitimate daughter; and he was photographed in a family group on the steps at Broadlands, wearing his hat at a rakish angle, and talking to the young women of the family. On his eightieth birthday in October, he spent the day inspecting the fortifications on the south coast. He left Broadlands at half-past eight in the morning, took the train from Romsey to Fareham, with his horse in the horse-box, and at Fareham mounted his horse and rode along Portsdown Hill, dismounting to walk around the Portsdown and Hilsea forts, and then crossed the water to Gosport to inspect the Anglesey forts, not reaching home until six o'clock in the evening. He was none the worse for his excursion, except that the sea breeze had removed the dye from his whiskers.

He met the new session of Parliament in February 1865; but everybody was now waiting for him to die, some with hope and some with anxiety. The Radicals no longer bothered to try to persuade him to introduce a Reform Bill: it was simpler to wait until he died. The Liberal Party organizers, who knew his power as a vote-catcher, were anxious as to what would happen after his death, which they feared would break up the party. ' "How does Lord Palmerston look?" was the question on a hundred lips', William White, the doorkeeper at the House of Commons, had written two years before, in February 1863, 'and as the noble Lord marched across the lobby a hundred eyes examined him keenly. For a time after he entered the House he was scarcely observed, for he entered at the back door and glided unseen into his place, as his manner is'. But soon he had to go to the table, and as he walked up, dressed in his close-fitting black frockcoat, with his dark trousers and black necktie, 'every eye was fixed upon him. Cheers burst forth from his supporters when they saw that he walked as firmly as ever. It was not surprising that we were anxious about this old man's health, for upon his shoulders rested the whole framework of our party arrangements. Like Atlas, he alone held up the structure; and we knew that when he failed, all would collapse and sink into temporary ruin. But the noble Lord had no thought of failing, for it was only the other day that he appeared in the hunting field with a new scarlet coat'.

But there were the increasing number of occasions when he was too ill to do business. He had his first serious breakdown in December 1861, when the cold weather and the strain of work – or, as some believed, the shock of the Prince Consort's death at the same time – caused him to fall seriously ill, and forced him to spend a few weeks in bed. He was ill on a number of occasions in the next three years. In November 1864 he went out for a two-hour walk at Broadlands, pulled a boat across a stream, and tripped over a tree-trunk as he returned home in the failing light, which again put him out of action and caused anxiety to the party whips; and at the end of April 1865, when he was ill again, it was rumoured in London that he was dying. His friends were also worried by his occasional mental lapses. Before leaving London in August 1864 he wrote a letter to Russell about the American Civil War, and then wrote to him a few days later from Delapré Abbey at Northampton to point out that in the first letter he had throughout written 'Bucharest' when he meant Richmond. Russell was more alarmed next year when Palmerston asked him whether France had been a party to the treaty that established the independence of Belgium in 1831. He fell asleep more often than formerly in the House and at Cabinet meetings. 'He is always asleep', wrote Greville, 'both in the Cabinet and in the House of Commons, where he endeavours to conceal it by wearing his hat over his eyes'. Clarendon, who returned to the Government as Chancellor of the Duchy of Lancaster in April 1864, told Greville that in the Cabinet 'one half of them seem to be always asleep, the first to be off being Lansdowne, closely followed by Palmerston and Charles Wood'. His Cabinet was the oldest that there has ever been in Britain, with only five members who were under sixty.

The Government introduced a new Poor Law Act in February 1865, which removed some of the harshest conditions in the workhouses. The President of the Poor Law Board, Charles Villiers, introduced the bill, in a speech in which he referred to the dreadful conditions of the workhouses in the past, which had provoked the agricultural revolts of 1830 in the South of England. The Prime Minister – a relic of the age which had accepted these conditions as desirable and inevitable – sat in silence beside Villiers on the Treasury bench; but he intervened in a series of debates on Ireland, regretting the human suffering involved in emigration, but declaring that tenant right was landlord's wrong, and asserting that more investment in Ireland by English capitalists was the only thing that could help the Irish people.

In the summer of 1865, he dissolved Parliament, which after six years had only a year to go, and a general election was held in July. The Liberals again pledged themselves to introduce some measure of reform which would give the vote to the urban working class; and though everyone knew that this would not be implemented until after Palmerston's death, the pledge was important, because it was not likely that Palmerston would survive till the next election. But the personality of Palmerston was still a great electoral asset, and the Liberals increased their majority in the House of Commons. At Tiverton, Palmerston had a closer contest than usual. The Conservatives put up one candidate, and unofficially told their supporters to cast one vote for him and the other for Palmerston's colleague, Heathcote, in the hopes of securing the election of their candidate and Heathcote, and defeating Palmerston. Rowcliffe voted for Heathcote and the Conservative; and Palmerston, who was present when Rowcliffe cast his vote, twitted him: 'Then you did not vote for me, friend Rowcliffe; you prefered voting for a Tory'. 'I did not vote for you, my Lord', replied Rowcliffe, 'for if I had, I should have voted for a Tory'. Many Liberals were afraid that Palmerston would be defeated, and countered the Conservative manoeuvre by plumping for Palmerston alone, with the result that Palmerston topped the poll, but the Conservative defeated Heathcote by three votes.

The Liberals also lost a seat at Oxford University, which

had been Gladstone's constituency for many years. Gladstone's High Church policies had made him very popular at Oxford in the past; but he had deeply offended many University voters by his recent conversion to electoral reform and his call to give the vote to the artisans in the towns, and had completely alienated them by his call for the disestablishment of the Anglican Church in Ireland. Before the general election, Gladstone was invited to stand as a candidate for the Radical industrial constituency of South Lancashire; but he decided to try to hold his University seat. Palmerston used all his influence to help Gladstone at Oxford. Apart from his sense of duty to his party and his Chancellor of the Exchequer, he thought that, as long as Gladstone was MP for Oxford University, he would to some extent be restrained by his constituents. 'He is a dangerous man', said Palmerston to Shaftesbury, 'keep him in Oxford, and he is partially muzzled; but send him elsewhere, and he will run wild'. But Palmerston's Low Church policies had made him less popular at Oxford than he would otherwise have been with the University voters, and he could not save Gladstone. Gladstone lost his seat, and next month was returned at the election for South Lancashire.

After the election, Palmerston received a letter from Mr. Macdonogh, the Conservative candidate in Sligo, who had been defeated by Sergeant Armstrong, the Liberal candidate. Macdonogh complained that Palmerston's agent and bailiff in Sligo had used threats to compel Palmerston's tenants to vote for Armstrong against Macdonogh. On 26 June Palmerston wrote to Macdonogh denying the allegations. 'I may without disrespect to yourself frankly avow to you that I take a great Interest in the Success of Sergeant Armstrong from whom I might hope that the Government would receive general support instead of yourself who sit on the opposite side of the House, but though I have desired that my wishes in regard to this matter should be made known to those who might be likely to be influenced by a knowledge of those wishes I have never authorized the employment of Threats which it would be inconsistent with my principles and practice to carry into effect'. On the same day he wrote to his agent at Sligo: 'I wish

you to make immediate Inquiry into this Matter and if Mr.
Fox and the Bailiff Smith have used the imputed Threats they
should be strongly admonished to desist from such objectionable Practices. I do not know Mr. Fox and cannot judge
whether he is likely to have overstepped the line of his
Duty in this matter, but as to Smith the Bailiff I believe him
to be a Man of No judgement and who is very likely to have
gone beyond his orders'. But he was still as opposed as ever
to secret ballot. Nor would he intervene to restrain other landlords who were more disposed than he to exercise arbitrary
power over their tenants. In 1861 a landlord in Donegal evicted all his three hundred and fifty tenants as a punishment for
the murder of his steward by an unknown person. Palmerston
refused to demand of MPs that an inquiry should be held.
'It would be a most outrageous and dangerous abuse of the
power of the House', he said, 'if it interfered with the private
transactions of any individuals within the limits of their legal
rights'.

Chapter Forty

The End of Palmerston

As soon as he had won the general election, Palmerston began preparing for the next session of Parliament. His first concern was about reform. The Chief Whip, Brand, whose report in 1861 that most Liberal MPs were unenthusiastic for reform had been Palmerston's chief excuse for doing nothing at that time, now told Palmerston that MPs were demanding that some measure of reform should be introduced in the new session next February; and Brand urged that steps should be taken at once to prepare for this. Palmerston replied on 3 August: 'My dear Brand, You are really almost equal to Bright in your zeal for Reform. No doubt the Cabinet when it meets in November must consider the question.... But it would be entirely premature to take at present any steps to obtain information, because to do so would imply a Decision made which had not been made to propose some measure next Session'. He had now thought out a new argument against reform: if the franchise were extended, there might be a demand for a dissolution and for the election of a new Parliament on the new franchise; and it would be unfortunate if this were to happen so soon after the last election.

In the middle of August, Palmerston left Broadlands for the last time, and went to Lady Palmerston's house at Brocket in Hertfordshire. Here he busied himself with a new and serious problem – the Fenian movement in Ireland. He directed the Viceroy, Lord Wodehouse, to take drastic measures to deal with the outbreak of violence, urging that a military man should be placed in charge of the police there, and that the authorities should consider the possibility of suspending trial by jury; and he ordered that a careful watch should be kept on all passengers arriving from America. He was sure that the Fenian outrages were instigated by the United States, and was delighted when the police caught 'a brace of Yankees'. On 27 September 1865, he wrote to the Secretary for War, Lord de Grey: 'The American assault on Ireland under the name of Fenianism may be now held to have failed, but the snake is only scotched and not killed. It is far from impossible that the American Conspirators may try and obtain in our North American Provinces compensation for their Defeat in Ireland'. He therefore urged that more armaments should be sent to Canada. Three days later, he wrote to the Home Secretary, Sir George Grey, urging that more troops should be sent to Ireland, because 'if there is any Rising it will be headed and directed by some of these American Fenians come over to Ireland, and such men are very likely to carry on their operations according to the Practice in the Civil War in America, that is to say by a system of Plunder, Burning of Houses and Property, murder of men and outrage of women'. He had accepted the most extravagant allegations of the Confederate propagandists about Sherman's march through Georgia and the character of the Northern soldiers in the Civil War.

At Brocket, during these last few weeks of his life, Palmerston not only gave sympathetic consideration to the suggestion of an MP that civil servants should have a half-holiday off from work every other Saturday afternoon, but also formulated his ideas about important new alignments of foreign policy. The American threat led him to contemplate a new tion of an MP that civil servants should have a half-holiday rapprochement with France. He approved of the friendly visit of the British Navy to Cherbourg in September 1865, because he thought that it would show the Americans that Britain and France could unite, and that it would be 'a sort of preliminary defensive alliance' against the United States. In Central Europe, he was pleased to see the rise of Prussia; and when Bismarck began his quarrel with Austria over Schleswig-Holstein and his preparations for the war of 1866, Palmerston did not share the Queen's anxieties and her sympathy with Austria. 'It seems to me', he wrote to Russell on 13 September, 'rather late for the Queen and Drouyn to have opened their eyes as to the injustice of the Proceedings of the Two German Powers'; and he was not at all surprised that the two wolves, having devoured the lamb, should now fall out over the spoils. 'The fact is as far as the Queen is concerned that so long as the Injustice committed appeared calculated to benefit Germany and the Germans it was all right and proper, but now that an example is about to be set of extinguishing petty States like Coburg, her sense of right and wrong has become wonderfully keen, and her mind revolts at the idea of consequences which flow naturally from the proceedings she approved of'.

But his support for Prussia was based on more important factors than a desire to spite the Queen. He warned Russell that Russia 'will in due time become a power almost as great as the old Roman Empire. She can become mistress of all Asia, except British India, whenever she chooses to take it; and when enlightened arrangements shall have made her revenue proportioned to her territory, and railways shall have abridged distances her command of men will become enormous, her pecuniary means gigantic, and her power of transporting armies over great distances most formidable. Germany ought to be strong in order to resist Russian aggression, and a strong Prussia is essential to German strength'. He therefore hoped that Prussia would take Schleswig-Holstein.

His doctors had been worried throughout the summer that he would catch a fatal chill when the colder weather came in the autumn; but he was still thriving during the warm weather at the beginning of October. Palmerston was in the habit of vaulting over the railings in the park at Brocket; and once, when he was visiting his Solicitor-General, Sir Robert Collier, at Monkswell in Devonshire, he had surprised his host by vaulting over some railings there. In the first week of October he insisted on climbing over the railings at Brocket when he thought that no one was looking, just to see if he could still do it, and suffered no ill-effects. A few days later the weather turned cold; but he would not take care, and went out on to the terrace without a hat, telling his remonstrating doctor that he was merely taking 'what bathers call a header'.

On 12 October Palmerston went out for a drive in his carriage, and his doctors feared that he had caught a chill; but instead of going straight to bed, he insisted on spending an hour and a half undressing and dawdling, and taking his bath as usual. This brought on a violent fever, and he was expected to die in the night. During the next two days his condition was critical, and on 15 October the Queen arranged that Russell should succeed him as Prime Minister when he died; but on that very day there was a marked improvement, and he seemed to be recovering. His appetite returned, and he ate his mutton and apple-tart with relish; and one morning he ate a hearty breakfast of mutton chops and port, telling Lady Palmerston that he had waited all these years before discovering what an excellent breakfast this was. 'He was plucky and Palmerston to the last moment', wrote Clarendon. He had with him at Brocket not only Lady Palmerston, but also Lady Shaftesbury; and he told Minnie, during these last days, that her presence in his room was like a sunbeam. Occasionally, his mind wandered; and once he suddenly began laughing hysterically about an incident when he had been caught throwing stones as a schoolboy at Harrow.

During the night of 17 October his strength rapidly declined, though he was in no pain, and by 4 a.m. his doctor knew that this was the end. He asked Palmerston whether he believed in the regeneration of the world through Jesus Christ. Palmerston replied: 'Oh, surely'. Nothing could have expressed more clearly Palmerston's lifelong attitude towards religion – a complete lack of religious zeal, combined with a respectful tribute to the established Church as a social institution. He died at 10.45 a.m. on Wednesday, 18 October 1865, two days before his eighty-first birthday. In his last delirium, his thoughts were on diplomatic treaties. His last words were 'That's Article 98; now go on to the next'.

He had asked to be buried in Romsey Abbey, but the Cabinet insisted that he be given a state funeral in Westminster Abbey, and Lady Palmerston agreed, on the understanding that when she died she could be buried with him. The state funeral took place on Friday, 27 October. The United States Minister, Adams, was impressed with the dignity of the occasion, but contrasted it unfavourably with the simple funeral of Abraham Lincoln which he had attended six months before, when great crowds had walked past the catafalque in

Washington with tears in their eyes. He did not see anyone outside Westminster Abbey whose face was wet with tears. He caustically noted in his diary that Palmerston had died leaving nothing behind him except a widow who would now have to reconcile herself to playing a less prominent part in public life. Adams was not the only person whose private comments on the deceased were sour. 'I wish there were more to be said in his praise', wrote Bright; while at the other end of the political spectrum Queen Victoria wrote that though she regretted his death, she had never liked him or had any respect for him. 'Strange, and solemn to think of that strong, determined man, with so much worldly ambition – gone', she wrote in her diary. 'He had often worried and distressed us, though as Pr. Minister he had behaved *very well*'. But Florence Nightingale was very unhappy. 'He will be a great loss to us', she wrote on the day that Palmerston died. 'Tho' he made a joke when asked to do the right thing, he always did it. No one else will be able to carry the things thro' the Cabinet as he did. I shall lose a powerful protector. . . . He was so much more in earnest than he appeared. He did not do himself justice'. On the Stock Exchange, Consols fell by $\frac{1}{4}$ per cent.

The public tributes were not lacking. The British press praised him to the full, led by *The Times* with an obituary article running to 13,000 words. The Continental press joined in the tribute to a man whom some regarded as a great ally and others as a respected enemy. The European Radicals remembered him as the patron of revolution in 1848; the Italians as the friend of Italian freedom; and the Belgians, with a little more justification, as the creator of Belgium.

On the Sunday after the funeral, the Dean of Westminster, Arthur Stanley, preached a sermon about Palmerston. It was a masterpiece of tact and good taste. He said that he would not attempt to inquire into the things that Palmerston had done 'in the unseen world which were known to God alone. He left them, as our Church left them, to that Holy and Merciful Saviour whose mighty working was able to subdue all things to Himself'. But he would speak about Palmerston as an English statesman who had 'unfailing trust in the greatness of England'. It was the honour and interests of England, rather than the Church of England, which fired Palmerston's admiration; but Palmerston had stood for everything that is meant by England – 'our marvellous history', 'our refuge for freedom', 'our temperate monarchy and Constitution', the English Prayer Book, the English Bible, and 'our pure domestic homes'. Dean Stanley was perhaps unaware that Palmerston had once tried to seduce his cousin's wife, Lady Stanley of Alderley.

Palmerston's world died with him. Six days before he died, a negro revolt broke out in Jamaica. The Governor of Jamaica, Edward Eyre, immediately ordered the arrest and trial by court-martial of William Gordon, a prominent negro clergyman and politician, who had had no direct connexion with the outbreak, and he was hanged within twenty-four hours; and in the suppression of the revolt hundreds of negroes were executed, and many more, including women, were flogged with wire whips. When the news reached London in November, the country divided into violent factions denouncing and supporting the action of Governor Eyre; for though Bright and the Radicals demanded that Eyre be prosecuted for murder, Carlyle and Lord Cardigan opened a fund for a testimonial to him. To the great anger of Eyre's supporters, Russell's Government dismissed him from his post. Lady Palmerston publicly contributed to the fund for Eyre – 'as if to indicate', wrote a spokesman for the Eyre Committee, the view which would have been taken by 'the great statesman who, whatever his errors of policy, was at all events a man of noble and generous character, and never, in the whole course of his long career, had betrayed a colleague, forsaken a friend, or sacrificed an honest servant of the Crown'. But the great statesman's successors acted differently.

In the eight years which followed Palmerston's death, many of those changes took place which he had always successfully resisted. In 1866 Russell's Government introduced a Reform Bill which greatly reduced the property qualification for the voters in the towns; and in 1867 Disraeli and the Conservatives gave the vote to nearly all the urban working class. In the same year in Mexico the Radical native leader of a backward country executed the Emperor of Austria's brother, who had been installed as Emperor of Mexico with the consent of the European powers – an event which shocked Conservative opinion in Europe almost as much as the execution of Louis XVI. In 1868 public executions were banned in Britain, and, to the disgust of Lady Palmerston, a Jew, Disraeli, became Prime Minister for the first time. In 1869 the Suez Canal was opened. In 1870 Britain allowed a major war to be fought in Western Europe without attempting to influence events, and Russia took the opportunity to build a Black Sea fleet in defiance of the terms of the treaty that Palmerston had imposed upon her; while in England compulsory education, which Palmerston had approved in principle but had refused to implement, was introduced, and the purchase of commissions in the Army was abolished. In 1871 the trades unions were granted protection for their funds and the other demands which Palmerston had refused to grant them in 1853. In 1872 secret ballot was introduced, and Britain paid damages to the United States for the depredations of the *Alabama* in obedience to an adverse award in an international arbitration. In 1873 the tenants in Prince Edward Island acquired the freehold of their land, and William Cowper, who had inherited Broadlands, held public prayer-meetings in the grounds and banned all blood sports on the Broadlands estate. It is not surprising that Bulwer, writing his biography of Palmerston in 1870, described his old superior and hero as a 'man of the old régime'.

These changes would all have come before long even if Palmerston had lived, and Palmerston would have accepted them, as he accepted all the changes which had occurred in the social and political life of Britain between 1784 and 1865. He had welcomed many of these changes but had always opposed those which weakened the ascendancy of the nobility and landowning class, whose predominance he considered essential if the British constitution and system of government was to survive. If he had lived fifty years later, he would have welcomed the motor car as he had welcomed the railway train, and would have opposed Lloyd George and his 'People's Budget' and the campaign against the House of Lords as resolutely as he had opposed John Bright and his attempt, as Palmerston saw it, to incite class against class; and he would have been an ardent supporter of the annexationist and imperialist policy which he rejected in 1859. If he had lived a hundred years later, he would have adapted himself to even greater changes. Palmerston, with his excellent judgment of the realities of the balance of power in any situation, would have adopted a very different policy towards the United States in 1970 than in 1865; and he would have treated the China of Mao Tse-tung with much more respect than the China of Commissioner Yeh.

But if Palmerston had lived in 1910 or 1970 he would not have been Palmerston. He lived in what has been called, by so many historians, 'the age of Palmerston'. The historians end their books, or their chapters, on 'the age of Palmerston' in 1865. In fact 'the age of Palmerston' ended a few years earlier, because Palmerston, unfortunately for his reputation, survived 'the age of Palmerston'. If he had died in 1860 he would have avoided the humiliations of the last few years, when Palmerstonian policies could no longer succeed either at home or abroad.

Philip Guedalla, in his vivid portrait of Palmerston, presented him as an eighteenth-century figure; but in fact he was a product of the Regency period, which was also the period of Wilberforce. This accounts for a great deal of the contradictions in Palmerston's attitude. It explains why he had many mistresses, and why he tried to prevent the working classes from drinking in public houses and the British Museum and the Edinburgh Botanical Gardens from opening on Sundays. It explains his gay, incisive letters and his turgid sanctimonious despatches. If he had been an eighteenth-century man, he would have been out of date and out of touch with the feelings of his contemporaries; in fact, he was in perfect harmony with them, though not at all with the ideas of the advanced intellectual élite. The intellectuals, on their side, had no sympathy for him. He was popular with aristocrats and landowners, with the middle-class industrialist and professional man, and last but not least with the working classes, except for the minority who were actively engaged in Chartist and Socialist politics; but not with the intellectuals. Carlyle,

Turgeniev, John Addington Symonds and Victor Hugo all had a low opinion of Palmerston; and Disraeli, though he respected him as a politician, thought his jokes were dreadful.

Palmerston remained largely unaffected by the humanism of the nineteenth century, and by the campaigns against injustice and hypocrisy which were inspired by such thinkers as Dickens and Ibsen. He had no sympathy with the sufferings of Oliver Twist, and was always ready to back Mr. Bumble whenever any tyranny of the Bumbles was publicly exposed. Despite his venture in penal reform when he was Home Secretary, his letters at the time of the garrotting scare in 1862 show that his reaction to the problems of a Jean Valjean were not much more sympathetic than that of Inspector Javert himself; and for all his love affairs, he could preach morality like a Pastor Manders. He sympathized sincerely, and indeed ardently, with the sufferings of the negro slaves on the slave-ships; but a horror of the slave trade was not limited to advanced minorities. The opinion of all the British aristocracy had changed on this question since the far-off days of 1806, when Palmerston had fought his first election as a spokesman for the supporters of the slave trade.

It is not surprising that Palmerston was often accused of shamelessly changing his political coat for his personal advantage. A politician who, in 1827, after being Secretary at War for eighteen years in a Tory Government, changed his party in order to remain at the War Office and then rejoined the Tories when they returned to power nine months later and still continued in the same office, had to expect such accusations. In 1852, when Palmerston had been dismissed from the Foreign Office after twenty-one years on the Whig front bench, he immediately began negotiations that very nearly resulted in his joining a Conservative Government. But though Palmerston changed his party allegiance, he did not change his fundamental political principles. He disliked the first Reform Bill after he joined the Whigs, just as he had disliked it when he was a Tory; and both as a Tory and as a Whig, he was prepared to accept the Reform Bill as a last resort, if there was no other way of avoiding revolution or serious disorder. No Conservative opposed the second Reform Bill more strongly than Palmerston; and he only headed a Radical Cabinet in 1859 in order to hoax the Reform Club.

Palmerston was described, during his lifetime, as a Conservative at home and a Liberal abroad, and future generations of schoolchildren were taught to regard this as an accepted maxim. But there was no contradiction between Palmerston's internal and foreign policy. He believed, like most Englishmen of his generation, that the British Constitution and social system, as it existed in 1830, was the best in the world, and as near to perfection as any merely human institution could ever be. He believed in constitutional monarchy, with a hereditary Sovereign who was by no means politically powerless, but who was subject to the law, respected the privileges of Parliament, and acted on the advice of his ministers. He believed in a Parliament in which one House was composed of the wealthiest landowners, and the other was elected on a franchise which gave the vote to only five per cent of the adult males in the country. He believed in the rule of law, which must at all times be scrupulously, and often mercilessly, enforced; but when the State was in danger, the rule of law included the Six Acts – which Palmerston supported so enthusiastically, despite what his biographer Bulwer says – and other lawfully-enacted statutes which drastically restricted the political freedom of the Opposition parties. He believed in the freedom of the press, but of a press whose circulation was restricted to the wealthier classes by the stamp duties and the paper tax.

Palmerston was a Conservative at home because he wished to preserve this system and prevent any developments in the direction of democracy. He was a Liberal abroad because he wished to see this system replace the absolutist monarchies of the Continent. He much preferred it if these absolutist régimes could be replaced by a gradual process and without revolutionary violence; but if necessary he was prepared to applaud a revolution which had this limited objective and went no further than the English Revolution of 1688; and he cheered the Revolution of 1830 in France and the revolutions of 1843 and 1862 in Greece. He welcomed them as conferring on foreign countries the blessings of the English system, which he believed was the only happy mean between the two hateful extremes of royal despotism and republican democracy.

Greville was right when he wrote that in politics Palmerston had never been anything but a Palmerstonian. But Lord John Russell was equally right when he said that Palmerston's heart beat always for the honour of England. Palmerston spoke excellent French, was on terms of intimate friendship with foreign aristocrats, and believed that the affairs of the world should be settled, if possible, by friendly agreements between a handful of international statesmen without consulting anyone else; but he was as sincerely, as intensely, and as aggressively patriotic as any other Englishman of his time. His patriotsim was much more ingrained than that of many other great nationalist leaders. Napoleon was not even a Frenchman by birth, nor was Parnell an Irishman. Garibaldi, Clemenceau and Masaryk married foreign wives. Bismarck despised Germans, and preferred French wines and the Russian climate to those which Germany provided. But Palmerston thought that the English climate, like the English Constitution, was the best in the world. He sincerely believed, as he told Sir Francis Acland in October 1857, that the French, unlike the British, had no sense of right and wrong, and that it was 'unreasonable to expect honesty in a Portuguese or a Frenchman'. When the Queen's messenger, Captain Johnson, became involved in an incident with a Russian customs' official on the quayside at St. Petersburg in 1850, and the Russian Government complained that Johnson had assaulted the Russian, Palmerston's first reaction was to inform Nesselrode 'that I must certainly take the positive denial of an English Gentleman against the assertion of a Russian Custom House Officer', though on second thoughts he altered this passage, before sending the despatch, to: 'I certainly must attach weight to the positive denial of an English Gentleman'. Palmerston was British to the core, or rather English, for 'Britain' and 'British' were words which he only rarely used. In 1889 Gladstone told Lord Rendel how on one occasion 'a Frenchman, thinking to be highly complimentary, said to Palmerston: "If I were not a

Frenchman, I should wish to be an Englishman"; to which Pam coolly replied: "If I were not an Englishman, I should wish to be an Englishman"'.

In foreign policy, Palmerston acted on a very simple principle: to advance the interests of England. All other things had to be sacrificed to this end. He once stated that it was in the interests of England that constitutional governments should be established abroad; but if England's interests required it, he was ready to sacrifice these constitutional governments, and even to help the cause of slavery, as he did during the American Civil War. He was prepared to use all his skills to uphold the honour of England – his mastery of detail and protocols at international conferences, his charm and courtesy to the ministers of great powers, his bullying tactics to those of small nations, and bluff, and threat of war. He rejected the view that Britain should never threaten to go to war unless she was prepared to do so; that would be throwing away the useful weapon of bluff. Cobden accused him of 'brinkmanship' a hundred years before the word was invented. 'Palmerston likes to drive the wheel close to the edge', wrote Cobden, 'and show how dexterously he can avoid falling over the precipice'. But brinkmanship was a different thing in 1850 than in the days of nuclear weapons. Palmerston in fact never went over the precipice, except in the Crimean War, and Britain might well have kept safely on the road if he had been in sole charge of the carriage on that occasion.

In 1837 Attwood accused Palmerston in the House of Commons of being a bully to the weak and a coward to the strong. This accusation was repeated on numerous occasions at every stage of Palmerston's career, and by critics as diverse as Prince Albert, Cobden, Lord Cardigan and Karl Marx. Sidney Herbert, who was Palmerston's colleague in the Cabinet for a number of years, wrote in November 1856: 'Palmerston can never resist shaking his fist in the face of anyone whom he is not afraid of. If they show fight he runs away'. Palmerston showed an even greater disposition to yield to superior power in English internal politics. Greville wrote that when Palmerston was confronted with determined opposition in the Cabinet, he always 'knocked under'. The British public never saw him in this light, though his popularity was perhaps due as much to his readiness to yield to popular pressure as to his staunchness in facing the foreigner.

Palmerston did not usually trouble to reply to the accusation that he was a bully to the weak and a coward to the strong. On one occasion, when he did so, he argued that no one could accuse him of capitulating to powerful states, because he had been in favour of going to war with Russia in defence of Turkey in 1853. But he would not really have considered the charge as a reproach. Although he read *Don Quixote* in Spanish when he was a boy at Harrow, he never took Quixote as his prototype. Even in private affairs he avoided rushing into unnecessary altercations, and despite all the political controversies and love affairs in which he was involved, he never fought a duel, as so many of his contemporaries did, though he defended duelling in the Army in a debate in the House of Commons in 1844. When he was conducting the affairs of England, he used England's power to the full, in England's interests, against weaker opponents, and prevented England from coming to grips with powerful states in contests in which England might be worsted, or badly mauled. To have done anything less would, in his view, have been failing in his duty to England. He had no trust in the friendship of any other country, or in international arbitration, but believed that England must enforce her own interests by her own strength. 'It would be very delightful if your Utopia could be realized', he told Cobden, 'and if the nations of the earth would think of nothing but peace and commerce, and would give up quarrelling and fighting altogether. But unfortunately man is a fighting and quarrelling animal; and that this is human nature is proved by the fact that republics, where the masses govern, are far more quarrelsome, and more addicted to fighting, than monarchies, which are governed by comparatively few persons'. The most important thing was to maintain British military superiority; for while the anger of a weaker power did not matter, the anger of a stronger power meant national humiliation. He applied this harsh rule to other nations, and expected them to apply it to Britain. 'Mackieson gave me the other day', he wrote to Layard on 23 October 1864, 'a Buffalo

Hide Whip from Africa called in those Regions a Peace Maker and used as Such in the Households of Chieftains. Our Peace Makers are our Armstrongs and Whitworths and our Engineers'.

This single-minded devotion to the interests of his country was something that his foreign adversaries could understand and respect. Thiers, who was thoroughly worsted by Palmerston in 1840, told Beauvale six years later that he considered Palmerston to be 'the first statesman of this age, and perhaps of any other'. The Germans, after their more successful encounter with Palmerston, had an equally high opinion of him. On 20 October 1865 the *Cologne Gazette* published an obituary notice of Palmerston. 'If anyone in future times wishes to sketch the portrait of an English statesman, he had better try to write Lord Palmerston's history', they wrote; and after stating that 'he was as indefatigable in the hunting field as at the desk, and exercised all the more influence over his nation because he was its genuine son', they looked into the future. 'Even if England still continues to increase in civilization and opulence, she may yet, as other stronger states also rapidly augment, perhaps not long retain her present commanding position in the world; and it may be that in future ages the name of Palmerston will be synonymous with her greatest glory. From one generation of Englishmen to another, the saying will be handed down: We are all proud of him'.

In thinking that in every generation all Englishmen would be proud of Palmerston, the German journalist was forgetting that English phenomenon, the Nonconformist conscience. In Palmerston's generation, and in every succeeding one, there have been people in Britain who believed in all the doctrines which Palmerston opposed. The supporters of what in Palmerston's day was called 'democracy', the believers in the settlement of international disputes by arbitration instead of by British power, the opponents of aristocratic government, of nationalism, of capital punishment and flogging, will not be proud of Palmerston. They will be inclined to agree with John Bright. In 1886, when Lord Rosebery became Foreign Secretary in Gladstone's Government, Bright asked him whether he had read, in Greville's memoirs, about Palmerston's actions at the Foreign Office. Rosebery said that he had. 'Then', said Bright, 'you know what to avoid. Do the exact opposite of what he did. His administration at the Foreign Office was one long crime'. Others will take the simple view of Palmerston's biographer, the Marquis of Lorne, the son of his old colleague the Duke of Argyll. 'He loved his country and his country loved him. He lived for her honour, and she will cherish his memory'.

Principal Events in Palmerston's Life

1784 Oct. 20. Born.

1789 Travels in Belgium and Germany.

1792–4 Travels in France, Switzerland, Italy and Germany, wintering in Naples.

1795–1800 At Harrow.

1800–3 At Edinburgh University.

1802 Death of his father; succeeds as 3rd Viscount Palmerston.

1803–6 At Cambridge University.

1805 Death of his mother.

1806 Feb. Defeated in Parliamentary by-election at Cambridge University.
Nov. Defeated at Horsham in General Election.

1807 Apr. Appointed a Junior Lord of the Admiralty.
May. Defeated at Cambridge University in the General Election.
June. Elected MP for Newport, I.o.W.

1808 Feb. Maiden speech in House of Commons on Copenhagen expedition.
Sept. Visits his estates in Ireland.

1809 Oct. Appointed Secretary at War.

1809–12 Controversy with Commander-in-Chief.

1811 Elected MP for Cambridge University.

1815 Visits Paris after Battle of Waterloo.

1818 Apr. Wounded in an attempt on his life.
Sept. Visits Allied Army manoeuvres in Eastern France.

1819 Supports the Six Acts.

1821 Visits France.

1822 Feb. Defends dismissal of General Wilson from the
Army.
Mar. Charles Smith the poacher executed for
wounding Palmerston's gamekeeper.

1826 Retains seat at Cambridge University in General
Election, defeating High Tory candidates with Whig
support.

1827 Apr. Scandal concerning Devon and Cornwall
Mining Company.
Apr. Joins Canning's Government as Secretary at
War.

1828 Jan. Rejoins Tories, remaining Secretary at War in
Wellington's Government.
May. Dismissed from Wellington's Government.

1829 Speeches in Parliament on Ireland and foreign
affairs.
Visits Paris in January and December.

1830 Nov. Appointed Foreign Secretary in Lord Grey's
Whig Government.

1831 Presides at Conference on Belgium in London
(Treaty signed in November).
Presides at Conference on Greece in London.
Revolutions in Italy. Palmerston mediates.
Russia crushes revolution in Poland.
French blockade Lisbon.
Palmerston defeated at Cambridge in General
Election; elected MP for Bletchingley.
Aug. French and Dutch armies invade Belgium.

1831–2 Palmerston tries to negotiate compromise over
Reform Bill.

1832 Aug.–Sept. Denounces suppression of constitutional
freedom in Germany.
Dec. Elected MP for South Hampshire.

1832–3 Holland blockaded by British Navy.

1832–4 Civil war in Portugal between Miguel and Pedro.
Dispute with Russia about appointment of
Ambassador.

1833 Britain refuses to help Sultan against Mehemet Ali.
Treaty of Unkiar Skelessi between Russia and
Turkey.

1834 Lord Napier's mission to Canton.
Apr. Quadruple Alliance between Britain, France, Spain and Portugal.
Prince and Princess Lieven leave England.
Nov. Fall of Whig Government. Palmerston leaves Foreign Office.

1835 Jan. Defeated in South Hampshire at General Election.
Apr. Appointed Foreign Secretary.
June. Elected MP for Tiverton (holds seat till his death).

1835–9 Civil war in Spain between Isabelinos and Carlists.

1836 Texan War of Independence against Mexico.
Tension with Turkey over assault on Mr. Churchill.
Sept. Septembrist revolution in Portugal.

1836–7 Tension with Russia over detention of the *Vixen* off the Circassian coast.

1837 Revolt in Canada. Increased tension on Canadian–U.S. border.
June. Accession of Queen Victoria.

1837–40 Conflict with Portugal over slave trade and debts to British subjects.

1838 French blockade of Mexico and River Plate.

1839 Final settlement of Belgian-Dutch conflict.
July. Vienna Conference on hostilities between Sultan and Mehemet Ali.
Nov. Outbreak of Opium War between Britain and China.
Dec. Palmerston marries Lady Cowper.
Brunnow and Neumann visit Broadlands at Christmas for talks on Levant crisis.

1840 Feb. Queen Victoria marries Prince Albert.
Apr. British fleet blockades Naples.
July 15. Treaty of London, excluding France from the settlement of the Levant crisis.
Oct. Danger of war between the Four Powers and France.
Nov. Mehemet Ali capitulates after defeat in Syria.

1840–1 Threat of war between Spain and Portugal; dispute settled by Palmerston.

1841 Convention respecting the Dardanelles.
        Danger of war with USA over trial of McLeod.
        Aug. Government resigns; Palmerston leaves
        Foreign Office.

1843 Denounces Webster-Ashburton Treaty.
        Supports Ten Hours Bill.

1844 Visits Wiesbaden, Berlin, Dresden and Prague.

1845 Grey's opposition to Palmerston as Foreign
        Secretary prevents formation of Whig Government.

1846 Apr. Visits Paris.
        July. Appointed Foreign Secretary in Lord John
        Russell's Government.
        July 19. Despatch to Bulwer about Spanish
        marriages, revealed to French Government.
        Oct. Outbreak of Septembrist revolt against Queen
        of Portugal.
        Nov. Austria, Russia and Prussia destroy Republic
        of Cracow.

1846-7 Collaboration of Britain and France against Rosas
        on River Plate.

1847 Don Pacifico's house burned in Athens.
        May. Palmerston intervenes against Septembrists in
        Portugal.
        Irish famine.
        July. Debate with Harney at Tiverton in General
        Election.
        Nov. Swiss Government defeat the Sonderbund.

1848 Feb. Revolution in France. Palmerston collaborates
        with Lamartine's Government.
        Feb. Anstey moves impeachment of Palmerston in
        House of Commons.
        May. Bulwer expelled from Spain by Narváez.

1848-9 War between Austria and Sardinia; Palmerston's
        anti-Austrian policy.

1848-51 Conflict between Prussia and Denmark over
        Schleswig-Holstein. Palmerston presides at London
        Conference.

1848-50 Tension with USA over Mosquito and Central
        America.

1849 Defeat of Hungarian revolution. Palmerston
prevents Turkey from surrendering refugees to
Austria and Russia.

1850 Blockade of Greece over Don Pacifico's case.
June 25. Palmerston's *'Civis Romanus sum'* speech.
Aug. Palmerston submits to the Queen's
memorandum about his management of the Foreign
Office.
Sept. General Haynau assaulted at Barclay's
Brewery.

1851 Oct. Kossuth arrives in London. Palmerston receives
deputation from Finsbury.
Dec. Louis Napoleon's coup d'état in France.
Palmerston dismissed from Foreign Office.

1852 Feb. Palmerston's 'tit for tat' with Lord John Russell.
Palmerston collaborates with Conservatives.
Dec. Appointed Home Secretary in Lord Aberdeen's
Government.

1853 Apr. Police raid factory manufacturing arms for
Kossuth.
The Eastern crisis.
Dec. Palmerston resigns from the Government, and
returns.

1854–6 The Crimean War.

1855 Feb. 5. Palmerston becomes Prime Minister.
Feb.–Apr. Layard's campaign against aristocratic
mismanagement of the war.
Sept. Capture of Sevastopol.

1856 Feb. Controversy over Wensleydale peerage.
Mar. Congress of Paris; peace signed.
British Minister expelled from United States.
Oct. The lorcha *Arrow* seized off Canton.

1857 Mar. Palmerston defeated in House of Commons
over his China policy, but wins General Election.
May. Outbreak of Indian Mutiny.
Aug. Divorce Bill passes House of Commons.

1858 Feb. Palmerston resigns after being defeated on the
Conspiracy to Murder Bill.
Nov. Visits Napoleon III at Compiègne.

1859 June 6. Meeting of Liberal Party at Willis's Rooms.
      June 12. Palmerston becomes Prime Minister.
      War between France and Austria in Italy.

1860 Gladstone's bill to repeal paper duties defeated in
      House of Lords.
      Garibaldi's expedition seizes Sicily and Naples.
      French troops intervene in Syria after massacre of
      Maronites.
      Anglo-French expedition to Peking. Burning of
      Summer Palace.
      Volunteer movement in Britain.

1861–5 The American Civil War.

1861 Gladstone's bill to repeal paper duties becomes law.
      Britain, France and Spain intervene in Mexico.
      Nov.–Dec. Threat of war with U.S.A. (North) over
      case of the *Trent*.
      Dec. Death of Prince Albert.

1862 June. Conflict with U.S.A. (North) over General
      Butler's order in New Orleans.
      July. The *Alabama* escapes from Liverpool.
      Nov. Garrotting scare in London.

1863 Revolution in Poland, crushed by Russia and
      Prussia.
      Mar.–Apr. Palmerston's visit to Glasgow and
      Edinburgh.
      July. Palmerston promises to aid Denmark if Prussia
      and Austria invade Schleswig-Holstein.
      Sept. Confederate rams seized at Liverpool.
      British Navy bombards Kagoshima in Japan.

1864 Apr. Garibaldi's visit to England.
      May. Palmerston's conflict with Gladstone about
      electoral reform.
      June. Britain fails to support Denmark against
      Prussia and Austria in war over Schleswig-Holstein.
      Aug. Palmerston's visit to Bradford and Tiverton.
      Oct. Conflict with Brazil over slave trade.

1865 July. Palmerston wins General Election.
      Oct. 18. Palmerston dies at Brocket.

References

These references give the authority for the statements made in the passages ending on the page and line stated. For the editions referred to, and the abbreviations used, see the Bibliography.

The folio numbers in Palmerston's letter books have usually not been given, as the letters are normally entered in chronological order, and it is easier to find them from the date of the letter than from the folio number in the letter book. In some cases, the folio number has been given to avoid confusion.

Unless otherwise stated, references to 'Hansard' are to the reports of the proceedings in the House of Commons, not the House of Lords.

In the nineteenth century, the Julian calendar used in Russia and Greece was twelve days behind the Gregorian calendar used in Western Europe. Where letters are dated in the Julian calendar, both the Julian and the Gregorian dates are given, e.g., 2/14 Oct. 1830, where the date is 14 October by the Gregorian calendar. In all cases where only one date is given, it is the date by the Gregorian calendar.

CHAPTER I

THE YOUNG HARRY TEMPLE

Page	Line	
15	28	Suckling, *Up and down Old Romsey*, p. 7; *Gentlemen's Magazine*, LIV.792.
17	3	Guedalla, *Palmerston*, p. 463; Connell, *Portrait of a Whig Peer*, pp. 156–7.
19	4	Connell, *op. cit.*, pp. 17, 127, 379.
20	27	Connell, *op. cit.*, pp. 17, 169, 213; Parish, *Victory with Vaccines*, pp. 7–9, 14.
	38	Connell, *op. cit.*, pp. 143–4.
21	25	Suckling, *Around Old Romsey*, p. 11; *Diaries of Sylvester Douglas*, II.93; Connell, *op. cit.*, pp. 166–7.
22	12	Elliot to Lady Elliot, 26 May 1787; Minto, *Letters*, I.98, 167; Connell, *op. cit.*, pp. 200–5.
	30	Lady Malmesbury to Lady Elliot, 24 Aug. 1791 (Minto, *Letters*, I.393).
23	8	Connell, *op. cit.*, pp. 208–9, 260.
24	4	Connell, *op. cit.*, pp. 264–6.
	22	Metternich, 'Autobiography' (*Mémoires de Metternich*, I.10).

Page	Line	
25	11	Connell, *op. cit.*, pp. 17, 267–75, 277.
	24	Connell, *op. cit.*, p. 277; Clarke and M'Arthur, *Nelson*, I.138 n.
26	2	Connell, *op. cit.*, pp. 284–7, 293.
	19	Connell, *op. cit.*, pp. 293, 296, 300–5.
27	11	Vesey, *Chancery Reports*, XVII.491–507.
	34	Thornton, *Harrow School*, pp. 202, 361–2; Howson and Warner, *Harrow School*, p. 64.
28	13	Clifford to Bulwer, 21 Sept. 1870 (Dalling and Ashley, *Life of Palmerston*, I.x–xi).
	38	Connell, *op. cit.*, pp. 323–4, 420; Guedalla, *Palmerston*, p. 47.
29	16	Connell, *op. cit.*, pp. 420–1; Thornton, pp. 219–20, 361; Guedalla, *op. cit.*, p. 40; Bell, *Lord Palmerston*, I.5; Lorne, *Viscount Palmerston*, p. 3.
	28	Harry Temple to 2nd Viscount Palmerston, 9 Dec., 1798; Connell, *op. cit.*, pp. 321, 420–1, 423.
30	23	Hare to Harry Temple, 5 Jan. 1798; Harry Temple to Hare, 29 Mar. 1798 (D. & A., I.6, 8).
31	6	Connell, *op. cit.*, pp. 422–3.
	22	Lady Palmerston's journal, 16 May 1803 (Connell, *op. cit.*, p. 462).

CHAPTER II

EDINBURGH AND CAMBRIDGE: THE FIRST ELECTIONS

Page	Line	
32	2	Howson and Warner, p. 171; Guedalla, *op. cit.*, pp. 40–1.
33	6	Palmerston to Howden, 11 Oct. 1853 (B.M.Add.48578).
	15	Horner, *Memoirs*, I.153–74.
34	14	Stewart to Blane, 27 Apr. 1801 (D. & A., I.11); Minto, *Letters*, III.118 n., 213–22.
	36	Harry Temple to 2nd Viscount Palmerston, 28 Nov., 10 Dec. 1800, 3 Feb. 1801; Harry Temple to Lady Palmerston, 8 Dec. 1800, 15 May 1801; Connell, *op. cit.*, pp. 431, 433–5, 438, 440–1, 444.
35	8	Minto to Lady Palmerston, 10 Jan. 1802 (Minto, *Letters*, III.234–5).
	39	Minto to Lady Minto, 19 Apr., 3 June 1802 (Minto, *Letters*, III.247, 251).
36	13	Minto, *Letters*, III.262; Lady Palmerston to Malmesbury, 29 Apr. 1802 (Connell, *op. cit.*, pp. 458–9); Guedalla, *op. cit.*, pp. 44, 47.
	35	Malmesbury to Palmerston, 23 Nov. 1802 (Connell, *op. cit.*, p. 461); Lady Malmesbury to Minto, 19 May 1801 (Minto, *Letters*, III.220).
37	16	Palmerston's autobiography (D. & A., I.367); Hansard, 9 May, 1845; Palmerston to Croker, 16 Oct. 1856 (*Croker Papers*, III.362–3).

CHAPTER III

THE ADMIRALTY AND THE WAR OFFICE

Page	Line	
59	12	For the offer of the Exchequer, and Palmerston's appointment as Secretary at War, see Palmerston to Malmesbury, 16, 18, 23, 25, 27 Oct., 9 Nov. 1809; Malmesbury to Palmerston, 17 Oct. 1809; Palmerston's autobiography (D. & A., I.90–108, 371); Phipps, *Memoirs of Plumer Ward*, I.249–51, 274, 279–80, 291; Broughton, *Memoirs*, V.204.
61	30	'Statements of the Particulars of the Several Public Departments. . . . Included in the Army Estimates for the year 1817'; Note on pay of Secretary at War; Palmerston to Lushington, 26 Nov. 1821, and enclosures (B.M.Add. 48431, ff. 60, 67; B.M.Add.48419, ff. 81–8).
62	6	Croker to Palmerston, 14 June 1850 (*Croker Pap*, I.17); Arbuthnot to Herries (Oct. 1809) (Herries, *Memoirs of Charles John Herries*, I.13); Lady Sarah Spencer to Lord Spencer, 26 Oct. 1809 (*Correspondence of Sarah Spencer Lady Lyttleton*, p. 85).
63	35	Dundas to Perceval, 12 Nov. 1810, 11 Jan. 1811; Dundas's memorandum to the Prince Regent, Feb. 1811 (B.M.Add.48417, ff, 40–2, 67, 79).
64	33	Dundas to Perceval, 12 Nov. 1810; Palmerston's memorandum to the Prince Regent, 16 Aug. 1811 (B.M.Add. 48417, ff. 69, 83, 115; see also D. & A., I.385).
65	14	Palmerston's memorandum to the Prince Regent, 16 Aug. 1811 (B.M.Add.48417, see esp. f. 128; the memorandum is published in part in D. & A., I.384–417).
66	4	Palmerston's memorandum, 23 Nov. 1811; Duke of York's memorandum, 19 Dec. 1811 (B.M.Add.48417, ff. 168, 209).
	20	Perceval's memorandum, 19 Dec. 1811; Eldon's memorandum; Liverpool's memorandum; Prince Regent's memorandum, 29 May 1812; Palmerston to Perceval, 31 Dec. 1811 (B.M.Add.48417, ff. 215–31, 235–6).

CHAPTER IV

LORD CUPID

68	13	Gronow, *Recollections*, I.31–2; Airlie, I.41; Monypenny & Buckle, *Life of Disraeli*, I.256.
	34	Airlie, I.50–1; Gronow, II.222.
70	15	Gronow, I.32.
71	14	Broughton, *Memoirs*, III, 107; Airlie, I.ix–x; II.42; Greville, *Memoirs*, II.229; Lady Clanricarde to Hayward, 24 Jan. 1865 (Hayward, *Letters*, II.111); Lady Granville to Devonshire, 22 June 1829; Lady Granville to Lady Carlisle, Sept. 1829 (*Lady Granville's Letters*, II.42, 46).

Page	Line	
72	2	Harriette Wilson, *Memoirs*, pp. 43–4, 625.
	9	Phipps, I.351, 363–4, 368, 385, 402.
	17	See, e.g., Palmerston's story 'The Regent's Court: Presentation of the Deputies from the Friendless Islands' (B.P., H.M.C., PRE/B/2); 'The Choice of a Leader' (published in *The Courier*, 9, 11, 20 Feb., 3, 6 Mar. 1815, and in *The New Whig Guide*; see especially pp. 2, 23–6, 32–3).
	37	Ritchie, *The Life and Times of Viscount Palmerston*, II.713.
73	16	Palmerston to Peel, 14 June 1816 (B.M.Add.40256); Lorne, pp. 14–15.
	33	Palmerston to Frances Temple, 4 Jan. 1810 (D. & A. I.114); Cooper, *Annals of Cambridge*, IV.495; Phipps, I.404.
74	10	Palmerston to Liverpool, 28 June, 15 Nov. 1820 (B. M. Add.38194); Gunning, *Reminiscences of Cambridge*, II.222; Hansard, 19 June 1817, 3 Mar., 17 Apr. 1818.
75	35	Hansard, 1 Mar. 1813.
76	39	Lady Cowper to F. Lamb, 18 Sept., 26 Oct. 1820; Airlie, I.27, 39. 49–50, 66, 72; Gronow, I.153.
77	24	Mackintosh's speech, in Hansard, 4 June 1822.
78	5	D. & A., I.143–4; Princess Lieven, 'Sketch of Palmerston' (Temperley, *The Unpublished Diary of Princess Lieven*, pp. 163–8).
	34	Hansard, 7 Aug. 1846.
80	37	Hansard, 6, 13, 16 Mar., 15 Apr. 1812.
81	24	Hansard, 29 Nov. 1813, 3 Mar. 1815.
82	22	Hansard, 21 June 1815.
	30	B.M.Add.48432, ff. 62–9.
83	24	Palmerston's memorandum, 3 July 1815; Torrens to Palmerston, 5, 22 July 1815; Prince Regent's order, 12 July 1815; Palmerston to Liverpool, 19 July 1815; Liverpool to Palmerston, 19 July 1815; Palmerston to Duke of York and Wellington, 27 July 1815; War Office circular No. 287, 31 July 1815 (B.M.Add.48418, ff. 96–108).

CHAPTER V

LORD PUMICESTONE

84	28	Palmerston, *Selections from private journals of tours in France in 1815 and 1818*, pp. 7, 38–59; Palmerston to Mrs. Sulivan, 25 Sept. 1815, 29 Oct. 1818 (Ashley, *Life of Palmerston*, I.81–2, 85).
85	19	Palmerston, *op. cit.*, pp. 22–5; Palmerston to Mrs. Sulivan, Sept. 1821 (Airlie, I.95–6).
	36	Hansard, 5 Apr. 1816, 2 June 1820, 30 Mar. 1821, 5 Feb. 1822.

Page	Line	
		Palmerston's autobiography (D. & A., I.372); Connell, *Portrait of a Whig Peer*, pp. 448–53; Palmerston to Liverpool, 30 Nov. 1821 (B.M.Add.38194).
	30	Phipps, I.341.
124	31	Hansard, 9 Apr. 1824, 10 May 1825.
125	15	Palmerston to Liverpool, 15 Nov. 1820; Wood to Palmerston, 6 Feb. 1823 (B.M.Add.38194); Palmerston's autobiography; Palmerston to Temple, 2 Dec. 1825 (D. & A., I.161, 373).
	39	Palmerston to Eldon, 26 Dec. 1825; Eldon to Palmerston, Dec. 1825 (B.P., H.M.C., GC/EL/1/1–2). Palmerston's autobiography (D. & A., I.373).
126	23	Palmerston to the Cambridge voters, 13 Dec. 1825; Sedgwick to Hobhouse, 8 Jan. 1826 (B.M.Add.36461); Palmerston to Sulivan, 4 Dec. 1825 (D. & A., I.146–6).
127	2	Palmerston's autobiography; Palmerston to Temple, 5 June, 17 July 1826 (D. & A., I.167–70, 373–4); Cooper, *Annals of Cambridge*, IV.552.
	28	Hansard, 26 Feb., 12 Mar. 1827.
128	13	Hansard, 8 Dec. 1826, 14 Feb. 1827, 15 Apr. 1836, 6 June 1837.
129	8	Hansard, 8 Dec. 1826, 14 Feb. 1827.
	29	Palmerston's autobiography; Palmerston to Temple, 19 Apr., 4 May 1827; Palmerston to Sulivan, 15 Aug. 1827 (D. & A., I.186–93, 196–7, 373–4).
130	6	Palmerston's autobiography (D. & A., I.375–6); *The Times*, 20 Aug. 1827; but see Herries, *Memoirs of John Charles Herries*, I.128–30, 153–94, 225.
	21	Connell, *Portrait of a Whig Peer*, p. 378; Palmerston's Account Book (B.M.Add.40584, see especially entries of 23 July 1806, Michaelmas 1810, 8 Oct. 1811, 19 Mar. 1813, 28 Jan. 1818, 19 Nov. 1822, Michaelmas 1826, 18 Feb. 1837, 15 May 1839); Mortgage of lands near Dublin, 21 July 1823 (Hants R.O.); Palmerston to Peel, 23 Dec. 1813 (B.M.Add.40232); Palmerston to Elizabeth Temple, 6 Feb. 1808 (D. & A., I.83); Wheatley, *London Past and Present*, III.302.
	35	Palmerston to Temple, 5, 8 Aug., 2 Dec. 1825, 17 July, 21 Oct. 1826, 19 Oct., 27 Nov. 1827 (D. & A., I.157–63, 172–8, 200, 203).
131	34	Hansard, 22 Mar. 1826, 9 Apr., 15 May 1827.
132	22	Cobbett, *Rural Rides*, pp. 483–4.

Page	Line	
133	6	Palmerston's autobiography (D. & A., I.376).
	21	Palmerston's autobiography; Palmerston to Temple, 4 May, 24 Aug. 1827 (D. & A., I.190–3, 200, 376, 379); Hardinge to Wellington, 13 Aug. 1827 (*Wellington Despatches*, IV.91). See also Harriette Wilson, p. 513.
134	5	Palmerston to Temple, 24 Aug. 1827; Palmerston's autobiography (D. & A., I.197–8, 377–9).
	28	Greville (Wilson ed.). I.318; Palmerston's autobiography (D. & A., I.379–80).
135	29	Palmerston to Temple, 18 Jan. 1828 (D. & A., I.217–20).
136	39	Palmerston's journal, 9 Mar., 4 Apr. 1828; Palmerston to Temple, 8 May 1828 (D. & A., I.255–31).
137	21	Hansard, 29, 31 Jan. 1828.
	25	Princess Lieven to Benckendorff, 16/28 Mar. 1828 (*Princess Lieven's London Letters*, p. 125).
138	1	Hansard, 26 Feb., 13, 14 May 1828.
	18	Palmerston's journal, 28 Mar. 1828 (D. & A., I.239–46).
139	22	Palmerston's journal, 19 May 1828 (D. & A., I.239–46); Broughton, V.203–4.
	38	Hansard, 27 June 1828.
140	21	Ellenborough, *A Political Diary*, I.107; Palmerston's journal, 20–29 May 1828; Palmerston's autobiography (D. & A., I.258–76, 380–1); Ellenborough's speech, in Hansard, H. L., 14 May 1855; Mrs. Arbuthnot, II.188.
141	1	Palmerston to Merry, 8 Feb., 11 Mar. 1828 (B.M.Add. 48420, ff. 100–2).
	15	Mrs. Arbuthnot, I.419; II.129, 162, 190.
	35	Greville, I.211.
142	10	Palmerston's journal, Dec. 1828 (D. & A., I.308–12).
	36	Hansard, 10 Feb., 18 Mar. 1829.
143	15	Hansard, 7 May 1829.
145	8	Hansard, 1 June 1829.
	13	Hansard, 25 Mar. 1830.
146	4	Hansard, 10 Mar. 1830.
	33	Palmerston's journal, 10, 17, 23 Jan. 1829; Palmerston to Sulivan, 13 Jan. 1829; Palmerston to Temple, 7 Jan., 30 Mar., 4, 9, 15 Dec. 1829 (D. & A., I.305, 313–33, 347–59); Broughton, III.300.
147	6	Bloomfield to Palmerston, 26 Nov. 1830 (B.M.Add. 48448).
	21	On this point, see Villiers to Palmerston, 28 May 1837 (B.M.Add.48540); Palmerston to Villiers, 15 June 1837 (B.M.Add.48537).
148	4	Webster, *The Foreign Policy of Palmerston*, p. 75; Airlie, I.173.

Page	Line	
	28	Palmerston's autobiography (D. & A., I.380–1); Palmerston to Sulivan, 7 Oct. 1829 (Lorne, pp. 56–62).
	38	Mrs. Arbuthnot, II.373.
149	37	Palmerston's autobiography (D. & A., I.381–3); Palmerston to ——, 21 Dec. 1838 (Lorne, pp. 62–4). Cf. Princess Lieven to Benckendorff, 25 Sept./7 Oct., 2/14 Oct., and two letters of 25 Oct./6 Nov. 1830 (*Princess Lieven's London Letters*, pp. 254–6, 262–3, 267).
150	34	Mrs. Arbuthnot, II.339; Princess Lieven, 'Sketch of Palmerston' (Temperley, pp. 163–8); Princess Lieven to Benckendorff, 7/19 May 1828, 8/20 Sept., Nov. 1830 (*Princess Lieven's London Letters*, pp. 132, 242, 410).
151	32	Princess Lieven to Benckendorff, 8/20, 11/23 Nov. 1830 (*Princess Lieven's London Letters*, pp. 276, 282).

CHAPTER IX

THE FOREIGN SECRETARY

152	6	In 1815, 1818, 1821, twice in 1829, in 1830, 1846, 1854, and twice in 1858.
155	7	West, *Recollections*, I.23–4; Lady Dorothy Nevill, *Under Five Reigns*, p. 92.
	14	Hertslet, *The Old Foreign Office*, pp. 24–5.
156	2	G. W. E. Russell, pp. 466–7; Tilley and Gaselee, *The Foreign Office*, p. 60–2; Hertslet, p. 61; anonymous letter to Palmerston, 31 Oct. 1832 (B.P., H.M.C., FO/A/10).
157	31	Hertslet, pp. 77–9; Palmerston to Plowden, 3 Jan. 1848 (B.M.Add.48553).
158	5	Lorne, p. 220.
	36	Hertslet, pp. 33–5, 77.
159	37	Walpole, *Life of Lord John Russell*, II.53 n.; Greville, III.136.
160	15	Duchess of Dino, *Memoirs*, I.116.
161	5	Webster, pp. 56–7; Palmerston to Victoria, 25 Feb. 1838 (*Queen Victoria's Letters*, I.(i).136); Palmerston to Bloomfield, 9 June 1840 (B.M.Add.48534); Milbanke to Palmerston, 3 Oct. 1838 (B.M.Add.48535); Palmerston to Pakenham, 15 Mar. 1837 (B.M.Add.49965).
	23	Palmerston's speech, in Hansard, 22 May 1855.
162	19	Palmerston to Lady Cowper, 21 Sept. 1831; Webster, pp. 46–54.
163	16	Fitzmaurice, I.46; Day, p. 214; Webster, pp. 56–75; Webster, 'Lord Palmerston at Work' (*Politica*, I.139); Dasent, *John Thaddeus Delane*, I.326.
164	20	Duchess of Dino, I.67. Webster, pp. 59 n., 409–10 n.; Greville (Wilson ed.) II.82–3; Malmesbury, *Memoirs of an ex-Minister*, p. 427.
	34	Leveson to Granville, 10 Mar. 1840 (Fitzmaurice, I.29).

Page	Line	
165	35	Webster, 'Lord Palmerston at Work' (*Politica*, I.139); Lady Lyttleton, p. 316; Day, p. 217; Fraser, *Disraeli and his Day*, p. 209; Broughton, V.67, 92; Vitzthum, *St Petersburg and London* I.230; Webster p. 538 n.
166	2	Hansard 12 Dec. 1837, 30 July 1860.
167	5	D. & A., II.17.
	22	Dino, I.37; Creevey, pp. 610–11; Lady Granville to Lady Carlisle, 7 Sept. 1835 (*Lady Granville's Letters*, II.196).
	39	Fortescue's journal, 14 Mar. 1860 (Hewett, . . . *and Mr. Fortescue*, p. 162); Praed, *Political and Occasional Poems*, p. 311.
168	18	Greville (Wilson ed.) II.83; Creevey, p. 618; Hewett, p. 135; Dino, I.126.
169	6	Palmerston to Victoria, 24 June 1837 (Connell, *Regina v. Palmerston*, p. 8); Palmerston to Erskine, 1 July 1834 (B.M.Add.48463); Palmerston to Granville, 3 Oct. 1834 (B.M.Add.48454).
	36	Palmerston to Wynn, 4 Feb. 1840 (B.M.Add.48503); Palmerston to Lamb, 14 Feb. 1834 (B.M.Add.48444); Palmerston to Murray, 30 Aug. 1849 (D. & A., IV.130); Palmerston to Gordon, 21 Mar. 1831 (B.M.Add.48492).
170	15	Dino, I.70, 110, 154.
	36	Talleyrand, *Mémoires*, III.406–7; Dino, I.74–5.

CHAPTER X

THE BELGIAN CRISIS OF 1831

Page	Line	
171	7	Hansard, 19 Mar. 1839, 1 Mar. 1848.
173	27	Foster to Palmerston, 10 Jan. 1831 (B.M.Add.48471).
174	16	Nelson to Dey of Algiers, 9 Jan. 1804 (Nelson, *Letters*, V.347–9).
177	32	Palmerston to Ponsonby, 1 Dec. 1830 (B.M.Add.48446).
178	7	Palmerston to Chad, 31 Dec. 1830 (B.M.Add.48480).
	39	Palmerston to Granville, 9 Mar. 1831 (D. & A., II.49).
179	27	Hansard, 18 Feb. 1831.
180	23	Palmerston to Granville, 21 Jan. 1831 (D. & A., II.29–31).
182	23	Palmerston to Granville, 8 Feb. 1831 (D. & A., II.38–9).
	38	D. & A., II.37.
183	8	Granville to Palmerston, 4 Feb. 1831; Palmerston to Granville, 8 Feb. 1831 (D. & A., II.38 and n.).
	23	D. & A., II.41, 43.
184	22	Palmerston to Ponsonby, 1 Dec. 1830 (B.M.Add.48446).
	25	Palmerston to Granville, 7 Jan. 1831 (D. & A., II.27).
185	16	Palmerston to Granville, 17 May 1831 (B.M.Add.48453).
	38	Palmerston to Bagot, 27 June 1831 (B.M.Add.48466).
186	23	Palmerston to Bagot, 5 Aug. 1831 (B.M.Add.48466).

Page	Line	
	29	D. & A., II.97.
187	7	Hansard, H.L. 9 Aug. 1831.
188	3	Hansard, 3, 6, 11, 12 Aug. 1831.
	21	Palmerston to Granville, 18 Apr. 1831 (D. & A., II.71–3); Bell, I.133.
189	9	Palmerston to Granville, 13, 17 Aug. 1831 (D. & A., II.105, 109).
	37	See, especially, Palmerston to Jerningham, 25 July, 12 Aug., 14 Oct., 16 Nov. 1834 (B.M.Add.48466); Palmerston to Minto, 26 Feb. 1834 (B.M.Add.48480).
190	9	Palmerston's journal, 31 Oct. 1831 (Lorne, p. 65).
191	2	Webster, p. 110.
	11	Palmerston to Chad, 30 Dec. 1831, 3 Feb. 1832 (B.M. Add.48480); Palmerston to Forbes, 30 Dec. 1831 (B.M.Add.48444); Palmerston to Heytesbury, 14, 31 Jan., 15 Mar. 1832 (B.M.Add.48483).

CHAPTER XI

1831: ITALY, POLAND, SPAIN

193	21	D. & A., II.50–1.
	36	Palmerston to Seymour, 7, 22 Mar., 8 Apr. 1832 (B.M. Add.48470); Palmerston to Cowley, 26 Dec. 1830, 22 Mar., 1 Apr., 19 June 1831, 7 Mar. 1832 (B.M.Add. 48444); Palmerston to Granville, 14 Jan., 15 Mar., 1 Apr. (No. 60) 1831, 6 Mar. 1832 (B.M.Add.48453).
194	26	Palmerston to Taylor, 23 June 1831 (B.M.Add.48470).
	39	Palmerston to Taylor, 2 Apr. 1831 (B.M.Add.48470).
195	28	Palmerston to Taylor, 2 Apr. 1831; Palmerston to Seymour, 20 Feb., 22 Mar. 1832 (B.M.Add.48470).
	37	Palmerston to Lamb, 15 Apr., 8 May 1832 (B.M.Add. 48444); Palmerston to Seymour, 21 Aug. 1832 (B.M.Add. 48470).
196	11	D. & A., II.47–8.
197	27	Chad to Aberdeen, 5 Dec. 1830; Palmerston's summary of Chad to Palmerston, 12 June 1831 (B.M.Add.48481).
198	2	D. & A., II.49.
	39	Webster, p. 184; Opinions of Cabinet ministers as to whether Czartoryski's letter should be received by the King, 21 Aug.–6 Sept. 1831; see especially Grant's reply, 2 Sept., and Palmerston's, 25 Aug. (B.P., H.M.C., CAB/ A/2–12); Hansard, 8 Aug. 1831.
199	28	Palmerston to Granville, 17 Jan., 22 July 1831 (B.M. Add.48453); Granville to Palmerston, 21 Jan. (No. 26), 11 Mar., 20 May, 1 June, 8 July (Nos. 296, 297), 15, 18 July 1831 (B.M.Add.44855), 25 July, 29 Aug., 24 Oct. 1831 (B.M.Add.48456).

Page	Line	
200	12	Palmerston to Heytesbury, 22 Mar., 23 Nov. 1831, 12 Mar. 1832; Palmerston to Durham, 3 July 1832 (B.M. Add.48483); Heytesbury to Palmerston, 21 Jan., 13 Apr., 15 June, 4 Aug., 1, 10 Oct., 18 Dec. 1831 (B.M.Add. 48484), 2 Jan. 1832; Durham to Palmerston, 22 Aug. 1832 (Nos. 14, 15) (B.M.Add.48485); Webster, p. 184.
	31	Czartoryski, *Memoirs*, II.323–5.
	38	Czartoryski, II.339–44.
201	10	Palmerston to Fox, 22 June 1836 (Nos. 23, 24) (B.M. Add.48496).
	22	Czartoryski, II.339–44.
202	4	Palmerston to Addington, 9 Feb. 1831 (B.M.Add.48486); Palmerston to Granville, 8 Mar., 5 July 1831 (B.M.Add. 48453).
	19	Palmerston to Lamb, 11 Feb. 1837 (B.M.Add.48496). For Palmerston's attitude, see also Hansard, 9 Aug. 1836.
	39	Palmerston to Addington, 9 Feb., 9 Dec. 1831 (B.M.Add. 48486); Addington to Palmerston, 24 Jan., 4, 14, 20 Feb. 24 Nov. 1831 (B.M.Add.48487).
203	34	Palmerston to Addington, 20 Dec. 1831, 27 Feb. 1832 (B.M.Add.48486).

CHAPTER XII

THE REFORM BILL: THE NEW FOREIGN POLICY

204	18	*State Trials* (*New Series*), II.803–74.
205	2	Hansard, 8 Feb. 1831.
	7	Greville, II.229.
	15	Broughton, IV.96.
206	16	Hansard, 3 Mar. 1831; Broughton, IV.90.
	32	Cooper, *Annals of Cambridge*, IV.570.
207	14	Broughton, IV.198.
208	2	Grenville, II.211–13; Mrs Arbuthnot, II.437; Broughton, IV.241; Torrens, *Memoirs of Melbourne*, I.401–6.
	14	Torrens, I.408; Greville, II.252–8.
209	6	*The Times*, 20 Nov. 1832.
210	2	*The Times*, 17 Dec. 1832.
211	21	Praed, pp. 201–3.
	34	Hansard, 17 July 1834.
212	35	Grant, *Random Recollections of the House of Commons*, I.218.
213	8	Fraser, *Disraeli and his day*, p. 7.
	30	*The Times*, 22 Feb. 1836; Webster, p. 48 n.; Hansard, 18 Aug. 1831.
	38	Webster, p. 43 n.
214	12	Webb, *History of Trade Unionism*, p. 166 and n.
215	6	Hansard, 28 June, 16, 20 July, 7 Aug, 1832.

CHAPTER XIII

THE QUADRUPLE ALLIANCE

Page	Line	
	34	Princess Lieven to Benckendorff, 5/17 Oct. 1833 (*Princess Lieven's London Correspondence*, p. 358); Dino, I.162.
237	4	Palmerston to Temple, 21 Apr. 1834 (D. & A., II.181).
	29	Dino, I.91–2; Palmerston to Backhouse, 13 June 1834; Palmerston to Villiers, June 1834 (B.M.Add.48486).
	38	Webster, pp. 399–400.
238	14	Webster, p. 400; Villiers to Palmerston, 8 Oct. 1834 (B.M.Add.48489); Palmerston to Villiers, 20 June 1834 (B.M.Add.48486).
	34	Barnard to Palmerston, 10 Jan., 12 Feb. (Nos. 6, 7), 12 Mar., 20 May, 22 June 1832, 25 May, 17 June, 2, 13 July, 23 Sept. 1833 (B.M.Add.48462); Lamb to Palmerston, 17 Apr. 1834 (Nos. 35, 38) (B.M.Add. 48445).
239	23	Morier to Palmerston, 21 June 1833, 30 Jan., 8, 17, 22 Feb., 4, 13 (Nos. 18, 19), 18, 24 Mar., 10, 14, 22 Apr., 21 May, 19 (Nos. 34, 35), 27, 30 June, 26 July, 25 Oct. 1834; Palmerston to Morier, 31 Oct., 16 Nov. 1834 (B.M.Add.48491); Palmerston to Lamb, 19 Nov. 1833 (B.M.Add.48444); Lamb to Palmerston, 15 Mar., 19 Apr., 12 May 1834 (B.M.Add.48445); Palmerston to Cartwright, 15 Apr. 1834 (B.M.Add.48459).
240	1	Palmerston to Cartwright, 20 Sept, 1833 (B.M.Add. 48459).
	13	Hansard, 21, 25 Mar. 1834.
	23	Hansard, 3, 9 June 1834, 27 July 1838, 3 Aug. 1840.
241	20	Cartwright to Palmerston, 12 Apr. 1834 (B.M.Add. 48461); Palmerston to Cartwright, 15 May 1834 (B.M. Add.48459).
	36	Cartwright to Palmerston, 11, 21 June 1834 (B.M.Add. 48461).
242	21	Palmerston to Cartwright, 20 May, 4, 13 July, 16 Nov. 1834 (B.M.Add.48459); Cartwright to Palmerston, 29 Sept., 1 Oct. 1834 (B.M.Add.48461).
	34	Palmerston to Cartwright, 7 July, 26 Nov. 1835 (B.M. Add.48514).
243	19	Palmerston to Abercrombie, 12, 27 Feb., 2, 22 Apr. 1839 (B.M.Add.48514); Molyneux to Palmerston, 2 Feb. 1839; Abercrombie to Palmerston, 19, 26 Feb., 16, 25 Apr. 1839 (B.M.Add.48516).
	26	Abercrombie to Palmerston, 16, 24 Apr. 1839 (B.M.Add. 48516); Palmerston to Abercrombie, 7 May 1839 (B.M.Add.48514).
244	3	Webster, p. 321.
	23	Palmerston to Lyons, 28 Sept. 1837 (B.M.Add.48517); Palmerston to Howard de Walden, 12 Dec. 1839 (B.M. Add.45176).

Page	Line	
246	23	For the controversy over Sir Stratford Canning's appointment to Russia, see Webster, pp. 321–32. See also Princess Lieven to Aberdeen, 11/23 Oct. 1834 (Correspondence of Aberdeen and Princess Lieven, I.19).
247	6	Palmerston to Temple, 27 June 1834 (D. & A., II.199); Webster, p. 331; Dino, I.141, 145.

CHAPTER XIV THE DIFFICULTIES WITH PORTUGAL

248	8	Palmerston to Temple, 9 July, 29 Sept. 1836 (D. & A., III.13, 15).
	20	Palmerston's note, at end of B.M.Add.48452.
	29	Webster, p. 409; Metternich to Hummelauer, 29 Nov. 1834 (Mémoires de Metternich, V.643).
249	15	Palmerston to Temple, 25 Nov. 1834 (D. & A., II.213); Webster, p. 417 and n.; Palmerston to Howard de Walden, 4 Nov. 1837 (B.M.Add.45176).
	39	Palmerston to Temple, 16 Nov. 1834 (D. & A., II.207–8).
250	14	Webster, p. 417 and n.; The Times, 14, 17, 23 Jan. 1835; Greville, III.197–8; Mrs Arbuthnot, II.190.
	33	Webster, pp. 418–21; Bell, I.203–4.
251	7	Hansard, 22 May 1835; Webster, p. 417 and n.
252	36	Palmerston to Howard de Walden, 10 May, 13 June 1835 (B.M.Add.48439).
253	15	Palmerston to Howard de Walden, 13 June 1835 (B.M. Add.48439).
	23	Palmerston to Howard de Walden, 18 Dec. 1835 (B.M. Add.48440).
254	6	Torrens, p. 380; Hansard, 13 July 1830.
	36	Hansard, 29, 30 Mar., 6 Apr., 22, 28 May 1838; Snell, Palmerston's Borough, p. 68.
256	6	Palmerston to Howard de Walden, 25 Apr. 1836 (B.M. Add.48526).
257	3	Palmerston to Howard de Walden, 14 Dec. 1835 (B.M. Add.48440), 23 Jan. 1836 (B.M.Add.48441).
258	14	Palmerston to Howard de Walden, 20 Feb. 1836; Howard de Walden to Palmerston, 23 Jan. 1836 (B.M. Add.48441).
	37	Howard de Walden to Palmerston, 10 Sept. (despatch and private letter), 17, 23 Sept., 3 Oct. 1836 (B.M.Add. 48442); 11, 12, 24, 28 Sept., 1, 8, 18 Oct. 1836 (Nos. 256, 257, 258) (B.M.Add.48528); Sulivan to Palmerston, 10, 12 Sept. 1836 (B.M.Add.48442).
259	18	Palmerston to Howard de Walden, 19 Sept., 1, 11 Oct. 1836 (B.M.Add.48442).
260	19	Howard de Walden to Palmerston, 3, 8 Oct. 1836; Palmerston to Howard de Walden, 19 Sept., 8, 13 Oct. 1836 (B.M.Add.48442); Palmerston to Howard de Walden, 8 Oct. 1836 (B.M.Add.48526).

Page	Line	
		48538); Palmerston to Granville, 14 Mar. 1836 (B.M. Add. 48506); Cowley to Palmerston, 24 Apr. 1835; Aston to Palmerston, 21 Sept. 1835; Granville to Palmerston, 25 Sept. 1835 (B.M.Add.48509).
	23	Webster, p. 429.
271	4	Hansard, 24 June 1835; H.L., 14, 18 Mar. 1836.
	24	Palmerston to Villiers, 20 June 1836, 26 Jan., 16 Nov. 1837, 9 Apr. 1838 (B.M.Add.48537); Palmerston to Granville, 18 Aug. 1837 (B.M.Add.48507).
	31	Palmerston to Villiers, 10 June 1836 (B.M.Add.48537).
272	34	Villiers to Palmerston, 1, 11, 18, 31 Aug., 19, 23, 27 Sept., 21, 28 Nov. 1835, 5 Apr. 1836 (B.M.Add.48539); Palmerston to Villiers, 12 Sept. 1836 (B.M.Add.48537).
273	20	Villiers to Palmerston, 25 Jan, 27 Feb., 7, 22 Mar. 1836 (B.M.Add.48539); Palmerston to Villiers, 21 July 1835 (B.M.Add.48537); Palmerston to Aston, 29 July 1836 (No. 22) (B.M.Add.48506); Webster, pp. 425, 432.
274	3	Webster, p. 469 n.; Hansard, 5, 26 Feb., 5, 15, 16 Aug. 1836, 10 Mar., 18, 19 Apr., 12 Dec. 1837, 13, 26, 27 Mar., 26 June 1838; H.L., 21 Apr. 1837, 22 May, 19 June 1838.
	33	Hansard, 5 Feb. 1836.
275	39	Hansard, 19 Apr. 1837.
276	33	Webster, p. 441 and n.; Palmerston to Villiers, 2 June 1836 (B.M.Add.48537); Palmerston to Granville, 2 June 1836 (No. 98) (B.M.Add.48506).
277	30	Palmerston to Villiers, 12 Sept., 31 Oct. 1836 (B.M.Add. 48537).
278	10	Palmerston to Howard de Walden, 17 Nov. 1838 (B.M.Add.48526).
279	2	Palmerston to Villiers (Clarendon), 21 Dec. 1835 (Nos. 49, 50), 25 Mar., 17 Nov. 1836, 6 Jan. (No. 3), 13, 27 July 1837, 22 Mar. 1838 (B.M.Add.48537), 7 Feb. 1839; Palmerston to Southern, 14 Nov. 1839; Palmerston to Aston, 11 June 1840 (B.M.Add.48538); Webster, p. 439.
	27	Palmerston to Villiers, 14 Sept. 1836, 4 May, 2 Sept., 24 Oct., 14 Dec. 1837 (B.M.Add.48537); Villiers to Mrs Lister, 16 Sept. 1837 (Maxwell, *Life of Clarendon*, I.133); Webster, p. 453.
280	5	Palmerston to Villiers, 22 Mar. (No. 58), 9 Apr., 3 May 1838; Palmerston to Hervey, 26 July, 16 Aug. 1838 (B.M.Add.48537).
	26	Palmerston to Villiers, 25 Jan., 4 Sept. 1838 (B.M.Add. 48537).
281	13	Milbanke to Palmerston, 26 Jan. 1839 (B.M.Add.48497); Palmerston to Villiers (Clarendon), 21 July 1835, 20 June, 14 July 1836 (No. 57), 19 Oct., 28 Dec. 1837,

5 May, 5, 13 July 1838 (B.M.Add.48537), 10 Jan. 1839 (B.M.Add.48538); Southern to Palmerston, 24 Aug., 7 Sept. 1839 (B.M.Add.48541).

| | 33 | Carr, *Spain 1808–1939* p. 239; Aston to Palmerston, 11 Oct. 1840 (B.M.Add.48542). |

282   23   Palmerston to Lord W. Russell, 4 Dec. 1840 (B.M.Add. 48531).

283   2   Palmerston to Southern, 11, 18 July, 8 Aug. 1839; Palmerston to Jerningham, 2 Apr. (No. 27), 14 May, 3 Sept. (No. 40), 29 Oct., 26 Nov. (Nos. 68, 77), 25 Dec. 1840 (No. 93), 21, 23 Jan., 19 Feb., 25 Mar. 1841 (B.M.Add.48538); Hansard, 26 June 1838, 22 July 1839.

        24   Palmerston to Aston, 5 Apr. (No. 43), 2 Sept. 1841 (B.M.Add.48538); Aston to Palmerston, 4 Apr. 1841 (No. 73) (B.M.Add.48542).

284   19   Palmerston to Aston, 17, 25 Dec. 1840 (No. 95), 14, 16 Feb. 1841 (No. 21) (B.M.Add.48538); Aston to Palmerston, 19 Oct. (No. 121), 14 Nov. 1840 (B.M.Add. 48542); Palmerston to Howard de Walden, 21 Nov., 5, 17 Dec. 1840, 23 Jan., 27 Feb. 1841 (B.M.Add.48527), 5 Dec. 1840 (B.M.Add.48443); Howard de Walden to Palmerston, 22, 25 Oct., 11, 14 Dec. 1840 (B.M.Add. 48530).

CHAPTER XVI

MEHEMET ALI: THE CRISIS OF 1839

286   37   Campbell to Palmerston, 25 June 1833 (B.M.Add. 48452); Palmerston to Campbell, 2 Oct. 1833 (B.M.Add. 48451); Hansard, 24 May, 28 Aug. 1833.

287   20   Bell, I.297.

288   29   Webster, p. 275.

289   5   Palmerston to Campbell, 3 Sept., 5 Oct. 1835 (B.M.Add. 38505); Palmerston to Ponsonby, 6 Feb. 1838 (B.M.Add. 48543).

290   2   Palmerston to Campbell, 23 Nov. 1833 (B.M.Add.48451).

291   5   Webster, pp. 340–1, 598–600, 605.

        39   Ponsonby to Palmerston, 15 May, 10 (Nos. 81, 32), 28 June, 14, 15 (Nos. 112, 115), 22 July, 20 Aug., 7, 14, 25 Sept., 18 Nov. 1836 (Nos. 215, 218, 219) (B.M.Add. 48545); Palmerston to Ponsonby, 11 Nov. 1836 (B.M. Add.48543); Webster, pp. 530–5.

292   25   Howard de Walden to Palmerston, 14 June, 26 Aug., 6 Nov. 1833 (B.M.Add.48450); Granville to Palmerston, 28 Oct. 1833, 17, 20 Jan., 24 Mar., 30 May 1834 (B.M. Add.48458); Palmerston to Granville, 7 Jan., 25 Feb., 3 June, 8 July 1834 (B.M.Add.48454); Palmerston to Bloomfield, 26 Apr., 17 May 1836, 13 Nov. 1838 (B.M.

Page	Line	
302	23	Airlie, I.xiii; II.30.
303	19	Palmerston to Beauvale, 28 June 1839; Palmerston to Clanricarde, 9 July 1839 (*Lev. Pap.*, I.117–19, 156–8).
304	15	Campbell to Palmerston, 28 July, 7 Aug. 1839; Campbell to Ponsonby, 6 Aug. 1839; Palmerston to Campbell, 26 Sept. 1839; Palmerston to Hodges, 27 Sept. 1839; Hodges to Palmerston, 23 Aug. 1840; Palmerston to Beauvale, 16 Oct. 1839 (*Lev. Pap.*, I.322–3, 339–40, 401, 425, 622–3, 633; II.173, 244).
	22	Webster, p. 629.
	38	Palmerston to Granville, 27 May 1839 (Bell, I.295); Palmerston to Murray, 30 Aug. 1849 (D. & A., IV.131).
305	24	D. & A., II.298–9.
306	24	Clanricarde to Palmerston, 15 July 1839 (No. 133); Pisani to Ponsonby, 22 July 1839; Ponsonby to Palmerston, 26 July 1839 (*Lev. Pap.*, I.177, 280, 292); Palmerston to Beauvale, 1 Aug. 1839 (B.M.Add.48496).
307	9	Ponsonby to Palmerston, 29 July 1839; Note of the Five Powers, 27 July 1839; Pisani to Ponsonby, 28 July 1839 (*Lev. Pap.*, I.292–5); Webster, pp. 633–6.

CHAPTER XVII

MEHEMET ALI: THE CRISIS OF 1840

308	6	Summary of the four Consuls' talk with Mehemet Ali, 14 July 1839; Mehemet Ali to Grand Vizier, 16 July 1839; Ponsonby to Reschid Pasha, 25 Oct. 1839 (*Lev. Pap.*, I.244–9, 296–7, 484–5).
	16	Webster, p. 46.
309	8	Webster, p. 657; Beauvale to Palmerston, 3 May 1841 (B.M.Add.48498).
310	17	Palmerston to Bulwer, 10 Sept. 1839; Palmerston to Beauvale, 12 Mar. 1840 (*Lev. Pap.*, I.366–70, 600–3).
	36	Palmerston to Beauvale, 26 July 1839 (B.M.Add.48496).
311	24	Palmerston to Beauvale, 1 Aug. 1839 (B.M.Add.48496).
312	4	Palmerston to Granville, 29 Oct. 1839 (B.M.Add.48507); Webster, pp. 653–4.
	32	Airlie, I.xiii; II.30–1; Bell, I.259; Trollope, *Lord Palmerston*, p. 75; Longford, *Victoria R. I.*, p. 185.
313	8	Lady Palmerston to Mrs Huskisson, 26 Dec. 1839, 19 Mar. 1840 (B.M.Add.39949); Lady Granville to Lady Carlisle, 7 Dec. 1839 (*Lady Granville's Letters*, II.296–7).
314	10	Neumann to Metternich, 30 Dec. 1839; Webster, pp. 660–3, 678, 867–72).
315	3	Neumann to Metternich, 31 Dec. 1839; Webster, pp. 663–4, 666–8, 876; Palmerston to Bulwer, 24 Sept.

Page	*Line*	

1839; Palmerston to Hobhouse, 27 July, 1843 (D. & A., II.302; III.428).

31 Palmerston to Temple, 27 Oct. 1837, 26 Jan. 1838, 31 Jan., 13 (Nos. 10, 11), 26 Mar. 1840; Palmerston to Kennedy, 28 Jan., 4 Feb. 1840; Kennedy to Palmerston, 1 Sept. 1838, 27 May 1839 (B.M.Add.48522), 4 Jan. 1840 (B.M.Add.48524); Temple to Palmerston, 26 Sept. 1837 (B.M.Add.48523).

316 10 Granville to Palmerston, 1 May 1840 (B.M.Add.48511).

317 6 Beauvale to Palmerston, 15 (Nos. 47, 48), 24 Apr. 1840 (Nos. 57, 58) (B.M.Add.48497); Palmerston to Beauvale, 28 Apr., 6 May 1840 (Nos. 57, 58) (B.M.Add.48496).

35 Palmerston to Granville, 10, 17, 23 Apr. (Nos. 152, 153), 26 May 1840 (B.M.Add.48507), 23 June, 31 July 1840; Palmerston to Bulwer, 9 July 1840 (B.M.Add.48508); Granville to Palmerston, 6, 10, 13, 17, 20, 27, 30 Apr., 2, 4, 11, 13, 22, 29 May 1840 (B.M.Add.48511), 5 June 1840; Bulwer to Palmerston, 6 July 1840 (B.M.Add. 48512); Palmerston to Temple, 14, 17, 20 Apr., 1, 5, 26 May, 26 Aug. 1840 (B.M.Add.48522); 13 Mar., 20 Apr., 13 May, 13 July 1840 (D. & A., III.31–3, 35–8, 40); Temple to Palmerston, 1 (Nos. 21, 22), 14, 18 (Nos. 18, 19), 19, 22 (Nos. 21, 22), 24, 25, 29 Apr., 11 May, 13 June, 19, 21, 30 July, 15 Aug. 1840 (B.M. Add.48524).

318 37 Palmerston to Bulwer, 21 July 1840 (*Lev. Pap.*, II.8–10); Webster, p. 683.

319 11 Webster, p. 686.

36 Palmerston to Melbourne, 5 July 1840 (D. & A., II.356–61).

320 24 Convention of London, and Separate Act, 15 July 1840 (D. & A., II.420–7); Webster, p. 695.

321 7 Palmerston's memorandum to Guizot, 15 July 1840; Palmerston to Bulwer, 22 July 1840; Bulwer to Palmerston, 20, 27 July 1840 (*Lev. Pap.*, II.1–3, 7–8, 10–13, 37–40); Granville to Palmerston, 9 Oct., 14 Dec. 1840 (B.M.Add.48512); Erskine to Palmerston, 19 Feb. 1841 (B.M.Add.48516); Lord W. Russell to Palmerston, 28 Oct., 25 Nov. 1840 (B.M.Add.48533).

27 Palmerston to Bulwer, 21, 22 July, 23 Aug., 22 Sept. 1840 (D. & A., II.315–21, 327); Barrington, 'Sketches of Men of Mark', f.15 (Lambton MS.).

322 2 Palmerston to Hodges, 18 July 1840 (*Lev. Pap.*, II.4–5).

27 Webster, pp. 694, 710; Melbourne to Russell, 19, 26 Aug., 16, 19 (two letters), 26, 28, 29 Sept., 23, 31 Oct., 1 Nov. 1840; Clarendon to Melbourne, 31 Aug. 1840; Ellice to Melbourne, 16 Sept. 1840 (Sanders, *Lord*

Page	Line	
		Melbourne's Papers, pp. 460–2, 467–75, 477–83, 485–7, 491–2); Lady Palmerston to Mrs. Huskisson, 19 Mar. 1840 (B.M.Add.39949); Guizot to Princess Lieven, 14, 16 Mar., 21 May, 17 Sept., 20 Oct. 1840 (*Lettres de Guizot et de la Princesse de Lieven*, II.25, 28, 146, 205, 267).
323	12	Palmerston to Bulwer, 22 July 1840 (D. & A., II.318); Palmerston to Melbourne, 16 Sept., 8 Oct. 1840 (Sanders, pp. 386, 475–6); Webster, p. 710 n.; Hodder, *Life of Shaftesbury*, I.315; Metternich to Frederick William IV, 9 Oct. 1840 (*Mémoires de Metternich*, VI.490).
	38	Hansard, 22 June 1840; Urquhart to Melbourne, 6 Aug. 1840 (B.P., H.M.C., CAB/A/47); Webster, p. 720.
324	5	Webster, p. 720.
	23	Granville to Palmerston, 15, 19 Oct. 1840 (B.M. Add 48512); Palmerston to Granville, 19 Oct. 1840 (B.M. Add.48508); Brief to Attorney-General, with enclosures; Opinion of Attorney-General and others, 18 Nov. 1840 (B.P., H.M.C., FO/H/79); Palmerston's Account Book (B.M.Add.48584, entries dated 15 Aug., 4 Sept. 20 Oct., 2 Dec. 1840).
325	9	Palmerston to Bulwer, 22 Sept. 1840 (D. & A., II.327–8).
	22	Minutes of the four Consuls' talk with Mehemet Ali, 17, 25 Aug. 1840; Hodges to Palmerston, 20 Sept. 1840; Ponsonby to Hodges, 16 Sept. 1840 (*Lev. Pap.*, II.154–7, 174–6, 249, 253).
326	16	Thiers to Guizot, 8 Oct. 1840; Palmerston to Ponsonby 15 Oct. 1840 (*Lev. Pap.*, II.270–4, 311–12); Palmerston to Bulwer, 3 Oct. 1840 (D. & A., II.333).
327	6	Webster, pp. 722–3; Palmerston to Melbourne, 25 Oct. 1840; Louis Philippe to Leopold I (Sanders, pp. 487–90, 492).
	20	Palmerston to Granville, 22 Apr. 1831 (D. & A., II.74–5).
328	3	Palmerston to Victoria, 11 Nov. 1840 (Connell, *Regina v. Palmerston*, pp. 25–7).
	11 /	Palmerston to Granville, 9, 16 May 1840 (B.M.Add. 48507); Webster, p. 683.
	15	Palmerston to Seymour, 10 July, 26 Aug., 11 Sept., 17 Dec. 1840, 20 Apr., 4 May, 7 June, 6, 13 Aug. 1841 (B.M.Add.48499); Seymour to Palmerston, 15, 21 July, 4 Sept., 15 Dec. 1840, 19 Jan., 13 (Nos. 56, 57), 20, 27 Apr., 11 May, 13, 16, 23 July, 7, 10, 17 Aug. 1841 (B.M.Add.48502); Palmerston to Granville, 22 Dec. 1840; Palmerston to Bulwer, Aug. (No. 132), 24 Aug., 2 Sept. 1841 (B.M.Add.48508); Granville to Palmerston, 25 Dec. 1840 (B.M.Add.48512); Bulwer to Palmerston,

CHAPTER XVIII

THE OPIUM WAR

Page	Line	
339	17	Morse, *International Relations of the Chinese Empire*, I.68, 88, 90–1.
	34	Morse I.49 54, 57, 68–72.
340	10	Morse, I.108–9.
341	19	Hansard, 9 Apr. 1840.
342	9	Palmerston to Elliot, 22 July 1836, 12 June 1837 (*China Papers*, pp. 124–2, 149).
343	18	Elliot to Palmerston, 25 Jan. 1836 (*China Pap.*, p. 136); Morse, I.155, 172, 175, 185–9, 196, 214–19.
344	3	Palmerston to Elliot, 22 July, 8 Nov. 1836, 15 June 1838 (*China Pap.*, pp. 121–2, 129, 260); Morse, I.208.
	15	Hansard, 28 July 1838.
	25	Palmerston to Robinson, 6 June 1836 (*China Pap.*, pp. 111–12); Morse, I.152–3.
345	5	Elliot to Palmerston, 8, 13 Dec. 1838; Palmerston to Elliot, 15 Apr. 1839 (*China Pap.*, pp. 325–7); Morse, I.197–9.
	25	Morse, I.215–33.
346	13	Morse, I.237–8, 243–7.
347	23	Palmerston to Minister of Emperor of China, 20 Feb. 1840 (Morse, I.621–6).
	37	Palmerston to Elliot and Elliot, 20 Feb. 1840 (Morse, I.626–30).
	39	Hansard, 7, 8, 9 Apr. 1840.
350	3	Hansard, 9 Apr. 1840.
	18	Morse, I.256.
	37	Hansard, 9 Apr. 1840.
351	22	Elliot to Auckland, 21 June 1841; Morse, I.266–71, 274–5, 283–6, 648–54; Palmerston to Victoria, 10 Apr. 1841; Victoria to Leopold I, 13 Apr. 1841 (*Queen Victoria's Letters*, I(i).260–1); Melbourne to Russell, 30 Apr. 1841 (Sanders, pp. 493–4).
352	10	Palmerston to Elliot, 21 Apr. 1841 (Morse, I.641–3).
	15	Morse, I.279–80.
	35	Hansard, 17 Mar. 1842, 4 Aug. 1843; Elliot to Auckland, 21 June 1841 (Morse, I.649).
353	12	Palmerston to Elliot, 26 Feb. 1841 (*Opium Trade Papers*, p. 1 n.); Palmerston to Pottinger, 31 May 1841 (Morse, I.658–9).
	39	Hansard, 4 Aug. 1843.
354	28	Palmerston to Bligh, 16 June 1834 (B.M.Add.48483); Bligh to Palmerston, 2 July 1834 (B.M.Add.48485); *Daily Telegraph*, 17 July 1969 (note on Florence Nightingale's letters).
	31	Palmerston to Elliot, 21 Apr. 1841 (Morse, I.642).
355	10	Webster, pp. 750–1.

Page	Line	
356	6	Hansard, 12 Apr. 1858.
	24	Motley to Layard, 7 Jan. 1862 (B.M.Add.38988).
357	24	Hansard, H.L., 7 Apr. 1843.
358	6	Bell, II.242–3; Palmerston's summary of Vaughan's despatch to Aberdeen, 20 Nov. 1830 (B.M.Add. 49964).
	28	Hansard, H.L., 11 May 1819.
	38	Palmerston's summary of Vaughan's despatch of 9 May 1831 (B.M.Add.49964).
359	15	Palmerston to Crampton, 13 July 1849 (B.M.Add. 48575).
360	17	Palmerston to Vaughan, 25 Feb., 21 Dec 1833 (B.M. Add.49963); Palmerston to Bagot, 9 Jan. 1831 (B.M.Add. 48466); McLane to Vaughan, 11 Mar. 1834; Vaughan to McLane, 20 Mar. 1834 (B.M.Add.49964); Hansard, 12 June 1849, 17 June 1851; Palmerston's memorandum, 20 Oct. 1862 (B.M.Add.38988).
361	3	Bankhead to Palmerston, 21 Oct., 5 Nov. 1831; Vaughan to Palmerston, 28 Oct. 1833 (B.M.Add.49964); Palmerston to Fox, 8, 22 July 1837, 6 Oct. 1838, 6 Apr., 17 Sept., 14 Oct. 1839, 19 Feb. 1840, 19 July 1841 (B.M.Add.48495); Hansard, 24 Apr. 1837; *Cambridge History of British Foreign Policy*, II.243.
	19	Bell, I.251; Hansard, H.L., 7 Apr. 1843.
362	27	Hansard, 11 Aug. 1843; Vaughan to Palmerston, 4 Jan. 1831; Bankhead to Palmerston, 21 May 1832 (B.M.Add. 49964); Palmerston to Bankhead, 20 Feb. 1836 (B.M. Add.48495); Bulwer to Palmerston, 29 Sept. 1850 (B.M.Add.48576).
363	27	Palmerston to Packenham, 2 Oct., 14 Nov. 1835, 15 Dec. 1836, 15 Mar. 1837; Palmerston to Ashburnham, 15 Jan. 1838 (B.M.Add.49965); Palmerston to Addington, 28 Dec. 1832 (B.M.Add.48486); Pakenham to Palmerston, 6 May 1833 (B.M.Add.49966).
364	22	Hansard, 5 Aug. 1836, 9 Mar. 1837; Palmerston to Pakenham, 15 Aug. 1836, 15 Feb. 1840 (B.M.Add. 49965); Palmerston to Fox, 15 Nov. 1836, 6 Feb. 1837 (B.M.Add.48495); Pakenham to Palmerston, 27 May 1836 (B.M.Add.49967).
	30	Palmerston to Pakenham, 16 Dec. 1839 (B.M.Add. 49965).
365	33	Palmerston to Bulwer, 21 Aug. 1841 (B.M.Add.48508).
366	23	Palmerston to Ashburnham, 11, 15 Sept. 1838, 12 Apr. 1839 (B.M.Add.49965); Ashburnham to Palmerston, 31 Jan., 5 May, 5 Nov., 10, 31 Dec. 1838 (Nos. 113, 114, 116); Pakenham to Palmerston, 3, 5 Jan. 1839 (B.M.Add.

Page	Line	
		49967); Palmerston to Aston, 11, 15 Sept. 1838; Palmerston to Granville, 19 Feb. 1839 (B.M.Add.48507.)
367	2	Palmerston to Ashburnham, 21 July 1838 (B.M.Add. 49965); Palmerston to Aston, 7 Aug. 1838 (Nos. 21, 25); Palmerston to Granville, 30 Oct. 1838 (B.M.Add. 48507); Hansard, 27 July 1838, 1, 11, 19 Mar. 1839, 31 Jan. 1840.
	36	Palmerston to Fox, 9, 13 Jan., 10 Mar., 22 Nov., 15 Dec. 1838, 19 Jan. 1839 (B.M.Add.48495); Doughty, 'Papineau' (*Encyclopaedia Britannica*, 13th ed.).
368	19	Palmerston to Fox, 19 Jan., 9 Feb. (Nos. 4, 5), 2 Apr. 1841 (B.M.Add.48495).
369	12	Palmerston to Wynn, 31 Dec. 1840, 18 Mar., Mar. (No. 5) 1841 (B.M.Add.48503).
370	10	Palmerston to Fox, 9 Feb. 1841 (despatch and letter) (B.M.Add.48495; D. & A., III.48–50).
	26	Palmerston to Temple, 9 Feb. 1841 (D. & A., III.46).
371	1	Webster to Fox, 24 Apr. 1841; Webster to Crittenden, 15 Mar. 1841 (*St. Pap.*, XXIX.1129–42); Palmerston to Fox, 5 Mar. 1841 (B.M.Add.48495).
	19	Bell, I.247–8; Hansard, 26 Aug. 1841.
	30	Palmerston to Fox, 3, 18 Apr., 29 June, 18 Aug. 1841 (B.M.Add.48495); Hansard, 8, 9 Feb., 5 Mar., 6 Apr., 6 May, 26 Aug. 1841; Lady Palmerston to Mrs Huskisson, 28 Aug. 1841 (B.M.Add.39949).
372	20	Bell, I.240–1.
	38	Bell, I.253; *Cambridge History of British Foreign Policy*, II.259 n.

CHAPTER XX

IN OPPOSITION: THE WEBSTER-ASHBURTON TREATY

Page	Line	
374	2	Praed, pp. 316–18.
	21	Disraeli, *Tancred*, Book III, chap. 6.
375	22	Greville (Wilson ed.) II.88; Fulford, *The Prince Consort*, p. 61 n.
376	37	Hansard, 16 July 1844; Palmerston to the Lords of the Admiralty, 28 July 1841 (*The Exchequer Reports*, II.180).
377	23	Hansard, 18 May 1841.
	38	Greville, V.1–2, 5; Broughton, VI.22–7; Hansard, June 1841; Snell, *Palmerston's Borough*, pp. 47–67, 71, 106–7.
378	36	Gregg, *Social and Economic History of Britain*, p. 183; Hansard, 21 May 1847, 16 July 1858; H.L., 7 Apr., 1 June 1837.
379	13	Hansard, H.L., 12 Mar. 1838, 24 Jan. 1840.

Page	Line	
	22	Hansard, 4 June 1834.
	34	*The Times*, 22 June 1841.
380	13	*The Times*, 27 July 1837; Snell, p. 79.
	30	Snell, p. 104.
381	2	Snell, pp. 96–7.
	30	*The Times*, 3 July 1841.
382	16	Bulwer to Palmerston, 13 Aug. 1841; Palmerston to Bulwer, 17 Aug. 1841 (D. & A., II.376–9, 383).
383	13	*The Times*, 30 June 1841.
384	3	Palmerston to Bulwer, 10 Aug. 1841; Bulwer to Palmerston, 13 Aug. 1841 (D. & A., II.375, 377); Princess Lieven to Guizot, 22 Aug. 1841; Guizot to Princess Lieven, 23 Aug. 1841 (*Lettres Guizot–Lieven*, III.14–17).
	12	Lady Palmerston to Mrs Huskisson, 18 Oct. 1841 (B.M.Add.39949); Palmerston to Temple, 26 Nov. 1841 (D. & A., III.86–9).
	26	Palmerston to Temple, 21 Apr. 1834, 19 Jan. 1842, 29 May, 25 Dec. 1843, 5 Jan. 1844; Shaftesbury to Ashley, 6 Jan 1876 (D. & A., II.185; III.89, 125, 133; V.322); Palmerston's Account Book (B.M.Add.48586, entry for 26 Jan. 1842); Hayward to Gladstone, 5 Nov. 1838 (*Hayward's Letters*, II.13); Lorne, p. 223.
385	26	D. & A., V.199–200; Day, pp. 213–15; Cook, *A History of the English Turf*, p. 498; Marquis of Exeter to Palmerston, 1845 (B.P., H.M.C., Calendar); Hansard, 14, 21 Feb., 4, 10, 11, 13 July 1844.
386	4	Airlie, II.121; Webster, p. 75; Lady Palmerston to Mrs Huskisson, 19 Mar. 1840 (B.M.Add.39949).
	19	Palmerston to Temple, 22 Mar., 6 Dec. 1842 (D. & A., III.101, 119).
387	5	Lady Palmerston to Mrs Huskisson, 1 Mar. 1841 (B.M.Add.39949); Palmerston to Temple, 1 Sept. 1842 (D. & A., III.109).
	23	Palmerston to Temple, 19 Jan. 1842 (D. & A., III.89–90); Lady Palmerston to Mrs Huskisson, 18 Oct. 1841, 6 Mar. 1843 (B.M.Add.39949); Lady Cowper to Lady de Grey, Jan. 1842 (Cowper, *Earl Cowper*, p. 5).
	26	Palmerston to Lewis, 1 Sept. 1861 (B.M.Add.48582).
	38	Palmerston to Temple, 1 Sept. 1842 (D. & A., III.109–10).
389	14	Talleyrand, *Mémoires*, III.406–7.
391	4	Palmerston to Temple, 1 Sept. 1842 (D. & A., III.110–11).
392	17	Hansard, 21 Mar. 1843; *The Times*, 22 Mar. 1843.
	20	Bankhead to Palmerston, 13 July 1831 (B.M.Add.49964).
	29	Bell, I.334–5.

Page	Line	
	38	Bell, I.335.
393	19	Hansard, 4 Feb. 1845; Longford, *Victoria R. I.*, p. 189 n.
	31	Palmerston to Temple, 30 May–5 June 1844 (D. & A., III.137–8).
394	12	Palmerston to Granville, 14 Feb. 1840 (B.M.Add. 48507); Hansard, 4 Feb. 1845.
	34	Palmerston to Temple, 5 Jan. 1844; D. & A., III.64, 135; Hansard, 28 July 1843.

CHAPTER XXI

THE TEN HOURS BILL: FOREIGN TRAVELS

395	14	Airlie, I.150–1.
396	8	Lady Dorothy Nevill, *Under Five Reigns*, p. 148.
397	12	Hodder, I.310–11.
	24	Hansard, 22 June, 4, 5 July, 4, 6 Aug. 1842.
398	3	Ashley, anonymous book review in *Quarterly Review*, LXVII.180 (Dec. 1840).
399	25	D. & A., III.127–9.
400	4	Hansard, 15, 18, 22, 29 Mar., 3, 13 May 1844.
	29	Hansard, 25 July 1842.
401	4	Hansard, 27 Feb. 1822, 27 May, 10 July, 6 Aug. 1840, 25 May 1841, 1 Mar. 1842; D. & A., I.2.
	30	Hansard, 23 June, 12 July 1843, 24 June, 1, 2, 18, 19 July 1844, 4, 18, 19, 20, 21, 28 Feb., 24 Apr., 7, 9 May 1845.
402	39	Hansard, 23 June 1843.
403	10	Hansard, 12 July 1843; Bell, I.347.
	39	Hansard, 16 July 1844.
404	23	Hansard, 8 July 1845.
405	19	Palmerston to Temple, 29 Aug., 11 Sept., 13 Oct., 10 Nov. 1844; Palmerston's journal, 20, 21 Aug. 1844 (D. & A., III.145–6, 150–1, 156, 158–60, 163–
	39	Palmerston to Temple, 29 May 1843, 13 Oct., 10 Nov. 1844 (D. & A., III.125, 158–63).
406	33	Hansard, 30 July, 4 Aug. 1845.
408	2	Hansard, 13 June 1845.
	12	Hansard, 20 June 1845; Palmerston's memorandum on national defences, Dec. 1846, 31 Dec. 1847 (B.P., H.M.C., Calendar; D. & A., III.390–402).
	20	Lady Palmerston to Mrs Huskisson, 26 Sept. 1845 (B.M.Add.39949).
409	10	Bell. I.355–9.
	31	Broughton, VI.167–8.
410	39	D. & A., III.192–3; Greville, V.388–9; Bell, I.366; Victor Hugo, *Choses Vues*, pp. 109–10; Princess Lieven to Aberdeen, 29 Apr. 1846 (*Correspondence of Aberdeen and Princess Lieven*, I.249–50).

Page	Line	
412	6	Hansard, 29 June 1846.
413	11	Palmerston to Pakenham, 18 July, 15, 18 Aug., 31 Oct. 1846; Pakenham to Aberdeen, 28 June 1846; Pakenham to Palmerston, 23 Nov. 1846 (B.M.Add.48575); Palmerston to Bankhead, 15, 24 Aug., 31 Oct. 1846 (Nos. 13, 14); Bankhead to Aberdeen, 10 Mar., 1 Aug. (and enclosure), 13 Aug., 7 Sept. 1846; Bankhead to Palmerston, 30 Dec. 1846 (B.M.Add.49968); Rives, 'Mexican diplomacy on the eve of war with the United States' (*American Historical Review*, XVIII.275–94 (Jan. 1913)).
414	3	Bankhead to Aberdeen, 13 Aug. 1846, and enclosure (B.M.Add.49968).
	27	Palmerston to Bankhead, 15 Aug., 31 Oct. 1846 (B.M. Add.49968); D. & A., III.328.
415	21	Palmerston to Bankhead, 15 Aug. 1846; Bankhead to Aberdeen, 7 May 1846; Bankhead to Palmerston, 30 Oct. 1846 (B.M.49968); Palmerston to Pakenham, 18 Nov., 1 Dec. 1846, 30 Jan., 19 Apr. (Nos. 23, 30), 12 June 1847; Palmerston to Crampton, 30 June, 19 July, 4 Oct. 1847, 25 Feb., 24, 41 Mar. 1848; Crampton to Palmerston, 30 Dec. 1847, 27 Jan. 1848, 5 Feb., 12 Nov., 10 Dec. 1849 (B.M.Add.48575), 6 Aug. 1850; Palmerston to Potts, 29 Nov. 1850 (after entry of 17 June 1850) (B.M.Add. 48576).
416	32	Palmerston to Granville, 12 June 1838, 18 Jan., 5, 27 Mar., 23 Apr., 28 June, 15, 26 July, 13, 30, 31 Dec. 1839, 3 Jan., 14, 18 Feb., 12 May 1840 (B.M.Add.48507), 27 June 1840, 23 Jan. 1841; Palmerston to Bulwer, 21 July 1840 (B.M.Add.48508); Granville to Palmerston, 15, 22 June, 24 Sept., 16 Nov. 1838, 4 Jan., 4 Feb. 1839, 27 Apr., 29 May 1840 (B.M.Add.48511), 29 June 1840 (No. 231 and 'Most Confidential'), 12, 15 Jan. 1841 (B.M.Add. 48512); Aston to Palmerston, 10 Sept. 1838 (B.M.Add. 48511); Hansard, 31 Jan., 12 June, 22 July 1840.
417	15	Hansard, 23 Mar. 1847, 28 Jan. 1847; Ouseley to Aberdeen, 17 May, 7 June 1846 (B.M.Add.48574).
	31	Palmerston to Rosas, 5 Jan. 1862 (B.M.Add.48582).
	20	D. & A., IV.247.
418	29	Hansard, 4, 14, Mar. 1842, 7 Aug. 1844; Palmerston to Temple, 19 Jan. 1842 (D. & A., III.90); Palmerston to Victoria, 2 July 1848 (Connell, *Regina v. Palmerston*, p. 88).
421	28	Palmerston to Bulwer, 19 July 1846 (P.R.O., F.O.694; published in *Spanish Marriage Papers*, pp. 8–9, without the passage referring to Narváez).

Page	Line	
422	4	Bell, I.378.
	24	Guizot to Princess Lieven, 16, 18, 19, 21, 24 July, 8 Aug. 1846; Princess Lieven to Guizot, 17, 24, 25, 27 July 1846 (*Lettres Guizot-Lieven*, III.221, 223–31, 247).
423	25	Palmerston to Bulwer, 22 Aug. 1846 (No. 18) (P.R.O., F.O.72/694, published in *Span. Marr. Pap.*, pp. 11–13, without the derogatory references to Francisco).
	29	Palmerston to Bulwer, 22 Aug. 1846 (No. 19) (*Span. Marr. Pap.*, p. 13).
424	32	Guizot to Jarnac, 5 Oct. 1846 (*Span.Marr.Pap.*, pp. 43–56).
425	13	Note to Spanish Govt., enclosed in Palmerston to Bulwer, 14 Sept. 1846; Isturiz to Bulwer, 29 Sept. 1846 (*Span. Marr. Pap.*, pp. 20–2, 56–9).
	39	Palmerston to Ponsonby, 1 Jan., 8 Feb. 1847 (B.M.Add. 48547); Ponsonby to Palmerston, 17, 19 Feb. 1847 (B.M.Add.48458).
426	7	Albert to Ernst of Saxe-Coburg, 2 Apr. 1847 (Bolitho, *The Prince Consort to his Brother*, p. 96).
	39	Palmerston to Bligh, 30 Aug. 1833 (B.M.Add.48483); Palmerston to Abercrombie, 22 Apr. 1839 (B.M.Add. 48514).
427	17	Princess Lieven to Guizot, 24 July 1846 (*Lettres Guizot-Lieven*, III.230–1).
	33	Palmerston to Russell, 10 Sept. 1846 (*Russell Later Corr.*, I.118); Bell. I.380–4.
428	17	Palmerston to Normanby, 23 Nov. 1846 (*Cracow Pap.*, p. 41).
	26	Palmerston to Ponsonby, 23 Nov., 7 Dec. 1846; Palmerston to Normanby, 23 Nov. 1846; Guizot to Flahaut, 3 Dec. 1846 (*Cracow Pap.*, pp. 39–42, 49, 50–4; B.M.Add 48577).
429	21	Bell, I.389; Czartoryski, II.348–9.
	32	Normanby to Palmerston, 23 Nov. 1846, 5 Feb. 1847 (B.M.Add.48554); Palmerston to Normanby, 7 Feb. 1847 (B.M.Add.48577); 7 Dec. 1846, 17, 23 Feb. 1847 (D. & A., III.324–9, 324–4, 450–3).
430	28	Howard de Walden to Palmerston, 26 Oct. 1846, and enclosures; Wylde to Palmerston, 16 Nov. 1846; Palmerston to the Lords of the Admiralty, 30 Oct., 4, 6 Nov. 1846; Southern to British Consuls in Portugal, 5 Nov. 1846; Palmerston to Southern, 16 Nov. 1846 (*Portuguese Papers*, pp. 8, 14, 33, 41–2, 47–9, 52–4).
	35	Palmerston to Wylde, 30 Oct. 1846 (*Port Pap.*, pp. 12–14).
431	25	Palmerston to Wylde, 11 Feb. 1847; Palmerston to Moncorvo, 1, 3 Feb. 1847; Palmerston to Seymour, 5 Apr. 1847; Johnston to Southern, 20 Nov. 1846; Southern to Palmerston, 3, 19 Dec. 1846, 11 Jan. 1847 and enclo-

Page	Line	
445	18	Eckinger, *Lord Palmerston und der Schweizer Sonder-bundskrieg*, pp. 80–1, 88; Palmerston to Peel, 3 Aug, 5 Oct. 1847 (*Swiss Papers*, pp. 158–9, 174).
446	4	Oechsli, 'The Achievement of Swiss Federal Unity' (*Cambridge Modern History* (1909 ed.), chap. VIII).
	30	Palmerston to Normanby, 11, 19 Nov. 1847 (B.M.Add. 48577).
447	17	Palmerston to Minto, 18 Sept. 1847 (*Italian Papers*, I.128–30), 29 Oct. 1847; D. & A., IV.34–41; Palmerston to Normanby, 11 Nov. 1847 (B.M.Add.48577).
448	7	Palmerston to Peel, 17 Nov. 1847 (Eckinger, pp. 112–13).
449	14	Bois-le-Comte to Guizot, 24 Nov. 1847; Guizot, *Mémoires*, VIII.505–6; Eckinger, pp. 113–21; Hansard, 30 Nov., 13 Dec. 1847, 25 June 1850.
	29	Palmerston to Canning, 27 Nov., 1, 21 Dec. 1847 (Nos. 254, 255) (*Swiss Pap.*, pp. 258–60, 267–8, 302–3).

CHAPTER XXIV

1848: FRANCE AND SPAIN

451	21	Hertslet, p. 73–4; Magarshack, *Turgenev*, pp. 183–5.
	25	Hansard, 28 May, 4, 11, 14, 15, 17 June, 5 July 1847.
452	18	Hansard, 8, 23 Feb., 1, 6 Mar. 1848.
453	11	Hansard, 1 Mar. 1848.
	31	Palmerston to Milbanke, 20 Apr. 1848 (B.M.Add. 48549).
454	5	Palmerston to Normanby, 26 Feb. 1848 (B.M.Add. 48555).
	30	Palmerston to Normanby, 29 Feb. 1848 (Nos. 65, 70) (B.M.Add.48555); Victoria to Palmerston, 8 Aug. 1848 (Connell, *Regina v. Palmerston*, p. 91); Palmerston to Russell, 10 Aug. 1848 (*Russell Later Corr.*, I.299–300).
455	4	Palmerston to Victoria, 10 Mar. 1848 (Connell, *op. cit.*, p. 69); Palmerston to Normanby, 4 Mar., 19 May 1848 (B.M.Add.48555).
	14	Monypenny and Buckle, I.1000.
456	2	Palmerston to Ponsonby, 29 Feb. 1848 (B.M.Add. 48547); Palmerston to Bloomfield, 29 Feb., 4 Mar. 1848 (B.M.Add.48563); Palmerston to Normanby, 28 Feb. 1848 (D. & A., IV.81–2).
	20	Palmerston to Normanby, 7 Mar. 1848 (B.M.Add. 48555); Bell, I.424; Palmerston to Ponsonby, 20 Mar. 1848 (B.M.Add.48547); Palmerston to Bloomfield, 18, 28 Mar. 1848 (B.M.Add.48563).
457	14	Palmerston to Normanby, 14, 22, 24, 27 Mar. (Nos. 125, 126), 7 Apr. 1848 (B.M.Add.48555).
	29	Normanby to Palmerston, 24 Mar. 1848 (P.R.O., F.O.

Page	Line	
		27/809); Palmerston to Normanby, 27 Mar. 1848 (B.M. Add.48555).
458	4	Palmerston to Normanby, 7 Már. 1848 (B.M.Add. 48555).
	21	Palmerston to Normanby, 28 June 1848 (Nos. 268, 269) (B.M.Add.48555).
459	13	Palmerston to Normanby, 5 Sept. 1848, 13 July 1849 (B.M.Add.48555).
	35	Disraeli to Lady Londonderry, 21 Aug. 1849 (Monypenny and Buckle, I.1008).
460	22	Palmerston to Normanby, 11 Apr. 1848 (D. & A., IV. 93–4); Lady Palmerston to Mrs. Huskisson, 14 Apr. 1848 (B.M.Add.39949).
461	7	Palmerston to Russell, 7 Apr. 1848 (*Russell Later Corr.*, I.227); Palmerston to Normanby, 11, 18 Apr. 1849 (D. & A., IV.94–5); Dillon, *Life of Mitchel*, I.253–73; Crampton to Palmerston, 3 July 1848; Palmerston to Crampton, 7 July 1848 (B.M.Add.48575).
462	1	Bulwer to Palmerston, 17 Oct., 7 Nov. 1847 (B.M.Add. 48569); 31 Mar. 1848 (*Spanish Papers*, p. 10).
	20	Palmerston to Bulwer, 16 Mar. 1848 (*Span. Pap.*, p. 3).
463	13	Bulwer to Sotomayor, 7 Apr. 1848; Palmerston to Bulwer, 19, 20 Apr. 1848; Sotomayor to Bulwer, 10, 15 Apr. 1848 (*Span. Pap.*, pp. 16, 18-23, 25, 27).
	37	D. & A., III.245–57; Hansard, 22, 23, 25, 26 May, 5, 15 June, 16 Aug. 1848; Walpole, *Life of Lord John Russell*, II.45.
464	8	Palmerston's note to the Spanish Govt., 4 Mar. 1850 (B.M.Add.48577).

CHAPTER XXV

1848–1849: ITALY, HUNGARY, SCHLESWIG-HOLSTEIN

466	2	Palmerston to Abercromby, 12 Feb. 1848; Scarlett to Palmerston, 17 Mar. 1847; Abercromby to Palmerston, 30 Mar. 1847 (*Ital. Pap.*, I.33; II.60–1); Palmerston to Ponsonby, 13 Aug., 8 Oct., 9 Nov., 28 Dec. 1847, 11 Feb. 1848 (B.M.Add.48547).
467	31	Palmerston to Ponsonby, 18, 20 Apr., 8 May 1848 (*Ital. Pap.*, II.350-2, 415-16), 30 June 1848 (B.M.Add.48547).
468	16	Palmerston to Normanby, 3, 7 Mar., 28 July, 22 Sept. 1848 (B.M.Add.48555); 7, 29 Aug. 1848; Palmerston to Hummelauer, 3 June 1848; Palmerston to Ponsonby, 20 June 1948; Palmerston to Abercromby, 8 May 1848 (*Ital. Pap.*, II.416, 531-3, 597-8; III.98-9, 235).
469	36	Palmerston to Normanby, 26 Sept. 1848 (*Ital. Pap.*, III.424), 10 Oct. 1848 (B.M.Add.48555); Palmerston to

Page	Line	
		Russell, 6 Mar. 1849 (*Russell Later Corr.*, I.351–2).
470	20	Victoria to Palmerston (May 1848) (*Q.V.L.* I(ii)207; Bell, I.435.
471	14	Palmerston to Ponsonby, 31 Aug. 1848 (D. & A., IV. 107–10).
	25	Palmerston to Ponsonby, 26 Sept. 1848 (B.M.Add. 48547).
472	4	Palmerston to Victoria, 22 May 1848; Victoria to Palmerston, 21, 22 May 1848 (Connell, *Regina v. Palmerston*, p. 74).
	23	Radetzky's proclamation, 11 Nov. 1848; Palmerston to Ponsonby, 14 Nov. 1848 (*Ital. Pap.*, III.570–1).
473	15	Palmerston to Ponsonby, 20 Nov. 1848 (*Ital. Pap.*, III. 584–5).
474	8	Ponsonby to Palmerston, 23 Nov. 1848 (B.M.Add. 48548); Palmerston to Ponsonby, 13 Dec. 1848 (B.M. Add.48547).
	38	Schwarzenberg to Werner, 4 Dec. 1848 (RA J24/96).
475	7	General Grey to Albert, 8 Jan. 1860 (RA J24/95).
477	17	Palmerston to Normanby, 9 Mar. 1849 (*Ital. Pap.*, IV.176–7).
	34	Palmerston to Abercromby, 27 Dec. 1848, 12, 19 Mar. 1849 (*Ital. Pap.*, III.682–3; IV.189–90, 203).
478	25	Greville, VI.282–3; Russell to Palmerston, 13 Apr. 1849; Palmerston to Russell, 20 July 1849 (*Russell Later Corr.*, I.357–61).
	33	Bell, I.436–7.
479	20	Freeborn to Palmerston, 2 May, 4 Aug. 1849; Palmerston's memoranda, 13 May, 20 July, 2, 13 Aug. 1849. (P.R.O., F.O.43/45).
480	14	Cook, *Delane*, pp. 51–2.
	32	Palmerston to Russell, 22 Jan. 1849 (Walpole, II.51–2).
481	23	Palmerston to Ponsonby, 20 Dec. 1848 (B.M.Add. 48547); Kossuth to Palmerston, 12 Nov. 1848; Szalai to Palmerston, 15 Dec. 1848; Eddisbury to Szalai, 13, 19 Dec. 1848 (Sproxton, *Palmerston and the Hungarian Revolution*, pp. 44–7); Pulszky, *Meine Zeit, mein Leben*, II.322.
482	13	Buchanan to Palmerston, 2 May 1849 (B.M.Add. 48566); Palmerston to Buchanan, 17 May 1849 (BM Add.48564); Palmerston to Russell, 14 Aug. 1849 *Russell Later Corr.* II.6).
484	12	Hansard, 19 Apr. 1849; Malmesbury, p. 181–2.
	30	*Cambridge History of British Foreign Policy*, II.522–41.
485	18	Victoria to Palmerston, 18 Nov. 1850; Palmerston to Victoria, 18 Nov. 1850 (Connell, *Regina v. Palmerston*, pp. 129–31).
	39	Baronness Bunsen, *Memoirs of Baron Bunsen*, II.152.

Page	Line	
486	23	Victoria to Russell, 14 Mar. 1847 (*Q.V.L.*, I(ii)141).
487	7	Clifford to Bulwer, 21 Sept. 1870 (D. & A., I.x–xi).
	23	D. & A., III.407–8.
488	17	Palmerston to Seymour, 29 Sept. 1840 (B.M.Add. 48499).
489	8	Palmerston to Seymour, 27 Oct., 20 Nov. 1840 (B.M. Add.48499).
490	2	Palmerston to Hill, 16, 26 Aug., 16, 20 Sept. 1831 (B.M.Add.48469) (Naples); Foster to Palmerston, 16 Aug., 14 Sept., 22 Oct., 2, 7, 19, Nov. 1831 (B.M.Add. 48471) (Turin); Palmerston to Addington, 30 Dec. 1831 (B.M.Add.48486) (Madrid).
	20	Palmerston to Hamilton, 10 Nov. 1835 (B.M.Add. 48499).
491	8	Seymour to Palmerston, 11 Dec. 1840 (B.M.Add. 48502); Palmerston to Hamilton, 10 Nov. 1835; Palmerston to Seymour, 10 June, 22 July, 19 Aug. (No. 23 and unnumbered), 16, 30 Sept., 7 Oct. 1836, 27 Oct. 1840 (B.M.Add.48499); Palmerston to Disbrowe, 15 June 1838 (B.M.Add.48520).
	21	Palmerston to Orme, 3 Sept. 1859 (B.M.Add.48581; this passage is cited, not wholly correctly, by Bulwer in D. & A., III.407); Palmerston to Lyons, 28 Sept. 1837 (B.M.Add.48517).
493	7	Palmerston to Ponsonby, 8 June 1838 (B.M.Add.48543).
	25	Murray to Palmerston, 30 Jan. 1847; Palmerston to Murray, 27 May 1847 (B.M.Add.48553).
494	9	Murray to Palmerston, 30 Apr., 18 July, 21 Oct., 17 Dec. 1847, 27 Feb., 18 Mar. 1848; Palmerston to Murray, 27 May, 30 Sept., 8 Nov. 1847, 9 Feb., 14 Mar., 5 Apr., 31 July 1848 (B.M.Add.48553).
	34	See, *supra*, pp. 176–7, 214–15.
495	11	Ponsonby to Palmerston, 26 Mar. 1834 (B.M.Add. 48493).
496	14	Palmerston to Sheil, 21 Oct. 1846 (B.M.Add.48559); Sheil to Aberdeen, 21, 31 May, 30 June, 15 Dec. 1846; Sheil to Palmerston, 12 Jan. 1850 (received 21 Mar.) (B.M.Add.48560); Palmerston to Bloomfield, 7 Aug. 1848, 20 Mar. 1849, 26 Feb., 26 Mar. 1850 (Nos. 127, 129) (B.M.Add.48563); Buchanan to Palmerston, 23 Apr. 1849 B.M.Add.48566).
497	6	Palmerston to Russell, 26 Oct. 1862 (*Russell Later Corr.*, II.300–1).
	38	Palmerston to Lyons, 31 Jan. 1837 (B.M.Add.48517); Palmerston to Erskine, 8 Feb. 1837 (B.M.Add.48514); Lyons to Palmerston, 31 Mar. 1840 (B.M.Add.48518); Hansard, 28 July, 11 Aug. 1836, 15 Aug. 1843.

Page	Line	
498	17	Palmerston to Lyons, 7, 12 Apr. 1838 (B.M.Add.48517).
499	14	Palmerston to Erskine, 17 Oct. 1834 (B.M.Add.48463); Palmerston to Lyons, 3 Apr. 1837 (B.M.Add.48517); Dawkins to Palmerston, 28 June 1835 (B.M.Add.48518); Palmerston to Milbanke, 16 Apr. 1847 (B.M.Add. 48549); Palmerston to Aston, 8 Dec. 1837 (B.M.Add. 48507).
	40	Lyons to Palmerston, 10 Aug., 20, 22 Nov. 1840 (B.M. Add.48518); Palmerston to Lyons, 30 Nov., 21 Dec. 1840 (B.M.Add.48517); Palmerston to Campbell, 3 Mar., 1 Aug. 1834 (B.M.Add.48451); Campbell to Palmerston, 22 May 1834 (B.M.Add.48452).
500	17	Lyons to Palmerston, 4 Jan. (Nos. 6, 7), 9, 15 Feb, 1841 (B.M.Add.48519); Palmerston to Lyons, 30 Jan., 13 Feb., 19 June, 14 Aug. 1841 (B.M.Add.48517); Palmerston to Ponsonby, 31 Aug. 1840, 10 Feb., 20 May, 15, 26 June (Nos. 162, 165), 20, 23 July, 3, 26 Aug. 1841 (B.M.Add.48544); Ponsonby to Palmerston, 21 Feb., 17 Mar. 1841 (B.M.Add.48546); Hansard, 4 June 1841.
	32	Hansard, 14 Mar. 1844; Palmerston to Normanby, 12, 31 Mar., 10 May 1847 (B.M.Add.48577); Palmerston to Milbanke, 20 May, 16 July, 17 Aug. 1847 (B.M. Add.48549).
501	14	Finlay to Aberdeen, 18 Oct. 1842 (*Greek Papers*, I.1–2).
502	9	Palmerston to Lyons, 7 Aug. 1846; Kolettes to Lyons, 23 Oct./4 Nov. 1846; Colocotronis to Lyons, 30 Sept./ 12 Oct., 8/20 Dec. 1848; Finlay to Lyons, 12 Jan. 1849; Finlay to Wyse, 15 Mar. 1850 (*Greek Pap.*, I.16–17, 20–1, 35–6, 42–5; III.249–50).
	39	Crowe to Lyons, 29 July 1846; Lyons to Palmerston, 15 Nov. 1846; Lyons to Kolettes, 10 Nov. 1846, 24 Feb. 1847; Palmerston to Lyons, 6 May 1847 (*Greek Pap.*, I.177–9, 191, 195, 206–8, 235).
503	23	Douglas to Lyons, 12 Oct. 1839; Douglas to Russell, 7 Nov. 1839; Lyons to Palmerston, 20 Nov. 1839; Palmerston to Wyse, 7 July 1849; Wyse to Glarakis, 19 July 1849 (*Greek Pap.*, I.323–5, 337, 341–2); *F.O. Confidential Memorandum on Cervi and Sapienza*, 31 Dec. 1849, p. 3.
504	20	Palmerston to Milbanke, 11, 20 May 1847 (B.M.Add. 48549).
505	17	Palmerston to Milbanke, 8, 20, 29 Oct., 9 Nov. 1847, 22 Jan., 3, 11 Feb. 1848 (B.M.Add.48549).
506	8	Ansted, *The Ionian Islands in 1863*, pp. 347–8, 374–7; Ward to Grey, 7 Apr. 1850; Whyte-Jervis, *The Ionian Islands*, pp. 80–90; *Punch*, XVIII.111 (Jan.–June 1850); Hansard, H.L., 17 June 1850.

Page	Line	
		Hayward's obituary of Lady Palmerston in *The Times*, 15 Sept. 1869 (Hayward, *Selected Essays*, II.355).
526	10	Palmerston to Temple, 8 July 1850 (D. & A., IV.225); Fagan, pp. 83–91; Greville, VI.362; Kingsley Martin, *The Triumph of Lord Palmerston*, p. 56.
	36	Palmerston to Temple, 8 July 1850; Palmerston to Normanby, 29 June 1850 (D. & A., IV.224–5).
527	2	Hansard, 24 June 1850.
528	5	*The Morning Post*, 26 Apr. 1850.
	23	Hansard, 29 Apr. 1850; *The Morning Chronicle*, 30 Apr. 1850.

CHAPTER XXVIII

THE DISMISSAL FROM THE FOREIGN OFFICE

Page	Line	
529	19	Bell, I.226–7; Longford, *Victoria R.I.*, p. 75; *Victoria's Diaries*, I.225, 227–8; II,13.
530	6	See *supra*, pp. 239, 241, 275.
	33	Bell, I.383–4; II.20; Victoria to Palmerston, 28 Nov. 1846, 21, 22 May, 1 July, 8 Aug. 1848; Albert to Palmerston, 28 Jan. 1847; Albert to Russell, 2 Apr. 1850 (Connell, *Regina v. Palmerston*, pp. 48, 53–4, 74, 83, 91, 116); Walpole, II.60.
531	10	Palmerston's memorandum, 10 June 1838 (Webster, 'Lord Palmerston at Work', in *Politica* (I.136).
532	6	Southgate, *The Most English Minister*, p. 195; Palmerston to Victoria, 22 May, 16 Oct. 1848; Victoria to Palmerston, 21 May, 8, 14 Oct. 1848; Victoria's journal, 19 Sept. 1848; Albert's memorandum, 3 Mar. 1850; Albert to Russell, 2 Apr. 1850 (Connell, *op. cit.*, pp. 74, 96–7, 102–4, 113, 115–17); Russell to Palmerston, 22 May 1850 (Walpole, II.60–1).
	28	Albert's memorandum, 11 July 1850 (Connell, pp. 120–1).
533	12	Albert's memorandum, 17 Aug. 1850; Victoria to Russell, 12 Aug. 1850; Palmerston to Russell, 13 Aug. 1850 (*Q.V.L.* I(ii)315–16); Sir T. Martin, *Life of Prince Consort*, II.249–55, 282.
	39	Victoria to Palmerston, 10 Sept. 1850 (Connell, *op. cit.*, p. 127); Palmerston to Sir G. Grey, 1 Oct. 1850 (D. & A., IV.239–41).
534	17	Victoria to Palmerston, 4 Oct. 1850; Palmerston to Russell, 13 Oct. 1850; Russell to Albert, 18 Oct. 1850 (Connell, *op. cit.*, pp. 127–9).
535	10	Palmerston to Canning, 10 Feb. 1851 (D. & A., IV.173–5); Greville, VI.413–14.
	22	Palmerston to Russell, 21 Oct. 1851 (*Russell Later Corr.*, II.18), 30 Oct. 1851; Russell to Palmerston, 30 Oct. 1851 (Walpole, II.133).

Page	Line	
536	11	Walpole, II.134–6; Greville, VI.415; (Wilson ed.) II.390.
	27	Londonderry to Russell, 14 June 1849 (*Russell Later Corr.*, I.302).
537	29	Argyll, *Memoirs*, I.344; Tennyson, 'The Third of February 1852'; Palmerston to Normanby, 3 Dec. 1851; Normanby to Palmerston, 6, 15 Dec. 1851; Palmerston to Russell, 16 Dec. 1851 (D. & A., IV.291, 296, 300).
538	16	Walpole, II.138; Palmerston to Normanby, 5 Dec. 1851; Normanby to Palmerston, 6, 15 Dec. 1851 (D. & A., IV.294–7); Victoria to Palmerston, 6 Oct. 1848 (Connell, *op. cit.*, p. 102).
	28	Palmerston to Normanby, 16 Dec. 1851; Russell to Palmerston, 17, 19 Dec. 1851; Palmerston to Russell, 23 Dec. 1851 (D. & A., IV.297–9, 307–8), 18 Dec. 1851 (Walpole, II.139–40).
539	12	Palmerston to Russell, 23 Dec. 1851; Palmerston to Temple, 22 Jan. 1852 (D. & A., IV.307–8, 315); Victoria's journal, 26 Dec. 1851 (Connell, *op. cit.*, pp. 135–7); Palmerston to Borthwick, 6 June 1852 (Lucas, p. 138); Lady Palmerston to Mrs Huskisson, 9 Jan. 1852 (B.M.Add.39949); 'England and Napoleon' (Kingsley Martin, pp. 72–3 n.).
	27	Greville (Wilson ed.) II.379–80; Phillips, 'Palmerston: what has he done?' (published in Coningham, *Lord Palmerston and Prince Albert*, pp. 17–31, and in *The Times* 24 Jan. 1854).
540	12	Palmerston to Lansdowne, Oct. 1852; D. & A., IV. 325–31; Greville, VI.446–7; Phipps to Victoria, 10 Mar. 1852 (*Q.V.L.*, II.458–9); Sir T. Martin, II.426 n.; Monypenny and Buckle, I.1156; Hansard, 3 Feb. 1852.
541	6	'Chobham Camp' (Kingsley Martin, p. 104 n.).
	16	Bell, I.399.
	36	Hansard, 16, 20 Feb. 1852; Broughton, VI.297–9; Palmerston to Temple, 24 Feb. 1852 (D. & A., IV.334).
542	36	Palmerston to Malmesbury, 24 Feb. 1852; Malmesbury, pp. 227, 229–30, 237–8.
543	29	D. & A., IV.362–4.
544	17	Lady Palmerston to Palmerston, 8 July 1852 (Airlie, II. 142); Monypenny and Buckle, I.1196; D. & A., IV.350–62.
	35	Whyte, 'Landlord Influence at Elections in Ireland 1760–1885' (*English Historical Review*, LXXX.749 (Oct. 1965)).
545	19	D. & A., IV.361–2; Rowcliffe's statement, in Snell, p. 103.
	39	Hansard, 23, 25, 26 Nov. 1852.

Page	Line	
546	14	Hansard, 16 Dec. 1852; Reeve, *Memoirs*, I.269.
	30	Bell, II.72–3; Reeve, I.269.
547	9	Palmerston to Sulivan, 31 Dec. 1852 (Airlie, II.151–3).

CHAPTER XXIX

HOME SECRETARY: THE EASTERN QUESTION

548	29	Argyll, I.374, 378, 383; Aberdeen to Palmerston, 10 Sept. 1853; Palmerston to Aberdeen, 5 Nov. 1853 (B.M. Add.43069); Lady Clarendon's journal, 12 Sept. 1853 (Maxwell, *Life of Clarendon*, II.21–2); Greville (Wilson ed.), II.88–9; Bell, II.93.
549	25	Hansard, 6 Apr., 4 May, 2 June, 5 July 1853, 16 Feb., 11 Apr. 1854; H.L., 5 Aug. 1853.
550	8	Hansard, 9, 10, 15 Mar., 13 June, 20 July, 9 Aug. 1853, 2 Mar., 17 May, 6, 7, 24, 31 July 1854, 23 July 1857.
	23	Hansard, 11 Feb., 18 Mar., 8 Apr., 17 June 1853, 3, 7 Mar. 1854; H.L., 27 Mar., 2 May 1854; *The Romsey Register*, June, July 1854, Jan. 1856.
551	5	Palmerston to Gladstone, 20 Oct. 1853 (Guedalla, *Gladstone and Palmerston*, pp. 95–6); Hansard, 10 Feb. 1853.
	27	Hansard, 12 June 1854.
552	22	Palmerston to Aberdeen, 20 May 1853 (B.M.Add.43069); Hansard, 9, 11, 12 Aug. 1853; H.L., 1, 4 May, 4 Aug. 1854.
	37	Hansard, 2 May 1853; see *infra*,, pp. 509–10.
553	18	Griffiths and Ingram, 'Juvenile Offenders' (*Encyclopaedia Britannica*, 13th ed.); Hansard, 1 Aug. 1853, 14 Mar. 1854.
	26	Palmerston's memorandum, 10 Oct. 1854 (B.P., H.M.C., HO/10).
	36	Ibid.
554	27	Hansard, 25 May 1841, 18 June 1849.
555	10	Hansard, 22 Feb., 7 Mar. 1854, 9 May 1856; Dillon, *Life of Mitchel*, II.11–14.
	17	Hansard, 11 Apr., 2, 27 June 1854.
557	7	For Kossuth's case, see Hansard, 15, 25, 29 Apr., 5 May 1853.
	25	Kingsley Martin, pp. 86–101.
	34	Palmerston to Normanby, 25 Nov. 1852 (D. & A., IV.274–8).
559	4	Reeve, I.271; Greville, VII.106.
	20	Palmerston to Buchanan, 27 Mar., 20 Apr. 1849, 6 Aug., 13, 16 Nov. 1850 (B.M.Add.48564).
	35	Hansard, 20 Feb., 31 Mar. 1854.
560	16	Maxwell, II.3.
561	4	Bell, II.85–6.

Page	Line	
	20	Palmerston to Aberdeen, 12 July 1853 (B.M.Add. 43069, D. & A., V.32–4).
	37	Palmerston to Russell, 24 Oct. 1853 (D. & A., V.51); Argyll, I.463; Maxwell, II.22–3.
562	21	Whitty, *St. Stephens in the Fifties*, p. 287.
563	10	Bell, II.88; Argyll, I.455–6; Palmerston to Clarendon, 31 July 1853 (Maxwell, II.16).
	17	Argyll, I.456–8.
564	4	Palmerston to Aberdeen, 7 Oct. 1853 (D. & A., V.41; B.M.Add.43069); Lushington's poem; Kingsley Martin, pp. 227, 238–9, 241; Marx, *The Eastern Question*, p. 19 (New York Tribune, 2 Apr. 1853); Tennyson, 'Maud', Part III, lines 1–59.
	7	Palmerston to Aberdeen, 7 Oct. 1853 (B.M.Add.43069, D. & A., V.41–2).
565	14	Palmerston to Aberdeen, 1 Nov. 1853 (B.M.Add.43069; printed in part in D. & A., V.43–9).
	23	Hansard, 17 Feb. 1854.
566	10	Greville, VI.414; Broughton, VI.294; Argyll, I.471–2.
567	2	Palmerston to Lansdowne, 8 Dec. 1853 (B.M.Add. 43069).
	14	Palmerston to Aberdeen, 10 Dec. 1853 (B.M.Add.43069).
568	4	Bell, II.97–8; Kingsley Martin, p. 196.
	24	Bell, II.98; Palmerston to Aberdeen, 14 Dec. 1853 (B.M. Add.43069); Kingsley Martin, p. 198.
569	3	Kingsley Martin, pp. 198–200; Palmerston to Borthwick, 16 Dec. 1853 (Lucas, p. 139); Monypenny and Buckle, I.1345.
	32	Palmerston to Aberdeen, 23 Dec. 1853; Aberdeen to Palmerston, 24 Dec. 1853 (B.M.Add.43069).
570	1	Reeve, II.352–6, 356 n.; Stanmore, *Aberdeen*, p. 273.
	12	See Kingsley Martin, p. 180; Pemberton, *Lord Palmerston* pp. 216–18; Bell, II.97. See also Southgate, pp. 333–8.
571	25	Marx, *Life of Lord Palmerston*, p. 10; Urquhart, *Materials for the true history of Lord Palmerston*, pp. 1–3; Palmerston to MacGregor, 29 Oct. 1855 (B.M.Add.48579).
572	14	Kingsley Martin, pp. 204–5; 'Lovely Albert' (broadsheet); Lady Clarendon's journal, 12 Jan. 1854 (Maxwell, II.37); Palmerston to Borthwick, 25 Jan. 1854 (Lucas, p. 140).

CHAPTER XXX

THE CRIMEAN WAR

| 573 | 22 | Palmerston's memorandum, 15 June 1854 (D. & A., V.60–5); Gladstone to Palmerston, 4 Oct. 1854 (Guedalla, *Gladstone and Palmerston*, pp. 99–100); Walpole, II.223. |

Page	Line	
574	19	Fagan, *The Reform Club*, pp. 93–103.
575	16	D. & A., V.57–8.
576	15	Hansard, 13 Mar. 1854.
	30	Trevelyan, *John Bright*, p. 234.
577	4	Hansard, 31 Mar. 1854.
	26	Palmerston to Russell, 22 Jan. 1854 (Bell, II.95), 29 Jan. 1854 (B.P., H.M.C., CAB/B/16).
578	31	Palmerston to Aberdeen, 12 Feb. 1854 (B.P., H.M.C., CAB/B/17).
579	29	Argyll, I.475–8.
581	8	Woodham-Smith, *Florence Nightingale*, p. 125.
	25	Argyll, I.499–500; Maxwell, II.49–50.
582	9	Hayward, I.225; D. & A., V.68–9; Argyll, I.500, 516, 543–4; Maxwell, II.64.
	37	Tennyson, 'The Charge of the Light Brigade'; Argyll, I.508–9, 519.
583	22	Bell, II.106; Argyll, I.516–17; Palmerston to Russell, 24 Jan. 1855 (D. & A., V.70–1).
	35	Hansard, 25, 26, 29 Jan. 1855; Argyll, I.520.
584	16	Maxwell, II.57; Palmerston to Derby, 31 Jan. 1855 (D. & A., 73–4).
	35	Maxwell, II.57–60.
585	14	Maxwell, II.60.
	39	Argyll, I.527–8; Maxwell, II.61.
586	14	Argyll, I.528–30.
	34	Palmerston to Shaftesbury, 7 Feb. 1855 (two letters); Shaftesbury to Palmerston, 7 Feb. 1855; Shaftesbury to Ashley, 28 Feb. 1855 (Hodder, II.490–3, 503–4); Argyll, I.541.
587	14	Palmerston to Clarendon, 8, 10 Feb. 1855; Maxwell, II.62–3.
	31	Hansard, 16 Feb. 1855; Argyll, I.536.
588	9	Argyll, I.536–7; Hansard, 16 Feb. 1855.
	24	Trevelyan, *Bright*, p. 252; Palmerston to Temple, 15 Feb. 1855 (D. & A., V.77).

CHAPTER XXXI

PRIME MINISTER: THE PEACE NEGOTIATIONS

589	11	Bright's journal, 14 Feb. 1855 (Trevelyan, *Bright*, p. 241); Lady Cowper to Cowper, 28 Feb. 1855 (Cowper, *Earl Cowper*, p. 50).
590	15	Bayne, in *St Paul's Magazine*, Aug. 1868, cited in Trollope, *Lord Palmerston*, pp. 205–6.
591	5	Disraeli to Lady Londonderry, 2 Feb. 1855 (Monypenny and Buckle, I.1383); Lady Cowper to Cowper, 28 Feb. 1855 (Cowper, p. 50); Greville, VIII.160.

Page	Line	
	28	Hansard, 19 Dec. 1854; Palmerston to Panmure, 10 June 1855 (*Panmure Papers*, I.232).
592	8	Palmerston to Panmure, 4 July, 16 Aug. 1855; Palmerston to Clarendon, 16 Aug. 1855 (B.M.Add.48579); Hansard, 12 Mar. 1857.
	31	Palmerston to Argyll, 13 Oct. 1855; Argyll, I.543–5, 585–7; Maxwell, II.64.
593	26	Palmerston to Panmure, 1, 8 May 1855 (B.M.Add. 48579).
594	4	Waterfield, *Layard of Nineveh*, pp. 159–60, 179, 181, 185, 191–2, 194.
	28	Victoria's journal, 5 Feb. 1855 (Connell, *Regina v. Palmerston*, pp. 162–3).
595	12	Hansard, 19 Feb. 1855.
596	14	Waterfield, pp. 264, 267; Hansard, 27 Apr. 1855; *Punch*, XXVIII.186.
	37	Hansard, 15, 18 June 1855.
597	19	Palmerston's statement to the Commission (Woodham-Smith, *The Reason Why*), p. 23. See also Palmerston to Taylor, 28 Oct. 1824 (B.M.Add.48420).
	31	Hansard, 2 Apr. 1833 (Palmerston's speech), 16 Feb. 1860 (division lists).
598	15	Atkins, *Life of Sir W. H. Russell*, I.261–2.
	30	Palmerston to Victoria, 27 Feb., 26 Apr. 1855 (Connell, *op. cit.*, pp. 173–4).
600	20	Palmerston to Clarendon, 20 May, 9 Oct. 1855 (B.M. Add.48579).
601	14	Czartoryski, II.349, 351, 353; Kingsley Martin, pp. 231–2.
602	9	Palmerston to Clarendon, 20 May 1855 (B.M.Add. 48579); Hansard, 24, 25 May, 4, 5, 7, 8 June 1855.
	24	Argyll, I.549–58; Maxwell, II.80–6; Palmerston to Clarendon, 27 June, 25 Sept. 1855 (B.M.Add.48579).
603	21	Palmerston to Panmure, 27 June, 27 Sept. 1855; Palmerston to Sumber, 16 Sept. 1855 (B.M.Add.48579).
604	2	Palmerston to Clarendon, 9 Oct. 1855 (B.M.Add. 48579).
	31	Palmerston to Clarendon, 23 Nov. 1855; Palmerston to Seymour, 24 Jan. 1856 (B.M.Add.48579).
	36	Palmerston to Clarendon, 17 Jan. 1856 (B.M.Add. 48579).
605	38	Palmerston to Granville, 8 June 1838 (D. & A., II.268); Palmerston to Clarendon, 25, 27 Feb., 4 Mar. 1856 (B.M.Add.48580); Argyll, II.23.
606	18	Argyll, I.597, 599; II.9, 21–3.
607	17	Palmerston to Clarendon, 25 Feb. 1856 (B.M.Add. 48580).

Page	Line	
608	4	Palmerston to Clarendon, 28, 29 Feb. 1856 (B.M.Add. 48580); Palmerston to Lewis, 7 Oct. 1855 (B.M.Add. 48579).
	27	Fitzmaurice, I.121; Palmerston to Clarendon, 7, 8, 9, 11 Mar. 1856 (B.M.Add.48580); Clarendon to Palmerston, 29 Feb., 3 Mar. 1856; Clarendon to Granville, 8, 12 Mar. 1856 (Maxwell, II.116–19).
609	17	Malmesbury, pp. 403–4; Riker, *The Making of Roumania*, pp. 29, 61–2 and n., 96, 130–40, 157.
610	27	Argyll, II.24; Fitzmaurice, I.178; Hansard, 5, 6, 8 May; H.L., 5 May 1956; Palmerston to Victoria, 17 Jan. 1856 (*Q.V.L.*, I(iii)211).
611	18	Palmerston's memorandum, 12 Aug. 1856 (D. & A., V.111–17).

CHAPTER XXXII

THE LORCHA *Arrow*

Page	Line	
612	7	Hodder, III.34.
	24	Lorne, p. 223.
613	29	Hansard, 29 Apr., 2, 19 May 1956; Hodder, III.30–2; Argyll, II.49; Palmerston to Victoria, 10 May 1856 (Connell, *Regina v. Palmerston*, p. 202).
614	12	Crampton to Palmerston, 25 June 1849 (B.M.Add.48575).
	36	Palmerston to Crampton, 13 July, 9 Nov. 1849; Palmerston to Lawrence, 13 Nov. (two letters), 19 Nov. 1849; Crampton to Palmerston, 1, 29 Oct. 1849; Lawrence to Palmerston, 8 Nov. 1849 (B.M.Add.48575); Bulwer to Palmerston, 6 Jan. (Nos. 5, 6, 12), 3 Feb., 2, 16 Mar., 28 Apr., 1, 8 July, 18 Nov. 1850; Palmerston to Bulwer, 8 Mar. (Nos. 17, 20, 21), 14 Mar. (Nos. 23, 25) 1850 (B.M.Add.48576).
616	4	Bell, II.141–3; Palmerston to Clarendon, 24, 25 Sept. 1855 (B.M.Add.48579).
	16	Bell, II.154–7; Palmerston to Clarendon, 25 Sept. 1855 (B.M.Add.48579).
617	4	Argyll, II.47–9.
	31	Palmerston to Bulwer, 11 Jan., 22 Feb., 6 Apr. 1850; Bulwer to Palmerston, 15, 18 Mar., 28 Apr., 6, 20 May, 19 July, 23 Sept. 1850 (B.M.Add.48576).
618	8	Palmerston to Sheil, 29 Aug., 6 Oct., 17 Nov. 1846, 8 Feb., 6 Dec. 1847 (B.M.Add.48559).
	29	Sykes, *History of Persia*, II.346–51.
619	5	Bell, II.142; Palmerston to Clarendon, 27 May 1956 (B.M.Add.48580).
620	5	Palmerston to the Sadr Azim, 8 Sept. 1857 (D. & A., V.131–2).

Page	Line	
	19	Palmerston to Elliot and Elliot, 26 Feb. 1841; Palmerston to Pottinger, 31 May 1841 (*Opium Pap.*, p. 1 n.).
621	15	Shaftesbury to Clarendon (undated, 1855); Memorial from missionaries at Ningpo, 5 June 1855; Dr Hobson to Bowring, 6 Nov. 1855; Dent and Co. to Bowring, 28 Dec. 1855; Lindsay and Co. to Bowring, 7 Jan. 1856; Bowring to Clarendon, 8 Jan. 1856; Davis to Palmerston, 15 May 1847 (*Opium Pap.*, pp. 28, 36–47 70–1, 73–82).
622	5	Morse, I.374–6, 381–2.
	33	Palmerston to Davis, 25 Jan., 24 Feb. 1847; judgment in *The Queen v. Compton*, 24 Nov. 1848; Addington to Compton, 11 Mar. 1847 (*Canton Riot Pap.*, pp. 84–7, 89–90, 97); Morse, I.383–4.
623	15	Palmerston to Davis, 9 Jan. 1847 (D. & A., III.377–8).
	34	Palmerston to Bonham, 12 May 1849 (*Insults in China*, p. 195); Morse, I.379, 395.
624	25	Palmerston to Davis, 12 Jan. 1847 (*Canton River Ops. Pap.*, p. 3); Alcock to Davis, 17, 25, 31 Mar. 1848; Bonham to Palmerston, 25 Mar. 1848; Bonham to Alcock, 27 Mar. 1848; Palmerston to Bonham, 5 July 1848 (*Insults in China*, pp. 92, 94, 123, 127, 138, 169), 16 Aug. 1849; Morse, I.387–9, 393–4, 398.
625	3	Norse, I.391, 410 n.
	39	Granville to Bowring, 19 Jan. 1852 (*Corr. on Entrance to Canton*, p. 3); Morse, I.345, 403.
627	33	Morse, I.424–5.
628	27	Argyll, II.67–9.
629	21	Hansard, 26, 27 Feb., 2, 3 Mar. 1857; H.L., 24, 26 Feb. 1857.
630	25	Hansard, 3 Mar. 1857.
	39	Argyll, II.70; Victoria to Palmerston, 4 Mar. 1847; Victoria's journal, 4 Mar. 1857 (Connell, *Regina v. Palmerston*, pp. 212–13).
631	14	Argyll, II.76.
	34	Argyll, II.70; *The Times*, 24 Mar. 1857.
632	26	Palmerston to Matthews, 9 Mar. 1857; Palmerston to Turner, 9 Mar. 1857; Palmerston to Duncan, 12 Mar. 1857; Palmerston to Meith, 17 Mar. 1857; Palmerston to Town Clerk of Wick, 17 Mar. 1857; Palmerston to Lord Provost of Glasgow, 25 Mar. 1857; Palmerston to Thornton, 9 Mar. 1857 (B.M.Add.48580); Malmesbury to Palmerston, 25 Mar. 1857 (B.P., H.M.C., GC/MA/193/1–3).
	35	Palmerston to Malmesbury, 25 Mar. 1857 (B.P., H.M.C., GC/MA/193/4).
633	26	*The Times*, 28 Mar. 1857; Hodder, III.43.

	Pine	
634	26	Argyll, II.77; Elgin to Yeh, 12, 24 Dec. 1857; Yeh to Elgin, 14 Dec. 1857; Loch to Elgin, 5 Jan. 1858; Elgin to Canning, 22 Feb. 1858 (*China Elgin Mission Papers*, pp. 95–6, 121–4, 128, 144–6, 214–15); Hansard, 12 Feb. 1858.
637	20	For the debates on the Divorce Bill, see Hansard, 11, 17 July 1856, 24, 30, 31 July, 4, 13, 14, 17, 18, 19, 21, 25 Aug. 1857.
638	19	Hodder, III.55.
639	15	Victoria's memorandum, 18 July 1857 (Connell, *op. cit.*, pp. 220–3); Clarendon's diary, 5 Sept. 1857; Clarendon to Lewis, 28 Sept. 1857 (Maxwell, II.149, 152–3); D. & A., V.140; Hansard, 10 Dec. 1857; Palmerston to Fitzwilliam, 9 Sept. 1857 (B.M.Add.48580).
640	7	Kaye, *History of the Sepoy War in India*, II.397–403; III. 635–41.
641	4	*The Times*, 17, 23, 29 Oct., 6 Nov. 1857.
	35	Granville to Canning, 24 Sept., 9 Nov. 1857; Canning to Granville, 11 Dec. 1857 (Fitzmaurice, I.260, 263–4, 296).
642	27	*The Times*, 3, 5 Nov. 1857; Granville to Canning, 10 Nov. 1857; Granville to Argyll, 19 Feb. 1887 (Fitzmaurice, I.265, 291–2); Palmerston to Clarendon, 6 Nov. 1857 (Maxwell, II.155).
643	16	D. & A., V.139–40; *The Times*, 10 Nov. 1857.
	37	Hansard, 4, 8, 10 Dec. 1857; Lady Canning to Granville, 24 Dec. 1857, 9 Jan. 1858 (Fitzmaurice, I.284, 286); Malmesbury, p. 411.
644	16	D. & A., V.138–40.
	39	Clarendon to Lady Clarendon, 7 Sept. 1857 (Maxwell, II.150); Argyll, II.86.
646	22	Palmerston to Grey, 12 Oct. 1855 (B.M.Add.48579).
	37	Hansard, 5, 8, 9, 16 Feb. 1858.
647	14	Greville (Wilson ed.) II, 563; D. & A., V. 142.
648	19	Hansard, 19 Feb. 1858; Gladstone to Mrs Gladstone, 21 Feb. 1858 (Bassett, *Gladstone to his Wife*, pp. 120–1).
	31	Gladstone to Mrs Gladstone, 22 Feb. 1858 (Bassett, p. 121); Fortescue's journal, 1 Nov. 1858 (Hewett, . . . *and Mr Fortescue*, p. 136).

Page	Line	
649	20	Palmerston to Argyll, 20 Aug. 1858 (Argyll, II.109); Hansard, 12, 26 Mar., 12, 26, 30 Apr., 3, 4, 7 May, 7, 11, 14, 17, 25 June, 1, 2, 6, 8, 9, 27, 30 July 1858; D. & A., V.149.
650	13	Magarshack, *Turgenev*, pp. 183–5.
	33	Fortescue's journal, 29, 31 Oct. 1858 (Hewett, pp. 135–6); Hayward to Gladstone, 5 Nov. 1858 (Hayward, II.13); Dallas to Markoe, 8 Oct. 1858 (Dallas, *Letters from London*, II.54).
651	14	Bell, II.193; Palmerston to Borthwick, 28 Oct. 1858 Lucas, p. 146).
	27	Palmerston to Clarendon, 31 Oct., 2 Nov. 1858 (Maxwell, II. 162–3); Hewett, p. 139.
652	10	Malmesbury, p. 455; Clarendon to Duchess of Manchester, 27 Nov. 1858; Lady Theresa Lewis to Clarendon, 24 Nov. 1858 (Maxwell, II.165, 167, 169); D. & A., V.69.
	30	Hansard, 31 Mar. 1859.
654	6	Lucas, pp. 181–2; *The Times*, 26, 30 Apr. 1859.
655	12	Disraeli to Palmerston, 3 May 1859; Palmerston to Disraeli, 3 May 1859 (Monypenny and Buckle, I.1635–7); Greville, VIII.245–9.
	36	Herbert to Granville, 27 May 1859 (Fitzmaurice, I.328); *The Times*, 7 June 1859; Stanmore, *Herbert*, II.198–9.
656	26	Gronow, I.221–3, 225–7; Lady Dorothy Nevill, *Reminiscences*, p. 305.
657	14	Victoria's journal, 11 June 1859 (Connell, *Regina v. Palmerston*, p. 255); Palmerston to Victoria, 11 June 1859 (D. & A., V.155–7); Russell to Granville, 12 June 1859 (Fitzmaurice, I.337).
	37	Palmerston to Ramsden, 26 June 1859; Palmerston to Napier, 27 June 1859 (B.M.Add.48581); Lady Clarendon's journal, 13 June 1859; Palmerston to Clarendon, 13 June 1859 (Maxwell, II.185–6); Victoria's journal, 12, 13 June 1859 (Connell, *op. cit.*, pp. 255–60).
658	21	Gladstone, anonymous book review in *Quarterly Review*, CIV.527–8 (Oct. 1858).
659	18	Palmerston to Cobden, 27 June 1859 (B.M.Add.48581).
	38	Trevelyan, *Bright*, p. 282 n.; Holyoake, *Sixty Years of an Agitator's Life*, I.228; II.279; Palmerston to Victoria, 2 July 1859; Victoria to Palmerston, 2 July 1859 (*Q.V.L.* I(iii)446).
660	22	Hart, *Man born to live*, pp. 104–5, 147–8, 155–6.

Page	Line	
661	8	Palmerston to Russell, 17 Oct., 14 Nov. 1859; Palmerston to Cowley, 6 Sept., 29 Nov., 15 Dec. 1859, 20 Jan. 1860 (B.M.Add.48581); Hansard, 12 Mar. 1860.
662	20	Palmerston to Russell, 17 May 1860 (B.M.Add.48581).
	41	Palmerston to Russell, 17 May, 10 July 1860 (B.M.Add. 48581).
663	15	Trevelyan, *Garibaldi and the Making of Italy*, pp. 104–9.
665	35	Tennyson, 'Riflemen Form!'; Palmerston to Grey, 5 June 1855 (B.M.Add.48579); Palmerston to Somerset, 29 Dec. 1860 (B.M.Add.48582); Suckling, *Around Old Romsey*, pp. 148–9; Suckling, *Up and down Old Romsey*, p. 63; Palmerston to Cardwell, 1 Dec. 1859 (B.M.Add. 48581).
666	10	Bell, II.262; Dasent, *Delane*, II.21.
668	13	Barrington, 'Sketches of Men of Mark', ff. 19–20 (Lambton MSS.); Palmerston to Victoria, 7 May 1860 (RA A28/70); Bell, II.259–60; Greville, VIII.310; Fitzmaurice, I.380.
	34	Greville, VIII.310; Gladstone's memorandum, 26 May 1860 (Morley, *Life of Gladstone*, II.33); Palmerston's memorandum on voting in Cabinet, 2 July 1860 (B.P., H.M.C., CAB/A/132).
669	30	Hansard, 22, 24, 25 May, 6 July 1860; Phillimore's journal, 6 July 1860; Gladstone's memorandum, 1898; Gladstone's journal, 10, 13 Apr., 13 May 1861 (Morley, *op. cit.*, II.33–4, 38–40); Palmerston's memorandum on voting in Cabinet, 12 Apr. 1861 (B.P., H.M.C., CAB/A/137–8).
	33	Gladstone's memorandum, 1898 (Morley, *op. cit.*, II.39).

CHAPTER XXXV

THE LAST PREMIERSHIP: INTERNAL AFFAIRS

671	25	Shaftesbury to Ashley, 28 Feb. 1855; Hodder, II.505; III.191–9.
672	12	Palmerston to Wood, 20 Nov. 1856 (B.M.Add.48580).
	20	*Lord Rendel's Personal Papers*, p. 120; Hodder, III.196.
673	26	Palmerston to Cardwell, 15 Sept. 1859 (B.M.Add. 48581); Palmerston to Minto, 3 Dec. 1847 (D. & A., IV.45); Palmerston to Aberdeen, 28 Aug. 1853; Aberdeen to Palmerston, 30 Aug. 1853 (B.M.Add.43069); Palmerston to Grey, 31 July 1865 (B.M.Add.48583); Palmerston to Peel, 23 Jan., 23 Feb. 1865 (H.M.C., B.P. Letter Book).
674	9	Palmerston to St Germans, 20, 24 (wrongly dated 23), 26 Feb., 2 Mar., 6 July 1853; Aberdeen to Palmerston,

Page	Line	
		24 Feb. 1853 (B.M.Add.48578); Hansard, 8 Apr. 1853; H.L., 11, 21 Feb., 18 Mar. 1853.
	19	Hansard, 18 Mar. 1851; Lucas, p. 134; Bell, II.36–7.
675	12	Palmerston to Romilly, 6 Nov. 1859; Palmerston to Newdigate, 6 Nov. 1859 (B.M.Add.48581).
	17	*Calendar of State Papers (Foreign Series) of the reign of Edward VI*, ed. W. B. Turnbull; pp. v–xxvii; *Calendar of State Papers (Foreign Series) of the reign of Mary*, ed. W. B. Turnbull, pp. vii–xvi.
676	10	Palmerston to Romilly, 23 Dec. 1860, 13 Jan. 1861 (B.M.Add.48582); Hansard, 15 Mar. 1861.
	27	Fitzroy to Moderator of Presbytery of Edinburgh, 19 Oct. 1853; D. & A., V.13–16; Lorne, pp. 224–5.
	38	Palmerston to Sumner, 15 July 1860 (B.M.Add.48581).
677	21	Hansard, 9 Apr. 1824, 11 July 1860; Palmerston to Lewis, 15 Apr., 24 June 1860 (B.M.Add.48581); Palmerston to Campbell, 13 Sept. 1860 (B.M.Add.48582); Skeats and Miall, *History of the Free Churches of England*, pp. 561–3.
	36	Airlie, II.120; Palmerston to Oranmore, 13, 16 Aug., 29 Oct. 1856, 25 Aug. 1857.
678	30	Palmerston to Oranmore, 13 Aug. 1856; Palmerston to Smith, 3 Sept. 1857; Palmerston to Cavendish, 3 Sept. 1857 (B.M.Add.48580).
679	20	Palmerston to Milnes, 6 Feb. 1856 (B.M.Add.48579); Palmerston to Newcastle, 19 Nov. 1856; Palmerston to Carlisle, 10 Feb. 1857 (B.M:Add.48580), 28 Dec. 1861 (B.M.Add.48582); Palmerston to Bedford, 9 Jan. 1860 (B.M.Add.48581); Palmerston to Denison, 15 Nov. 1864 (B.P., H.M.C., Letter Book).
680	4	Argyll, II.10, 20; Hansard, H.L., 7, 25 Feb. 1856; Anderson, 'The Wensleydale Peerage Case' (*English Historical Review*, LXXXII.486 (July 1967)).
	30	*Goschen Letters*, p. 58.
	38	Hansard, 12 June 1855.
681	27	Palmerston to Gibson, 5 May 1864 (B.P., H.M.C., Letter Book).
682	5	Palmerston to Gibson, 27 Dec. 1860; Palmerston to Caithness, 24 Jan. 1861 (B.M.Add.48582); Palmerston to Grey, 22 Aug. 1964; Palmerston to Bessborough, 28 Aug. 1864 (B.P., H.M.C., Letter Book).
	18	Irving, *Annals of our Time*, 27 Aug. 1861; Palmerston to Lewis, 1 Sept. 1861 (B.M.Add.48582).
	39	Gregg, pp. 506–8; Bell, II.158; Walpole, II.283–4; Palmerston to Victoria, 14 June 1855 (Connell, *Regina v. Palmerston*, pp. 180–1); Palmerston to Elcho, 16 Feb. 1860 (B.M.Add.48581).

CHAPTER XXXVI

OLD PAM

Page	Line	
	22	Palmerston to Fox, 22 June 1855 (B.M. Add. 48579); Palmerston to Lewis, 9 Apr. 1862 (B.M.Add. 48582).
695	3	Palmerston to Molesworth, 8 July 1855; Palmerston to Hall, 25 Sept. 1855 (B.M.Add.48579).
	28	Palmerston to Hall, 29, 31 Oct., 3, 12 Nov. 1857 (B.M. Add.48580).
696	10	Webster, 'Lord Palmerston at Work' (*Politica* (Aug. 1934), p. 144); Palmerston to Scott, 26 July 1859 (B.M. Add.48581); Bell, II.286-8; Hansard, 18 Feb., 4 Aug. 1859.
	28	Suckling, *Up and down Old Romsey*, pp. 13, 31; Suckling, *Around Old Romsey*, pp. 39, 50, 67.
697	11	Woodham-Smith, *Florence Nightingale*, pp. 275-7; Hansard, 9 June, 23 July 1857.
	24	Greville, III.136; Argyll, II.77.
698	2	Albert to Ernst of Saxe-Coburg, 4 Aug. 1850 (Bolitho, *The Prince Consort to his Brother*, p. 117).
	31	Lady Palmerston to Palmerston, undated, 1848 (Airlie, II.122); Russell to Victoria, 9 Feb. 1860; Victoria to Palmerston, 10 Feb. 1860; Palmerston to Victoria, 10 Feb. 1860 (Connell, *op. cit.*, pp. 279-81).
699	35	Sir T. Martin, II.429, V.355, 359-62; Bell, II.296-8; Granville to Canning, 16 Dec. 1861 (Fitzmaurice, I.405); Hodder, III.132; Clarendon to Duchess of Manchester, 17 Dec. 1861 (Maxwell, II.253); Palmerston to Phipps, 12 Dec. 1861; Palmerston to Victoria, 2 Mar. 1863 (Connell, *op. cit.*, pp. 316, 335-6); West, *Recollections*, I.298.
700	18	Palmerston to Phipps, 7 June 1862 (B.P., H.M.C., Letter Book); Palmerston to Aberdeen, 18 Apr. 1853 (B.M.Add.43069); Malmesbury's journal, 25 Jan. 1858 (Malmesbury, p. 415); Hansard, 26 Feb. 1863.
701	8	Barrington, 'Sketches of Men of Mark', ff. 14, 16 (Lambton MSS.).
	25	Clarendon to Granville, 16 Sept. 1855 (Fitzmaurice, I.120); Greville, VI.415; Argyll, II.49.
	36	Herbert to Granville, 27 May 1859 (Fitzmaurice, I.328); Trevelyan, *John Bright*, p. 281.
702	21	Wheatley, *London Past and Present*, I.318; Fortescue's journal, 31 Aug. 1860 (Hewett, p. 168).
703	10	Fraser, *Disraeli and his Day*, p. 76; Palmerston to the Editor of *The Globe*, 9 July 1849 (B.P., H.M.C., Pre/A/12); Malmesbury, p. 211; Victoria to Palmerston, 6 Oct/1855; Palmerston to Victoria, 9 Oct. 1855 (Connell, *op. cit.*, pp. 186-7).

Page	Line	
	32	Lorne, p. 215; Airlie, II.172; Fraser, p. 10; Hayward's obituary of Lady Palmerston, in *The Times*, 15 Sept. 1869 (Hayward, *Selected Essays*, II.352–3).
704	13	Holyoake, I.227; II.80–1.
705	8	Holyoake, II.80; Harney's account, 10 Mar. 1894 (in Snell, pp. 87–8).
	36	Wolff, Rambling Recollections, I.113–15.
706	13	Palmerston to Cowley, 16 Oct. 1859 (B.M.Add.48581); Palmerston to Carlisle, 27 Feb. 1861 (B.M.Add.48582).
707	10	Palmerston to Russell, 4 Dec. 1863, 18 Feb. 1864 (B.P., H.M.C., Letter Book).
	30	Palmerston to Russell, 18 Feb. 1864 (B.P., H.M.C., Letter Book); Palmerston to Mrs. Cobden, 27 May, 11 June 1865 (B.M.Add.48583, f. 1).
708	31	Palmerston to Delane, 24 July 1861; Delane to Dasent, 4 Apr. 1864 (Dasent, *Delane*, II.29, 101).
709	2	See *supra*, p. 153.
	18	Grant, *The Newspaper Press*, II.205–7.
710	2	Ossington, *Notes from my Journal when Speaker of the House of Commons*, p. 116; Barrington, f. 16 (Lambton MSS); Palmerston to De Grey, 14 Aug. 1860 (B.M.Add. 48582); Bright to Cobden, 25 Oct. 1860 (B.M.Add. 43384, f. 229).
	32	*Punch*, 8 Oct. 1853, 10 Jan. 1852, 20 Aug. 1859, 19 July 1862; D. & A., V.260; Holyoake, II.77; Disraeli's memorandum (undated) (Monypenny and Buckle, II.157).
711	15	Denison's journal, 6 Feb. 1865 (Ossington, p. 174); Disraeli's memorandum (Monypenny and Buckle, II.156); Merimée to Fanny Longdon, 19 July 1864 (*Correspondance Génerale de Prosper Merimée*, XII.184).
	32	White, *The Inner Life of the House of Commons*, I.152–5; Lorne, p. 226; Obituary of Palmerston in *The Times*, 19 Oct. 1865.
712	29	Day, pp. 213–16; Hansard, 23 May 1848, 15 May 1860, 28 May 1861; D. & A., V.198–9.
713	3	*Punch*, 7 Mar. 1857; West, II.196.
	32	*The Times*, 18 Apr. 1860; Hansard, 20 Apr., 15 May 1860; Snell, p. 93.
714	8	Irving, *Annals of our Time*, 19 Nov. 1863; Cobden to Lady Dorothy Nevill, 29 Oct. 1863 (Lady Dorothy Nevill, *Under Five Reigns*, p. 81); *Correspondance de Merimée*, XI.506 n.
	28	Clarendon to Cowley, 4 Nov. 1863 (Cowley, *The Paris Embassy during the Second Empire*, pp. 253–4); Merimée to Panizzi, 9 Nov. 1864 (*Correspondance de Merimée*, XI.506–7); Gladstone to Mrs. Gladstone, 10, 11 Nov. 1863 (Bassett, pp. 157–8); Blake, *Disraeli*, p. 434.

Page	Line	
	39	Irving, *Annals of our Time*, 19 Nov. 1863.
716	6	Webb to Palmerston, 3 May 1864 and enclosure (B.P., H.M.C., GC/WE/2/1–2.
	28	Palmerston's draft reply to Webb (undated) (B.P., H.M.C., G.C./WE/2/3–4).

CHAPTER XXXVII

THE LAST PREMIERSHIP: FOREIGN AFFAIRS

717	20	Palmerston to Russell, 4 Nov. 1859 (B.M.Add.48581, printed in part in D. & A., V.187–8).
718	18	Palmerston's memorandum of his talk with Flahaut, 27 Mar. 1860 (D. & A., V.190–2); Palmerston to Victoria, 29 Mar. 1860 (Connell, *Regina v. Palmerston*, pp. 281–3).
719	21	Palmerston to Russell, 19, 22, 26, 30 July, 8 Aug. (two letters) 1860; Palmerston to Cowley, 31 July 1860 (B.M. Add.48581); Bell, II.268–70.
721	8	Palmerston to Cowley, 25 Nov. 1859 (B.M.Add.48581).
	32	Hansard, 25 June, 1 Aug. 1861, 16, 22 May, 1 Aug. 1862, 15 May, 12 June, 28 July 1863, 12 Apr. 1864.
722	40	Palmerston to Herbert, 12 Sept., 5 Oct. 1860 (Stanmore, *Herbert*, II.296, 299).
723	16	Elgin to Russell, 25 Oct. 1860 (*China Papers, 1859–60* pp. 213–15).
	34	Palmerston to Herbert, 20 Dec. 1860 (Stanmore, *Herbert*, II.350).
724	2	Palmerston to Herbert, 20 Apr. 1860 (Stanmore, *Herbert*, II.314–15).
	24	Hansard, 6 July 1863, 4 Mar. 1864.
725	4	Palmerston to Elliott, 21 Apr. 1841 (Morse, I.642).
	26	Palmerston to Brooke, 23 Feb. 1848 (B.M.Add.48556); Palmerston to Elgin, 8 Oct. 1859 (B.M.Add.48581); Palmerston to Russell, 13 Aug. 1862 (B.P., H.M.C., Letter Book; other parts of this letter are printed in D. & A., V.227–8); Palmerston to Cardwell, 8 Sept. 1864 (B.P., H.M.C., Letter Book).
726	11	Hansard, 10 Aug. 1842, 12 Feb. 1844, 23 July 1845, 25 Feb. 1848, 15 Apr. 1851, 21 May 1858, 18 Mar. 1859; Broughton, VI.78; Palmerston to Whalley, 22 Feb. 1860 (B.M.Add.48581); Palmerston to Lewis, 9 Jan. 1861; Palmerston to Glenelg, 31 Aug. 1861 (B.M.Add.48582).
	30	Palmerston to Ward, 26 Dec. 1850, 19 Nov. 1851 (D.& A., IV.266, 269); Palmerston to Normanby, 10 May 1847 (B.M.Add.48577).
727	9	Bell, II.335; Hansard, 10 Feb., 5 June, 21, 23, 24, 28 July 1863, 25 Feb., 18 Mar. 1864.

CHAPTER XXXVIII

THE AMERICAN CIVIL WAR

Page	Line	
743	5	C. F. Adams, pp. 217–18; Bell, II.294–5; Palmerston to Victoria, 12 Jan. 1862 (Connell, *op. cit.*, p. 322); Bright to Sumner, 14 Dec. 1861 (Trevelyan, *Bright*, pp. 315–16).
744	9	Hansard, 17 Feb. 1862; Bright to Sumner, 14 Dec. 1861 (Trevelyan, *Bright*, pp. 315–16); E. D. Adams, I.229; Bell, II.296; Palmerston to Victoria, 5 Dec. 1861 (Connell, *op. cit.*, p. 311); Fitzmaurice, I.401.
	23	Cobden to Paulton, Jan. 1862 (Morley, *Life of Cobden*, II.389); Bright to Mallet, 23 Dec. 1861 (Trevelyan, *Bright* p. 316); E. D. Adams, I.229; Palmerston to Victoria, 17 Feb. 1862 (RA A30/25).
745	3	Hansard, 17 Feb. 1862.
	27	C. F. Adams, pp. 243–7.
746	19	Palmerston to Adams, 11 June 1862 (B.P., H.M.C., Letter Book).
747	13	Palmerston to Russell, 14 June 1862 (*Russell Later Corr.*, II.325–6); Palmerston to Adams, 15, 19 June 1862; Adams to Palmerston, 12, 16, 20 June 1862; C. F. Adams, pp. 246–60; Hansard, 13 June 1862.
	38	C. F. Adams, pp. 306–15; Layard's memorandum, 14 Mar. 1865 (B.M.Add.38991).
748	14	Bell, II.317.
749	10	Granville to Russell, 27 Sept. 1862; Granville to Stanley of Alderley, 1 Oct. 1862 (Fitzmaurice, I.442–4); Bell, II.315; Maxwell, II.264–5.
	34	Clarendon to Lewis, 26 Oct. 1862; Palmerston to Clarendon, 20 Oct. 1862 (Maxwell, II.266–7); Granville to Stanley of Alderley, 1 Oct. 1862 (Fitzmaurice, I.442).
750	12	Russell's memorandum, 13 Oct. 1862; Palmerston to Russell, 2 Nov. 1862 (E. D. Adams, II..60–1, 101–2); Henry Adams to Charles F. Adams Jr., 23 Jan. 1863 (*Adams Letters*, I.243); C. F. Adams, pp. 260, 291–3.
	37	H. Adams to C. F. Adams Jr., 27 Jan. 1863 (*Adams Letters*, I.243–4); E. D. Adams, II.130–1, 294–5.
751	15	D. & A., V.233, 236; Vincent, *The Foundation of the Liberal Party*, p. 149 n.
	30	Argyll, II.195–7.
752	25	Hansard, 30 June, 10 July 1863.
753	8	E. D. Adams, II.143–50; Russell to Palmerston, 4 Sept. 1863; Palmerston to Layard, 5 Sept. 1863 (B.M.Add. 38989); Palmerston to Somerset, 13 Sept. 1863 (B.P., H.M.C., Letter Book).
	23	Hansard, 27 Mar. 1863; 12 Feb. 1864.
754	24	E. D. Adams, II.206–17, 250; Hansard, 1 May 1865.

Page	Line	
755	17	Monypenny and Buckle, I.1415.
	23	Magnus, *Gladstone*, p. 394.
756	16	Gregory, *Autobiography*, pp. 239–40; Granville to Canning, 26 July 1860 (Fitzmaurice, I.386); Bell, II.261–2.
	29	Palmerston's memoranda, 2 July 1860, Feb. 1861, two of 12 Apr. 1861, 25 June 1864 (B.P., H.M.C., CAB/A/132, 137–8, 157).
757	4	Bell, II.255–6; Brand's memorandum, 9 Feb. 1861 (B.P., H.M.C., CAB/B/23).
	22	Hansard, 11 May 1864; Palmerston to Gladstone, 11, 12, 13, 14 May 1864 (Guedalla, *Gladstone and Palmerston*, pp. 279, 281–4).
758	8	Palmerston's memorandum, 15 May 1864 (B.P., H.M.C., PM/A/16).
	15	Hodder, III.187.
	38	Hansard, 26 Apr. 1858; Hewett, p. 128.
759	22	Magnus, *Gladstone*, pp. 381, 418; D. & A., IV.359; Hodder, III.187.
760	21	Webster, pp. 233–4; Bell, I.224–5.
761	2	Macdonald to Russell, 15 Sept. 1860; Crossthwaite to Russell, 21 Sept. 1860; Bloomfield to Russell, 29 Sept 1860; Schleinitz to Bloomfield, 9 Oct. 1860; Russell to Louther, 11 Feb. 1861 (*St Pap.*, LII64–6, 70, 73, 80–3, 117–19); Hansard, 26 Apr. 1861; Bell, II.309–11.
	33	Palmerston to Leopold I, 13 Mar. 1863 (D. & A., V.232).
762	8	Palmerston's draft despatch to Napier on Polish affairs, 'read to the Cabinet but thought too Strong', 25 July 1863 (B.P., H.M.C., MM/PO/14).
763	7	Hansard, 10, 20, 23, 27 Feb., 20, 23, 27 Mar., 17, 21 Apr., 19 May, 22, 26 June, 6, 20 July 1863, 4 Feb. 1864.
	24	Hansard, 19 Feb. 1863.
764	14	Palmerston to Leopold I, 15 Nov. 1863 (B.P., H.M.C., Letter Book; other parts of this letter are printed in D. & A., V.236–42).
	33	Palmerston to Victoria, 4 Jan. 1864; Victoria to Leopold I, 25 Feb. 1864 (Connell, *Regina v. Palmerston*, pp. 341, 350).
765	24	Palmerston to Ponsonby, 4 Aug. 1837 (B.M.Add.48543); Lord W. Russell to Palmerston, 17 May 1837 (B.M.Add. 48532); Palmerston's memorandum, 27 June 1863 (B.M.Add.38989).
	36	Hansard, 23 July 1863.
766	14	Palmerston to Russell, 7 Jan. 1864 (*Russell Later Corr.*, II.304).
	32	Palmerston to Russell, 13 Feb. 1864 (D. & A., V.247–8).

Page	Line	
767	25	Palmerston to Russell, 13 Feb., 1 May 1864 (D. & A., V.247–52); Granville to Russell, 6 May 1864; Russell to Granville, 6 May 1864; General Grey to Granville, 9 May 1864 (Fitzmaurice, I.463–5); Palmerston to Victoria, 10 May 1864; Victoria to Palmerston, 11 May 1864; Victoria to Leopold I, 12 May 1864 (*Q.V.L.*, II(i)186–8).
768	5	Fitzmaurice, I.471.
	22	Palmerston's memorandum of voting in Cabinet, 25 June 1864 (B.P., H.M.C., CAB/A/157); Malmesbury, p. 598.
769	10	Hansard, 27 June 1864.
	31	E. D. Adams, II.206–17; Hansard, 4 July 1864.
770	15	Hansard, 8 July 1864.
	22	Monypenny and Buckle, II.139.
771	7	Malmesbury, pp. 593–4; Hibbert, *Garibaldi and his Enemies*, pp. 341–6, 349–51; Holyoake, II.119–22; *The Times*, 12 Apr. 1864.
	31	Lorne, p. 216; Hibbert, pp. 347–9, 351; Hansard, 19, 21 Apr. 1864.
772	13	Brougham to Lady Westmorland, 21 Apr. 1863 (*Lady Westmorland's Letters*, p. 466); Herbert to Gladstone, 10 Nov. 1856 (Stanmore, *Herbert*, II.56); Vincent, *The Foundation of the Liberal Party*, pp. 145, 149, 231; D. & A., V.123, 258–9; Suckling, *Around Old Romsey*, p. 14.
	30	Holyoake, II.78; Greville, I.426; D. & A., V.9.
773	6	Holyoake, II.78–80; *The Times*, 10 Aug. 1864.
	26	*The Times*, 24 Aug. 1864; Snell, pp. 71–2, 94–6.
774	3	*The Times*, 6, 22 Sept. 1864; Suckling, *Up and down Old Romsey*, p. 5; Suckling, *Around Old Romsey*, p. 3; Palmerston to Temple, 2 May 1836; Palmerston to Normanby, 2 Apr. 1847 (D. & A., III.11, 369).
	19	Suckling, *Up and down Old Romsey*, p. 46; Clarendon to Cowley, 2 Oct. 1861 (Cowley, p. 221); D. & A., V.260.
775	7	White, *The Inner Life of the House of Commons*, I.173–4.
	36	Southgate, pp. 526–7; Irving, *Annals of our Time*, 28 Apr. 1865; Palmerston to Russell, 4 Aug. 1864 (B.P., H.M.C., Letter Book); Bell, II.414; Hodder, III.178–9; Greville, VIII.160.
776	13	Hansard, 20, 27 Feb. 1865.
	38	Snell, pp. 107–12.
777	17	Magnus, *Gladstone*, p. 170; Hodder, III., 187–8.
778	18	Palmerston to Macdonogh, 26 June 1865; Palmerston to Kincaid, 26 June 1865 (B.M.Add.48583); Hansard, 2 July 1861.

Page	Line	
779	20	Palmerston to Brand, 3 Aug. 1865 (B.M.Add.48583).
780	18	Palmerston to Grey, 13, 17, 20 Sept. 1865; Palmerston to Wodehouse, 17 Sept. 1865; Palmerston to De Grey, 27 Sept. 1865 (B.M.Add.48583, ff. 45–8, 54–7).
781	9	Hansard, 12 June 1865; Palmerston to Gladstone, 23 Aug. 1865 (Guedalla, *Gladstone and Palmerston*, pp. 341–2); Palmerston to Victoria, 4 Sept. 1865 (*Q.V.L.*, II(i)275–6); Palmerston to Russell, 13 Sept. 1865 (B.M. Add.48583).
	22	*Ibid.*; this part of the letter is printed in D. & A., V.270–1.
	36	Lady Cowper to Cowper, 19 Oct. 1865 (Cowper, *Earl Cowper*, pp. 135–6); D. & A., V.272; Reeve, II.120; personal information from Mr. William Collier.
782	18	Victoria to Leopold I, 15 Oct. 1865 (*Q.V.L.*, II(i)277–8), Lady Cowper to Cowper, 19 Oct. 1865 (Cowper, *op. cit.*; pp. 135–6); Lucas, p. 154; Lady Palmerston to William Cowper, 16 Oct. 1765 (Lever, *Letters of Lady Palmerston*, pp. 364–5); Clarendon to Granville, 21 Oct. 1865 (Maxwell, II.298); Airlie, II.149; D. & A., V.273.
	30	Airlie, II.272–3; Lady Cowper to Cowper, 19 Oct. 1865 (Cowper, *op. cit.*, pp. 135–6); Reeve, II.120.
783	21	Gladstone to Mrs. Gladstone, 22 Oct. 1865 (Morley, *Gladstone*, II.153); C. F. Adams, pp. 373–6; Trevelyan, *Bright*, p. 344; Victoria's journal, 18 Oct. 1865 (Connell, *op. cit.*, p. 360); Florence Nightingale to Dr. Walker, 18 Oct. 1865 (Woodham-Smith, *Florence Nightingale*, p. 439).
	24	*The Times*, 19 Oct. 1865.
784	6	*The Times*, 31 Oct. 1865.
	8	See *supra*, p. 118.
	31	Finlason, *History of the Jamaica Case*, p. 368 ss.
785	26	Lever, *Lady Palmerston's Letters*, p. 366; Suckling., *Up and down Old Romsey*, p. 47; D. & A., I.4.
786	28	Palmerston to Victoria, 21 Feb. 1856 (Connell, *op. cit.*, pp. 201–2); Hansard, 20 Mar. 1855, 21 Feb. 1856, 8 June 1863; Gregory, p. 221.
787	3	See *supra*, pp. 302, 483, 508–9; Wilson, *Carlyle at his zenith*, pp. 254, 401–2; Monypenny and Buckle, I.1415.
788	2	Cf. Disraeli, *ibid.*
790	3	Greville, VIII.100; *Annual Register, 1865*, Chron., p. 160; Palmerston to Temple, 10 Nov. 1844 (D. & A., III.163); Hansard, 31 July 1854 (Palmerston's speech); Palmerston to Acland (between 23 and 29 Oct. 1857) (B.M.Add.

Page	Line	
		48580); Bell, II.411; Palmerston to Bloomfield, 1. Aug. 1850 (B.M.Add.48564); *Personal Papers of Lord Rendel*, p. 60.
	21	Hansard, 2 Aug. 1832, 20 July 1863; Cobden to Chevalier, 14 Dec. 1861 (Morley, *Cobden*, II.389).
	39	Hansard, 14 Dec. 1837; Albert to Stockmar, 11 Sept. 1847 (Martin, I.427); Albert to Russell, 2 Apr. 1850; Albert's notes on article in *Westminster Review*, 14 July 1852 (Connell, *op. cit.*, pp. 115, 143); Herbert to Hayward, 1 Nov. 1856 (*Hayward's Letters*, I.295); Greville (Wilson ed.), II.390.
792	4	Hansard, 11 Mar. 1844, 12 June 1849, 17 June 1851, 3 Mar. 1857; Harry Temple to Hare, 29 Mar. 1798; Palmerston to Cobden, 8 Jan. 1862 (D. & A., I.8; V. 221, 226); Palmerston to Layard, 23 Oct. 1864 (B.M.Add. 38990).
	26	Beauvale to Lady Palmerston, 5 Jan. 1846 (Airlie, II.105); *Cologne Gazette* of 20 Oct. 1865, as quoted in translation in *The Times*, 21 Oct. 1865.
793	9	Rosebery's journal, 17 Mar. 1886 (Rosebery MSS.); Lorne, p. 235.

Bibliography

MANUSCRIPT SOURCES

Aberdeen MSS. (B.M. Additional Manuscripts, 43069).
Bright Papers, vol. II (B.M. Add. 43384).
Broadlands Papers: Palmerston MSS. (B.M. Add. 48417–48589, 49963–49969).
Broadlands Papers, Historical Manuscripts Commission.
Broughton Correspondence, vol. VI (B.M. Add. 36461).
Dr. Samuel Butler's Correspondence, vol. VI (B.M. Add. 34588).
Church Papers: Correspondence of Lt. Col. Church, vol. I (B.M. Add. 36543).
Egerton MSS.: Hoppner's correspondence (B.M. Egerton 2343).
Foreign Office Papers (Public Record Office, F.O. 27/809; F.O. 72/694; F.O. 43/45).
Hampshire County Record Office, Calendar.
Hardwicke Papers, vol. LXXVI, CCCV (B.M. Add. 35653, 35424).
Howard de Walden MSS: Letters to Lord Howard de Walden 1835–1868 (B.M. Add. 45176).
Huskisson Papers, vol. XXIII, Supplementary vol. II (B.M. Add. 38756, 39949).
Jeune MSS: A letter in the possession of Capt. R. D. Jeune.
Lambton MSS.: 'Sketches of Men of Mark', by C. G. Barrington.
Layard MSS., vols. LVII–LXII (B.M. Add. 38987–38992).
Liverpool MSS., vols. V, CLXXXI (B.M. Add. 38194, 38370).
Miscellaneous Original Letters (B.M. Add. 19242).
North Baddesley MSS. (manuscript copies) in North Baddesley Vicarage.
Peel MSS., vols. LII, LIV–LV (B.M. Add. 40232, 40234–40235).
Pointing MSS.: two letters in possession of Mr. J. Pointing.
Rosebery MSS.: journal of 5th Earl of Rosebery, in possession of Earl of Rosebery.
RA: The Royal Archives at Windsor.

PRINTED SOURCES

ABERDEEN, Earl of: *Correspondence of Lord Aberdeen and Princess Lieven* (Camden Society, 3rd Series, Nos. 60, 62) (London, 1938–9).

ADAMS, C. F.: *A Cycle of Adams Letters 1861–1865* (ed. W. Chauncey Ford) (London, 1921).

ADAMS, C. F. Junr.: *Charles Francis Adams,* (London, 1900).

ADAMS, E. D.: *Great Britain and the American Civil War* (London, 1925).

ADAMS, Sir W.: *A Treatise on the Artificial Pupil,* (London, 1819).

AIRLIE, Mabel, Countess of: *Lady Palmerston and her Times* (London, 1922).

ALBERT, Prince Consort: *The Prince Consort to his Brother: Two hundred new Letters* (ed. H. Bolitho) (London, 1933).

ALBERY, W.: *A Parliamentary History of the Ancient Borough of Horsham 1295–1885* (London, 1927).

ANDERSON, Q.: 'The Wensleydale peerage case and the position of the House of Lords in the mid nineteenth century' (*English Historical Review*, vol. LXXXII, London, July, 1967).

Annual Register 1865 (London, 1866).

ANSTED, D. T.: *The Ionian Islands in the year 1863* (London, 1863).

ARBUTHNOT, Mrs. H.: *The Journals of Mrs. Arbuthnot 1820–1832* (ed. F. Banford and the Duke of Wellington) (London, 1950).

ARGYLL, George Douglas, 8th Duke of: *Autobiography and Memoirs* (London, 1906).

ARGYLL, 9th Duke of: See Lorne.

ASHLEY, Anthony, Lord (later 7th Earl of Shaftesbury): Anonymous book review in *Quarterly Review*, vol. LXVII (London, December 1840).

ASHLEY, E.: *The Life and correspondence of Henry John Temple, Viscount Palmerston* (London, 1879) (cited as 'Ashley'). See also Dalling and Ashley.

ATKINS, J. B.: *Life of Sir William Howard Russell* (London, 1911).

BAKER, T.: *History of the College of St. John the Evangelist, Cambridge* (ed. J. E. B. Meyer) (Cambridge, 1869).

BARRINGTON, C. G.: 'Sketches of Men of Mark' (*History Today*, London, March 1961) (see Manuscript sources, Lambton MSS).

BASSETT, A. T.: See Gladstone.

BELL, H. C. F.: *Lord Palmerston* (London, 1936).

BLAKE, R.: *Disraeli* (London, 1966).

BOLITHO, H.: See Albert, Prince Consort.

BRIGGS, Asa: *Victorian People: some reassessments of people, institutions, ideas and events 1851–1867* (London, 1954)

BROUGHTON, Lord (Sir J. C. Hobhouse): *Recollections of a long life* (ed. Lady Dorchester) (London, 1910).

BULWER, Sir H. L.: See Dalling and Ashley.

BUNSEN, Frances, Baroness: *A Memoir of Baron Bunsen* (London, 1868).

BYRON, Lord: *The Poetical Works of Lord Byron* (London, 1855–6 ed.).

Calendar of State Papers (Foreign Series) of the reign of Edward VI (ed. W. B. Turnbull) (London, 1861).

Calendar of State Papers (Foreign Series) of the reign of Mary (ed. W. B. Turnbull) (London, 1861).

Cambridge History of British Foreign Policy 1783–1919 (ed. Sir A. W. Ward and G. P. Gooch) (Cambridge, 1922–3), vol. II.

Cambridge Modern History (ed. A. W. Ward, G. W. Prothero, S. Leathes) (Cambridge, 1907–10), vols. VII, IX–XI.

Canton: *Correspondence relative to entrance into Canton 1850–1855* (Parliamentary Papers, 1857).

Canton: *Further Papers relative to the Proceedings of Her Majesty's Naval Forces at Canton* (Parliamentary Papers, 1857).

Canton Riot Papers: *Papers relating to the riot at Canton in July 1846* (Parliamentary Papers, 1847).

Canton River Operations Papers: *Correspondence relative to the operations in the Canton River, April 1847* (Parliamentary Papers, 1847).

CARR, R.: *Spain 1808–1939* (Oxford, 1966).

CECIL, Lord Robert (later 3rd Marquis of Salisbury): Anonymous book review in *Quarterly Review*, vol. CXVII (London, April 1865).

Cervi: *Confidential Memorandum on the Answer of the Government of Greece to that of Great Britain respecting the Islands of Cervi and Sapienza* (Foreign Office, London, 31 December 1849).

China Elgin Mission Papers: *Correspondence relative to the Earl of Elgin's Special Missions to China and Japan 1857–1859* (Parliamentary Papers, 1859).

China Papers: *Correspondence and Papers relating to China* (Parliamentary Papers, 1840).

China Papers 1859–60: *Correspondence respecting Affairs in China 1859–60* (Parliamentary Papers, 1861).

China: See also Canton; Insults in China; Opium Trade.

Chinese Service: *Correspondence relative to Lieutenant-Colonel Gordon's position in the Chinese Service* (Parliamentary Papers, 1864).

CLARKE, J. S., and M'ARTHUR, J.: *The Life of Admiral Lord Nelson, K.B.* (London, 1809).

COBBETT, W.: *Rural Rides* (ed. G. D. H. and M. Cole) (London, 1930 ed.).

COBBETT, W.: *Cobbett's Weekly Register* (London, 6 Apr. 1822).

COLLINS, Treacher: *The History and Traditions of the Moorfields Eye Hospital* (London, 1929).

CONINGHAM, W.: *Lord Palmerston and Prince Albert* (London, 1854).

CONNELL, B.: *Portrait of a Whig Peer* (London, 1957).

CONNELL, B.: *Regina v. Palmerston* (London, 1962).

COOK, Sir E.: *Delane of the Times* (London, 1915).

COOK, T. A.: *A History of the English Turf* (London, 1901–4).

COOPER, C. H.: *Annals of Cambridge* (Cambridge, 1843).

The Courier (London, 1 April 1814–2, January 1816).

COWLEY, Lord: *The Paris Embassy during the Second Empire* (ed. F. A. Wellesley) (London, 1928).

COWPER, Katrine Cecilia, Countess: *Earl Cowper, K.G., A Memoir* (privately printed, 1913).

Cracow Papers: *Papers relative to the Suppression by the Governments of Austria, Prussia and Russia of the Free State of Cracow* (Parliamentary Papers, 1847).

CREEVEY, T.: *The Creevey Papers* (ed. Sir H. Maxwell) (London, 1923).

CROKER, J. W.: *Correspondence and Diaries of John Wilson Croker* (ed. L. J. Jennings) (London, 1884).

CZARTORYSKI, Prince A.: *Memoirs of Prince Adam Czartoryski* (ed. A. Gielgud) (London, 1888).

DALLAS, G. M.: *A Series of Letters from London written during the years 1856, '57, '58, '59, and '60* (Philadelphia, 1869).

DALLING and ASHLEY: *The Life of Henry John Temple, Viscount Palmerston*, by Sir Henry Lytton Bulwer (Lord Dalling), edited by E. Ashley (London, 1870–4) (cited as 'D. & A., vols. I–III').

The Life of Henry John Temple, Viscount Palmerston 1846–1865, by E. Ashley (London, 1876) (cited as 'D. & A., vols. IV and V').

See also ASHLEY, E., *The Life and Correspondence of Henry John Temple, Viscount Palmerston* (London, 1879) (cited as 'Ashley').

DASENT, A. I.: *John Thadeus Delane* (London, 1908).

DAY, W.: *William Day's Reminiscences of the Turf* (London, 2nd ed., 1891).

DENISON, J. E.: See Ossington.

Dictionary of National Biography (Oxford, 1921–2 ed.).

DILLON, W.: *Life of John Mitchel* (London, 1888).

DINO, Duchess of: *Memoirs of the Duchesse de Dino, afterwards Duchesse de Talleyrand et de Sagan* (ed. Princess Radziwill) (London, 1909).

DISRAELI, B.: *Tancred, or The New Crusade* (London, 1847).

DOUGHTY, A. G.: 'Papineau' (*Encyclopaedia Britannica*, vol. XX, 13th ed., London, 1926).

DOUGLAS, S. (Lord Glenbervie): *Diaries of Sylvester Douglas* (ed. F. Bickley) (London, 1928).

DUNN, P.: 'Sir William Adams' (*British Journal of Ophthalmology*, vol. II, London, January 1918).

ECKINGER, K.: *Lord Palmerston und der Schweizer Sonderbundskrieg* (Berlin, 1938).

ELLENBOROUGH, Earl of: *A Political Diary 1828–1830* (ed. Lord Colchester) (London, 1881).

Encyclopaedia Britannica, 9th and 13th editions (London, 1875, 1926).

The Evening Star (London, 11 January–28 June 1809).

The Exchequer Reports: Reports of Cases argued and determined in the Courts of Exchequer and Exchequer Chamber, vol. II (London, 1849).

FAGAN, L.: *The Reform Club* (London, 1887).

FINLASON, W. F.: *The History of the Jamaica Case* (London, 1869).

FITZMAURICE, E.: *Life of Granville George Leveson Gower, Second Earl Granville, K.G.* (London, 1905).

FRASER, Sir W.: *Disraeli and his Day* (London, 1891).

FULFORD, R.: *The Prince Consort* (London, 1949).

Gentleman's Magazine, vol. LIV (London, 1784).

GLADSTONE, W. E.: Anonymous book review in *Quarterly Review*, vol. CIV (London, October 1858).

GLADSTONE, W. E.: *Gladstone to his wife* (ed. A. T. Bassett) (London, 1936).
See also Guedalla.

GOSCHEN, Letters: *Lord Goschen to his Friends* (ed. P. Colson) (London, 1946).

GRANT, J.: *Random Recollections of the House of Commons* (London, 1836).

GRANT, J.: *The Newspaper Press* (London, 1871).

GRANVILLE, Harriet, Countess: *The Letters of Harriet, Countess Granville* (London, 1894).

Greek Papers: *Correspondence respecting the demands made upon the Greek Government and respecting the islands of Cervi and Sapienza* (Parliamentary Papers, February 1850) (cited as 'Greek Pap., vol. I').

    Correspondence respecting Mr. Finlay's claim upon the Greek Government. Additional to the Papers presented to Parliament on the 22nd of February (Parliamentary Papers, April 1850) (cited as 'Greek Pap., vol. II').

    Further Correspondence respecting the Demands made upon the Greek Government (In continuation of Papers presented to Parliament on the 22nd February 1850) (Parliamentary Papers, 17 May 1850) (cited as 'Greek Pap., vol. III').

    Further Correspondence respecting the Demands made upon the Greek Government (In continuation of Papers presented to Parliament on the 17th of May 1850) (Parliamentary Papers, May 1850) (cited as 'Greek Pap., vol. IV').

    Further Correspondence respecting the Demands made upon the Greek Government (In continuation of Papers presented to the House of Lords on the 27th of May 1850) (Parliamentary Papers, 14 June 1850) (cited as 'Greek Pap., vol. V').

    Further Correspondence respecting the Demands made upon the Greek Government (In continuation of Papers presented to both Houses of Parliament on the 14th of June 1850) (Parliamentary Papers, 18 June 1850) (cited as 'Greek Pap., vol. VI').

    Further Correspondence respecting the Demands made upon the Greek Government (In continuation of Papers presented to the House of Commons on the 18th of June 1850) (Parliamentary Papers, 24 June 1850) (cited as 'Greek Pap., vol. VII').

GREGG, Pauline: *A Social and Economic History of Britain 1760–1960* (London, 1962).

GREGORY, Sir W.: *Autobiography* (London, 1894).

GREVILLE, C. C. F.: The Greville Memoirs:

    A Journal of the reigns of King George IV and King William IV (ed. H. Reeve) (London, 1875 ed.) (cited as 'Greville, I–III').

A Journal of the reign of Queen Victoria from 1837 to 1852 (ed. H. Reeve) (London, 1885) (cited as 'Greville, IV–VI').

A Journal of the Reign of Queen Victoria from 1852 to 1860 (ed. H. Reeve) (London, 1887) (cited as 'Greville, VII–VIII').

The Greville Diary (ed. P. W. Wilson) (London, 1927) (cited as 'Greville (Wilson ed.)').

GRIFFITHS, A., and INGRAM, T. A.: 'Juvenile Offenders (*Encyclopaedia Britannica*, 13th ed.) (London, 1926).

GRONOW, R. H.: *The Reminiscences and Recollections of Captain Gronow* (ed. J. Grego) (London, 1892).

GUEDALLA, P.: *Gladstone and Palmerston: being the correspondence of Lord Palmerston with Mr. Gladstone 1851–1865* (London, 1928).

GUEDALLA, P.: *Palmerston* (London, 1926).

GUIZOT, F.: *Mémoires pour servir à l'histoire de mon temps* (Paris, 1858–67).

Guizot–Lieven Letters: *Lettres de François Guizot et de la Princesse de Lieven* (ed. J. Naville) (Paris, 1963–4).

GUNNING, H.: *Reminiscences of the University, Town and County of Cambridge from the year 1780* (London, 1854).

HAMMOND, J. L. and B.: *The Town Labourer 1760-1832* (London, 1949 ed.).

HAMMOND, J. L. and B.: *The Village Labourer* (London, 1948 ed.).

Hampshire Independent (Winchester, 1849–53).

Hansard: *Parliamentary Debates: Official Report* (London, 1807–66).

HART, Elizabeth: *Man born to live* (London, 1953).

HAYDON, B. R.: *Life of Benjamin Robert Haydon from his Autobiography and Journals* (ed. Tom Taylor) (London, 1853).

HAYWARD, A.: *Selected Essays* (London, 1878).

HAYWARD, A.: *A Selection from the Correspondence of Abraham Hayward, Q.C.* (ed. H. E. Carlisle) (London, 1886).

HERRIES, E.: *Memoirs of John Charles Herries* (London, 1880).

HERTSLET, Sir E.: *Recollections of the Old Foreign Office* (London, 1901).

HEWETT, O. W.: *. . . and Mr. Fortescue* (London, 1958).

HIBBERT, C.: *Garibaldi and his Enemies* (London, 1965).

HOBHOUSE, Sir J. C.: See Broughton

HODDER, E.: *The Life and Work of the Seventh Earl of Shaftesbury* (London, 1886).

HOLYOAKE, G. J.: *Sixty Years of an Agitator's Life* (London, 3rd ed., 1893).

HORNER, F.: *Memoirs and Correspondence of Francis Horner, M.P.* (ed. L. Horner) (London, 1843).

HOWSON, E. W., and WARNER, G. Townsend: *Harrow School* (London, 1898).

HUGO, Victor: *Choses Vues* (Paris, 1887).

Insults in China: *Correspondence respecting Insults in China* (Parliamentary Papers, 1857).

Ionian Papers: *Papers respecting recent changes in the Constitution of the Ionian Islands* (Parliamentary Papers, 1850).

IRVING, J.: *The Annals of our Time 1837–71* (London, 1871 ed.)

Italian Papers: *Correspondence respecting the Affairs of Italy 1846-1849* (Parliamentary Papers, 1849).

KAYE, Sir J. W.: *A History of the Sepoy War in India* (London, 1864–76).

LABORDE, E. D.: *Harrow School, yesterday and today* (London, 1948).

LAYARD, Sir H.: *Sir Henry Layard's Autobiography* (ed. W. Bruce) (London, 1903).

LE MARCHANT, Sir D.: *Memoir of John Charles Viscount Althorp, Third Earl Spencer* (London, 1876).

Levant Papers: *Correspondence relative to the Affairs of the Levant* (Parliamentary Papers, 1841).

LEVER, Sir T.: *Correspondence of Lady Palmerston* (London, 1957).

LIEVEN, Princess Dorothea: *Letters of Princess Lieven during her residence in London 1812–34* (ed. L. G. Robinson) (London, 1902).
     See also Aberdeen; Guizot; Temperley.

LONGFORD, Elizabeth: *Victoria R.I.* (London, 1964).

LORNE, Marquis of (later 9th Duke of Argyll): *Viscount Palmerston, K.G.* (London, 1892).

Lovely Albert (broadside ballad) (London, 1854).

LUCAS, R.: *Lord Glenesk and the Morning Post* (London, 1910).

LYTTLETON, Lady: *Correspondence of Sarah Spencer Lady Lyttleton* (London, 1912).

MAGARSHACK, D.: *Turgenev* (London, 1954).

MAGNUS, Sir P.: *Gladstone* (London, 1963 ed.).

MAGNUS, Sir P.: *King Edward the Seventh* (London, 1964).

MALMESBURY, 3rd Earl of: *Memoirs of an ex-Minister: an Autobiography* (London, 1885).

MARTIN, Kingsley: *The Triumph of Lord Palmerston* (London, 1924).

MARTIN, Sir Theodore: *Life of H.R.H. The Prince Consort* (London, 1875).

MARX, Karl: *The Eastern Question* (London, 1897).

MARX, Karl: *The Story of the Life of Lord Palmerston* (London, 1899).

MAXWELL, Sir H.: *The Life and Letters of George William, Fourth Earl of Clarendon* (London, 1913).

MERIMÉE, P.: *Correspondence Générale de Prosper Merimée* (Paris and Toulouse, 1941–64).

METTERNICH, C. von: *Memoires, Documents et Écrits Divers laissés par le Prince de Metternich* (ed. Prince R. Metternich) (Paris, 1880–4).

MINCHIN, J. G. C.: *Old Harrow Days* (London, 1898).

MINTO, Earl of: *The Life and Letters of Sir Gilbert Elliot, First Earl of Minto* (ed. Countess of Minto) (London, 1874).

MONYPENNY, W. F., and BUCKLE, G. E.: *The Life of Benjamin Disraeli, Earl of Beaconsfield* (London, 1929 ed.).

MORLEY, J.: *The Life of Richard Cobden* (London, 1881).

MORLEY, J.: *The Life of William Ewart Gladstone* (London, 1903).

MORSE, H. B.: *The International Relations of the Chinese Empire* (London, 1910–18), vol. II.

NELSON, Lord: *The Despatches and Letters of Vice Admiral Lord Viscount Nelson* (ed. Sir N. H. Nicolas) (London, 1845–6).

NEVILLE, Lady D.: *The Reminiscences of Lady Dorothy Nevill* (London, 1906).

NEVILLE, Lady D.: *Under Five Reigns* (London, 1910).

NEVILL, Ralph: *The Life and Letters of Lady Dorothy Nevill* (London, 1919).

NEWTON, Lord: *Lord Lyons* (London, 1913).

The New Whig Guide (London, 1819).

Opium Papers: *Papers relating to the Opium Trade in China 1842–1856* (Parliamentary Papers, 1857).

OSSINGTON, John Evelyn Denison, Viscount: *Notes from my Journal when Speaker of the House of Commons* (London, 1900).

PALMERSTON, 3rd Viscount: *Selections from private journals of tours in France in 1815 and 1818* (London, 1871).

PANMURE, Lord: *The Panmure Papers* (ed. Sir G. Douglas and Sir G. D. Ramsay) (London, 1908).

PARISH, H. J.: *Victory with Vaccines* (Edinburgh, 1968).

PEEL, Sir R.: *Sir Robert Peel from his private correspondence* (ed. C. S. Parker) (London, 1891).

PEMBERTON, W. B.: *Lord Palmerston* (London, 1954).

PHILLIPS, S.: 'Palmerston: what has he done?' See Coningham.

PHIPPS, E.: *Memoirs of the Political and Literary Life of Robert Plumer Ward, Esq.* (London, 1850).

Portuguese Papers: *Correspondence relating to the Affairs of Portugal* (Parliamentary Papers, 1847).

PRAED, J. M.: *Political and Occasional Poems* (ed. Sir G. Young) (London, 1888).

PULSZKY, F.: *Meine Zeit, mein Leben* (Pressburg, 1880–3).

Punch (London, 1841–65).

PUTNAM, G. H.: *Memories of my youth* (New York, 1914).

REEVE, H.: *Memoirs of the Life and Correspondence of Henry Reeve, C.B., D.C.L.* (ed. J. K. Laughton) (London, 1898).

RENDEL, Lord: *The Personal Papers of Lord Rendel* (ed. F. E. Hamer) (London, 1931).

RIKER, T. W.: *The Making of Roumania* (Oxford, 1931).

RITCHIE, J. E.: *The Life and Times of Viscount Palmerston* (London, 1866).

RIVES, G. L.: 'Mexican diplomacy on the eve of war with the United States' (*American Historical Review*, vol. XVIII, London, January 1913).

RODKEY, F. S.: 'Lord Palmerston and the Regeneration of Turkey 1830–41' (*Journal of Modern History*, vols. I and II, Chicago, December 1929 and June 1930).

The Romsey Register (Romsey, April 1854–October 1856).

RUSSELL, G. W. E.: *Collections and Recollections by one who has kept a diary* (London, 1898).

RUSSELL, Lord John: *The Later Correspondence of Lord John Russell 1840–1878* (London, 1925).

ST HELIER, Lady: *Memories of Fifty Years* (London, 1909).

SALISBURY, 3rd Marquis of: See Cecil.

SANDERS, L. C.: *Lord Melbourne's Papers* (London, 1889).

SHELLEY, Frances: *The Diary of Frances Lady Shelley* (ed. R. Edgcumbe) (London, 1912–13).

SKEATS, H. S., and MIALL, C. S.: *History of the Free Churches of England 1688-1891* (London, 1891).

SNELL, F. J.: *Palmerston's Borough* (Tiverton, 1894).

SOUTHGATE, D.: '*The Most English Minister . . .*': *the Policies and Politics of Palmerston* (London, 1966).

Spanish Marriage Papers: *Correspondence relating to the Marriages of the Queen and Infanta of Spain* (Parliamentary Papers, 1847).

Spanish Papers: *Papers relative to the Affairs of Spain and Correspondence between Sir Henry Bulwer and the Duke of Sotomayor* (Parliamentary Papers, 1848).

SPROXTON, C.: *Palmerston and the Hungarian Revolution* (Cambridge, 1919).

STANMORE, Lord: *Sidney Herbert, Lord Herbert of Lea: a Memoir* (London, 1906).

STANMORE, Lord: *The Earl of Aberdeen* (London, 1893).

State Papers: *British and Foreign State Papers*, vol. XXIX (1840–1), and LII (1861–2) (London, 1857, 1868).

State Trials: *Reports of State Trials, New Series*, vol. II, 1823–31 (London, 1889).

SUCKLING, Frances: *Around Old Romsey* (reprints from *The Romsey Register*, etc., 1910–16).

SUCKLING, Frances: *Up and down Old Romsey* (reprints from *The Romsey Register*, etc., 1906–12).

Swiss Papers: *Correspondence relative to the Affairs of Switzerland* (Parliamentary Papers, 1847–8).

SYKES, Sir P.: *A History of Persia* (London, 1921).

TALLEYRAND, Prince de: *Memoires du Prince de Talleyrand* (ed. Duc de Broglie) (Paris, 1891).

TEMPERLEY, H.: *The Unpublished Diary and Political Sketches of Princess Lieven* (London, 1925).

TENNYSON, Lord: *The Poetical Works of Alfred Lord Tennyson* (London, 1926 ed.).

THORNTON, P. M.: *Harrow School and its Surroundings* (London, 1885).

TILLEY, Sir J., and GASELEE, S.: *The Foreign Office* (London, 1933).

The Times (London, 1784–1865).

TORRENS, W. M.: *Memoirs of the Right Honourable William second Viscount Melbourne* (London, 1878).

TREVELYAN, G.: *Garibaldi and the Making of Italy* (London, 1911).

TREVELYAN, G.: *John Bright* (London, 1925 ed.).

URQUHART, D.: *Materials for the true history of Lord Palmerston* (London, 1866).

URQUHART, D.: *The Queen and the Premier* (London, 1857).

VESEY, F.: *Reports of Cases argued and determined in the High Court of Chancery from the year 1789 to 1817*, vol. XVII (London, 1827).

VICTORIA, Queen: *The Girlhood of Queen Victoria: a selection from Her Majesty's diaries 1832–40* (ed. Viscount Esher) (London, 1912).

VICTORIA, Queen: *The Letters of Queen Victoria 1837–61* (ed. A. C. Benson and Viscount Esher) (London, 1907) (cited as 'Q.V.L., I (i–iii)'.

The Letters of Queen Victoria. Second Series 1861–85 (ed. G. E. Buckle) (London, 1926–8) (cited as 'Q.V.L., II (i–iii)').

VINCENT, J.: *The Formation of the Liberal Party 1857–1868* (London, 1966).

VITZTHUM von ECHSTAEDT, Count C. F.: *St. Petersburg and London* (London, 1887).

WALPOLE, S.: *Life of Lord John Russell* (London, 1889).

WARD, R. P.: See Phipps.

WATERFIELD, G.: *Layard of Nineveh* (London, 1963).

WEBB, Sidney and Beatrice: *History of Trade Unionism* (London, 1920 ed.).

WEBSTER, Sir C.: 'Lord Palmerston at Work' (*Politica*, London, August 1934).

WEBSTER, Sir C.: *The Foreign Policy of Palmerston 1830–1841* (London, 1951).

WELLINGTON, 1st Duke of: *Despatches, Correspondence and Memoranda of Field-Marshal Arthur Duke of Wellington* (ed. 2nd Duke of Wellington) (London, 1867–80).

WEST, Sir. A.: *Recollections: 1832 to 1886* (London, 1899).

WESTMORLAND, Countess of: *Correspondence of Priscilla Countess of Westmorland 1813-1870* (London, 1909).

WHEATLEY, H. B.: *London Past and Present* (London, 1891).

WHITE, W.: *The Inner Life of the House of Commons* (ed. Justin McCarthy) (London, 1897).

WHITTY, E. M.: *St Stephens in the Fifties* (London, 1906).

WHYTE, J. H.: 'Landlord Influence at Elections in Ireland 1760–1885' (*English Historical Review*, vol. LXXX, London, October 1965).

WHYTE-JERVIS, J.: *The Ionian Islands during the present century* (London, 1863).

WILBERFORCE, R. S. and S.: *Life of William Wilberforce* (London, 1838).

WILKS, W.: *Palmerston in three epochs* (London, 1854).

WILLIAMS, J. F.: *Harrow* (London, 1901).

WILSON, D. A.: *Carlyle at his zenith* (London, 1927).

WILSON, Harriette: *Harriette Wilson's Memoirs* (ed. J. Laver) (London, 1929).

WOLFF, H. D.: *Rambling Recollections* (London, 1908).

WOODHAM-SMITH, Cecil: *Florence Nightingale 1820-1910* (London, 1950).

WOODHAM-SMITH, Cecil: *The Great Hunger* (London, 1962).

WOODHAM-SMITH, Cecil: *The Reason Why* (London, 1953).

Index